Europe and Northern Asia

NC STATE UNIVERSITY

Europe and Northern Asia

HUMANITIES EXTENSION/PUBLICATIONS PROGRAM

North Carolina State University

Raleigh, North Carolina

Dedicated to the memory of Joseph P. Mastro, Ph.D.,
professor of Political Science & codirector of
Humanities Extension/Publications Program,
North Carolina State University.

Cover: Gold Hill, Shaftesbury, England. Photo by British Tourist Authority,
courtesy of Ogilvy & Mather.

Design and Production: DECODE, Inc.

ISBN 1-885647-00-X
Printed in the United States of America.
  2 3 4 5 6 7 8   BN   04 03 02 01 00 99 98

Contents

UNIT 7
Russia and Its Neighbors Today 476

Skill Lessons

EYEWITNESS TO HISTORY

Maps

LIVING IN...

CONNECTIONS

The British Isles

CHAPTER 1

A Journey Through Europe and Russia

The mothers of Jared Sizemore and Angela Maris are taking them to Europe. Jared's mom is a doctor. Angela's mom is an air quality control engineer. Both women work for the Environmental Protection Agency, which is doing a study on air quality in Europe and Northern Asia, including the lands that once were parts of the Soviet Union.

Their teacher, Mr. Calvert, suggested Jared and Angela keep a travel journal. He asked that they bring back souvenirs, take pictures, and write about the countries they visit. Here's what Jared and Angela found and described.

Trooping the Colour ceremony at the palace

England

Dear Travel Journal,
   We left Raleigh-Durham and landed in London! Wow! The guards at the royal palace look serious. Traffic is crazy here compared to home. Cars on the left side of the street make it look strange.
   Angela

Jan. 4, 9:00 A.M. *London time*
   We ride red buses all over the city. We're going to take the train to Liverpool so Mom, or rather Mum, as they say it here, can see where the Beatles got their start. Distances here seem shorter compared to home. I hope I get to see the Parliament. We went to a court for an air pollution case. The judges wear wigs, long white ones!
   Jared

Dear Travel Journal,

We've seen ruins of old Roman roads. Excavation has uncovered some Roman baths. I had never thought of the Romans here. Jared went on and on about Parliament. I liked walking in the city more. People everywhere. The cities are crowded and filled with people of many different nationalities.

Jan. 9, 6:00 P.M. London time

We had tea. I thought tea was a drink. It's a meal with lots of sweets. Cookies are called biscuits. Interesting. The parks in the cities are small, but nice. Lots of people stand on soapboxes to yell about things. Soccer games are everywhere! I'm glad I brought my cleats. Angela says she'll play.

English soccer match

Dear Travel Journal,

Liverpool and Manchester are industrial cities. Both have high unemployment. Unemployed teenagers and college-age kids hang out during the day. Lots of dirty air. Why can't something be done to get people work? One thing I noticed, there are lots of nightclubs. People go to hear bands and to dance. We couldn't go because we weren't eighteen.

Jan. 12, 7:00 P.M.

Glad to be out of Liverpool and Manchester. Crowded and dirty. Liked the old buildings though. Mom and I visited a school. Their school days are ten hours long. Not as crowded as our schools at home.

London double-deck bus

Scotland

Scottish hotel

Dear Travel Journal,

We've left for Scotland. I think of countries as being far apart, but here everything is so close. Lots of sheep around, too. Jared tells me there is a monster around here somewhere.

Now we're at a hotel where there is only one bath per hallway. Its raining outside so hard you can't see anything. The hotel served haggis for supper. I don't want to know what it is.

Dear Travel Journal,

Gross! Haggis is sheep's stomach!

No television, no computer, no lights on after midnight. Sometimes I do miss the U.S.A. Tomorrow we hike up a hill and view some of the lochs, or lakes. Mom says looking at the sky will be different here. She says the ocean breeze keeps the pollution away. The sea is all around us. We're on Scotland's western coast. It looked like the end of nowhere in the rain today.

Jan. 14, 8:00 A.M.

There are many deep lakes in Scotland, which the Scottish call "lochs." Told Angela to expect to see the Loch Ness monster. But wouldn't it be great to spot it? Ancient animal left over from prehistoric times trapped in a land-locked lake! It would beat looking at sheep. Flocks and flocks of them. We had to wait 15 minutes while they crossed the road we were on.

Jan. 15, 6:00 P.M.

Rain has kept us inside. The electric heat is warm, but the peat fires in the fireplace are smoky. The kitchen is tiny. The houses are painted white mostly. The pubs and stores are painted blue and pink and green. Streets are so narrow here the cars have to be tiny to go through them.

Loch Tummel

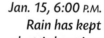

Ireland

Dear Travel Journal,

Doogin, near Donegal. A tiny town on the coast with streets as narrow as they are in Scotland. The people here play music everywhere. I think everyone has a fiddle or guitar. Lots of bicycles. We're going riding this afternoon while the weather is clear.

Irish coast at Donegal

Jan. 16, 5:00 P.M.

Bicycle riding around here takes work. These hills are steep. We have to be careful as we ride along the coastline. It's wild to watch the waves crashing up over 100 feet and see the rock crumble away. We couldn't do this in a winter storm. It would be too dangerous.

The best part about the bike ride is when we come back and have tea. Irish soda bread and jam! Tomorrow we go to Belfast in Northern Ireland.

Dear Travel Journal,

There has been fighting in Northern Ireland. The checkpoint in Belfast didn't seem as threatening as I thought it would be. People cross through a checkpoint to go to work every day. I'm glad we don't have to have guards at each state line when we travel at home.

We're going to the really cold countries next.

Belfast checkpoint guard

3

Iceland

Jan. 18, 7:00 P.M.

What a strange country. Fire and ice. Steam rises from the water because the air is frigid. People swimming in January outdoors. Snowmobiles are the favorite method of transportation in the northern snowfields. What a difference from the British Isles, where bicycles and cars got us everywhere. It was dark here by 3:00 P.M.

Dear Travel Journal,

Mom couldn't believe it. We had to take a snowmobile from one medical clinic to another. We all had to ride! It was fun zooming across the fields. Jared and I each drove one. Fast, like a boat on water, and cold. Good thing we had wool caps and earmuffs. We wore goggles, too. The snow is several feet deep in Raufarhofn, above the Arctic Circle. We saw people walking using snowshoes. It looked as if they were walking with tennis rackets on their feet.

Norway

Jan. 20, 9:00 A.M.

I try to imagine the fields in summer, but its hard to think of this place without snow. I like Norway and Sweden. I can say Hej (Hello) and Hej da (Bye). Winter sports everywhere. It's ice skating for me at the rink in Lillehammer. It was used in the Olympic games.

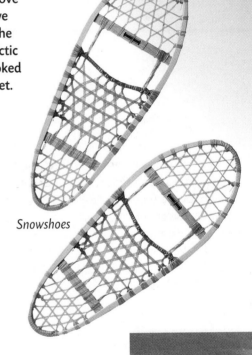

Snowshoes

Snowmobiling

Dear Travel Journal,

Norway combines old and new. Snowmobiles and old churches. Vikings once sailed out to sea on fjords. Now cruise ships filled with tourists churn through the fjords. The glaciers and blue water must sparkle in the summer, but much of the day is like dusk. It is strange. Next, we go to Tampere in Finland.

Raufarhofn

ICELAND

Reykjavík

Finland

Jan. 23, 8:30 A.M.
 Here in Finland, everybody skis. Even tiny children! I had to try it. I didn't go fast, but I could get from one place to another. We watched an icebreaker being built at Turku. Lots of industry here, but the pollution isn't bad. These countries seem to have few pollution problems. They have few coal-burning industries. They have more water for power than some other countries.

FINLAND
Tampere
Turku

NORWAY
Lillehammer

Inverness
SCOTLAND

Donegal Belfast
Liverpool
Manchester
IRELAND
ENGLAND London

Berlin
GERMANY

Germany

Dear Travel Journal,
 Castles on the Rhine. Inside they are cold and spooky. The wind whistles around and makes awful sounds. The fireplaces are big enough for the four of us to walk into and sit down. We looked off the highest point of the castle, the parapet, and saw huge barges on the river. We're going to a beer garden for lunch. We won't have beer, but we'll have about 30 kinds of sausages.

Smashing the Berlin Wall

Jan. 25, 9:30 P.M.
 Berlin looks like most large cities. We saw the remnants of the Berlin Wall. The schools are great. They only go from 8:00 in the morning to 1:00 in the afternoon. But they do have homework every day. I wanted to go to the Black Forest, but I learned that the forest has problems. So much acid rain from industry has damaged the trees, the forest isn't as thick as it used to be.

*Stahlech Castle, Germany,
on the Rhine River*

Benelux Countries

Double tulips

Dear Travel Journal,

Such a small country, but what great things they have in Belgium. Chocolate and flowers. Two of my favorite things. Brussels is filled with old, old buildings and greenhouses full of flowers. Chocolate shops on every corner.

The **Belgian**
ZEEVRUCHTEN • SEASHELLS • FRUITS DE MER
MEERESFRÜCHTE NUSS-NOUGAT-PRALINEN
POIDS NET WEIGHT 75g ℮ (2.6 oz.)

Jan. 27, 10:00 A.M.

Although Belgium is okay, I liked The Netherlands better. Amsterdam rocks with music and parties. We had to be careful not to get tangled up with the partygoers. But it is exciting. Ice skating takes place when the canals are frozen over. There is a race on a canal today. We won't have time to go to Luxembourg, the third country of Benelux.

France

Jan. 29, 9:00 A.M. France, southeastern border

We went up into the mountains. Wow! It took several hours to make a 100-mile trip because the mountains are steep and the snow causes problems. We went to a ski resort town in the Alps as we made our way through France. One snowslide blocked a road for an hour. The ski resort town had tourists from all over the world. People skied day and night.

Mont Blanc, the highest mountain in the French Alps, is also the highest in Europe!

French Alps

Amsterdam
GERMANY
Berlin
Brussels ● BENELUX
Reims
FRANCE
Madrid
Barcelona
SPAIN

Dear Travel Journal,

Met Laurie, who is my age. She invited me to go riding at her grandfather's farm, near Reims. We had fun riding around their large farm. She lives an hour or so away from the mountains. Her grandfather grows vegetables for the markets in the city. The people here grocery shop every day. Even in winter fresh vegetables and animals are brought into the city every morning for people to buy. When Laurie stays with her grandparents in the summer, she gets up at 4:00 A.M. to go into the city. She has a small garden. She sells things from it and gets to keep the money.

Spain

Jan. 29, 9:30 P.M.

More crowded cities. Right in the middle of Spain is Madrid. Huge squares called plazas are great places to shop and eat. It's easy to find. The wind blows here, and it is chilly. The high temperature in the summer is around 100 degrees. I guess that's why people take a siesta, a rest in the afternoon. What else could you do? It's almost 10:00 P.M., but we've just finished dinner. Tomorrow we go to one of the world's largest museums, the Prado. Then we leave for Barcelona on a high-speed train.

Barcelona market

Dear Travel Journal,

At the market in Barcelona we saw oranges, lemons, limes, sunflowers, onions, garlic, grapes, and olives. People come in from the countryside all year to sell their products. The sunflowers came from the coast. I saw a picture of a coastal resort, and it looked like pictures of Miami Beach. We ate paella, which is a coastal dish of fish, rice with saffron, and vegetables. We're taking a boat from here across the Mediterranean. I'm nervous about it. I haven't been on the open sea before.

Plaza de Cibeles, Madrid

Italy

Feb. 6, 7:00 P.M. Near Milan

Factories and other businesses crowd around Milan. Most of the people in Italy live in cities or near cities. There are still small villages around, especially in the mountains. Italy is a mountainous country. Angela nearly got sick as we drove up and down the mountains and through the villages.

Dolomite Alps, Italy

Italian leather book cover

Dear Travel Journal,

Being in Italy is like being on a ride at the fair. Up and around and down in a valley and back up a mountain. We stopped and looked at a field of poppies near Florence. Red flowers as far as your eye could see. I was glad we stopped. Jared says he wants to go rock climbing. It would be the thing to do around here because there are so many mountains.

We are taking the train and then a car to the Adriatic coast.

Greece

Feb. 9, 12:00 noon, Patras

Great food here! A sandwich with ham and cheese in Greek pita bread tastes great. I see lemon trees and grapevines and olive orchards. Food here comes with olives, large green ones, black ones, and tiny olives as small as the end of my finger. Olives are in all the salads. I like baklava, a pastry with honey and walnuts. They serve it in triangle shapes. I'm having it again today at lunch, right now!

Dear Travel Journal,

The coast of Greece looks like it did from the travel pictures. Bright blue skies and water here in Patras. Lots of boats. Fishing seems to be a big industry here. Wonder what would happen if the water became polluted . The tiny fishing villages would disappear. I noticed that many of the schools are large. Mom says that children from outside the small towns come in to the schools.

Greek fishing boat

Hungary

Dear Travel Journal,

Budapest houses crowd one another. The streets go from wide to so narrow only one car can pass. Snowfall is thick and heavy. It covers the houses like ice cream. There are high-rise apartment houses, too. Most people like to live in the large buildings in the city. We bought postcards to see how Hungary looks during the summer.

Summer in Budapest

Feb. 11, 9:30 P.M.

We went to a concert here in Budapest because there were people from the medical clinic playing in it. Mom said that music is important to many families here. The people work during the day and practice music every night. Some people work for two orchestras. One family we visited had two cellos and three guitars in the living room.

Amsterdam
Berlin
GERMANY
Brussels
BENELUX
Reims
FRANCE
Budapest
HUNGARY
Milan
Florence
Barcelona
ITALY
Madrid
GREECE
SPAIN
Patras

Dear Travel Journal,

In the countryside near Budapest, the land seems to go for thousands of miles. So flat it seems endless. Not much to look at except farms and small villages. I see children playing in the snow. They wear bright colors. I'm buying postcards of summer scenes.

Hungarian vineyard in summer

Feb. 13, 7:00 P.M.

The wind freezes me if I try to go without a hat. We've seen many small farms. Goats with long horns and thick fur grazed near the back door of one farm. We had goat cheese and home-made bread at that farm. Saw some old castles in the forested areas.

Poland

Dear Travel Journal,

So far, Poland looks like Hungary. Part of Poland gets lots of snow. Some parts, near the coast, are warmer. We see the great plains of Poland as well. It is a flat country. I like all the colorful clothes. The tights the girls wear are bright splotches of color.

Feb. 15, 6:30 P.M.

We walked along the older parts of the city where thousands of Jews once lived. It wasn't right for people to be persecuted because of their religion. This part of the city is crowded. Many buildings here were destroyed in World War II. They have been rebuilt to look like the originals. We found a rock music station on a radio.

Rebuilt Jewish Quarter of Kraków

Dear Travel Journal,

We went to a museum and a cathedral in Kraków. The gold and jewels shine and sparkle. Those people must have been rich. The cathedral's stained glass windows gleamed in the afternoon sun. Most images were of the Virgin and child. I try to pronounce the artist's names. I trip over the consonants in their long names.

Feb. 17, 9:00 P.M.

One museum had the scepters of the rulers of Poland in the 1400s. All three were made of gold! The tops of the scepters looked like crowns. Each one had different engravings on it. One had the coats of arms of Poland, Lithuania, and the House of Anjou. It tells you how connected all these country's rulers were. There were many countries, but most were ruled by related families.

Cathedral in Kraków

Moldova

Dear Travel Journal,

In Tiraspol after a short stop in Tarnow. I see lots of dead trees. Mom says the pollution rate is high here. I see some people in the cities wearing masks. There were pollution warnings in Budapest and in Warsaw. Tiraspol is smaller. We went to a puppet play at a local school. They used puppets they had sewn themselves.

Feb. 21, 7:30 A.M.

Watched a chess tournament at a local school yesterday. There were about 40 kids playing at one time. Angela and I played one round with other kids. I drew a girl as a partner. We didn't have to speak the same language. We both knew the rules of chess.

Ukraine

Feb. 25, 7:00 P.M.

Kiev was once part of Russia until Ukraine won its independence. It is a resort town because the river attracts tourists during the summer. There are amusement parks that are shut down now. We will take a train to Moscow. It's too snowy and icy to drive now.

Dear Travel Journal,

We took a plane to Kiev. We didn't want to drive over the mountains, even though they're not as high as some of the other mountain ranges we've seen. Flying over the mountains is scary. Kiev in winter isn't too cold. It's on the Dnepr River. The river goes to the Black Sea. There are many barges on this river. I've seen barges in every river that's not frozen.

Rally for Ukrainian independence

Russia

Dear Travel Journal,

The train was good for looking at Russia's farmland in winter. I saw miles and miles of empty fields. The temperature in and around Moscow can go down to below freezing for a long time in the winter. Springtime doesn't happen here until May.

We took the subway, or Metro, around the city. We saw the apartment buildings where most of the people live. Some children have to travel on the Metro to get to school, the way we do on school buses.

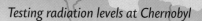

Dear Travel Journal,

Yesterday I met Margotta. She used to live in Chernobyl, but her family had to move after the nuclear accident there. Her older brother died from radiation sickness. Margotta hopes she will not get sick, but her family is not sure yet. Her grandparents who lived in Chernobyl both died after the accident. Margotta likes rock music and wants to be able to buy more blue jeans.

Testing radiation levels at Chernobyl

Feb. 28, 8:00 P.M.

Russian soldiers still march around Red Square. The Kremlin looks like a forbidding place. The domes in the city look like they belong in Turkey or Budapest. Some of the domes appear to be gold.

I asked about the wolves in the country. Older people tell about wolf attacks during the hungry times after World War II. There are still wolves in the forests.

St. Basil's Cathedral

Winter Farewell Festival, Moscow

Anchorage **ALASKA**

• Vladivostok

Dear Travel Journal,

Margotta gave me a picture of a lady measuring radiation in Chernobyl. Ugh! I'm going to send Margotta a pair of blue jeans. I'll write to Laurie in France. I'm glad to be going home. Surprise! I'm even looking forward to going back to school. First, we fly from here to Vladivostok, a city with a big naval base. From there we'll fly to Anchorage, Alaska, U.S.A.!

March 1, 9:00 P.M.

Tomorrow we begin the journey home. I have to pack all my souvenirs. I'm going to write some of the people I met here after I get back to North Carolina. I will be glad to get home, but I won't ever see the names of these countries in the news again and think of those places as I did before.

We fly out and go through eight time zones!

The Kremlin, Moscow

Harbor of Vladivostok

Using Geography's Five Themes

Suppose that Jared and Angela are your classmates and that you are in school the day they return to class. The first questions everyone asks are about the people, places, and things they saw.

Jared and Angela use one of the school's maps to show where they have been. They discuss their travel journals, pictures, and souvenirs. The teacher tells everyone to listen closely, because they will have an assignment based on Jared's and Angela's experiences. Here is the class assignment.

Getting Organized

You will serve on one of five teams. Each team will collect data for oral reports on "The Land and People of Europe and Northern Asia." You may use some reference books, but Jared's and Angela's travel journals, pictures, and souvenirs will provide the main source material.

Five Themes and Key Questions

Remember that you have studied the **Five Themes of Geography** in earlier grades. Geographers use the themes to ask **key questions** that help them understand places and the people who live there. These questions help them gather facts and organize those facts into ideas.

To understand how these key questions and themes can be used, the Five Themes of Geography are reviewed below.

Do not be too concerned if you cannot answer everything. You will be studying geography's themes again in weeks to come.

Team No. 1
Theme of Location

Your assignment: Apply the geographers' first theme to Jared and Angela's trip. Ask a key question, "Where is this place?" Use a classroom map or atlas to describe the location of Europe and Northern Asia as well as the places your classmates visited. Do you recall that geographers describe location in two ways?

(1) *Absolute location* is given with parallels of latitude and meridians of longitude. For example, what is the absolute location of Kiev, Ukraine? (2) *Relative location* can be described by telling where a place is found in relation to other places. For example, how can you use Greenland and Norway to describe Iceland's location?

Team No. 2
Theme of Place

Your assignment: Use the geographers' second theme to ask "What is this place like?" Again, remember that geographers try to find facts that answer this question in two ways.

(1) *Physical characteristics.* How do landforms, bodies of water, and climate describe a place? (2) *Cultural characteristics.* How do

all parts of the lives of the people—language, religion, food, sport, or customs—describe a place?

Can you find in Jared's and Angela's journals, pictures, and souvenirs enough information for you to say how each place they visited might be similar to or different from others? What changed most as they traveled—physical or cultural characteristics? Why?

Team No. 3
Theme of Human-Environmental Interaction

Geographers usually ask a series of questions when they use this theme. In what ways have people living in a place adapted (or adjusted) their ways of life so they can live in cold, hot, dry, or other types of environments? How have people tried to change their environment? What have been the consequences of these efforts?

Jared and Angela made their trip in midwinter. Your assignment: Answer the following questions about the theme of *human-environmental interaction.* Did they find people adapting to different climates? Did they see any evidence of people's having changed their environments? Did these efforts seem to improve people's lives? Did they see changes that made life worse?

Team No. 4
Theme of Movement

When geographers think about this theme, they most often have in mind the *movement* of people, goods, and ideas. Geographers, for example, want to learn how a place is affected by the flow of industrial raw materials into the factories of a city and the shipment of finished products to world markets. They might also ask how the character of a place can be affected by barriers or aids to movement.

Your assignment: Look closely at Jared's and Angela's materials for evidence of movement. How do they describe movement in their journals? What pictures show movement? Does there seem to be more exchange of people, goods, and ideas in some places than in others?

Team No. 5
Theme of Region

Geographers define a region as a group of places bound together by one or more characteristics. For example, places that are located in mountains and have much the same climate and vegetation would be part of a region. Do Jared and Angela describe places that have things in common? Do they describe places that are quite different? Are Europe and Northern Asia part of one big region, or are they divided into many regions?

Jared and Angela do not speak of regions as geographers might. Yet their journals and pictures give clues that they have been traveling sometimes within a *region.* Did they sometimes move from one *region* to another? Your assignment is to find that out.

Team Reports

Teams will report on the results of their assignments. Use maps, charts, reports, and illustrations to show how geography's themes help you organize information. Who will prepare and gather materials? Who will make the reports to the class?

Europe: An Introduction

Around 100 years ago, wealthy people in the United States wanted to live like Europeans. They collected European art and took long trips to Europe. Such families as the Vanderbilts of Biltmore House copied the mansions of Europe when they built their American homes.

Have you visited Biltmore House in Asheville, North Carolina? It is built in the style of a French Renaissance chateau. It looks like the great houses French nobles constructed 700 to 800 years ago.

UNIT PREVIEW

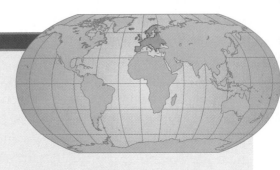

CHAPTER 2
Europe's Lands and People
Europe's people, ideas, and languages have come to the United States. Today, there remain strong connections between Europe and the United States.

CHAPTER 3
Europe's Foundations
Europe's foundations in ancient Greek and Roman civilizations and in its own Middle Ages have given shape to the continent as we know it today.

CHAPTER 4
Modern Europe Takes Shape
The Renaissance and Reformation, the building of nations, and worldwide exploration and expansion have also contributed to Europe's character.

CHAPTER 5
Europe in the Twentieth Century
World Wars I and II seriously weakened Europe, but most countries, especially in Western Europe, have made a remarkable recovery.

Biltmore House

Europe's Lands and People

Nearly a dozen bagpipers in tartan kilts stand in a semicircle on the green lawn. When they start to play, a twelve-year-old girl, also in Scottish dress, dances the Highland fling, her feet darting nimbly to the music.

This is not Scotland, though. The bagpipers and dancer are performing on the lawn of North Carolina's Capitol Building in Raleigh, on the afternoon of the Fourth of July. As the festivities show, North Carolina's customs partly come from a European heritage.

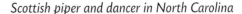

Scottish piper and dancer in North Carolina

Europe—Political

Reykjavik ✪
ICELAND

Arctic Circle

N
W · E
S

Norwegian Sea

ATLANTIC
OCEAN

FINLAND

Helsinki ✪

Oslo ✪

NORWAY

Stockholm ✪
SWEDEN

Tallinn ✪
ESTONIA

St. Petersburg ●

RUSSIA

Moscow ✪

FAROE IS.
(Den.)

SHETLAND IS.
(U.K.)

Scotland

North Sea

No. Ireland

Dublin ✪
IRELAND

**UNITED
KINGDOM**

Wales

England

London ✪

NETHERLANDS

Amsterdam ✪
✪ The Hague

Brussels ✪
BELGIUM

DENMARK
Copenhagen ✪

Gulf of Bothnia

Baltic Sea

Riga ✪
LATVIA

LITHUANIA

RUSSIA
Vilnius ✪

Minsk ✪

BELARUS

Berlin ✪

POLAND

Warsaw ✪

Kiev ✪

GERMANY

LUXEMBOURG

Prague ✪
CZECH REP.

SLOVAKIA
Bratislava ✪

UKRAINE

MOLDOVA
Kishinev ✪

Paris ✪

FRANCE

LIECHTENSTEIN

Bern ✪
SWITZ.

Vienna ✪
AUSTRIA

Budapest ✪
HUNGARY

ROMANIA

*Bay of
Biscay*

Ljubljana ✪
SLOVENIA

Zagreb ✪
CROATIA

Belgrade ✪

Bucharest ✪

*Black
Sea*

MONACO

SAN MARINO

**BOSNIA–
HERZEGOVINA**
Sarajevo ✪

ANDORRA

ITALY

Adriatic Sea

SERBIA
Podgorica ✪

BULGARIA
Sofia ✪

PORTUGAL

Madrid ✪

Rome ✪

CORSICA
(Fr.)

MONTENEGRO

ALBANIA
MACEDONIA
Skopje ✪

Istanbul ●

Lisbon ✪

SPAIN

SARDINIA
(It.)

Tiranë ✪

TURKEY

BALEARIC IS. (Sp.)

Mediterranean Sea

GREECE

*Aegean
Sea*

*Strait of
Gibraltar*

Gibraltar (U.K.) ●

SICILY
(It.)

MALTA

Athens ✪

CRETE (Gr.)

✪ National Capital
— International boundary

0   250   500 mi.
0   250   500 km

AFRICA

Europe's Lands and People **19**

Discovering Europe in North Carolina

LESSON PREVIEW

Key Ideas

- North Carolina's early settlers included English, Scots, Scotch-Irish, Swiss, and Germans. The traditions of these early settlers remain alive in the state.
- Almost all of Europe is represented in the population and ways of life in North and South America.
- These European traditions are reminders of the Americas' close cultural links to Europe.

*There's a little group of isles beyond the wave,
So tiny, you might almost wonder where it is…*

These lines about the British Isles come from *Utopia, Limited,* a comic opera written by Sir William S. Gilbert and Sir Arthur Sullivan. In spring 1995, the Durham Savoyards, Limited, could have been singing that tune as they flew across the Atlantic Ocean toward Europe.

The Savoyards usually sing the operas of Gilbert and Sullivan in North Carolina. That spring they performed in Durham, England. They helped their sister city celebrate the 1,000th anniversary of the dedication of their cathedral.

Carolina Connections

The English settlers of Durham, North Carolina, named their new town after Durham, England. Years later, the architects of Duke University Chapel continued the English connection. They designed the church in the style of English cathedrals.

Other Europeans who settled in North Carolina honored their European heritage in their new home. They named their settlements for European people and places.

The state capital, Raleigh, is named for Sir Walter Raleigh, a key figure in the court of Queen Elizabeth. Raleigh founded the first English settlement in North Carolina. Rockingham, North Carolina, shares the name of the English Marquis of Rockingham, an early supporter of the colony.

Duke Chapel in Durham, North Carolina, is built in the style of an English cathedral. *What buildings in your county show a European connection?*

The city of Charlotte, in Mecklenburg County, honors Queen Charlotte of Mecklenburg, the wife of King George III. Bath, North Carolina, recalls the resort city of Bath, England. The capital of Switzerland, Bern, gave its name to New Bern, a town settled by Germans and Swiss in 1710.

Settlers from many parts of Europe moved to North Carolina. Moravians from today's Czech Republic began a community in Salem. Germans settled to the south. The Scotch-Irish—people who moved from Scotland to Ireland, then to North America—found homes in the Piedmont. Several thousand Scottish Highlanders came to Fayetteville and along the shores of the Cape Fear River.

The richness of this European heritage is still alive and helps give the state its distinctive character. The Highland Games, a celebration of Scottish tradition, are held on Grandfather Mountain the weekend after July 4; in Red Springs, early October; and in Waxhaw, late October.

During the Highland Games, descendants of the original Scottish Highlanders dress in colorful kilts and dance to tunes played on bagpipes. Men compete in the stone toss and the caber toss. A caber is a heavy wooden pole.

It is this European heritage that the Durham Savoyards traveled to Britain to celebrate. Today, as in the past, North Carolina continues to share culture, trade, and ideas with Europe.

Queen Charlotte (c. 1762) by Allan Ramsay. The names of Charlotte and Mecklenburg County honor her and her German home, Mecklenburg. *What other North Carolina towns are named for people and places in Europe?*

Europe in the Americas

Such close ties with Europe are common everywhere in the Americas. Christopher Columbus touched off a scramble among Europeans to conquer North and South America. The Americas became European colonies. Spain built an empire in Middle and South America that lasted 300 years. Portugal's rule in Brazil was also that long.

The French and English became the chief rivals for control of North America. The English drove the French out, but France left a community of colonists in Quebec, Canada. Quebec still maintains strong ties with France.

In 1783, England's 13 colonies along the Atlantic coast won their independence and became the United States of America.

♦♦♦♦ GAMES ♦♦♦♦
People Play

Highland Games Scotland's open lands are ideal for golf, soccer, and the Highland Games. The games combine music with physical skills.

Tossing the caber requires great strength. Contestants pick up a telephone-pole-size log weighing about 180 pounds (81 kilograms) and throw it as far as they can.

♦♦♦♦♦♦♦♦♦♦♦♦♦♦♦♦

Canada, England's colony to the north, gained independence gradually. In both countries, the English left behind their language, customs, and ways of governing.

Europeans have continued to come to the Americas, especially to the United States and Canada. North Carolina is not the only place where people named towns after their homelands. You can find Munich in North Dakota as well as in Germany. Dublin, the capital of Ireland, is a more modest town in Pennsylvania. Eau Claire, French for "clear water," is the name of towns in Wisconsin and South Carolina.

Clues to our European connections lie hidden in names of our food and families. What was the nationality of Americans who first ate baklava? Dvořák and Szymczyk are Eastern

Leaving Europe for North Carolina

Throughout the 1700s, thousands of people moved to the Carolinas to start new lives. They were farmers, merchants, and indentured servants bravely seeking new lives in North America. The story of their sea crossing and their settlement is important to the history of our state.

VIRGINIA

Salem •

Salisbury •

Charlotte •

SOUTH CAROLINA

Edenton

Blount pitcher

Colonists were attracted to coastal towns, such as Edenton and New Bern, by stories like this one: "No place that we have seen is better furnished with grain, fish, sugar, melons, and roots.... We think that any that ... comes here and settles and is industrious may have a very ... comfortable way of living in a few years."

Tryon Palace, New Bern

European names. Swensen sounds Swedish. The Ramirezes trace their origins to Spain. Names of people and places remind us of our close ties with Europe.

LESSON 1 REVIEW

Fact Follow-Up

1. What are some North Carolina connections to Europe?
2. Does your county's name or its cities' names show connections with Europe? Which European nation's heritage is most noticeable?

Think These Through

3. Are North Carolina's ties to Europe strengthening or weakening? Explain your answer.
4. Which European nation's heritage is most influential in the area where you live? Why? How is it celebrated?

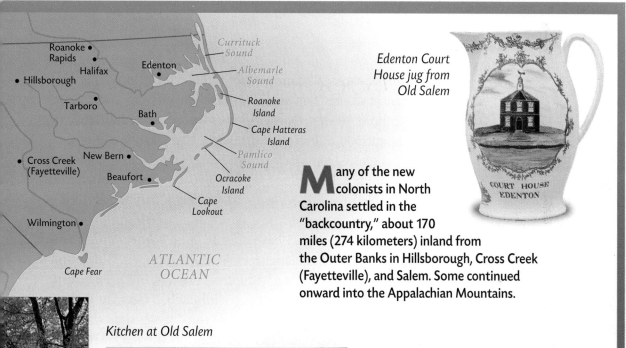

Edenton Court House jug from Old Salem

Many of the new colonists in North Carolina settled in the "backcountry," about 170 miles (274 kilometers) inland from the Outer Banks in Hillsborough, Cross Creek (Fayetteville), and Salem. Some continued onward into the Appalachian Mountains.

Kitchen at Old Salem

While crossing the Atlantic, most colonists were given a handful of oatmeal for breakfast, a piece of meat and some cheese for lunch, and a biscuit with molasses for dinner. Storms often swept the ships off course. Water poured into open holds, soaking passengers, and putting out cook fires. Colonists' possessions were often lost at sea during the dangerous crossing.

Europe's Lands and People **23**

European Homelands

LESSON PREVIEW

Key Ideas

- Europe is divided into many small nations and many groups of people with different languages and customs.
- Europe is the third most populous continent.
- Americans, accustomed to the huge size of their own nation, are often surprised by the smallness of European nations.

Key Terms

dialects, ethnic group, peninsula

An outline map of the United States shows that Europe is slightly larger. Compare this map with the one on page 19. *About how many European countries would fit into the continental United States?*

During spring vacation, a Raleigh family entertained a French exchange student. They drove to Charlotte, a trip that took about three hours. When they arrived, the thirteen-year-old French girl was delighted to get out of the car.

"Where are we?" she asked.

"Charlotte," she was told.

"But what country is this?" she wanted to know.

When she discovered she was still in North Carolina, she laughed. From her home in France, a three-hour drive would take her family through Belgium and into Germany.

People

Europe is a small continent of many nations. Imagine that the French student visiting Charlotte had driven from North Carolina's western border to the Outer Banks, a distance of about 500 miles (805 km). If she had taken a trip of that distance from northeastern France, through Luxembourg and Belgium, she could have traveled through the Netherlands, a corner of Germany, and almost to the Danish border.

She would have crossed four borders and heard four different languages—French, German, Dutch, and Flemish—and many different dialects. In Luxembourg, she would have heard Letzeburgesch, a German dialect.

Europe is only about one third larger than the continental United States (see the map on the left). Yet more than 580 million people live in Europe. (The estimated United States population in 1995 was 263 million.)

Europeans speak 50 different languages and more than 100 **dialects**, or similar language variations. Europe counts among its inhabitants about 150 ethnic groups. An **ethnic group** is made up of people with the same cultural background, united by language, religion, or ancestry.

This diverse population occupies only 6 percent of the

Europeans Talk About Europe

How do Europeans describe the people and world around them? If you could go to Europe, these are comments you might hear:

"There are a lot of cities," a Belgian dockworker observes. "Many people in Europe work in factories or offices," says a French student.

"Dozens of different languages are spoken in Europe. Many Europeans speak two or even three languages fluently," mentions a linguist from Italy.

"One person in ten in the world is European," says a market researcher in the Czech Republic.

A Swedish journalist describes the health of Europeans. "They eat well and live long."

"Europeans are well educated," says a construction worker in Finland.

"People from all over the world live in Europe. Some of them are from places nearby. Others come from places that Europeans colonized," says a university professor living in Germany.

An immigrant from India captures the importance of

Islamic bookstore in Paris, France

Europe. "Events in Europe have affected the rest of the world."

world's land—4,033,000 square miles (10,485,000 square kilometers). Europe has the smallest area of any continent except Australia. Yet only Asia and Africa exceed it in population.

Location and Landforms

Europe occupies a huge peninsula extending west from Asia. A **peninsula** is a body of land surrounded by water on three sides. The Atlantic Ocean borders Europe to the west. To the north lies the North Sea and the Arctic Ocean. The Mediterranean and Black Seas wash its southern and southeastern coasts. To the east, the Ural Mountains separate Europe from Asia.

Almost everywhere in Europe, you are within 300 miles (483 km) of a coast, that includes many peninsulas and natural harbors. Europe has so much seacoast, geographers have called it a peninsula of peninsulas. Europe's coastline stretched out could be wrapped around the earth one and a half times.

Europe contains an immensely varied landscape. Nowhere else in the world will you find extremes so close, from the heights of the snowcapped Alps to the below-sea-level coastline of The Netherlands.

What would **YOU** do?

Imagine you are traveling Europe by rail. In one week you might cross the borders of up to a dozen countries, each with a different language. What ways can you think of to communicate with the people living there? What might you talk with them about?

The landforms of Europe influence where and how people live. Mountains tend to divide people and slow their movement. Plains encourage both migration—movement of people—and settlement. Rivers provide a means of travel, trade, and communication.

The crowded Dutch city of Amsterdam and a French vineyard are part of the Northern European Plain. *How do rivers and the flat land of the plain affect how people live?*

The Northern European Plain

The Northern European Plain extends from Russia through France and includes Southwest England. It measures 1,500 miles (2,415 km) from north to south in Russia, stretching from the Arctic Ocean to the Caucasus Mountains.

The plain narrows in Poland and Germany, widens in western France, and is most narrow in Belgium, where it spans only 50 miles (81 km). The Northern European Plain lies flat or rolls gently. It includes fertile farmland and Europe's largest cities.

European Highlands

European highlands rise north and south of the Northern European Plain (see map, page 27). The northern mountains—with different names—run through northwest France, Ireland, northern Britain, Norway, and Sweden. The ranges contain some of the oldest rock formations on earth. Because of the thin

Europe–Physical

30°W 20°W 70°N 10°W 0° 10°E 20°E

ICELAND

Arctic Circle

Norwegian Sea

60°N

FAROE IS.

KJØLEN MOUNTAINS

SCANDINAVIAN PENINSULA

Gulf of Bothnia

SHETLAND IS.

ATLANTIC
OCEAN

Baltic Sea

North Sea

JUTLAND
PENINSULA

BRITISH ISLES

50°N

Thames R.

English Channel

NORTHERN EUROPEAN PLAIN

Ruhr
Valley

Elbe R.

Oder R.

Vistula R.

Dnepr R.

Rhine R.

Seine R.

Loire R.

Bay of
Biscay

Danube R.

CARPATHIAN MTS.

Dniester R.

ALPS

Rhône R.

Garonne R.

Po R.

PYRENEES

Ebro R.

40°N

IBERIAN PENINSULA

Tagus R.

Guadiana R.

CORSICA

APENNINES

ITALIAN PENINSULA

Adriatic Sea

DINARIC ALPS

Danube R.

Black
Sea

BALKAN MTS.

BALKAN PENINSULA

Bosporus

BALEARIC
ISLANDS

SARDINIA

PINDUS MTS.

*Aegean
Sea*

Dardanelles

ASIA MINOR

Strait of
Gibraltar

Mediterranean Sea

SICILY

*Ionian
Sea*

AFRICA

CRETE

30°N

0 250 500 mi.

0 250 500 km

Land Elevation

Feet	Meters
13,333	4000
6,667	2000
3,333	1000
1,667	500
667	200
0	0

Place The physical characteristics of Europe include mountains, plains, rivers, islands, and peninsulas. *What are some ways they affected settlement in Europe?*

soil, which is poor for farming, fewer people live here.

Low mountains and high plateaus rise in the central Iberian Peninsula. The Alpine Mountain system—also with several names—stretches across Southern Europe. The Pyrenees between Spain and France are part of the Alpine system. So are the mountain ranges in Italy, Switzerland, Austria, and the Balkan peninsula. The eastern Alpines include the Carpathian Mountains of Slovakia and Romania (see map, page 27).

The Swiss and Italian Alps in the central Alpines, with their high elevations and deep snowfall, are popular for skiing and winter sports. The lower slopes and valleys offer good land for farming and grazing.

Sheep produce wool for their Basque herders. The Pyrenees Mountains allow the Basques to live in isolation. *Where are the Pyrenees?*

Rivers

Europe's many rivers provide transportation to inland cities and access to seaports. The rivers also serve as sources of hydro-electric power and irrigation for farmland.

The Danube, one of Europe's longest rivers, flows from southern Germany through Austria, Slovakia, Serbia, Bulgaria, and Romania, and empties into the Black Sea. With the help of connecting canals, the Danube provides a water route from Eastern Europe all the way to Germany. The Danube flows past 35 major ports, linking them by water and giving them access to the Black Sea.

Other important European rivers include the Oder and Vistula in Poland. The Elbe and Rhine are in Germany. The Po flows through Italy. The Rhône and the Seine are in France, the Tagus in Spain and Portugal, and the Thames in England. These rivers form a network of transportation and trade.

LESSON 2 REVIEW

Fact Follow-Up

1. What are the major landforms of Europe?
2. Why is the ocean important to Europeans?
3. What mountain ranges are in the Alpine Mountain systems?
4. What are the major rivers of Europe?

Think These Through

5. Is river transportation more or less important to Europe than to the United States? Explain your answer.
6. In what ways does the Northern European Plain benefit Europe?

Europe's Environment

LESSON 3

" I live in Rome, and I have a cousin who lives in New York City," explains thirteen-year-old Gina. "He always thought I lived farther south than he did, because we have such a warm climate here. But if you look on a globe, you'll see that Rome is just as far north as New York City."

Climate—A Key to Europe

The cousin's confusion is understandable. Distance from the Equator is a major influence on climate. So why don't two cities on the same latitude, such as New York and Rome, have similar climates?

When you examine the map below, other questions may puzzle you. The southernmost part of Europe lies north of North Carolina. In fact, much of Europe occupies the same latitudes as Canada.

LESSON PREVIEW

Key Ideas

- Much of Europe is located on the same latitudes as Canada, but Europe's climate is generally more moderate than Canada's.
- Europe's nearness to warm ocean waters is the chief reason for Europe's moderate climate.
- The geography and history of Europe shaped the continent to play a major role in world affairs.

Key Terms

Gulf Stream, North Atlantic Drift, Western Civilization

....

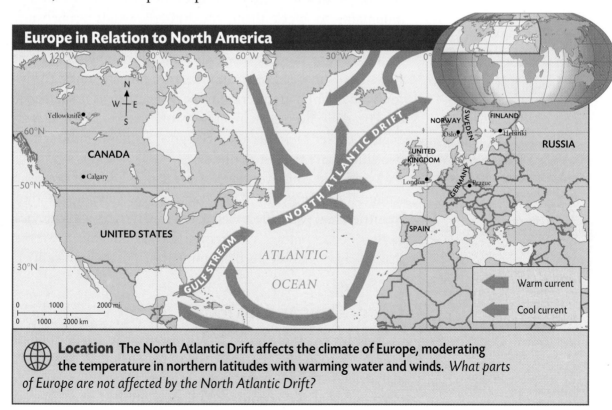

Europe in Relation to North America

Location The North Atlantic Drift affects the climate of Europe, moderating the temperature in northern latitudes with warming water and winds. *What parts of Europe are not affected by the North Atlantic Drift?*

The extremes of climate in Europe are shown by the continental climate of Moscow and the Mediterranean climate of Nice, France. *Why is Nice warmer in winter?*

Look at the map on page 29. Why are cities in Canada much colder than cities in Europe, even though they are located on similar latitudes? *Why is Prague colder than London?*

Average Temperatures in Canada and Europe		
Cities near 50°N	Jan.	July
Calgary	10°F	50°F
London	40°F	64°F
Prague	20°F	70°F
Cities near 60°N	Jan.	July
Yellowknife	-10°F	60°F
Oslo	25°F	65°F
Helsinki	21°F	64°F

Yet Europe's population is much greater than Canada's, and many Europeans live much farther north than most Canadians do. Despite its northerly location, most of Europe enjoys milder weather than North American regions at the same latitude.

Europe's mild climate comes partly from winds blowing eastward off the Atlantic Ocean's Gulf Stream. The **Gulf Stream** (called the **North Atlantic Drift** as it passes into northern waters) is an ocean current that carries warm water from the Gulf of Mexico to the western coast of Europe. With no high mountains to block them, the westerly winds bring warm weather and moisture to most of Europe.

In Western Europe, where the winds have the most effect, winters are short and mild. Summers are cool and rainy. Farther from the Atlantic in eastern Europe, the climate is much harsher. The daily average temperature of Moscow, Russia, is 24 degrees cooler in winter than Glasgow, Scotland, although the two cities share the same latitude.

Winds blowing over the North Atlantic Drift do not reach nations bordering the Mediterranean Sea. Climates in these countries, however, reflect their southerly latitudes and closeness to the Mediterranean. Winters are shorter and much warmer than in nations to the north. Summers are hot and much drier.

Geography and history

Geography and history have combined to shape modern Europe. Europe's people have lived in regions divided by natural barriers—rivers, mountains, and seas. Over thousands of years these barriers encouraged the development of a variety of languages and customs. Yet these barriers were not too great to prevent Europeans from exchanging ideas, trading with one another, or fighting one another in terrible, destructive wars.

Despite all its wars, Europeans brought together special combinations of ideas, institutions, religious faiths, and ways of life that came to be called **Western Civilization**. Europeans first carried Western Civilization to the Americas. Eventually, Western Civilization became influential throughout the world. All European nations, parts of Asia closely connected to Europe by Russia, and the Asian countries of the Pacific connected to Europe by trade, share in the history which created Western Civilization.

All European nations inherited their ideas from the past. Those ideas still shape modern Europe today.

Some of the most powerful influences shaping modern Europe date back hundreds of centuries. Ancient Greece and Rome collapsed long ago, but ideas from these ancient civilizations continue to live in Europe's culture today. Forms of government and commerce reflect those ancient ideas. Other influences on today's Europe sprang from the Middle Ages and the Renaissance. Modern influences come from Europe's contact with the world.

Europe's place in the world meant it became a great power. It also nearly destroyed itself in the twentieth century during World Wars I and II. Europe rebounded from the destruction of those wars and plays a major role in world affairs.

The double-deck bus in the Asian city of Hong Kong shows how European ways of life affect the rest of the world. *What is this European culture called?*

LESSON 3 REVIEW

Fact Follow-Up

1. Most of Europe has milder climate than the part of North America at the same latitudes. Why?
2. Describe the Mediterranean climate.
3. Define the term Western Civilization. Of what importance has it been to people in the Americas?

Think These Through

4. What is the importance of the Gulf Stream (North Atlantic Drift) to Europe? Is the Gulf Stream more important to Europe or the United States? Explain.
5. Why is Glasgow, Scotland, warmer than Moscow, though both are at the same latitude.

The Five Themes of Geography

Using Geography's Themes: Location

As geographers use the theme of **location** to describe where a place is on earth, you can too. All places on earth can be located in at least two ways.

Absolute Location

Absolute location describes the global address of a place on the surface of the earth. This global address may be stated in degrees of latitude and longitude.

Lines of **latitude** are imaginary circles drawn east and west around the globe. The **Equator** is the longest line of latitude, ringing the earth at its middle. The Equator is given the latitude measurement of 0°. The symbol "°" is used for **degree**, the unit for measuring latitude and longitude.

The Equator divides the earth into two equal parts. The area of the earth north of the Equator to the North Pole is the **Northern Hemisphere**. The area of the earth south of the Equator to the South Pole is the **Southern Hemisphere**. There are 90 degrees of latitude between the Equator and the North Pole and 90 degrees between the Equator and the South Pole. Europe is in the Northern Hemisphere.

All the other lines of latitude are called **parallels** because all points on any single line are the same distance from the Equator. The parallels give distance from the Equator in degrees. Each degree is equal to about

70 miles (113 km).

Remember that the Equator is 0°. So the greater the number of degrees, the farther the place is from the Equator.

The North Cape of Norway is at latitude 71° North. We write the location as 71° N, which means the northern part of Europe is 71 degrees north of the Equator.

Knowing how far north or south a place is from the Equator gives us only half the information we need to find its absolute location. Lines of **longitude** give us the other piece of information.

Lines of longitude are like lines of latitude because they are measured in degrees. But instead of being drawn parallel to the Equator, each meridian line runs north to south from the North Pole to the South Pole.

The **prime meridian** is the starting point for measuring longitude. It is assigned the longitude of 0°. Like the Equator, the prime meridian also splits the earth in half. The area of the earth west of the prime meridian is the **Western Hemisphere**. The area of the earth east of the prime meridian is the **Eastern Hemisphere**. Look at the map on page 19. In what hemisphere is most of Europe?

The other meridian lines around the globe give longitude measurements. These give distance in degrees east and west of the prime meridian. Meridian lines to the west of the prime meridian are longitude degrees west. Lines to the east of the prime meridian are longitude degrees east.

Together, the parallels of latitude and the meridians of longitude create an imaginary grid on the surface of the planet. With this grid we can exactly locate any spot on the earth's surface.

Relative Location

Relative location is not as precise as absolute location. The relative location of any place is described in relation to other earth features or places. For example, on page 20, Durham, England, is described as being "across the Atlantic from Durham, North Carolina." What other places could also be described as being "across the Atlantic from Durham, North Carolina"?

Consider the locations of two places near the prime meridian, London in England and Brussels in Belgium. Locate the two on the map on page 19. What is the global address (the absolute location) of each? The absolute locations of London and Brussels belong only to them. No other place on earth can share these locations.

Their relative locations can be stated in more general terms: (1) London is located in the southeast of England. (2) London is on the banks of the Thames River. Is that enough information to find London? Other places will fit the two facts that you have been given.

When a third item of information is added—that London is a huge city while other places are are much smaller—you will have all the information that is necessary.

If relative location is so much less precise, why use it? One answer is that you may not need a map. If you say that you will vacation

Geography's Themes: Location	
	Data
Absolute	
a) latitude	
b) longitude	
Relative (reference points or other information)	
a)	
b)	
c)	
d)	

near Moscow, Idaho, most will know that you are not headed for Russia.

In many instances, relative location is more helpful than absolute location. For example, you read that the Northern European Plain is one of the key places for food production, but you are not told its absolute location. What information would most quickly tell you where it is—its latitude and longitude? Or its relative location from deep in Russia all the way to southwest England?

Tourists use relative location in a variety of ways. If you are in London for one day of touring, do you want the absolute location of Edinburgh, Scotland, or information that the city is a five-hour train ride away? Such information could prompt you to visit nearby Oxford University instead.

To practice using the geographic theme of location, examine the map on page 19 and choose three different places in Europe. Begin making notes about the three places on three graphic organizers like the one above. Describe on each the absolute and relative locations of the places you have chosen.

Chapter 2 Review

LESSONS LEARNED

LESSON 1   European influence on life in the Americas can be seen almost every day in family names, the names of towns and cities, and traditions that are observed here in North Carolina and throughout the Americas.

LESSON 2   Europe is the third largest population center in the world. Yet its landmass is only a third larger than the United States, excluding Alaska and Hawaii. It is occupied by many mostly small nations each with its distinct language and customs.

LESSON 3   Europe is located in the northerly latitudes. Much of it is in the same latitudes as Canada, but winds blowing toward Europe over warm Atlantic Ocean water maintain a temperate climate for much of the land.

TIME FOR TERMS

dialects
peninsula
North Atlantic Drift

ethnic groups
Gulf Stream
Western Civilization

FACT FOLLOW-UP

1. What are five places in North Carolina named for people or places in Europe? Why do these North Carolina places have their names?
2. What portion of the world's population lives in Europe?
3. What portion of the earth's land lies in Europe?
4. Describe the relative location of Europe in relation to other places on earth.
5. What are the major landforms of Europe?
6. What are some major rivers in Europe?
7. How is the Mediterranean climate different from the climate of Western Europe?
8. What is the Gulf Stream (North Atlantic Drift), and what is its importance to Western Europe?

THINK THESE THROUGH

9. Why are there such close ties between Europe and the Americas? between England and North Carolina?
10. Which is more important for Europe—its coastline or its mountains? Explain your answer.
11. Europe has been described as being a giant peninsula of Asia. Is this description accurate or not? Explain.
12. Describe the relative location of Europe in as many ways as you can.
13. Which is more important for Europe—its coastline or its rivers? Explain.

SHARPENING SKILLS

14. Define the following terms found in the skill lesson:

location
latitude
degree
Southern Hemisphere
longitude
Western Hemisphere
relative location

absolute location
Equator
Northern Hemisphere
parallels
prime meridian
Eastern Hemisphere

15. Write a paragraph describing the location of a country in Europe, using at least half of the terms in the skill lesson.

PLACE LOCATION

Use the letters on the map to locate and name the following places in Europe:

16. the oceans and seas bordering Europe.

17. major city in England.

18. the mountain range that divides Spain and France.

19. the mountain range that runs south through Italy.

20. part of this range is found in Switzerland.

21. three letters showing the location of the Northern European Plain.

22. mountains found throughout Norway and in part of Sweden.

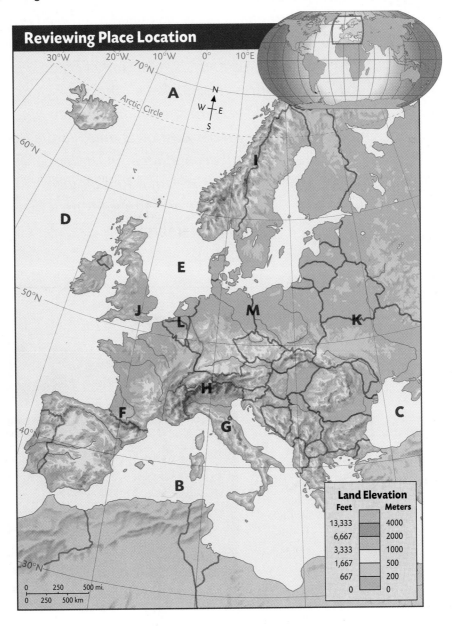

Reviewing Place Location

Land Elevation		
Feet		**Meters**
13,333		4000
6,667		2000
3,333		1000
1,667		500
667		200
0		0

CHAPTER 3

Europe's Foundations

The next time you take a quarter out of your pocket, look closely at the coin. Just above the eagle's head are three Latin words: E Pluribus Unum—"Out of Many, One." That motto of our country expresses the diversity and unity of the United States.

The Latin phrase also makes a connection to ancient Rome, where Latin was the spoken and written language. Our representative government owes much to the Roman republic, and an even earlier Greek democracy. Before Greek and Roman ideas reached the Americas, Europeans used them in building their own nations.

CHAPTER PREVIEW

LESSON 1
Europe's Foundations in Ancient Greece
Ancient Greece is the place where many of modern-day Europe's ideas began.

LESSON 2
Europe's Foundations in Ancient Rome
The Roman Empire expanded into Europe. Through Rome, Europe learned about Greek ideas and Christianity.

LESSON 3
Europe After the Fall of Rome
After the Roman Empire collapsed, Europe had to begin building its own civilization. The building began in a time called the Middle Ages.

Acropolis in Greece

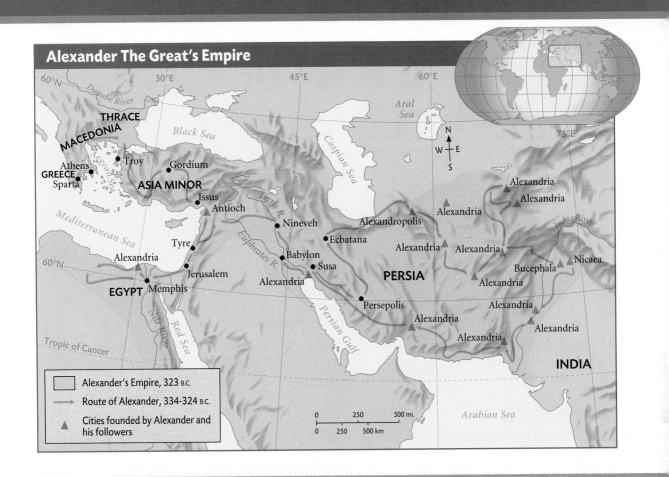

Alexander The Great's Empire

THRACE
MACEDONIA
GREECE
Athens
Sparta
Troy
Gordium
ASIA MINOR
Issus
Antioch
Tyre
Jerusalem
EGYPT Memphis
Alexandria
Nineveh
Babylon
Susa
Alexandria
Persepolis
Alexandropolis
Ecbatana
PERSIA
Alexandria
Alexandria
Alexandria
Alexandria
Alexandria
Alexandria
Alexandria
Alexandria
Alexandria
Bucephala
Nicaea
INDIA

Danube River
Black Sea
Aegean Sea
Mediterranean Sea
Tigris R.
Euphrates R.
Caspian Sea
Aral Sea
Red Sea
Nile River
Persian Gulf
Arabian Sea
Indus River

60°N 30°E 45°E 60°E 75°E
Tropic of Cancer

N W E S

Alexander's Empire, 323 B.C.

Route of Alexander, 334-324 B.C.

Cities founded by Alexander and his followers

0   250   500 mi.
0   250   500 km

Europe's Foundations in Ancient Greece

Ancient Greek artists painted images of important events on vases. *What does this vase show?*

A crowd of mourners slowly gathered in Athens, Greece, as men lifted coffins from funeral carts. As the workmen finished, a man named Pericles (PERH·uh·kleeze) stepped forward and began to speak. He praised the dead and spoke of their defense of Greek democracy.

O ur constitution is called a democracy because power is in the hands not of a minority but of the whole people.... Future generations will wonder at us, as the present age wonders at us now.

Pericles' Funeral Oration—his speech honoring the dead—reflected the pride that Greeks took in governing themselves. He also was right in predicting that future generations would not forget what Greeks had accomplished. Today, about 2,500 years after Pericles spoke, ideas from ancient Greece shape our world.

The Greek World of City-States

Most early civilizations were united under a single ruler. The ancient Greeks lived in small, independent areas that were constantly at war with one another.

Greeks organized these independent areas around cities. Together, a city and surrounding countryside was called a **city-state**. Greeks called a city-state *polis*, which forms the root of our word "metropolis."

The independence of each city-state was always threatened by other city-states seeking to gain strength. In this struggle to keep their cities free, the Greeks developed a deep concern for the rights and responsibilities of individual citizens.

The Greek city-states could remain independent because some were located on islands and those on the rugged indented coast were isolated. The mountains that reached down to the sea

Greek Alphabet

Phoenician	⟨A⟩	⟨⊘⟩	⟨⊃⟩	⟨△⟩	⟨ⰶ⟩		⟨#⟩	⟨Ⅎ⟩	⟨Ⅎ⟩	⟨L⟩
Greek	A	B	Γ	Δ	Ɛ	F	Θ	⟨⟩	K	Λ
Modern	A	B	C	D	E	F	H	I	K	L

discouraged farming and internal trade. The rough mountain slopes also made movement on land difficult. City-states did not unite until Athens grew to dominate the hundreds of Greek city-states.

Greece's islands and coasts created many natural ports (see map below). The Greeks built ships and sailed throughout the Mediterranean. They proved to be good sailors and merchants. They made money by trading such products as olive oil for wheat.

As they traded, the ancient Greeks learned and shared ideas. From the Phoenicians, another trading people in the Mediterranean, the Greeks adopted an alphabet and learned to use coins for money. They brought home ideas from others about government, religion, and nature.

The Greeks used the alphabet of the Phoenicians to create their own. That alphabet influenced our modern way of writing. *Which Greek and Phoenician letters are most like our own?*

Greek Democracy

The exchange of ideas was easy in a city-state. A mild, dry climate encouraged people to spend time outside, where they became acquainted.

At the center of each city-state was an **acropolis** (uh · KRAHP · uh · liss), or hilltop fortress. Men gathered here for conversations about the latest gossip and serious matters of politics, government, and religion.

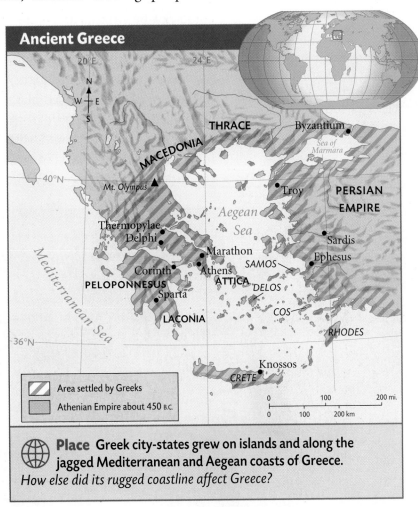

Ancient Greece

Area settled by Greeks

Athenian Empire about 450 B.C.

🌐 **Place** Greek city-states grew on islands and along the jagged Mediterranean and Aegean coasts of Greece. *How else did its rugged coastline affect Greece?*

The connections between ancient Greek architecture such as the Parthenon, and modern buildings, such as the state capitol building in Raleigh (inset), are clear. *How else has ancient Greece affected the modern world?*

Athens was one of the first city-states to develop democratic government. Democracy, as practiced there by the time of Pericles in 450 B.C., was **direct democracy**. In this system, all citizens participated directly in government. Citizens of small New England towns in the United States still engage in direct democracy.

Citizens of Greek Democracy

Greek popular wisdom taught that for direct democracy to work, a city-state should be small enough to walk across in a day. Aristotle—a famous Greek philosopher—insisted that all citizens of a polis should know one another by sight.

This requirement was not as difficult as it might seem. Not everyone living in a polis was a citizen. A citizen was a free man whose father had been a citizen. Women, foreigners, and slaves could not be citizens and were excluded from government. In the fifth century B.C., the population of Athens totaled 350,000. Only 20,000 of this number enjoyed the rights of citizenship.

The citizens of a polis gathered to make political decisions in the *ecclēsia* (ay·CLAY·see·ah), or assembly. Every citizen had an obligation to take part in the debates and vote on public issues. Not everyone could vote in the polis. Yet the idea of individual responsibility in government became a powerful tradition shaping democracy throughout the world.

The Visual Arts

The Greeks built the Parthenon when ancient Athens was in her glory. Stately marble columns supported a rectangular roof. The columns still stand, glittering in the sun, creating a sense of lightness and height.

Visitors to Athens want to see the Parthenon. Greek achievements in architecture, sculpture, and pottery making continue to be admired in Europe and the Americas. Countless public buildings and even private houses modeled on Greek designs are still being built.

Greek sculptors and potters also loved balance and beauty. This idealism is reflected in whatever they did. Greek statues of human figures, for example, never display anyone with an ounce of extra fat or a crooked nose. Sculptors gave everyone the perfect body.

Many museums today display statues carved by Greeks, usually from a wonderfully white marble. Some museums contain Greek pottery decorated with heroic warriors, athletes, or chariot races.

Other Greek Contributions

Doctors today take the Hippocratic oath before they begin to practice medicine. Most teachers know about the Socratic method of teaching. Advanced math students learn the Pythagorean theorem. These examples of learning are Greek contributions to world knowledge.

Ancient Greece was a place where people were intensely curious about the world and the role of humans living in it. Greek thinkers, or **philosophers**, believed that individuals could discover important truths by investigating the world and by reasoning. Greek philosophers laid the foundations of modern scientific methods and made basic discoveries in medicine, mathematics, and astronomy.

The Survival of Greek Achievements

Before Greek civilization collapsed, its achievements spread around the eastern Mediterranean Sea and even reached India.

Greek sculptors wanted to show flawless human forms, as this statue of a discus thrower illustrates. *In what other forms of art did Greeks portray their ideals of beauty and balance?*

Drama and Literature

Politics and government were not the Greeks' only interests. If you visited Athens today, you would find the ruins of a huge outdoor theater that seated 20,000.

Because theaters were so large, actors wore huge masks so audiences could see the character and emotions they were portraying. A funnel was built into the mouth of the masks to amplify the actors' voices.

The plays performed so long ago became part of another tradition handed down to later centuries. When you reach high school, you might read parts of a Greek **tragedy**, a play in which a major character suffers a disaster, or a **comedy**, a play that poked fun at famous people, ideas, or social customs.

Antigone is one of the most famous examples of Greek tragedies. It tells the story of a courageous young woman, Antigone, whose brother has been killed while disobeying the king. Antigone is determined to bury her brother, but her action violates the king's law. The king has said that anyone burying a traitor shall be executed.

Antigone decides to disobey the king, because she believes that her duty to her brother is greater than her duty to the king. Antigone

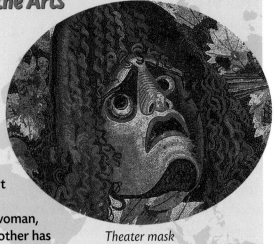

Theater mask

is executed for disobeying the law.

Antigone raised questions that we still debate. What must a person do if his or her duty to the government conflicts with deeply held personal beliefs?

For that reason, the play continues to be read and performed.

An extraordinary Greek general, Alexander the Great, built an empire that spread eastward to the edges of India (see map, page 37). But the Greeks themselves did not carry their accomplishments into Europe. Much of that work would be done by the people of the Roman Empire.

LESSON 1 REVIEW

Fact Follow-Up
1. What was a city-state? How did the physical characteristics of Greece encourage the independence of city-states?
2. How was the invention of direct democracy linked to the city-state?
3. What were some Greek accomplishments?

How did relative location influence those accomplishments?

Think These Through
4. Which Greek ideas do you think have been most important? Explain why.
5. How did the physical characteristics of Greece influence its culture? Explain how.

Europe's Foundations in Ancient Rome

"Greece has conquered her rude conqueror," wrote the Roman poet Horace. By "rude conqueror," Horace meant his own city of Rome.

When Roman forces conquered Greece, they shipped home thousands of Greek statues. Roman architects studied and then copied the design of Greek buildings. Roman writers adopted Greek literary forms, adapting the Greek style to their Latin language. Wealthy Romans employed educated Greek slaves to tutor their sons.

No wonder Horace thought that in winning control of Greece, Rome itself had been conquered. On every side he saw Greek influences.

Founding the Roman Empire

At the height of its power 2,000 years ago, Rome ruled a vast area (see the map on page 44). Roman lands surrounded the Mediterranean and Black Seas. To the north in Europe, Rome governed territories that now are the Balkans, Austria, some of

A Roman frieze, or picture carved into a wall, shows Roman activity. *What do you think is happening in this frieze? Compare it to the Greek vase on page 38.*

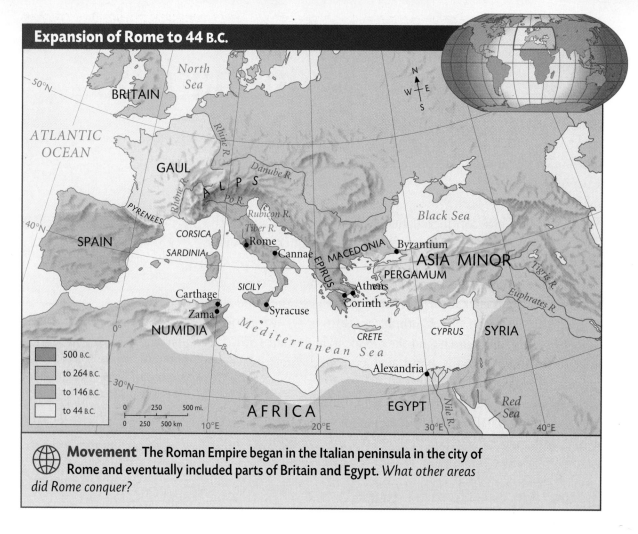

Expansion of Rome to 44 B.C.

Legend:
- 500 B.C.
- to 264 B.C.
- to 146 B.C.
- to 44 B.C.

Movement The Roman Empire began in the Italian peninsula in the city of Rome and eventually included parts of Britain and Egypt. *What other areas did Rome conquer?*

Germany, all of France, Belgium, The Netherlands, and the southern half of Britain.

Yet Rome, much as ancient Greece, rose from humble beginnings. About 2,750 years ago, some bands of people moved from the North into the Italian peninsula. They settled in several small villages that grew together to form Rome, the city that eventually built the empire.

The people who founded Rome were farmers and shepherds. Their struggles with neighboring groups of people shaped a belief in duty, discipline, and patriotism. Roman armies grew into a strong fighting force.

Rome's founders also recognized that they could use ideas from more advanced civilizations. Early in their history they came into contact with the Greeks, who had built a colony on the Italian peninsula. Roman leaders ordered careful study of Greek ideas, architecture, and government.

An Expanding Roman World

The powerful Roman army defeated one enemy after another. Soldiers were trained in the use of slings, javelins, spears, and swords. These forces were divided into **legions**, army units that numbered about 6,000 men each. The legions were divided into smaller units that could be moved around swiftly. This freedom of movement usually gave Roman forces an advantage over the massed troops of its enemies.

Rome began to build its empire in Italy. Roman forces battled rivals for control of the peninsula. By 264 B.C., Rome commanded the Italian peninsula. Rome then turned to conquests in North Africa, Spain, Gaul (modern-day France), Greece, and the lands at the eastern ends of the Mediterranean.

Rome organized its foreign lands into provinces. Each was headed by a governor who directed tax collections and organized the defense of the province. The new rulers did not try to change local customs, religions, or government. This policy made Roman domination less painful to the conquered people.

Each conquered province, however, was expected to help make Rome richer and more powerful. Spain became for Rome a source of wine, fruit, gold, silver, iron, and horses. Gaul produced glass, pottery, wool, wine, and precious metals. In this way, Rome drew on an amazingly varied quantity of raw materials and luxuries.

Roman rulers organized the defense of conquered lands. Hadrian's Wall, built in A.D. 122 to defend against northern invaders, still stands in Britain. *What other duties did Roman leaders have?*

To bring these treasures home—and to help keep control over the empire—Rome built a remarkable communications network. Roman ships sailed regularly to ports of conquered lands. Goods and people moved by land on new Roman roads. Some of these roads were built so well that they are still in use today.

Roman Government

Our nation's government contains Roman influences. Rome was too big to be governed by direct democracy. Therefore, the Romans built democratic principles into a **republic**. This meant the people elected representatives to carry out their wishes in the government. Both the Roman republic and Greek democracy were governments of the people.

Timeline of Greek and Roman Civilizations

800 B.C. Greeks adopt Phoenician alphabet.

Greek temple at Delphi

700 B.C. Greeks set up colonies.

447 B.C. Construction of the Parthenon begins.

323 B.C. Alexander the Great dies at 33.

| 900 B.C. | 800 B.C. | 700 B.C. | 600 B.C. | 500 B.C. | 400 B.C. | 300 B.C. |

750 B.C. Emergence of Greek city-states.

509 B.C. Romans establish a republic. Women enjoy more rights in Rome.

350 B.C. Macedonia invades Greece.

✓The Roman Republic lasted 500 years (see time line, below). During that time Rome grew from a city-state into a world power. The republic's government came to be centered in two representative bodies, including an upper house called the Senate. The representatives gathered for debate and decision making. Every year the Senate chose two consuls, or officials, to administer the laws that had been passed. Europe's modern-day cabinet system had its origins in this practice.

Rome made still another important contribution to modern government. In 451 B.C., Rome's first written law code was carved on 12 stone tablets. This began the development of law codes that defined people's responsibilities and rights. These codes contributed to the development of **constitutional government**, or government under law, in Europe. Then the idea traveled to the rest of the world.

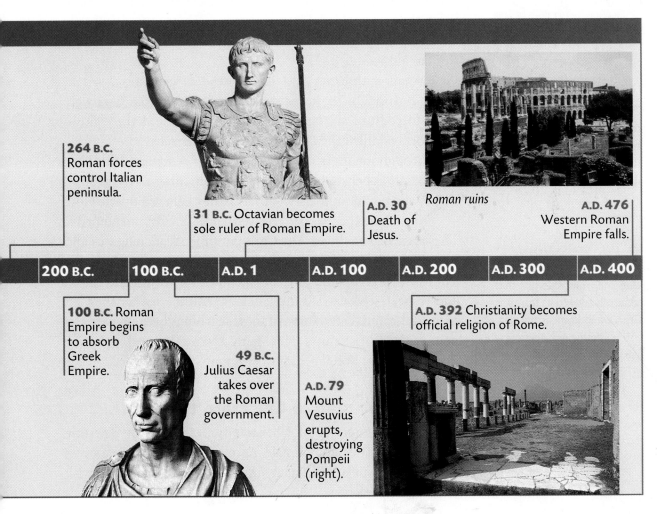

264 B.C. Roman forces control Italian peninsula.

31 B.C. Octavian becomes sole ruler of Roman Empire.

A.D. 30 Death of Jesus.

Roman ruins

A.D. 476 Western Roman Empire falls.

200 B.C.	100 B.C.	A.D. 1	A.D. 100	A.D. 200	A.D. 300	A.D. 400

100 B.C. Roman Empire begins to absorb Greek Empire.

49 B.C. Julius Caesar takes over the Roman government.

A.D. 79 Mount Vesuvius erupts, destroying Pompeii (right).

A.D. 392 Christianity becomes official religion of Rome.

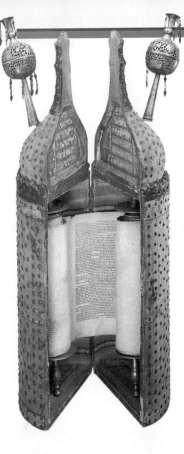

The Torah is Jewish Scripture. It contains laws and wisdom of Jewish faith, including the Jews' covenant with God. *What was their covenant?*

What would YOU do?

One important tradition that comes directly to us from ancient Greece and Rome is the idea of voting. Voting gives people who live in a democratic society a say in how their society is run.

Imagine that you could run for office in an election. How would you get people to vote for you?

Judaism

You have read that Rome allowed conquered peoples to practice their religions within the empire. This included Judaism, the great religious tradition followed by Jewish people.

The Hebrews, or Jews, had come to believe long before the Roman Empire existed that they had a **covenant**, or binding agreement, with God. They had accepted God as the ruler of Heaven and Earth. In return, God had made the Jews the chosen people on Earth.

Jews once had been wandering shepherds from Palestine, an area at the eastern end of the Mediterranean Sea. In about 1025 B.C. they formed the kingdom of Israel in Palestine. The kingdom flourished for many years under two great rulers, David and Solomon.

After Solomon's death, Israel was defeated. The Jews had to leave their homeland for many years. They were eventually allowed to return to Israel. It was then that they came under Roman authority.

Roman authorities and Jewish leaders generally lived in peace. But in A.D. 70, Rome crushed a Jewish revolt. Jews were again forced to leave Israel. The scattering of Jews throughout the world is called the **Diaspora** (dy·AS·peh·rah).

Throughout all their troubles, the Jews remained faithful to their religious beliefs. Judaism differed from other early religions. The Jews were monotheistic—that is, they believed in one God.

From Moses the Jews had received God's Ten Commandments. These guided their lives. The Commandments are religious and moral laws. They forbid stealing, lying, cheating, and murder. They also urge people to treat one another with justice, love, and respect. Jews carried these beliefs with them after they left their homeland. Later, some of these teachings became part of a new faith, Christianity. This faith spread beyond Palestine throughout the Roman Empire (see map, page 49).

Rise and Spread of Christianity

Jesus, the founder of Christianity, was born in Palestine while it was under Roman rule. According to Christian sources called the **Gospels**, Jesus as a young man studied with Jewish scholars and teachers.

When he was about thirty, Jesus began to preach. His message was rooted in the Jewish faith in one God, the God of the Hebrews. He also upheld the Ten Commandments as God's law. Jesus taught about God's goodness and mercy. He spoke of a forgiving God. God was the loving father of all people, rich and poor, Jew and non-Jew.

Jesus urged repentance, which means to ask for forgiveness of sins. He told the Jews, according to the Gospels, that "no one can come to the Father, except through me."

Jesus attracted many followers. As Jesus' following grew, Roman officials worried that he might provoke an uprising. In A.D. 33 Jesus was arrested and sentenced to die by crucifixion, a Roman method of execution.

Jesus' followers believed that he was the Son of God and that

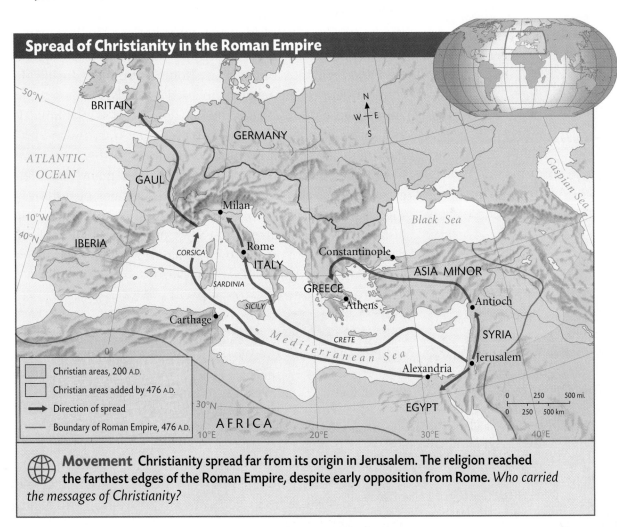

Spread of Christianity in the Roman Empire

Christian areas, 200 A.D.
Christian areas added by 476 A.D.
Direction of spread
Boundary of Roman Empire, 476 A.D.

Movement Christianity spread far from its origin in Jerusalem. The religion reached the farthest edges of the Roman Empire, despite early opposition from Rome. *Who carried the messages of Christianity?*

Roman coins showed images of Roman emperors and Roman gods. *How did Christians look upon Roman gods? How did this affect Rome's treatment of Christianity?*

he rose from the dead, or resurrected, three days after his crucifixion. Paul, an early convert, traveled in the Roman Empire, spreading Jesus' message. Those who followed Jesus' teachings became known as Christians, or followers of Christ. That name came from the Greek word *Christos,* or messiah.

Rome became increasingly suspicious. Christians refused to show respect for Roman gods. As a result, thousands of Christians suffered persecution and death. Then Rome suddenly supported Christianity's growth.

In A.D. 312, on the eve of battle, the Roman Emperor Constantine dreamed of a cross. In his dream, Constantine understood that if he took the cross as his symbol, he would win the battle. After his victory, Constantine converted to Christianity and allowed Christians freedom of worship.

In the late 300s, Christianity became the official religion of the Roman Empire. Under Roman rule, Christianity spread throughout the Mediterranean and northward into Europe (see map, page 49).

Other religious practices in Rome continued during the Christian era. These religions focused on gods, goddesses, and animal and natural spirits. These religions had special holidays and feast days. Christian leaders placed their holidays and feast days on the same days. Eventually, people stopped practicing the older religions. Christianity developed over many years and grew stronger through a well-organized system of authority. The highest Christian officials were bishops. Eventually, the bishop of Rome became the head of the Church. He took the name of **pope**, or father of the Church. It was this Church that carried the Christian faith into Europe.

LESSON 2 REVIEW

Fact Follow-Up

1. How would you describe the lands of the Roman Empire at its height?
2. In what ways did the Romans learn from the Greeks?
3. How does a republic differ from direct democracy?
4. What characteristics of Judaism made it different from other major religions?
5. What characteristics of Christianity linked it to Judaism? set it apart from Judaism?

Think These Through

6. Was it true that "Greece... conquered her rude conqueror"? Why or why not?
7. In what ways did the Roman Empire contribute to the spread of Christianity?

Europe After the Fall of Rome

No land without a lord, and no lord without land.

This saying sums up Western Europe in the **Middle Ages**—the period of about 1,000 years between the decline of Rome in the A.D. 400s and the beginning of the modern European world in about A.D. 1450.

The Fall of Rome

The once mighty Roman Empire did not suddenly collapse. By the A.D. 200s, it had become so large that Rome could no longer provide needed leadership. Rival leaders battled one another for power. Remote areas began to govern themselves. A Germanic tribe called the Goths took advantage of the confusion and invaded Roman territory.

In an effort to save the empire, Rome divided its territory into eastern and western halves. By reducing the empire's size, Rome hoped that its empire would be easier to manage. This step was only partly successful. The eastern half, ruled from Constantinople, survived for 1,000 years. The western half governed by Rome collapsed.

The areas of Europe under Roman authority soon felt the impact. No longer was there a single governmental authority. Europe became a collection of small parcels of land, each ruled by a different **lord**, or nobleman with military power. The unity of the ancient world had disappeared by A.D. 500.

LESSON PREVIEW

Key Ideas
- The Roman Empire's collapse left part of Europe in disorder and without protection.
- The Roman Catholic Church remained a strong unifying force.
- The feudal system became a new form of government.

Key Terms
Middle Ages, lord, barter, feudalism, vassals, knights, serfs

This tapestry shows lords and ladies at an outdoor banquet. After the fall of Rome, many lords controlled small areas of land throughout Europe. *How was this different from how the Roman Empire controlled land?*

Disorder in the Middle Ages

Rome had provided part of Europe with protection. After Rome's collapse, invaders took over territory that had been in the Roman Empire. Roman roads, once the connections for communication and commerce, were no longer safe to travel. Cities and towns became isolated.

Without trade, people in the towns had no work. They drifted to the country, where they could grow enough food to feed themselves. In rural areas, small communities survived on the crops they raised and the goods they traded with neighbors.

People stopped using money almost completely. Instead, they bartered. To **barter** is to exchange goods. A farmer with

---

EYEWITNESS TO HISTORY

Charlemagne

From 768 to 814, Charlemagne ruled an empire in Western Europe that included all of today's France, Belgium, and Switzerland and parts of Italy, Austria, Germany, and Poland. For a few years, Charlemagne brought peace and prosperity. He was a hero in Europe.

BRITAIN

CHARLEMAGNE'S EMPIRE

ATLANTIC OCEAN

SPAIN

The most famous description of Charlemagne and one of his bravest knights is *The Song of Roland.* This great poem was written during the Middle Ages. It describes the heroic actions of Charlemagne's knights during a battle.

This great poem was written in French, not Latin. Europe's knights memorized it and sometimes sang some of its verses as they went into battle. Roland's bravery and loyalty became the goals of knights everywhere. Charlemagne's empire ended with his death. Europe was again split into many small units.

Charlemagne is crowned emperor

crops would trade some of his crops for wool he needed for weaving into clothing, for example. There was no law and no protection against crime. When raiders attacked isolated farm communities, the farms were defenseless.

People also had no defense against the bubonic plague, spread by disease-carrying fleas. The "Black Death" swept through Europe from port cities inland to other cities and the countryside.

Feudalism

Much of the western European mainland was briefly reunited around A.D. 800 under a Germanic king named Charlemagne (SHAHR·luh·mayn). The king established an efficient govern-

Charlemagne's empire reflected life in the Middle Ages. Charlemagne was a warrior king. His knights, skilled horsemen loyal to the emperor, were important in building and defending the empire.

In the poem, Roland commands knights who are surrounded and killed by the enemy. Roland himself prepares to die, but he wants Charlemagne (Charles) to see how brave and loyal he is even as he faced death.

The death of Roland

He turns his face toward the infidel
For greatly he desires that Charles should say,
With all his men: 'Roland, the noble count,
Roland the brave has died a conqueror.'

Fourteenth century French tapestry showing knights at battle

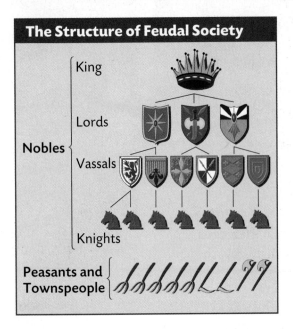

The Structure of Feudal Society

King

Nobles
- Lords
- Vassals
- Knights

Peasants and Townspeople

Every person knew his or her place in feudal society. *Who had the most power? Who had the least? Which group do you think had the most people?*

ment. He encouraged the spread of Christianity and helped improve education. Although his kingdom broke up after his death, Charlemagne helped lay the foundations of civilization in the Middle Ages.

The people of the Middle Ages came to be dominated by feudalism. **Feudalism** was a system of government under a local nobleman, or lord, who was bound with other local lords by ties of loyalty to a king (see chart at left).

Under feudalism, the lord governed only the people on his own land. Sometimes the king united the local nobility in a common defense against invading forces. This was an improvement over having each lord attempt to act alone in defending his land and people.

In a feudal society, each person had a fixed place. Powerful local lords acted independently of the king, but they recognized his leadership and their duty to serve him. The local lords divided their land among **vassals**, or lesser nobles. Vassals then divided their land among **knights**, or still lesser nobles, who served in war as mounted warriors.

The common people, mostly peasant farmers, tilled the land in return for the lord's protection. Sometimes peasants were called **serfs**. They were not slaves, but had to stay on the land and serve their lords.

The Roman Catholic Church

When Europe divided into small independent feudal states, the Roman Catholic Church became the single unifying force on the continent. The Catholic Church played a powerful role in nearly everyone's social and personal life. Most Europeans were baptized, married, and buried by Catholic priests.

The Church preserved the tradition of classical learning. Classical learning consists of the literature, philosophy, and science of ancient Greece and Rome. In monasteries throughout Europe, monks studied and transcribed manuscripts containing the work of the ancient scholars, so that their ideas would not be lost. Later, the Church also founded the first universities in Europe.

The Church also held great political power. If a lord refused to obey the commands of the Church, the pope might punish him with excommunication, which kept him from Church activities. All of the churches on his land would be closed, and neither he, his family, nor anyone within his territory could be baptized, married, or buried with the Church's blessing.

Jewish communities lived under discrimination and persecution in Europe. They were forbidden to own land. They could work only in certain professions. Christians often blamed Jews when disease or natural disasters struck. Yet Jewish communities remained intact and preserved their traditions. Jewish scholars continued to make contributions to learning for all Europeans.

During the Middle Ages, Europeans spent a lot of time and money building church buildings, such as the abbey at Mont-Saint-Michel in France. *How did the Church hold power during this time?*

LESSON 3 REVIEW

Fact Follow-Up
1. Describe reasons for the fall of Rome.
2. How did feudalism serve the needs of Europeans after Roman authority was gone?
3. Describe the activities of the Roman Catholic Church in Europe during the Middle Ages.
4. What part did Jews play in European society during the Middle Ages?

Think These Through
5. The feudal system lasted about 1,000 years after Rome fell. How were Europeans served by the feudal system and the Church in these years? Explain.
6. Which group seems to have been more powerful in Europe's Middle Ages—the great lords or the Church's clergy? Explain your answer.

The Five Themes
of Geography

Using Geography's Themes: Place

Place, one of the Five Themes of Geography, asks the questions "What is special about this place? What makes this place different from all other places on earth?" In this chapter you have read about two special places: Athens and Rome. To learn more about the theme of place, we will explore the physical and cultural characteristics of the two cities.

Physical Characteristics of Place

The physical characteristics of the two places include their climate, landforms, and vegetation. Look at the map of Europe on page 27 and at the maps of the Greek and Roman Empires on pages 39 and 49. Find clues about the physical characteristics of Athens and Rome.

What do these maps tell you about the landforms and bodies of water of the two places? What information can you get from reading the text about climate and vegetation? What can you learn from the photos on pages 37 and 57 about the physical characteristics of Athens and Rome?

Once you have gathered information about the physical geography of Athens and Rome, you might display this information in a graphic organizer like the one at the top of the next column. Or, you could organize the information by category: landforms, climate, and vegetation.

Physical Characteristics	
Athens	**Rome**

Cultural Characteristics of Place

Another way of answering the questions ("What is special about this place? What makes this place different from all other places on earth?") is to examine the cultural characteristics of places. Culture is generally defined as the way of life of a people.

The cultural characteristics of Athens and Rome would include the ethnic make-up of the cities, religion, foods, economic activity, family life, education, language(s),

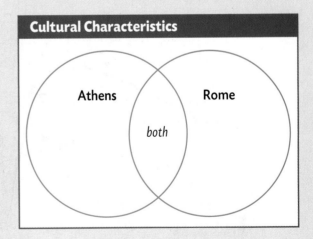

Cultural Characteristics

Athens   Rome

both

political organization, forms of government, and so forth. Information about the cultural characteristics of places can come from maps and charts and from a careful reading of text materials. Graphic organizers similar to the one at the bottom of page 56 (called a Venn diagram) can be constructed for Athens and Rome. Whenever you find the cultural characteristics of the two places are alike, enter those items in the organizer marked "both."

Now that you have identified the physical and cultural characteristics of place for Athens and Rome, you are ready to bring your findings together in a graphic organizer like the one on the right. Compare the notes that you have made with those of a classmate. Have you found the same things or are your findings different?

You may wish to add information from other sources. Other chapters in the text will be of help. Consult the table of contents and index to find the information you need.

Encyclopedias, atlases, and other library references can also help you. Your graphic organizer should now look like the one below:

Geography's Themes: Place		
Characteristics	Athens	Rome
I. Physical		
A.		
B.		
C.		
II. Cultural		
A. Similar		
1.		
2.		
3.		
B. Different		
1.		
2.		
3.		

Chapter 3 Review

LESSON 1 Two ancient Mediterranean civilizations contributed vital institutions and ideas to the building of modern Europe. Their ideas help you understand today's Europe.

LESSON 2 Ancient Greece laid foundations for basic institutions of government. In other areas, the Greeks explored many fields of knowledge—medicine, science, math, and the arts. The Romans absorbed these ideas and made contributions of their own. It was from Rome that Europe learned what these ancients had accomplished. It was also through Rome that Europe learned about Judeo-Christian religious traditions.

LESSON 3 After Rome fell, Europe invented a new social and political order called feudalism during the Middle Ages. Yet the Roman Catholic Church remained a strong presence. It helped preserve Christianity and much of the classic learning of Greece and Rome.

TIME FOR TERMS

city-state
direct democracy
tragedy
legions
constitutional government
Diaspora
pope
lord
feudalism
knights

acropolis
philosophers
comedy
republic
covenant
Gospels
Middle Ages
barter
vassals
serfs

FACT FOLLOW-UP

1. Show the differences and similarities between Greek democracy and Roman republicanism in a Venn diagram.
2. How did the physical features of Greece affect the development of the city-states?
3. What did it mean to be a citizen of Athens?
4. What were some of the rights and responsibilties of the citizens of Athens? In what ways are the ancient Greek ideas about citizenship similar to ours?
5. How did Rome expand into an empire?
6. What characteristics of democracies originated in the Roman Republic?
7. What happened to Europe after the collapse of Rome?
8. Why was the Church so powerful during the feudal period?

THINK THESE THROUGH

9. Imagine that you could have lived in ancient Greece or Rome. Which would you have chosen, and why?
10. Use *Antigone* or some other Greek art form to explain how the people of ancient Greece placed great importance on the individual.
11. All citizens took part in the government's decisions in ancient Greece. Rome is described in the text as having preserved democracy as a republican form of government. Can you explain why this was done? Was the Roman idea in your opinion a good one, or should the Romans have used the Greek form of direct democracy? Explain.
12. "The Church united Europe during the feudal

age." Is this statement accurate? Explain.

13. Which had the more "civilized" society, Greece, Rome, or feudal Europe? Explain.

14. What has been the most important legacy of Greece? of Rome? Explain.

15. Was Rome conquered, or did Rome fall because of its own actions? Explain.

SHARPENING SKILLS

16. Which is more important in contrasting Athens and Rome—physical or cultural characteristics of place? Explain.

17. Athens was very near the sea and Rome was not. How did these physical characteristics affect their societies?

18. How did the Venn diagram help you organize the cultural characteristics of place? What other graphic organizers could you have used?

PLACE LOCATION

Use the letters on the map to locate the following places linked to the spread of Christianity:

19. Jerusalem.

20. the city that became the headquarters of the Christian Church.

21. the modern nation where the headquarters of the Catholic Church is located.

22. the country that is modern-day France.

23. the body of water that was closest to the Roman Empire.

24. Britain.

25. Black Sea.

26. Greece.

27. the area where Christianity did not spread.

28. Spain.

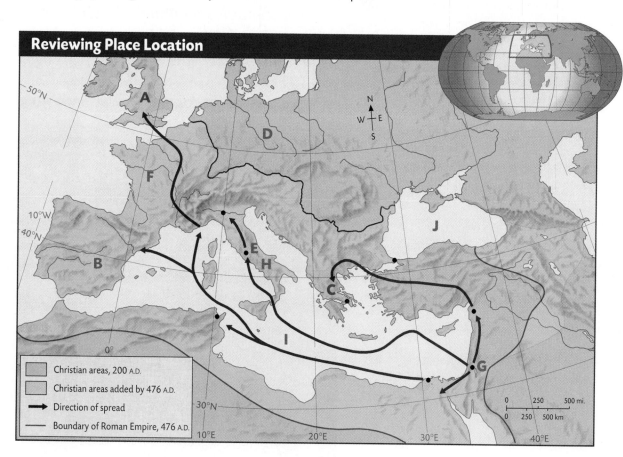

Reviewing Place Location

Christian areas, 200 A.D.

Christian areas added by 476 A.D.

Direction of spread

Boundary of Roman Empire, 476 A.D.

Modern Europe Takes Shape

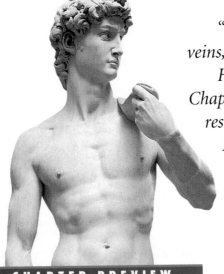

"You can see the blood flowing through their veins," exclaimed Pier Giorgio Bonetto.

High on a scaffold above the altar of the Sistine Chapel in the Vatican, Bonetto was carefully restoring a painting that covers the ceiling, Michelangelo's Last Judgment. *The painting's human figures seemed to come alive as the grime of centuries fell away.*

Michelangelo's paintings and sculptures still have the grandeur and power that this Renaissance master gave them 500 years ago.

CHAPTER PREVIEW

LESSON 1
Renaissance and Reformation
Modern Europe was shaped by the Renaissance—when Greek and Roman ideas were revived—and the Reformation—the birth of Protestantism.

LESSON 2
The Rise of Modern Nations
Europe's modern nations began to take shape 500 years ago. Ambitious kings extended their rule over larger and larger areas of land.

LESSON 3
The Expansion of Europe
The emerging nations explored the world and conquered North and South America. They opened trade with other parts of the world.

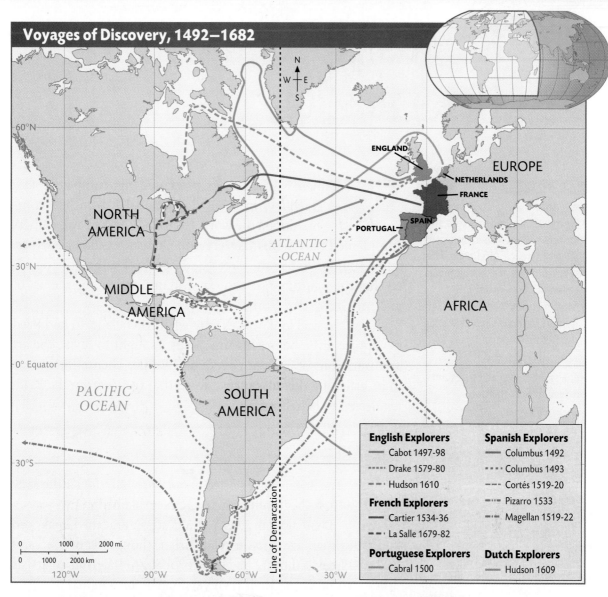

Voyages of Discovery, 1492–1682

N
W · E
S

60°N

ENGLAND
NETHERLANDS
FRANCE
PORTUGAL — SPAIN

EUROPE

NORTH
AMERICA

ATLANTIC
OCEAN

30°N

MIDDLE
AMERICA

AFRICA

0° Equator

PACIFIC
OCEAN

SOUTH
AMERICA

30°S

Line of Demarcation

| 0 | 1000 | 2000 mi. |
| 0 | 1000 | 2000 km |

120°W   90°W   60°W   30°W

English Explorers
— Cabot 1497-98
···· Drake 1579-80
– – Hudson 1610

French Explorers
— Cartier 1534-36
–·– La Salle 1679-82

Portuguese Explorers
— Cabral 1500

Spanish Explorers
— Columbus 1492
···· Columbus 1493
– – Cortés 1519-20
–··– Pizarro 1533
–·– Magellan 1519-22

Dutch Explorers
— Hudson 1609

*Left to right:
Michelangelo's* David; *detail from* Last Judgment; *detail from Sistine Chapel ceiling.*

Renaissance and Reformation

LESSON PREVIEW

Key Ideas

- By the 1300s, Italian artists and writers had revived ideas from ancient Greece and Rome. This rebirth of classical learning was called the Renaissance.
- Martin Luther's challenge to the Roman Catholic Church started the Reformation.

Key Terms

Renaissance, secular, Protestants, Protestant Reformation

When Michelangelo presented his completed *Last Judgment* in 1541, Pope Paul III, who had commissioned the work, fell to his knees in awe. Others complained that the saints were nude, the angels had no wings, and Jesus looked like the Greek god Apollo. These critics decided that the painting was too classical, too much like the art of ancient Greece and Rome.

That classical look was exactly what Michelangelo had tried to capture. Even before his time, artists sought to revive the art and traditions of ancient Greece and Rome. Their efforts came to be called the **Renaissance**, a word that comes from the Latin *rinascere*, "to be reborn."

Renaissance

The Renaissance started in northern Italy during the early 1300s. Its beginnings there can be explained in two ways.

First, Italian artists could study ancient Greek and Roman art. As you read earlier, thousands of pieces of Greek sculpture had been brought to Italy. Italian artists could create their own versions of ancient art.

The Medici family (right) paid Renaissance artists to produce great works, such as Botticelli's *The Adoration of the Child* (above). *What artistic sources did the artists use?*

From Renaissance Through Reformation

1215 Magna Carta is signed.

1469 Lorenzo de Medici rules Florence.

1337 Hundred Years' War begins.

1517 Martin Luther writes his 95 Theses.

1534 Henry VIII establishes Church of England.

1100	1200	1300	1400	1500	1600

1066 William the Conqueror invades England.

1232 Inquisition begins.

1455 Gutenberg Bible printed.

1505 Michelangelo paints Sistine Chapel.

Renaissance art also flourished in Italy because Italy had become one of the wealthiest places in Europe. The Catholic Church had money to pay artists. So did hundreds of wealthy Italian merchants and bankers. Michelangelo took four years to complete *The Last Judgment*. Yet the Church could afford to pay him.

The Italian peninsula in the 1300s contained about 250 city-states, most of them controlled by powerful families. Florence, a wealthy banking city, became the center of the Renaissance in Italy. It was ruled by the Medici family.

The Medicis sent agents to monasteries and private libraries all over Europe, to search for classical manuscripts. Two of the Medici representatives, the poets Petrarch and Giovanni Boccaccio, studied those ancient writings. They decided to imitate the clear and elegant style of the classics.

Renaissance writers and artists also admired the Greek and Roman emphasis on the importance of the individual and on life in this world. For that reason, Michelangelo portrayed Jesus in Heaven as a human being in *The Last Judgment*.

As the Renaissance spirit spread beyond Italy, still more artists and writers used these themes. William Shakespeare, England's great poet and playwright, explored the whole range of human emotions—love, greed, jealousy, and ambition. He had his title character in *Hamlet* express a Renaissance view of the individual:

> *What a piece of work is man! How noble in reason! How infinite [unlimited] in faculties. In apprehension [understanding] how like a god.*

The time line illustrates when the Renaissance, the Reformation, and growth of European kingdoms occurred. *Did these events influence each other? How?*

What would **YOU** do?

Imagine you were living in the Renaissance. Talented people were developing new skills. Some people were good at music or painting. Others enjoyed mathematics, science, or writing. Still others excelled in athletic skills. What talents of your own would you develop? How would you go about developing them?

The Reformation

By reviving the work of ancient Greeks and Romans, Renaissance artists and writers introduced a concern for **secular**, or earthly, affairs to European thought. This did not mean that interest in the Roman Catholic Church or its teachings had declined.

Yet many Church leaders became concerned about the effect of the Renaissance on the Catholic Church. Some criticized the Church for spending too much on richly decorated buildings. Others opposed the rich lifestyles of some Church officials. Several leaders called for the Church to go back to simpler ways.

Martin Luther, a Catholic monk and professor of theology, wrote his "95 Theses," a condemnation of corruption and abuses in the Church. He posted his theses on the door of the Castle Church in Wittenberg, Germany, on October 31, 1517. Printing presses soon spread copies of Luther's criticisms throughout Europe. Others read Luther's arguments and added their own criticisms.

The Catholic Church defended its authority. The fierce debate split Christians in Europe into two large groups, Catholics and **Protestants**. "Protestant" comes from the Latin word *protestans*, or one who protests.

Luther had begun the **Protestant Reformation**, a movement against the Catholic Church's domination. Several Protestant church groups began spreading throughout Western and Northern Europe (see map, page 65).

The Spread of Protestantism

Before the moveable-type printing press was introduced, only the Catholic Church distributed religious literature. The Bible had been printed only in Latin, the language of Church leaders.

Luther translated the Bible into German so that more people could read and understand it. Soon editions of the Bible were appearing in other languages, along with literature interpreting the Scriptures. Printing presses turned out copies that were read throughout Europe.

Several of the new Christian churches in Europe traced their origins to John Calvin, a French refugee living in Switzerland.

Martin Luther began the Protestant Reformation. *What invention helped to quickly spread Luther's ideas?*

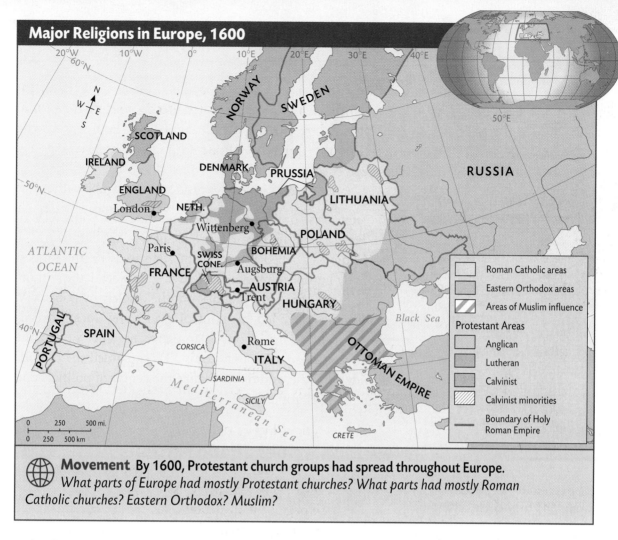

Major Religions in Europe, 1600

Legend:
- Roman Catholic areas
- Eastern Orthodox areas
- Areas of Muslim influence

Protestant Areas
- Anglican
- Lutheran
- Calvinist
- Calvinist minorities
- Boundary of Holy Roman Empire

Movement By 1600, Protestant church groups had spread throughout Europe. *What parts of Europe had mostly Protestant churches? What parts had mostly Roman Catholic churches? Eastern Orthodox? Muslim?*

Calvin's writings attracted many followers. In France, they were known as Huguenots. In the British Isles, his followers were Puritans and Presbyterians. In some countries, such as England and Sweden, the spread of Protestantism was encouraged by political leaders.

LESSON 1 REVIEW

Fact Follow-Up

1. Define the Renaissance. Why was it important?
2. Why was the printing press so important to the Protestant Reformation?
3. What conditions in the Catholic Church led to the Protestant Reformation?

Think These Through

4. Would the Reformation have been possible without the Renaissance? Explain.
5. The leaders of the Renaissance believed that there was no conflict between secular concerns and deep religious conviction. Can you think of specific examples?

The Rise of Modern Nations

King Louis XIV ruled France from 1643 to 1715. He began the process of creating a nation. *What was his title?*

"L'etat, c'est moi—I am the State," boasted Louis XIV of France. Calling himself *le Roi Soleil*—"the Sun King"—Louis XIV ruled France from 1643 to 1715, the longest reign of any European monarch. He was so powerful, the authority of the State—the government—was held solely by Louis XIV.

Louis XIV extended his control over many local governments. He drew people from a large area together under one powerful central government. Louis XIV expanded the boundaries under his rule, and made France the center of political and cultural life in Europe.

New Monarchies Shape Nations

Louis XIV and other powerful monarchs in the 1500s and 1600s created strong central governments called New Monarchies. **New Monarchies** replaced the feudal system of the Middle Ages. In a New Monarchy the ruler brought together small areas of land ruled by lords into larger territories. The monarch drew boundaries around the land and people he or she governed. The monarchs saw themselves as vital to their kingdoms' survival.

Europe during the Middle Ages had been a region of hundreds of small, weak governments (see map, page 67). Earlier, part of Europe was unified by Rome's empire. With Rome's collapse, scores of feudal territories ruled by lords sprang up throughout Europe. These lords formed alliances with each other to protect their lands and people.

New Monarchies emerged in Europe after the Renaissance, when powerful kings began replacing local lords as the governing authorities. Louis

XIV represented this type of New Monarchy.

The Renaissance helped Louis XIV and other ambitious monarchs unify their kingdoms. The Renaissance had encouraged thoughts about the individual and his or her place on earth.

In this atmosphere, these New Monarchs could turn to a book by Niccolò Machiavelli (mahk · ee · uh · VEHL · ee). Machiavelli's *The Prince* gave practical, but sometimes brutal, advice on how to succeed in politics. He advised rulers to use whatever means necessary to achieve their goals: "It is much safer to be feared than to be loved, if it is necessary to choose."

The Reformation also strengthened the New Monarchs by weakening the Roman Catholic Church as the only authority on religious life. Some ambitious monarchs had adopted a Protestant faith partly as a way of reducing the Catholic Church's interference in their kingdoms. Other monarchs found ways of cooperating with the Catholic Church.

WORD ORIGINS

The word **castle** entered the English language from French, the language spoken by Norman invaders who conquered England in 1066. The Norman French word *castel* comes from the Latin word *castellum*, which means "fortress."

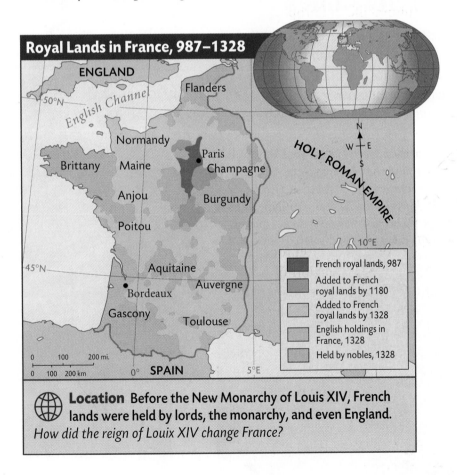

Royal Lands in France, 987–1328

Legend:
- French royal lands, 987
- Added to French royal lands by 1180
- Added to French royal lands by 1328
- English holdings in France, 1328
- Held by nobles, 1328

Location Before the New Monarchy of Louis XIV, French lands were held by lords, the monarchy, and even England. *How did the reign of Louix XIV change France?*

Rise of Nationalism

New Monarchies became forerunners of modern-day nations. A **nation** is inhabited by people who share a sense of belonging to a large community. These people occupy territory defined by borders and controlled by a central government.

From the Middle Ages, through the era of New Monarchies, and into the time of modern nations, Europeans expanded their loyalties. Under feudalism in the Middle Ages, Europeans had felt a sense of loyalty to their lord and to the Church. They also felt a kinship with all the Christians in the world through the Catholic Church.

As you have read, people began to feel loyal to such New

Louis XIV at Versailles

There is no better illustration of the wealth and power of Europe's New Monarchies than Louis XIV's palace at Versailles. The palace is more than half a mile (0.8 km) long with enormous wings. The building and grounds around it proclaim the king's glory.

No one knows exactly what the palace cost. Work on it began in 1661. Only the best architects, sculptors, and landscape gardeners were permitted to work on it. Design and construction required 20 years. The king used the palace to strengthen his rule. Powerful nobles moved to Versailles. By having these lords in the palace, Louis XIV made it impossible for the nobles to plot against him.

Versailles gardens

Monarchs as Louis XIV. These monarchs drew people together into larger kingdoms. The monarchs would have agreed with Louis XIV's statement that he was the state. His subjects were loyal to Louis XIV, the person and king.

Loyalties developed among people who had been brought together by a monarch. They felt a sense of belonging to those who spoke the same language and shared the same history and customs. People took pride in their nation's culture. Loyalty to the ruler as an individual gradually was replaced by a sense of pride in the nation itself. This sense of pride is called **nationalism**.

In England, the dramatist William Shakespeare expressed this feeling of nationalism with his history plays. *Henry IV, Richard II, Henry V,* and other plays tell stories of the country's

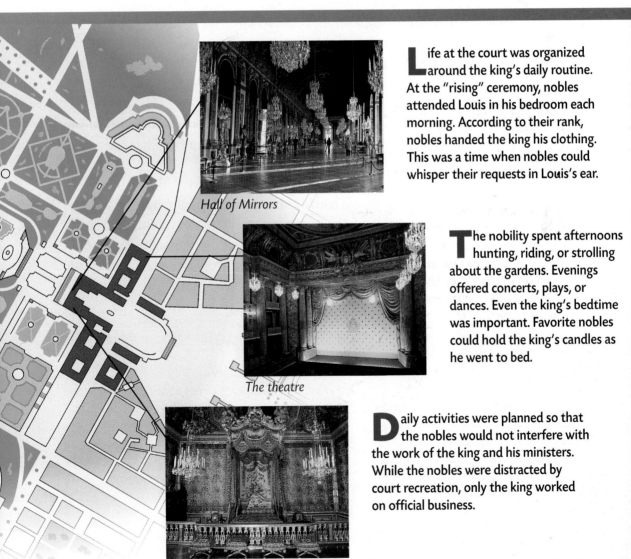

Hall of Mirrors

The theatre

The Queen's Bedroom

Life at the court was organized around the king's daily routine. At the "rising" ceremony, nobles attended Louis in his bedroom each morning. According to their rank, nobles handed the king his clothing. This was a time when nobles could whisper their requests in Louis's ear.

The nobility spent afternoons hunting, riding, or strolling about the gardens. Evenings offered concerts, plays, or dances. Even the king's bedtime was important. Favorite nobles could hold the king's candles as he went to bed.

Daily activities were planned so that the nobles would not interfere with the work of the king and his ministers. While the nobles were distracted by court recreation, only the king worked on official business.

Actors produce a play written by William Shakespeare. *How did Shakespeare's history plays support nationalism?*

great and glorious past. Shakespeare's poetic language presents England as a country blessed above all others:

> *This royal throne of kings, this sceptered isle,*
> *This earth of majesty, this seat of Mars,*
> *This other-Eden, demi-paradise …*
> *This blessed plot, this earth, this realm, this England.*

Shakespeare was one of the earliest advocates of nationalism. This sense of belonging to a nation did not become widespread in Europe until the late 1700s.

By then, England, France, Spain, Portugal, the Netherlands, Prussia, and Russia had become great national powers in Europe. The struggles of these nations affected every other European country and the world for 200 years. By the 1800s and 1900s, **patriots**—the name used to describe people who take great pride in their nation—were to be found everywhere.

LESSON 2 REVIEW

Fact Follow-Up
1. Define nationalism.
2. What was the difference between the feudal system and the nation-state?
3. List some of the early European nations.
4. Some monarchs expanded their power by reducing the influence of the Catholic Church in their kingdoms. Why did they do this?

Think These Through
5. Reread Shakespeare's lines about England. How do they express his feeling of nationalism?
6. From what you have read about empires, the feudal system, and nations, do you think that nations were an improvement over other forms of government? Explain.

LESSON 3 The Expansion of Europe

An Italian nobleman, Antonio Pigafetta, recorded these memories of crossing the broad waters of the Pacific in 1520:

> *We remained 3 months and 20 days without taking on any food or other refreshments. We ate only old biscuits reduced to powder and full of grubs, and we drank water that was yellow and stinking.*

The Italian nobleman had sailed from Spain aboard one of five small ships commanded by Ferdinand Magellan. The voyage lasted two years, and only 18 of the original crew of 268 returned to Spain. These 18, however, were the first Europeans to sail around the world.

LESSON PREVIEW

Key Ideas
- Emerging European nations began to explore the world.
- These nations conquered overseas territories and opened trade wherever they could.
- Europe's first major conquests were in the Americas.
- Europe conquered more foreign territory in the 1800s. Europe's empires reached around the world.

Key Terms
Age of Exploration

Beginning an Age of Exploration

Magellan's voyage was only one of many daring exploits by European sailors in the age of the Renaissance and Reformation. While artists and scholars rediscovered the classics, others explored lands Europeans never knew existed.

Two of Europe's new nations, Portugal and Spain, led the way across the oceans. Soon, other nations followed. Through these voyages Europe opened trading routes to Asia halfway around the world. Through their search for faster routes, explorers learned of two huge continents—North and South America.

This **Age of Exploration**, as the years 1450 to 1750 came to be called, marked a change in European thinking about the world. During the Middle Ages, Europeans had been scarcely interested in distant places. Now Europe's new monarchs became curious about faraway lands. They realized that the unknown world might offer riches for their treasuries.

Religious controversies stirred by the Reformation also encouraged the monarchs to pay for explorations. Voyages to Asia, North America, and South America promised to open the

Navigation equipment, such as this astrolabe from a seventeenth-century ship, helped sailors plot their course over the ocean. *Which two countries led the way in exploring North America and South America?*

The time line below shows key events in Europe's exploration and expansion to the Americas. *How does the time line show the rise and decline of Spain?*

world to the Christian Gospel. Some monarchs hoped to win new converts for the Roman Catholic Church. Others supported the spread of Protestant faiths.

Prince Henry of Portugal became one of the earliest Europeans to encourage exploration. At his own observatory in Sagres, near Cape St. Vincent, Prince Henry established a school to teach new navigation and sailing techniques. Using his knowledge of mathematics and astronomy and his influence with his father, King John, Henry gathered together mapmakers, astronomers, and mathematicians. The school became an early center for the age of exploration.

With Henry's royal backing, Portuguese explorers began sailing along Africa's northwest coast in 1419. Henry planned 50 voyages along Africa's coast, although he never sailed on any himself. His support of sea exploration earned him the name Prince Henry the Navigator.

After Prince Henry's death, Portugal continued to sponsor voyages farther south along the African coast. Portuguese explorers believed that the shortest water route to India lay around Africa. Spain, on the other hand, was persuaded by Columbus to look west. Columbus convinced Spanish royalty that a passage across the Atlantic would take trade ships to Asia faster.

Europe and the Americas

We usually think of the voyage of Christopher Columbus in 1492 as the story of contact between Europeans and the people of the Americas. But the idea behind his expedition,

European Expansion and Rivalries

	1521 Cortés conquers Aztec Empire.	1607 First English settlement at Jamestown.		1803 U.S. purchases the Louisiana Territory from France.	1914 World War I begins.
1500		**1600**	**1700**	**1800**	**1900**
1492 Columbus reaches the Bahamas.	1564 William Shakespeare is born.	1643 Louis XIV begins rule of France.	1762 Catherine the Great begins rule of Russia.	1880 Scramble for Africa begins.	

sponsored by King Ferdinand and Queen Isabella of Spain, was to establish sea trade with India.

Columbus calculated it would take him two months to reach Asia by sea. Spanish scholars disagreed, because they believed the earth was much larger than Columbus thought. According to their calculations, it would take a ship four months to reach India.

The difference meant life or death. At the time, ships could carry only enough fresh water and provisions for a two-month voyage. Fortunately for Columbus, who was wrong in his calculations, the Americas lay halfway to India. Just as their two months of provisions ran out, Columbus and his crew reached land, where they found riches beyond their dreams.

Columbus's discoveries touched off a race for control of the Americas (see map, page 61). Spain and Portugal led the way. They divided almost all of Middle and South America between them, and began building colonies there. England and France competed for control of North America. In this struggle, the English were the winners.

European conquests nearly destroyed Native American civilizations. Native Americans died by the thousands from diseases carried by Europeans. Native American populations in the Caribbean Islands were destroyed. In North America, they died in warfare or fled from European settlements. Elsewhere, Native Americans were more numerous in western South America and

Christopher Columbus believed he would reach India by sailing west. He sailed to the Americas instead. *What four countries competed to gain control of the Americas?*

on the Middle American mainland. They survived to help shape the nations that grew in those places.

The Americas' impact on Europe was equally powerful, though generally more positive. Spanish explorers struck gold, silver, and other treasures that helped boost Spain into a European power. Other Europeans found little or no gold, but they profited from trade in furs, timber, cotton, and tobacco. All Europeans benefited from a more varied diet as new foods—chocolate, corn (maize), potatoes, and tomatoes—flowed in from the Americas.

European Expansion

The conquests of the Western Hemisphere suggest that Europe's nations had become great world powers. In reality, they were no match in the 1500s for such ancient kingdoms as China.

European nations in the 1500s and 1600s made no significant conquests in Asia or Africa that matched those they made in the

LIVING IN EUROPE

Explorers Bring New Foods to Europe's Tables

Explorers of the Americas brought their kings and queens gold and entertained them with stories of the great empires they had visited on their travels.

For most Europeans, contact with the Americas meant they began eating new foods.

From about 1600, corn, sugar, and potatoes from the Americas provided Europeans with new kinds of food in their diet. Some new foods gained popularity quickly. Others found a place on European tables many years after their introduction.

Farmers in the Mediterranean found that corn grew easily in their region. When dried and ground, corn made a fine alternative to wheat.

Cane would not grow in the colder climate of Europe, but after tasting sugar from the Americas, Europeans began trading for it in great quantities. Soon sugar replaced honey as the popular sweetener.

But the distance and the expense of importing cane from the Americas proved to be difficult. After a time, Europeans learned to extract sugar from beets, which grow easily in many climates.

At first, Europeans did not eat the potato. Instead they fed potatoes to livestock. Eventually, people developed a taste for potatoes. This new food became one of Europe's most important crops.

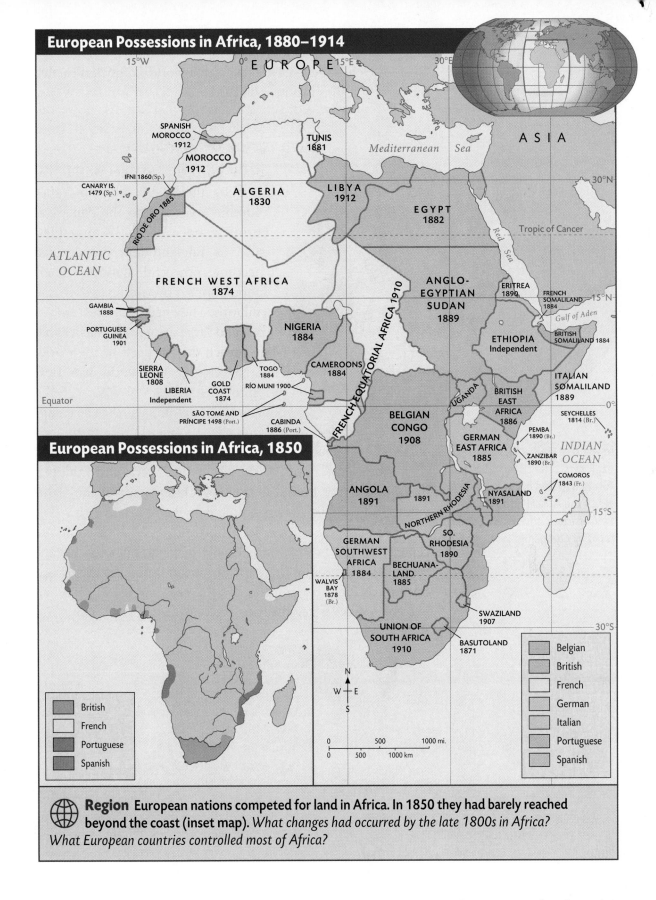

European Possessions in Africa, 1880–1914

EUROPE

ASIA

SPANISH MOROCCO 1912

TUNIS 1881

Mediterranean Sea

MOROCCO 1912

IFNI 1860 (Sp.)

CANARY IS. 1479 (Sp.)

ALGERIA 1830

LIBYA 1912

EGYPT 1882

RÍO DE ORO 1885

Tropic of Cancer

Red Sea

ATLANTIC OCEAN

FRENCH WEST AFRICA 1874

FRENCH EQUATORIAL AFRICA 1910

ANGLO-EGYPTIAN SUDAN 1889

ERITREA 1890

FRENCH SOMALILAND 1884

Gulf of Aden

GAMBIA 1888

PORTUGUESE GUINEA 1901

NIGERIA 1884

ETHIOPIA Independent

BRITISH SOMALILAND 1884

SIERRA LEONE 1808

LIBERIA Independent

GOLD COAST 1874

TOGO 1884

RÍO MUNI 1900

CAMEROONS 1884

UGANDA

BRITISH EAST AFRICA 1886

ITALIAN SOMALILAND 1889

Equator

SÃO TOMÉ AND PRÍNCIPE 1498 (Port.)

CABINDA 1886 (Port.)

BELGIAN CONGO 1908

GERMAN EAST AFRICA 1885

SEYCHELLES 1814 (Br.)

PEMBA 1890 (Br.)

ZANZIBAR 1890 (Br.)

INDIAN OCEAN

ANGOLA 1891

1891

NORTHERN RHODESIA

NYASALAND 1891

COMOROS 1843 (Fr.)

GERMAN SOUTHWEST AFRICA 1884

SO. RHODESIA 1890

BECHUANA-LAND 1885

WALVIS BAY 1878 (Br.)

SWAZILAND 1907

UNION OF SOUTH AFRICA 1910

BASUTOLAND 1871

N / W–E / S

0   500   1000 mi.
0   500   1000 km

	Belgian
	British
	French
	German
	Italian
	Portuguese
	Spanish

European Possessions in Africa, 1850

	British
	French
	Portuguese
	Spanish

Region European nations competed for land in Africa. In 1850 they had barely reached beyond the coast (inset map). *What changes had occurred by the late 1800s in Africa? What European countries controlled most of Africa?*

Western Hemisphere. In the rest of the world Europeans carried on trade, but they conquered little land.

Dominance of Europe

In the late 1800s, European explorers, scientists, and adventurers traveled by any means to reach the African interior. *What two African nations were not ruled by Europeans?*

Both Europe and the world had changed by the 1890s, 400 years after Columbus's voyages to the Americas. Europe's once infant monarchies, such as England and France, had become powerful nations. Their populations now numbered in the millions. They had built great industries and large armies and navies that could reach distant parts of the world. Power to change the world was now within Europe's grasp.

Look at the map on page 75. The smaller inset map shows that in 1850 European nations claimed only small territories along Africa's coasts. The larger map shows how all of Africa, except for Liberia and Ethiopia, had come under European control. Other maps of the 1890s would show extensive European colonial empires in Asia.

These great empires reflected how Europe had become the center of world power. But what the maps do not show are the bitter rivalries among the great European powers as they raced for control of these empires. By the early 1900s, Europe had become a powder keg ready to explode.

LESSON ③ REVIEW

Fact-Follow-Up
1. What was Prince Henry's role in laying foundations for Europe's exploration of the world?
2. Why did emerging European nations develop an interest in the Americas?
3. Why was Columbus so determined to sail westward across the Atlantic?

4. What nations became involved in a contest for control of the Americas?

Think These Through
5. Is it likely that Native Americans and Europeans had different views of Europe's conquests in the Americas? Imagine a debate between a European colonist and a Native American. How would they differ?

The Five Themes of Geography

Using Geography's Themes: Human-Environmental Interaction

Human-environmental interaction is the third of the Five Themes of Geography.

This theme asks three questions:

1. What happens when people occupy a location?
2. What happens to humans because of their environment?
3. What happens to the environment because of humans?

To practice answering these questions, think about the human-environmental interactions described in this chapter.

Imagine that you can go back to France in the time of Louis XIV. You will visit Versailles before the palace was built (at a place where there was a hunting lodge and forest). You will visit again while the palace is being built and then spend time there after the king has moved his court to the palace. Reread the Eyewitness to History section and study the pictures on pages 68-69.

Now how would you answer the first question? In what ways do you think the palace and grounds changed the place where they were located? How would the palace change nearby villages and roads?

Next, turn to question 2. The feature describes the daily lives of nobility at the palace. In addition to the lords and ladies, hundreds of servants, cooks, and gardeners worked at the palace. Do you think the palace's environment changed their lives? How?

Finally, think about and try to answer

Human-Environmental Interaction	
Questions	**Data**
1. What happens when humans occupy a place?	
2. What happens to humans because of their environment?	
3. What happens to the environment because of humans?	

question 3. You have already given part of the answer with the first question by describing how Versailles changed the place where the palace was located. Another part of the answer is that the building of Versailles and the life there changed the environment in other places. Might the quarrying, or digging, of the stone for the palace have had an impact on the environment? Would feeding all of those people and dressing them in fine clothes have touched off changes beyond the palace grounds? Would the gathering of a large number of people in one place change the environment? How would density of population cause water or land pollution? Can you think of other ways Versailles might have changed the environment?

Record your answer on a graphic organizer in your notebook. A model is given above.

Compare your answers with those of some of your classmates.

Chapter 4 Review

LESSON 1   Two great upheavals in ideas and religious beliefs—the Renaissance and the Reformation—contributed to the shaping of modern Europe.

LESSON 2   Europe is divided into many nations. The building of these nations became an important feature of Europe's development by 1500.

LESSON 3   As modern Europe took shape, Europeans began to explore and conquer lands in other parts of the world. Europe's first successful conquests were in the Western Hemisphere. By the late 1800s, European nations had gained control of colonies throughout Africa and Asia.

TIME FOR TERMS

Renaissance	secular
Protestants	Protestant Reformation
New Monarchies	nation
nationalism	patriots
Age of Exploration	

FACT FOLLOW-UP

1. In what ways did the Reformation help shape modern Europe?
2. What ideas were contributed to modern-day Europe by the Renaissance?
3. Define the words nationalism and nation. Why did the development of nationalism and nations become so important?
4. What role did Prince Henry of Portugal play in Europe's explorations and conquests in the 1500s and 1600s?
5. Why were infant European monarchies so interested in trying to reach Asia? How did Columbus's voyages reflect this interest in Asia?
6. In what ways did the conquest of the Americas by European nations help change Europe?
7. Describe the differences that marked Europe's efforts to conquer foreign lands in the 1600s and the late 1800s.

THINK THESE THROUGH

8. How did the Renaissance help bring about the Reformation?
9. "The spread of the Protestant Reformation was due to the invention of the printing press." Do you think that this statement of cause and effect is completely accurate? Explain.
10. Why did Martin Luther's posting of the 95 Theses lead to the Protestant Reformation? Explain.
11. The description of Louis XIV at Versailles portrays a king determined to live in splendor and focus everyone's attention on him. How would you analyze the king's behavior? Was he simply a pleasure-loving, self-centered man, or were there other reasons for his behavior? Explain.
12. The rulers of Europe's new nations became the chief sponsors of early voyages of exploration. Why were the monarchs interested in exploring beyond Europe?

13. Louis XIV's construction of Versailles is presented as a case study in a human-environmental interaction that changed the land of the palace grounds, the lives of the people, and human-environmental interactions in places beyond the palace.

a. Can you think of some new construction—an apartment complex, a highway intersection, a factory, an agribusiness, or a school—in or near your home that might be described in similar terms?

b. In what ways has the new facility changed the environment in its immediate vicinity?

c. Has the new facility changed the lives of those using or working in it?

d. Can you cite any changes in human-environmental interaction far away from the new facility?

Use the letters on the map to identify the locations of the following:

14. Portuguese voyages of exploration.

15. England's voyages of exploration.

16. Voyages sponsored by The Netherlands (the Dutch).

17. Spanish voyages of exploration.

18. French voyages of exploration.

19. The continent(s) and/or region(s) where the Spanish explored.

20. The continent(s) where the Dutch explored.

21. The continent(s) where the English explored.

22. The continent(s) where the French explored.

23. The continent(s) where the Portuguese explored.

24. The continent divided by Europe in the 1890s.

Reviewing Place Location

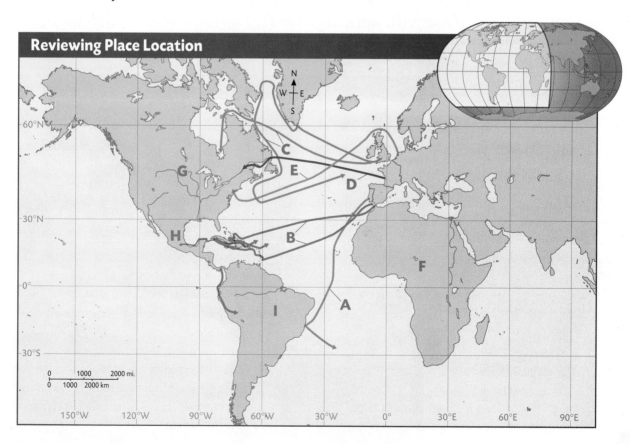

CHAPTER 5

Europe in the Twentieth Century

Gavrilo Princip

On a brilliantly sunny summer day, the Archduke Franz Ferdinand, heir to the Austrian throne, rode through the streets of Sarajevo, the capital of Bosnia-Herzegovina. His wife, the Archduchess Sophie, sat beside him. It was June 28, 1914.

When the royal car made a wrong turn, nineteen-year-old Gavrilo Princip rushed from the crowd, drew a pistol, and fired twice, killing the archduke and the archduchess.

By the end of the summer, war had engulfed all of Europe. Even worse, the war that erupted in 1914 would be only the first of two great wars. Together they threatened to destroy 500 years of European achievement.

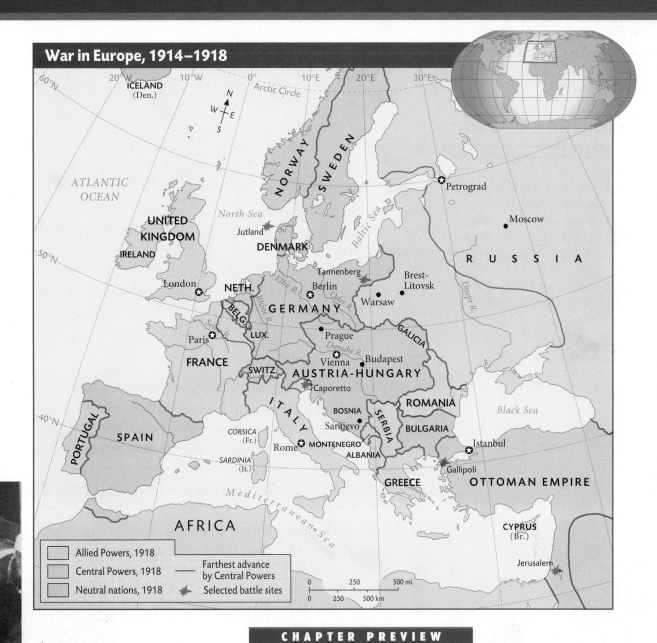

War in Europe, 1914–1918

ICELAND (Den.)

Arctic Circle

ATLANTIC OCEAN

NORWAY

SWEDEN

Petrograd

Moscow

UNITED KINGDOM

IRELAND

North Sea

Jutland

DENMARK

Baltic Sea

RUSSIA

London

NETH.

BELG.

Elbe R.

Tannenberg

Berlin

Oder R.

Warsaw

Brest-Litovsk

Dniepr R.

GERMANY

Rhine R.

Seine R.

Paris

LUX.

Prague

Danube R.

Vienna

Budapest

GALICIA

FRANCE

SWITZ.

AUSTRIA-HUNGARY

Caporetto

ITALY

BOSNIA

Sarajevo

SERBIA

ROMANIA

Black Sea

BULGARIA

Istanbul

PORTUGAL

SPAIN

CORSICA (Fr.)

Rome

MONTENEGRO

ALBANIA

Gallipoli

SARDINIA (It.)

Mediterranean Sea

GREECE

OTTOMAN EMPIRE

AFRICA

CYPRUS (Br.)

Jerusalem

☐ Allied Powers, 1918	
☐ Central Powers, 1918	— Farthest advance by Central Powers
☐ Neutral nations, 1918	★ Selected battle sites

0   250   500 mi.

0   250   500 km

The Austrian archduke and archduchess

World War I

LESSON PREVIEW

Key Ideas

- At the time, World War I was the largest war ever fought.
- Despite early hopes that the war would be short, it was long and bloody. New weapons took millions of lives.
- The war cost billions of dollars and weakened European nations.

Key Terms

alliances, trenches

"You'll be home before the leaves have fallen from the trees," Germany's Kaiser Wilhelm told his troops as they departed for war in August 1914. The kaiser, or emperor, might have really believed this promise. Europe had not had any big wars for 100 years. Most had been short and had not taken many lives.

The kaiser soon discovered how wrong he was. The great powers fought battles for four bloody years. The war cost millions of lives and billions of dollars.

Causes of World War I

The killing of the archduke and archduchess started World War I, partly because the European powers had lined up against one another in rival **alliances**, or partnerships. Austria-Hungary, Germany, and Italy previously had agreed to support one another through the Triple Alliance, also called the Central Powers. Russia and France had a similar agreement. When the United Kingdom joined them, the combination was called the Triple Entente, also called the Allied Powers.

Statesmen thought that these alliances would keep the peace. They believed war between these great powers would be so terrible that no one would dare fight. To their surprise, the alliance system pushed nearly all of Europe into war.

After the archduke was killed by Princip, a Serbian nationalist, Austria-Hungary set out to punish the Serbs. Russia, Serbia's ally, then called up its troops. Soon all the powers declared war, as the map on page 81 shows.

Events in Serbia had set off a chain reaction. Europe's alliance system had failed to keep the peace. Instead, the system had turned a local dispute into a world war involving every great power.

World War I—The Western Front

Soon after the fighting started, all hopes for a short war disappeared. German troops marched quickly through Belgium. They were stopped in fierce fighting as they approached Paris, the French capital. British troops from the United Kingdom and French forces prevented Germany from conquering France, but they could not force the Germans back into Germany.

Both sides dug **trenches,** deep ditches, into French soil and spent weeks shelling enemy lines with heavy artillery fire. When the time seemed right, troops were ordered "over the top." Soldiers scrambled out of their trenches and headed toward the enemy.

The attacking troops sometimes seized their opponents' trenches a few hundred yards away. A few days later enemy troops would seize the land again. In this type of warfare, thousands of men were killed every day. In one 11-month battle, Germany lost 330,000 men. The other side's losses were equally heavy.

Technology of War

New weapons pouring out of Europe's industrial plants caused the large numbers of deaths. Soldiers going "over the top" faced enemy machine-gun fire. Two men handling this rapid-firing weapon could kill dozens of the enemy in minutes. Before the war ended, both sides were using tanks that sent high explosive shells into enemy trenches.

Soldiers of World War I dug deep trenches to protect themselves from heavy artillery fired by tanks. *What countries fought in World War I?*

Russian Red Guards fought in Petrograd during the Communist revolution of 1917. *How did the difficulties of World War I lead to the founding of a Communist government in Russia?*

United States involvement made the difference in the outcome of World War I. Posters like this called Americans to fight. *Who is the man in the picture?*

World War I on Other Fronts

While the British and French battled the German forces in France, German and Austrian-Hungarian armies fought the Russians along lines that stretched from the Baltic to the Black Sea.

Russia had by far the largest armies to throw into this fighting. Yet these troops were poorly trained and led. In some battles Russian troops went into the fight without any guns. Men in the rear were told to arm themselves by picking up the guns of fallen comrades. Despite heavy Russian losses, the fighting on the eastern front produced no decisive results until November 1917.

At that point, Russia dropped out of the fighting. The Russian government that had taken the nation into the war was overthrown. The country's new Communist rulers were determined to have peace. They believed that defeating Germany was less important than turning Russia into a Communist government.

France and the United Kingdom were deeply troubled by the Russian peace. They feared German troops would be transferred from the Russian front back to the western front in France. This did not happen. Neither France nor the United Kingdom could break through German lines. The best news they received came in April 1917, when the United States declared war on Germany.

Final Months of World War I

The United States could not offer much immediate help with the fighting in France. An army had to be recruited, trained, and transported to France. The United States Navy did help with the destruction of German submarines in the Atlantic. The United States Treasury loaned funds for the purchase of war materials to be used against Germany.

By late 1917, the United States presence in the war was making a difference. Every month, 50,000 American troops landed in France. American ships attacked German submarines in the Atlantic Ocean. France and the United Kingdom were receiving badly needed aid. Meanwhile, Germany was rapidly running out of manpower and military supplies.

Early in 1918, a fierce German offensive was stopped. A counteroffensive was launched that broke German lines and drove the German forces back. Germany's problems multiplied as its ally, Austria-Hungary, fell apart and dropped out of the war. In November 1918, Germany, now alone, asked for peace.

The Versailles Peace Treaty ending World War I was signed in King Louis XIV's Hall of Mirrors. Peace came at a great expense of lives and land. *What were some costs of the war?*

Costs of World War I

Europe sacrificed 30 million dead and wounded soldiers to the slaughter of World War I. The war also destroyed much of Europe's industry. The fighting nations spent about $337 billion—most of it borrowed. For both the countries who won and those who lost, these enormous national debts prevented economic growth. The war devastated the land, with bombardments ripping up the farmland and poisoning the soil.

The war destroyed Europe's confidence that the years ahead would be better. "We do not know what will be born, and we fear the future," wrote French writer Paul Valery.

LESSON 1 REVIEW

Fact Follow-Up
1. Where was the western front and who fought there?
2. Why did Austria-Hungary drop out of the war? Why did Russia?
3. How did the United States contribute to Germany's defeat?

4. Explain why the machine gun was so deadly.
Think These Through
5. The alliance system was supposed to prevent war, but it turned a local conflict into a general European war. Why did it fail so badly?
6. Why do you think Paul Valery worried about Europe's future?

The Road to World War II

LESSON PREVIEW

Key Ideas

- By 1939, Europe was back at war. Asia had already gone to war, so fighting went on all over the world until 1945.
- World War II was bigger and more costly than World War I.
- Europe, once the center of world power and wealth, seemed almost destroyed by the war's end.

Key Terms

Nazis, Axis, Allies, Cold War

At the Paris Peace Conference, United States President Woodrow Wilson (front row, far right) helped form an organization that he hoped would prevent another war. *What was the organization? Was it successful?*

Woodrow Wilson, president of the United States, said that World War I must be "a war to end all wars." Everyone agreed. When the shooting stopped, statesmen tried to lay a solid foundation for peace.

The United Kingdom, France, and Italy joined the United States and Japan in treaties limiting naval weapons. A League of Nations was established as the world's first effort for nations to keep peace internationally.

Dictators Gain Power

The League could not help the many nations overwhelmed by the economic and political problems left by World War I. Poverty, shame over war losses, and fear of communism encouraged people to turn to powerful leaders. Italy welcomed Benito Mussolini. Germans looked to Adolf Hitler as the man to lead their nation.

Mussolini came to power when workers in cities were on strike and peasants in the countryside were seizing the property of wealthy landowners. He acted decisively to end the upheaval. He denounced communism and condemned democracy. Free

elections, he said, destroyed national unity.

Mussolini ruled Italy as a dictator. No one could speak out against his government. Schools were placed under tight government supervision. Armed forces were expanded so that Italy might rule a great empire.

Hitler gained a national following much the same way as Mussolini. He founded a political party called the National Socialists, or **Nazis**. He and his followers won support by attacking the peace treaty signed at the end of World War I. That treaty, Hitler said, had treated Germany unfairly. He said Jews had plotted Germany's defeat in World War I and had created the nation's postwar economic problems. He claimed that true Germans belonged to a superior "Aryan" race that was destined to rule the world.

Under Hitler, Germany quickly became a dictatorship that controlled every aspect of life. Secret police arrested anyone suspected of opposing Hitler. Schools, the press, and even churches were used to spread Nazi propaganda. A particularly violent campaign was waged against Jews. Millions of Jews were sent to concentration camps. These camps later became horrifying places of mass murder.

Adolf Hitler claimed Germany had been badly treated by the victors of World War I. He said he and his party would regain for Germany what had been lost in the war. *What was the name of Hitler's party?*

World War II in Europe

German forces invaded Poland on September 1, 1939, touching off war in Europe. Japan and Germany drew the United States into the war in December 1941. Japan bombed the American naval base at Pearl Harbor. Germany, because of a treaty with Japan, then declared war on the United States.

The **Axis** powers (Germany, Italy, and Japan) fought the Allies. The **Allies** included the United Kingdom, France, the Soviet Union, United States, China, and 45 other nations.

In Europe and Asia, the Axis at first won most battles. France, Denmark, Norway, and The Netherlands fell quickly to the Germans. Italy and Germany jointly occupied the Balkans and parts of North Africa (see map, page 89).

After France fell in 1940, German bombers began hammering airfields near the English coast. London and other cities suffered heavy damage from bombing raids. Germany was preparing to invade the British Isles. Then suddenly, Hitler changed course. His troops invaded the Soviet Union, pushing deep into that country.

Late in 1942, the momentum shifted. German and Italian forces were defeated in North Africa and Allied invasions of Italy were launched. In 1942-1943, the Russians won a costly, but vital, victory over the Germans at Stalingrad.

By 1944, Italy was out of the war and Germany was in retreat. The Allies invaded France and started drives that took them deep into Germany. Meanwhile, Russian forces advanced into Eastern Europe and Germany. Hitler committed suicide rather than face defeat. Germany surrendered on May 7, 1945.

World War II in the Pacific

World War II ended in the Pacific and Asia in August 1945, shortly after the United States dropped two atomic bombs on Japan. Before surrendering, Japan had fought China across a long front. Japanese troops had held for a time all of Southeast Asia. Japan's forces had established a line of defense that reached far out into the Pacific.

Japanese naval forces suffered serious losses to its navy in 1942. Men and equipment were in low supply. Still, the Japanese continued to fight. American forces were preparing to invade Japan when the atomic bombs were dropped.

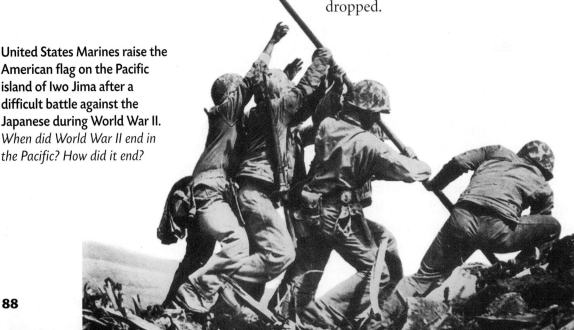

United States Marines raise the American flag on the Pacific island of Iwo Jima after a difficult battle against the Japanese during World War II. *When did World War II end in the Pacific? How did it end?*

World War II in Europe and North Africa, 1942–1945

Legend:
- Main Axis powers, 1937
- Maximum extent of Axis control, 1942
- Neutral nations, 1942
- Allied territory, 1942
- → Allied advances

0   250   500 mi.
0   250   500 km

Movement During World War II, nearly all of Europe was a battleground as the Axis powers of Italy and Germany tried to take over territory. *How far did Axis control extend during World War II? What nations were neutral in World War II?*

Costs of World War II

The human price of World War II was the highest in history. Some have estimated that more than 30 million people died in Europe alone. Another 30 million died in other parts of the world. Hundreds of European cities lay in ruins.

This second great war further reduced Europe's impact on world affairs. Germany had been stripped of its colonial empire at the end of World War I. Soon after World War II, all of

Europe's colonial holdings in Africa, Southwest Asia (the Middle East), and Asia would be gone. World leadership passed to two new superpowers—the Soviet Union and the United States.

Germany Divided

As Hitler's military was collapsing at the end of the war, the Soviet Union occupied Germany from the east. American, British, and other Allied forces moved toward Berlin from the west. After Hitler's suicide, Germany surrendered.

With World War II over, the four Allies divided Germany—including Berlin—into four occupation zones. The division was supposed to be temporary, but Germany remained split for

---

CONNECTIONS

Geography & Science

How Nuclear Energy Works

When someone says the word "nuclear," we might think of the nuclear weapons invented by American scientists near the end of World War II. But another use for nuclear energy is in the production of power—power that can run our televisions, heat our homes, and drive the machines in our factories.

Nuclear energy production starts with atoms of uranium or plutonium. Because these elements are radioactive, people who work with them are shielded by such protective devices as lead sheets and special kinds of glass.

The uranium and plutonium are placed into tubes called fuel rods. The rods are loaded into a large water-filled vessel, or nuclear reactor (right). When enough of the fuel rods are placed into the reactor, a nuclear reaction begins that heats the surrounding water.

The water turns to steam and goes through a heat exchanger. On the other side of the heat exchanger is more water, which also turns to steam. The steam spins huge turbines, and electricity is produced.

Today, nuclear power is responsible for more than

17 percent of all electricity produced in the United States. France gets more than 70 percent of its electricity from nuclear power.

nearly a half century. Quarrels broke out among the occupying powers. In 1949, Britain, France, and the United States agreed to permit the German sectors under their control to unite as West Germany. The Soviet Union refused to allow its sector, called East Germany, to join in the reunification. The Soviet Union also attempted to take over the Allied section of Berlin—West Berlin—with a military blockade around the city. An airlift of food and supplies kept West Berlin free from Soviet control.

This set the stage for many years of tension, a time when all of Europe would be divided into east and west. The United States and the Soviet Union squared off as superpowers in a dangerous rivalry called the **Cold War**.

East Germany and its industries were closely linked to the Soviet Union after World War II. *What happened to the rest of Germany?*

LESSON 2 REVIEW

Fact Follow-Up
1. Describe the events that led to World War II.
2. Where were the battlefronts in Europe?
3. Why do you think the Axis powers believed in 1941 that they would win the war?
4. Describe the major military operations that defeated Italy and Germany.
5. How did the Cold War begin?

Think These Through
6. The Cold War broke out in 1949. How did events at the end of World War II indicate that this new conflict might be coming?
7. Would it be accurate to say that Europe's loss of colonial empires after World Wars I and II reflected Europe's decline? Explain.

Europe Rebounds

Key Ideas
- After World War II, Europe was dominated by two new superpowers, the United States and the Soviet Union.
- Western European nations soon began to revive. Governments rebuilt and economies expanded.
- By the 1990s, a new Europe, uniting and developing, was becoming a superpower.

Key Terms

containment, NATO, Warsaw Pact, European Union

Winston Churchill, who led the United Kingdom as prime minister in World War II, warned of the Soviet Union's desire to spread communism. *Was the Soviet Union successful?*

"An iron curtain has descended across the Continent," announced Winston Churchill in March 1946. Churchill had been prime minister of the United Kingdom during World War II. He was speaking of the Soviet Union's steps to install Communist-led governments in East Germany and all the other countries of Eastern Europe.

The Cold War Years

Churchill was only one of many in Western Europe who believed the Soviet Union was preparing an advance into the remainder of Europe. He also feared that the Soviet Union would support Communist-led independence movements throughout the world. By making his speech in 1946, he hoped to arouse the people of the United States to new dangers.

The United States was alerted to Soviet expansion. The United States began a policy called **containment** to stop the Soviet advance. In 1947, Secretary of State George C. Marshall announced a massive economic aid program designed to assist European nations in rebuilding their economies. By restoring economic prosperity, Marshall hoped that democratic governments in Europe would grow strong.

Two years later, the United States, Canada, and eight Western European nations, as well as Greece and Turkey, formed the North Atlantic Treaty Organization (**NATO**). The members pledged to protect one another from a Communist-led attack. The Soviet Union, in turn, led Eastern European governments in signing the **Warsaw Pact** to defend themselves against invasion.

The two rival alliances soon developed huge arsenals of tanks, airplanes, missiles, and nuclear weapons. From the 1940s through the 1980s, the armed forces on both sides remained in a constant state of readiness for war. Repeated crises raised fears that war might come at any time.

These Cold War tensions finally lifted in the 1980s. Tremendous changes had taken place in the Soviet Union and Eastern Europe. Most amazing of all was the collapse of the once mighty Soviet Union. In East Germany, a series of economic and political crises led to the fall of its Communist-led government. Both Washington and Moscow announced that the Cold War was over. A new era of international cooperation had begun.

Rebuilding Western European Governments

Even while Cold War tensions tested the world's nerves, parliamentary governments were being rebuilt in Western Europe. Nations such as the United Kingdom and France had strong traditions of parliamentary government.

Cologne, Germany, was destroyed during World War II. In 1945, Europe lay devastated by bombs and fires. Rebuilding buildings was only part of the work; rebuilding governments was harder. *How did the United States help Europe do both?*

In 1946, Italy established a republic in the place of the dictatorship headed by Benito Mussolini. Economic assistance from the United States helped revive democracy there.

After World War II, Spain and Portugal remained under the rule of longtime dictators. Both countries became democracies after their dictators died in the 1970s. Greece, where democracy had been born, also made a change in the 1970s. After several years under military rule, the Greeks established a democratic government.

A parliamentary government had been established in West Germany soon after World War II ended. By October 1990, the Communist-led East German government was gone. Citizens of East Germany and West Germany began tearing down the wall

The 1956 Hungary Crisis

One important part of the Soviet Union's strength was its willingness to use power. Joseph Stalin, the Soviet dictator, used his army in 1956 against Hungary, which wanted the right to rule itself. Soviet troops put down a major revolt after several days of bitter fighting. Many thousands died, and more than 200,000 people fled the country.

Imre Nagy

Hungary's leader, Imre Nagy, sent his last message to his people shortly before he was captured: "This fight is ... for freedom by the Hungarian people against the Russian intervention. I [will] only be able to stay at my post for one or two hours. The whole world will see how the Russian armed forces are crushing the Hungarian people." Nagy was taken prisoner and later executed.

dividing Berlin. East Germans voted to merge with fellow Germans in the West. Germans in every part of the reunited country celebrated wildly.

The merger presented Germany with major problems. East Germans had little experience with democracy. They would now have the difficult task of learning how to work within the parliamentary government in the German capital.

East Germans demonstrate in Dresden in December 1989 for the reunification of their country with West Germany. The merger occurred in October 1990. *What problems did this cause?*

Economic Recovery

Western Europe's economic recovery after World War II was as amazing as the rebirth of its political strength. War-devastated factories and transportation systems were repaired. Cities were

To explain its actions, Stalin's government said that Hungary had actually asked the Soviets to help them. The Soviets said "[We] regret that the development of events in Hungary has led to bloodshed. On the request of the Hungarian People's government, the Soviet Government consented to the entry into Budapest of Soviet Army units to ... establish order."

Joseph Stalin

Clearing the rubble in Budapest

Hungarians celebrate the capture of a Soviet tank

Hungarian weapons were no match for Soviet troops and tanks.

Life in Hungary became difficult under Soviet-led rule. Soviet leaders installed a Hungarian leader who followed their orders. That leader, Janos Kadar, came down harshly on the Hungarians. Hungarians could not publicly express their views about the new government. Those who dared to were imprisoned or executed.

rebuilt. Farms returned to full production.

Europe's rate of economic growth varied from nation to nation. West Germany led the way with factories that manufactured cameras, electronic goods, chemicals, and automobiles. Although production was less spectacular elsewhere, Western Europe as a whole was producing more by 1963 than it had produced in the 1930s.

Economic aid from the United States helped restart Europe's economy. As you have read, Europeans had led the world in the industrial revolution in the 1700s and 1800s. This meant that Europeans were rebuilding on an already well-established industrial and agricultural base. The people were experienced workers and managers.

Steps Toward Economic Unity

In the Cold War years, while western Europeans cooperated in defense against the Soviet Union, they also began to lower trade barriers. In 1951, France, West Germany, Belgium, Luxembourg, The Netherlands, and Italy formed the European Coal and Steel Community. They pooled their coal and steel resources and abolished tariffs on these vital industrial materials. This proved to be a first step toward forming what would become the **European Union**, an organization of full economic cooperation.

WORD ORIGINS

Sending people into space was one of the most dramatic times of the United States-Soviet rivalry. The space travelers were called astronauts.

The word **astronaut** is a recent addition to our language. Invented in 1929, it comes from two Latin words: *astro*, meaning "star," and *naut*, meaning "sailor."

High-speed trains entering a French station are symbolic of Europe's postwar industrial surge. *Why did Europe's economy recover so quickly?*

In 1957, for example, several nations formed a "Common Market." This agreement lowered trade barriers. This brought once rival nations together in a giant marketplace.

In 1991, a treaty was signed that provided for closer economic unity. By the mid-1990s, as the map on the right shows, 15 nations had joined the European Union. The countries trade freely and are working under a single system of currency.

Despite two terrible wars and the loss of empires, Western Europe had rebounded. As the world moved toward a new century, the continent had again emerged as an economic and political powerhouse.

The Soviet Union and Eastern Europe were not as fortunate. Under communism, their economies did not grow as quickly. The Soviet Union used the resources of Eastern European countries under Soviet control.

European Union, 1995

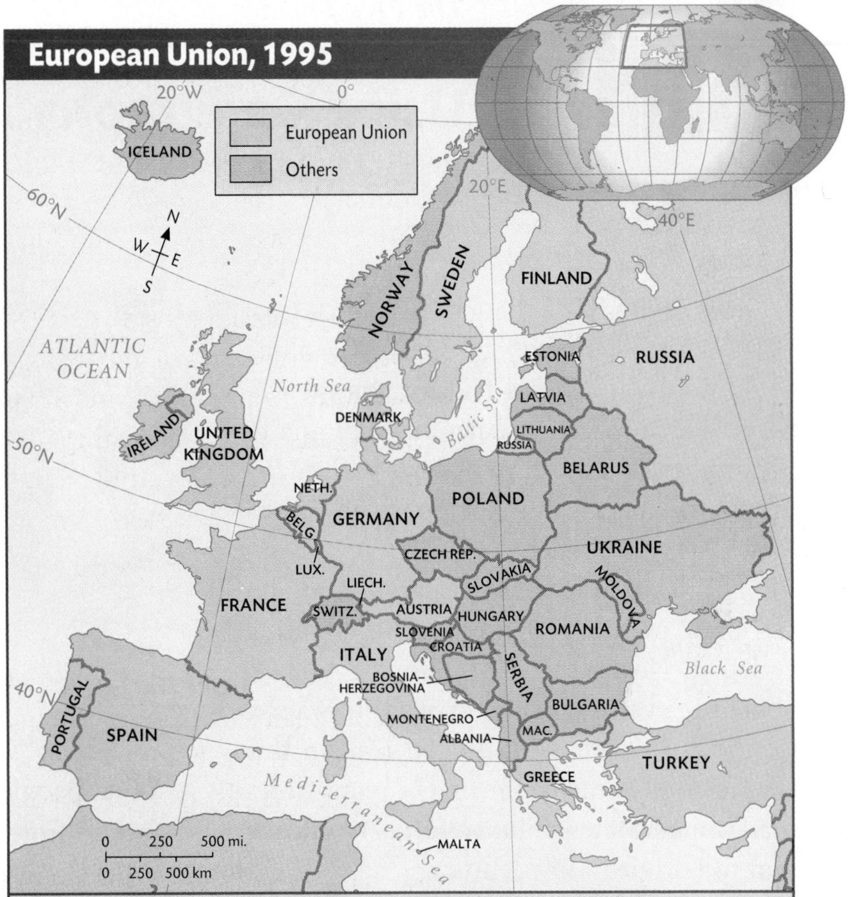
European Union
Others
20°W
0°
20°E
40°E
60°N
50°N
40°N
N
W
E
S
ICELAND
ATLANTIC OCEAN
North Sea
Baltic Sea
NORWAY
SWEDEN
FINLAND
ESTONIA
RUSSIA
LATVIA
LITHUANIA
RUSSIA
DENMARK
IRELAND
UNITED KINGDOM
NETH.
BELG.
LUX.
GERMANY
POLAND
BELARUS
UKRAINE
CZECH REP.
SLOVAKIA
MOLDOVA
LIECH.
FRANCE
SWITZ.
AUSTRIA
HUNGARY
SLOVENIA
CROATIA
ROMANIA
ITALY
BOSNIA–HERZEGOVINA
SERBIA
Black Sea
BULGARIA
MONTENEGRO
ALBANIA
MAC.
PORTUGAL
SPAIN
TURKEY
GREECE
Mediterranean Sea
MALTA
0 250 500 mi.
0 250 500 km

Region **Economic strength through the European Union might mean lasting peace for Europe.** *What nations have become a part of the European Union?*

LESSON 3 REVIEW

Fact Follow-up

1. Winston Churchill used the phrase "an iron curtain." What did he mean by it?
2. Describe NATO and the Warsaw Pact. Who established them? Why?
3. How did Europe's experience with industrialism help its economic recovery?
4. Why were the United States and the Soviet Union called "superpowers"?

Think These Through

5. In what ways did both world wars reduce Europe's economic and political power?
6. How did Europe rebound in the years since World War II?

The Five Themes of Geography

Using Geography's Themes: Movement

Tom Wilkins, of the graduating class of 1918 at the University of North Carolina, could not be in Chapel Hill for commencement. The university mailed his diploma to his mother because Tom—along with many of his classmates—was serving in the United States Army in France.

The United States declared war on Germany in 1917. By the time the fighting ended in November 1918, about 1 million United States troops had arrived in France. Of these, 100,000 died. As you read in this chapter, this would be the first of many times that United States military forces would be sent to Europe in this century.

Your reading in this chapter on the United States in World War I illustrates **movement**, one of the Five Themes of Geography.

Note that Tom Wilkins was in Chapel Hill in 1917. When his class graduated the next year, he was in France. He had "moved" with hundreds of thousands of other young Americans about a quarter of the way around the earth. The United States sent many things with these men—guns, artillery, ammunition, uniforms, food, and medical supplies.

The movement of such a huge force and its supplies in such a short time was a major achievement. You can understand how it was done and the results by using the questions that geographers use to analyze movement:

Tar Heel troops left home to fight in World War I

1. What people, goods, and ideas are moved from one place to another?
2. What event or events prompt the movement?
3. How are people, goods, and ideas moved?

Movement: Organizer 1

Things to be Moved

↓

Event

↑

How Things Are Moved

Make a graphic organizer like the one on page 98 and begin to fill it out. You should already have enough data from this skill lesson and the lesson on World War I in this chapter to fill in the sections "Things to be Moved" and "How Things Are Moved."

You also know that United States troops and supplies moved on ships across the Atlantic Ocean. But that is only part of the story. How might Tom Wilkins have moved from Chapel Hill to an army training camp in the United States? How would he have moved from the training camp to a port such as New York? How might he have moved from a port on the French coast to camps in France and then on to a battlefield? Hint: Think about transportation systems in the early twentieth century. What might have been available?

Geographers also ask questions about why movement may sometimes be impossible, difficult, or slow. When people, goods, or things move rapidly, they ask what speeded movement. The graphic organizer above should help you list your answers to these questions in an orderly fashion.

First, think about barriers to movement. Look at the world maps in Chapter 1 or the Atlas. Refer also to the map of France on page 81. About how far was it from Chapel Hill to New York, from New York to France, and from the French coast to battle lines in eastern France? Might distance have been a barrier? Imagine what other barriers might have stopped or slowed movement? Hint: Reread what is said about submarines. What "aids" or "helps" might have speeded the movement of men and war supplies?

Now you are ready for the last question geographers ask. What was the result or effect of the movement? The answer to that is in the lesson on World War I. Did the United States help defeat Germany? Put your answer—along with items already recorded—on the organizer below. When you have done that, you will have a well-thought-out and organized explanation of how Tom Wilkins and all the other men and supplies contributed to the defeat of Germany.

Movement: Organizer 2	
Barriers to Movement	Aids to Movement

Movement: Organizer 3				
Things to be Moved	How Things Are Moved	Barriers to Movement	Aids to Movement	Effects/Results of Movement

Chapter 5 Review

LESSON 1 At the time, World War I, 1914-1919, was the bloodiest and most costly conflict in Europe's history. Germany lost its colonial empire. Austria-Hungary broke into many smaller countries. Czarist Russia collapsed and came under Communist rule. The victorious British, French, and Italians suffered heavy losses.

LESSON 2 World War II broke out in Europe in 1939. After the Japanese attack on Pearl Harbor in 1941, the United States joined fighting that was worldwide. When the fighting stopped in 1945, almost every European power lay in ruins. The last of Europe's once vast world empires were lost.

LESSON 3 The United States and the Soviet Union dominated Europe. By the 1950s, however, the British Isles, Norden, and the nations of Western and Mediterranean Europe had begun to rebound. Generous economic assistance from the United States, Europe's own resources, and international cooperation combined to restore Europe as a center of world power.

TIME FOR TERMS

alliances	trenches
Nazis	Axis
Allies	Cold War
containment	NATO
Warsaw Pact	European Union

FACT FOLLOW-UP

1. How did an assassination in Sarajevo lead to World War I?
2. Describe the ways that trench warfare contributed to a long, bloody war.
3. Name the key nations fighting one another in World War I.
4. How did technology influence warfare in World War I? in World War II?
5. What were the most important results of World War I?
6. Italy under Mussolinii and Germany under Hitler were dictatorships. After studying these governments, how would you describe a dictatorship?
7. What was the lineup of warring nations in World War II?
8. How were World Wars I and II alike and different?
9. What were some causes of the Cold War?

THINK THESE THROUGH

10. After World War II, West Germany's recovery was encouraged to help check communism's expansion. Some European leaders feared that a healthy West Germany might be dangerous. What might have been the reason for these fears?
11. The European part of World War II was fought partly to check the spread of German Nazism and Italian dictatorships. Why do you think that such democracies as the United Kingdom and the United States might have been concerned about the spread of these political and economic ideas?

12. The United States played a much larger role in World War II than in World War I. Between 1941 and 1945, our nation contributed to the war in Europe by moving millions of men and military supplies to North Africa, the British Isles, and the European continent. Using the map of the war and the text, demonstrate how geography's theme of movement helps you understand the challenges solved by the United States. Fill out three graphic organizers as you did for World War I.

Use the letters on the map to locate and name the following places:

13. The European members of the Axis powers.

14. Major European powers opposed to the Axis.

15. Countries or areas occupied by Axis powers in Europe.

Reviewing Place Location

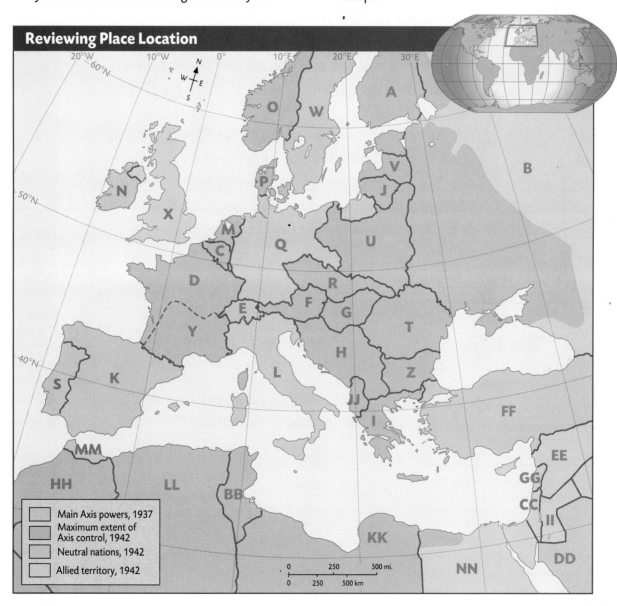

Main Axis powers, 1937
Maximum extent of Axis control, 1942
Neutral nations, 1942
Allied territory, 1942

UNIT 2

The British Isles and Norden

How would you like to try bicycling on this street? This is Shaftesbury, located near England's southern coast. It is one of many old villages in Europe. Steep streets and small villages offer one view of life in the British Isles and Norden.

Stockholm's throngs of people and London's office workers crowding the "tube" (subway) offer another. Factories and governments employ thousands of people. Fashions, theater, and historical landmarks bring tourists. Europe influences the world's culture, economy, and politics.

UNIT PREVIEW

CHAPTER 6
Lands and People
The British Isles and Norden are two distinct regions, differing in landforms and people.

CHAPTER 7
People and Their Environment
The British Isles and Norden are places of changing human-environmental relationships.

CHAPTER 8
Economy and Government
The economies of both regions are strong and growing. All nations in

these regions are deeply committed to democracy.

CHAPTER 9
Society and Culture
Although the British Isles and Norden have much in common, daily lives reveal differences in language, customs, religious faiths, and recreation.

Shaftesbury, England

CHAPTER 6

Lands and People

From a hill in Sweden high above the Baltic Sea, hang gliders take off, soaring over the shining waters. On the hill sits a monument, called Ale's Stones, made of huge half-buried stones that form the shape of a ship. The ship's prow points to the place in the sky where the sun appears at the winter solstice, the shortest day of the year.

For centuries, the Ale's Stones have served as a landmark for sailors. Today, the monument symbolizes the importance of the sea and sun to the people of two European regions—the British Isles and Norden.

Ale's Stones

Countries of Norden
Iceland
Denmark
Norway
Sweden
Finland

Countries of the British Isles
United Kingdom
Ireland

Five Regions of Europe

30°W 20°W 10°W 0° 10°E 20°E 30°E

70°N

Barents Sea

Reykjavik ✪ **ICELAND**

Arctic Circle

60°N

Norwegian Sea

FINLAND

Helsinki ✪

FAROE IS. (Den.)

SHETLAND IS. (U.K.)

ATLANTIC OCEAN

Oslo ✪   **SWEDEN** ✪ Stockholm   ✪ Tallinn   **RUSSIA**
NORWAY   **ESTONIA**

Gulf of Bothnia

Baltic Sea

Scotland

No. Ireland

North Sea

Riga ✪ **LATVIA**

DENMARK   **LITHUANIA**

✪ Copenhagen   **RUSSIA**   Vilnius ✪

Dublin ✪   **UNITED**   **NETHERLANDS**   ✪ Minsk
IRELAND   **KINGDOM**

Wales   Amsterdam ✪   Berlin ✪   **POLAND**   **BELARUS**
England   ✪ The Hague   **GERMANY**   Warsaw ✪

London ✪   Brussels ✪   ✪ Kiev
BELGIUM

LUXEMBOURG   Prague ✪   **UKRAINE**
CZECH REP.

Paris ✪   **LIECHTENSTEIN**   **SLOVAKIA**
Bratislava ✪   Budapest ✪   **MOLDOVA**
FRANCE   Bern ✪   Vienna ✪   ✪ Kishinev

Bay of Biscay

SWITZ.   **AUSTRIA**   **HUNGARY**
Ljubljana ✪   **ROMANIA**
SLOVENIA   Zagreb ✪
MONACO   **CROATIA**   ✪ Bucharest
SAN MARINO   **BOSNIA-**   ✪ Belgrade   *Black Sea*
ANDORRA   **HERZEGOVINA**
40°N   Sarajevo ✪   **SERBIA**   **BULGARIA**

PORTUGAL   ✪ Madrid   *CORSICA* (Fr.)   **ITALY**   Podgorica ✪   Sofia ✪
Lisbon   Rome ✪   **MONTENEGRO**   Skopje ✪
SPAIN   **ALBANIA**   **MACEDONIA**   **TURKEY**
SARDINIA (It.)
BALEARIC IS. (Sp.)   Tiranë ✪
Aegean Sea
GREECE

Strait of Gibraltar   Gibraltar (U.K.)

M e d i t e r r a n e a n   S e a

Athens ✪

SICILY (It.)

MALTA

CRETE (Gr.)

30°N

AFRICA

▢	The British Isles
▢	Norden
▢	Western Europe
▢	Mediterranean
▢	Eastern Europe
✪	National Capital
—	International boundary

0   250   500 mi.
0   250   500 km

Location Influences Life

LESSON PREVIEW

Key Ideas

- The United Kingdom and Ireland are in the British Isles. Norden includes Iceland, Norway, Sweden, Finland, and Denmark.
- The British Isles and Norden's latitudes are about the same as Canada's.
- These nations are warmed by winds blowing over the ocean.

Women in the Shetland Islands contribute to family income by knitting sweaters. *Why are the sweaters made of woolen yarn?*

heep outnumber people on the Shetland Islands. The islanders knit wool into sweaters valued worldwide for their warmth and beauty.

By an electric hearth in their modern home in the Shetland Islands, eighty-year-old Laura Malcolmson teaches her great-grandniece Romaine Kemp how to knit a sweater. One of the most challenging patterns Romaine will learn, the fisherman's knit, imitates the weave of a fishing net. The fishing image symbolizes the islanders' attachment to the sea. They depend on the sea for food, trade, and connections to other parts of the world.

The Shetland Islands are part of the British Isles (see page 105), one of Europe's five regions. The British Isles are located west of the European mainland and are occupied by the United Kingdom and Ireland. A second region, Norden, includes Iceland, Norway, Sweden, Finland, and Denmark. Norden means "the north." It is the word used by Europeans for the region located to the north and east of the British Isles.

The other three regions of Europe are Western Europe, the Mediterranean, and Eastern Europe. The map on page 105 shows the location of Europe's five regions.

Location on Water

Nations of Norden and the British Isles contain long stretches of shoreline along the Atlantic Ocean, the Norwegian Sea, the North Sea, the Baltic Sea, and the English Channel.

Wherever you are in these lands, you're never far from the sea. This nearness to water influences how people live, work, and spend their leisure time.

Northern Latitudes

Every year, on the last Friday in June, fourteen-year-old Matti celebrates the beginning of summer at a festival in Finland's capital city, Helsinki. Fortune-tellers stroll and folk dancers weave patterns to welcome the days of light. Matti and his friends cheer the end of months spent in near-darkness. They watch the lighting of a 60-foot (18-meter)- high bonfire, then rush to devour roasted sausage.

Helsinki is located only a few hundred miles south of the Arctic Circle, which cuts across the northernmost part of the region. Norden and the British Isles are quite far north. In fact, the southernmost tip of England is at 50° N, the same latitude as Winnipeg, Canada. That's farther north than any place in the United States except Alaska.

Living so far north means seeing little of the winter sun. In Norway, Sweden, and Finland, midwinter nights last for 20 or 21 hours out of every 24. As the chart shows, the Northern Hemisphere is tilted away from the sun during winter.

In the summertime, the exact opposite happens. The Northern Hemisphere is tilted toward the sun. In Oslo, Norway, the sun is still up at 11:15 P.M. in late June. In northern Norway, Sweden, and Finland, the sun never sets during May, June, and July.

Young people in Helsinki, Finland (above), dance during the summer festival. *Why does summer mean a return to the long days of sunlight, according to the illustration below?*

The Northern Hemisphere is tilted toward the sun in the summer, so places in the Northern Hemisphere receive longer hours of sunlight. During the winter, beginning on December 21, the Northern Hemisphere, is tilted away from the sun. *How does this affect Norden?*

Vernal equinox (March 21)

Summer solstice (June 21)

Winter solstice (December 21)

Autumnal equinox (September 21)

To locate the lands of the British Isles and Norden on the map on page 105, look for the prime meridian, the line of longitude marked 0°. The prime meridian runs through England (part of the United Kingdom), passing through the city of Greenwich, near London. East of the prime meridian are Finland, Norway, Sweden, and Denmark.

Climate

Despite being close to the Arctic Circle, most of the British Isles and Norden enjoy a moderate climate. The North Atlantic Drift, the current of warm water that begins in the Gulf of Mexico, influences the climate.

A City on the Arctic Circle

Imagine living in a place where a day lasts for two and a half months and where a night lasts for two months. That is life in the Norwegian town of Hammerfest, the northernmost city in Europe.

Hammerfest, which lies almost four degrees north of the Arctic Circle—less than 1,400 miles (2,254 km) from the North Pole—has been called "the city of one day and one night." The sun shines from May 17 to July 29. There is no sunlight at all from November 21 to January 21. "At first, it's confusing, not seeing the sun rise every morning," says one resident. "But we still know it's there because we see it for two months in the summer."

Even though Hammerfest is so far north, temperatures there usually remain above freezing for most of the year because of the warming effects of the North Atlantic Drift. Hammerfest's harbor remains free of ice year-round, allowing residents to earn a living by fishing the Norwegian Sea.

Temperatures stay warm enough for Norwegians to raise cattle and pigs.

Another key industry of the town is tourism. People from all over Europe come every year to experience life north of the Arctic Circle.

The drift flows north through the Atlantic Ocean into the North Sea, then along the Norwegian coast. A branch of the drift flows near Iceland.

Because of this warming current of water, the Atlantic Ocean and the North Sea never freeze. The North Atlantic Drift also moderates the climate of the British Isles and Norden.

Warm, wet winds blow eastward off the drift across all of the British Isles, Denmark, and southern Sweden. Even southern Finland benefits from winds blowing from the Atlantic Ocean and Baltic Sea (see climate maps on pages 125 and 580). These winds produce the cool summers and mild winters of a moderate climate. Rain falls in every season of the year.

Even in Iceland and Norway, the weather along the coast remains relatively mild due to the North Atlantic Drift. But inland, away from the moderating winds, the climates are humid continental or subarctic. Winters in these areas can be bitterly cold, with the Arctic winds bringing frigid temperatures and heavy snows. Sweden and Finland also experience these climates.

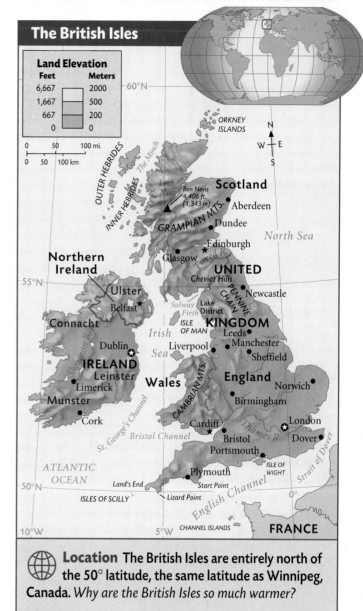

The British Isles

Land Elevation

Feet		Meters
6,667		2000
1,667		500
667		200
0		0

0   50   100 mi.
0   50   100 km

Location The British Isles are entirely north of the 50° latitude, the same latitude as Winnipeg, Canada. *Why are the British Isles so much warmer?*

(see climate maps on pages 125 and 580)

LESSON 1 REVIEW

Fact Follow-Up
1. How do sun and sea affect Norden?
2. What is the importance of the North Atlantic Drift for people living in Norden and the British Isles?
3. Describe the location of Norden and the British Isles relative to North America.

Think These Through
4. Which—sun or sea—affects Norden and the British Isles most? Explain.
5. Describe what Norden and the British Isles would be like without the North Atlantic Drift.

Describing Norden and the British Isles

"We like our hills green," says Halla Svavardottir, as she shovels black volcanic ash from the side of a cliff in the village of Vestmannaeyjar, Iceland. "Look where we have planted grass," Halla points to the slope near the village. "Once that was black. Now it is green."

Teenage Halla and her friends have worked three summers cleaning up the hillside after the eruption of the volcano Eldfell (Fire Mountain). They scooped the black ash into a chute connected to a truck that hauled it away. Where the ash was too deep to shovel away, Halla and her friends fertilized the area and planted grass.

Iceland

About 75 percent of Iceland—an island about the size of Virginia—is covered with volcanic lava, huge glaciers, and snow-capped mountains. A range of volcanic mountains runs north to south through the center of the island and continues underwater.

Iceland sits on a spot where the earth's crust is slowly separating. This means that volcanoes erupt frequently, both above ground and underwater. Iceland has earned its nickname, "The Land of Frost and Fire."

Despite these limitations, about 265,000 Icelandic people live comfortably in or near their capital city, Reykjavík (REY·kjah·vik), or in smaller towns along the coast. There summers are cool and winters are mild. Ports remain free of ice, and enough grass grows to feed sheep.

A harsh land of cold glacier lakes, Iceland also has hot volcanic eruptions. How does Iceland's nickname describe these conditions?

The Scandinavian Peninsula

Norway and Sweden make up the **Scandinavian peninsula**. The peninsula is a long, narrow stretch of

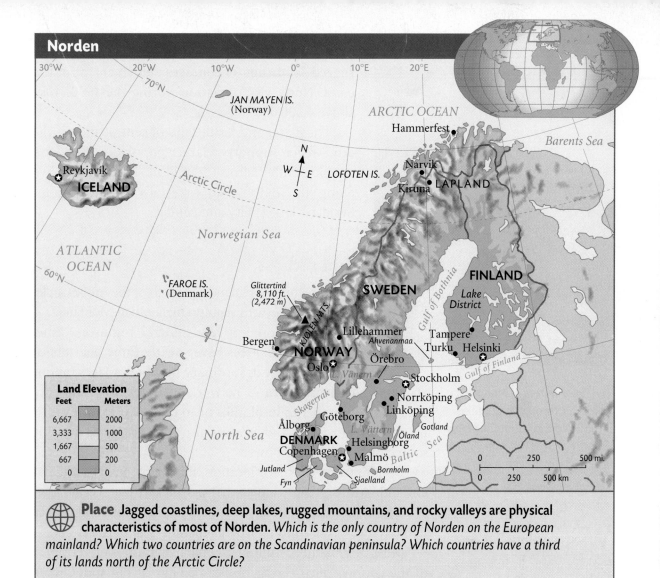

Norden

Land Elevation

Feet	Meters
6,667	2000
3,333	1000
1,667	500
667	200
0	0

Place Jagged coastlines, deep lakes, rugged mountains, and rocky valleys are physical characteristics of most of Norden. *Which is the only country of Norden on the European mainland? Which two countries are on the Scandinavian peninsula? Which countries have a third of its lands north of the Arctic Circle?*

land with a jagged coastline (see map above).

A high mountain range in the west, the "mountainous spine" of Scandinavia, dominates the peninsula. The land south and east of the mountains slopes gently.

Norway's coast is jagged with **fjords** (fyords), inlets with steep sides carved by huge glaciers during the Ice Age. From Norway's northern coast on the Arctic Ocean to the Skagerrak Strait, 1,000 miles (1,610 km) of coastline actually measures 5,000 miles (8,050 km) if you include the fjords. Fjords give Norway natural ports. Their beauty attracts tourists.

In addition to fjords, Ice Age glaciers also formed the rugged landscape, scraping away most of the topsoil. Left behind was rocky, flinty earth not very good for farming. As in Iceland, the

The deep waters of Norway's fjords cut through mountains into the country's interior. *How does the picture explain why little farming is done in Norway?*

rugged landscape encourages settlement near the coast. Norway's population during the 1990s rose above 4,300,000.

The flatter and fertile land of central and southern Sweden supports a larger population. Sweden's people number almost 9 million. The majority live along the Baltic Sea, especially in Stockholm, Sweden's largest city and capital.

Finland

One third of Finland lies north of the Arctic Circle. Finland has an area slightly smaller than Montana.

The nation has few mineral resources. Pine, spruce, and fir trees cover nearly three quarters of Finland. The extraordinary number of lakes (about 60,000) and streams form a network of waterways. They are used to float lumber to local mills or to the seacoast for export. In recent years, rivers and streams also have served as a major source of hydroelectric power.

Despite its far northern location, Finland contains some flat lowlands with soil and climate that permit farming. Fertile lowlands in southwestern Finland rise into an area of forests and lakes in the center of the country, where Finlanders go on vacation.

Most of Finland's 5 million people live in the southern part of the country, near the Baltic Sea or Gulf of Finland. Others cluster around the shores of the many lakes.

Denmark

Denmark is the only country of Norden located on the European mainland. It includes several large islands, many smaller ones, and the Jutland peninsula, which extends into the North Sea toward the Scandinavian peninsula. The country is surrounded by water, except for a 42-mile (68-km) boundary with Germany.

The low-lying, flat land of Denmark forms part of the European Plain. Denmark's productive farmland makes it the only country in Norden able to grow enough food to feed its population. The other countries of the region must import food.

Denmark's population is about equal to Finland's 5 million. The people, however, live mostly in cities and towns located in a land much smaller than Finland, Norway, or Sweden.

The British Isles

About 5,000 islands make up the British Isles. The largest is Britain, about the size of Minnesota. Ireland is the second largest. The other islands are small.

Britain consists of three once independent nations—Scotland, England, and Wales—now under a single government centered in London. Britain and Northern Ireland form a nation called the United Kingdom. Its official name is the United Kingdom of Great Britain and Northern Ireland. About 80 percent of the nation's 58 million people live in England.

The southern part of Ireland is an independent nation, the Republic of Ireland (also called Eire). It is much smaller than the United Kingdom in size and population. Today, less than 4 million people live in Ireland.

The United Kingdom's Southeast is grassy plains. To the west and north, the land turns to low, wooded hills. Along the northern coast are granite highlands. The western coastline offers many natural ports. The Thames River in eastern England made London a major port city despite its inland location.

A green plateau rises in central Ireland, with gently rolling hills and mountains near the coast. Ireland's western coast is rugged, with bays and inlets.

Houses crowd along the water in Nyhavn Harbor, Denmark. *Why do most Danish people live close to the sea?*

◆ ◆ ◆ ◆ **GAMES** ◆ ◆ ◆ ◆
People Play

Cricket, a sport popular throughout Britain, looks like a combination of baseball, croquet, and bowling. The game is played when a bowler runs and tosses a ball toward a batsman, who tries to hit the ball with a long paddle. The bowler wins points if his ball strikes a goal called a wicket.

◆ ◆ ◆ ◆ ◆ ◆ ◆ ◆ ◆ ◆ ◆ ◆ ◆ ◆ ◆

LESSON 2 REVIEW

Fact Follow-Up
1. Using the theme of place, describe the physical characteristics of Norden.
2. How is Denmark similar to other nations in Norden? How is it different?
3. Compare the physical characteristics of Norden and the British Isles.

Think These Through
4. Pick one place in Norden or the British Isles that you would like to visit. Why?
5. How do landforms affect movement in the regions of Norden and the British Isles?

People of the British Isles and Norden

LESSON PREVIEW

Key Ideas
- The British, Irish, and Norden's people share similar ideas about democratic government, and, except for the Irish, most are Protestants.
- Many languages are spoken in the regions.
- A variety of cultural traditions are honored.

Key Terms
Vikings, Lapps

This statue of a Celtic warrior is a rare image from a group of people who settled in England. *When did the Celts come to England?*

Tan y'n cunys lemmyn gor uskys—"Now set the pyre at once on fire." In ancient Cornish, the proclamation rings out at sunset on Midsummer's Eve. Around a bonfire on the English hill, everyone sings while the children dance in a circle to the right, the direction the sun travels.

These celebrants are members of the Federation of Old Cornwall Societies. The group works to keep alive the traditions of the Celts, who were the ancestors of many now living in the British Isles.

"I have learned to speak Cornish because I am Celtic," explains Janet Fennell, who wears the pleated skirt of the traditional kilt. "I taught my daughter to speak it, so she will feel Celtic, too. We are Celts, not English, not Anglo-Saxons. We must make our heritage live, as must the Irish, the Welsh, the Bretons, and the Scots." These groups have lived in the British Isles for thousands of years.

The British Isles

Most of the people living in the British Isles today are descended from those different groups of ancient Europeans. The first of these groups, the Celts, reached the islands almost 3,000 years ago. Today, the Celtic traditions and those of other ancient people remain.

The Scots, for example, are especially proud of their centuries of independence. Scotland has preserved many of its old laws and has its own education system. Most Scots have not joined the Church of England. They remain Presbyterian.

Wales flies its own flag and prints its own postage stamps. Even more important has been the people's determination to hold on to their traditional language.

CROESO
I GYMRU
WELCOME
TO WALES

Everyone speaks English, but about 20 percent of the people still use Welsh first and English second.

Despite these differences, the people of the United Kingdom today share a commitment to democratic government and a sense of belonging to the same nation. They have served together in war and peace.

Divisions between Ireland and the United Kingdom run deeper and have caused many wars. When English kings began to rule in Ireland hundreds of years ago, the Irish resisted. English-Irish conflicts became even worse when the English broke with the Roman Catholic Church and established the Church of England. Most Irish remained faithful Catholics.

Much of Ireland won its independence from Great Britain in 1921. Six counties in the Northeast, where most people were Protestants, split away to form Northern Ireland, which remains part of the United Kingdom. This arrangement, however, has not brought peace. Protestants and Catholics have continued to fight each other in Northern Ireland.

The people of the British Isles are descended from many different European groups. The Highland dancers are Scottish. The sign shows the Welsh language. *What other groups live in the British Isles?*

Norden

The people of Norden share more than homelands with similar climates and location. They also have a shared history.

From about A.D. 800 to 1050, fierce warriors called **Vikings** sailed from Denmark, Norway, and Sweden to raid towns in other parts of Europe. Iceland, Norway, and Sweden have been united in the past under Danish rule. Sweden and Finland once lived under a common government.

People of Norway, Sweden, Finland, Denmark, and Iceland share similar political and economic beliefs. All five of these northern nations are democracies. All have generally tried to avoid involvement in the quarrels of the great powers. Their people support peaceful solutions to international crises.

Most residents of Norden are Lutheran. Lutheran ideas and traditions are celebrated every year in Christmas festivals, worship services, and other ceremonies.

WORD ORIGINS

The word **Viking** might have come from the Old Icelandic word *vik*, meaning "bay or creek," referring to one who sails in shallow water. The people of Norden never called themselves Vikings. Early European writers used the name, and it stuck.

EYEWITNESS TO HISTORY

The Canterbury Tales

Writing about history is like solving a mystery. Archaeologists, historians, and other scholars look for clues to help them piece together how people lived during a certain period. Often they rely on books that were written by people living at that time.

Geoffrey Chaucer described people living in his own time and place in *The Canterbury Tales.* Scholars think the *Tales* give a good picture of life in the British Isles, during the Middle Ages. Read Chaucer's description of two of his 29 characters. What can you learn from these descriptions about daily life?

Canterbury Cathedral (below) and pilgrims (right)

Page from Chaucer's Tales

Common Ties

Another shared tradition of people living in Denmark, Sweden, and Norway is language. The languages of Danish, Swedish, and Norwegian have individual characteristics. Yet a Danish-speaking person can understand someone who is speaking Swedish, and both of them might be able to have a conversation with someone who's speaking Norwegian.

Both English and the languages of Scandinavia share the same root in an old language called North Germanic. English branched off early and developed in its own way. By A.D. 800, the Vikings spoke common Scandinavian, which later developed into Danish, Norwegian, Swedish, Faroese (spoken in the Faroe Islands, see map, page 111), and Icelandic.

A good wife there was from beside [the town of] Bath (below, right). Of cloth-making she had such a skill, she surpassed them in Ypres and Gaunt [towns famed for their fine woven cloth]. Gap-toothed she was, soothly for to say. Upon a saddle-horse she sat, covered in a cloth, and on her head was a hat as broad as a buckler or a shield; a skirt about her waist, and on her feet a pair of sharp spurs.

A Yeoman ... was clad in a coat and hood of green (right). A sheaf of peacock arrows bright and keen, under his belt he bore thriftily, and in his hand he bore a mighty bow. Of woodcraft much he knew. Upon his arm he had an arm-guard, and by his side a sword and a buckler, and on that other side a dagger, well-adorned and sharp as a spear. A forester was he, truly.

Morgunbladid

STOFNAD 1913

The language that Icelanders speak today sounds basically the same as the language the Vikings spoke more than 1,000 years ago. Icelanders joke that if the original Vikings returned suddenly, they might be surprised by all the changes they would see, but they would still be able to understand the language spoken today.

The Icelanders resisted borrowing words from other languages. For example, instead of adopting the new word "telephone," Icelanders call it "simi," which means "cord" in Icelandic. Rather than calling a military tank by a foreign name during World War II, Icelanders invented their own descriptive term. It translates as "creeping dragon."

Icelanders speak and write much the same language as their ancestors spoke 1,000 years ago. *Why is that important?*

Finland

No one can say for certain who were the ancestors of the modern Finns. There are some clues about their origins.

Today, Finns speak and write a language entirely different from the other languages of Norden. Finnish most closely resembles languages used in neighboring Estonia and more distant Hungary.

Scholars who study the origins of languages think that the ancestors of all these people migrated from the region that is present-day Russia. Many Finnish people today speak and write Swedish as well as their own language.

Lapland

Finland shares with Norway, Sweden, and some of neighboring Russia a region called Lapland. The region is bordered on the north by the Arctic Ocean. While the region has no definite southern border, all of it is located north of the Arctic Circle.

The region's inhabitants, the **Lapps**, probably moved into the far North about 9,000 years ago from central Russia. Their ancestors and those of the Finns may have been related, but the Lapps speak a language of their own. They have traditionally lived apart from their southern neighbors. Their lives have been different from the Finnish, Swedish, and Norwegians because their homelands are so cold and dark much of the year.

Lapland is a bleak, barren tundra region with few trees and not much other vegetation. The trees seldom grow more than a few feet high. Reindeer live in this forbidding environment. Most Laplanders have survived by breeding reindeer and following their herds as the animals search for lichen (reindeer moss) to eat. Because of this harsh lifestyle, Lapps had little contact with other groups of people.

Today, the Lapps see more outsiders. Ever-increasing numbers of tourists visit Lapland during the short summers. Most Lapps have joined Finnish, Swedish, and Norwegian people in becoming members of the Lutheran Church. Lapps living in Finland sometimes work in lumber mills, and in Sweden they work in northern iron mines. On a few occasions they have flown in helicopters to help round up reindeer herds. Others earn their living from the sea by fishing in the Norwegian Sea, Arctic Ocean, and Barents Sea (see map, page 111).

Lapland in northern Norway, Sweden, and Finland is the home of the Lapps. They herd reindeer and adapt in other ways to the cold environment. *How has life changed for Lapps?*

LESSON 3 REVIEW

Fact Follow-Up
1. What similar characteristics are shared by the nations of Norden that make it a region?
2. What characteristics are shared by the different parts of the United Kingdom that make it a region?
3. How is Finland similar to and different from other areas of Norden?

Think These Through
4. In which region—Norden or the British Isles—is culture a major characteristic that brings people together? Explain.
5. Does language bring people together or divide them in Norden? Explain.

Using Geography's Themes: Region

Geographers identify the British Isles and Norden as two regions of Europe. The Five Themes of Geography define a **region** as "a large area with one or more common features that set it apart from other regions." In the weeks ahead you will continue to study Europe and Northern Asia by region—Western Europe, Mediterranean Europe, Eastern Europe, and Russia.

Each region occupies a part of land that stretches thousands of miles from the Atlantic Ocean to the Pacific Ocean. Millions of people speaking different languages, holding different beliefs, and living in different ways inhabit this vast land.

Geographers discovered long ago that they could not learn about all of these lands and people unless they organized their data carefully. They discovered that the job could be done if they focused on one region at a time. Then they could fit together what they had learned, much like assembling a jigsaw puzzle.

The geographers' approach is one that you might already use. Imagine, for example, that you collect trading cards in four sports—basketball, football, baseball, and ice hockey. You might have started this hobby by collecting cards in only one sport, perhaps because you discovered that you could not learn about every sport all at one time. By looking closely at one sport, you are studying a "region" of sport.

In this skill lesson you will discover why the British Isles and Norden are defined as separate regions. By organizing facts about the British Isles and Norden, you will understand how they have different characteristics. When you finish, you will have learned how to compare these regions.

The British Isles and Norden are first defined by their physical features. Each has its own location, mix of landforms, waterways, and climate. Review Chapter 6 for the *physical* characteristics of the British Isles that set them apart from Norden.

To record these characteristics, create two graphic organizers—one for the British Isles and one for Norden—that look like the one to the left. Complete the lines by describing the region's landforms, climate, waterways, and location.

Within a region the mix of landforms, waterways, and climate are usually similar.

Physical Characteristics

Landforms   Climate

1.
2.
3.
4.

Waterways   Location

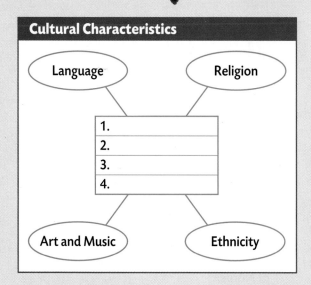

Cultural Characteristics

Language

Religion

1.
2.
3.
4.

Art and Music

Ethnicity

Do not be surprised, however, if you discover that the physical characteristics of some areas within a region are different. Geographers do not insist that everything in a region be exactly the same.

Denmark is a good example. Review the description of that country in Lesson 2. In what physical ways does Denmark differ from the rest of Norden? If Denmark is physically different, why is it in Norden?

You would find the answer if you also knew that geographers also define regions by *culture*. Cultural characteristics include language, religious beliefs, styles in art and music, and ethnicity (a shared origin of a group of people). To record these characteristics, create two graphic organizers—one for the British Isles and one for Norden—that look like the one to the left.

Keep in mind that you are looking for a mix of cultural features that makes a large area stand apart from others. As with physical characteristics, not everything has to be exactly the same.

That is also true of regions. What are the differences between the British Isles and Norden? Are there also similarities? You can answer these questions by taking the information from your graphic organizers to complete the Comparing Regions chart below. The chart helps you organize your findings to describe two of Europe's regions and to understand why Northern Europe is separated into these two regions.

Comparing Regions	Norden	British Isles
1. Physical Characteristics		
a) landforms		
b) climate		
c) waterways		
d) location		
2. Cultural Characteristics		
a) language		
b) religion		
c) ethnicity		
d) art and music		

Chapter 6 Review

LESSON 1 The British Isles and Norden—two of Europe's regions—have seven nations located in the northern latitudes. Winds blowing over warm ocean currents provide all of the British Isles and parts of Norden with a moderate climate. Northern and interior areas of Norway, Sweden, and Finland do not receive as much benefit from these warming winds. In Norden, winter nights are long. Summers with many hours of daylight are short.

LESSON 2 Islands, peninsulas, and protected harbors give almost everyone in the British Isles and Norden access to the seas. Except in Denmark, poor soil limits farming in Norden. Forests cover much of Sweden and Finland. The British Isles provide more opportunity for farming.

LESSON 3 English is the common language in the British Isles. In much of Norden—Iceland, Norway, and Sweden—people use languages that are related. The Finnish and Lapp languages are not related to others in the region. The people of the British Isles and Norden share a commitment to democratic government. Except for the Irish, most in both the British Isles and Norden are Protestant Christians. Lapps have their own language and live in a region that crosses borders.

TIME FOR TERMS

Scandinavian peninsula   fjords
Vikings   Lapps

FACT FOLLOW-UP

1. How does geographic location influence life in the British Isles? in Norden?
2. Describe patterns of human-environmental interaction in Lapland.
3. How does the sea contribute to the movement of people, goods, and ideas in any two nations of Norden?
4. Describe the cultural characteristics of the United Kingdom.
5. Describe the physical characteristics of Norway and Sweden.
6. Describe the relative and absolute locations of the British Isles and Norden.

THINK THESE THROUGH

7. Which seems more important in defining the British Isles and Norden as regions—the physical or cultural characteristics of place? Explain.
8. Which season of the year characterizes Norden best—summer or winter? Explain.
9. Some groups in Finland have urged that businesses be allowed to cut more trees each year than they now may cut under Finnish law. Can you think of reasons that this idea might benefit Finland? What arguments might be used against the idea?

SHARPENING SKILLS

10. Your reading suggests that the people of the British Isles often think of themselves as quite different from one another. Yet geographers say the islands are a region. Are the geographers right or wrong? Explain.

11. If a nation could be eliminated from Norden to make it a more unified region, which nation would it be? Explain.

12. Which region–Norden or the British Isles–is most unified by similar characteristics? Explain why.

13. Which is more important in defining Norden as a region–its physical or cultural characteristics? Would your answer be the same for the British Isles? Explain.

14. After filling out the large chart, were you convinced that geographers are right in defining the British Isles and Norden as separate regions? Or did you find that they had enough in common to belong to the same region?

15. Use the numbers on the map key to identify Europe's five regions.

16. Use the letters on the map to associate nations with regions. Under the heading "The British Isles," write the identifying letter and name of each nation in this region. Under the heading "Norden" write the identifying letter and name of each nation in this region.

17. Use the letters on the map to locate the major bodies of water surrounding the British Isles and Norden.

Reviewing Place Location

People and Their Environment

About 1,000 years ago, Aelfric, a monk, described life on an English farm:

Farm plow

> *I work very hard. I go out at dawn and I drive the oxen in the field…. Every day I have to plough a full acre or more. I have a boy who drives the oxen with a goad…. I fill the ox-bins.*

Few in the British Isles or Norden today would recognize that kind of life. Farmers do not till the soil as Aelfric did. Most people live in cities. New ways of life have changed the relationships of people to their environment.

CHAPTER PREVIEW

LESSON 1
Before Industry
Early Europeans had few ways to control their environment. Most were farmers and lived in small villages.

LESSON 2
An Industrial Revolution
Improvements in farming and the invention of steam-powered machinery brought industry and changed cities in the United Kingdom.

LESSON 3
The Twentieth Century
Industry and growth of cities came later to Norden. The nations in this region have enjoyed success in solving some of the problems brought by industry.

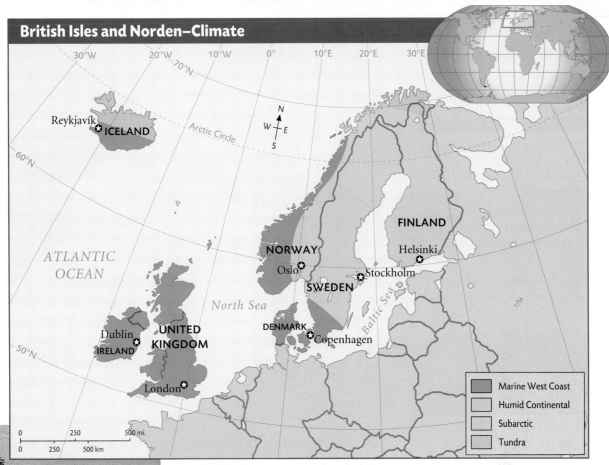

30°W   20°W   10°W   0°   10°E   20°E   30°E

70°N

Reykjavík **ICELAND**

Arctic Circle

60°N

N
W E
S

FINLAND

Helsinki

NORWAY

ATLANTIC
OCEAN

Oslo   Stockholm

SWEDEN

North Sea

Baltic Sea

50°N

Dublin **UNITED
KINGDOM**

DENMARK

IRELAND

Copenhagen

London

◼	Marine West Coast
◻	Humid Continental
◻	Subarctic
◻	Tundra

0   250   500 mi.

0   250   500 km

City life today in Norden and the British Isles, as shown in Oslo, Norway (above), contrasts with the hard rural life of the past, as shown in the seventeenth-century painting (left), Summer Harvest, *by Pieter Brueghel the Younger.*

People and Their Environment   **125**

Before Industry

LESSON 1

LESSON PREVIEW

Key Ideas
- Early settlers in Europe lived in small, self-sufficient communities.
- Improved farming and cloth manufacturing laid foundations for industry.

Key Terms
three-field system, crop rotation, peasants, manor, cottage industry

Early inhabitants of Norden and the British Isles used whatever resources they found simply to survive. The environment shaped their lives, determining their food, clothes, and work.

Describing England in the first century, Strabo, the Roman geographer, wrote that "the greater part of the island" was "level and wooded." He also noted that the people there minted their own crude coins, each of which showed an ear of barley on its face.

These coins suggest the importance of farming to early Europeans, but for many years farmers did not produce much. Farmers scattered grain on plowed fields where birds gobbled much of what had been sown. Only a few plants grew and harvests were small.

By Aelfric's time 1,000 years ago, however, farmers had already discovered how to increase production. Improved farming methods changed the Europeans' relationship with their environment.

Farming Improved

People settling in southern England found good farming land. They cut down the forests and cleared brush to plant food and graze cattle. As the population grew, farmers cut and cleared more of the forest until nearly all of the South had become farmland.

Farmers raised crops in a **three-field system**. One field would be planted in the fall with wheat or rye. A second field would be planted in the spring with such summer crops as oats, peas, beans, or barley. The third field was left fallow, or uncultivated, to permit the soil to rest. The following

Leeds Castle in England is an example of a manor house. Manor houses were the centers of rural communities during the Middle Ages. *Who lived in the manor houses?*

year the crops were rotated, and a different field was left fallow.

This system made farms more efficient by spreading planting and harvesting throughout the year. **Crop rotation** improved yields.

Still other improvements came from new inventions. Aelfric's big plow proved ideal for breaking heavy soils and preparing the ground for planting seed. When iron mining began, sturdier iron tools replaced wooden farm tools. As you will discover later, innovations such as these led to other dramatic changes in the British Isles.

Change in Norden

These improved farming methods from the British Isles were tried in Denmark where there was good farmland. But as the climate map on page 125 shows, most of Norden was too cold for farming. Norden's soils were also thin and rocky, and mountainsides were steep.

Settlers left the forests standing and turned to the sea for survival. They sailed from coastal villages to catch cod and herring. They also hunted seals.

Between the 700s and 1100s, some Norwegians, Swedes, and Danes, known as Vikings, added to their income by raiding the British Isles—Great Britain and Ireland—as well as the

A Viking raid shows why they were feared by people of the British Isles and the European mainland. *Where did Vikings originate?*

European mainland. They built boats that moved swiftly through both deep ocean or shallow river waters. Each carried 30 or 40 well-armed men, who could attack quickly, gather treasure, and disappear.

Most Vikings usually farmed or fished. Farmers, for example, planted crops, joined neighbors in raids, and then returned home to harvest their crops. The Vikings' victims, however, did not regard these raiders simply as men earning a living.

People throughout Europe feared Viking attacks. The inhabitants of tiny coastal communities seldom could defend themselves. They knew that Viking raiders would take whatever they wanted and would kill without mercy anyone who stood in their way.

The Vikings began raids in Ireland, Scotland, and England in the late eighth century. The scholar Simeon of Durham described their attack on the monastery, a religious community, at Lindisfarne:

> *They came to the church of Lindisfarne, laid everything waste with grievous plundering, trampled the holy places with polluted feet, dug up the altars, and seized all the treasures of the holy church. They killed some of the holy brothers; some they took away in fetters; many they drove out, naked and loaded with insults; and some they drowned in the sea.*

The drawing of a typical manor shows the three-field system of crop rotation. Each manor was run by a lord. *Who did the work of a manor?*

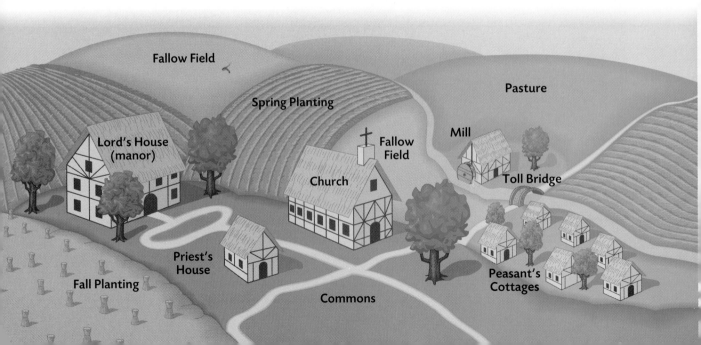

Fallow Field

Spring Planting

Pasture

Lord's House (manor)

Mill

Fallow Field

Church

Toll Bridge

Priest's House

Fall Planting

Peasant's Cottages

Commons

Living in the Middle Ages

By Europe's Middle Ages (about A.D. 500 to 1450), most people lived in places where crops could be grown. **Peasants**, the common laborers, worked in large fields belonging to a lord or nobleman. Peasants farmed the lord's land. In return, they received a portion of the food they raised and the protection that the lord could give them.

The largest crop in the British Isles and Norden was grain. Wheat, rye, and barley all were grown to make bread, which was the most important food. The lords ate the light, soft wheat bread. Everyone else ate coarser bread made from barley or rye.

The lord set aside pasture land. Here everyone could graze animals, usually pigs, cattle, and sheep. The peasants could grow grain, beans, and peas for themselves on strips of land in the fields and in gardens near their houses. Floods, drought, or unseasonable heat or cold could wipe out everyone's food supplies.

Peasants and the lord and his family made up a village community known as the **manor**. Manors could be large or small, but most had similar features, as the drawing on page 128 shows.

The lord's residence was the manor house. Depending on the lord's wealth and power, the manor house might be simply a large, fortified wooden building. A few lords lived in huge stone castles.

The peasants' houses clustered together for protection. The houses were small, one or two rooms at most. They were built from whatever materials were available. Where trees were plentiful, as in Britain or Norden, then houses were constructed of wood. Where wood was scarce, as in Ireland, people built houses using mud, clay, and stone. Roofs were usually thatched, that is, covered with tightly packed straw.

During most of the years between 500 and 1450, manors were scattered and largely self-sufficient. Located among the peasant houses were a church and village workshops. Few people traveled or conducted trade between the manor communities.

Sometimes a local fair brought some entertainment to the community. The church gathered people for worship and important religious holidays such as Easter. These occasions lightened lives that were hard and uncertain, often cut short by war or disease.

Ainwick Castle in Northumberland, England, is surrounded by fields of crops, similar to a manor of the Middle Ages. *What were the major crops grown on manor lands?*

Beginnings of Commerce

Life on a manor was cooperative. People ate what they grew. Since the fall of Rome, Europeans had no monetary system. To get items they needed, they would barter, or make a fair exchange. For example, if one family had a good crop of beans but no sheep and another family grazed several sheep but needed food, the two would barter wool for food.

Trade eventually expanded beyond manors. Trade encouraged people to specialize in what they produced. For example, English and Scottish lords who owned hundreds of sheep could sell their wool to merchants in small cities. The merchants then sold the wool in Flanders, the most important cloth-making

EYEWITNESS TO HISTORY

Attending a Fair in the Middle Ages

Fine eagle textile, Auxerre, France

"Is not your work very hard?" a priest asked a peasant in 1305. "Indeed, indeed, it is very hard," replied the peasant. One escape was the fair—a yearly gathering of merchants and entertainers. Peasants and lords could relax and have some fun.

Europe's fairs did not begin as a place to go for entertainment. Merchants gathered near a sea or river port to sell items from faraway places. Church leaders also displayed religious articles (left) during festivals. People were in a holiday mood.

Lords could look at and perhaps buy from tables crowded with spices or rich silks from Asia, glass from Venice, or Russian-made cloaks of fine fur. Sometimes merchants had medicines for some dread disease. Local merchants often purchased some of these goods to sell at other fairs. As people mixed, they swapped stories about new farming methods or ways of making things. Because the fairs were along trade routes (see map, page 131), merchandise and ideas spread throughout Europe.

Illuminated manuscript of a fair at Rouen, France

center in mainland Europe. English wool sold there brought a good price.

As the profits from wool rose, the lords began to turn their farmlands into grazing land for sheep. The more sheep they raised, the more wool they sold. The merchants who bought the wool also decided to keep more of it in England. They kept the wool and hired workers to spin and weave it. The merchants could make a better profit selling the finished cloth than they could selling the raw wool.

The English merchants paid people on the manors to spin and weave cloth at home. With this money, people could buy what they needed or wanted, instead of bartering or doing without. They could survive without farming.

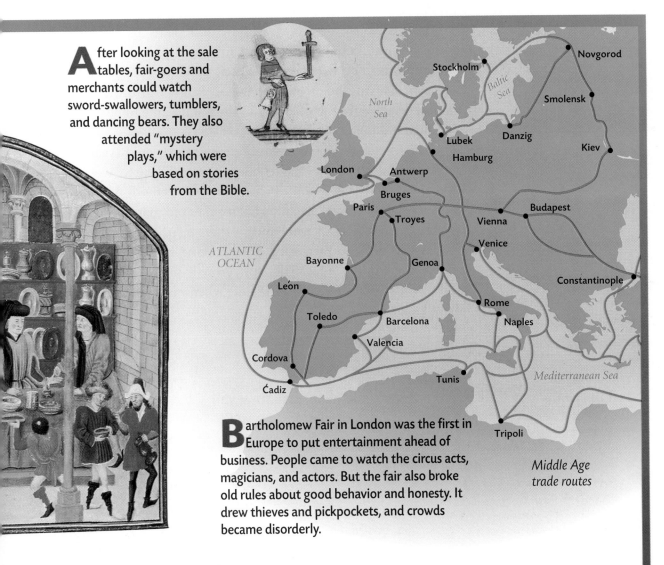

After looking at the sale tables, fair-goers and merchants could watch sword-swallowers, tumblers, and dancing bears. They also attended "mystery plays," which were based on stories from the Bible.

Bartholomew Fair in London was the first in Europe to put entertainment ahead of business. People came to watch the circus acts, magicians, and actors. But the fair also broke old rules about good behavior and honesty. It drew thieves and pickpockets, and crowds became disorderly.

Middle Age trade routes

Families worked together at home to create textiles with a foot-operated spinning wheel and a hand loom. *What is the name for this home-based system of work?*

Cloth Manufacturing

Making cloth at home was slow and painstaking work. Entire families, including children, had to lend a hand. One person spun thread on the spinning wheel, which was propelled by a foot pedal. Another wove the thread into cloth on a hand loom. This system of work based in the home came to be called a **cottage industry**.

Textile, or cloth, manufacturing expanded for many years as a cottage industry. The market for the manufactured woolen cloth grew slowly. Gradually, efficient farming methods provided more food to feed workers and wool for them to manufacture.

The good supply of wool and workers helped England and Scotland to develop their own cloth-making industries by the end of the Middle Ages. The slow growth in manufacturing and commerce set the stage for a time when machines powered manufacturing.

LESSON REVIEW

Fact Follow-Up
1. Describe a peasant's life on a manor.
2. What caused the Viking raids? How were other Europeans affected?
3. Describe the beginnings of trade. Why did it start?
4. Define the term "cottage industry." Explain.

Think These Through
5. Describe human-environmental interaction by answering the following: How could people living on a manor control their environment? Describe the ways in which people could not exercise control. Why was their control limited?

LESSON 2
An Industrial Revolution

I n the novel *Hard Times*, Charles Dickens, a writer living in London during the Industrial Revolution, describes "Coketown" as characteristic of a nineteenth-century industrial city:

> *It was a town of machinery and tall chimneys, out of which…serpents of smoke trailed themselves forever and ever….It had a black canal in it, and a river that ran purple with ill-smelling dye, and vast piles of buildings full of windows where there was a rattling and a trembling all day long, and where the piston of the steam-engine worked monotonously up and down like the head of an elephant in a state of…madness.*

The **Industrial Revolution** began between 1750 and 1800 in the textile industries of England and Scotland when machines provided power for manufacturing. During this period of great change, machines and workers were brought together in buildings called factories. This new **factory system** enabled workers to produce far more cloth than they could in their homes.

What Machines Could Do

The power-driven machines worked faster than the old hand-operated or foot-operated machines. A worker also produced more because each worker specialized in doing only one task to produce cloth. This specialization, or **division of labor**, meant workers doing different tasks cooperated to create a finished product.

Cloth could be produced more efficiently in factories by bringing together machines and workers with special skills. So factories gradually replaced cottage industries. People began moving from rural areas to work in city factories. The new machines created new jobs for the new urban dwellers.

LESSON PREVIEW

Key Ideas
- The Industrial Revolution started in the United Kingdom.
- Factories with power-driven machinery became a key to greater control over the environment.
- Industrial cities provided new environments.

Key Terms
Industrial Revolution, factory system, division of labor, urbanization

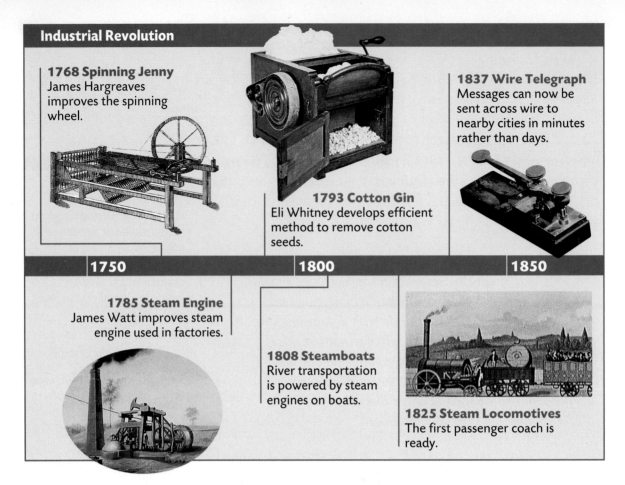

Industrial Revolution

1768 Spinning Jenny
James Hargreaves improves the spinning wheel.

1793 Cotton Gin
Eli Whitney develops efficient method to remove cotton seeds.

1837 Wire Telegraph
Messages can now be sent across wire to nearby cities in minutes rather than days.

1750   **1800**   **1850**

1785 Steam Engine
James Watt improves steam engine used in factories.

1808 Steamboats
River transportation is powered by steam engines on boats.

1825 Steam Locomotives
The first passenger coach is ready.

From Home to Factory

In *Hard Times*, Dickens describes the owners of the factories as wealthy and privileged. They lived well, but they knew little about the lives of the factory workers. The owners thought of the workers as little more than human machines who kept the factory running. They even talked about the people who worked for them as "the Hands."

Most children learned to spin and weave at home. Mothers taught their boys and girls the simplest parts of the cloth-making process. Many families worked at the mill together making cloth. Twelve-year-old Hands worked the same hours as adults. This young person could prepare wool for the spinning wheel, spin thread, and even help the men at the hand loom, where thread was woven into cloth.

At first, a foot pedal drove the spinning jenny. Then water, and later steam power, took over the task. This meant five threads were spun at a time, instead of only one. Either the young spinner had quick hands or was quickly out of a job.

Every morning at 7:00 A.M. all Hands arrived for work. Everyone worked without stopping in a large room filled with loud machines. A whistle shrieked at noon to announce the lunch break. Some companies gave people a half-hour to eat, some an hour. Regardless, 1:00 P.M. meant everyone must be back at their tasks. The chimes rang out at 1:00 P.M., not once, but thirteen times so everyone would hear the hour. A few minutes late meant lost pay.

New Sources of Power

The first factories used water power to run their machines. The machinery worked because water flowed through a water wheel. Machinery drew power from the movement of water. So the first factories were located beside streams or rivers. Early industrial towns did not have tall chimneys pouring out black smoke.

Tall chimneys became part of the industrial landscape when James Watt developed his improved steam engine in 1785 (see time line, page 134).

Steam engines were powerful. The steam engine ran on coal, which was abundant in northern England and Wales. Factories could be built almost anywhere. Burning coal created clouds of thick, black smoke, which poured into the air through factory chimneys.

Because factories needed fuel, coal mining expanded. Coal production doubled between 1750 and 1800. In the nineteenth century production increased 20 times.

Steam power also revolutionized transportation in Britain. Manufacturers could move large quantities of raw materials to factories and products to markets.

Before the Industrial Age, people and goods moved by foot, horse, or

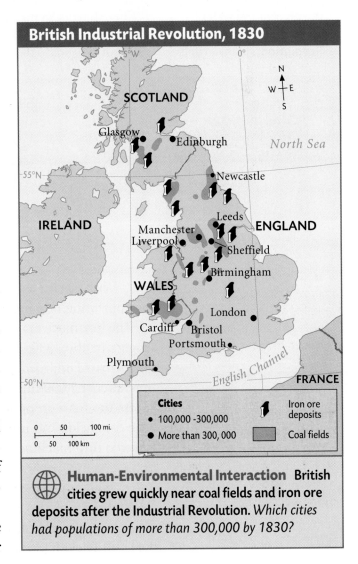

British Industrial Revolution, 1830

SCOTLAND
Glasgow
Edinburgh
North Sea
Newcastle
IRELAND
Leeds
ENGLAND
Manchester
Liverpool
Sheffield
Birmingham
WALES
London
Cardiff
Bristol
Portsmouth
Plymouth
English Channel
FRANCE

0   50   100 mi.
0   50   100 km

Cities
• 100,000 - 300,000
● More than 300,000

Iron ore deposits

Coal fields

Human-Environmental Interaction British cities grew quickly near coal fields and iron ore deposits after the Industrial Revolution. *Which cities had populations of more than 300,000 by 1830?*

How a Steam Engine Works

Imagine driving to the service station with your father and hearing him say, "Ten pounds of coal. And fill our water tank, please." If you had lived during the first few years of the twentieth century, coal and water, not gasoline, might have fueled automobiles. Most engines were steam engines which ran on coal and water.

Early in the Industrial Revolution, steam engines supplied power to English factories. Later, inventors harnessed steam power to drive ships, locomotives, and even tractors, cars, and trucks.

The process of converting steam into mechanical power begins with heated water. The water is converted to pressurized steam by a hot fire. Then the steam travels through pipes to the piston-cylinder. The pressurized steam expands in the cylinder and pushes a piston forward. Once the pressure is released, the piston is pushed back to its original position. In this way, a steam-driven piston can turn a gear, a wheel, or a belt.

Steam engines were used first in England to power textile looms. Later, an inventor named Richard Trevithick had the idea of using a steam engine to turn the wheels of a railcar. From this was born the modern steam-locomotive.

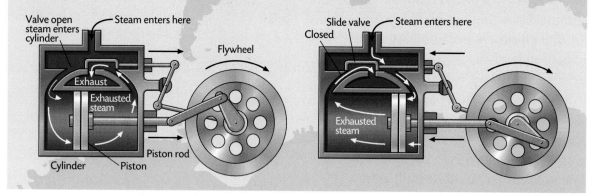

boat. With steam engines powering trains and steamboats, transportation became faster and cheaper.

The locomotive, a steam engine on wheels, first carried passengers in the 1830s. At that time, there were only 500 miles (805 km) of railroad track in Britain. Within 20 years, there were almost 7,000 miles (11,270 km) of track.

As the map on page 135 shows, factory cities were located near coal fields and iron ore deposits. The iron ore was manufactured into machinery, locomotives, and rails.

Industry's Advantages and Disadvantages

During the industrial age, the British used the resources of the land. They shaped their environment to their needs, digging coal from deep mines, laying track across the countryside, and building factories.

Greater control over the environment changed every aspect of life. Expanding transportation routes meant that more raw materials and finished products could be shipped into and out of factory towns. Workers produced more goods. People of the middle and upper classes could buy items that would have been beyond the dreams of the lords of even the greatest manors.

Cities with stores, restaurants, and theaters seemed more pleasant than isolated villages. Good cloth woven by powered looms provided a greater variety of clothing. Vegetables, fruit, and meat were brought to the cities by rail, so city dwellers were free to do other work besides farming. Iron and steel made much of life easier, from the labor-saving machines in the factories to the railroads themselves. Change also endangered the environment and people's lives.

During the Industrial Revolution, children worked in factories. *What dangerous conditions can you see that might have inspired countries to outlaw child labor?*

An Era of Growing Cities

The Industrial Revolution also fueled the fast growth of large cities in Great Britain. Textile mills became surrounded by warehouses, smelters, railroad tracks, and crowded homes.

People moved from working on farms or in their rural homes to working in factories located in crowded cities. The new industries created new jobs for a growing population.

The **urbanization**, or the spread of cities, contributed to environmental challenges which Europeans still face.

LESSON 2 REVIEW

Fact Follow-Up

1. What were some of the major inventions of the early years of the Industrial Revolution?
2. What changes did the development of the factory system make in people's lives?
3. In what ways did the application of the steam engine to transportation change human-environmental interaction?

Think These Through

4. Imagine that you are a young peasant living on a manor. Then imagine that you are a part of a factory worker's family during the Industrial Revolution. In what ways might your life have been different? During which of these two times would you have preferred to live? Explain.

The Twentieth Century

LESSON PREVIEW

Key Ideas
- The nations of Norden industrialized later than those of the British Isles.
- Newer industrial technologies and cleaner energy sources have reduced Norden's environmental problems.
- Both the British Isles and Norden are facing and resolving environmental problems.

Key Terms
geothermal energy

A Swedish demonstrator holds up a sign for the TV cameras. In blue and yellow, the colors of the Swedish flag, he has written: "Atomkraft? Nej, Tek!"—"Nuclear Power? No thanks!"

The demonstration for the press symbolizes Norden's attempt to balance energy and environmental needs. Nuclear power, supporters say, is a clean way to produce energy because it does not cause air pollution. Opponents charge that this energy source is as bad as, or worse than, fossil fuels. Nuclear power may not pollute the air, but nuclear waste remains toxic for centuries.

Throughout the British Isles and Norden, people have been aware that any use of the environment's resources carries risks. They have tried to resolve such conflicts with solutions that increase benefits and cut down risks.

Norden's Industries and the Environment

Norway, Sweden, Finland, Denmark, and Iceland have followed the British lead in agricultural improvements, industrialization, and urbanization. Because Norden began to industrialize much later than the British, these nations used newer and cleaner technologies.

Icelanders benefit from geothermal energy because it generates electricity and warms recreational lakes. *What other "clean energy" sources can be found in Norden?*

Electricity as a clean energy source did not exist when the British Isles began to industrialize. British industry burned coal in factory steam engines. Neither Norway nor Sweden had coal, but both had plenty of rivers rushing down steep mountains. This abundant source of hydroelectric power is clean and renewable.

Iceland also uses hydroelectric power—and a newer technology that is even more remarkable. Iceland taps the earth's **geothermal energy**, heat from the earth's interior. The movement of the earth's crust permits superheated lava, or molten rock, from deep in the earth to come to the surface. The lava heats water that engineers use to heat houses and office buildings.

Icelanders also have built greenhouses that cover about 35,800 acres (14,320 square hectometers). These indoor farms, heated by geothermal energy, produce food and flowers for Iceland and for export. Bananas grown in greenhouses are less expensive than imported bananas on sale in the United States. Strawberries picked in Iceland are flown to Stockholm, where they are sold the next day.

Helsinki, Finland, is one of many large cities in Norden. *Why do most people of Norden live in the cities?*

Modern Urban Life

Today, industry and commerce have drawn about eight out of every ten of Norden's people into cities. In the United Kingdom the figure is even higher. By comparison, about five out of every ten North Carolinians live in cities.

Some 1,000 years ago, the British and people in Norden lived in small, self-sufficient communities. Modern cities, however, are neither small nor self-sufficient. Every day, city dwellers require water, food, fuel, and electricity to carry on their lives. Factories require raw materials to manufacture and markets for their products. Wastes from homes, offices, and factories must be treated and sent away.

All of these daily requirements place heavy demands on resources located beyond the cities. Sometimes, whatever is needed can be found within a nation's own lands or waters.

The energy needs of the United Kingdom and Norway have been eased in recent years by the discovery of oil in the North Sea. Other needs can be met only by looking to other countries.

What would YOU do?

In recent years, oil fields in the North Sea have become important sources of energy. Oil-drilling there has created thousands of jobs. But fishermen and many others worry that oil spills will hurt the ocean life in the North Sea.

Imagine you are put in charge of managing the North Sea oil fields. Would you risk oil spills to preserve jobs? Or would you cut jobs by stopping undersea drilling?

The United Kingdom, Ireland, Denmark, Finland, and Sweden have joined other European nations in an economic community called the European Union. Each member gains access to one another's raw materials and markets. Also, Iceland, Norway, Sweden, and Finland have taken steps to find the raw materials and markets they require by easing trade barriers with other European nations.

The United Kingdom and Norden's nations also have been active in searching for solutions to urban problems. Many cities have been working hard to deal with the congestion and air pollution that comes from automobiles. Although these problems have not been solved, the number of private automobiles on city streets has been reduced.

The London subway system, called the "tube" or the "underground," moves people throughout the city of 7 million. *How does mass transit help solve problems in cities?*

Mass transit systems have become much more popular than in most cities in the United States. London boasts of a subway system (Londoners call it the "underground" or "tube") that is fast, clean, and safe. Above ground, special lanes in city streets have been set aside during rush hours for the exclusive use of the famed double-deck buses.

Stockholm, Sweden's capital city, uses a computer-aided bus scheduling system that cuts the waiting time of passengers. In Göteborg, Sweden's second largest city and main port, a modern version of the old street trolley system is popular.

Through planning and cooperation, Northern Europeans show a determination to grow economically while preserving their environment.

LESSON 3 REVIEW

Fact Follow-Up
1. Why have the nations of Norden faced fewer problems with pollution than the United Kingdom?
2. Compare the industrialization of Norden and the British Isles.
3. How have people in the British Isles and Norden overcome some environmental problems?

Think These Through
4. In which of the two regions that you have been studying does human-environmental interaction now seem to be working with greatest benefit to humans and least harm to the environment? Explain.

CAROLINA SOCIAL STUDIES SKILL GOALS NORTH CAROLINA

Skill

*Acquiring Information from
a Variety of Sources*

Using Globes

Has anyone told you about flying from North Carolina to Tokyo, Japan, or Hong Kong off the coast of China? On such a trip the person might have started in Charlotte or Raleigh/Durham, flown to Chicago, and then stopped in Alaska for refueling before going on to Asia.

That may sound strange, but it is the shortest way to reach the other side of the earth. The pilot was flying what is called the Great Circle Route.

Pilots flying from North Carolina to London or Rome in Europe use another Great Circle Route. They head northeast toward Greenland and Iceland. Then they turn southeast.

Why is it shorter to fly north and then south to reach distant parts of the earth that are west or east of us? You need to follow these routes on the globe in your classroom. The maps on your classroom wall or in this book will not be as helpful.

Only a globe can give a correct picture of the earth. A globe is round like the earth's surface. Because it is shaped like the earth, it represents all parts of the earth true to scale. The size and relation of lands and oceans can be shown as they really are. When the curved earth is shown on a flat map, some distances and sizes cannot be shown accurately.

On a flat map, a straight line between two points appears to be the shortest distance. Yet the flat map does not really tell you why this

is not true. The two maps on this page suggest an answer to this problem, but you really need to study the globe in your classroom to discover what is missing.

Can you and your classmates solve the puzzle? Here is a clue. Does the curve of the earth add or subtract from the distance you must travel east or west across oceans or between continents?

Here is a final question. Imagine that you are to fly between a North Carolina airport and Rio de Janeiro, South America. Is there a Great Circle Route that will help you shorten the distance on this north-south trip?

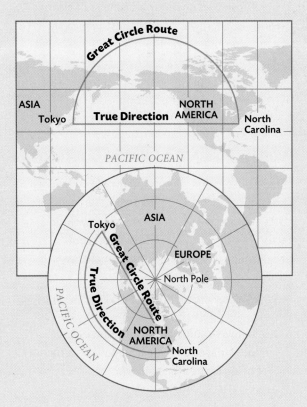

Chapter 7 Review

LESSON 1   One thousand years or more ago, most people lived in small, self-sufficient communities called manors. As agricultural methods improved and production increased, people turned to cottage industries and trade. These were key steps toward the Industrial Revolution.

LESSON 2   The factory system improved transportation, expanded trade, provided jobs, and developed cities. Cities offered living conditions different from those found in small country villages. For some, city life could be quite comfortable. For others, it could be grim.

LESSON 3   Norden industrialized later than the British Isles and took advantage of cleaner forms of energy to power industry, such as hydroelectric and geothermal energy. Norden and the British Isles are solving current environmental problems through cooperation. Mass transit helps ease air pollution.

TIME FOR TERMS

three-field system	crop rotation
peasants	manor
cottage industry	Industrial Revolution
factory system	division of labor
urbanization	geothermal energy

FACT FOLLOW-UP

1. What were some of the advantages and disadvantages of being a peasant on a manor? of being lord of the manor?

2. In what ways did the development of trade help end the self-sufficent life of the manor?

3. Describe changes brought about by the decline of cottage industries and the development of the factory system.

4. During the Industrial Revolution, how did human-environmental interactions change? Give specific examples to explain your answer.

5. Compare the industrialization of the United Kingdom with the industrialization of Norden?

THINK THESE THROUGH

6. Which social groups benefited the most from the manorial system? the Industrial Revolution? Which groups benefited the least? Give reasons why.

7. Draw a line from top to bottom through the middle of a sheet of paper. On the top on one side write "Industrial Revolution, United Kingdom, Advantages." On the other side write "Industrial Revolution, United Kingdom, Disadvantages." How many things can you list on both sides? Compare your list with a classmate.

8. If your parents were offered an opportunity to work with a United States company either in Helsinki or London, which position would you hope that your parents might take? Why? Or would you hope that your parents might be given another choice in the British Isles or Norden? What would that be and why?

9. Is a Great Circle Route always the shortest distance between two points? Explain your answer.

10. Is it possible for ships at sea to use Great Circle Routes? Explain why or why not.

11. Airline pilots flying between the United States and Europe use Great Circle Routes for reasons other than distance. What might one of those reasons be?

12. Globes might be more useful than commonly used maps for determining Great Circle Routes. In what other ways might globes be more useful than maps? Give some examples.

13. Which of these journeys would use a Great Circle Route—New York to Santiago, Chile, or New York to Moscow? Why?

Use the letters on the map to locate and name the following places:

14. area inhabited by nomadic reindeer herders.

15. areas where mountains or climate permit either grasslands or forests but little or no farming.

16. nation in Norden with good farmland.

17. area that led in the Industrial Revolution.

Use the numbers on the map to locate and name the following places:

18. the capital city of Denmark.

19. the capital city of Sweden.

20. the capital city of Iceland.

21. the capital city of the United Kingdom.

22. the capital city of Ireland.

23. the capital city of Finland.

24. the capital city of Norway.

Reviewing Place Location

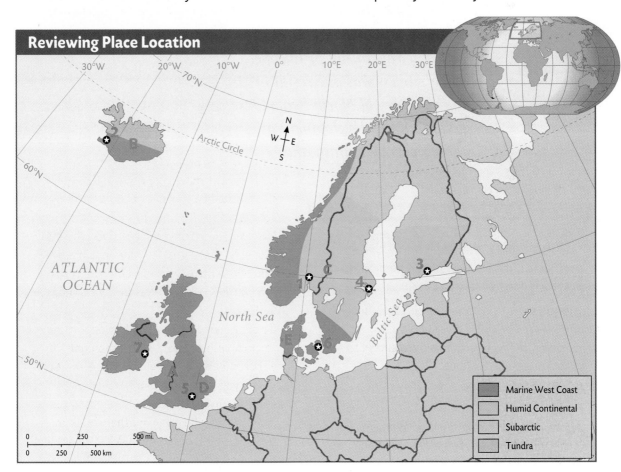

CHAPTER 8

Economy and Government

When oil was discovered in the North Sea in the 1960s, Britain saw a chance to improve its economy. Since then, oil companies have built more than 150 oil platforms there.

In the 1970s, David Bond was a crop duster working outside Aberdeen, Scotland. One day he was hired to fly a helicopter to an oil rig.

By 1992, Bond's family owned the second-largest helicopter operation in Europe. Their success was one result of the discovery of North Sea oil fields and the development of those fields by Britain and Norway.

CHAPTER PREVIEW

LESSON 1
Economies of the United Kingdom and Ireland
The United Kingdom's economy is bouncing back. Ireland's economy has been expanding.

LESSON 2
Norden's Economies
In Norden, skillful use of limited resources has created prosperous nations.

LESSON 3
Government
Democratic and constitutional governments are deeply rooted in the British Isles and Norden.

British Isles and Norden–Population Density

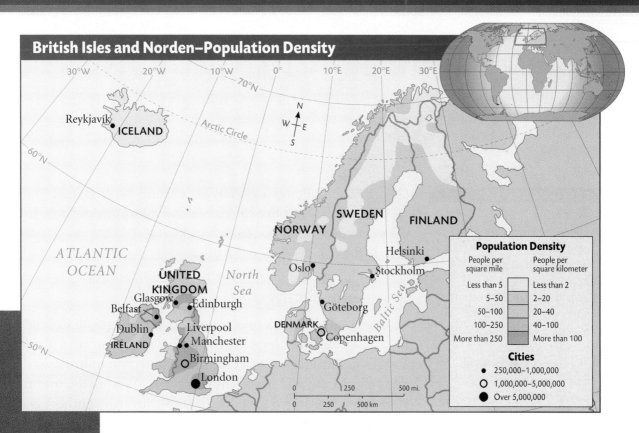

Population Density

People per square mile	People per square kilometer
Less than 5	Less than 2
5–50	2–20
50–100	20–40
100–250	40–100
More than 250	More than 100

Cities

- 250,000–1,000,000
- 1,000,000–5,000,000
- Over 5,000,000

On the deck of a North Sea oil rig

North Sea oil rig

LESSON 1

Economies of the United Kingdom and Ireland

LESSON PREVIEW

Key Ideas
- The United Kingdom is rebounding by improving old factories and building high-tech industries.
- Ireland is expanding economic opportunities to slow the migration of educated youth to other countries.
- The United Kingdom and Ireland have benefited by joining the European Union.

Key Term
Blitz

Industry in the British Isles made many cities grow. When factories close, a country loses economic strength and cities such as Liverpool, England (right), suffer. *What happens to cities when there are no jobs?*

I n 1992, the Bonds were already expanding their helicopter business beyond the North Sea and into other parts of the world. Bond Helicopters was bidding for contracts as far away as the Middle East and Asia.

Economic Change

In a family business or a nation, economic growth depends on responding to change. In the last chapter, you read about changes in life and work as the United Kingdom industrialized in the eighteenth and nineteenth centuries. Now, in the twentieth century, the United Kingdom is going through another period of economic change.

More than one hundred years ago, the United Kingdom became one of the world's most powerful nations. It was the center of a global empire. Its navy dominated the world's oceans. Its people led the world in building modern industry.

The British in those years could easily import food and raw materials. Raw materials could be manufactured in British factories and exported around the world. These advantages kept the British economy strong for generations.

Challenges to the United Kingdom

In the twentieth century, the United Kingdom began to lose its advantage. Other nations industrialized. Two world wars weakened the economy of the United Kingdom. Its colonial empire began to collapse as African and Asian colonies gained their independence from the United Kingdom.

Today, the United Kingdom has fallen behind the world's strongest economies—those of the United States, Japan, and Germany. Yet its industrial output remains impressive. The United Kingdom ranks sixth among the world's top 40 industrial powers.

Troubled Economic Areas

Find two cities on the map of England (see page 109)—Norwich, northeast of London, and Bristol, west of London. The United Kingdom's most troubled economic areas are located northwest of a line drawn between Norwich and Bristol. Here, millions of people still live in once booming industrial cities.

Birmingham led the world in iron and steel production. Manchester became famous for its cotton textiles. Leeds produced woolen textiles. Many of the factories are closed now or operate only part of the time. The area is troubled by high unemployment.

This is also true of Liverpool, once one of the world's busiest ports. Fewer ships dock in Liverpool now. During the 1980s, the city lost about 50,000 jobs. It is especially hard for young people to find work after they finish school. Fifty percent of inner-city youth are unemployed. Many of them will live on welfare for their entire lives.

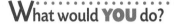

What would YOU do?

The United Kingdom's once prosperous industrial regions now face high unemployment. The low-skill jobs are gone and unlikely to come back. Many young people are not qualified to work in high-tech jobs that might come to the area.

Imagine that you have been asked by city officials to lower unemployment. The city will improve schools. Your job is to suggest ways of encouraging young people to study for high-tech jobs. What would you do?

The United Kingdom has attracted some new industries to these depressed areas. These efforts, however, have not resolved basic problems. The once abundant supplies of coal and iron from nearby mines are now nearly exhausted. Old factories cannot compete with modern plants in other countries. Run-down factory buildings and housing show the United Kingdom's decline.

Areas of Economic Growth

Such depressing scenes tell only part of the story. Some factories now have up-to-date machinery. New ones have been built. Workers skilled in modern technologies have helped revitalize old industries and develop new ones.

London During the Blitz

*Anyone visiting London today finds it hard to believe that a half-century ago the city was in ruins, the victim of heavy German bombing raids. The **Blitz**, as the air raids in 1940 and 1941 came to be called, was Adolf Hitler's attempt to weaken the United Kingdom's defenses against invasion during World War II.*

Crippled by Germany's attack, the British air force was unable to defend London. German aircraft pounded London every night for nearly three months. Londoners took cover in subway stations (above, right), schools, steel shelters, or anything else that would offer them protection.

One survivor, Lily Wilkins, remembered one attack. "We sat in the school all night and heard the bombs. In the morning ... the streets were just piles of rubble (far left)."

Buckingham Palace, the residence of the British royal family, was hit. The queen of England (left), said to one shaken Londoner, "I'm glad we've been bombed. It makes me feel as though we can look the East End in the face." The East End had been the hardest hit.

Britain continues to produce, as it has for generations, fine steel cutlery, porcelains, and textiles. The British also manufacture advanced aircraft, automobiles, space-exploration equipment, and many kinds of machinery. British banks and other financial institutions play key roles in the world's economy.

Some of this economic growth is taking place in the old industrial cities, but much of the United Kingdom's rebounding economy has been centered in Scotland and south of the Norwich-Bristol line, in England's lowlands.

Some of the lowlands are farmed intensively, producing grain, potatoes, and sugar beets. Much of the remaining open land is used as pasture by the dairy industry. Enough food is produced here—or brought into port by British fishermen—to

Londoners refused to let the German attack keep them from their daily routines. One storefront sign read: "This store is only closed when there is danger overhead and is reopened immediately when our spotters give the Danger Past signal."

Extensive bomb damage around St. Paul's Cathedral, which was saved from destruction.

Liverpool Street subway station was turned into an underground shelter.

The East End, the site of many vital shipping docks and warehouses, was most heavily bombed.

Though many other London landmarks were destroyed, Tower Bridge survived the air raids.

Buckingham Palace, the residence of the royal family, was hit.

Thames River

German bombers destroyed many buildings but failed to break the British determination to continue fighting. Then the Soviet Union and the United States joined the war. Germany surrendered in 1945.

St. Paul's Cathedral from the Thames today

Entire city blocks were destroyed in London

The British economy is growing stronger again because of productive farms in the lowlands and high-technology businesses in London, such as Glaxo Wellcome. *What is another economic center of the British Isles?*

provide about a third of what the United Kingdom's 58 million people consume.

Even more impressive are the thriving high-technology and service industries in the lowlands. These businesses provide good jobs and high living standards for about 20 million people. London, with a population of about 7 million, is the center of finance, engineering, communications, and energy-related businesses.

The second thriving economic center is in Scotland. The map on page 145 shows Glasgow on the west coast and Edinburgh on the east coast. There are extensive coal fields and nearby iron deposits between the two cities. The North Sea oil fields are not far off Scotland's east coast. These resources provide a basis for manufacturing goods, including oceangoing ships and electronic devices.

A Mixed Economy

The United Kingdom's economy mixes state-owned businesses and private enterprise. Shortly after World War II ended in 1945, the Labour Party was voted into office. The new government quickly claimed ownership of the nation's key industries—railways, steel plants, and health care.

Britain's Conservative Party returned to power in the late 1970s. It restored many of the businesses to private hands. A large part of the population, however, continues to use the nationally funded health service for medical care.

The United Kingdom cooperated with other nations in forming an economic community that since 1994 has been called the European Union. As members of the Union, the British have access to the resources and markets of 15 (the membership may grow) other European nations. Membership in the Union has helped the United Kingdom rebound from its earlier troubles.

Republic of Ireland

Ireland's informal name, the Emerald Isle, provides clues to its economy. If you flew over Ireland, you would look down upon mile after mile of misty green countryside. Villages are scattered through rolling farmlands.

You would not see many large cities. Dublin, Ireland's capital, is home to slightly more than 500,000 people. The nation's population of nearly 3.6 million is tiny compared to the United Kingdom's population of 60 million people.

Ireland does not have resources for much large-scale agriculture or industry. The production of field crops is limited by heavy rains that keep the soil too wet to grow much except potatoes. The island has few mineral resources.

Cattle, sheep, and horses thrive on the pasturelands. Seafood comes from ocean waters surrounding the island. Families or small businesses usually operate cattle farms and fishing boats.

Beautiful small villages dot the landscape in Ireland. Ireland keeps its rural traditions, but does not have the resources for large-scale agriculture. *How has this affected the Irish population?*

Potato Famine

About 150 years ago, 8 million people lived in Ireland's countryside. Most were farmers or fishermen. In the 1840s, however, heavy rains and plant disease wiped out potato crops. The Irish faced starvation. A million people died in those terrible years, and nearly twice that number left the country. Many of these emigrants found new homes in the United States.

Today, potatoes are thriving again, but the population of the Republic of Ireland remains less than half the size that it was before the famine. Young men and women, especially those who are well educated, continue to leave Ireland. They leave because they find few economic opportunities at home. The map on page 145 shows a low population density in Ireland.

Glass manufacturers, such as Waterford Crystal, and other businesses that turn out finished goods have helped Ireland's economy. *How has Ireland attracted such companies?*

Improving Ireland's Economy

Ireland's leaders have searched for ways to overcome the lack of resources. Ireland's businesses gained access to a growing European market after Ireland joined the European Union.

Ireland recruited foreign industries. The Irish government offered to give them low taxes and low labor costs. Companies responded by moving hundreds of factories to Ireland. They import raw materials, turn the materials into finished products, and sell them in Europe.

By the 1990s, Ireland was exporting manufactured goods and farm products. Thousands of new jobs have been created. Despite these successes, unemployment remains a major national problem.

LESSON 1 REVIEW

Fact Follow-Up
1. Why have the United Kingdom's once booming industries declined?
2. What evidence can you give that the United Kingdom remains a major industrial power?
3. How has Ireland tried to enlarge economic opportunities for its people? How successful has it been?

Think These Through
4. Both the United Kingdom and Ireland are troubled with high unemployment. Explain why.
5. Do you think Ireland and the United Kingdom have benefited by joining the European Union? Explain.
6. Using examples, show how the United Kingdom remains an industrial power.

LESSON 2 — Norden's Economies

Have you ever heard of white coal? Coal from the earth is black, of course. "White coal" is Norway's nickname for its most important energy source: hydroelectric power.

Resources of Water

Glaciers from the Ice Age still stand in northern Norway. About 12,000 years ago, the glaciers began to melt, forming fast-flowing rivers. The rivers run so swiftly that the water seems white. They are ideal locations for hydroelectric dams to produce energy.

Everywhere you look in Norden, water is an abundant resource. Under the North Sea lie oil and gas. Fishing has provided food and work for Norden's people over thousands of years.

Compared with the rest of Europe, Norden has few other natural resources. This shortage has been offset by populations who are well educated and work hard. The people living there enjoy high standards of living because of strong economies.

Norden's Economies Today

As you have read, Norden did not industrialize in the nineteenth century. Because most of these northern nations had no coal, manufacturing developed slowly.

Early in the twentieth century, hydroelectric power became an important energy source for Europe's northern nations. Norway, Sweden, and Finland especially had plenty of rivers for generating electricity.

As Norden industrialized, people began moving from the country to the cities to find manufacturing jobs. The industrial cities are located mostly on the southern coast.

A Norwegian tanker ships oil from the North Sea around the world. *What other energy resource has strengthened Norden's economy?*

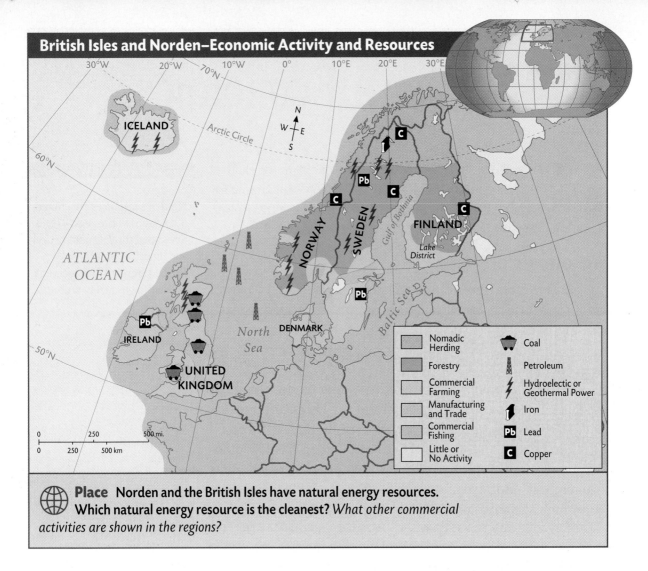

British Isles and Norden–Economic Activity and Resources

Legend:

- Nomadic Herding
- Forestry
- Commercial Farming
- Manufacturing and Trade
- Commercial Fishing
- Little or No Activity
- Coal
- Petroleum
- Hydroelectric or Geothermal Power
- Iron
- Lead (Pb)
- Copper (C)

Place Norden and the British Isles have natural energy resources. Which natural energy resource is the cleanest? *What other commercial activities are shown in the regions?*

♦♦♦♦ **GAMES** ♦♦♦♦
People Play

Third Man Out A favorite game in Denmark is Third Man Out. Two players stand about ten feet (3 m) apart and toss a ball back and forth. A third player, who is "It," tries to intercept the ball. If he or she does, the last player to yell "Third Man Out" is "It," and the game starts again.

♦♦♦♦♦♦♦♦♦♦♦♦♦♦

As the map above shows, half of the manufacturing in Norway today occurs in southern Norway. Half of Denmark's manufacturing is located in, or near, Copenhagen. Port locations enable manufacturers to import fuel and raw materials, process the raw materials, and ship high-quality goods to world markets. Each country in Norden has found ways to take advantage of its location and resources.

Swedish Iron Sweden converts its iron into high-quality steel for precision tools and instruments. Sweden's skilled workers manufacture farming equipment, aircraft, ships, and automobiles that are welcomed in foreign markets.

One of Sweden's largest markets for cars is the United States. Nearly half of all luxury cars made in Sweden are exported here every year.

Danish Shipping Denmark's location between the North Sea and the Baltic Sea makes the nation a shipping hub. In Copenhagen, the nation's capital, goods are collected, stored, and shipped to other ports. Much of Copenhagen's income comes from its location at the southern entrance to the Baltic Sea. It serves as a transfer point between Baltic ports and the world.

The Danes also manufacture stereos and televisions, as well as fine furniture and porcelain. They make diesel engines and industrial machinery. Denmark's farms produce dairy products and Danish hams for export.

Norwegian Petroleum Norwegian oil pumped from the North Sea is the source of many petroleum products. Norway manufactures fuel oil, rubber, and plastics. The country also produces clothing, electrical machinery, and furniture. Norway is one of the world's largest processors of aluminum, a metal that requires large amounts of electricity to manufacture.

The Norwegian fishing industry is large and operates in all oceans. Another major ocean-based industry is the Norwegian merchant marine. Ships from this fleet carry freight from other nations throughout the world.

Finnish Timber Timber is Finland's most abundant raw material. It is made into furniture, paper, and plywood.

Finland's skilled labor and business management have built profitable industries in a nation with few resources. Other products include farm machinery, electric motors, generators, and machinery for paper and lumber industries. Finland's shipbuilders make high-quality icebreakers and ferries.

Icelandic Fish Processing Iceland's most important industry is fish processing. The country also produces aluminum, cement, clothing, and electrical equipment. Iceland's underground supply of geothermal energy may soon encourage greater industrial development.

Service Industry In Norden, **service industries** make up about 70 percent of each country's economy. Service industries are businesses that supply services, such as education, health care, government administration, transportation, banking, or trade. A growing service industry in the region is tourism. Sweden, Norway, and Denmark especially attract tourists.

Sweden's automobiles and Finland's timber products are sold worldwide. *What natural resources do these industries use?*

Mixed Economies

The economies of Norden's countries are mixed, having both government-owned enterprises and privately owned farms and businesses. Most of the industries listed above are privately owned.

Education and national health-care services are tax supported. In Norway, about half the income of Statoil, the government-owned oil business, pays for public services.

North Sea Oil Since Norwegians first struck oil in the North Sea in 1969, "black gold" has become as important as "white coal" to the economies of the British Isles and Norden. The largest source of energy in Norway continues to be hydroelectric power, but North Sea oil has provided the country with a valuable export.

Soon after the discovery in the United Kingdom's North Sea fields, British Petroleum started pumping large quantities

LIVING IN SWEDEN

A Student's Daily Life

Mia Sahlander is a sixteen-year-old high school student from the Swedish town of Falun.

"I like school. It's a nice place. Most of the teachers are very friendly and I have some good classmates. I study English, Swedish, German, math, natural sciences, and humanities. English is my favorite subject and the one which will probably be of most use to me.

"School starts at 8:20 A.M. and finishes at 4:00 P.M. I have about six periods per day and get between five and six hours of homework per week. We have a students' recreation room where we can read, play billiards, or just sit around and chat.

"I always have lunch at school. Every school in Sweden has to provide school meals. The food is not so good—the meatballs [a Swedish speciality] bounce on the table! There are always vegetables and salad, milk, water, or orange juice, and bread with butter.

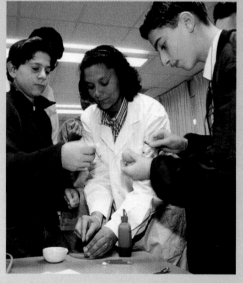

Swedish classroom

"There are no exams in our school system. We get grades for every piece of work we complete during the year. If you want to get a high average grade, it means you have to be good at everything in a Swedish school. One weak subject can ruin your chances [to advance to a university]."

of oil. Norway's Statoil started more slowly but soon caught up. By 1991, Norway was producing 100,000 more barrels a day than the United Kingdom.

Norway's biggest customers for oil are the United States and Canada. Statoil now looks to Eastern Europe for new business. In a partnership with British Petroleum, Statoil has also found buyers in Russia, Africa, and Asia.

An oil tanker spilled millions of gallons of oil after running aground in the Shetland Islands. *Why do the people of Norden and the British Isles want to protect nearby waters?*

New Challenges

North Sea oil has brought new prosperity to Norway and the United Kingdom. It has also raised environmental challenges.

In 1993, an oil tanker off the coast of the Shetland Islands spilled 21 million gallons of crude oil. Shetland's otters and seals were saved from the oil by a hurricane that broke up the spill. But the oil spread to other shores.

Waters of the North Sea are as important for fishing as they are for oil. Environmental ministers of the regions' governments have begun to work together to protect the natural resources of the North Sea and Baltic Sea.

LESSON 2 REVIEW

Fact Follow-Up

1. How have Norden's nations developed industries without many essential raw materials?
2. In what ways has the sea been an important resource in Norden?
3. After examining the map on page 145, write a statement about the distribution of population within the British Isles and Norden.

Think These Through

4. Reading about the economies of the British Isles and Norden helps you understand the distribution of population in these regions. Explain how.
5. Explain how the United Kingdom and Norden show a link between a well-educated population and economic development.

3 Government

Key Ideas

- Monarchs once were powerful in the British Isles and Norden. Their activities are now largely ceremonial.
- Democratic and constitutional governments are now well established in these two regions.

Key Terms

absolute monarchs, constitutional monarchs, democracy

King George III of England was an absolute monarch. Today Queen Elizabeth II is a constitutional monarch. *What is the difference between the two kinds of monarchy?*

Every summer morning at 11:30, crowds gather to see the changing of the guard in front of Buckingham Palace, the residence of the queen of England and the royal family. Sentries in red coats and tall bearskin hats march in ceremonial splendor.

Nearby, a helmeted bobby, or London policeman, stands guard alone at the door of 10 Downing Street. This is the official residence of the British prime minister.

One scene is regal, the other businesslike. Together, they suggest the balance between traditional admiration for royalty and a respect for representative democracy in the governments of the British Isles and Norden.

Constitutional Monarchies

Most of the countries of the British Isles and Norden are constitutional monarchies. The United Kingdom, Norway, Denmark, and Sweden all have governments that have a king or queen who acts as the formal head of state.

Hundreds of years ago, the monarchs of the British Isles and Norden were **absolute monarchs.** This means they held almost total power over the people of their countries. Today, both countries have constitutional monarchs. **Constitutional monarchs** are monarchs whose powers are limited by law. Royal activities are mainly symbolic.

The monarch does perform important ceremonies. The king or queen attends the opening of the nation's parliament, or legislature. In some parliamentary democracies, the monarch asks the leader of the majority party to form a government after an election. The request is symbolic, since the monarch has no real political power.

Denmark is the oldest monarchy in Norden. There has been a Danish royal family for more than 1,200 years. Today, Queen Margrethe II is the monarch of Denmark.

158 *Chapter 8*

Each of the constitutional monarchies has its own traditions. All are governed under constitutions by democratically elected parliaments. All operate much like the one in the United Kingdom.

The United Kingdom's Constitutional Monarch

Queen Elizabeth II is the current monarch of the United Kingdom. She is queen of England, Scotland, Wales, and Northern Ireland. She serves as an important symbol of the nation's traditions and unity.

Laws in the United Kingdom are made by Parliament, a legislature that has two branches. One of these branches, the House of Lords, has limited powers. When people today say "Parliament," they usually mean the House of Commons, where the important debates take place and laws are made. The members of the House of Commons (called M.P.'s, for "members of Parliament") are chosen in elections open to all adults.

In the United Kingdom, the party that wins the most seats in Parliament chooses a leader who will be the prime minister. The prime minister chooses members of his or her own party for positions in the cabinet. Together, the prime minister and the cabinet perform the day-to-day tasks of government.

WORD ORIGINS

Bobby is a slang term used in England for a policeman or policewoman. It comes from the name of Sir Robert "Bobby" Peel, who was the home secretary when England's Metropolitan Police Force was created in 1829.

This chart shows the organization of government in the United Kingdom. The dashed lines show that the prime minister and cabinet are part of the legislative branch. The dashed lines to the judiciary show that judges are appointed by the monarch with advice from the prime minister. *Who is the chief executive of government?*

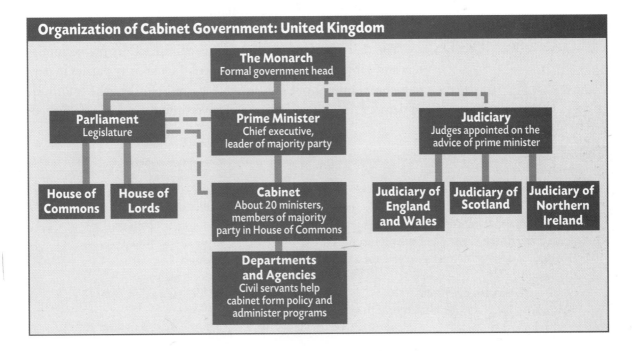

Organization of Cabinet Government: United Kingdom

The Monarch
Formal government head

Parliament
Legislature

Prime Minister
Chief executive, leader of majority party

Judiciary
Judges appointed on the advice of prime minister

House of Commons

House of Lords

Cabinet
About 20 ministers, members of majority party in House of Commons

Judiciary of England and Wales

Judiciary of Scotland

Judiciary of Northern Ireland

Departments and Agencies
Civil servants help cabinet form policy and administer programs

As part of its work, the majority party proposes bills to be voted on in Parliament. If the votes turn against the policies of the prime minister and the cabinet, a new election is held.

Two things should be remembered about a government that works in these ways. It is a **democracy** because the lawmaking is done by freely elected representatives of the people. The government is also constitutional because it operates under laws that protect the rights of the people.

This government of law is reflected in Parliament's acceptance of election results. Prime ministers and cabinets change peacefully when voters say that they no longer approve of government policies.

Parliament is the lawmaking body of government in Denmark. *Who chooses the members of parliaments in Norden and the United Kingdom?*

Republican Governments

Three nations—Ireland, Finland, and Iceland—live under republics, or representative democracies. They have elected presidents rather than kings or queens. Their parliaments are also elected.

In practice, these governments do not differ much from constitutional monarchies. In these countries the elected presidents serve in largely ceremonial roles. They are, like the monarchs, symbols of national unity and tradition.

The daily work of government is conducted by prime ministers and cabinets elected as members of the majority parties in parliaments. Throughout the British Isles and Norden, the traditions of democratic and constitutional government are well established.

LESSON 3 REVIEW

Fact Follow-Up
1. What are the differences between the direct democracy of the Greeks and the representative democracies that you have read about in this lesson?
2. Some governments discussed in this lesson are called constitutional monarchies and others republican governments. What are the differences between the two?

Think These Through
3. Does a democracy have to be *constitutional* to be truly a democracy? Explain.

Using Maps: Part I

Your last skill lesson pointed out that globes furnish some of our most accurate information about the earth. Well, if they are so useful, why don't we use them all the time?

Imagine for a moment that a globe is the only map that you have. How big would it have to be to show you the roads from Maggie Valley, west of Asheville, North Carolina, to Morehead City, on the coast? Would it fit into the glove compartment of your parents' car?

Size, however, is only one consideration. How many huge globes would you need to show you all the things that you have already seen in this book on small, flat maps?

To discover all that a map has to say, you need to review carefully the special language used by mapmakers.

Determining Directions

You will find on most maps a **north arrow**, a small arrow that points in the direction of the North Pole. By using a north arrow to indicate the direction of the North Pole in these maps, you also learn other directions.

North, east, south, and west are called **cardinal directions**—the major or principal directions. Halfway between each of the cardinal directions are the **intermediate directions**—northeast, southeast, southwest, and northwest.

Check again the map on page 29 and review the lines in the text (page 30) that tell you about the Gulf Stream and the North Atlantic Drift. Use the map, the north arrow, and the text to describe the directions of these ocean currents.

Using Scale

Every map in this book, of course, is much, much smaller than the area that it represents. To show distances accurately, every map is drawn to **scale**. That means that on some maps an inch may represent 50 miles (81 km). On another map, one inch may represent 500 miles (805 km).

Study the two maps on pages 105 and 109 showing the British Isles drawn to different scales. Check the scale of each map. Use the scale on page 109 to determine the distance in miles between London and Dublin. Now use the map on page 105 to determine the distance between the same two points. Are your measurements the same or different? On which map is it easier to determine the exact distance? Why?

You have now taken the first step in understanding how maps drawn to different scale can provide different information. Take the second step by making two lists. One list should contain information you can discover only by reading the map on page 105. The second list should contain information from the map on page 109.

Chapter 8 Review

LESSON 1 Despite serious blows to its economy in the early years of this century, the United Kingdom has bounced back. Although it is no longer the leading world power, its economy makes it one of Europe's leaders. Ireland has enjoyed some success in building its economy.

LESSON 2 Norden is composed of nations with smaller populations and fewer resources than the United Kingdom, but all have built thriving economies. Their people enjoy high standards of living.

LESSON 3 The governments of the British Isles and Norden differ in matters of detail. All have long traditions of democratic and constitutional government.

TIME FOR TERMS

Blitz
absolute monarchs
democracy
service industries
constitutional monarchs

FACT FOLLOW-UP

1. How does the European Union help the economy of the United Kingdom?
2. The United Kingdom has suffered many economic blows but has been able to recover. Explain how.
3. What sources of energy are used in Norden? What are the advantages and disadvantages of each?

4. Define "constitutional monarchy." What is the role of a monarch in a constitutional government?
5. Define a republic. How does it differ from direct democracy?
6. How does a parliamentary or cabinet government differ from the presidential system of the United States?
7. Compare the economic roles of the governments in Norden and the United Kingdom.

THINK THESE THROUGH

8. Demonstrate how you might use geography's themes of human-environmental interaction and movement to help you organize a discussion of changing economies in the British Isles and Norden.
9. Which of the two regions that you have studied here—the British Isles or Norden—seems to have better prospects for continued economic expansion? Explain.

SHARPENING SKILLS

10. In your daily life, how might you use cardinal and intermediate directions?
11. Why do mapmakers draw a north arrow on maps?
12. You want to give a friend the distance between your home town and Billings, Montana. Which would help you most, a globe or map? Why?
13. Work with a friend in selecting three maps from different parts of this book. Then pick five sets of two cities, for example, Oslo and Helsinki, London and Glasgow, and so on.

Each of you use the mileage/kilometer scale to determine the distance between the cities. Compare answers.

14. Foreign visitors in Greensboro suggest that they would like to drive to Disney World the next afternoon. How could you use a map to show how difficult this would be?

PLACE LOCATION

Colors are used on the map below to indicate types of economic activity. Name the nations or waters (oceans or seas) where the following can be found:

15. The color for forestry is **B**. In what nation(s) is this industry found?
16. **E** is the color for commercial fishing. Name the waters where this occurs.
17. The color for manufacturing and trade is **D**. In what nations are there centers of manufacturing and trade?
18. The color for commercial farming is **C**. In what areas can this be found?

Symbols are used to locate resources.

19. Letter **I** is the symbol for hydroelectric power. What nations have this resource?
20. **G** is the symbol for coal. Where is this resource?
21. Letter **H** is the symbol for petroleum. Describe the location of important petroleum fields.
22. Letter **J** is the symbol for iron ore. Does iron ore appear to be an abundant resource?
23. Letter **L** is the symbol for copper. Explain why you think copper is more or less abundant than iron ore.
24. Does the map indicate any economic activity or resources for Iceland? If so, what letter(s) would you choose?

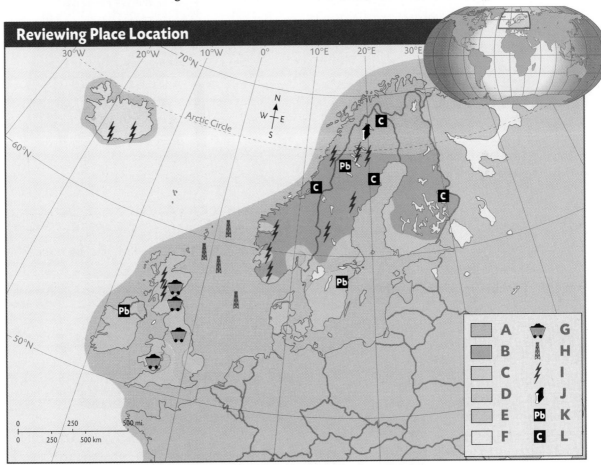

Reviewing Place Location

CHAPTER 9

Society and Culture

A beefeater, in his colorful red uniform, locks the Tower of London gates at 10:00 P.M. Keys in hand, he turns and approaches another sentry guarding the gates. The sentry challenges the beefeater:

"Halt! Who comes there?"

"The Keys."

"Whose Keys?"

"Queen Elizabeth's Keys."

The Ceremony of the Keys is almost 700 years old and is one of many traditions in the British Isles and Norden.

CHAPTER PREVIEW

LESSON 1
A Tale of Three Cities
London, Stockholm, and Copenhagen show the variety of life in the British Isles and Norden.

LESSON 2
The Tradition of Religion
Protestant and Roman Catholic faiths are deeply rooted in the British Isles and Norden. Lives in each country are influenced by these traditions.

LESSON 3
Recreation
Outdoor sport and recreation reflect the variety of environments in the British Isles and Norden.

Tower of London

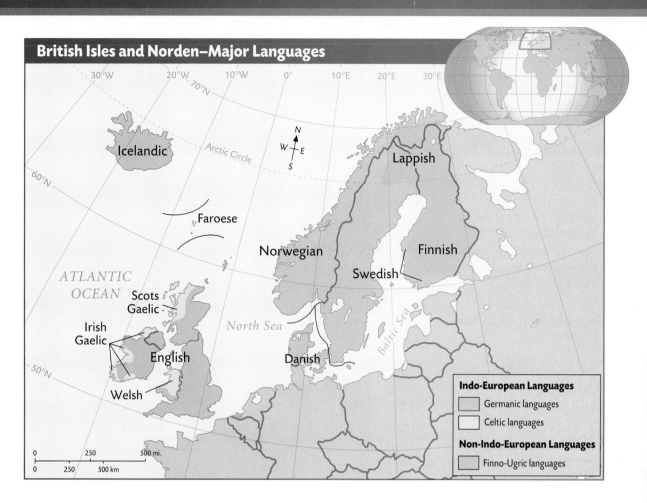

British Isles and Norden–Major Languages

Icelandic

Arctic Circle

Faroese

Lappish

Norwegian

Finnish

Swedish

ATLANTIC
OCEAN

Scots
Gaelic

Irish
Gaelic

North Sea

Baltic Sea

English

Danish

Welsh

0   250   500 mi.

0   250   500 km

Indo-European Languages

Germanic languages

Celtic languages

Non-Indo-European Languages

Finno-Ugric languages

The crown jewels of England.

LESSON 1

A Tale of Three Cities

LESSON PREVIEW

Key Ideas

- Even brief visits to three capital cities provide glimpses of the variety in the lives of the British, Swedes, and Danes.
- The different ways of life reflect the environment and history of each place.

Key Terms

Swedish Modern architecture, Nobel Prize

The London skyline includes new skyscrapers and the domes and spires of ancient cathedrals. *What river runs through the city?*

If you walk through the streets of a city in the British Isles or Norden, you'll find a surprising mixture of old and new. You will wander down winding, narrow streets from the Middle Ages and then look up to see a modern skyscraper. You will emerge from an underground train station, turn a corner, and find a royal palace.

Take a look at three cities and see how change and tradition have helped shape the character of these two European regions.

London

If you fly to London, you will land at one of two large airports, Heathrow or Gatwick. Many business people who travel to the United Kingdom never leave London because it is a world financial center. For tourists, London is an excellent starting point for a trip through the British Isles. Passenger trains run in every direction from the city.

London has been developing for centuries as the center of life in the British Isles. Although the city is located miles from the sea, the broad, deep waters of the Thames River enable ships from all over the world to reach its docks.

For about 300 years, the United Kingdom and its worldwide empire was governed from London. These were also the years of British leadership in the Industrial Revolution. As the center for government and finance, London grew into one of the largest and wealthiest cities in the world.

The British world empire and industrial leadership are gone today, but London remains a major economic and cultural force in world affairs. London's banks and businesses still have worldwide influence. Many of these firms are housed in tall modern buildings that stand side by side with London's older buildings.

It is this older London that draws tourists. Crowds gather at Buckingham Palace to watch the Ceremony of the Keys or the changing of the guards. There are other great buildings to visit, such as the Parliament Building with more than 1,000 rooms, and Westminister Abbey, the cathedral where kings and queens are crowned. Museums and libraries hold paintings and books of both ancient and modern times.

Away from the great buildings are brick homes or businesses that may be 300 years old. The buildings are built next to each other in unbroken rows.

Moving along the streets are immigrants from London's former empire—people from India, Pakistan, Egypt, the West Indies, Hong Kong, and various African nations. Their accented English mixes with the speech patterns of the Irish, Scots, Welsh, and native English. They all make up the city's population of about 7 million.

London is often the starting point of a journey through the British Isles. An old city, London holds the history of its people. *What would you like to see in London?*

Copenhagen

Copenhagen, the capital of Denmark, is a lively city of pointed spires and copper-green roofs. The city is built on two islands, Sjaelland and Amager, that are connected by drawbridges.

Copenhagen serves as Denmark's chief port and political center. About a fourth of Danish people—nearly a million and a half—live in and around Copenhagen because of job opportunities in government and trade. Most of them regularly commute to school or work by bicycle.

Copenhagen began as a small fishing village about A.D. 1000. Within 100 years, it had grown into an important port because of its good harbor and location on the Baltic Sea. Today, the Lurblaeserne monument in downtown Copenhagen honors early Scandinavian traders. At the top of the Lurblaeserne, two Vikings cast their gaze over the Radhus Pladsen, or City Hall Square. Radhus Pladsen is the city's business center. Major streets extend from it.

A short distance east is Christiansborg Palace. It stands on the exact spot where Copenhagen's first fortress was built. The palace is now the meeting place of the Folketinget, the Danish

A Visit to Tivoli Gardens

Map of Tivoli Gardens, 1937

When Tivoli Gardens opened in August 1843, Copenhagen's citizens turned out to hear music, to dance, to eat, and to see the gardens. "Where a street carnival may come to an American town once every few years, in Tivoli Gardens it is continuous ... from May to mid-September," noted one early visitor.

"The attractions range from riotous fun fairs to symphony orchestras and deluxe restaurants," said another. "Dance halls ... abound. It costs nothing to enjoy the outdoor performances of famous European trapeze artists and acrobats. The most lonely person is infected with the crowd's friendliness and gaiety."

Danish author Hans Christian Andersen visited Tivoli Gardens during its first season and claimed that "here I was given the idea for my Chinese story" (*The Nightingale*). Walt Disney visited the park twice to get inspiration for Florida's Disney World.

Tivoli Gardens, 1850s

parliament. Behind the palace stands the Borsen, Copenhagen's stock exchange. This was built in the sixteenth century by King Christian IV. Atop its spire four copper dragons, their tails intertwined, appear to be standing on their heads.

The people of Copenhagen, as in the rest of Denmark, are well educated. Almost everyone has a basic education in language arts, science, and math. At some point, most Danes attend "folk high schools," which are really places of learning for advanced studies in Danish history, literature, folklore, and methods of democracy.

Christiansborg Palace in Copenhagen houses the Folketinget. *What is the Folketinget? What happens there?*

Tivoli Palace (far left), Tivoli restaurant (left), and Tivoli Gardens Pagoda (below)

Today, more than 4 million visitors pass through the gardens each season. They still come to hear music, to dance, and eat. Today, they also come to enjoy many exciting rides. For nearly all, "Denmark is Copenhagen, and Copenhagen is the Tivoli."

Copenhagen University has been teaching students since 1479. The Royal Library, founded in 1673, has the largest collection of books in Norden.

Copenhagen is also known for its entertainment. On the other side of the Radhus Pladsen, you'll discover Tivoli Gardens, a world-famous amusement park.

In the summer, everyone comes to Tivoli. They find something to enjoy, whether it's food, rides, circuses, outdoor concerts, or pantomime. The excitement continues late into the evening. A display of fireworks ends the night when the great bell in the Radhus tower strikes midnight.

The people of Copenhagen are as proud of their gift for entertainment as they are of their commerce. At the water's edge of Copenhagen's harbor, amid ships from all nations, a statue honors a character who is known and loved all over the world— *The Little Mermaid*, created by Copenhagen's author of fairy tales, Hans Christian Andersen.

Stockholm

Stockholm is Sweden's capital, largest city, and a major port. Much of its business involves government and trade. The city lies on the east coast, facing the Baltic Sea.

Stockholm is built on 14 islands connected by 50 bridges. Because the waterways are the heart of the city, people sometimes compare Stockholm to Venice, Italy, a city of lovely canals. More than 1 million people live in Stockholm.

Stockholm was founded in 1250 by Birger Jarl. Jarl built a castle in the city center, now called Gamla Stan ("Old Town"). The royal palace also stands in Gamla Stan. The Swedish legislature meets in the parliament building nearby, on a separate island.

To the north of Gamla Stan are the business and theater districts, where most people work. Here the city has broad streets and buildings made of white granite, brick, or stone. The area has a clean, uncrowded appearance. Buildings are designed in a plain, unadorned style that has become known as **Swedish Modern architecture**.

The Little Mermaid **watches ships come into Copenhagen's port.** *Who wrote that fairy tale?*

Stockholm is Sweden's largest industrial center. Its industries include metal and machine manufacturing, paper and printing, chemicals, and food processing.

The city also is the nation's educational and cultural center. There the Nobel Foundation selects Nobel Prize winners. The **Nobel Prize** is one of the world's highest awards for lifetime achievements in literature, medicine, and science. (The Nobel Peace Prize is awarded in Oslo, Norway.)

The Royal Theater and the Stockholm Philharmonic Orchestra perform excellent opera and symphony music. Royal academies offer training in music, painting, sculpture, and architecture, plus instruction in science and agriculture.

Because of its northern latitude, Stockholm never is fully dark on summer nights. With the midnight sun sparkling on its canals, Stockholm deserves its Swedish nickname, "Beauty on Water."

The Nobel Prize in medicine in 1995 was awarded to North Carolina's Martin Rodbell (inset left). The Nobel Prizes awarded in Stockholm (top) are one way the city leads in Swedish education and culture. *What are other examples of Stockholm's cultural leadership?*

LESSON 1 REVIEW

Fact Follow-Up
1. Give two examples of tradition and change in each of the three cities studied.
2. In what ways are the three cities much the same? How are they different?
3. What is the importance of water to each city?
4. What tells you that the people living in Norden are well educated?

Think These Through
5. If you could visit only one of these cities, which one would you choose? Why?
6. Access to the seas was important in the founding of these cities. Is it still as important today? Explain.
7. Explain how tradition, or its history, has given each city a special character.

The Tradition of Religion

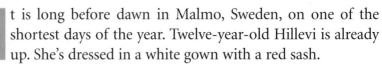

LESSON PREVIEW

Key Ideas

- Religious faiths have been—and continue to be—important in shaping the lives of people in Norden and the British Isles.
- In all of Norden the Lutheran Church predominates. The British Isles are home to several Protestant faiths as well as the Catholic Church.

Key Terms

summer solstice, winter solstice, monasteries, convents

• •

St. Lucia's Day honors the Italian saint whose name means light. A girl is chosen to represent St. Lucia. *What do you think the candles represent in this Swedish religious holiday?*

It is long before dawn in Malmo, Sweden, on one of the shortest days of the year. Twelve-year-old Hillevi is already up. She's dressed in a white gown with a red sash.

Hillevi carefully picks up a tray of coffee, saffron bread, and ginger cookies she has prepared for her parents. As she walks toward their room, she looks in the mirror and sees her crown of lighted candles glowing in the darkness.

As the eldest daughter, Hillevi plays a dramatic role on St. Lucia's Day, December 13. Hillevi is the Lucia girl, honoring the Italian saint whose name means "light." Her brilliant crown of candles brings magical light into the long, dark winter. With a festive breakfast, she officially begins the Christmas season.

Religion in Norden and the British Isles plays an important part in social as well as spiritual life. People mark the seasons of the year and the special days of their lives with religious rituals.

Norden's Countries

"We use our holidays to celebrate the sun. We celebrate the sun on the **summer solstice** (the longest day of the year). On the day we miss it most, because it is farthest away (the **winter solstice**), we cheer ourselves with a Christmas feast," says a Norwegian living in the North.

Religious celebrations in Norden do tend to occur around the longest and shortest days of the year. The rituals almost always involve lighting fires in the darkness.

St. John the Baptist is honored with evening bonfires on June 23, the longest day of the year. The Swedish people burn the candles of St. Lucia during the darkest time of the year to light the way into Christmas.

In Finland, lighted candles are set on Christmas tree branches. Finnish families sing a Christmas carol around the tree: "Oh, has summer come in the midst of winter?"

Early Nordens performed rituals to make sure the sun returned after winter. These customs existed before the arrival

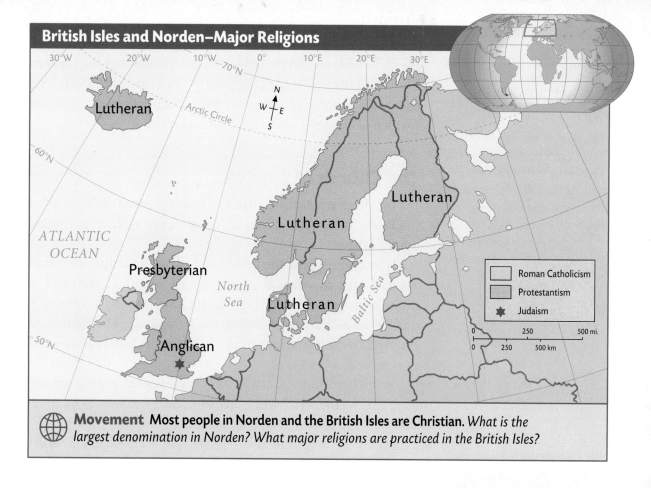

British Isles and Norden–Major Religions

Legend:
- Roman Catholicism
- Protestantism
- ★ Judaism

ATLANTIC OCEAN

North Sea

Baltic Sea

Arctic Circle

Lutheran (Iceland)
Presbyterian
Anglican
Lutheran (Norway)
Lutheran (Sweden)
Lutheran (Finland)
Lutheran (Denmark)

0   250   500 mi.
0   250   500 km

Movement **Most people in Norden and the British Isles are Christian.** *What is the largest denomination in Norden? What major religions are practiced in the British Isles?*

of Christianity in the ninth century. People added the old rituals to Christian beliefs to create new traditions.

Today, about 90 percent of the people of Norden are Lutheran. Church members marry in church and their children are baptized, but many attend services only on holidays. Religious celebrations often take place at home, among family and friends.

All citizens are guaranteed freedom of religion, but the Lutheran Church is the official church of all Norden countries (see map above). The governments support the church and appoint bishops and pastors. In Norway and Sweden, the monarch is the head of the church.

Christianity has been important in Norden for more than 1,000 years. Missionaries from France, the British Isles, and Germany laid the foundations of the Roman Catholic Church, beginning in Sweden in the ninth century. Norden remained Catholic until the sixteenth century, when news of Martin Luther's ideas about Protestantism spread from Germany.

Gustav Vasa, Sweden's king, agreed with Luther's teachings.

Traditional wedding clothes in Lapland are worn at a modern-day wedding ceremony. *Why would people continue to wear traditional clothing?*

He declared the Church of Sweden independent of the Catholic Church in Rome. By the king's decree, the Bible and church rituals were translated into Swedish. Then other countries in Norden also converted to the Lutheran faith.

The Church of England

In the sixteenth century, Luther's ideas also reached England. The English monarch, King Henry VIII, became interested in them.

For several years, the pope had refused to annul, or cancel, Henry VIII's marriage to Catherine of Aragon. Frustrated by Rome and influenced by Luther, the king forced Parliament to declare him head of the church in England. The Church of England, with the monarch as its head, carried Protestantism into Britain.

Just as in Sweden, the Latin ritual was changed. Services were conducted in English, according to *The Book of Common Prayer*, written by Henry's archbishop, Thomas Cranmer. The beauty of the language in the prayer book enriched the development of English.

About half of the population of England today belongs to the established church, which is also called the Anglican Church. Elsewhere in the United Kingdom, other Protestant faiths have attracted many followers.

The Presbyterian Church is particularly strong in Scotland. Nearly all of the Welsh are Protestant. The Methodist Church in Wales has the most members, but other faiths—Anglican, Baptist, Congregationalist, and Presbyterian—have large followings.

The Catholic Church in Ireland

More than 95 percent of the people in the Republic of Ireland consider themselves Roman Catholic. The Roman Catholic Church has strong roots in Ireland. The church has influenced Ireland's culture and history for centuries.

In the fifth century, a British-born priest

King Henry VIII followed the beliefs of Martin Luther, leading England in a break with the Roman Catholic Church. *What denomination did he begin?*

named Patrick arrived in Ireland to convert the people to Christianity. His missionary work was a great success. Now he is remembered as St. Patrick, the patron of Ireland.

The Irish Catholics built religious communities—**monasteries** for men and **convents** for women. Both strengthened the Church in Ireland. The monasteries especially became important centers of learning and culture.

The monks of the Irish monasteries copied books in Latin. They decorated the pages with elaborate lettering and colorful illustrations. These books are called illuminated manuscripts. The most famous Irish illuminated manuscript, completed in the eighth century, is the *Book of Kells*, which contains passages from the New Testament.

In 1534, Henry VIII started a campaign to bring all of Ireland into his kingdom. The king also insisted that the Irish abandon their Catholic faith. This touched off an Irish resistance movement—often marked by fierce warfare—that lasted until the Republic of Ireland won its independence in 1921.

As you have read, only the northeastern corner of Ireland, where many Protestants settled, swung over to the British. This region, named Northern Ireland, became part of the United Kingdom.

Northern Ireland was not to be a peaceful place. Catholic and Protestant groups battled there in what seemed to be a never-ending war. By the mid 1990s, people on both sides had become weary of the fighting and the loss of family and friends. Peace negotiations started slowly, but years of bitter struggle have made compromise difficult.

Copied by monks, the Book of Kells combines beauty and Scripture. *What is that kind of book called?*

WORD ORIGINS

Monasticism is the way of life for people who leave worldly affairs behind and move into monasteries or convents. They step away from everyday life to devote their lives to prayer and religious work. The name comes from the Greek word *monos*, meaning "alone."

LESSON 2 REVIEW

Fact Follow-Up
1. What is an established church? How did the Lutheran Church become the established church in Sweden? the Anglican (Church of England) in England?
2. What is the significance of St. Patrick's Day in Ireland?
3. What is the *Book of Kells? The Book of Common Prayer?*

Think These Through
4. What may be the advantages and disadvantages of living in a country with an established church?
5. Norden's religious celebrations cluster around the longest and shortest days of the year. Explain why.

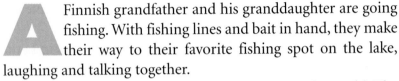

Recreation

LESSON PREVIEW

Key Ideas

- The environment is an important factor in determining what kinds of outdoor recreations people will choose.
- Skiing is favored by people of the far North. Bicycling is favored by the Danes. Field sports are favored by the English. All are examples of the relationships between environment and recreation.

In a land of ice and snow, ice fishing is a favorite form of recreation in Finland and throughout Norden. *In the past, why was it important for the people to know how to ice fish?*

A Finnish grandfather and his granddaughter are going fishing. With fishing lines and bait in hand, they make their way to their favorite fishing spot on the lake, laughing and talking together.

It is a picture that could be from any place in the world. The one detail that makes this fishing trip extraordinary is the lake. It is entirely frozen.

Grandfather walks carefully on the ice, looking behind to make sure the girl is following. When he finds his spot, he kneels. His granddaughter watches closely.

The grandfather then takes a large drill from his pack and begins to bore holes in the thick lake ice. When he's made an opening, he and his granddaughter will drop their lines in the water and hope for good luck, just like all the other fishermen in the world.

Ice fishing once was a survival skill in Finland. Fish were an important food during long winter months. Now ice fishing is a recreational sport. Yet people of Norden preserve the tradition. It is handed down to their children and grandchildren as part of a national heritage.

As you have read in earlier chapters, the working life of a country depends on its land, climate, and resources. Land, climate, and resources also affect the ways people enjoy themselves in Norden and the British Isles.

Norden

Probably the most popular form of recreation in Norden, except for Denmark, is skiing. The name comes from the Norwegian word *ski* (pronounced shee), meaning "piece of wood."

Centuries ago, skiing was the best way that folks in Norden could travel in winter. People learned that by carving skis carefully and by performing certain maneuvers, they could move quickly through the snowy woods and down steep mountainsides. Now skiing is a sport for both enjoyment and competition.

The Finns especially enjoy cross-country skiing and ski jumping. Many towns in Finland have their own ski jump. Finns learn to ski as soon as they can walk.

Summers are short and cool in Norden. Everyone tries to be outside often to enjoy the sunshine and warmer temperatures. It is common for Swedish families to take a walking vacation in summer along marked trails through the countryside. As they walk, Swedes often pick mushrooms or berries. They teach their children about the plants and animals they see on the way.

In Sweden, there is a tradition called Allemansratt (AHL·ler·mahns·RAT), or "every person's right." This tradition permits

The Music of Jean Sibelius

Jean Sibelius (1865-1957) is known to the world as a great composer of symphonies. To Finnish people he is remembered for much more than his music. The huge statue standing in Finland's capital, Helsinki, honors him as a great patriot.

Finland suffered under the hard rule of Russia during the first half of Sibelius' life. His music, which was based on Finnish myth and literature, aroused his country's desire for independence. Later, as an internationally acclaimed composer, his music gave Finns reasons to be proud of their country.

As a student, he loved to read stories of his nation's heroes. He also demonstrated an early talent for music. These interests came together in his studies at the Helsinki Conservatory. In 1892, he won instant fame among Finns for his symphonic poem, "Kullervo," which was based on a famous Finnish epic.

In 1897, Finland gave him funds so that he could spend all of his time composing music. Two years later he completed "Finlandia," a highly patriotic composition. The Russians, fearing that the piece would inspire opposition to their rule, refused to allow "Finlandia" to be performed. Symphony orchestras in Berlin and Paris played it anyway.

After Finland gained independence in 1917,

Jean Sibelius

"Finlandia" became the new country's national anthem. It is today probably the world's longest national anthem and the only one that is regularly played in concert halls all over the world.

Golf probably developed in Scotland about 1,000 years ago. The game was played with a bent stick and a leather ball filled with feathers. In 1457, King James II of Scotland ordered his people to stop playing. The king feared it kept men from practicing archery, or shooting with bows and arrows.

♦♦♦♦♦♦♦♦♦♦♦♦♦♦♦♦

Rugby is one of the most popular sports in the British Isles. *What other sports are popular there?*

people to walk and camp on private property as long as they don't disturb the owner or destroy the land. Allemansratt is cherished by the Swedes, and its rules are carefully observed. After the long, dark winter, this tradition allows everyone to enjoy sunlight and nature.

The land and resources of Iceland and Denmark offer other opportunities for play. Because of Iceland's underground geothermal energy, heated swimming pools are open year-round. Icelanders take advantage of the pools, and all children learn to swim in school.

Denmark's flat landscape makes the country ideal for bicycling. About half the Danes use bicycles for transportation and enjoyment. Many roads in the country and the city have separate lanes especially for bicycles.

The United Kingdom and Ireland

The temperate climate and rolling land of the United Kingdom and Ireland are ideal for field games and golf, a sport invented in Scotland. The British love rugby, a form of football developed at Rugby School. The British also enjoy cricket, a sport played with a bat and ball, but different from baseball. Soccer, which the British call football, is their most popular sport.

Soccer and Irish football are popular in Ireland. Another favorite sport is camogie, a form of field hockey played by women.

The Irish also enjoy riding horses in the countryside and up into the hills. Irish horse racing draws national and worldwide attention. The two most famous yearly races are the Irish Derby and the Irish Grand National.

LESSON 3 REVIEW

Fact Follow-Up
1. What are some of the winter and summer recreational activities in Norden?
2. Outdoor activities in the British Isles are different from those in Norden. Explain why.
3. Which sports mentioned in this lesson are also popular in the United States?

Think These Through
4. How does outdoor recreation in the British Isles and Norden illustrate geography's theme of human-environmental interaction?
5. Would Allemansratt be a good idea to adopt in the United States? Why or why not?

Using Maps: Part II

Your practice in using geography's themes required you to make use of latitude and longitude as you studied absolute location. You might have used the north arrow as you worked with relative location. And you might also have used the Europe Physical map as you researched the theme of place in Chapter 3.

Symbols

If you have used maps in these ways, you have learned already how to interpret some of the mapmaker's language. Other maps require that you learn map terms.

Many maps (see page 154) use a variety of symbols to convey information with few words. In that map, all you need to do to discover resources of a place is match a symbol in the boxed **key** with one or more that you find on the map. For example, the key on page 154 tells you that a lightning bolt is the symbol for hydroelectric or geothermal power. When you see that symbol, you find the locations of hydroelectric and geothermal power in the British Isles and Norden. What other symbols are used on that map? How is color used as a symbol?

Political Maps

Political maps show boundaries of nations or provinces and states within nations. They show capital cities and the locations of parks, highways, and waterways.

A highway map of North Carolina offers political information. The state's boundaries stand out, because the neighboring states are printed in different colors. State maps show the boundary lines of counties and the towns where county governments are located.

A political map helps you learn absolute and relative locations of places on the map. Political maps, when used with scales, give the distance between places. Map keys on political maps give information about capitals, recreation areas, and historical sites.

Physical Maps

What if you are asked whether a nation has many mountains? Sometimes maps with political and physical information are combined. The map of Norden (page 111) is such a map. Colors help show land elevation and rivers are labeled. Boundaries, cities, and countries also are plainly marked.

Sometimes you may need to consult two maps. The Europe Physical map on page 27 outlines national boundaries, but it does not give the names of nations. So first you may need to consult a map with political information, such as the one on page 105, to find a nation's location. Then, by examining the key for the colors giving the land's elevation, you can answer the question.

Chapter 9 Review

TIME FOR TERMS

Swedish Modern architecture
summer solstice
monasteries

Nobel Prize
winter solstice
convents

FACT FOLLOW-UP

1. Describe the absolute and relative locations of London, Stockholm, and Copenhagen.
2. In what ways are the three cities alike? different?
3. In what ways are religious celebrations in Norden related to the environment?
4. How did the Lutheran Church become linked with the government as the established church in Sweden? How did the Church of England become established in England?
5. What role did monasteries play in preserving the Catholic Church in Ireland?
6. What recreational activities in today's Norden were once necessities?

THINK THESE THROUGH

7. Which seems to have been more important in shaping the special character of each of the three cities studied in this lesson—environment or tradition?
8. In what ways can the growth of the three cities be described in terms of geography's theme of movement.
9. You are attempting to describe Norden as a region. Do the religious faiths professed by the people there help or make more difficult the identification of the region as a place that has many common features? Can you also say that religion is a unifying characteristic in identifying the British Isles as a region? Explain.
10. All of the countries in Norden today have abundant supplies of electricity. In what ways do you think daily life in that region has been made easier by the coming of electric power? (Don't limit your answer to the growth of economic opportunities and jobs! Think of the routines of daily life in the far North).

SHARPENING SKILLS

11. Use a physical map to describe the landforms in Sweden.
12. Describe how you might use a political map of the British Isles to identify some of the cultural characteristics of the United Kingdom.
13. Would you most likely use a physical or a

political map to describe the relative location of Helsinki? Explain.

14. Which map symbols do you think may be most often used in everyday life? Why?

15. Some maps have both physical and political features. When would a map with only physical features be more useful? Why?

PLACE LOCATION

Note to students: In preparing for this review you may need to reread the map on page 165 of this chapter and Lesson 3 of Chapter 6.

Use the letters on the map to answer the following questions:

16. What are the names and locations of the countries with a common religious faith?

17. What is the name and location of the country where the language indicates the original settlers came from deep in Russia?

18. What is the name and location of the country marked by conflict between Catholics and Protestants?

19. What is the name and location of the country where people speak much the same language as the Vikings?

20. What are the names and locations of three nations where the people speak different, but closely related, languages and can usually understand one another?

21. What is the name and location of the country where the people were converted to the Roman Catholic faith by St. Patrick?

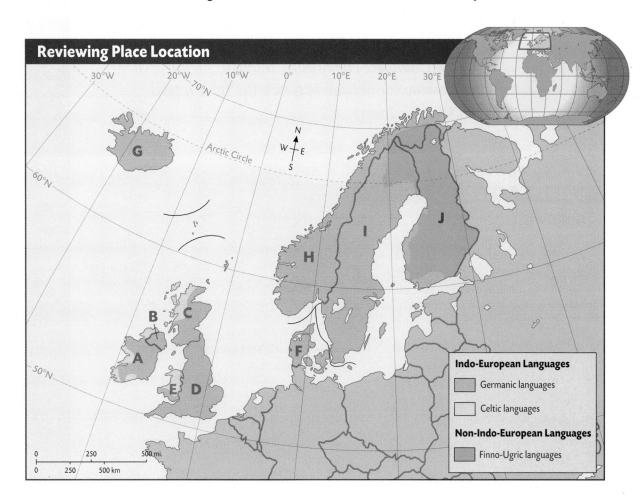

Reviewing Place Location

Indo-European Languages
- Germanic languages
- Celtic languages

Non-Indo-European Languages
- Finno-Ugric languages

The Region of Western Europe

In July 1994, hundreds of bicyclists competing in the Tour de France sped into Portsmouth, England. This marked the first time the world's most famous bicycle race had been run outside the European mainland.

The bikers had ridden through the Eurotunnel— or Chunnel. They were the first (except for freight trains) to travel the 31 miles (50 km) beneath the English Channel. The historic moment highlighted the growing connection between the British Isles and Western Europe.

UNIT PREVIEW

CHAPTER 10
People and Lands
Although the nine nations occupying this region have much in common, Western Europe has much variety in its people and lands.

CHAPTER 11
People and Environment
Human–environmental interaction in today's Western Europe is quite different from the interaction of centuries ago.

CHAPTER 12
Economy and Government
Western Europe has taken giant steps toward economic and political union. The cooperation helps strengthen the region's democracies.

CHAPTER 13
Societies and Cultures
Three great cities, different religions, and different social traditions illustrate the region's variety.

Eurotunnel (Chunnel) under construction (right) and train exiting Chunnel (inset)

People and Lands

"All my life I've been thinking in German," said twelve-year-old Hans, who lives in Lucerne, Switzerland. "But this year in school I'm going to have to start thinking in French."
Switzerland has three official languages: German, French, and Italian. All Swiss schools teach students in the most frequently used languages, German and French. For example, if you speak German with your family, as Hans does, then you must study French.
"It's fair, because the kids who speak French at home learn German, too," Hans said. "In Switzerland, everyone speaks more than one language. It's just the way things are."

School books are written in several languages in Western Europe.

CHAPTER PREVIEW

LESSON 1
People of Western Europe
Traditions and languages have divided Western Europe in the past. Now the region is drawing together.

LESSON 2
Lands of Western Europe
Western Europe today continues to enjoy the benefits of easy access to the world's seas. A variety of landforms characterize the region.

LESSON 3
Climate and Vegetation
Climate varies throughout the region, but, generally speaking, it is moderate. Abundant rain supports the variety of natural vegetation.

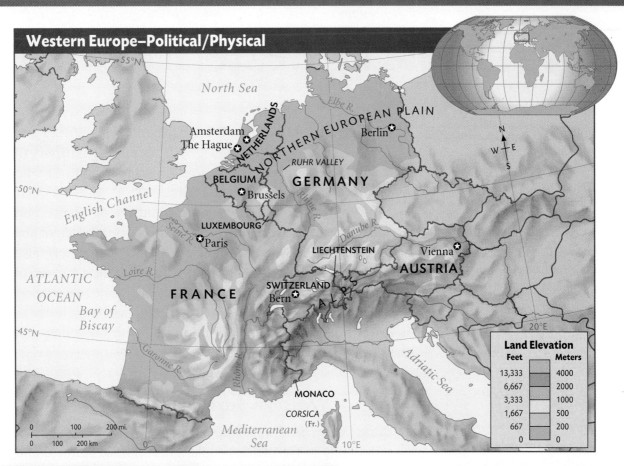

Western Europe–Political/Physical

North Sea

Elbe R.

Amsterdam
The Hague
NETHERLANDS
NORTHERN EUROPEAN PLAIN
Berlin

BELGIUM
RUHR VALLEY
GERMANY

Brussels

Rhine R.

English Channel

Seine R.

LUXEMBOURG

Paris

Danube R.

LIECHTENSTEIN

Vienna
AUSTRIA

ATLANTIC
OCEAN

Loire R.

FRANCE

SWITZERLAND
Bern

A L P S

Bay of
Biscay

Garonne R.

Rhône R.

Adriatic Sea

Land Elevation

Feet		Meters
13,333		4000
6,667		2000
3,333		1000
1,667		500
667		200
0		0

MONACO

CORSICA
(Fr.)

Mediterranean
Sea

0   100   200 mi.
0   100   200 km

Western Europe
Austria
Belgium
France
Germany
Liechtenstein
Luxembourg
Monaco
The Netherlands
Switzerland

*Swiss sixth
graders study
three languages.*

People of Western Europe

LESSON 1

LESSON PREVIEW

Key Ideas
- Western Europe is composed of nine countries of various sizes.
- Differing traditions and languages have caused conflicts among Western Europeans.
- Since World War II, Western Europe has been moving toward increased cooperation.

Key Terms
Benelux countries, Flemish, Walloon

The people of Western Europe live in nine countries and speak even more languages. It seems that citizens of smaller countries speak more languages than those who live in the large countries of the region.

The residents of the two large countries of France and Germany speak French and German, of course. People of the smaller nations of Switzerland, Belgium, The Netherlands (also called Holland), Luxembourg, and Austria speak a variety of languages within each country. Citizens of two of the smallest countries in the world, Liechtenstein and Monaco, learn as many as four languages to communicate with one other and their neighbors.

Roots of Western Europeans

Most Western Europeans can trace their ancestry back to early Celtic or Germanic people. These nomads hunted and farmed on the European plains in ancient times.

Julius Caesar and his Roman soldiers conquered Gaul (present-day France) in 51 B.C. The Roman army did not defeat the Germanic groups living beyond the borders of Gaul. As a result,

An ancient aqueduct in the south of France shows the influence of the Roman Empire in Western Europe. *What part of Western Europe did Rome not conquer?*

the German language today shows little Latin influence. Modern French does reflect the deep influence of Latin, just as the French legal system takes Roman law as its model.

France

Most French are descended from the Celts and later the Roman, German, and Norse invaders. One Germanic group called the Franks gave its name to France.

The French trace their language back to a dialect spoken only in Paris around 1500. At that time, people in other regions of France spoke a variety of dialects, such as Basque, Breton, Dutch, Walloon, Picard, and Provençal.

Over the centuries, the French have worked hard to unite their country through language. They have discouraged and even forbidden the use of dialects other than Parisian French. More recently, France has tried to preserve its language by banning foreign words—especially American expressions such as "weekend"—from newspapers and television.

The Mirapolis, an amusement park near Paris, competes with Disneyland Paris for customers. *Why do the French want to protect their culture from outside influences?*

Germany and Austria

Germany has the largest population of any country in Europe, but the German people have had a united nation for only a small part of their history. The Germans descended from the nomads that fought the Roman armies in the first century and then later invaded Rome itself. The Romans called these nomads *Germani* and their lands *Germania*.

For centuries, Germany consisted of many small territories ruled by nobles. These small territories came together under a single government more than a century ago. By 1870, the boundaries of Germany outlined a nation even larger than the country today. Germany, however, has not been a single nation for all this time.

After World War II, Germany was divided into two nations. East Germany became a Communist country with close ties to its huge eastern neighbor, the Soviet Union. West Germany took

The Imperial Palace in Vienna housed emperors of Austria-Hungary. *What kind of government does Austria have now?*

What would **YOU** do?

Only 13 percent of the world's people speak English as their first language. Since the language is common in the United States, we have few difficulties speaking with others. But people in business work in a world where English is not spoken every-where. Europeans solve such problems by learning two or three languages. Would you recommend that students in the United States learn other languages? Why or why not?

shape under a democratic government with close ties to France, the United Kingdom, and the United States.

Creation of the two Germanys was largely the product of the Cold War, the intense rivalry between the Soviet Union and the United States. That rivalry, as you read earlier, faded away in the late 1980s. The end of conflict permitted Germany to come together again. Since 1991, Germans have been reunited into one nation.

Austria's people have a rich heritage. Austrians count among their ancestors not only the Germanic groups and the Celts, but also Romans, Asians, and Magyars (Hungarians). Most Austrians speak German or one of its dialects.

Austria once was the heartland of a large empire called Austria-Hungary. Vienna, the empire's capital city, became a major European political and commercial center. Austria-Hungary fell apart in 1918 as World War I was ending.

Austria emerged as a much smaller independent nation. The new Austria had lost much of its earlier importance as a center of European affairs. Yet its people preserved their cultural heritage. Vienna's beautiful old buildings, its art and music, and its grand churches continue to draw tourists.

The Benelux Countries

Belgium, The Netherlands, and Luxembourg border one another and share many resources. They are called the **Benelux countries**.

Belgium's people have a divided ancestry. The Flemings, descendants of the Franks, live in the North, in a region known as Flanders. The Flemings speak **Flemish**, a language much like Dutch, which is spoken in The Netherlands. The Walloons, descendants of the Celts, live in the South. They speak a French dialect called **Walloon**.

The Dutch spoken in The Netherlands is a Germanic language similar to Finnish. Luxembourg, the smallest of the Benelux countries, shares an ancestry with the peoples of Belgium, Germany, and France. Nearly all Luxembourgers speak three languages: French, German, and their own dialect, Letzeburgesch.

The *Luxembourger Wort* (Luxembourger Voice), the country's largest daily newspaper, illustrates the mixture of languages, offering articles in French, German, Letzeburgesch, and English. Many European newspapers print separate editions in different languages, but in the *Luxembourger Wort,* articles in French and German appear side by side, on the same page.

The newspaper of Luxembourg reflects the mixed cultures of that country. *What languages are found in the paper?*

WORD ORIGINS

The name of Liechtenstein comes from the ruling family. Johann-Adam Liechtenstein, a prince from Vienna, bought two adjoining pieces of land in 1699 and 1712. He and his descendants have served as heads of government (now a constitutional monarchy) since that time.

Switzerland and Liechtenstein

As you have read, Switzerland has three official languages: German, French, and Italian. About 1 percent of the population speaks another language, Romansh, which is similar to Latin.

In 58 B.C., the Roman armies led by Julius Caesar conquered the Celts living in what is now Switzerland. It became a Roman province called *Helvetia*. Today, the Swiss print "Helvetia" on their postage stamps.

The people of Liechtenstein, who are closely related to the Swiss, speak their own language, a German dialect called Alemannic. They enjoy an open border with neighboring Switzerland, and use the Swiss franc as their official currency.

"The people are quite satisfied with this union," explained Prince Franz Josef II, the constitutional monarch of Liechtenstein, in 1981. "It does well for our economic life. Our position without the union would be very weak."

Swiss stamps show the name the country had as a province of the Roman Empire. *What was that name?*

Liechtenstein occupies 62 square miles (161 sq km), making it smaller than Washington, D.C. Despite its small size, Liechtenstein is actively involved in Europe's economic growth and is one of the richest countries in Europe. Low taxes have encouraged hundreds of corporations to establish their headquarters there.

Monaco

Monaco is even smaller than Liechtenstein. Occupying less than 1 square mile (2.6 sq km), Monaco is one of the smallest countries in the world.

Only about one seventh of Monaco's 31,000 people are

EYEWITNESS TO HISTORY

A European Union

Look again at the map on page 24 that shows Europe to be about the same size as 48 of our nation's 50 states. In Europe, as in the United States, the land offers a rich variety of resources. When these are combined, they give Europe what it needs to become one of the world's economic giants.

George C. Marshall (left) and U.S. Ambassador Lewis Douglas

Until World War II, Europe's resources were divided among many nations. That division began to fade after the war. Robert Schuman and other European leaders worked to unite Europe's economy. They were encouraged by United States Secretary of State George C. Marshall, who engineered the Marshall Plan of aid to Europe.

In just half a century, 15 European nations (see map on page 191) have made remarkable progress. Their borders are open to free trade with one another. People may now cross one another's borders with freedom (right). The Rhine River and its connecting canals are only part of a system that makes easy the transfer of goods throughout Europe.

actually Monegasque (natives of Monaco). Most of the rest are French. Other residents are mainly wealthy Americans, Belgians, British, and Italians.

Monaco has often been in the news, but it plays no vital role in Western Europe's affairs. It exists simply as a playground for the rich. Monaco offers a beautiful beach on the Mediterranean Sea. A good harbor for yachts, fine hotels and restaurants, and a world-famous gambling casino attract many visitors.

Many people in the United States first heard of Monaco in 1956. That year, Grace Kelly, an American movie star, left Hollywood to marry Monaco's constitutional monarch, Prince Ranier III. Princess Grace died in 1982. The country continues to be in the news as a playground for the celebrities.

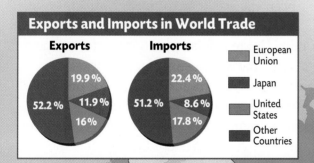

Exports and Imports in World Trade

Exports

- 19.9% European Union
- 11.9% United States
- 16% Japan
- 52.2% Other Countries

Imports

- 22.4% European Union
- 8.6% United States
- 17.8% Japan
- 51.2% Other Countries

Legend:
- European Union
- Japan
- United States
- Other Countries

In 1995 European Union members chose the *euro* as the name of the Union's currency. But many Europeans believe that economic cooperation will survive only if the members form a common government, a United States of Europe. In economic terms, a united Europe equals the United States (see chart at left).

European Union

A move toward a common European coin and paper money has led to arguments over what the money should be named and what it would look like. The French have designed a coin for the European Monetary System, but no one has ever used it. On one side of the coin is Charlemagne. They wanted to name it the "ecu," an abbreviation for European Currency Unit, but also the name of an old French coin. EU members finally decided to call the coin the "euro."

Euro currency

Conflict and Cooperation

Western Europe includes people of many nationalities and backgrounds. Unlike the British Isles, Western Europe lacks a common language. In contrast with Norden, Western Europe lacks a common cultural heritage. Frequently, the differences among the people of this region have led to conflict.

World War I and World War II erupted in large part because of the tensions among the countries of Western Europe. The two largest countries in the region, France and Germany, opposed one another in both wars. A divided Germany later became the political battleground for the Cold War.

Perhaps because Western Europe has been the scene of so much conflict, leaders today are searching for ways to unify the region. The European Union offers opportunities for cooperation among nations that have been rivals for centuries.

While the countries of Western Europe work for unity, they also want to maintain their own national identities. For example, Luxembourg is a founding nation of the European Union. However, like all the countries of Western Europe, Luxembourg does not want to lose its individual sense of nationhood. Its national anthem is "We Want to Remain What We Are." Similarly, the national anthem of Spain—another member of the Union—is "Viva España," "Long Live Spain."

Nazi armies destroyed buildings in Belgium and throughout Western Europe. *How are Western Europeans dealing with conflict today?*

LESSON 1 REVIEW

Fact Follow-Up
1. What are the nations of Western Europe?
2. Why are there so many languages in Western Europe?
3. Which is the "newest" nation of Western Europe?
4. Did the nations of Western Europe cooperate or fight more during the 500 years of modern European history? Why?

Think These Through
5. In what ways does France seem to be different from other Western European nations?
6. Why have most Western European nations been willing to cooperate on economic matters in recent years?

Lands of Western Europe

LESSON 2

Jean-Marc Degrave, age seventeen, lives aboard his family's home—a barge on the Seine River in France. Jean-Marc and his younger brothers and sisters attend school in Rouen. During the summer months they live and work aboard their parents' cargo craft, the *Notre Dame de Lourdes II*, traveling the 5,000 miles (8,050 km) of French rivers and canals that link up with waterways throughout Europe.

Western Europe offers a variety of settings for its people's homes. Canals float Jean-Marc's barge. Western Europeans also live on the rolling plains of Germany, the mountains of Austria, and even land reclaimed from the sea by the Dutch.

Location

When you look at the map of Western Europe, you'll notice that the prime meridian, at 0° longitude, runs through western France, very near the port city of Le Havre. Most of Western Europe, then, extends east of the prime meridian and is in the Eastern Hemisphere.

Much like the British Isles and Norden, Western Europe enjoys a long coastline, which gives the region access to world trade routes by ocean and sea. The Atlantic Ocean and the Bay of Biscay border the western coast of France. The North Sea lies north of Germany, Belgium, and

LESSON PREVIEW

Key Ideas
- Western Europe occupies only a small part of the earth's land. Yet its location and resources have been important factors in the region's major role in world affairs.
- Western Europe's excellent ports, navigable rivers, and canals provide easy access to the world's seas.
- The rich soils of the Northern European Plain furnish a base for productive farming.

Inland harbors are the home of a family's river barge (inset). The harbor of Hamburg, Germany (below), welcomes river barges as well as oceangoing ships. *Why is this important?*

The Netherlands. Northeastern Germany borders the Baltic Sea.

The English Channel, which the French call *La Manche* (The Sleeve), separates the continent and the British Isles. The southern coasts of France and Monaco border the Mediterranean Sea.

Western Europe has dominated European life and history mainly because of its commanding position on the continent. The region lies south of Norden, east of the British Isles, and north of the Mediterranean countries. Western Europe forms the core of continental Europe.

Western Europeans live in a region of rich resources and varied landforms. The land has shaped the lives of the peoples living in this region.

People enjoy outdoor dining in an old square in Cologne, Germany. *How did Cologne's location attract settlers early in Germany's history?*

The Northern European Plain

A large, flat, and fertile area, the Northern European Plain extends east to west across northern Western Europe (see map, page 185).

In ancient times, the Northern European Plain attracted settlers because of its excellent farmland. Since then, with progress in agriculture, the plain has supported a growing population, especially in Germany, Belgium, and France.

The river valleys in the southern part of the plain in Germany include highly fertile soil that is good for farming. People settled there early and founded two of Germany's oldest cities, Bonn and Cologne. The larger, northern part of the plain in Germany has soil mixed with sand and gravel left behind by Ice Age glaciers. These areas support forests, and such hardy grain crops as flax, barley, oats, and rye.

In Belgium, the Northern European Plain runs through the center of the country. Belgians farm this area intensively. The Northern European Plain widens in France. In northern France, farms on the plain produce enough wheat to export.

Rivers, Canals, and Coastlines

Years ago, students studying European geography memorized these lines:

The Rhine, the Rhône, the Danube, and Po,
Rise in the Alps and away they go.

The rhyme reminded students of a reason for Europe's influence. Western Europe's ready access to the Atlantic Ocean, through waterways from the interior, made the region a center of world trade.

The principal river of Western Europe, the Rhine, runs along the border between France and Germany before emptying into the North Sea in The Netherlands. With its branches, the Rhine forms the busiest river system in Europe.

The Rhône, the Seine, and the Loire Rivers carry boat traffic through France towards the Atlantic Ocean. The Elbe and the Danube are key rivers of Germany, flowing in opposite directions. The Elbe flows into the North Sea. The Danube winds through Austria and Eastern Europe before emptying into the Black Sea.

Western Europe's many canals link smaller rivers to one another and to the larger waterways, enabling people and goods to travel easily and cheaply by water. The North Sea Canal in The Netherlands is one of the world's deepest and widest canals. Fifty feet (15 m) deep and 525 feet (158 m) wide, the canal links the port of Amsterdam to the North Sea.

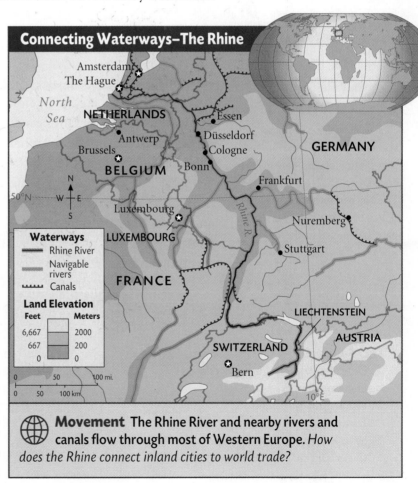

Connecting Waterways—The Rhine

Waterways
— Rhine River
— Navigable rivers
⊔⊔⊔ Canals

Land Elevation

Feet	Meters
6,667	2000
667	200
0	0

Movement The Rhine River and nearby rivers and canals flow through most of Western Europe. *How does the Rhine connect inland cities to world trade?*

When cold weather freezes the canals of The Netherlands, the Dutch take winter vacations to skate. *Which two Dutch cities are world ports because of the canals?*

Like Norden, Western Europe's long coastline supports a prosperous water trade. The northern coast—washed by the Atlantic Ocean, the English Channel, the North Sea, and the Baltic Sea—contains many busy ports. Some ports are away from stormy coasts, a few miles upstream on deep rivers. Bordeaux and Nantes in France, Antwerp in Belgium, Rotterdam and Amsterdam in The Netherlands, and Hamburg in Germany are all several miles inland.

Only the important ports of Le Havre and Marseilles in France lie on the seacoast. Le Havre is the major French port of the English Channel. Marseilles plays an important role in Mediterranean trade on the southern coast of France.

The Alps

With snowcapped peaks rising 6,000 to 8,000 feet (1,800 to 2,400 m), the Alps are the highest mountains in Europe. Located south of the Northern European Plain, the Alps separate Germany, Austria, and Switzerland from Italy and the Mediterranean.

Although Alpine land is too rocky and steep for much farming, the mountains aid the economy of Western Europe through tourism. The Matterhorn on the Swiss-Italian border and Mont Blanc in France have drawn visitors for centuries. In Germany, Austria, and Switzerland, the Alps offer mountain climbing and skiing.

LESSON 2 REVIEW

Fact Follow-Up
1. Describe Western Europe's relative location.
2. Use the map on page 185 to give Western Europe's absolute location.
3. Why are Western Europe's ports, navigable rivers, and canal system so important?

4. How is the Northern European Plain an important resource?

Think These Through
5. Which best describes Western Europe—its absolute or relative location? Explain.
6. How can the Alps be both an advantage and a disadvantage to Western Europe? Explain.

Climate and Vegetation

uring *Fasching*, the Austrian spring festival, mountain villages come alive after the long winter. Marchers in *lederhosen*—traditional leather shorts—and elaborately flowered and feathered headdresses perform the phantom dance to celebrate the beginning of spring.

Although the snow on the high peaks of the surrounding mountains will remain all summer, *Fasching* makes it official. Winter has finally ended.

Moderate and Alpine Climates

The spring celebrations in Austria's mountains reflect the climate characteristic of Europe's interior. Summers tend to be warm, and winters—depending on the location—can be very cold.

As you move eastward away from the Atlantic, the influence of warming winds off the ocean fades. The differences between summers and winters become more noticeable. In most of Western Europe the seasons change, but people do not experience extremes of heat and cold.

Western Europe enjoys a generally moderate climate, with long growing seasons and abundant moisture for agriculture. Summers are mostly cool and humid. The winters are about as chilly as North Carolina's.

For example, Germany's average temperature in January usually remains above 30° F (−1° C). In July, the hottest month, the temperature averages a mild 64° F (18° C). The country receives anywhere from 20 to 40 inches (51 to 102 cm) of precipitation (rain and snow) a year. Farming regions receive plenty of moisture for crops to thrive.

Westerly winds blowing off the Atlantic Ocean bring mild winters and cool summers

LESSON PREVIEW

Key Ideas

- Much of Western Europe's climate is temperate with abundant rain. This supports agricultural production and abundant natural vegetation.
- Two areas in the region offer different climates. The Alps in Austria, Liechtenstein, Switzerland, and southeastern France have a highlands climate. Southern France's climate is Mediterranean: dry and warm.

Sidewalk cafés, such as this one in Aix-en-Provence, France, are favorite gathering spots. *How do the climates of France allow outdoor eating?*

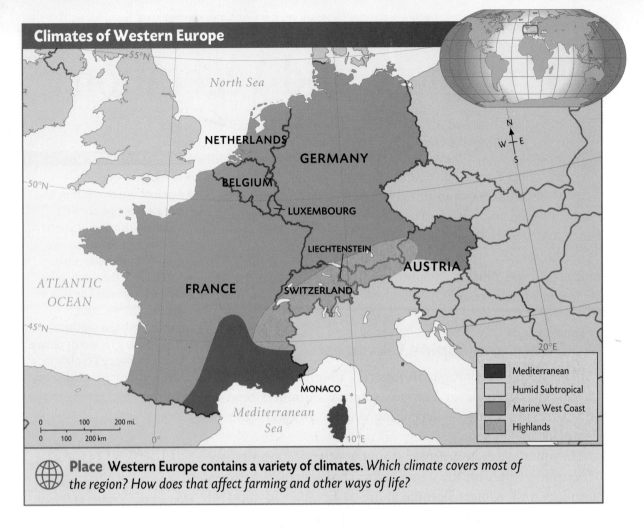

North Sea

NETHERLANDS

GERMANY

BELGIUM

LUXEMBOURG

LIECHTENSTEIN

AUSTRIA

SWITZERLAND

ATLANTIC
OCEAN

FRANCE

MONACO

Mediterranean
Sea

	Mediterranean
	Humid Subtropical
	Marine West Coast
	Highlands

Place Western Europe contains a variety of climates. *Which climate covers most of the region? How does that affect farming and other ways of life?*

to the coastal areas of northern France, Belgium, and The Netherlands. Southern France and Monaco enjoy the Mediterranean climate of hot, dry summers and mild winters.

The drier, warmer Mediterranean climate in southern France proved centuries ago to be ideal for cultivating vineyards. Grapes could be grown in abundance in a region with enough rain (but not too much) and where the sun shone much of the time. Grapes, unlike most other crops, also grew well where the soil was stony and poor.

In time, the many combinations of soil and climate in southern France were recognized for producing special kinds of grapes. Each type of grape yielded wine that was different from the others. French winegrowers often named their wines for the places where the grapes grew. Some wines are named for the vineyards around the busy seaport of Bordeaux (bor·DOH). The Champagne district gives its name to sparkling wines.

Avalanche!

"I'm okay! I'm alive!" said Anna Conrad, as searchers and dog teams discovered her after she was buried in an avalanche. Anna, a ski-lift operator, had been trapped suddenly by the fast-moving river of snow. When rescuers found her, she had been buried five days in snow and the wreckage of her office.

Avalanches occur when snow piles up high on a mountain. In general, mountains catch moisture from the winds. If the mountains are high enough (temperatures drop about three degrees with each 1,000 feet of elevation), snow may fall at any season. Snow really piles high in the winter, the season when many avalanches occur.

Living in an area with avalanches can be difficult and dangerous. Without warning, avalanches moving upwards of 100 miles an hour (161 kph) can fall, burying people, houses, and even entire villages under tons of snow. Avalanches are dangerous because they can be set off easily, by something as simple as a strong gust of wind.

The architecture of many older alpine buildings reflects the reality of avalanches. Most older buildings have thick walls. The walls join in corners shaped liked a ship's prow. They are called splitter wedges, and their purpose is to divert the avalanche away from the rest of the building.

Another protection against avalanches are stands of trees above alpine villages. The trees are called bannwalds, or forbidden forests, and no one—especially children—is supposed to enter them. But extensive tree cutting has left many of the bannwald stands too depleted to fend off avalanches. For this reason, artificial barriers of steel have been constructed at high places in the Swiss Alps. The barriers help stabilize the snow before it becomes too heavy and begins to fall in an avalanche.

When avalanches do come in Alpine areas, most are stopped by other barriers built on the lower slopes. But Alpine skiers still know when to get off the slopes—and children know to stay out of the bannwalds.

Higher elevations in Austria and Switzerland experience the highlands climate. Overall temperatures become cooler, enough to maintain year-round snow on the mountaintops.

Vegetation

At one time, most of the lowlands and plains of Western Europe were covered with forests of broadleaf deciduous trees, such as birch, oak, and beech. People cleared the forests for farming and housing. The climate of Western Europe still supports deciduous forests, such as the Ardennes in Belgium and the Black Forest of Germany.

In the Alpine regions, above 4,000 feet (1,200 m), there are coniferous trees. The most plentiful are spruce, fir, larch, and pine. Still higher, above the timberline in the mountains, no trees grow because of the thin soil, short summers, and low temperatures. At this altitude, only a few wildflowers appear.

The small, hardy Alpine flowers—gentian, primrose, buttercup, monkshood, and edelweiss—have adapted to the strong winds, cold temperatures, and snow of the high mountains. As soon as the snow melts, they pop up to bloom briefly.

The Black Forest (above) contains beautiful birch, oak, and beech trees growing among meadows. *Where would edelweiss (inset) grow?*

LESSON 3 REVIEW

Fact Follow-Up
1. Describe the climate of Western Europe.
2. Where in Western Europe are deciduous and coniferous forests found?
3. How does climate change as you travel from northwestern Germany to Switzerland and into southwestern France?
4. Why are the seasons of inland Western Europe more distinct than those areas on the Atlantic Ocean?

Think These Through
5. Where in Western Europe would the climate enable you to enjoy your favorite outdoor activities?
6. Compare the Alps with the Rocky Mountains in the United States and Canada.

Skill

Using Information for Problem Solving, Decision Making, and Planning

Using Maps to Locate New Businesses

Mark with slips of paper the loca-tion of four maps on Western Europe—"Politi-cal/Physical," page 185; "Climates," page 198; "Population Density," page 205; and "Eco-nomic Activity and Resources," page 223. You will practice using these maps to help you find solutions to practical problems.

A real estate developer, for example, will consult different types of maps in searching for locations where a shopping center might be located. The developer wants a large piece of land for stores, offices, and parking. The land should be located where it can draw many shoppers from a distance of 50 miles.

A political/physical map might suggest where good land for construction may be located. A population density map tells where people (potential customers) live. An economic activity map might show where other businesses—suppliers or competing shopping centers—are located. Maps help the developer locate possible sites.

Using Western Europe's Maps

Imagine that you are president of a com-pany that helps other businesses from the United States locate branch offices in Western Europe. You start your search by using your file of maps. Here are some busi-nesses that want your recommendations about where to locate. You will use the maps on Western Europe to help you make the recommendations. As you find one or more possible locations for each business, write brief descriptions of each relative loca-tion. Then, write a short paragraph stating the reasons why those locations are best for each business.

1. *Winter Sports Equipment Manufacturer—desires location near or in center of winter sport—skiing, skating, sled racing. Raw materials for equipment may be transported by highway or rail. Wants factory near large population with potential customers.* You would consult political/physical, climate, and population density maps to make a recommendation.

2. *Farm Machinery Manufacturer—wants location near iron/steel producer but also near commercial farming operations. Needs good rail and water (river or canal) transportation.* Consult political/physical and economic activity maps.

3. *Water Sport Equipment/Swim Wear Wholesale Dealer—wants location near popular beaches easily reached by large population. Wants place where water sports are played most of the year. Wholesaler wants to open retail stores in several towns and cities.* Consult political/physical, population density, and climate maps.

Check your suggestions with your class-mates. Are there a variety of ideas? Why?

Chapter 10 Review

LESSON 1   Nine countries make up the region of Western Europe. People in this region have long been divided by strong national traditions and different languages. More recently, however, Western Europe has moved toward economic and political unification.

LESSON 2   Western Europe's location gives it easy access to the world's seas through many excellent ports, navigable rivers, and a well-developed system of canals. Western Europe's location also gives its people access to another important resource, the rich agricultural lands of the Northern European Plain.

LESSON 3   Western Europe enjoys other advantages coming from its temperate climate. Abundant rainfall, mild winters, and warm summers encourage farming and the growth of natural vegetation. The snow–covered peaks of high Alpine mountains offer a contrast to Western Europe's generally temperate climate. Another exception is southern France, which has a Mediterranean climate.

TIME FOR TERMS

Benelux countries   Flemish
Walloon

FACT FOLLOW-UP

1. Which two countries in Western Europe are the largest? the smallest?
2. Through which nations does the Rhine River pass?

3. Describe the type of natural vegetation to be found in Western Europe.
4. List three types of climates found in Western Europe and describe the characteristics of each.
5. How have Europeans met the problem of Western Europe's many languages?
6. Do Western Europe's steps toward economic and political unification mean that Europeans have abandoned their old loyalties to their own nations?
7. Describe the relative location of Austria , Liechtenstein, and Luxembourg.
8. Which country in Western Europe has the most navigable rivers? Name them.
9. How do Western Europe's canals serve the people of the region?

THINK THESE THROUGH

10. Canals and rivers were the major means of transportation in the United States for part of the nineteenth century. Water transportation is no longer nearly as great as it once was. In Western Europe, canals were first built centuries ago. Their number and size have steadily increased. Why do you think that canals have remained so important in Europe and have declined in importance in the United States?
11. Geographers agree that the nine countries discussed in this chapter make up a *region* in Europe. Describe their similar characteristics. What characteristics make them unlike one another? Explain.
12. In your studies of Western Europe from the time of the Roman Empire to the present, you

have learned how the *movement* of people, goods, and ideas have contributed to the region. Select three examples of movement from different periods. Describe the movement and how it helped shape today's Western Europe.

SHARPENING SKILLS

13. From the map, identify physical features shared by two or more Western European nations. How do these shared physical features affect each nation's wealth?

14. From your examination of the map, which Western European country (or countries) appears not to have access to river transportation? Which countries benefit most from the rivers of the region?

PLACE LOCATION

Use the letters on the map to locate and name the following places:

15. one of the world's smallest countries.
16. a small country linked to Belgium and The Netherlands.
17. another small nation that once was home to the capital of a large empire.
18. where the people speak two languages, Flemish and Walloon.
19. a nation located in the heart of the Alps.
20. the site of Rotterdam and Amsterdam.
21. a small state between Switzerland and Austria.
22. Germany's one-time enemy but now Germany's partner in the European Union.
23. an industrial giant that depends heavily on a port in another country for exports and imports.

Reviewing Place Location

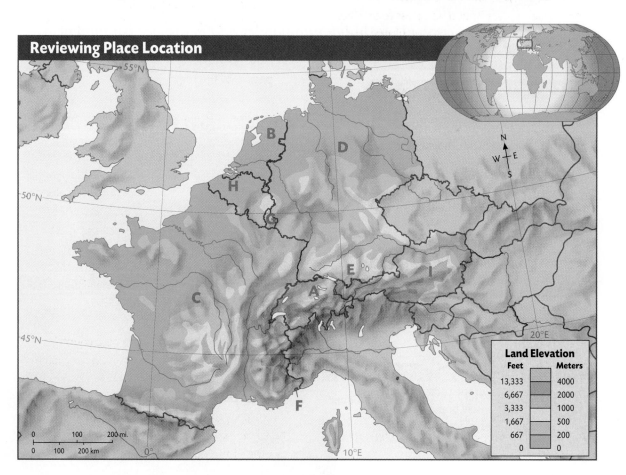

Land Elevation

Feet	Meters
13,333	4000
6,667	2000
3,333	1000
1,667	500
667	200
0	0

People and Environment

A horse-drawn hay wagon creaks near a farm field (left) north of Bordeaux, France. This scene of the time-honored harvest of the land could be from the Middle Ages. Yet in the distance a nuclear power plant looms, providing electricity for the area.

Over the last 20 years, this rural region has surged into the technological age. Nearby, new plants build automobiles and aerospace equipment. Other plants process petroleum and nuclear energy.

CHAPTER PREVIEW

LESSON 1
The Agricultural Revolution
Improved farming methods and new machines started the Agricultural Revolution. Population increased as people lived longer.

LESSON 2
Transportation and Industry Grow
Improved agriculture brought changes in human–environmental interaction. The interaction changed still more as modern transportation and industry appeared.

LESSON 3
The Environment of Western Europe Today
Much of Western Europe today is industrial, urban, and densely populated. Human–environmental interaction has changed over 1,000 years.

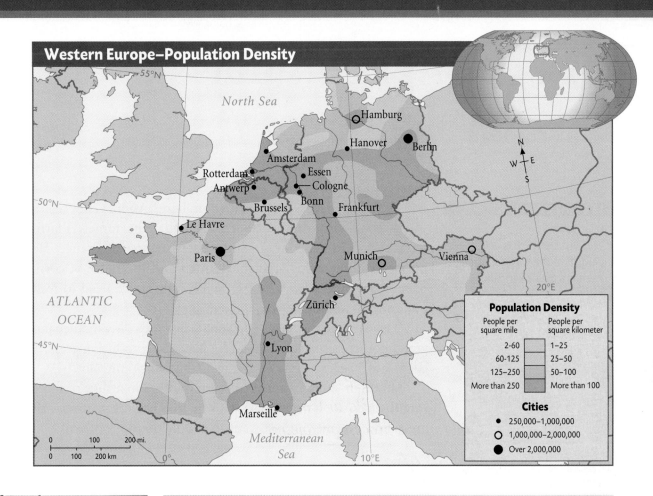

Western Europe–Population Density

North Sea

Hamburg
Hanover • Berlin
Amsterdam
Rotterdam • Essen
Antwerp • Cologne
Brussels • Bonn
Frankfurt
Le Havre
Paris
Munich
Vienna
Zürich
Lyon

ATLANTIC OCEAN

Marseille

Mediterranean Sea

55°N
50°N
45°N
20°E
10°E
0°

N
W E
S

0   100   200 mi.
0 100 200 km

Population Density

People per square mile	People per square kilometer
2-60	1–25
60-125	25–50
125–250	50–100
More than 250	More than 100

Cities

- 250,000–1,000,000
○ 1,000,000–2,000,000
● Over 2,000,000

French nuclear plant

Bordeaux vineyard

The Agricultural Revolution

LESSON
1

Key Ideas

- Western Europe has only 4 percent of the world's farmland. Yet it is a major agricultural producer.
- The Agricultural Revolution happened in Western Europe and the British Isles at the same time.
- The Agricultural Revolution changed human-environmental interactions in Western Europe. Population increased and cities grew.

Key Terms

scythe, sickle, enclosure, philately, polder

"We have a private kingdom here," Andre Galey tells a visitor to his 30-acre (12-square hectometer) farm in Gascony, a southwestern region of France. He points proudly to his vegetable garden and the fields of corn, oats, barley, and wheat. "We grow everything we need to feed our animals and ourselves."

"I take care of the geese," Madame Galey adds. "My mother and grandmother raised geese. So do I. I have 15 reproducing geese. A goose lays 50 eggs a year; we average 750 goslings annually."

Although she sells most of the goslings when they're three months old, she hates to part with them. "They're so pretty, all green and downy, you just want to cuddle them."

Farming in Western Europe

Western Europe includes only about 4 percent of the world's farmland. Still, the region is one of the world's most productive farming areas, especially for wheat, such as the Galeys raise. The region also produces potatoes, sugar beets, and dairy products.

Successful farming in Western Europe has depended on the fertile soil of the Northern European Plain and the moderate climate. Also, as farmers there learned new ways to produce more food, they improved farm harvests.

This farm in Normandy, France, is part of Western Europe's productive farming region. It produces grain, potatoes, dairy products, and wine. *What makes the region productive?*

The Agricultural Revolution

As you have read, late in the Middle Ages European farmers began using crop rotation to keep the soil fertile. At first, they used a three-field system, cultivating two fields and leaving one unplanted to rest the soil. Later, by the 1700s, farmers could keep all fields in use. Food yields increased.

Improvements began on both sides of the English Channel. In the 1700s, Charles Townsend in England found a way of keeping all fields in production. Townsend's plan called for planting turnips in the field that farmers had been leaving unplanted. "Turnip" Townsend—as he came to be called—discovered that turnips put nutrients back into the soil. They also provided good food for cattle and sheep during the winter.

New methods such as these gradually spread through Western Europe. In 1727, German King Frederick William I opened an agricultural school where new farming methods could be studied. In 1747, the Swiss founded an agricultural society to encourage farmers to put the ideas into practice.

As Western European farmers tried the fresh ways of farming, food production rose and the quality of farm products improved. Farmers who used the new techniques produced good feed for their cows even in winter months. As a result, cows produced better milk and meat. Increased animal fertilizer in the fields also improved crop yields. Western Europeans had more high-quality food to eat.

In 1727, German King Frederick William I opened a school for his people. *What was taught there? How did the school help Germany and Western Europe?*

New Tools for Agriculture

In the nineteenth century, the farmers of Western Europe began using better farming tools. The steel plow could shovel through hard-packed soil and required less effort to pull than the older wooden and iron plows. The seed drill enabled farmers to plant seeds in regular rows rather than scattering them. Another new machine, the reaper, greatly reduced the time needed to harvest grain.

Even farmers who could not afford a mechanized reaper discovered more efficient means to cut their crop. By the end of the nineteenth century, these farmers stopped using the sickle and switched to the **scythe** to cut grain.

The old-fashioned **sickle**, with a hooked blade, required the reaper to stoop low and cut only about a handful of grain at a time. With the scythe's long blade and handle, the reaper could stand and cut a much wider swath of grain. Four times more grain could be harvested with a scythe.

Farmers in The Netherlands, Germany, and Belgium developed methods for draining wetlands for farming. Farmers began laying manufactured clay pipes to drain water. This innovation put more land in production.

Enclosure

Along with these improvements, farmers adopted the practice of **enclosure**. They made farms and grazing lands private by

The Dutch Claim Land from the Sea

The Dutch like to boast a bit. "God created the world," they say, "but the Dutch created Holland." If you look closely at the physical map on these pages, you can see why they feel proud. They have pumped the sea out of about 40 percent of their land—and kept it out!

The land the Dutch "created" is some of the most valuable in the nation. The soil makes wonderful farmland. It can be cultivated intensively, producing tulip bulbs (right) that can be sold profitably in world markets. Rotterdam and Amsterdam, two of Western Europe's most important ports, are built on land below sea level.

North Sea

Amsterdam • **NETHERLANDS**
The Hague • • Utrecht
Rotterdam

Lek River
Waal River
Rhine River
Maas River

Land above sea level

Land below sea level

BELGIUM   **GERMANY**

enclosing their fields. This was a major change from the custom of the Middle Ages, when all animals grazed in common areas and roamed freely in the fields.

With enclosure, each farmer knew that only his animals would eat his turnips. The farmer also could make certain that his animals would fertilize his soil and not somebody else's. Every farmer who made the effort and investment to adapt to the new methods could reap the benefits.

In order to increase grain production and improve the breeding of livestock, Frederick the Great ordered his German farmers to adopt the new system. He saw an opportunity to export wheat to Britain, where more people were working in factories and fewer on farms.

The drained land is called a *polder*, a word the Dutch invented in 1604. To make a polder, the Dutch build a dike—a strong, waterproof wall (inset, below)—around an area to be drained. Water is then pumped from the area into canals that drain into the North Sea. Since the polders are below sea level, water must be pumped constantly to keep the land dry.

Kinderdijk, The Netherlands

Electric motors run the pumps now, but windmills (above) furnished power during the early years. Reclaiming the land began about 400 years ago. The Dutch have lost some battles. In 1953, fierce storms broke some dikes, flooding 375,000 acres of land and drowning 1,800 people. The Dutch still keep their dikes strong and pumps running.

Amsterdam canal

People and Environment **209**

Agriculture in Western Europe and British Isles
Late Middle Ages, 1000–1500
• Feudalism (manors)
• Three-field system of crop rotation introduced
• Heavy wooden plows used in the fields
Modern Europe Begins to Take Shape, 1500–1700
• Feudalism fades
• Enclosure movement spreads
• Dutch discover new ways of draining water from farm lands
• New crops, especially potatos, introduced from the Americas
Agricultural Revolution, 1700–1800s
• Improved crop rotation
• Better agricultural tools and machinery introduced, increasing production
• European governments promote adoption of new agricultural methods

The chart above shows agricultural progress through European history. *What farming improvements occurred before the Agricultural Revolution?*

The Agricultural Revolution

Crop rotation, improved farming tools, and enclosure made farms more efficient. Western European farms produced more grains and foods high in protein, such as meat, milk, and cheese. When these foods became a regular part of the diet, the health of Western Europeans improved. They were able to resist disease and live longer lives. The population grew in Western Europe.

These farming innovations also meant that more food could be produced from the same amount of land with fewer workers. Not as many people were needed to farm.

As the population increased and the demand for workers on farms decreased, people moved from the country to the cities. The new city dwellers found work in the new industries of Western Europe.

As you have read, the Industrial Revolution began in England and Scotland with the textile industry. It expanded into Western Europe, especially in Germany, after advances in transportation made widespread industrialization possible.

LESSON 1 REVIEW

Fact Follow-Up
1 What was the Agricultural Revolution?
2. How did people in Western Europe contribute to the Agricultural Revolution?
3. What were some of the results of the Agricultural Revolution?
4. How did the Agricultural Revolution

contribute to the Industrial Revolution?
Think These Through
5. Why is Western Europe one of the most productive agricultural regions in the world?
6. Would the Industrial Revolution have been possible without the Agricultural Revolution? Explain.

Transportation and Industry Grow

Johann, age twelve, enjoys a train ride on the InterCity Express, which hurtles along at 120 miles per hour (193 kph). He and his parents have left their home in Hamburg, Germany, for a vacation in the Austrian Alps. Tomorrow they'll be mountain climbing, but for now Johann watches the passing scenery out the train window while enjoying an American treat—a Big Mac hamburger.

"The Hamburg-to-Berchtesgarden train is the first InterCity Express with a McDonald's on board," Johann explains excitedly. "The train takes us right to the Austrian border, and along the way we can see all of Germany from north to south. I told my father we had to try it."

LESSON PREVIEW

Key Ideas
- Human-environmental interactions in Western Europe changed with construction of transportation and factory systems.
- Places in Western Europe were linked by rivers, canals, railways, and highways.
- The factory system developed later in Western Europe than in the British Isles. Yet nations such as Germany soon caught up with the British.

Transportation

Western Europe today enjoys one of the best rail systems in the world. These railroads, together with deep ports, navigable rivers, and canals form an interlocking network of transportation that has made the region a center for European and world trade.

The modern transportation system began with rivers and canals. Extra food raised by farmers after the Agricultural Revolution was moved by boat to city markets. Then, with the development of the steam engine, railroads spread through the countryside, reaching places untouched by canals and rivers.

As commerce increased, towns and cities grew, usually at intersections of railroad lines and water routes. People began to take more control over their environment, using more products from farms, forests, and mines. More factories and cities were built. Everything was connected by the complex network of transportation that crossed through the countryside.

The TGV Express from France speeds through Western Europe. Fast trains mean more than convenient transportation for people. *How else have railroads affected Western Europe?*

Trains of the nineteenth century, such as this one in King's Cross Station in London, were powered by steam. *What fuel was used in steam engines?*

Early Rail Transport

The first steam-driven trains in Western Europe began running in 1835. Their purpose was to transport coal from the coal fields of Belgium and southern Germany to the manufacturing cities.

About the same time, the French built a rail system from Paris to small towns. Like the Belgian and German lines, the French railway supported industry by carrying raw materials. The trains also shipped food from the rural areas to the city.

Roads, Canals, and Ports

Western Europeans made railways, roads, canals, and rivers work together. Roads and canals were improved to carry more traffic. By the time the railroad system covered much of Western Europe, the roads and canals were in excellent condition.

The railroad could carry goods cheaper and faster than roads, but the roads could provide reliable routes to the railroads. Farmers and tradespeople who shipped their goods by train needed the good roads to get to the railway.

Canal barges moved slowly, but they carried heavier, bulkier goods more cheaply than railways. Water transport was ideal for moving heavy raw materials, such as coal. The Ruhr and Rhine Rivers, along with connecting canals, became the main highway from the rich coal fields of the Ruhr valley. Trains carried lighter and more perishable goods, such as food crops, that needed quicker transport.

Western Europe's improved transportation system promoted world trade. Hamburg, Rotterdam, and Le Havre had been important ocean ports for many years because their location on rivers connected them to inland cities. With connections to new factory and farm centers, they became even more important. By the late 1800s, Western Europe was linked to the world through those cities.

Increased trade led to more jobs and increased population. Hamburg and four other cities in Western Europe now have more than 1 million people. Two of those cities—Paris and Berlin—have more than 2 million people (see map, page 205).

Beginnings of Industry

After Britain, Belgium was the second nation to industrialize. In 1799, William Cockerill, an English carpenter, moved to Belgium and began making textile machinery. Belgium's textile businesses used his new machinery and modernized the centuries-old methods of making cloth.

German industrialization came after the railroad system had developed. German industry emerged in many areas at once, instead of just in the region nearest the coal fields, as it had in Britain. German trains could transport coal for factories all around the country. Eight of those cities now have populations greater than 250,000 each (see map, page 205).

Rivers form connections from inland cities to the sea. Cities such as Hamburg have large ports to hold oceangoing ships. *How did that help trade in Western Europe?*

LESSON 2 REVIEW

Fact Follow-Up
1. Why did a modern transportation system develop in Western Europe?
2. How do canals contribute to the operation of Western Europe's transportation system?
3. Name three important ports in Western Europe and the nations they serve.
4. Describe how railroads contributed to Germany's industrial development.

Think These Through
5. How are the Agricultural Revolution, the building of modern transportation systems, and the Industrial Revolution connected?
6. Which was most important in changing Western Europe's transportation systems—canals, railroads, or highways? Explain.

The Environment of Western Europe Today

LESSON PREVIEW

Key Ideas
- Revolutions in agriculture, transportation, and manufacturing contributed to increases in Western Europe's population and improved living standards.
- Those same revolutions have created serious environmental problems that Europeans are now trying to solve.

Key Terms

life expectancy, standard of living, toxins, the Greens

When the Rhine River flooded in the spring of 1995, causing widespread damage along its banks, there seemed to be one sign of hope. Swimming in the river was a single salmon—a kind of fish absent from the Rhine for more than 40 years because of pollution.

At first, people took the salmon sighting as a sign that the Rhine had become a healthy habitat again. But Dutch biologists disagreed. The salmon, they explained, probably drifted into the Rhine from one of the cleaner tributaries, where researchers had released young fish as part of an experiment. There was no proof that mature salmon were returning to the Rhine for good.

Environment Today

The pollution of Western Europe's waters is a serious problem that makes newspaper headlines. It is only one of the dramatic changes in the region's environment. Western Europe's agricultural and industrial revolutions have transformed the land.

Think for a moment about Europe's early Middle Ages. Europe 1,000 years ago was thickly forested and thinly populated. Most people lived in small, self-sufficient communities. How different Europe looks today!

The three Benelux nations (Belgium, The Netherlands, and Luxembourg) are only slightly larger than West Virginia. Yet, their combined population is more than 25 million. That is almost as many people as live in all of

Amsterdam shows how crowded parts of Benelux are. It is one of the most densely populated areas in Europe. *What are the three nations of Benelux?*

Canada. The combination of small land area and large population makes the Benelux countries one of the most densely settled areas in Europe (see map, page 205).

Despite the small land area, most enjoy the benefits of good housing, ample food, and fine medical care. The average life span (**life expectancy**), as it is in the rest of Western Europe, ranges between 74 and 77 years. All of these qualities of life contribute to a high **standard of living**, which is a way of measuring the basic needs and comforts of life. Even in cities with populations more than 250,000 each, people enjoy comforts and luxuries.

CONNECTIONS

Geography & Science

How a Microscope Works

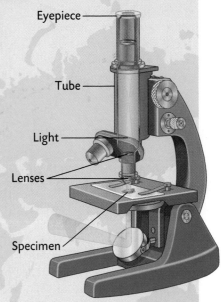

Eyepiece

Tube

Light

Lenses

Specimen

After peering into a lens pressed between two metal plates, Anton van Leeuwenhoek wrote "wretched beasties" in his notebook. Later, he observed that the small animals he was looking at moved about "very nimbly, because they had incredibly thin feet!"

Van Leeuwenhoek, of The Netherlands, is regarded as the founder of the scientific field of microbiology. It is important in solving today's environmental problems.

Van Leeuwenhoek used a microscope to discover and describe tiny living things—**microorganisms**—invisible to the naked eye. The microscope changed forever how people looked at their world. Van Leeuwenhoek helped people understand that diseases might come from things that they could not see.

Today's microscopes are basically the same as the one used by van Leeuwenhoek in 1671. Light reflected from the object under the microscope travels until it hits a lens at the bottom of the microscope. The lens bends the rays of light, spreading them out and making a small image appear much bigger. Other lenses expand the image more and correct the light's angle. The image then hits the eye.

In this way, scientists can study bacteria and disease-causing viruses.

Some modern-day microscopes use beams of electrons instead of rays of light. Called electron microscopes, these instruments are capable of showing images in three dimensions. Some of them have even been modified to show objects as small as a single atom.

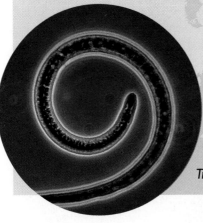

Trichivella Spiralis

Water Pollution

Such skillful use of resources is typical of much of Western Europe. Most nations in the region have well-developed agriculture, industry, and commerce. Even though these nations suffered through two terrible wars, they have recaptured much of their lost prestige and wealth.

Yet they have not been able to escape many of the environmental costs of well-developed agriculture and industry. For example, the Rhine River is called "the great open sewer of Western Europe." It flows 820 miles (1,320 km) from the Alps to the Dutch coast, through the most populated and industrialized areas of Europe.

About 20 million people depend on the Rhine and its tributaries for their drinking water, which must be cleaned with filters and chemicals. In the crowded cities, engine exhaust leaves heavy metal and soot in the water. Farms drain pesticides, herbicides, and animal manure into the river. Recently, scientists have discovered new pollutants that can cause illnesses, and that are passed down from one generation to the next.

In recent years, strict pollution-control laws and expensive waste-water treatments have helped to improve the water quality. The amounts of metals and pesticides in the Rhine have decreased. More work must be done to restore the river to its original health.

In Germany, river otters still show dangerous levels of **toxins**—poisons—in their kidneys, liver, and fatty tissues. And cormorants

German factories, such as this steel mill in the Saar Valley, help the German economy. Factories located near rivers also can cause pollution.
What are other sources of water pollution in Western Europe?

nesting near the Dutch Rhine estuary have been laying fewer eggs and the eggs have thinner shells. Scientists worry that the pollution also threatens human life.

Air Pollution

Elsewhere, other types of pollution present serious problems. Western Europe's thriving industries burn coal, fuel oil, or natural gas to run their factories.

These fuels produce smoke containing sulfur dioxide and nitrogen oxide, chemicals that become sulfuric acid and nitric acid. These chemicals often are carried great distances by the winds. Scientists believe that when they fall to the ground again with precipitation, they damage forests and wildlife.

Southern Norway in particular feels the impact of acid rain carried from the British Isles, the Benelux countries, and Germany. Acid rain falls onto forests and lakes there. Trees have been damaged or killed. Many fish in the lakes have died.

What would **YOU** do?

As trading between Western and Eastern Europe has increased, boat traffic along the Danube River has skyrocketed. Some people favor building canals. Others think that expanding the canals would be too expensive. Products that are now shipped by canal could be shipped instead by truck or railroad. Which do you think might be better from an environmental standpoint—canals or other forms of transportation?

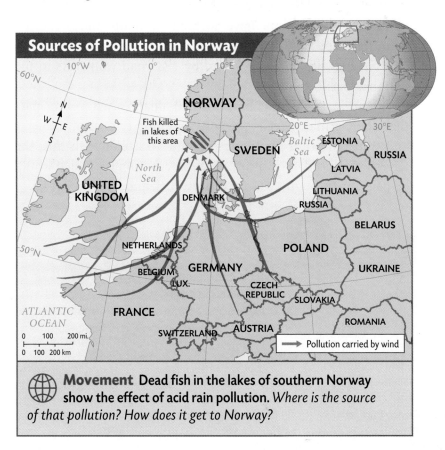

Sources of Pollution in Norway

Fish killed in lakes of this area

Pollution carried by wind

Movement Dead fish in the lakes of southern Norway show the effect of acid rain pollution. *Where is the source of that pollution? How does it get to Norway?*

Increased air pollution in East Germany created problems for the environment. Trees died because of acid rain. *What is the source of air pollution in a country with few heavy industries?*

Germany inherited serious environmental problems when its western and eastern regions were reunited. Under its Communist government, East Germany had industrialized without regard to the environment. Factories poured smoke into the skies. Air pollution caused acid rain. Soil and groundwater around factories were sometimes loaded with dangerous chemicals. Years of hard work and great sums of money will be required to repair the damage.

Even the once-clean mountain air of Switzerland did not escape damage. Tunnels were dug through the rugged Alps to provide easy travel by rail and automobiles. By the 1990s, some 100 million people annually were traveling in Switzerland.

The traffic caused air pollution and acid rain that damaged mountain forests. Building roads and constructing ski resorts, critics claim, destroyed once-beautiful mountain scenery.

Environmentalism and Politics

In response to environmental dangers, political parties known as **the Greens** have formed in many industrialized countries, especially in Western Europe. In Germany, *die Grunen* (the Greens) began in 1979, and by 1983 had won seats in the national legislature.

Recently, the Greens have formed alliances with other parties. The German Greens propose sweeping reform of industry and transportation for better ecology. To accomplish this, the Greens support conservation and new technologies, which would be paid for through taxes on energy, fuel, and waste disposal.

LESSON 3 REVIEW

Fact Follow-Up
1. What are key sources of pollution in Western Europe?
2. What efforts are being made to control pollution?
3. Environmental pollution in Western Europe is a problem that reaches across national boundaries. Explain.
4. What area—or areas—of Western Europe are most densely populated?

Think These Through
5. Compare and contrast the revolutions in agriculture, transportation, and manufacturing. Which is greater—the advantages or disadvantages?
6. If you cared deeply about living in a clean environment, in which Western European nation would you choose to live? Explain.

Skill

*Acquiring Information
From a Variety of Sources*

Changing Uses of the Environment

Chapters 7 and 11 are filled with information about changes in Europe's economy and human-environmental relations. To help you understand and remember these events, you can reorganize this information in graphic ways. Look at the data retrieval chart on page 210. This pulls together information on agriculture from chapters 7 and 11. You can expand this chart to show other changes.

Below you will find a time line that shows how changes in agriculture can be linked to changes in other areas. Draw five columns on a sheet of paper, leaving enough room for a blank column on the right side of the paper. Divide the columns into four rows. Be sure to make the spaces large enough so that you will have plenty of room to write.

Note that each column below gives an example or two of the type of information to enter. The examples in the column labeled "Agriculture" are taken from the chart on page 210. The others come from chapters 7 and 11. Examine these two chapters and find information to add to each of the columns. When you have finished, compare your time line with two or three classmates.

Be sure to put as much information as you can on your time line. With a time line of several columns, you can now see more readily how changes in agriculture, transportation, and industry helped change each other.

Complete one more column, using the blank space on the right side of the paper. At the top, put "Human-Environmental Interaction." Add here information on changes that took place while Europe changed—movement of people to cities, population increases, changes in ways of making a living, and pollution problems. After examining this time line, write two or three paragraphs on "Economic Change and Human-Environmental Interaction."

Human-Environmental Interaction: Sources of Change				
Agriculture	**Transportation**	**Years**	**Industry**	**Human–Environmental Interaction**
Feudalism (manors)	Foot, horse, boat	1000	Home spinning and weaving	
		1500		
New crops		1700		
	Railways	1800		
		1900	Auto assembly by robot	

Chapter 11 Review

LESSONS LEARNED

LESSON 1 The Agricultural Revolution in Western Europe and the British Isles took place about the same time. Good climate, good farmland, and improved farm methods brought population increases. More people could live in cities. All these trends caused large changes in human–environmental interaction.

LESSON 2 Human–environmental interaction changed still more as Western Europe's modern transportation and industrial systems emerged. People's lives changed as they moved to cities.

LESSON 3 Human–environmental interactions in Western Europe have changed greatly in 1,000 years. Western Europe had been thinly populated in the late Middle Ages. Most people lived in scattered, rural communities. Today, the region's modern economy supports a huge urban population. High living standards are common. At the same time, Western Europe suffers from serious environmental problems.

TIME FOR TERMS

scythe

enclosure

polder

standard of living

the Greens

sickle

philately

life expectancy

toxins

FACT FOLLOW-UP

1. With only 4 percent of the world's farmland, how does Europe manage to be one of the most productive agricultural regions in the world?

2. Describe the effects of the Industrial Revolution on Western Europe.

3. How did an increasingly modern transportation system contribute to changes in agriculture and to the Industrial Revolution?

4. Since Western Europe's nations are small, both air and water pollution created in one country passes into others. What special problems does this create in environmental cleanups?

5. How are such countries as The Netherlands and Switzerland able to have prosperous economies without many agricultural or industrial resources?

THINK THESE THROUGH

6. Western Europe has a good system of rivers, canals, railways, and highways. How did the development of such a transportation system help the development of agriculture, commerce, and industry?

7. Germany's industrialization began later than Great Britain's. Yet by 1900, Germany was outproducing Great Britain in such key areas as iron and steel. How could this have happened?

8. If you were developing a Top Ten list of reasons for Western Europe's economic development, which of the following would rank highest on that list—the enclosure movement or invention of the railway? Explain.

9. Imagine another Top Ten list of Western Europe's environmental problems. What item is at the top of your list? Why is its solution more pressing than any other problem?

10. Chapters 3, 4, and 5 described Europe's foundations: (a) From ancient Greece and ancient Rome came key ideas and institutions; (b) from the Jewish and Christian traditions came religious faiths; (c) from the Roman Empire came secular and religious ideas into Europe; (d) from early modern Europe came the beginnings of nations; and (e) from World Wars I and II came near destruction. Make a time line to show these events.

11. Time lines can be used to plan for the future. For example, time lines are often used by government and business people. Design a time line that could have been used to plan Western Europe's transportation system.

12. What if you had about eight things to do next Saturday? You knew that each one would require anywhere from a half-hour to two hours. Would a time line be helpful? Explain.

Use the letters on the map to locate and name the following places:

13. the city in Austria with a population of between 1 million and 2 million.

14. the city in France with a population over 2 million.

15. the city in Germany with an ocean port and a population over 1 million.

16. the city in Germany with a population over 2 million.

17. the city in central Belgium with a population over 250,000.

Reviewing Place Location

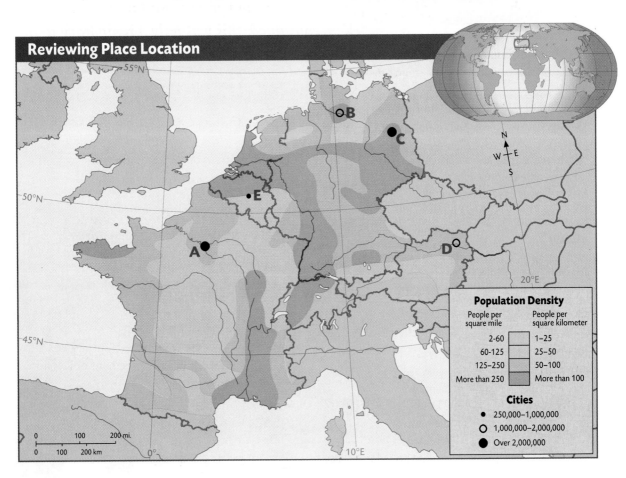

Population Density

People per square mile	People per square kilometer
2-60	1–25
60-125	25–50
125–250	50–100
More than 250	More than 100

Cities

- 250,000–1,000,000
○ 1,000,000–2,000,000
● Over 2,000,000

Economy and Government

*Kees Rijnvos (far right)
with his sister and brothers*

In 1951, six years after World War II ended, Dutch teenager Kees Rijnvos entered a contest that challenged young people to predict their country's future. Kees' essay began with a description of his parents and nine brothers and sisters as they sat in a single room playing cards. As usual, their evening meal had been potatoes and gravy—and nothing else. But, Kees continued, this was only a temporary result of World War II. Life would soon be better.

CHAPTER PREVIEW

LESSON 1
Western Europe Rebounds
Western Europe has once again become an economic giant. High-level technology is used in production. Manufactured goods are high quality.

LESSON 2
Foundations of Growth
Behind this return to economic power are nations willing to cooperate with one another in sharing resources. Each specializes in what it best produces.

LESSON 3
Government
Western European governments are constitutional democracies. They cooperate easily on economic matters. Political cooperation has been harder.

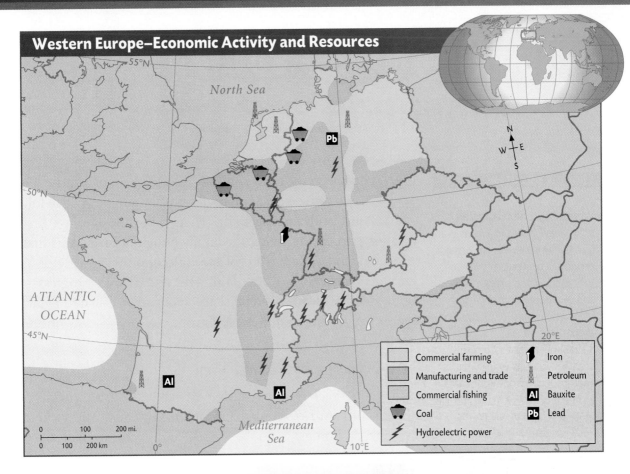

North Sea

Pb

ATLANTIC
OCEAN

Mediterranean
Sea

Commercial farming	Iron
Manufacturing and trade	Petroleum
Commercial fishing	Al Bauxite
Coal	Pb Lead
Hydroelectric power	

0   100   200 mi.
0   100   200 km

The Netherlands had a difficult recovery from World War II because of destruction suffered in such cities as Rotterdam (above) and Nijmegen (left).

LESSON 1

Western Europe Rebounds

LESSON PREVIEW

Key Ideas

- Western Europe rebounded from heavy losses in World War II to become once again a major economic center.
- Western Europe's new power and prosperity comes partly from a new spirit of international cooperation.
- Success also comes from the construction of modern plants and production of high-quality products.

Kees won the essay contest, and his dream of a better life also came true. Soon his family had a radio, a flush toilet, and a refrigerator. Then came the family's first vacation trip. In the 1960s, the family bought a car and its first television. Today, Kees is a professor of economics and rector of Erasmus University, Rotterdam. His remarkable progress—along with his family's—represents an experience shared by his generation throughout Western Europe.

The Effects of World War II

Looking back on those early postwar years, it is difficult to understand how Kees could have been so confident. Everywhere he looked, homes, schools, stores, and factories had been

A cheese market in The Netherlands today shows the productivity of the Dutch economy, especially in comparison to its economy of the 1960s. *What did the Benelux countries do to help their economy?*

224 *Chapter 12*

destroyed. Everyone—not just his family—suffered from shortages of food and clothing. Western Europe was in ruins.

Yet Kees may have realized that rebuilding had already started in his own country and some others. In 1949, the United States Marshall Plan made large sums of money available to European countries that were not under the control of the Soviet Union. With this aid, transportation systems were repaired, and farms and factories were restarted.

Meanwhile, some key European countries had already taken the first steps to cooperate rather than compete with one another. Even before World War II ended, the Benelux countries had agreed to lower trade barriers. As you have read, this was a first step in the creation of today's European Union.

The Postwar Boom

Soon after World War II, Europe west of the Iron Curtain had launched an ambitious program of economic development. European leaders did not attempt to rebuild their countries as they had been before the war. The ruined factories and transportation systems had once served Europe well, but the machinery had become out-of-date. Many of Europe's products seemed out-of-date as well. As a result, Europe's postwar industries were redesigned to make products for the postwar years.

For centuries, France's industry had produced quality goods by hand. French wine, fine china, and perfume brought high prices, but their quantity was limited. After World War II, France decided to turn out more goods by mass production, using assembly lines in large factories. For example, such French firms as Citroen,

◆◆◆◆ GAMES ◆◆◆◆
People Play

Tour de France The most popular sporting event in France is the annual Tour de France, a professional bicycling race. The three-week race is contested in daily stages and covers from 1,900 to 2,200 miles (3,059 to 3,542 km). Bicyclists compete over flat, hilly, and mountainous land on the way to Paris. The cyclist with the shortest overall time wins the race. The Tour de France winner in 1986, 1989, and 1990 was an American, Greg LeMond.

◆◆◆◆◆◆◆◆◆◆◆◆◆◆◆◆

Peugeot, and Renault began manufacturing cars in great numbers. France's reputation for high-quality goods helped make the cars popular worldwide. France soon became a major industrial power.

Just seven years after losing World War II, West German factories were back in business. They stopped producing weapons and began turning out machine tools and cars. Such cars as Mercedes-Benz and Volkswagen sold especially well abroad. Germany became the third largest producer of automobiles in the world.

German industries soon created a trade surplus as the country sold more products abroad than it bought. In the 1960s, this trade surplus grew to 20 times the size it was in the

Changing Patterns of Immigration

Millions of people have left Europe in the last 400 years. These Europeans settled in the Americas, Australia, and other parts of the world. Now the flow of immigrants has been reversed. By the mid-1990s, about 15 million immigrants had settled in Europe.

In the Americas and Australia, Europeans created societies that were much like the ones they left behind. The Spanish and Portuguese transported many of their ways to Middle and South America. Visitors to Quebec, Canada, find a knowledge of French useful. The rest of Canada and the United States reflect the influence of the British Isles as well as other European regions.

Quebec political rally shows French influence in Canada

Many fled Europe to escape religious or political persecution. The New England colonies in the United States were founded in the early 1600s by English seeking freedom to worship. In the twentieth century, Albert Einstein, a world-famous scientist, settled in the United States to escape Hitler's campaign against Jews.

Immigrant registration in New York, 1866

Albert Einstein

early 1950s. Everyone marveled at the economic miracle—the *Wirtschaftswunder*—of West Germany.

Because of Belgium's location, the war took a terrible toll on the country's industries. During the 1950s, many Belgian textile businesses moved to other parts of the world, where workers' wages were lower. Belgium turned from making lace to manufacturing steel. Today Belgium ranks as a major steel-producing nation.

Belgium has also earned an international reputation for mechanical engineering—the planning and building of large-scale projects. Belgians have built railways and factories in countries as far away as Argentina, China, Egypt, Mexico, and Russia.

Before World War II, tiny Liechtenstein was a farming

Europe's economic boom began to draw immigrants in the 1960s and 1970s. Some of these newcomers came from countries that had been European colonies. Others, such as Turks, came as "guest workers" to work in jobs that Western Europeans did not take. As Communist governments crumbled in Eastern Europe, people moved from that region to work in Western Europe.

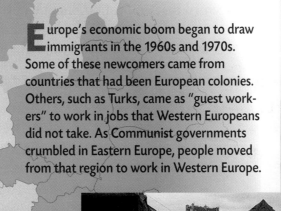

"Guest worker" in Germany (above) and immigrants in France (left)

Immigrants were generally welcomed at first. There were plenty of jobs and not enough immigrants to attract much attention. In the 1990s, competition for jobs became more intense. The immigrants became the target of demonstrators in Germany and some other countries. European leaders began to search for ways of controlling this reverse flow of people.

Turkish immigrants protest in Germany against prejudice

country, with nearly half of its people working the land. Now only about 4 percent of the population farms. As Europe's economy boomed, Liechtenstein industrialized for the first time. By 1979, its total exports amounted to $18,000 for every citizen in the country—the highest in the world and 20 times that of the United States. Moreover, Liechenstein's economy profited by attracting foreign deposits into its banks.

Western Europe's Economy Today

Unexpected difficulties have sometimes challenged Western Europe's leaders. German planners did not anticipate either the difficulties or the expense of uniting the economies of East Germany and West Germany. East Germany's economy had been shaped by a Communist-led government. West Germany thrived through its capitalist economy. In the early 1990s, it seemed that unification might take only a year or two.

But East Germany was in worse shape than anyone expected. Its roads, railways, telecommunications, and factories hardly

This Coca-Cola plant in Brussels, Belgium, shows that small countries in Western Europe have major industry. *What economic activity dominated in Belgium before World War II?*

worked. Massive environmental problems had to be solved. Ways had to be found to bring millions of workers into a modern industrial system.

All these difficulties forced German leaders to make new estimates. The work will not be finished until after the year 2000. The cost will run more than $750 billion. Yet German leaders have pushed ahead. A fully reunified Germany promises to strengthen a nation that already has the strongest economy in Europe.

Germany's determination to resolve its reunification problems seems typical of Western Europe's determination to rebound from near disaster. As Western Europe—along with the British Isles and nations in Norden and Mediterranean Europe—enters the twenty-first century, Europe seems close to becoming even more important in the world than in the past. Together, the 15 members of the European Union have a population of almost 350 million. The region is one of the world's richest markets. Its factories produce nearly 40 percent of the world's exports. More European nations want to belong to this powerful organization.

Differences in the region are still present. Many European leaders continue to hope that economic connections created by the European Union will overcome cultural barriers and perhaps bring greater political unity.

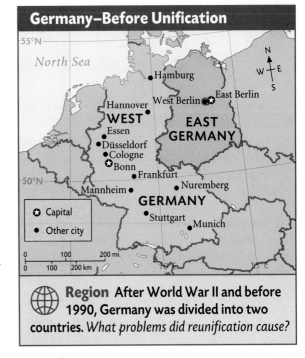

Germany–Before Unification

Region After World War II and before 1990, Germany was divided into two countries. *What problems did reunification cause?*

LESSON 1 REVIEW

Fact Follow-Up
1. Describe the problems facing Western Europe just after World War II.
2. Describe Germany's "economic miracle."
3. How did Western Europe's industries change after World War II?
4. What economic problems has Germany faced since reunification?
5. How has Belgium's economy changed?

Think These Through
6. Some economists say that the destruction of Western Europe's factories in World War II contributed to the region's economic rebound. Do you agree or disagree? Explain.
7. Do you think that the term Second Industrial Revolution is an accurate name for the changes in Western Europe's economy since 1945? Why or why not?

Foundations of Growth

LESSON PREVIEW

Key Ideas

- People in Western Europe have prospered by adapting to change.
- Nations have dropped ideas of economic independence. They now specialize in the production of things best suited to available resources and skills of their people.

Stand on Friedrichstrasse, a broad avenue in what was once Communist-controlled East Berlin. The Communists are gone and Germany is united.

Rather than empty streets, construction workers swarm about. Luxury apartments, offices, restaurants, and shops rise out of the once-drab buildings. Berliners see hope where there was despair.

A united Germany's government moved from Bonn to its old capital city of Berlin. The city's reunification has brought economic hope.

The avenue's location encouraged business leaders to open new shops and restaurants. Government workers, foreign delegations, and native Berliners may make these new businesses successful. One of Berlin's finest old streets now hums with new life.

Friedrichstrasse, a main street in East Berlin, had little to offer before reunification (above). *What changes occurred on the street after reunification (right)?*

Human Ingenuity

Business in Communist East Berlin had been government owned and managed. Under the newly united Germany government, Berlin's businesses were free to rebuild the Freidrichstrasse. Their decision illustrates how Western Europe has rebounded from two devastating world wars and the loss of colonial empires. Berlin's leaders believed that they could succeed. Like Europe's earlier generations, they must use their resources wisely.

East Berliners are reminders of how Western Europeans faced the destruction of war. They were not content with rebuilding Europe exactly as it had been before the war. New ways of doing business were adopted. National rivalries were replaced by a willingness to cooperate with one another in reviving Europe's economic and political power.

Pooling Resources

Neither terrible wars nor the loss of empires destroyed the advantages that Europe enjoyed because of its geographic location. It remained a large peninsula extending westward from Asia into waters that link nearly all its parts with the world. It also was a place with a remarkable mix of resources—good agricultural land and climates that favored farm production, forests, and a variety of mineral resources. Finally, its people had rich experience in farming, trade, and industry.

The division of Europe centuries ago into rival nations had established barriers to the movement of these resources. France, the largest nation in Western

Europe, had good farms and Germany had iron and coal mines. Each needed the resources of the other. Yet in a time of intense national rivalries, trade was slow to occur. After World War II, trade connections grew. The European Union encouraged trade among its members.

Agricultural Specialization

The European Union encourages nations to promote types of agricultural production that are best suited to their land and climate. Some members of the European Union have only limited agricultural resources. That means they must import more food. In these nations, people make their living from other industries that pay for these imports.

European nations do not try to produce for themselves all of their own agricultural and industrial products. As members of the European Union they concentrate on what they can do best.

French farmers still produce for French markets. Substantial profits also come from sales in Europe and throughout the world. Northern France is well suited for production of wheat and sugar beets. Other regions—Alsace, Bordeaux, Burgundy, Champagne, and the Loire Valley—are known for their wine-producing grapes. France produces and exports more wine than any country except Italy.

France also produces substantial quantities of meat and dairy products. Most of the milk goes into butter and many kinds of cheese that are exported.

The Netherlands produces large quantities of cheese for export, also. In other ways, Dutch farmers operate quite differently from the French. Much of The Netherlands' soil is fertile, but in such a small, densely populated country there is strong competition for land. Dutch farmers fertilize their land intensively and use modern machinery to increase crop yield.

Tulip farming provides the world with millions of beautiful flowers. *What country supplies the word with these bulbs?*

More than half of The Netherlands' farmland serves as pasture for 5 million cattle. Climate-controlled greenhouses occupy additional land, providing fresh vegetables and flowers for nearby markets. Even more notable are the acres used for the production of millions of tulip bulbs, one of the nation's major exports.

The Alps limit farming in Austria. In a few low-lying areas, such as the Vienna Basin, farmers grow potatoes and sugar beets. Cattle graze in the mountains, where the land is too cold and rocky for crops. Through this practical arrangement, Austria's cattle and dairy farmers produce all the meat, eggs, and milk the country needs. Austria, however, has no agricultural products to export. Both the Austrians and Dutch import food.

Cattle graze on high, rocky ground outside of Kitzbuhl, Austria. *How does mountain cattle raising contribute to well-planned use of agricultural land?*

Variety in Industry and Commerce

Germany is the leading industrial power of Western Europe. Germany's Ruhr Valley has been the nation's center of manufacturing since the Industrial Revolution. Here Germany produces the iron and steel used to manufacture cars, trucks, factory and farm machinery, ships, and tools.

The nation also uses the latest technology to manufacture cameras, computers, and scientific instruments. About 30 percent of Germany's overall wealth comes from manufacturing. This is a much higher percentage than in any other Western European country.

Among Western Europe's smaller nations, Luxembourg is the only one that has heavy industries. Iron deposits in the northern part of Luxembourg provide the raw material for a busy steel industry.

Other small nations, such as The Netherlands, have limited natural resources. Yet the Dutch have found ways of maintaining high standards of living. The Netherlands enjoys a small but thriving agricultural economy. Also, The Netherlands' two

WORD ORIGINS

French fries, one of our own nation's favorite foods, really did originate in Europe. Those "fries," however, came from Belgium, not France. The Belgians called them *patates frites*. The French say *pommes frites*.

port cities, Rotterdam and Amsterdam, handle the overseas trade of neighboring countries. Dutch manufacturers use their seaports to bring raw materials into the country and to convert them into high-tech products, such as computers.

Switzerland has no seaports and few raw materials. This inspired the Swiss to specialize in manufacturing very small, expensive items, such as watches, precision instruments, and knives. The metal, glass, and other materials needed to make those items are relatively cheap. Swiss workers can manufacture and export the products for a much higher price. The skilled, precise work creates the higher value.

LIVING IN SWITZERLAND

Swiss Chocolate

So, you think that you like chocolate? The Swiss like it even more. Each year the average United States citizen consumes 2 to 10 pounds (0.9 to 4.5 kg) of chocolate. The average Swiss consumes 22 pounds (9.9 kg).

The word *chocolate* comes from two Mayan words meaning "warm beverage." If we all lived in the high, snowy Alps we might drink more hot chocolate than we already do.

Switzerland manufactures large quantities of the product. Most of what they produce is exported throughout the world.

Chocolate travels a long way to reach Switzerland. Cacao beans—the source of chocolate—come from trees that grow on land located 20° north or south of the Equator. Almost all cacao beans are exported from Africa, South America, or Middle America.

The Swiss manufacture chocolate because it fits their formula for economic success. The cacao beans are hardy and can be shipped long distances to Switzerland without much spoilage. The beans can be made into chocolate products in typically small Swiss factories. The finished products—chocolate candies, cocoa, and baking chocolate—are transported out of the country. Because the Swiss specialize in producing high-quality goods, the exports bring good profits.

Swiss sixth graders eat chocolate during recess

This Berlin TV factory is an example of how German industry provides that nation with much of its wealth. *Name some other products Germany makes.*

Working Together

In some important ways, Western Europe's economy now works like the economy of the United States. In our nation, each of the 50 states has its own special mix of agriculture, industry, and commerce. By trading with one another across state lines, the United States has become an economic giant. European Union members trade across national lines in similar ways.

LESSON 2 REVIEW

Fact Follow-Up
1. How has the European Union's lowering of trade barriers among nations spurred Western Europe's economic development?
2. Describe agricultural specialization in Western Europe.
3. How has Switzerland become prosperous without seaports and many raw materials?

4. In what ways does Western Europe's economy operate like the economy of the United States?

Think These Through
5. Specialization in agricultural production in Western Europe is obvious. Is there evidence of similar trends in manufacturing? Cite evidence for your answer.

Government

LESSON PREVIEW

Key Ideas

- Western Europe's governments are constitutional democracies.
- Western Europe's long tradition of independent nations is still alive. Nations cooperate on economic matters but are less eager to join a political union.

Key Terms

Reichstag, single Europe, European Parliament

As Berliners and tourists marveled, "Wrapped Reichstag" billowed in the wind next to the Brandenburg Gate, looking like a silver-gray cloud that had floated down to earth.

New York artist Christo had wrapped the monumental **Reichstag** building in more than a million square feet (90,000 square meters) of fabric. A work of art and cultural event in 1995, "Wrapped Reichstag" symbolized Germany as a nation in transformation, struggling to emerge from its reunification with a new identity.

Built in 1884, the Reichstag housed the parliament of the unified German empire. Now, at the end of this century, it again serves as the parliament of a united Germany.

Democracy in Western Europe

Just as in the British Isles and Norden, the governments of Western Europe uphold democratic principles. Forms of government are similar to those in the British Isles and Norden.

All Western European nations have constitutions that define what powers governments shall have and how they will operate. These constitutions provide the people guarantees of such basic rights as freedom of speech, religion, and the press. The people of Western Europe have the right to choose their representatives and leaders in government through elections.

Some Western Europe nations —Liechtenstein, Luxembourg, Belgium, The Netherlands, and Monaco—have kings, queens, or princes as heads of state. All of these monarchs, however, perform mostly ceremonial duties. As in the British Isles and Norden, these governments are constitutional monarchies.

Artists have different ways of expressing important events. Christo wrapped the Reichstag to symbolize an event in Germany. *What did that work of art symbolize?*

Some other governments are headed by elected officials. In France, for example, that official is called the president. The French president's duties are more like those of a constitutional monarch than the duties of our own president. The French expect their president to be a ceremonial head of state.

Throughout Western Europe the power of central governments rests with elected national legislatures. These legislatures enact laws and choose an official to head a cabinet. As you have read, in the United Kingdom the official is called the prime minister. In Germany he or she is named chancellor. Despite the variety of names, these governments are really cabinet governments. They operate much like those that you studied earlier.

Grand Duke Jean (left), the monarch of Luxembourg, greets a Roman Catholic bishop. *What kind of government does Luxembourg have?*

Creating Government for the European Union

Do you recall what the artists hoped that their "Wrapped Reichstag" symbolized? They had wrapped the old German parliament building like a gift box. What would the government of a reunited Germany—the gift—be like when the wrapping was removed?

Questions like this one were raised about national governments everywhere in Western Europe. Many questions arose after an agreement signed in 1991 outlined steps for changing the European Union.

The agreement called upon each member of the European Union to take steps that would create a **single Europe**, a kind of United States of Europe. In this new system, Europe's nations would become part of a larger governmental system.

This was not a new idea in 1991. A **European Parliament** had already been established. Elections in the nations belonging to the European Union had sent delegates to meetings of that body in Strasbourg, Germany. In its early years, the European Parliament did not have many powers, but it was to receive substantial powers under the 1991 agreement.

Just as voters debated the design of a single European

What would **YOU** do?

Europeans against a common currency often do not reject the idea. They say that a common currency will be fine if it has a certain design.

The Dutch and the Belgians want a portrait by Rembrandt, but the French and the Italians disapprove. When the French proposed the Eiffel Tower, the Germans rejected the idea. The British say that they will accept any design if it includes a picture of their queen. How would you solve the argument?

Austrians celebrated after their country joined the European Union on January 1, 1995. Finland and Sweden also joined the EU that day. *How might the European Union solve some economic problems for new members?*

currency, other questions have been raised. What might a European flag be like? Such concerns—along with other more serious ones about losing national identity—aroused widespread opposition to a single Europe. In France and Denmark, the agreement of 1991 was approved in national elections, but with only a few votes to spare.

The growing debate on a single Europe did not threaten Europe's pooling of its economic resources. Western Europe's people soon after World War II had warmly supported steps to build a more unified Europe. They had no trouble believing that close cooperation would help revive Europe's economy and end the hardships they were suffering. A strong economy also seemed an important defense against the threat of Communist expansion into Western Europe. By the 1990s, Western Europe was enjoying prosperity. Communism no longer seemed a threat after the Soviet Union's collapse. In place of the old fears came new ones.

People everywhere worried that their own special identities might be forgotten or—worse—destroyed. You read earlier that in the British Isles some people were working hard to keep ancient traditions alive in Wales, Scotland, and Ireland. Across the English Channel, Belgium was threatened by a possible split of the country. The Flemish–speaking people in the North and the Walloons in the South believed that they would be better served by separate governments.

Western Europeans worry that their nations will be forgotten in a single Europe. Some Western European leaders believe that a "United States of Europe" may be many years away.

LESSON 3 REVIEW

Fact Follow-Up
1. How are governments in Western Europe alike? How are they different?
2. What are the duties of constitutional monarchs in Western Europe?
3. What are some of the reasons that nations do not support the European Union?
4. What are some of the forces threatening to divide European nations?

Think These Through
5. How can a nation be both a constitutional monarchy and a democracy?
6. How are cultural differences a threat to peace and prosperity in Western Europe?
7. How does a European Union help keep the countries of Western Europe whole?

Using Information for Problem Solving, Decision Making, and Planning

Locating a Factory in Western Europe

Western Europe's Industrial Revolution created factories that changed nations. Most of the early factories took shape without much planning. Factory owners had to act without much information to guide them.

Big corporations today open new factories only after they have done planning and research. As you learned from the skill lesson in Chapter 10, business people think carefully about where they will locate their factories. After they have found possible locations, they look for answers to other questions:

• How much should we spend for the land we need? Are land costs in one location higher than in another?

• Can we find enough workers in an area to meet our needs? Do workers in the area have the skills that we need?

• Will we be able to reach the raw materials and the products of other companies that we need? Can we move everything easily?

• Can we ship our products to market quickly and without great costs?

The questions that business leaders ask depend on their business. Below is a decision-making grid that was drawn up for people interested in building an entertainment theme park. If you were deciding on the park's location, where would you put it?

Now pick another business, three possible locations in Western Europe, and questions that will help you select a site. Make a grid similar to the one below. Fill in the spaces. Use maps on pages 185, 198, 205, and 223. Review the text. These sources will supply your needs.

Decision Making Grid: Locating a Theme Park			
Needs	**Near Paris**	**Near Berlin**	**Near Vienna**
land cost	high	high	low-to-moderate
skilled workers to build and maintain park	variety of skilled craftspeople	skilled workers	skilled workers available but large number not available
customers	major population center; easy transportation from distant areas; another theme park near Paris	heavily populated, prosperous area; nearest competition is Tivoli Gardens	not as heavily populated as areas farther west; population has less income than other areas
park staff	large pool of well-educated young people; speak several languages	large pool of well-educated young people; speak several languages	moderate-to-large pool of young people; many speak two or more languages

Chapter 12 Review

TIME FOR TERMS

Reichstag
European Parliament

single Europe

FACT FOLLOW-UP

1. How did World War II change Western Europe's economy?
2. In what ways did the Cold War help Western European nations start their economic recovery?
3. Define what is meant by economic specialization. How does that term apply to the economies of postwar Western Europe?
4. What factors have once again made Germany Western Europe's industrial leader?
5. How do you explain the prosperity of small nations, such as the Benelux countries?
6. What are some of the similarities and differences among Western European governments?
7. Explain why some of Western Europe's leaders have been urging more political cooperation under a European Union.
8. What factors discourage hopes for more political cooperation in the European Union?

THINK THESE THROUGH

9. Some United States corporations have established one or more factories in countries belonging to the European Union. Explain why these companies would move to Europe instead of manufacturing products at home before exporting them to Europe.
10. Imagine you are in charge of attracting foreign companies to build factories in your country. What arguments would you use to convince local leaders to accept a new factory?
11. You read in Chapter 8 that Ireland—a member of the European Union—encourages foreign companies (especially those from the United

States) to open factories on its land. What benefits do Ireland and other nations in Western Europe hope to receive from this type of foreign investment?

12. Some European critics of the European Union argue that membership in the Union will destroy the members' national identities. Does this seem to be a valid argument? Why?

13. If you could live and work in one of these Western European nations for a year or two, which one would you choose? Explain.

SHARPENING SKILLS

14. Imagine that you are part of a team that is to develop a plan to clean up the Rhine River. Your team has several different ways of doing the job. What kind of a decision-making grid would you draw to make this decision?

15. Have you begun to think about what you might like to do in your life? Can you draw a decision-making grid that might help you think about possibilities?

PLACE LOCATION

Use the map key to name the countries where the following resources are located:

16. commercial farms.

17. major coal deposits.

18. iron mining.

19. petroleum.

20. hydroelectric power.

21. bauxite.

22. lead.

23. manufacturing and trade.

24. commercial fishing.

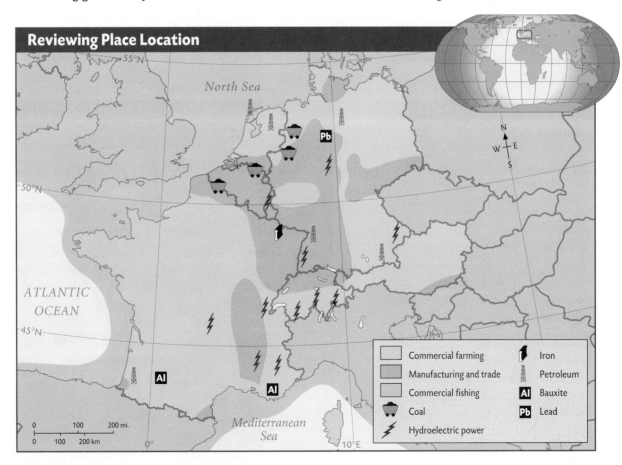

Reviewing Place Location

Key:
- Commercial farming
- Manufacturing and trade
- Commercial fishing
- Coal
- Hydroelectric power
- Iron
- Petroleum
- Bauxite (Al)
- Lead (Pb)

Economy and Government **241**

Societies and Cultures

Bois de Boulogne

"Of course I go to school on Saturday morning!" explains thirteen-year-old Henri. "Saturday morning is schooltime for everyone in France. But Wednesday afternoon . . ." His eyes light up as he describes the weekly half-holiday from school. Henri and his friends play soccer at le Bois de Boulogne, one of the large, beautiful parks in Paris.

The parks of Paris are like outdoor living rooms for Parisians. They spend as much time as they can walking through gardens, sitting by small lakes, or, like Henri, playing sports in the city's parks.

CHAPTER PREVIEW

LESSON 1
A Tale of Three Cities
Paris, Vienna, and Berlin illustrate Western Europe's rich past and its determination to recover from earlier disasters.

LESSON 2
Religion in Western Europe
Religious beliefs continue as a force shaping life. Most people are Protestant or Catholic Christians. Jews and Judaism remain important.

LESSON 3
Food and Leisure
Because Western Europe has excellent transportation, people have access to variety in recreation. The region's many styles in food reflect traditions.

Western Europe—Major Languages

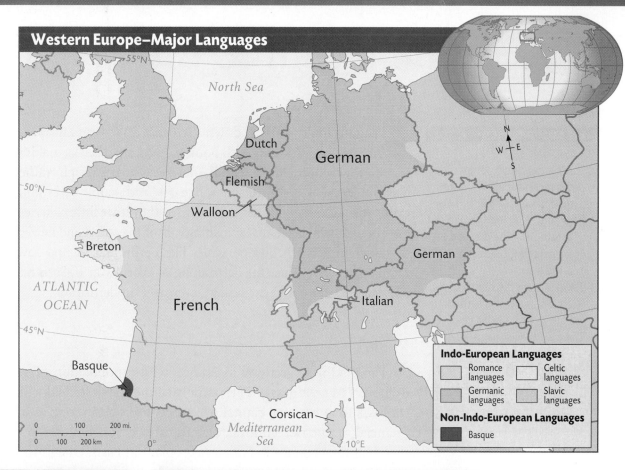

North Sea

Dutch

German

Flemish

Walloon

Breton

ATLANTIC
OCEAN

French

German

Italian

Basque

Corsican

Mediterranean
Sea

55°N

50°N

45°N

0°

10°E

0   100   200 mi.

0   100   200 km

Indo-European Languages

Romance languages

Germanic languages

Celtic languages

Slavic languages

Non-Indo-European Languages

Basque

The Parc de Bagatelle (middle and left)

A Tale of Three Cities

LESSON 1

LESSON PREVIEW

Key Ideas

- Three great cities capture the character and spirit of Western Europe.
- Paris and Vienna mix reminders of greatness in the past and a determination to push ahead into the future.
- Berlin is again the capital of Germany and works hard to reunite a once divided city. The city reflects the nation's determination to put past disasters behind.

Panthéon of the Place Edmond Rostand on Paris's Left Bank exhibits the charm and beauty of Paris. *What are other sites to visit in Paris?*

Imagine you're walking down a street in a Western European city. You see students with book bags on their backs making their way home from school. Bicycles weave through traffic. Customers drink coffee in sidewalk cafés, and people carry long crusty loaves of bread under their arms as they leave little bakeries.

You would also see an astonishing mix of the oldest and newest buildings in Western Europe. Cities like Berlin and Vienna have rebuilt themselves since the destruction of World War II. Paris has preserved and restored its heritage, even as it modernizes.

Paris

Paris is the largest city in France, with a population of 12 million. The greatness of Paris simply cannot be described with statistics. The national capital of France, Paris also serves as its financial, industrial, cultural, and transportation center. More than half the business in France takes place in Paris. One fourth of the nation's labor force lives and works there.

Hosting 2 million tourists each year, Paris also deserves its reputation as one of the most beautiful cities in the world. Every night, Paris earns its nickname, The City of Light, as floodlights illuminate its many magnificent buildings and monuments. Even before electricity, artists called Paris by that name because of the quality of the light they portrayed in their paintings.

The heart of the city lies on the *Ile de la Cité* (Island of the City) in the Seine River. On this narrow island, Paris began as a fishing village about 2,000 years ago, and then grew outward. The Cathedral of Notre Dame, built in the thirteenth century, stands on the island.

North of the Seine, on the *Rive Droite* (Right Bank), you can stroll by office buildings, shops, formal gardens, and small factories. To the south, on the *Rive Gauche* (Left Bank),

stands the part of the University of Paris called the Sorbonne. Nearby are student neighborhoods called the Latin Quarter.

Paris escaped much of the destructive bombing of the war by declaring itself an "open city"—one not defended by military forces and not allowed to be bombed under international law. Most Parisian buildings and neighborhoods were left untouched. These older buildings still serve the people of Paris.

Paris played a key role in shaping modern France. French monarchs (see map, page 67) unified France from Paris. As the kingdom expanded, the king's subjects were required to speak French as it was spoken in Paris.

Today, the city continues to be a major force shaping France. Paris is a remarkable magnet drawing to it people from all over the world. Fashion conscious people everywhere regard Paris as a clothing design capital. The city attracts artists of every kind—painters, sculptors, musicians, composers, and writers. Scholars in the arts, sciences, and technologies come to Paris for study and research. Few other cities in the world can match the art treasurers of the Louvre or the millions of books collected in the Bibliothèque Nationale (National Library). France continues to have a reputation for its cultural achievements. In modern times, as in ancient times, Paris attracts people for cultural and economic reasons.

Notre Dame Cathedral beckons people from all over the world to see its beauty. It stands on an island in the center of Paris. *What river flows around the island?*

WORD ORIGINS

The world-famous University of Paris and its famous division, the Sorbonne, trace their origins to the Middle Ages. Centuries ago, university students spoke in Latin, the common language of scholars. The neighborhood where they lived became known as the **Latin Quarter**.

Vienna

Vienna, or Wien (VEEN), as Austrians call their capital, was once one of the most important cities in Europe. From 1273 to 1918 it was the center from which the Hapsburg royal family ruled a large empire covering much of central Europe.

The city today is no longer a great political center. Vienna serves as an administrative center for the United Nations and provides meeting places for international conferences. Austria is

The Music Of Vienna: A City of Song

"When we are young," a gentleman from Vienna remarked, "we would all like to be Vienna Choirboys. After we are much older, we all wish that we could move like those dancing horses."

The gentleman was speaking about two of Vienna's respected institutions. The Vienna Boys Choir tours the world, singing in the most famous concert halls. Boys join the choir when they are six or seven. They leave it in their teens when their voices begin to change.

Those "dancing horses" are Lipizzaners–beautiful, spirited animals. They came to Austria from Spain in the 1500s. Today they are trained in Vienna's Spanish Riding School to do graceful jumps and dance steps to traditional Viennese music. They, too, are known around the world.

Did you notice how music was one thing our Viennese friend most admired? That was no accident. Vienna has been called a City of Song.

Music entered Viennese life in the early 1700s when Vienna was the capital of the Hapsburg Empire. The royal family loved music. Emperor Leopold I wrote operas. His son, Charles VI, liked to conduct. A nobleman in this court might choose a servant based on his skill playing a cello.

Much of today's classical music was composed in Vienna between the 1780s and 1820s. Haydn, Mozart, Beethoven, and Shubert all lived and composed there.

Johann Strauss, Sr., and his three sons brightened Viennese life with light dance

Vienna Boys Choir

music. The father wrote more than 250 waltzes, polkas, and marches for his orchestra. Almost certainly you have heard his son's "The Blue Danube."

The Vienna Boys Choir and the Lipizzaner horses capture the cultural appeal of Vienna.

one of Europe's smaller nations and plays only a modest role in world affairs.

Yet Vienna remains for tourists one of the most important of Europe's cities. Great buildings—such as Saint Stephen's Cathedral with a graceful spire that rises 450 feet (135m) above the ground—are among the most beautiful Gothic-style and Renaissance-style buildings to be found anywhere. Visitors also like to join local people in the relaxed, friendly coffeehouses.

Vienna today is much more than a tourist center. It is an important river port on the Danube River and a vital commercial and industrial center. The University of Vienna, the Academy of Oriental Languages, and the Conservatory of Music are among the world-famous institutions that make the city an important center for research and education. Finally, Vienna's State Opera, concert houses, and orchestras continue centuries of music tradition.

Berlin

Berlin reflects much of Germany's modern history. Before World War II, it was Germany's largest city, capital of the entire nation, and a major industrial center. All of this was changed by Germany's total defeat and by the city's complicated involvement in Cold War tensions after 1945.

Recall that Germany was split into two nations after World War II. It remained divided until 1990. East Germany was ruled by a Communist dictatorship with close ties to the Soviet Union. West Germany emerged as a democracy linked to Europe's western nations and the United States. In this new setting, Berlin became an island deep inside East Germany.

Much like Germany itself, Berlin was divided. The Communists held the city's eastern half and made it the capital of East Germany. Under international agreement, Berlin's western sector was tied to West Germany. The city's division lasted

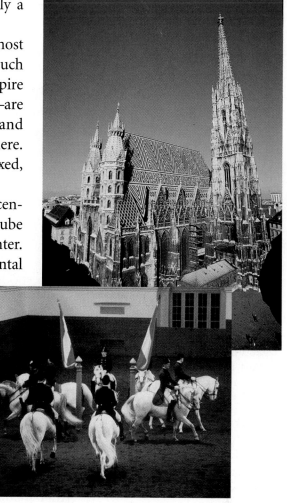

St. Stephen's Cathedral and the Lipizzaner horses are part of the rich cultural heritage of Vienna. *What else makes Vienna a center of culture?*

The Berlin Airlift in 1948-49 brought supplies to West Berlin after a blockade by the Soviet Union of roads into the city. Later, the Berlin Wall was built in 1961, dividing East and West Berlin. *Why did the Soviet Union build the wall?*

45 years, until Germany was reunited.

The two sectors of divided Berlin developed quite differently. Despite its distance from West Germany, West Berlin was rebuilt and enjoyed an economic revival. Its city government, much like that of West Germany, became a democracy.

East Berlin, like East Germany, suffered from poverty and dictatorship. By 1961, about 1,000 East Germans were escaping every day to the West by crossing the boundary dividing Berlin. Once they had crossed the line, these escaped people could stay in West Berlin or continue to West Germany. East Germany responded by building the Berlin Wall. They posted armed guards with orders to shoot anyone trying to escape. Many Germans were killed trying to climb the wall.

East Germany tried to speed the economic development of its sector behind the wall. Bombed buildings were rebuilt, new industries opened, and some of the city's beautiful old parks and streets were restored. Yet, Communist-run industries did not provide the kind of prosperity enjoyed by West Berliners.

In November 1989, crowds pushed past East German troops and smashed the Berlin Wall. The Cold War was over, and the East German government had collapsed. Berlin soon became the capital once again of a united Germany.

After living apart for nearly half a century, West and East Berliners found that everyone would have to make changes. In their newly united country, Germans who grew up under different systems of government would have to learn to work together.

LESSON 1 REVIEW

Fact Follow-Up
1. How is Paris like and different from Washington, D.C.?
2. Age-old buildings in Paris escaped destruction in World War II. How does this make a difference in Paris today?
3. Why was Berlin a divided city?
4. Compare and contrast Vienna and Paris.

Think These Through
5. If you had the opportunity, which of the three cities—Paris, Berlin, or Vienna—would you visit? Why?
6. Which of these cities seems most representative of its nation? Why?
7. Which city most deserves to be called "Europe's capital"? Why?

Religions in Western Europe

LESSON 2

In a northern German town, a child is carried to the baptismal font of a Lutheran church. In a French village, girls in white dresses and boys in their best dark suits walk in procession to a Catholic church to celebrate their first communion. In Antwerp, a twelve-year-old Jewish boy reads a passage from the Scriptures in Hebrew at his bar mitzvah. In Vienna, a gathering of Turkish children hear stories from the Koran at a Muslim school.

Throughout Western Europe, religion plays an important part in personal and cultural life. Protestants, Catholics, Jews, and Muslims cherish their religious traditions while acknowledging the rich diversity of their region.

Catholics and Protestants

As you have read in Chapter 4, Western Europe was once a predominantly Catholic region. During the sixteenth century, German theologian Martin Luther opposed some Catholic Church practices and inspired the Protestant Reformation.

LESSON PREVIEW

Key Ideas

- Daily life for the majority of Western Europeans is influenced by the Protestant and Catholic faiths.
- Before the 1930s, Western Europe was home to many Jews. Nazi Germany's campaign to exterminate Jews killed millions and caused others to flee.
- Muslims have become Western Europe's newest religious minority.

Key Term
Holocaust

A Roman Catholic Baptism in France is among many ceremonies celebrated by the religiously diverse people of Western Europe. *What other religions are practiced in Western Europe?*

Societies and Cultures **249**

After the Reformation, Western Europe became both Protestant and Catholic. At times, conflict arose between members of both traditions, even to the point of war. In recent years, though, Western Europe's Protestants and Catholics have accepted one another's beliefs.

Today, about 45 percent of Germans describe themselves as Protestants and about 37 percent as Catholics. Most Protestants live in the North. Catholics live mainly in the South.

The Protestant Reformation began in Germany when the writings of Martin Luther became widely available. Luther's translation of the Bible from Greek into German encouraged more people to learn to read, so they could learn scripture for themselves. The dialect Luther used in his translation—

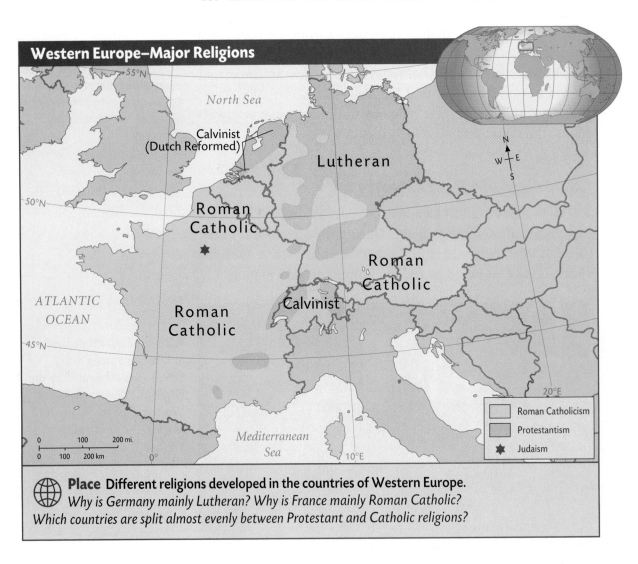

Western Europe—Major Religions

Place Different religions developed in the countries of Western Europe. *Why is Germany mainly Lutheran? Why is France mainly Roman Catholic? Which countries are split almost evenly between Protestant and Catholic religions?*

In France, couples marry in church before they have an official ceremony in a government office. *Why does this occur?*

Hochdeutsche, or High German—became the common written language of Germany.

The government today provides financial support to both the Protestant and Catholic churches in Germany. The two churches offer day care, preschool, and other social services to their members.

Switzerland's population is also divided almost equally into Protestants and Catholics. Today, despite their differences, Swiss Protestants and Catholics pride themselves on their religious tolerance.

In France, 90 percent of the people are Catholic. Protestants make up only 2 percent of the French population. The French government supported the Catholic Church financially until 1905. Since that time, the French have carefully separated the powers of church and state. For instance, a French couple who marry in a church service must also go through a civil ceremony in a government office to make their marriage official.

About 27 percent of the Dutch describe themselves as Protestant, and 36 percent call themselves Catholic. Nearly 25 percent belong to no church. This is the largest percentage of unchurched people in all of Western Europe.

The Reformation took strong hold in The Netherlands, but Catholic loyalty remained high as well. After centuries of struggle, the Dutch developed their own answer to religious conflict. Protestants and Catholics agreed to live completely separate social lives. Schools, hospitals, newspapers, and even television stations served either Protestants or Catholics, but not both.

By the 1960s, the Dutch had come to believe that social separation was unnecessary. Protestant and Catholic Dutch discovered that they often agreed on many public issues. Now, they often join forces to deal with such problems as pollution, housing, and women's rights. The religious barriers that had once divided them continue to break down.

Western European nations have discovered that religious tolerance leads to strength. By working together, people of different faiths can better face economic and political problems.

Jews in Europe

The Roman Empire carried Judaism as well as Christianity to much of Europe. Jews in Europe often suffered persecution. Yet they were warmly welcomed by many European rulers. Jewish merchants and bankers helped strengthen Europe's new monarchies.

Jews found life to be especially attractive in The Netherlands during the seventeenth century. The Dutch were competing for a share of world trade and colonies. Jewish bankers and merchants helped the Dutch. This painting of a rabbi (right), well known as a Jewish religious leader and scholar, is by the famed Dutch artist Rembrandt van Rijn.

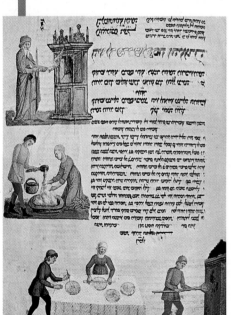

In the Renaissance, Jews lived all over Europe. In most towns and cities they were required to live together. These Jewish neighborhoods were crowded. By living together they kept their traditions alive. An illuminated manuscript (left) written in 1466 shows Jews celebrating Passover in Italy.

Jewish Life

Jews have lived in Western Europe since the time of the Roman Empire. Over the centuries, Jews have suffered persecution. During the Holocaust, Hitler's Nazis tried to kill all the Jews in Europe. Six million Jews died as a result.

Before the 1930s, more than 190,000 Jews lived in Vienna, contributing to the vibrant artistic and intellectual life of the city. After World War II, only 2,000 Jews remained. Today, about 12,000 Viennese are Jews.

Throughout Western Europe there are fewer Jews than there were before World War II. In the Belgian cities of Brussels and Antwerp, only 35,000 residents are Jewish. Before the rise of Hitler, about 530,000 Jews lived in Germany. Now only 30,000

A large Jewish community settled in Vienna. This painting of a large Viennese synagogue, or temple (left), was completed in 1922. Jewish life in Vienna came to an end when Hitler seized Austria. The Nazis killed most of the city's Jews during World War II.

You will read later about Russia. In the 1800s and early 1900s, the Russian government encouraged its people to stage *pogroms,* or organized massacres of helpless people, against Jews. Many left their homes and businesses. Jewish women and children, fleeing from their village, have stopped for a brief rest (right).

The German Nazis stirred hatred of Jews. The German poster (left) blames Jews for World War II. The message printed on the poster reads "Behind the enemy the Jew." Such hatred led to the **Holocaust**, the mass slaughter of 6 million Jews and countless other European civilians.

Hinter den Feindmächten: der Jude

Muslims live in Germany and other parts of Western Europe. Some are workers and some are refugees. *What countries might the refugees come from?*

remain, mostly in Berlin and Frankfurt.

Despite their smaller numbers, the Jews of Western Europe continue to practice their religious traditions. Many Jewish rituals, like the *seder,* a ceremonial meal, take place at home among families. At other times, the community gathers in a synagogue to pray and to hear scripture read and interpreted.

Muslims in Western Europe

In recent years, many Muslims have moved to Western Europe. They have added their Islamic traditions to the region's religious diversity. The majority of Muslims now living in Western Europe have come from North Africa and Turkey. Millions arrived to work in Germany and France. Muslim refugees from war-torn Bosnia also have fled to Western Europe.

Today, about 1,700,000 Muslims live in Germany. About the same number have settled in France. European reaction to these new arrivals has varied. At first, Muslims were welcomed, because additional labor was needed in a booming economy. In 1978, Vienna opened an Islamic Center to help the city's Muslim community. The center provided a mosque (a place of worship), a school, and aid for families. In 1996, Muslims confronted the police in Paris when France began sending some Muslim immigrants home.

LESSON 2 REVIEW

Fact Follow-Up
1. How do the governments of France and Germany support religions in their countries?
2. Describe how government and religious relationships changed in The Netherlands.
3. How has Jewish religious life in Western Europe changed since the 1930s?
4. Which religious group recently appeared in high numbers in Western Europe?

Think These Through
5. Which of Western Europe's nations seems to have been the most accepting of religious diversity? Give reasons for your answer.
6. Which Western European nation appears to make the greatest effort to separate church and state? Why?

Food and Leisure

As you sit on the beach in Belgium, making the most of the sunshine, you suddenly see a sailboat breezing along on the sand near the shoreline.

Walking to the water's edge for a closer look, you will find that the craft is not a sailboat after all. It is a sand yacht—a kind of bicycle rigged with a mast and a large sail, propelled by the wind.

Sand sailing, a popular Belgian beach sport, combines sailing and bicycling in a unique way. With their sand yachts, young Belgians can bicycle without pedaling and sail without getting wet.

On Vacation

Not long ago, Tracy and Biff, two American college students studying in Europe, discovered Europeans' enthusiasm for taking annual vacations. When the two young Americans arrived in Paris in August, they found about half of the little shops and restaurants closed. The sidewalks were not as crowded as they usually were. Even the street traffic was light.

Yet their hotel was crowded, mostly with visitors from other European countries or the United States. The museums in Paris also were crowded. Tourists were in Paris, but a lot of Parisians were missing.

When Tracy and Biff boarded a train headed for Nice, a French city on the Mediterranean coast, they found some of the people of Paris. All the passengers on the overcrowded train were headed out of the city on vacation. Many were loading bicycles into the train's baggage car. Everyone, it seemed, had backpacks strapped to their shoulders.

Europe's excellent transportation system, temperate climate, and varied geography encourage people to spend their free time outdoors. French families frequently take their five-week summer

LESSON PREVIEW

Key Ideas
- Western Europeans use their region's excellent transportation system to enjoy recreational activities.
- Disneyland Paris has encouraged the building of United States-style theme parks. Traditional national games remain popular.
- Food and methods of preparing it continue to link people to their national traditions.

A Belgian beach offers a new way to sail. Sand sailing! *What two sports are combined in sand sailing?*

vacations at the seashore, where they swim and fish. The Dutch also fish and sail in the warm weather. The lakes and rivers offer Austrians summers of boating, canoeing, and waterskiing.

Bicycling is most popular in countries with a level terrain, such as The Netherlands, France, and Belgium. The Netherlands offers 600 miles (966 km) of bicycle paths. Families frequently bicycle together on weekends.

The Alps in France, Switzerland, Germany, and Austria are as easy to reach as the seashore. Hiking through the mountains is a favorite activity. Teenagers frequently hike on vacations, camping out or stopping overnight at inexpensive inns called youth hostels. Sometimes families will venture out into the snow on a pleasant day for a picnic on a sunny mountainside.

You have already read about Tivoli, Denmark's famous amusement park. A few years ago, Disneyland Paris, a theme park much like Disney World in Florida, opened outside of Paris. Europeans did not seem to care much for Disneyland Paris at first. But today people are flocking to Disneyland Paris in such numbers that other theme parks are opening in the Benelux countries, the British Isles, and Spain.

Sports

In every country of Western Europe, professional soccer continues to be the most popular sport. Each nation eagerly follows the World Cup Soccer competition, hoping that their team will be champion.

Western Europeans also enjoy games and competitions that are tied to their national traditions. The French play at *boules,* a form of outdoor bowling. The Austrians compete at *curling,* a game on ice in which players slide flat stones toward a target.

In the Swiss game *hormussen,* one team uses long clubs to hit a disk toward the other end of the field while the opposing team tries to knock the disk down. *Pelote,* a fast-paced variation on handball, is popular in Belgium.

Hikers enjoy walking in the spectacular Swiss Alps. The Alps cross into three other Western European countries. *What are they?*

A Swiss family enjoys the main meal of their day at noon. The evening meal in Western Europe is more like our lunchtime. *How are school schedules adjusted for this?*

Dining in Western Europe

Visitors to Europe from the United States can easily find fast food similiar to home. Hamburgers and cola drinks seem to be everywhere. Yet there is no danger that Europeans will abandon their traditional dishes.

Western Europe is home to some of the world's most famous styles of cooking. Each country's tradition is different, and people take pride in their ways of preparing food.

Most Western Europeans sit down to their main meal at noon. Schools allow a break of one and a half or two hours in the middle of the day so families can eat together. Breakfast usually includes rolls, jam, and coffee or milk. The evening meal, which resembles our lunch, is served as late as 7:30 P.M.

Foods Reflect Tradition

Germans enjoy hearty dinners of veal, pork, chicken, or beef with vegetables and potatoes. Lighter meals include sausage, bread, and cheese.

Many familiar German dishes began as ways of protecting food from spoiling. Cabbage soaked in vinegar became *sauerkraut.* Beef preserved in the same way produced *sauerbraten.* Ground spiced meat could keep for weeks as sausages and frankfurters.

Like the Germans, Austrians enjoy pork, veal, chicken, and beef. Instead of potatoes, Austrians are more likely to include dumplings or noodles in their meals. Austria's unique contribution to cuisine is the *wiener schnitzel,* breaded veal cutlet fried

What would **YOU** do?

Imagine that someone in your family has offered to take you on a two-week trip to one country in Western Europe. Which country would you pick? What would you want to see and do?

Belgians enjoy eating fresh fish. They cook it many different ways. *Why is it so easy for the Belgians to get fresh fish?*

lightly in butter. Cooks served this dish first in Vienna. In the afternoon, Austrians frequently drop in at a *Kaffeehaus* (coffeehouse) for a pastry snack and coffee or hot chocolate.

In France, cooking is regarded as an art rather than as a routine. The most complex kind of French cooking, *haute cuisine* (oat kwee·zeen), has maintained the interest and respect of cooks all over the world since the 1700s. Haute cuisine literally means "high cooking," expressing the importance of artful cooking to French life.

But haute cuisine is not for every day. In most French homes, families gather around relatively simple meals in several courses. Dinner may begin with onion soup, or raw vegetables, called *crudités*. A main course usually includes roast chicken, steaks, or chops with potatoes. Salad comes next, followed by cheese and fresh fruit, and, on special occasions, a rich dessert.

Belgians insist that their cuisine is just as delicious as French cooking. Many people visiting Belgium agree. Belgians enjoy seafood, especially mussels and eels. They cook fish with fresh vegetables, or even seaweed. *Waterzooi,* a popular chowder, is made with fish or chicken and includes the favorite Belgian vegetables of endive, leeks, and asparagus. Brussels sprouts, vegetables shaped like tiny cabbages, also come from Belgium.

The Dutch usually enjoy uncomplicated meals of meat or fish, cheese, and vegetables. *Hutspot,* a dish with potatoes, carrots, and onions, often accompanies herring, shrimp, or sole.

LESSON 3 REVIEW

Fact Follow-Up

1. The physical characteristics of place influence recreation. Explain how this works in Western Europe.
2. Describe how Western Europe's recreation is affected by the rest of the world. What traditional games or recreational activities are still popular?
3. Give examples of the foods and cooking methods in Western Europe.

Think These Through

4. Imagine that your family is host to a Western European student. You want to introduce the student to American recreation and food. What would you show him or her? What food would you include in a daily menu?

Acquiring Information from a Variety of Sources

Comparing Three Cities in Western Europe

Do you recall the following passage from Chapter 13?

> *Y*ou see students with book bags on their backs making their way home from school. Bicycles weave through traffic. Customers drink coffee in sidewalk cafés, and people carry long crusty loaves of bread under their arms as they leave little bakeries.

The passage was included to compare Western European cities. Now that you have read about three of Western Europe's cities, are you prepared to say exactly what makes all of them the same in some ways and quite different in others?

Probably you have some general answers to such a question, but you are not prepared to be *exact*. The retrieval data diagram below will help you refine your thoughts. Draw a similar diagram on a sheet of paper.

Note that the lines under the left column, "Characteristics," are blank. As you start, think first about items that you can put on the lines under "Characteristics." What political roles are played by each city? What historic buildings can be seen? Are there religious similarities and differences? What commercial and industrial roles does it play? To these characteristics you may wish to add such other items as language, food, recreation, schools and universities, and museums. The number and type of items on these lines will influence how you compare these cities.

You will find basic information about each city in this text, but your teacher may want you to do further research. The *World Almanac*, an encyclopedia, magazines such as the *National Geographic*, and books about France, Germany, and Austria will provide much more information. Now you have data to compare.

Once your data retrieval chart is complete, you can analyze in organized ways how the cities are alike and different. You have brief sketches of each city in this chapter. You should also skim through Chapters 10, 11, and 12. Those chapters also have information that you can use.

Ready? *Exactly* how similar—and different—do you find the three cities?

Comparing Cities			
Characteristics	**Paris**	**Berlin**	**Vienna**

Chapter 13 Review

LESSONS LEARNED

LESSON 1 Three of Western Europe's great cities—Paris, Vienna, and Berlin—provide glimpses of the region's unity and variety. Paris and Vienna are old cities. Paris played a leading role in bringing France together and shaping the nation's culture. Vienna was the capital of a much larger country that has now broken into many smaller pieces. The city itself, however, continues to be a place where many of Europe's great achievements in music, art, and architecture are on display. Berlin is once again the capital of Germany and leads a vigorous effort to reunite a nation that was divided for nearly 30 years under different economic and political systems.

LESSON 2 Western Europe remains mostly Christian. Daily life is influenced by Protestant and Catholic faiths. Jewish congregations, once numerous and often influential, have never recovered from the German Nazi Party's efforts to exterminate all Jews. Muslims have been drawn to Western Europe by the region's prosperity. They are the region's newest religious and ethnic minority.

LESSON 3 Western Europe offers a remarkable variety of choices for vacationers. Many places can be reached quickly on the region's transportation system. Depending on the season, vacationers can hike or ski in mountains, or swim in the warm Mediterranean. United States-style theme parks are gaining popularity, but they have not overshadowed traditional games. Finally, dining offers a great variety of food prepared in traditional styles.

TIME FOR TERMS

Holocaust

FACT FOLLOW-UP

1. How important are Paris, Berlin, and Vienna to Western Europe? Which is most important? Why?
2. In what ways do relationships between government and religion vary throughout Western Europe?
3. Where do most Protestants live in Germany? Where are most Catholics found? Are the geographic divisions between religious faiths as sharply defined in any other part of Western Europe?
4. Think about the physical characteristics of place in Switzerland and The Netherlands. What effect do these differences have on recreation in those two countries?
5. Are there differences between the vacations taken by Western Europeans and the people of our country? If so, what are they?

THINK THESE THROUGH

6. Suppose you were to write a short sketch of a fourth Western European city. Your aim would be to show still another side of Europe's character. Which city would you choose and why?
7. Which city (you need not limit yourself to the three described in this chapter) do you think is the greatest in Western Europe? Explain your choice.
8. Make a prediction! What influence on European life might be made by the growing number of Muslims?

9. A traditional Western European family vacation may last five weeks. This is longer than most family vacations in the United States. Do you think the longer vacation together is about right, too long, or too short? Explain your thinking.

SHARPENING SKILLS

10. How did the data retrieval chart help your ability to discuss *exactly* the ways the three cities were alike and different? Write a short paragraph about how it helped.

11. The chart can be used to assist you with a close comparison of other things. How would a data retrieval chart help you in a friendly disagreement with friends over which NFL team is the most interesting football team to watch? Do you think you could overwhelm the opposition?

PLACE LOCATION

Use the letters on the map to name and locate the following places:

12. where Dutch is spoken.
13. the home of Breton speakers.
14. German is spoken here.
15. where the language of Paris became the national language.
16. Basque is the language here.
17. Flemish is spoken here.
18. Walloon is spoken here.
19. Italian is spoken in this part of this mountainous country.
20. the Corsican language is spoken here.
21. a German-speaking nation that once was the seat of government of the Hapsburg Empire.

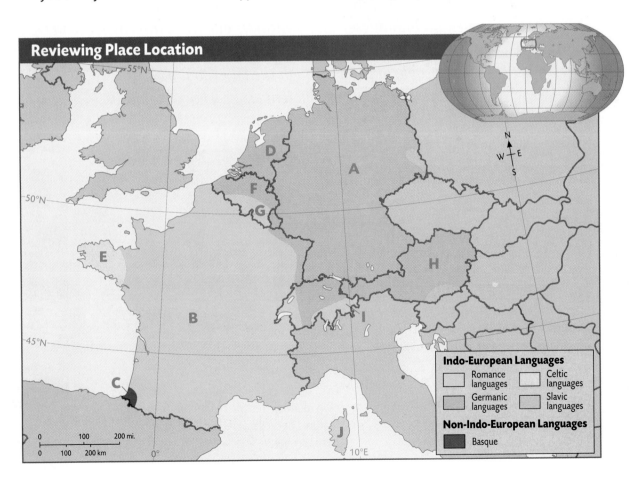

Reviewing Place Location

Indo-European Languages
Romance languages
Celtic languages
Germanic languages
Slavic languages

Non-Indo-European Languages
Basque

The Region of Mediterranean Europe

Venice, Italy's third largest port, is not built on solid ground. Instead it lies on a cluster of small islands at the edge of the Adriatic Sea. With canals for streets, splendid buildings—most centuries old—rise directly out of the water. Beautiful old bridges everywhere allow people to stroll through the city. Gondolas, or flat-bottomed boats of different sizes, serve as taxicabs.

UNIT PREVIEW

CHAPTER 14
People and Lands
Portugal, Spain, Italy, and Greece are nations of the Mediterranean region. Landforms vary from volcanic islands to deserts.

CHAPTER 15
People and Environment
Much of the Mediterranean until recent times has been behind the rest of Europe in economic development.

CHAPTER 16
Economy and Government
Mediterranean Europe's economy today builds on a lively tourist industry and

manufacturing. Democratic governments are taking root.

CHAPTER 17
Society and Culture
Each of the region's four nations has its own identity. Yet the region has common features because of its location near the Mediterranean Sea.

Grand Canal, Venice

People and Lands

Lava stream

Mount Vesuvius in eruption arouses fear and wonder. Great clouds of volcanic dust are blown high in the air. Lava—melted rock—pours over the lip of the volcano onto the land below. A French painter, Pierre-Jacques Volaire, captured the drama of people fleeing from danger in 1777 (below).

Vesuvius is the only active volcano on the mainland of Europe. It has erupted so often and so violently that it has become a major tourist attraction. Vesuvius rises only a few miles from Naples, an area that travelers can easily reach. Hundreds of thousands of tourists are drawn to the Mediterranean region every year by more than the wonders of nature. They also come to see wonders created by ancient civilizations.

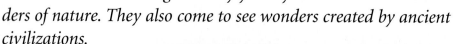

CHAPTER PREVIEW

LESSON 1
People of Mediterranean Europe
Greece, Italy, Spain, and Portugal are the largest of eight nations making up the Mediterranean region.

LESSON 2
Lands of Mediterranean Europe
The Mediterranean Sea has served since ancient times as a highway linking people in the region.

LESSON 3
Climate and Vegetation
The Mediterranean climate throughout the region limits variety in natural vegetation.

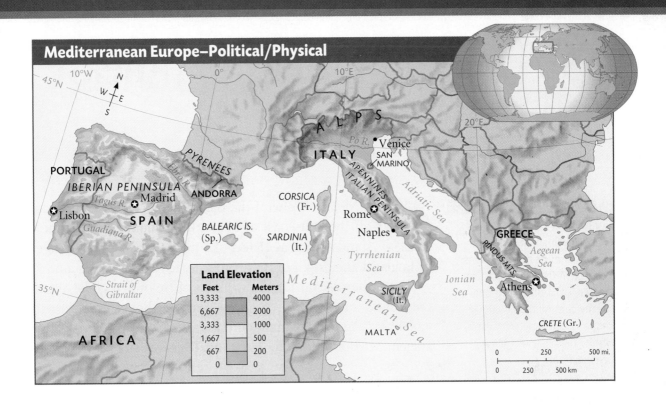

Mediterranean Europe–Political/Physical

45°N 10°W 0° 10°E 20°E

ALPS
ITALY
Po R.
Venice
SAN MARINO
PORTUGAL
PYRENEES
IBERIAN PENINSULA
Ebro R.
Tagus R.
Madrid
ANDORRA
APENNINES
ITALIAN PENINSULA
Adriatic Sea
CORSICA (Fr.)
Lisbon
SPAIN
Guadiana R.
BALEARIC IS. (Sp.)
Rome
Naples
GREECE
RINDUS MTS.
Aegean Sea
SARDINIA (It.)
Tyrrhenian Sea
Athens
35°N
Strait of Gibraltar
Mediterranean Sea
Ionian Sea
SICILY (It.)
CRETE (Gr.)
AFRICA
MALTA

Land Elevation

Feet	Meters
13,333	4000
6,667	2000
3,333	1000
1,667	500
667	200
0	0

0   250   500 mi.
0   250   500 km

Mediterranean Europe
Portugal
Spain
Italy
Greece
Andorra
Malta
San Marino
Vatican City

The Eruption of
Mount Vesuvius,
(1777)

People of Mediterranean Europe

LESSON PREVIEW

Key Ideas

- Portugal, Spain, Italy, and Greece are the major nations located in the Mediterranean region, or Southern Europe.
- Many cultural ties link these nations. The languages used in the region reflect those connections.

Key Terms

Latin, Romance languages, Iberians

Romans left their mark throughout the region, including Spain. *What evidence of Roman culture can you see in this picture from Merida, Spain?*

On Menorca, one of the Balearic (bah·LEER·ik) Islands off the east coast of Spain, huge hand-carved stones stand as high as 15 feet (4.5 m). Much like Stonehenge in England, the origin of these prehistoric rocks is uncertain.

Were they meant for the worship of unknown gods? Were they altars for sacrifice? Whatever purpose these stones served 4,000 years ago, today they stand as mysterious monuments to ancient Mediterranean people whose lives we can only imagine.

Mediterranean Europe

Most people of Mediterranean Europe live in four countries: Greece, Italy, Spain, and Portugal. A small fraction of the region's population inhabit some of the world's tiniest countries—Andorra, Malta, San Marino, and Vatican City.

These Mediterranean people have been in contact from early times. Their cultures have affected one another. The ancient Greeks influenced the Romans. The Romans took their own language and culture throughout their empire. That empire included all of Mediterranean Europe.

Greece

Ten million people live in Greece today. About 98 percent of Greeks trace their ancestry to the region's first settlers who came from northern and eastern Europe. A small minority of Turks have settled along the southern and eastern coasts.

The people of Greece speak *demotic* (modern) Greek. Demotic Greek developed from the dialects spoken thousands of years ago in the Greek city-states. Of these dialects, the one that appeared most often in ancient writing was *koine* Greek. Early Christian writers used it to compose the New Testament.

Greek letters have a special look about them (see page 39). They became the basis of the alphabet later developed by Rome. The Roman alphabet would eventually spread throughout much of Europe and to the Americas. The letters that we use in writing English can be traced through Rome to Greece. Even the English word "alphabet" has in it the first two letters of the Greek alphabet, *alpha* and *beta*.

Demotic Greek includes words from the English, French, Italian, Slavic, and Turkish languages. Although it is used less often, Greeks today can read texts in *koine* Greek with little difficulty.

People of Santorini, Greece, whitewash their houses just as others do in the Mediterranean region. *Why do people of the region share such characteristics of culture?*

Italy

Many of the 58 million people living in Italy today are descended from the Etruscans (ih·TRUHS·kuhnz) and Romans, the original inhabitants of the region. Germans, French, and Slovenes, most of whom live along the northern borders, form a small minority within the country.

The Etruscans were Mediterranean traders from the Middle East. They settled in Tuscany (near present-day Florence) about 3,000 years ago. As their numbers grew, they moved southward, where they met and conquered the early Romans. The Romans, however, eventually overthrew the Etruscans. This victory enabled them to establish the Roman republic and later the Roman Empire.

The Roman Empire passed along to Europe achievements of ancient Mediterranean civilizations. One of these achievements—the **Latin** language—came from Rome itself. Roman soldiers and merchants used it wherever they went. For hundreds of years Latin was spoken by a majority of Europe's population.

After the Roman Empire fell, people in different parts of Europe—including Italy—began to change the everyday Latin that they spoke and wrote. In this way, the modern-day Italian language grew from Latin. Latin also became the basis of French, Spanish, and Portuguese.

All of these languages are called **Romance languages**. The name reminds us that these languages came from Rome and Latin, the language the Romans used (see map, page 270).

Pompeii

On August 24, in A.D. 79, Mount Vesuvius erupted and quickly buried the nearby Roman settlement of Pompeii under volcanic ash and molten lava. After centuries of excavation, Pompeii provides a ghostly glimpse into ancient Mediterranean life.

Pompeii (below) lies 15 miles (24 km) southeast of Naples on the western coast of Italy, very near where the African tectonic plate and the Italian peninsula grind together. This constant geological friction forms volcanoes and causes earthquakes.

Because the destructive ash fell so suddenly, completely burying the town, excavators in the eighteenth century found streets and buildings preserved almost as they were in the first century. Today, more than three fifths of the city has been excavated, revealing its forum, temples, baths, theaters, and many homes. Excavators also discovered pots, jewelry, and even the remains of someone's breakfast.

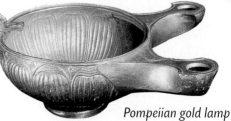

Pompeiian gold lamp

Spain and Portugal

More than 95 percent of all Spanish and Portuguese trace their ancestry back to the original **Iberians**. These people settled in this southern European peninsula called Iberia as far back as 5,000 years ago.

The heritage of Spain and Portugal also reflects the many conquerors, traders, and settlers who lived in the area at different times over thousands of years. About 100 B.C., the Romans conquered the region. The Iberians took Latin as their language. The Spanish and Portuguese languages developed from Latin and from the Arabic language brought by invaders from North Africa.

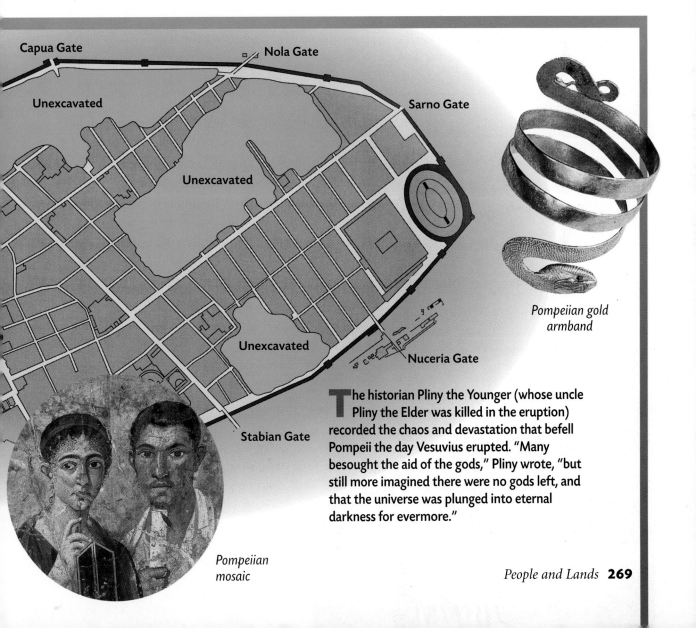

Capua Gate

Nola Gate

Unexcavated

Sarno Gate

Unexcavated

Unexcavated

Nuceria Gate

Pompeiian gold armband

Stabian Gate

The historian Pliny the Younger (whose uncle Pliny the Elder was killed in the eruption) recorded the chaos and devastation that befell Pompeii the day Vesuvius erupted. "Many besought the aid of the gods," Pliny wrote, "but still more imagined there were no gods left, and that the universe was plunged into eternal darkness for evermore."

Pompeiian mosaic

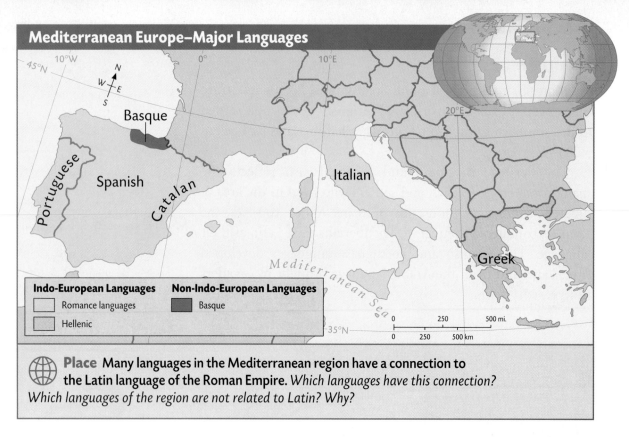

Mediterranean Europe–Major Languages

Indo-European Languages
- Romance languages
- Hellenic

Non-Indo-European Languages
- Basque

Place Many languages in the Mediterranean region have a connection to the Latin language of the Roman Empire. *Which languages have this connection? Which languages of the region are not related to Latin? Why?*

In the twelfth century, Portugal became an independent country. The Portuguese language grew out of Spanish. It came to have its own distinctive sounds and grammar. The Portuguese colonized Brazil in South America in the sixteenth century. Portuguese became the major language of Brazil.

Spain also took language to various parts of the world as it colonized its empire in the sixteenth century. Now, more than 300 million people speak Spanish, making it the most commonly used Romance language.

LESSON 1 REVIEW

Fact Follow-Up
1. What nations make up Mediterranean Europe?
2. What are some common characteristics of the nations of Mediterranean Europe?
3. Which nations occupy the Iberian Peninsula? Which group of people from the past influenced this peninsula?

Think These Through
4. How has the culture of ancient Greece affected the Mediterranean European nations of today?
5. Explain why Rome so greatly influenced other nations of Mediterranean Europe.
6. Why do many people living in the Americas today speak Spanish and Portuguese?

Lands of Mediterranean Europe

I n 1970, while exploring the sea floor of the Mediterranean, the crew of the ship *Glomar Challenger* made an astounding discovery. At one time there was no Mediterranean Sea. About 6 million years ago, it suddenly dried up and became a desert.

The change came as a result of moving landmasses. Over thousands of years, Arabia had been swinging northward, and finally closed off the sea to the east. At the same time, Africa and Europe joined at Gibraltar, blocking out the flow of water from the Atlantic.

The Mediterranean Reappears

For half a million years, the desert stretched between Africa and Europe, broken only by briny lakes and green oases at the mouths of coastal rivers. Then, without warning, the sea filled up again.

Scientists believe that an earthquake tore an opening at Gibraltar. Water poured in from the Atlantic with a force hundreds of times greater than the most powerful waterfall. In about 100 years, the Mediterranean was a sea once more.

Scientists believe if the waterway between Gibraltar and Africa closed today, the Mediterranean would again disappear. The Mediterranean would evaporate faster than rainfall or rivers could fill it.

LESSON PREVIEW

Key Ideas
- The Mediterranean Sea has served for thousands of years as a highway, connecting the people of Southern Europe.
- Before modern transportation systems helped break down natural barriers, travel inside Mediterranean countries was often more difficult than travel across the seas.

Key Term
navigable

The Straits of Gibraltar link the Mediterranean Sea and the Atlantic Ocean. *What would the Mediterranean be like without the straits?*

Location

To define the region of Mediterranean Europe, look on the map (p. 265) for the Mediterranean Sea. The Latin word *Mediterranean* means "in the middle of land." Notice that land surrounds this sea: Africa to the south, Asia to the east, and continental Europe to the north and west.

Look for three peninsulas—bodies of land surrounded on three sides by water—jutting southward into the Mediterranean from continental Europe. These are the lands of Mediterranean Europe.

Greece pushes southward between the Aegean and Ionian Seas into the eastern Mediterranean. Italy looks much like a boot kicking the football of Sicily in the central Mediterranean. The Iberian Peninsula in the western Mediterranean is occupied by Spain and Portugal.

Landforms

Because the four countries of the region form peninsulas, they all have long coastlines. Since ancient times, people living near the coasts of these countries have been able to make use of one of the world's chief trading routes—the Mediterranean Sea.

Within each country movement across land has been much more difficult than trade and transportation by sea. People were often divided by mountains. In recent times, rail, good roads, and the airplane made travel easier within these countries.

Mediterranean seaports such as Capri (below) linked people of the region. *How does the picture of the Abruzzi Mountains of Italy (right) show the difficulty of overland travel?*

Greece

According to a Greek legend, when the gods created the world, they carefully sifted earth through a strainer. The good soil went to make all the other countries. The stones left behind became Greece.

Most Greek soil has always been poor and stony, with the exception of some coastal areas and river valleys. One region, Thessaly, for example, grows grain, especially wheat, on its fertile plains in the shadow of Mount Olympus, the highest peak in Greece.

Stony mountains cover 70 percent of Greece, and many of these are high. Mount Olympus rises 9,570 feet (2,871 m). Other areas have elevations over 3,000 feet (900 m). The Pindus Mountains divide Greece into east and west. Other mountains in the Northeast form a border with Bulgaria.

In the South, the Gulf of Corinth and the Gulf of Patrai nearly cut off the lower portion of Greece, known as Peloponnesus (pel·uh·pohn·KNEE·sus). Peloponnesus forms its own peninsula on the peninsula of Greece.

Wherever you are in Greece, you will find yourself always within 85 miles (137 km) of the sea. In fact, some 1,450 islands make up 20 percent of Greece's land area.

WORD ORIGINS

The word **peninsula** comes from two Latin words: *paene*, meaning "almost," and *insula*, or "island." Together, the Latin words combine to describe a landform that is "almost an island."

Italy

Italy occupies a peninsula and two nearby islands, Sicily and Sardinia. Altogether, Italy possesses 5,000 miles (8,050 km) of coastline. Mountains or hills cover about 75 percent of the country. The Alps in the North form a border with France, Switzerland, and Austria. The highest point in the Alps is Italy's Mont Blanc at 15,787 feet (4,736 m).

The Apennines (AP · uh · nighnz) divide Italy into east and west, and are the source of most of the rivers of Italy. Many short streams flow down the steep slopes of the east side. Longer rivers (the Arno, Tiber, Volturno, Garigliano) begin on the west side. The Appenines are about 838 miles (1,349 km) long and from 25 to 80

miles (40 to 129 km) wide. They occupy much of the peninsula. Despite its long coastlines, Italy has few flat coastal plains.

The North Italian Plain is the largest flat region of the country. It contains the richest soil and the longest river, the Po. Rising in the Alps, the Po waters the plain for 405 miles (652 km), emptying finally into the Adriatic Sea. Farther south is the Tiber, Italy's second longest river at 252 miles (406 km). It eventually flows through Rome, which is 16 miles (26 km) from its mouth at Ostia on the Tyrrhenian Sea.

Italy's mainland mountains include Mount Vesuvius, an active volcano. Mount Etna, on the island of Sicily, last erupted in 1985.

Spain

The Spanish people have lived under a central government for 500 years. Yet they retain a strong identification with their home regions. Most seem to think of themselves first as Basque, Catalan, or Castilian.

Such internal divisions are partly a product of the country's geography. As in Greece and Italy, there are many natural barriers to movement.

Spanish castles, such as this one in Valencia, were built to offer protection from invaders. *What landform found in Spain provided steep sides for castle builders?*

Much of Spain is covered by the high plateaus that rise sharply from waters around the Iberian Peninsula. The largest of these is the central plateau called the Meseta (may·SAY·tuh), which means "little table." Several rivers rise in these highlands and flow between mountains. Only one of these rivers is **navigable**, or deep enough for travel by boats. Dangerous rapids make most rivers unsuitable for transportation.

To the north of the Meseta rise the Pyrenees (PIHR·uh·neez) Mountains, where transportation is difficult. Along one stretch of railway, trains run through 22 mountain tunnels in just 21 miles (34 km). The Pyrenees, 5,000 to 11,000 feet (1,500 to 3,300 m) high, form the border with France.

Spain also includes two groups of islands. The Balearic Islands lie to the east in the Mediterranean. The Canary Islands are off the northwestern coast of Africa.

Portugal

Portugal, the westernmost country in Mediterranean Europe, shares the Iberian Peninsula with Spain. Portugal also includes two volcanic island groups in the North Atlantic: the Madeiras, famous for its wine, and the Azores.

Unlike Greece, Italy, and Spain, Portugal faces the Atlantic Ocean rather than the Mediterranean Sea. Its coastline drops sharply to the ocean, with steep seaside cliffs as high as 3,000 feet (900 m).

Also, unlike the other countries of the region, Portugal is mostly flat and low-lying, although it shares a portion of the Meseta plateau with Spain. The Serra da Estrela mountain range rises about 6,000 feet (1,800 m) in the central region of the country.

Portuguese built this village on cliffs overlooking the Atlantic Ocean. Portugal faces the Atlantic, not the Mediterranean Sea. *How else is Portugal different from other Mediterranean countries?*

An Ancient Fishing Village

Portuguese fisherman have been setting out to sea since before recorded history. Today, in coastal towns such as Aveiro and Estoril, the ancient tradition continues to be an essential part of the local economy.

In Portugal, fishing is a family business, with connections going back generations. The boats are small and simple. Few have engines or outboard motors.

The people of Aveiro live in houses built close to the sea, in a ring formation around a harbor. Fishermen leave their homes for the sea before dawn.

At the end of the day, the crew of each fishing boat brings its catch to the market, where the fish are sold by auction. A day's catch may include shrimp, lobster, crab, eel, octo-pus, squid, sardines, tuna, cod, and whiting. Some fish, such as sardines, are specially dried in the sun on huge racks.

The Portuguese have developed another valuable business from the sea. They gather and sell seaweed, which is a good fertilizer. Workers collect the seaweed on the beaches with wide wooden rakes and sell it to local farmers.

Estoril harbor

The Douro River flows east to west across Portugal, emptying into the Atlantic Ocean. The Douro divides the country into north and south. In the densely populated North, you find cooler weather and small farms. In the sparsely populated South, hotter weather and huge grain farms prevail.

LESSON 2 REVIEW

Fact Follow-Up

1. What three peninsulas jut into the Mediterranean Sea to make up Mediterranean Europe?
2. How have sea and mountains affected the development of Mediterranean Europe?
3. What is the Meseta? Where is it located?
4. Which nation of Mediterranean Europe does not border the Mediterranean Sea? What body of water does it border?

Think These Through

5. Which is more important to Mediterranean Europe: mountains or long coastlines? Explain.
6. Why is the Mediterranean Sea itself important to the region?

LESSON 3 Climate and Vegetation

The rain in Spain falls mainly in the plain.

This saying may be a good exercise in pronunciation. As a weather report for Spain, it turns out to be entirely wrong. Spain's inland plain—the Meseta plateau—receives little precipitation.

In fact, the Spanish describe the weather on the plain as *nueve meses de invierno y tres meses de infierno* ("nine months of winter and three months of an inferno").

The Mediterranean Climate

Near the coasts, mild, wet winters and hot, dry summers characterize the climate named for the Mediterranean region (see map, page 285). The westerlies, winds from the Atlantic Ocean, bring rain in the winter. During the summer, the **sirocco** (sih·ROCK·oh), a wind pushing north from the Sahara Desert, brings dry, hot weather. Throughout most of the year, the coastal areas remain moderately warm.

Inland, extreme changes in weather from summer to winter characterize the mountainous Highlands climate. Northern Spain enjoys a Marine West Coast climate—pleasant, but wetter than the Mediterranean climate.

Greece

During the summers, Greece sees months of cloudless skies, and nearly all of its rivers dry up. About three fourths of all rain in Greece falls in the winter, mostly in the mountainous Northwest. The plains of the Southeast get little rain.

Most trees, including firs, beeches, and pines, grow in the Pindus Mountains and the highlands of Peloponnesus. At higher

Spring and summer in Greece means dry weather. Greeks and tourists enjoy an outdoor cafe in Athens. *What time of year does Greece get most of its rain?*

Mont Blanc, known as Monte Bianco in Italy, sits on the border of France and Italy.
The highest mountain in Europe is in what mountain range?

altitudes, alpine lichens (mosses) and flowering plants flourish.

The forests that once covered Greece have almost disappeared over the centuries. People cut down the trees for wood to build houses and ships. Low shrubs now cover much of Greece.

Italy

"Sunny Italy" describes the Italian climate part of the year. Winters are cloudy and rainy. In the North, winter days are chilly.

Winter regularly brings snow to the higher slopes of the Alps and the Apennines. At the same time, the lower regions of the mountains enjoy mild temperatures.

Evergreens grow in the Alps and Apennines. On the rolling hillsides, chestnut, beech, oak, pine, and olive trees thrive. Only prickly pear, agave, and eucalyptus trees can endure the dryness in the South. On the coastal plains, warm, moist winds support oleanders and palm trees.

Spain

Spain's southern coastal plain enjoys the typical Mediterranean climate: mild, rainy winters alternating with hot, dry summers. Oleander, myrtle, poplar, palm, bougainvillea,

cork trees, and olive trees thrive here. Farther inland, only pine and scrub trees can survive in the dry central plateau.

In northernmost Spain, winds blowing over the North Atlantic Drift bring mild, wet weather throughout the year. The higher peaks in the Pyrenees receive much snow in winter. This area enjoys a climate much like that of Western Europe. Its weather supports deciduous forests of oak, beech, ash, birch, and chestnut trees.

Wild cork, juniper, and wild olive trees once covered all of Spain. As in Greece, Spain's forests have disappeared, especially in the Meseta, where scrubby bushes now grow in their place. In southern Spain, cork and olive trees are raised in orchards. Their products are important contributors to Spain's economy.

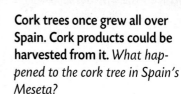

Cork trees once grew all over Spain. Cork products could be harvested from it. *What happened to the cork tree in Spain's Meseta?*

Portugal

Like northern Spain, Portugal enjoys the benefits of the North Atlantic Drift. Although there is plenty of rain, snow falls only on the highest peaks.

North of the Tagus River, Portugal experiences humid and cool winters, and warm (but not hot) summers. Pine and oak trees grow here. In the mountains where rain is plentiful, trees, bushes, vines, and mosses thrive. In the south of Portugal, drier weather prevails. Mild winters and warm summers support olive and cork trees.

Unlike Spain, Portugal remains heavily forested. Centuries ago, Portuguese kings established laws to preserve the forests from being cut down for ships and houses. Today, forests cover about a third of Portugal.

What would YOU do?

A beautiful climate and Mediterranean beaches draw millions of tourists to Southern Europe each year. The region has come to rely on the tourist trade to boost its economy. But the enormous crowds threaten the environment.

Imagine you're an environmental minister in Southern Europe. Would you put limits on tourism, even if it means your country will make less money?

LESSON 3 REVIEW

Fact Follow-Up
1. Describe the climate of Mediterranean Europe.
2. What effects do extensive coastlines have on the climate of Mediterranean Europe?
3. Compare the vegetation of Spain, Portugal, Greece, and Italy.
4. In what ways are the climate and vegetation

of Greece and Spain alike?

Think These Through
5. Why is the tourist trade so successful in Mediterranean Europe?
6. In which nation of Mediterranean Europe do you feel it would be most difficult to make a living from farming? Explain your answer.

Maps, Tables, and Descriptions Teach About Landforms

Each of us probably has a preference as to the way information is presented. Yet being able to use information that is presented in a variety of ways is important.

Here are some statements describing Mediterranean Europe taken from Chapter 14:

- Because the four countries of the region form peninsulas, they all have long coastlines.
- Stony mountains cover 70 percent of Greece, and many of these are high.
- Mountains or hills cover about 75 percent of the country (Italy).
- Much of Spain is covered by the high plateaus that rise sharply from waters around the Iberian Peninsula.
- Its coastline drops sharply to the ocean, with steep seaside cliffs as high as 3,000 feet (900 m).

In this skill lesson, you may examine two other sources, giving information about physical characteristics of the Mediterranean region. They present the information in three different forms.

Each form is useful. Written descriptions, such as those that you have just read, help people who learn best by reading, since words paint verbal pictures. For people who learn best by seeing, the map may be better. For others, the elevation table is useful because, unlike a map, it can give exact information about specific places in Mediterranean Europe.

But can any one of these sources tell you all that you might want to know about the Mediterreanean region? Pretend that the statements at the beginning of this lesson are all that you have in writing about Spain and Portugal.

If you study them carefully, you will discover that they tell you two important things: (1) The two nations are located on a peninsula, giving them long coastlines; (2) the coasts of Spain and Portugal drop sharply from a plateau to the sea.

The physical map gives you some of this information in a different form. The map confirms that the two nations are on a

Mediterranean Europe–Highest and Lowest Elevations		
Nation	**Highest Elevation**	**Lowest Elevation**
Greece	9,570 feet (2,871 m)	sea level at coast
Italy	15,787 feet (4,736 m)	sea level at coast
Spain	11,407 feet (3,422 m)	sea level at coast
Portugal	6,532 feet (1,960 m)	sea level at coast

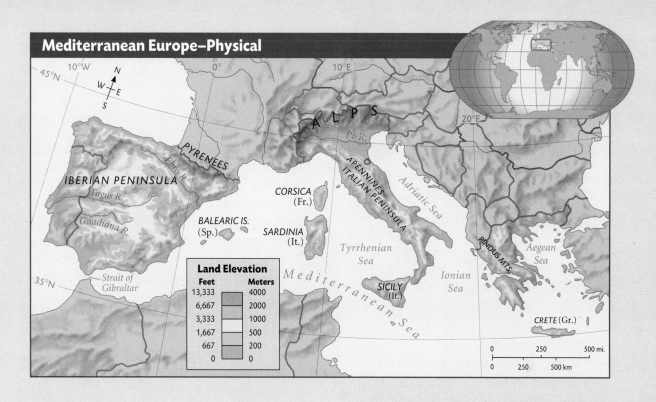

Mediterranean Europe–Physical

Land Elevation

Feet	Meters
13,333	4000
6,667	2000
3,333	1000
1,667	500
667	200
0	0

peninsula, that their land is a high plateau, and that they have long coastlines. Note, however, that the map gives you additional detail about the information you read. It gives you the location—absolute and relative—of the peninsula and tells you the peninsula's name. By reading the map's key, you can determine about how high the Iberian plateau really is.

The map also offers information that you did not have in your reading. It tells you that Spain's border runs along a range of mountains called the Pyrenees and gives you an idea of the mountains' height. You can spot the location and names of major rivers. You can measure—roughly anyway—the length of the coastlines. You can identify the name of the ocean to the west and sea to the east. And, finally, you can discover how close the Iberian Peninsula is to Africa.

Does that leave anything to be learned from the elevation table? You will quickly discover that this source provides two pieces of information that is not given any other place—the exact elevation of the highest points in Spain and Portugal. Your reading mentioned mountains in Italy and Greece, and described peaks in Spain and Portugal. The elevation indicates that the second highest mountain in the Mediterranean region is in Spain.

Note that each of the sources on Spain and Portugal offered information not found in any other source. How much more could you add to your store of data if you added one or two photographs of Spain and Portugal?

Practice using the variety of sources that you have in this chapter to describe the physical features of another Mediterranean nation. When you have finished, exchange papers with a classmate and compare descriptions. What can you learn from each other? Can you summarize your description?

Chapter 14 Review

TIME FOR TERMS

Latin
Iberians
sirocco

Romance languages
navigable

FACT FOLLOW-UP

1. How are the landforms of the nations of Mediterranean Europe similar?
2. How has nearness to the sea affected the nations of Mediterranean Europe?
3. Describe seasonal climatic changes in Mediterranean Europe.
4. Describe the landforms of Greece.
5. From what groups are most people in Italy and Spain descended?
6. How did Latin become the leading language of Europe for hundreds of years?
7. What are the Romance languages?
8. Describe how the Portuguese language came to be different from Spanish.
9. How did mountains and sea affect the economic development of Mediterranean European nations in earlier times?
10. Identify the mountains that have isolated Iberia from Western Europe.
11. What is the importance of the Po River and its plain for Italy?
12. How do the landforms of Spain differ from that of Greece?

THINK THESE THROUGH

13. How has the Mediterranean Sea been beneficial to the region? Explain.
14. Suppose the Mediterranean Sea were to close once again. How would the modern nations of Western Europe be affected?
15. In which nation of the region have mountains seriously slowed economic development? Explain your choice.
16. Which nation of Mediterranean Europe has landforms that are least helpful to economic development? Explain your answer.
17. Which nation of Mediterranean Europe has landforms that are most helpful to economic development? Explain your answer.
18. Which nation of the region do you think is most dependent on its long

coastline? Explain your choice.

19. Which has been more important for the economic development of Mediterranean Europe: climate or landforms? Explain your answer.

20. Which mountain range has been more important in the history of Mediterranean Europe: the Pyrenees or the Apennines? Explain your answer.

21. Based on vegetation, in which nation of Mediterranean Europe would a furniture-making factory be most likely to locate? Explain.

22. Compare the climate and vegetation of Mediterranean Europe with your home county.

23. Which do you think had the more important influence on Mediterranean Europe: Greece or Rome? Explain your choice.

SHARPENING SKILLS

24. When in your daily life might you use the skill of translating information from one source to another?

25. Is it easiest for you to acquire information from a written description, an elevation table, a map, or a photograph? Why?

26. Use the information from the elevation table to write a description of Mediterranean Europe.

27. Which source (map, written description, elevation table) used in the skill lesson provides the most precise information?

PLACE LOCATION

Use the letters on the key to locate and name the following:

28. a language that is not related to any other in the Mediterranean.

29. nations where Romance languages are used.

30. a nation whose ancient alphabet supplied some of the letters in the Latin alphabet.

31. the nation whose language evolved from the language of a neighboring country. The language is spoken in the largest nation in South America.

32. the place where Latin originated.

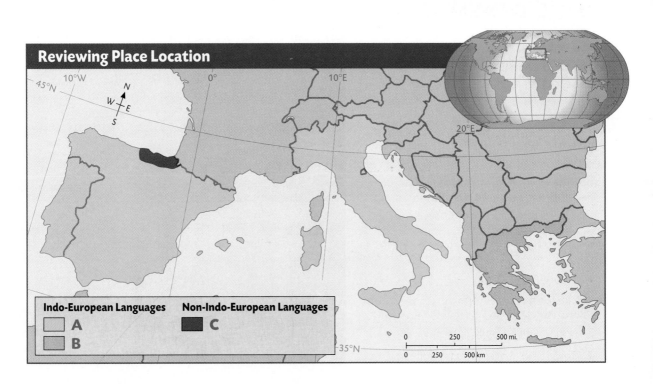

Reviewing Place Location

Indo-European Languages	Non-Indo-European Languages
A	C
B	

CHAPTER 15

People and Environment

In Portugal, people sometimes still crush grapes for wine the old-fashioned way. Rather than use a mechanical press, they stomp the grapes with their bare feet.

"The press crushes stems and seeds as well as the fruit, and gives the juice a slightly bitter taste," said the chief steward at a large family vineyard. "The human touch is gentler. It is slower, but in my opinion it is worth it."

This method of crushing grapes is only one of many things done the old-fashioned way. Mediterranean Europe has changed more slowly than nations to the north.

CHAPTER PREVIEW

LESSON 1
Before the Coming of Industry
The Greeks and Romans established trade routes among Mediterranean countries. Trade increased the resources of their homelands.

LESSON 2
Industrialization After World War II
Except in Italy, Mediterranean Europe had little industry until after World War II. Portugal still does not have much industry.

LESSON 3
The Consequences of Industrialization
Industrialization has speeded the growth of cities, changing ways of life and increasing environmental problems.

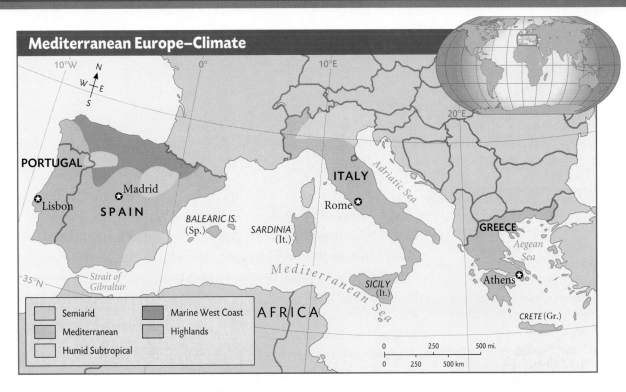

Mediterranean Europe–Climate

10°W   0°   10°E   20°E

PORTUGAL

Lisbon

Madrid

SPAIN

Strait of Gibraltar

35°N

BALEARIC IS.
(Sp.)

SARDINIA
(It.)

ITALY

Rome

Adriatic Sea

GREECE

Aegean Sea

Athens

Mediterranean Sea

SICILY
(It.)

CRETE (Gr.)

AFRICA

Legend:
- Semiarid
- Mediterranean
- Humid Subtropical
- Marine West Coast
- Highlands

0   250   500 mi.
0   250   500 km

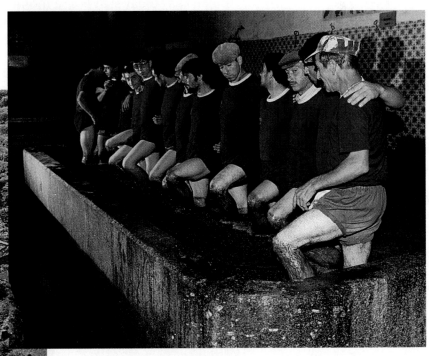

Stomping grapes in Portugal

Vineyards on hillside terraces in Portugal.

Before the Coming of Industry

LESSON 1

LESSON PREVIEW

Key Ideas

- Ancient Greeks and Romans built thriving trade networks based in the Mediterranean.
- Spain and Portugal were valuable trading partners of Rome. Later, both nations began world trade.
- Trade brought more resources to Mediterranean countries.

Key Terms

Appian Way, quarried, irrigation, terrace farming

Today, you can still travel parts of the ancient Roman road, *Via Appia*—the **Appian Way**. In the days of the Roman Empire, the Appian Way carried goods from distant ports to Rome. The route also served as a marketplace for rural people to trade their own goods.

Built of green-gray volcanic stone, the Appian Way started in Rome and ran through the Apennines to southern Italy. Along its 360-mile (580-km) course, the road passed along three seas—the Tyrrhenian, the Ionian, and the Adriatic. It took no more than 15 days to travel the road's entire length. The Appian Way today stands as a monument to the Roman understanding that trade was vital to the ancient Mediterranean.

Early Farming and Trade

For many centuries, the people of the Mediterranean region worked for food by herding goats and sheep and fishing in the rivers and the seas. They farmed wherever they could find flat and fertile land.

Jacob Conjuring Laban's Sheep (c. 1612-1622) by Pedro Orrente of Spain shows how many people of the region worked for centuries. *How else did they make a living?*

As their numbers grew, Mediterranean people found the supply of food limited by rocky soil and summer heat that dried up rivers and scorched crops. They relied upon the sea for food and trade. From their many harbors on the coasts, they sailed throughout the Mediterranean and beyond.

Trade by sea improved life in the Mediterranean, as more food and better tools became available. Whenever the Greeks, the Romans, and the Iberians traded with one another, they exchanged not only goods but also ideas. This contact among Mediterranean people led to innovations in architecture, agriculture, diet, and manufacturing that changed the region forever. Trade also spread religions throughout the region.

Greece

With little farmland, the Greeks became Mediterranean traders when nearly 5,000 years ago (3000 B.C.), merchants on the island of Crete began trading throughout the region. They were looking for resources their small island could not provide.

Later, the Greek Empire depended on trade. Greek colonies in southern Italy, Spain, France, and Northern Africa supplied wheat for city-states on the Greek peninsula.

With a reliable supply of bread, the Greeks could use their farming and grazing land to increase or vary their diet. They grew olives in protected groves and herded goats for milk and cheese. Greeks also fished the surrounding waters. They cut down nearly all their forests to build wooden ships for trade and fishing. The ships required a large amount of wood.

The Greeks built public buildings from high-quality marble. Marble was **quarried**, or cut in large blocks, from their rocky land. For centuries, traders throughout the Mediterranean prized Greek marble and used it for their important buildings. Later, many of Rome's great landmarks were constructed of Greek marble.

Trade by sea led to losses. Underwater wrecks await divers who can explore and recover them. *What do you think artifacts from sunken ships might tell us about ancient people?*

Greek wool also gained a reputation for quality. Greek shepherds tied sheep skins over their sheep to keep the fleece clean.

Italy

Rome emerged as the center of Mediterranean trade after the decline of Greece. The city's population topped 1 million at the height of the Roman Empire. It was one of the largest and most densely populated cities in the ancient world.

Supplying such a large population with food required many farms. Ninety percent of the people of the Roman Empire worked on farms outside of Rome. Farmers grew wheat, barley, and rye. They cultivated grapes and olives on the hillsides in valleys north and south of Rome. Farther south, they herded sheep, goats, pigs, and oxen. The name "Italy" comes from *Italia*, meaning "land of oxen" or "grazing land."

As Rome grew, farms became larger and more specialized. Many of the larger farms grew only grain, usually wheat. To increase efficiency, Romans introduced into their colonies throughout Europe and North Africa the oxen-drawn plow. The Romans also began using new **irrigation**, or crop-watering, systems.

In Italy, farmers developed **terrace farming**. Flat fields were

Farmers in Italy adapted their ways of growing crops to the land. *What kinds of crops do Italians grow on hillsides? on flat land?*

cut into hillsides. The terraces looked like steps going up the fertile hills, where they grew grapes and olives.

Despite Italy's good farm and grazing land, Rome needed trade to support its growing population. To connect towns throughout the empire, the Romans built nearly 50,000 miles (80,500 km) of roads. They also maintained the largest fleet of cargo ships in the ancient world.

CONNECTIONS
Geography & Science

Engineering

How did the ancient Romans manage to build the Appian Way and many other roads so well without any modern construction equipment?

First, they planned carefully, so that the road would be as straight as possible. Using an instrument called a *groma*, a surveyor found the most direct path through the land ahead.

Then large numbers of slaves, convicts, and soldiers prepared the ground. Along the Appian Way, these workers filled in valleys and swamps to level the roadbed. They then pounded the earth to make it smooth and flat.

Next, the workers laid a foundation of rubble, usually a thick bed of rough stone. Then came two more foundation layers. Flat rocks were laid carefully over the rubble, and crushed stone mixed with concrete was placed on top of those.

Finally, the road was paved. The paving stones had been cut so the pieces had flat surfaces and fitted tightly together. The road of the Appian Way is made of green-gray volcanic stone. No mortar held the stones in place. Instead, workers shaped them carefully so they would fit together like the pieces of a puzzle.

All this work was accomplished with the simplest tools, including pickaxes, chisels, hammers, and levers. The labor was backbreaking. The Appian Way, like so many

other Roman roads, has survived centuries of travel by foot, horse, and even armies in tanks. Skill and hard work made Roman engineering a worldwide success.

Appian Way

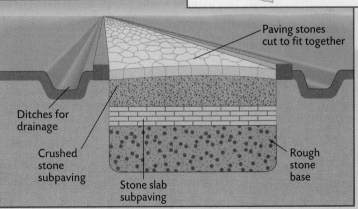

Paving stones cut to fit together

Ditches for drainage

Crushed stone subpaving

Stone slab subpaving

Rough stone base

Rome exported wine and olive oil. The city imported food, horses, gold, silver, and such building materials as marble, bricks, and lead for pipes. The city also imported manufactured goods, including pottery, glassware, weapons, tools, and textiles.

The Iberian Peninsula

The Iberians were the last to join in the Mediterranean trade because their peninsula lies so far to the west. The Greeks had traded actively since 3000 B.C., but the Iberians did not participate in the commerce of the Mediterranean Sea for another 2,000 years.

The Iberians offered farm crops and animals for sale. They

Muslims in Europe

The Muslims in Spain and Eastern Europe were followers of Islam (IHS·lam), one of the world's important religions. The Prophet Mohammed first preached Islam in the seventh century A.D. It soon spread to other parts of the world from its center in Mecca in the Arabian Peninsula.

Madrid
IBERIA

*ATLANTIC
OCEAN*

Córdoba

☐ Center of Muslim world, seventh century
☐ Muslim expansion, 700–1500

Muslim armies—called the Moors—conquered most of the Iberian Peninsula in the 700s. Armed with superb weapons such as the swords being made in an Iranian workshop (left), the invaders overwhelmed local princes. Spanish and Portuguese armies regrouped and fought back. The Moors, however, continued to rule parts of Iberia for almost 800 years.

Despite the fighting, European and Moorish scholars met peacefully in Spain. Europeans discovered that they could learn many things from the Moors. Europeans found Muslim medical manuscripts (right). These included what the Greeks, Arabs, and Muslims had learned about the diagnosis and treatment of disease. Pictured is a drawing of how to make medicine from honey.

also mined copper and tin that could be worked into bronze tools and weapons. Iberians traded their metalwork, wheat, and olives with Greeks and North Africans. Later, Rome traded with the Iberians for iron, silver, gold, and exceptionally fine horses.

Rome's influence changed the Iberian Peninsula. The Romans built roads to carry people and goods to and from isolated areas. They also constructed aqueducts to transport water to drier regions. As a result, people moved from mountain villages and formed towns on the plains to take advantage of the roads and the water.

Muslim invaders in the eighth century made still more changes. They improved the aqueducts with new ditch systems for irrigation and waterwheels for power. The Muslims

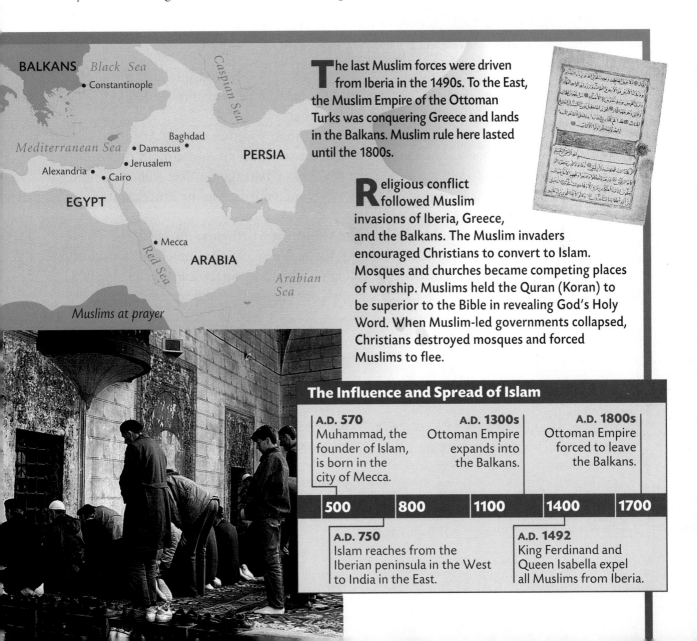

The last Muslim forces were driven from Iberia in the 1490s. To the East, the Muslim Empire of the Ottoman Turks was conquering Greece and lands in the Balkans. Muslim rule here lasted until the 1800s.

Religious conflict followed Muslim invasions of Iberia, Greece, and the Balkans. The Muslim invaders encouraged Christians to convert to Islam. Mosques and churches became competing places of worship. Muslims held the Quran (Koran) to be superior to the Bible in revealing God's Holy Word. When Muslim-led governments collapsed, Christians destroyed mosques and forced Muslims to flee.

Muslims at prayer

The Influence and Spread of Islam

A.D. 570 Muhammad, the founder of Islam, is born in the city of Mecca.	**A.D. 1300s** Ottoman Empire expands into the Balkans.	**A.D. 1800s** Ottoman Empire forced to leave the Balkans.

500	800	1100	1400	1700

A.D. 750 Islam reaches from the Iberian peninsula in the West to India in the East.	**A.D. 1492** King Ferdinand and Queen Isabella expel all Muslims from Iberia.

Prince Henry the Navigator encouraged Portuguese exploration of Africa during the fifteenth century. *Where else did the Portuguese explore?*

WORD ORIGINS

Portugal is a name that has roots in Latin words. *Portus Cale* means the "harbor of Cale." The harbor was located on the Douro River.

also introduced African crops, including pomegranates, oranges, figs, dates, rice, sugarcane, and cotton.

With more food and goods for trade, population increased. Towns grew into cities. Córdoba, the Muslim capital in Iberia, became the largest and wealthiest city in Mediterranean Europe.

By the fifteenth century, two nations—Spain and Portugal—had taken shape on the Iberian Peninsula. Both began searching for trade in the world beyond the Mediterranean region.

The Spanish looked west—across the Atlantic Ocean—for a route to Asia. In 1492, Queen Isabella and King Ferdinand of Spain supported Christopher Columbus in his search for a trade route by sea to Asia. His voyage, paid for by Ferdinand and Isabella, helped to expand the Spanish Empire into the Americas. After colonization of the Americas, Spain traded with its colonies there.

The Portuguese used their location on the Atlantic as an advantage in developing a sea route to Asia around the southern tip of Africa. In 1500, a Portuguese fleet sailing around Africa to Asia lost its way and ended up in the Americas, too, on the coast of what is now Brazil.

Both the Spanish and the Portuguese brought back new crops and gold from the Americas. Just as Rome had once ruled the Mediterranean through trade, Spain and Portugal established empires based on the wealth and resources of their worldwide colonies.

LESSON 1 REVIEW

Fact Follow-Up
1. What was the Appian Way?
2. Why did people in the Mediterranean region begin to trade among themselves? Why was this important?
3. What were some products the Greeks traded with other peoples?

4. Describe agriculture in ancient Rome.

Think These Through
5. What would Greek life have been like without trade?
6. Why is it said that "Rome changed the Iberian peninsula"?
7. How did Muslims change Iberia?

Industrialization After World War II

"The young move away," explained a Spanish farmer in 1978. "They'd much rather go and work in factories." Since the 1940s and 1950s, Spain has experienced a shift in population from rural areas to the cities. Farmers' sons no longer wanted to inherit the family's land. Instead, they chose to move to the cities, particularly Madrid and Barcelona, where they could find jobs in manufacturing or construction.

A Spanish newspaper reported in 1984 that more than 2,000 villages had been abandoned, and 3,500 more were nearly uninhabited.

Industry

Since the 1960s, three countries of the Mediterranean region—Greece, Italy, and Spain—have experienced rapid industrialization and economic growth. Portugal's economy has been changing much more slowly.

These changes resulted partly from the large amounts of aid provided by the United States in the late 1940s for the postwar reconstruction of Europe. As you have read, the Marshall Plan spurred Europe's economic growth.

Even more important in recent years has been the success of the European Union. Mediterranean nations belong to the Union and have shared in the economic growth enjoyed by its members.

Most of the Mediterranean region had lacked many of the necessary conditions for early industrialization. Coal was scarce, for example, and the mountainous terrain slowed the development of a modern transportation system.

LESSON PREVIEW
Key Ideas
- Except in Italy, industry came late to the Mediterranean region. Despite a well-established trade network, the region lacked the resources that had spurred industrial development elsewhere in Europe.
- Post-World War II aid from the United States and the formation of the European Union have encouraged industrial development.

A factory in Barcelona, Spain, encourages its workers to remember quality in their production of TVs. *How has modern industry changed where people live in Spain?*

Most people lived in the rural villages of Greece until the 1960s. Now much of the population resides in urban areas. *What is the largest city in Greece?*

The Agricultural Revolution of the British Isles and Western Europe did not reach Mediterranean farms outside of nothern Italy. People who remained on the land farmed with old-fashioned methods. With few industrial jobs, farm people remained in the countryside, living in poverty. The rocky soil and dry climate also kept Mediterranean farms from becoming as efficient as those on the Northern European Plain.

Greece

World War II and a civil war nearly destroyed the economy of Greece. During the 1950s, the nation's economy expanded. Aid came from the United States, and a profitable trade with the Middle East developed. Greek cities began to grow.

Earlier, the majority of people lived in the countryside. Many were poor, living on mountain farms that produced barely enough to keep them alive. These families moved when jobs were available in coastal cities.

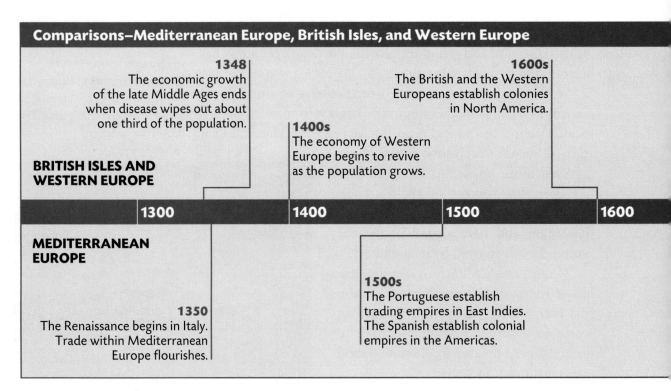

Comparisons—Mediterranean Europe, British Isles, and Western Europe

BRITISH ISLES AND WESTERN EUROPE

1348
The economic growth of the late Middle Ages ends when disease wipes out about one third of the population.

1400s
The economy of Western Europe begins to revive as the population grows.

1600s
The British and the Western Europeans establish colonies in North America.

1300	1400	1500	1600

MEDITERRANEAN EUROPE

1350
The Renaissance begins in Italy. Trade within Mediterranean Europe flourishes.

1500s
The Portuguese establish trading empires in East Indies. The Spanish establish colonial empires in the Americas.

Today, two thirds of the Greek population reside in urban areas. About 30 percent live in Athens and its suburbs, with another 7 percent in Thessaloníki, the second largest city.

Greek cities today reflect this rapid growth. New neighborhoods of tall apartment buildings and wide streets border older neighborhoods with low buildings, narrow streets, and few sidewalks.

Italy

Since World War II, Italy's industry has grown quickly. In 1953, for example, one third of the population still worked in farming. Today, only 10 percent of the workforce remains employed in agriculture. By the 1960s, Italy had achieved a rate of industrial production twice its prewar level. Its economic growth ranked among the highest in Europe.

Italy has become highly urbanized, with nearly 70 percent of the population living in cities. Most people live in the industrialized North. Northern cities such as Milan are among the wealthiest in Europe. Southern Italy remains rural and sparsely populated because of its rugged, mountainous landscape.

♦♦♦♦ **GAMES** ♦♦♦♦
People Play

Tavli is a board game enjoyed by Greeks of any age. With its circular pieces and triangular board designs, tavli resembles backgammon. Many tavli boards fold up, securing the pieces inside, so that players can take the game wherever they wish. Many adults enjoy tavli in the park, and children often play it on the steps outside their homes.

♦♦♦♦♦♦♦♦♦♦♦♦♦♦♦♦

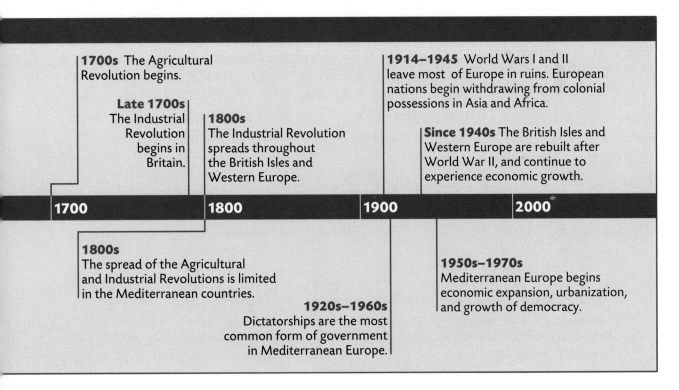

1700s The Agricultural Revolution begins.

Late 1700s The Industrial Revolution begins in Britain.

1800s The Industrial Revolution spreads throughout the British Isles and Western Europe.

1914–1945 World Wars I and II leave most of Europe in ruins. European nations begin withdrawing from colonial possessions in Asia and Africa.

Since 1940s The British Isles and Western Europe are rebuilt after World War II, and continue to experience economic growth.

1700 | **1800** | **1900** | **2000**

1800s The spread of the Agricultural and Industrial Revolutions is limited in the Mediterranean countries.

1920s–1960s Dictatorships are the most common form of government in Mediterranean Europe.

1950s–1970s Mediterranean Europe begins economic expansion, urbanization, and growth of democracy.

Spain

Until after World War II, Spain remained one of the poorest countries in Europe. In the 1950s and 1960s, Spain's industry and trade rapidly expanded. Its economic growth rate became one of the world's highest.

As in Greece and Italy, Spain's population shifted quickly from the country to the cities. Today, most people—80 percent of the population—live in such urban centers as Madrid and Barcelona. They enjoy a much higher standard of living than they did before industrialization.

Portugal

Before World War II, Portugal's economy depended on farming and fishing. A half-century later, the nation's economy remains heavily agricultural. Farming often does not provide families with enough income to live on. So many people have moved away from the farms to work in new factories.

About one third of the population now live in or near the two major cities, Lisbon and Oporto. These cities have begun to assume the same characteristics as other growing cities in the region. New office and apartment buildings have popped up in neighborhoods that are hundreds of years old.

As more people moved to Lisbon and Oporto for work, those cities changed to provide services, such as mass transit, for their residents. *Why is it important for cities to offer such services?*

LESSON 2 REVIEW

Fact Follow-Up
1. Contrast the Industrial Revolution in Mediterranean Europe and in the British Isles.
2. Describe population changes in Mediterranean Europe since World War II.
3. Describe economic changes in Mediterranean Europe since World War II.

Think These Through
4. Compare the industrialization of Italy and Portugal.
5. How was World War II, in the long run, beneficial to the industrialization of Mediterranean Europe? Explain your answer.
6. Why did Mediterranean Europe lag behind Western Europe in agriculture?

The Consequences of Industrialization

LESSON 3

ntonio Paolucci, an art restoration expert, worries about the effects of pollution on the Renaissance art of his native Florence, Italy. He points out statues where the marble has become soft and powdery, blurring fine details.

"We first became aware of the problem in the 1960s," Dr. Paolucci explained. "In just that short time, so much more damage has been done. The major cause is pollution from automobiles and fumes from home heating systems."

Life in Changing Economies

Most Mediterranean people once followed the regular rhythms of rural life. The relationship between people and their environment changed in the region of Mediterranean Europe after industrialization.

Since World War II, these countries (see table, next page) have experienced increasing population. People have moved from rural areas to cities, as they have left work in farming to take city jobs. With a growing demand for trained workers who

LESSON PREVIEW

Key Ideas
- Before World War II, much of the Mediterranean region was rural. Now, except for Portugal, the region is urban.
- With industrialization and a booming tourist trade, population has increased and standards of living have improved.
- Economic change also has brought severe urban overcrowding and pollution.

Modern equipment is needed to preserve the Mediterranean region's ancient structures, such as the Parthenon in Athens. Air pollution causes ancient columns to crumble. *What else can be done to preserve these buildings?*

297

can read and write, literacy–the ability to read–has increased. Higher education has become more available. People now live longer and enjoy a higher standard of living. Electricity and transportation are a common part of daily life.

Modern life has become more convenient, but people have paid a price for this convenience. Cities have become overcrowded, with housing shortages and traffic congestion. Pollution threatens water and air.

Most European countries face the same environmental challenges of overcrowded cities. Because urban growth only recently came to the Mediterranean region, problems of overcrowding and pollution developed quickly.

Greece

As late as the early 1960s, Greece lacked many of the advantages of modern life. Today, Greeks enjoy every modern convenience.

In 1961, nearly half of all the houses and apartments in Greece had no electrical power. People living in those areas had no electric lights, refrigerators, or televisions. Now only a few remote areas remain without electricity.

There are fewer farms, but they have become more profitable because of mechanized equipment and improved efficiency. Country life is more comfortable, with central heating, plumbing, and electricity in most houses. Paved roads link once isolated farms to the towns.

Because of the recent industrialization, Greeks have moved in large numbers from farms to cities in search of new opportunities. Cities are now crowded with many people unable to find adequate housing. Abandoned farms dot the countryside.

As population grew in the large countries of the Mediterranean region, many people moved to cities. *Why?*

Population Trends in the Mediterranean Region				
Year	Portugal	Spain	Italy	Greece
1961	8,851,000	30,431,000	49,904,000	8,387,000
1995	10,293,000	39,303,000	58,138,000	10,565,000

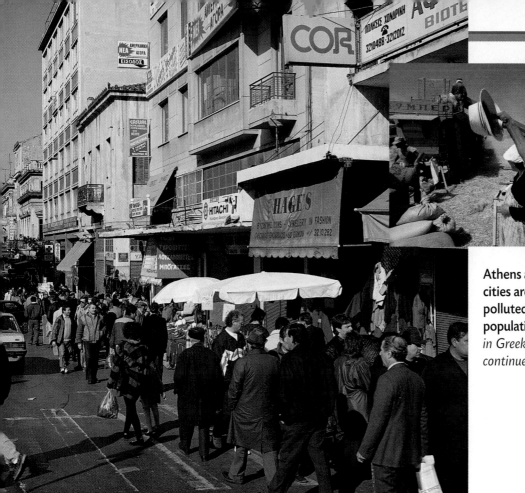

Athens and other Greek cities are overcrowded and polluted. Rural areas are losing population. *Despite the problems in Greek cities, why do Greeks continue to move to cities?*

As Greeks seek a higher standard of living in the cities, they also find many of the modern problems of urban life. Higher wages allow many more Greeks to buy cars, but traffic congestion makes driving in the cities difficult.

Because of car exhaust and industrial waste, Athens has become one of the most polluted cities in Europe. Greek officials have placed tightened pollution controls on industry. They also have limited the number of cars allowed within its city limits during the day. In some sections of Athens, cars may not enter at all.

Italy

Postwar industrialization has enabled Italy's cities on the northern plains to pull far ahead of the rural, mountainous South in population and wealth. Life in the peninsula has become sharply divided. A drive from the highly urbanized North into the South, with its small farms and dirt roads, seems like a journey into Italy's past.

Rural Italy has the flavor of older times. A bustling city like Milan reflects modern-day city life. *Which do you think Italian children prefer?*

As in Greece, Italy's rural population has declined, especially in the mountains. Its cities have become crowded. Bologna and other urban centers have banned cars from city centers to fight air pollution.

What would YOU do?

The Madrid garbage dump has become a feeding ground for storks, egrets, and teals. But Madrid planners want to close the dump and burn the garbage in a new incinerator.

Environmentalists argue that the dump should be declared a bird sanctuary.

What do you recommend for Madrid—bird sanctuary or incinerator?

The Iberian Countries

Spain's standard of living in the cities has increased steadily since industrialization began in the 1950s. Portugal has remained one of Europe's poorest countries.

Spaniards have eagerly accepted the modern ways of urban life, while letting go of many of the old customs. For example, fewer people observe the *siesta,* a midday rest once considered an essential part of Spanish life.

About two thirds of Portugal's people still live in the countryside. In Lisbon and Oporto, the two major cities, people use cars, buses, and electric street cars for transportation. In rural areas people still travel by oxcart or mule.

LESSON 3 REVIEW

Fact Follow-Up
1. How has urbanization helped the people of Mediterranean Europe?
2. In what ways has urbanization damaged the quality of life in Mediterranean Europe?
3. Describe life in rural areas in Mediterranean Europe.

Think These Through
4. Imagine that you are a young person living in Italy today. Which of the traditional ways of life would you most dislike giving up? Explain your choice.
5. Which nation of Mediterranean Europe do you believe has the brightest future? Explain.

Analyzing Cause and Effect

Do you remember dyeing eggs? If you didn't have purple dye and you wanted purple eggs, you simply combined red and blue dyes to create purple dye. Mixing the two colors caused them to change to purple.

The change can be expressed this way:

Blue + Red = Purple

Changes in dyeing eggs are fairly simple and uncomplicated. Causes of the changes—differing amounts of blue and red—can result in various shades of purple, but some tint of purple is always the result.

When we begin to analyze the causes and effects of changes like those in Mediterranean Europe in this century, we are dealing with considerably more complexity. These social and economic changes do not have one cause. Nor do they have only one result.

In the next chapter, you will read more about the coming of industry to the Mediterranean region. Yet if you review what you have already read about industrialization in the British Isles, Norden, and Western Europe, you already can draw up a list of probable causes. Foreign economic assistance, the transfer of ideas from industrialized countries into the Mediterranean, and the lowering of trade barriers within the European Union may be causes of change. What other causes of social and economic change have been at work in the Mediterranean?

Economic growth in the Mediterranean

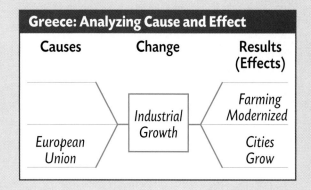

brought about several results. Here are three: (1) the movement of people from the countryside to cities; (2) rising standards of living; and (3) environmental pollution. How many more can you name after reviewing the chapter?

A graphic organizer like the one on this page can help you organize your thinking. After reading this chapter, study economic change in Greece. Enter the words, "economy" in the center of your organizer under the Change category.

On the left—under Causes—make room to list all the causes for economic change in Greece that you can find in this chapter. Leave room for more that you may find in Chapter 16. On the right—under Results (Effects)—list what happened as the economy developed.

Now that your data is organized, report your findings in a short essay titled "Economic Change in Greece—Some Causes and Effects of Growth."

Chapter 15 Review

TIME FOR TERMS

Appian Way   quarried
irrigation   terrace farming

FACT FOLLOW-UP

1. Describe ancient Rome's contributions to new agricultural methods.
2. Compare ancient and modern agriculture in Mediterranean Europe.
3. What caused nations of the region to trade in ancient times? What causes them to trade today?
4. Describe the ways that Rome's roads and easy access to the sea helped the development of trade.
5. How did construction of the Appian Way contribute to strengthening Rome as the center of an empire?
6. Why have more people moved to cities in Mediterranean Europe since World War II?
7. What are advantages and disadvantages of urbanization in the region?
8. How did the Muslims influence life in the Iberian Peninsula?
9. Compare rural and urban life in Mediterranean Europe today.
10. What causes young people to leave rural areas and flock to the cities of Mediterranean Europe?
11. In what ways did ancient Rome influence much of Mediterranean Europe?
12. What were the effects of World War II on the nations of Mediterranean Europe?
13. How have urbanization and industrialization affected the physical environment of Mediterranean Europe?

THINK THESE THROUGH

14. What have been the lasting effects of the Muslim conquest of much of Spain and Portugal?
15. Which was more important in the development of ancient Mediterranean Europe—Greece or Spain? Explain your answer.
16. Identify and discuss the factors that have contributed to the growth of cities in Mediterranean Europe.

17. How has the growth of cities in Mediterranean Europe affected ways of life? Explain.
18. Why has Mediterranean Europe changed more slowly than the nations of Western Europe?
19. The theme of human-environmental interaction is evident in recent changes in Mediterranean Europe. Explain.
20. Which is more important in explaining how Greece has changed over time: the physical or cultural characteristics of place? Explain your answer.
21. Why has Portugal seemed to change less than other nations of the region?

SHARPENING SKILLS

22. Use a graphic organizer like the one on page 301 to show the causes and effects of a political change.
23. How can a similar graphic organizer be used to show the multiple causes and effects of a
change in physical geography, such as the eruption of a volcano or a devastating hurricane?
24. What are some other ways a graphic organizer like the one on page 301 can be used?

PLACE LOCATION

The map "Europe and Northern Asia–Climate," pages 580-81, will help with the definitions required for the questions below.

25. Describe the characteristics of a Marine West Coast climate and identify the area of a Mediterranean nation that enjoys this climate.
26. Describe where a humid subtropical climate prevails in the Mediterranean region. What are the characteristics of this climate?
27. Describe the characteristics of a Mediterranean climate. Identify the nations where this climate is most frequently found.
28. Identify semiarid areas in the Mediterranean region. Describe their relative locations.

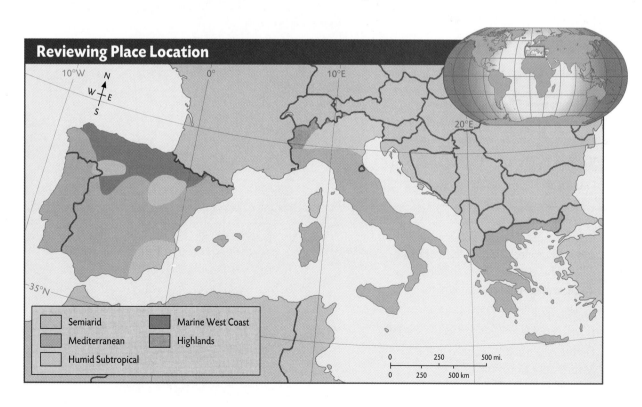

Reviewing Place Location

Legend:
- Semiarid
- Mediterranean
- Humid Subtropical
- Marine West Coast
- Highlands

0   250   500 mi.

0   250   500 km

Economy and Government

Costa del Sol, Spain

In Almansa, Spain, a Ferris wheel spins its riders near a Moorish castle. In Barcelona, circus performers create a human castle.

Like the other countries in the Mediterranean region, Spain uses its historic past, its present entertainment, and its lovely landscapes to attract tourists. Money from tourism supports industrialization in the Mediterranean region.

CHAPTER PREVIEW

LESSON 1
The Mediterranean Economies
Mediterranean Europe's economies have been changing and growing. Nations depend heavily on the tourist trade to boost income.

LESSON 2
The Mediterranean and the European Union
Italy has been a leader in the movement toward European unity. Mediterranean nations have gained from membership in the emerging European Union.

LESSON 3
Government
Democracy has been reborn in the Mediterranean region.

Amusement park in Almansa, Spain

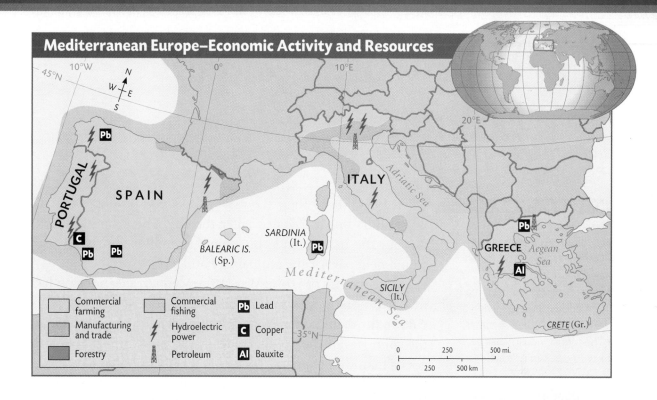

Mediterranean Europe—Economic Activity and Resources

45°N 10°W 10°E 20°E 35°N

PORTUGAL

SPAIN

ITALY

Adriatic Sea

SARDINIA (It.)

BALEARIC IS. (Sp.)

Mediterranean Sea

SICILY (It.)

GREECE Aegean Sea

CRETE (Gr.)

Pb Lead
C Copper
Al Bauxite

Commercial farming
Commercial fishing
Manufacturing and trade
Hydroelectric power
Forestry
Petroleum

0   250   500 mi.
0   250   500 km

"Human castle" in Barcelona

The Mediterranean Economies

LESSON PREVIEW

Key Ideas
- Mediterranean Europe has limited resources to support agriculture and industry.
- Some progress has been made in modernizing production and expanding national incomes.
- The tourist industry has been key to economic growth.

Key Terms
gross national product, trade deficit

The Piazza San Marco (St. Mark's Square) in Venice brings tourists from all over the world. *If every visitor had to buy a ticket to see Venice, what might happen?*

I n 1984, Mario Rigo, the mayor of Venice, proposed that all visitors buy a ticket to enter the city. The proposal failed, but the mayor made his point: 15 million tourists a year would help pay for the annual city budget.

Since the end of World War II, the Mediterranean region has invested more money in manufacturing while improving agriculture through modern farm machinery and irrigation. Yet all the countries of the Mediterranean still must import far more goods than they export.

Petroleum remains the most essential and most expensive import for Greece, Italy, Spain, and Portugal. Expanding industry and agriculture help them pay for imports. Tourism also earns money to pay for expensive imports.

Greece

Almost all tourists visiting Greece first see Athens. Many probably expect to see an ancient place. What they find is a city of 3 million people. Athens has few parks, terrible air and noise pollution, and frequent traffic jams.

Even so, few ever forget the sight of the Acropolis atop a hill overlooking the city. This cluster of Greek monuments includes the Parthenon and the temple of Athena.

Tourism Such spectacular sights keep the tourists coming. Service industries, especially those associated with tourism, make up 60

percent of the Greek **gross national product**—the total of a nation's annual production of goods and services. Every year about 8 million tourists visit Greece, a country of 10.5 million people. These visitors spend billions of dollars while in Greece.

Other service industries benefit from tourism. Manufacturing of souvenirs, construction of hotels and restaurants, and increased use of transportation systems earn money for a nation's economy.

Agriculture The farms of rural Greece average only about 8 acres (3.2 sq hm), although the number of large farms is increasing. These farms in northern and western Greece grow wheat, corn, and tobacco. Greece leads the world in growing olives. The country is the leading cotton producer in Europe.

Farmers also raise chickens, sheep, goats, hogs, and cattle. Feta cheese and yogurt come from the milk of these sheep and goats. Still, Greece must import much of its meat and dairy products from abroad.

Manufacturing, Mining, and Industry Most Greek manufacturing takes place in or near the cities of Athens and Thessaloníki. These factories make food, cement, chemicals, petroleum products, clothing, and cigarettes. Greece exports about 80 percent of the cigarettes manufactured there.

Greeks continue to mine marble, which is still prized worldwide, as it was in ancient times. In the Pindus Mountains, workers dig for lignite, a brown coal used for fuel.

Most of Greece's energy comes from imported petroleum. The flow of water down the nation's mountains dries up in the summer. The Greek rivers are a poor source of hydroelectric power. Greek engineers have begun to experiment with geothermal, solar, and wind energy.

Greek Shipping Besides tourism, Greece depends on shipping to support its economy. The Greek merchant fleet ranks as one of the world's largest, and includes oil tankers, cargo carriers, and passenger ships. Piraeus (py·REE·us), Greece's largest port, has three harbors and serves as an international shipping center.

Many people in the Mediterranean work in olive production. *What country in the region leads the world in growing olives?*

WORD ORIGINS

The name for the seedless raisin called the **currant** comes from *Corinth*, the Greek city where the processing of currants takes place. Europeans use currants as we do raisins, enjoying them in cookies, on cereal, or just by themselves.

Italy

Italy contains many tourist attractions. As in Greece, tourism in Italy is the most important part of its economy. Italy is also fortunate in having a strong manufacturing base to support a healthy economy.

Italy must import petroleum to meet half of the country's energy needs. This one item contributes heavily to a **trade deficit**, which occurs when a country imports more than it exports.

Manufacturing Geographers sometimes say that Italy seems to be two countries. Northern Italy's climate is similar to Western Europe's climate. Northern Italy also is much like Western Europe in terms of its strong economy. The North is Italy's manufacturing center. The South is much more agricultural, benefiting from the mild Mediterranean climate. Southern Italy has much less prosperity than the North.

Northern Italy contains few raw materials required for industry. It imports iron ore, coal, and other minerals. It does have ample hydroelectric power and skilled labor.

The people of northern Italy use resources and imports to produce high-quality products. Italy sells its products for substantial profits. Milan, for example, is one of Europe's wealthiest cities.

Northern Italy has a strong economy that is based on manufacturing, yet it lacks raw materials. *How has the area come to be a center of car production?*

Agriculture   Rich soil and ample water make the Po Valley Italy's chief agricultural region. The farms here are small, about three fourths of them measuring less than 12 acres (4.8 sq hm). Yet many of the crops raised in Italy are sold in world markets.

Italian olive oil and wine are the nation's best-known exports. Italy also exports more than half of the world's artichokes and ranks as one of the leading growers of sugar beets.

Italian farmers cultivate fruit, potatoes, and grain—chiefly wheat, corn, and rice. In the South, farmers raise cattle, hogs, chickens, and sheep, although most of the meat eaten in Italy comes from Argentina.

Italian Tourism   More tourists visit Italy than any other country in the world except the United States. As in Greece, tourists are drawn by the still magnificent remains of an ancient civilization. Others visit to see the art of the Renaissance or to hear Italian opera. Vatican City, the administrative and spiritual center of the Roman Catholic Church, receives millions of visitors every year. Still others come to enjoy the Italian countryside or ski in the Italian Alps.

The country hosts 50 million tourists a year, with Rome, Venice, and Florence attracting the most people. Hotels, restaurants, and other travel businesses all benefit from the tourist trade. These service businesses help offset Italy's trade deficit.

Spain

Spain also relies on tourism to balance its trade deficit. Spain's churches, castles, seaside beaches, and art museums attract visitors. Spain's high-grade iron ore supplies the raw materials for rapidly growing industries.

Manufacturing   With auto plants located in Madrid, Valencia, and Saragossa, Spain ranks as one of the world's leading producers of cars. Spain exports more automobiles than any other country in Europe, including Germany, France, and Italy.

Northern Spain produces iron and steel for export and excels

Visitors crowd the Spanish Steps and other sites in Rome. Good food and the Alps also are among the attractions of Italy. *Why is tourism important to the country?*

◆◆◆◆ **GAMES** ◆◆◆◆
People Play

Bocci is a popular game throughout Italy. Enjoyed outdoors, bocci is a lot like bowling without pins. Players alternately roll a large ball toward a target, which is either a smaller ball or a peg in the ground. The player whose ball comes closest to the target scores a point. Bocci started in Egypt, where Roman soldiers learned it in 50 B.C. It became a favorite pastime among Caesar's troops, who played the game in army camps all over the Roman Empire.

◆◆◆◆◆◆◆◆◆◆◆◆◆◆◆

Spain builds ships and exports iron and steel. *Where does the iron ore used in shipbuilding and steel manufacturing come from?*

in shipbuilding. Spanish products manufactured for the average consumer include refrigerators, furniture, televisions, and toys. Madrid produces electronics, and Barcelona specializes in textiles and shoes.

Agriculture and Fishing Spain ranks among the world's leading producers of cork, oranges, lemons, olives, and wine. Farmers grow most of Spain's leading crops on large farms in the South and East, where the government has helped pay for irrigation. Small farms in the North produce barley, wheat, and potatoes.

Spain is one of Europe's leading fishing countries. Most of Spain's catch comes from the Atlantic coast, in the Bay of Biscay. The country also experiments with breeding fish in ponds and then releasing them in the ocean. In this way, Spain hopes to replenish its supply of hake, sardines, and tuna.

Portugal

The Portuguese economy is not as strong as the economies of its Mediterranean neighbors. Traditional ways of making a living, such as fishing and farming, remain important but do not produce a lot of income.

Fishing and Farming Portuguese fishermen venture into the Atlantic in boats that look a bit like those used by the ancient Phoenicians. The traditional Portuguese fishing boat features a high prow, often decorated with a painted eye to ward off danger.

These boats return with catches of cod, sardines, and tuna. Because the Atlantic is still relatively clean, the fish caught there are safer to eat than those taken from the increasingly polluted Mediterranean Sea.

In contrast with Spain, Portugal receives ample rainfall for farming. Grains such as wheat, corn, and barley are produced on southwestern plains. Grapes grow in northern valleys. The wine produced from these grapes, plus olive oil and cork, are major agricultural exports.

Manufacturing Portugal's economy has been changing rapidly. Farmers are leaving the land to work in new factories. Manufacturing now produces about one third of the nation's income.

Portugal's most important manufacturing industry is textiles, especially the production of cotton fabric. Other manufactured goods include processed food (such as canned tuna), paper products, and electrical machinery. Lisbon and Setubal also have shipyards for building and repairing oceangoing vessels.

Services As in other Mediterranean countries, tourism is a growing industry. Along with government employment, tourism accounts for much of the service part of the economy. About 16 million tourists—12 million from Spain—visit Portugal each year. Many Europeans find Portugal a quiet and economical place to vacation.

Despite these changes, Portugal remains much poorer than its neighbors. It will probably have a hard time catching up with them. Neither fishing nor agriculture are big income producers in Portugal. Many of the factory jobs require few skills and wages are low. Unfortunately, 15 percent of the population cannot read. These Portuguese cannot perform high-tech jobs in high-tech industry.

Portuguese fishing boats display traditional designs. Yet the country's fishermen support modern food production. *What other goods are produced in Portugal?*

LESSON 1 REVIEW

Fact Follow-Up
1. What is the essential product that all nations of Mediterranean Europe must import? How do they pay for it?
2. Describe the economy of Greece.
3. Compare agriculture in Italy and Portugal.
4. What is gross national product?

Think These Through
5. How might Greece's economy be different without a tourist industry?
6. How is tourism an example of the geographic theme of movement?
7. Which of the Mediterranean European economies seems strongest? Explain.

The Mediterranean and the European Union

LESSON PREVIEW

Key Ideas

- Italy under a democratic government has been a leader in the movement toward European unity.
- As members of the European Union, Greece, Spain, and Portugal are forming close economic ties to Europe and are benefiting from the Union's economic assistance.

Greece has used funds from the European Union to restore its cities' neighborhoods.
What other countries in the Mediterranean have joined the Union?

I n 1995, the Greek Finance Ministry began setting up a computer network to modernize tax collection. Before then, tax officials relied on outdated tools of record keeping, using carbon paper, ink pads, and worn rubber stamps.

Because of this inefficiency in the Greek tax system, as much as 40 percent of all economic activity in the country had remained untaxed. The money lost through this huge "underground" economy could have helped pay for government services and economic development in the neediest parts of Greece.

The Greek government now has begun to reform its tax collection under pressure from the European Union. Greece, a member of the Union, has received generous economic assistance from more prosperous members. Greece recognizes that all Union members must work under the same economic rules—including tax collection.

Italy and the European Union

Italy helped start the European Union. Early in the 1950s, the newly established democratic Italian government joined France, West Germany, and the Benelux countries in taking the first steps toward European unity. Italy shared with these other nations the conviction that economic cooperation was vitally important. Through cooperation, they believed, democracy could be strengthened and another terrible war prevented.

Italy played an important role, leading European nations toward cooperation with one another. In 1991, when the treaty providing for the European Union was completed, Italy promptly joined the organization.

Meanwhile, Italy's economic growth gave it a strong voice in world affairs. It met regularly with the United States, Canada, Germany, France, the United Kingdom, and Japan—the world's richest nations—in efforts to solve international economic problems.

Greece, Spain, and Portugal became members of the emerging European Union later than Italy. Along with Ireland, these three Mediterranean nations were the poorest members of the European Union. The wealthier nations pledged economic assistance to the new members. Greece, Spain, and Portugal in turn promised reforms that would promote economic growth.

LIVING IN ITALY

Golden Triangle

Like the cities in North Carolina's Triangle and Triad, the cities of Italy's Golden Triangle—Milan, Turin, and Genoa—have been working together to improve business and life in their region. The three cities remain very different places to work and live, but they cooperate and share resources.

Turin has been a growing factory town since the Fiat automobile company opened there more than 100 years ago. Now Turin workers produce one of the most popular cars in Europe. Other Turin workers assemble the bodies of one of the finest luxury cars in the world, the Ferrari. Ferraris are assembled in Modena, north of Bologna.

Many people in Milan work for banks, insurance companies, and the stock exchange in old, elegant buildings in the center of town. Others earn their living in high fashion, designing and manufacturing fine clothes. Milan's fashion shows draw photographers, reporters, and celebrities from around the world several times a year.

Because Genoa is a port city, most of its people work in jobs related to shipping, such as loading cargo, building and repairing docks, and refueling ships. Genoa's businesses transport necessary raw materials to Milan and Turin, and then ship the finished goods to other ports in Italy and the rest of the world.

Ferrari

Greece

Since the 1980s, Greece has used the money it receives from the European Union to encourage the growth of agriculture and industry. By providing money for building irrigation dams, expanding the road system, and bringing electricity to isolated areas, the European Union has helped make Greece a more productive and competitive nation.

Greece is an important economic partner in Europe. It conducts half its international trade with other European Union nations. Greek ships make up 70 percent of the European Union's commercial fleet.

Spain

Before joining the emerging European Union, Spain had few close ties with other European nations. As a member, it has strengthened connections and found European markets for its

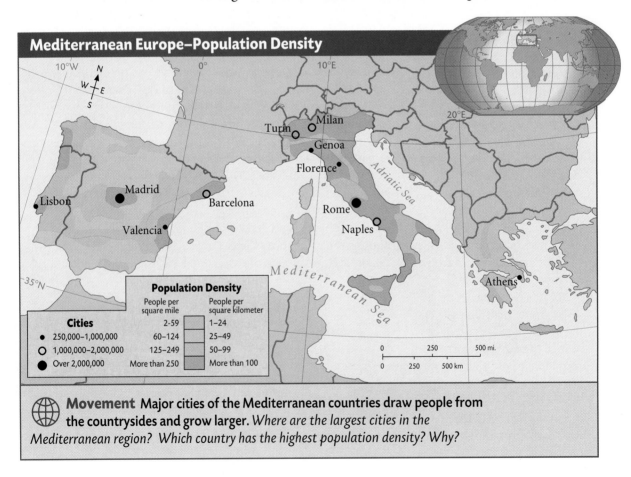

Mediterranean Europe–Population Density

Population Density

	People per square mile	People per square kilometer
	2-59	1–24
	60–124	25–49
	125–249	50–99
	More than 250	More than 100

Cities
- ● 250,000–1,000,000
- ○ 1,000,000–2,000,000
- ● Over 2,000,000

0   250   500 mi.
0   250   500 km

Movement Major cities of the Mediterranean countries draw people from the countrysides and grow larger. *Where are the largest cities in the Mediterranean region? Which country has the highest population density? Why?*

products. Spain also has benefited from financial aid that has helped improve farming, fishing, and communications. Loans are helping Spain bridge the gap between its economy and the rest of Europe's economies.

At one time, travel to and from Spain by rail was difficult, because Spanish trains ran on wider tracks than trains in the rest of Europe. With help from the European Union, Spain developed the Talgo train. The wheels of the train can be changed easily to run on different track widths. This innovation increased transportation of goods by rail and provided Spain with a valuable export.

In 1989, a media poll revealed that Spaniards highly approved of their country's economic expansion. The Spanish believe the European Union helped promote prosperity.

Spanish Crown Prince Felipe de Borbon (left) helps American Amtrak officials unveil a photograph of the Spanish-built Talgo train used in Seattle, Washington. *How is Talgo important to Spain?*

Portugal

Portugal receives more financial aid from the European Union than any other member country. The assistance encourages the improvement of every part of the Portuguese economy. Farming, manufacturing, services, communications, and transportation are growing stronger in Portugal. Portugal also uses money from the European Union for education. It is training more doctors, engineers, and teachers.

LESSON 2 REVIEW

Fact Follow-Up
1. What changes came to Greece as a result of its membership in the European Union?
2. What has been Italy's role in the European Union?
3. How has Spain benefited from membership in the European Union?
4. How do Spaniards feel about the European Union?

5. How is membership in the European Union changing Portugal?

Think These Through
6. Suppose Portugal had not joined the European Union. How would its economy have been different?
7. What is the most important advantage for Mediterranean nations that are members of the European Union? Explain.

Every government-built project in Rome, from a bridge to a manhole cover, bears the inscribed letters SPQR. The initials stand for the Latin words *Senatus Populusque Romae,*—"The Senate and People of Rome."

The Roman government began this tradition more than 2,000 years ago as a way of reminding people of Rome's accomplishments. Today, the ancient letters continue to express the pride that the people of Rome and their city's government take in community improvements.

From Dictatorship to Democracy

Ancient Greece and ancient Rome gave birth to the ideas of democracy and republican forms of government. Yet both democracy and republican government faded away in the Mediterranean region. They did not reappear until after World War II.

Dictators ruled nations in the Mediterranean for many years. Benito Mussolini, Italy's dictator (right), was an ally of Adolf Hitler (left), Germany's dictator. *In what war was Mussolini an ally with Hitler?*

After the Roman Empire fell, the Mediterranean region broke up into many small territories. Other empires seized control of what had been Roman territory.

Muslim armies—called Moors by the Spanish—invaded and conquered much of the Iberian Peninsula. Greece became part of two empires based in the eastern Mediterranean—first the Byzantine Empire and then later the Ottoman Empire. Meanwhile, the Italian peninsula broke up into many tiny city-states. Democracy could not survive in any of these new environments.

Mediterranean Dictatorships

In the twentieth century, Greece, Italy, Spain, and Portugal emerged as independent countries. All fell, however, under governments headed by dictators. A **dictator** heads a government that exercises total authority over its people.

Benito Mussolini ruled Italy as a dictator beginning in 1925. With the support of his political party, the **Fascists**, Mussolini controlled the press, schools, and all organized groups. He permitted no opposition to his government.

In World War II, Mussolini became an ally of Hitler. Near the end of the war, Italians who opposed fascism caught the dictator and shot him. Soon after, in 1946, Italy held free elections for the first time in 20 years.

In Spain, a group of generals led by General Francisco Franco started a war in 1936 against their own government. Franco's followers called for a Fascist dictatorship, a government much like those headed by Hitler in Germany and Mussolini in Italy.

Both Germany and Italy soon came to Franco's aid. Those countries supplied arms and manpower. Later you will read (page 329) about a famous painting called *Guernica*. This picture expressed the horror of an air attack by Nazi German

General Francisco Franco became the leader of Spain in 1939 after a civil war. *How long did he rule Spain?*

planes on a defenseless Spanish town. Nine waves of Nazi planes bombed the town. Then they flew back to machine-gun defenseless people in the streets.

After winning the Spanish Civil War, Franco established a dictatorship much like Mussolini's. He held power until his death in 1976. During his last years, Franco arranged for a descendant of Spain's royal family to take his place. Franco believed that the king would rule as he had. Instead, King Juan Carlos supported the establishment of democracy.

Portugal's dictator, Antonio de Oliveira Salazar, also did not provide for the continuation of his type of government. Salazar ruled in Portugal for about the same length of time as Franco controlled Spain.

EYEWITNESS TO HISTORY

The Unearthing of Knossos

In 1898, British archaeologist Sir Arthur Evans (1851-1941) discovered the ruins of a lost civilization on Crete that influenced early Greece. Evans called the culture "Minoan," after the mythical characters of King Minos and his Minotaur, the half-man and half-bull monster who roamed the maze beneath the palace.

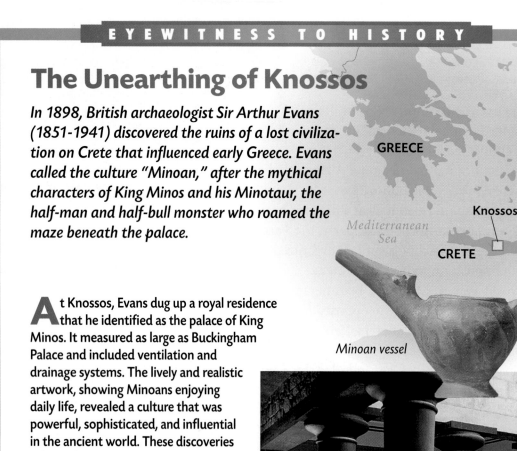

GREECE

Mediterranean Sea

Knossos

CRETE

Minoan vessel

At Knossos, Evans dug up a royal residence that he identified as the palace of King Minos. It measured as large as Buckingham Palace and included ventilation and drainage systems. The lively and realistic artwork, showing Minoans enjoying daily life, revealed a culture that was powerful, sophisticated, and influential in the ancient world. These discoveries tell us what an extraordinary civilization ancient Greece really was.

Palace of Minos at Knossos

Salazar came to power earlier (in 1932) than Franco , but he died sooner (in 1970). As dictator, Salazar ruled with the help of a secret police force. In 1974, an army revolt cleared the way for free elections.

Also in 1974, a Greek military dictatorship collapsed when it failed to force Turkey to back down in a dispute over control of Cyprus, an island in the eastern Mediterranean. As in Portugal, democratic elections followed the government's collapse.

Mediterranean Democracies

Years of dictatorship did not prepare the region for establishing democratic government. Democracy's success in the

What would YOU do?

Most countries in the European Union are industrialized and have strong economies. But four members—Portugal, Spain, Greece, and Ireland—have needed financial help. The European Union's assistance drains the members' resources.

Other economically weak countries want to join the Union. What would you require for membership in the Union?

The most famous mural that Evans discovered was a fresco depicting the ritual of bull-dancing (right). This picture shows three youths leaping over a bull's back. This exciting, dangerous ritual may have been the source of the Minotaur myth.

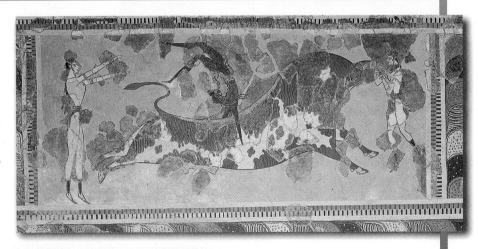

Evans also discovered 2,000 small clay tablets (left) with writing in an unknown language, later called Linear B. When scholars finally deciphered the tablets in 1953, they found that the language of the Minoans was an early version of ancient Greek.

Palace of Minos at Knossos

319

King Juan Carlos succeeded Franco as head of Spain. But he did not follow Franco's lead in ruling a dictatorship. *What kind of government does Juan Carlos lead in Spain?*

Mediterranean region became linked to economic progress within the European Union.

The Union's leadership had decided as early as the 1950s that membership would be limited to democratic governments. This requirement strengthened the demand for democratic government in nations outside the Union. No European nation could expect much prosperity or influence if it did not belong to the European Union.

As in Western Europe, democratic government in the Mediterranean countries takes different forms. Of the four nations, only Spain has a king, who serves as a constitutional monarch. In the other three nations, the presidents serve as heads of state, but these presidents are chosen in different ways and have different duties.

The parliaments are of different sizes and are known by different names. Some parliaments have one house, others have two.

All of these governments, however, are shaped by constitutions that limit governmental power. The rights of individuals are guaranteed, especially such vital rights as freedom of speech, freedom of the press, and the right to vote. These are the essentials of constitutional and democratic government.

LESSON 3 REVIEW

Fact Follow-Up
1. Who were Benito Mussolini, Francisco Franco, and Antonio de Oliveira Salazar?
2. What role do the people have in a dictatorship?
3. Which nation in Mediterranean Europe is a constitutional monarchy?
4. What are the necessary parts of constitutional and democratic government?

Think These Through
5. Why do you think the European Union required that all members have democratic governments?
6. Of all the rights taken away from people by dictatorships, which do you think was most important? Explain your answer.

Using Information for Problem Solving, Decision Making, and Planning

Planning for Change in Mediterranean Europe

Have your teachers ever told you to plan your work? Of course they have! And when you plan your work—your homework or a unit project, for example—what do you do? Probably you make a list of everything that must be done, decide what needs to be done first, and get on with the job.

Nations of Mediterranean Europe have gained new wealth by industrializing and promoting the tourist business. All want those businesses to grow. Yet too much industry and too many tourists could ruin everything. Millions of tourists create traffic jams and damage historic sites. Automobile traffic and industry create pollution. If the nations don't plan wisely, their future will not be bright.

Keep in mind these words that open Chapter 16:

S pain uses its historic past, its present entertainment, and its lovely landscapes to attract tourists. Money from tourism supports industrialization in the Mediterranean region.

If you looked closely at the pictures in this unit, you probably have an understanding of the problems tourism can create. The photographs on pages 306, 309, and 315 show what tourists can experience.

Look through these pages for other pictures that reflect damage being done by too many tourists and too much industry.

Tourists don't want to visit ruined sculptures or breathe the exhaust of automobiles. How can Mediterranean Europe balance its traditional and industrialized aspects so that neither is destroyed? Its leaders will have to plan for a future that can include both.

Planning for the future includes these steps:

1. Planners must have a vision of what they want the future to be like. This is a step that many people forget to take. Without a plan for the future, it is difficult to reach goals.
2. They must then decide what tasks are to be done to achieve those goals. They make lists in the order in which each task must be done.
3. They then decide who will work on each task and who will pay for each part of the work.
4. After the work starts, they should remember to refer often to the vision of the future that was created in Step 1. Any work that varies from that vision should encourage planners to reconsider either their work or their goals.

Use these steps to make a plan for Mediterranean Europe that will preserve both traditional treasures and the benefits of industrialization. Compare your plan with a classmate's plan.

Chapter 16 Review

TIME FOR TERMS

gross national product   trade deficit
dictator   Fascists

FACT FOLLOW-UP

1. What is a trade deficit?
2. How do countries in Mediterranean Europe offset their trade deficit?
3. How did the European Union encourage the formation of democratic governments in Mediterranean Europe?
4. What is the Golden Triangle of Italy? Why does it have that name?
5. What natural resource not found in other nations of Mediterranean Europe supplies raw materials for Spanish manufacturing?
6. Why are Spain and Portugal known for fishing?
7. Why do tourists visit each nation of Mediterranean Europe?
8. What is the poorest nation of Mediterranean Europe? Explain.
9. Why have the nations of Mediterranean Europe chosen to join the European Union?
10. How does membership in the European Union strengthen the economies of Mediterranean Europe?
11. Describe the Mediterranean region after the fall of the Roman Empire.
12. Describe the kind of government of each country in the Mediterranean during most of this century.
13. Describe the characteristics of governments in Mediterranean Europe today.

THINK THESE THROUGH

14. What strengths can nations such as Italy bring to the European Union? Explain.
15. Which nation of Mediterranean Europe would be most hurt in the case of a worldwide oil shortage? Explain your answer.
16. What economic problems does Portugal need to overcome to catch up to its Mediterranean neighbors?

17. Which benefits of the European Union will prove most helpful to nations of Mediterranean Europe—economic assistance or the requirement that government be democratic? Explain your choice.

SHARPENING SKILLS

18. Use the four-step model to plan a school field day or a class party.

19. List all the kinds of planning that are used in your community. Is there any community planning similar to the planning needed to preserve tradition and encourage industrialization in Mediterranean Europe?

20. Which step of the process do you think is most difficult to accomplish? Explain why.

21. Suppose you read the following headline: "Local Industry Plans Expansion That Will Provide 1,000 New Jobs." What plans will your community need to make to support the expansion?

PLACE LOCATION

Use the map key to answer the following questions:

22. Reading the symbols on this map, what seems to be the greatest source of power in the Mediterranean region? Where is most of it found?

23. The text indicated that no Mediterranean nation had enough resources to build modern industry. Which resources do you find in the region that might contribute to industrial development?

24. Thinking back to earlier studies of industrial development elsewhere in Europe, which resources are missing altogether? Which are in short supply?

25. Identify the industrialized areas of the Mediterranean.

26. According to the map symbols, what are the region's most important nonmanufacturing industries? Describe the relative location of each.

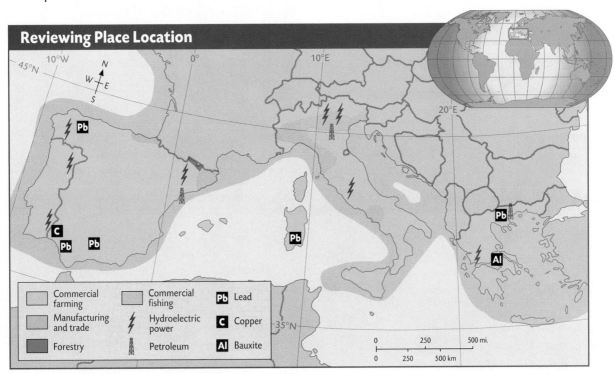

Reviewing Place Location

Commercial farming
Manufacturing and trade
Forestry
Commercial fishing
Hydroelectric power
Petroleum
Pb Lead
C Copper
Al Bauxite

CHAPTER 17

Society and Culture

On a warm summer evening in Athens, twelve-year-old Nikos waits for his friends on the stone bench of the Odeon Herod Atticus, an outdoor theater 1,800 years old. The Odeon once was a stage for ancient drama and dance, but tonight Nikos and his friends will hear a rock concert. The concert is part of the Athens Festival, an annual event that draws audiences from all over Greece and around the world.

"Sometimes they have opera and ballet here," Nikos says to tourists sitting next to him. "I like the rock concerts best."

CHAPTER PREVIEW

LESSON 1
A Tale of Three Cities
Three major cities in the Mediterranean reflect the region's similarities and differences.

LESSON 2
Religious Traditions
The Greek Orthodox Church and Roman Catholic Church greatly influence daily life.

LESSON 3
Food and Leisure
The people of the Mediterranean eat similar foods, but styles of preparation differ. Water sports and soccer are popular.

The Herod Atticus theater

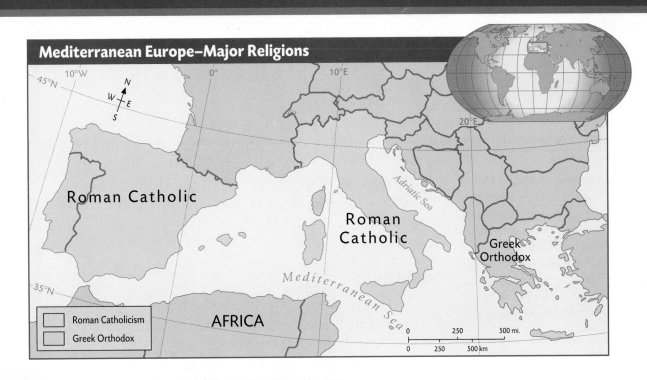

Mediterranean Europe–Major Religions

45°N   10°W   0°   10°E

Roman Catholic

Roman Catholic

20°E

Adriatic Sea

Greek Orthodox

Mediterranean Sea

35°N

AFRICA

□ Roman Catholicism
□ Greek Orthodox

0   250   500 mi.

0   250   500 km

The Odeon Herod Atticus ruins

A Tale of Three Cities

LESSON PREVIEW

Key Ideas

- Athens, Rome, and Madrid offer a mixture of sights— buildings and art reflecting ancient glories and modern accomplishments.
- This mixture of the old and new provides clues to the special nature of nations in the Mediterranean region.

What would **YOU** do?

Some of the most famous ancient Greek art is actually in London, England. In the nineteenth century, Lord Elgin took several huge pieces of the Parthenon back home with him to England, where they are still on display in the British Museum.

The Greeks want the art returned, but the British refuse, saying that the pieces have been protected in the museum. Whose claim seems to you to be most valid? How would you mediate between the two sides?

If you grow up in Athens, Rome, or Madrid, you expect tourists to visit your city. These cities hold the wonders of the ancient world and the beauty of the modern Mediterranean. Millions of people visit each city every year.

Athens

The Greek name for Athens is *Athinai*. Today, about a third of all Greeks, more than 3 million people, live in or near Athens, the capital of Greece.

Part of Athens, the home of the great philosophers Socrates and Plato, is thousands of years old. In the southwest corner of Athens stand the ruins of the old city.

Modern Athens dates from the middle of the nineteenth century, when the city became the capital of an independent Greece. Architects planned the new Athens with straight streets and large public squares. Today, three main public squares, each having a distinctive atmosphere, form the center of Athens.

Syntagma (Constitution) Square serves as the center of government. The parliament stands here, surrounded by other government buildings. At lunch, Athenians who work in the government offices gather at tables in the outdoor restaurants to talk and drink coffee. In the evenings, families come here to relax near the National Gardens, a large park.

Omonoia (Concord) Square is the chief shopping center of Athens, with many department stores and expensive shops. Tourists enjoy strolling in this district and buying souvenirs to take home.

Athenians shop every day at *Monastiraki* Square, the old marketplace of the city. This part of Athens shows Turkish influence, from the time when Greece was part of the Ottoman Empire. Small shops line the narrow lanes here, and street vendors crowd to hawk their goods. On hot afternoons, the butchers

Monastiraki Square (above) is the old marketplace of Athens. Syntagma Square (left) is the center of Greek government. *What is Athens' third major square and what happens there?*

stretch out for naps on their washed and cool marble slabs.

Most Athenians today live in apartments or small houses on the outskirts of the city. Although many own cars, city law strictly limits driving to cut down on air pollution. To avoid driving, Athenians ride buses, trolleys, or the subway to work.

Rome

Rome, the capital of Italy, is often called the Eternal City because its history and influence in the world have endured for thousands of years. Recall how Rome once served as the capital of a huge empire. Later, Rome became the center of the Roman Catholic Church. Vatican City, the headquarters of the Catholic Church, is an independent nation. It is located in northwest Rome.

Rome's busiest area is the *Piazza Colonna,* where there are banks, offices, restaurants, and theaters. Through the Piazza Colonna runs the *Via del Corso* (Way of the Course), the main street of Rome. Its name comes from the Middle Ages, when Romans used the road as a horse race course.

Many Roman parks were once large, private estates, called villas. The Villa Borghese, which opened to the public in 1902, offers people green countryside right in the middle of the city. The Villa Borghese includes a zoo.

Romans enjoy camping in the Villa Ada, where the kings of Italy used to live. There is even a park in the ruins of the *Domus Aurea* (Golden House), where the Emperor Nero resided.

Most Romans live in apartment buildings. They work in businesses, government offices, and in the many restaurants that cater to tourists. Unlike Athens, Rome is not an industrial city. Only one in five Roman workers goes to a factory job.

To get to work, many Romans take buses, streetcars, trolleys, or the subway. Since 1973, Rome has banned cars from the ancient section of the city to avoid pollution and vibrations that might wear down the ruins.

At the end of the day, Roman families enjoy *la passeggiata,* an evening stroll. Teenagers often go to the movies or meet friends for a snack.

Madrid sits high on a plateau in central Spain. A city 1,000 years old, Madrid became the capital of Spain about the time this street was built. *When did that happen?*

Madrid

One of the highest capitals in Europe, Madrid sits on a plateau 2,150 feet (645 m) above sea level. Madrid is located at the geographical center of Spain.

In downtown Madrid, the main streets meet at the *Puerta del Sol* (Gate of the Sun), a long, crescent-shaped plaza. To the southwest lies the old section of Madrid. Here are narrow streets dating from the sixteenth century.

To the north, Madrid's business district is filled with banks, hotels, restaurants, theaters, and stores. Nearby are the Retiro, one of the city's largest parks, and the Prado, a world-famous art museum. Among its more than 3,000 paintings are works of such great Spanish artists as El Greco, Francisco de Goya, and Diego Velázquez.

The Moors founded Madrid as a fortress in the tenth century. Madrid remained an unimportant town, however, until it became Spain's capital in the 1500s. From then until the 1800s, Madrid was one of the great European cities.

As you have read, Spain missed the Industrial Revolution and lagged behind the British Isles and the nations of Western Europe. Madrid went into decline. During the Spanish civil war (1936-39), the capital was moved out of Madrid because of the fierce fighting there. At the end of the conflict, General Francisco Franco, the head of the victorious Fascist forces, made Madrid the capital of Spain again. He ordered the destroyed city rebuilt.

CONNECTIONS
Geography & the Arts

Picasso's *Guernica*

Pablo Picasso (1881-1973) was a Spanish artist who developed the painting style called Cubism. In his Cubist paintings, Picasso attempted to present his subjects from all sides at once—a view possible only in art. His masterpiece is *Guernica*.

On April 26, 1937, during the Spanish civil war, German Nazi airplanes bombed the defenseless town of Guernica, traditional capital of the Basque region. The bombing and the fires that followed destroyed the town. The planes machine-gunned people—mostly women and children—who sought safety in nearby fields.

When Picasso, then living in Paris, heard about the terrible destruction of Guernica, he began making sketches of the event. Picasso drew 45 studies. He completed the painting on June 4, 1937.

In black, white, and gray, on a canvas measuring 11.5 feet by 25.7 feet, *Guernica* presents the horror of a peaceful town suddenly destroyed in war. Picasso's depiction includes people trying to escape, a wailing woman holding her dead child, and the tragic figures of the bullfight—the horse and the bull.

Society and Culture **329**

Francisco Goya's *Threshing* hangs in the Prado. This spectacular art museum in Madrid houses more than 3,000 paintings. *What are other attractions in Madrid?*

In the 1950s, Spain began its postwar industrialization. Madrid's population boomed and the city expanded. Since then, Madrid's population has more than doubled.

Today, nearly 3 million people live in Madrid. Most Madrileños, as they are called, live in apartments. The typical workday begins at 9:00 A.M., with a long lunch break between 1:00 and 4:00 P.M. Most Madrid offices and businesses close at 7:00 P.M.

In the early evening, Madrileños enjoy a stroll (*el paseo*, the walk) and a light snack called *tapas* at a restaurant with friends. Dinner in Madrid comes much later, between nine o'clock and midnight.

Madrid has become a large, busy metropolis, but it still prides itself on its atmosphere of *comodidad*—an easy, leisurely pace.

LESSON  REVIEW

Fact Follow-Up
1. How many of the 10 million Greeks live in Athens and its surrounding areas?
2. How do Athenians deal with problems of air pollution?
3. Why is Rome called the Eternal City?

Think These Through
4. Which city would you most like to visit–Athens, Rome, or Madrid? Explain why by naming characteristics of the city.
5. Which city do you think has changed most? Explain your choice.

Religious Traditions

On the night before Easter, twelve-year-old Diana stands with her father and mother in their crowded Greek Orthodox church in the suburbs of Athens. It is nearly midnight, and everyone in the darkened church holds an unlighted candle.

On Holy Thursday, Diana and her mother had dyed eggs red and coated them with olive oil until they shone. On Good Friday, they baked *tsoureki*—Greek Easter bread, topped with the red eggs—which they will eat on Easter.

But for now, on Holy Saturday, the family stands in the dark, waiting for the light. Suddenly, a priest in golden robes appears with a single lighted candle.

One of the congregation lights his candle from the flame and passes it to the person on his right, who passes it again. The light begins to illuminate the church.

Diana carefully lights her own candle and then passes the flame to her mother. By midnight, the church is filled with candlelight—the sign that Easter has finally come.

Establishment of the Greek Orthodox Church

Most people living in the Mediterranean region belong to the Greek Orthodox or Roman Catholic Church (see map, page 325). Greek Christians were once part of the Roman Catholic Church. About 1,000 years ago, Greek Eastern Orthodox Churches were established.

After the Roman Empire fell, Christian bishops in Constantinople (now Istanbul, Turkey) became church leaders in Greece and the eastern half of what was the Roman Empire. Rome remained the center of Christianity in the West.

In 1054, church leaders in Rome and Constantinople argued bitterly over their differences in understanding the Bible. Christianity split into two parts. The Roman Catholic Church represented the beliefs in the West. The Orthodox Church

---

LESSON PREVIEW

Key Ideas

- The Greek Orthodox and Roman Catholic Churches play major roles in the daily lives of Mediterranean people.
- The Greek Orthodox and Roman Catholic Churches differ in ceremonies and beliefs.
- Differences in religious practices in Italy, Spain, and Portugal reflect differences among the people of the region.

A Greek Orthodox priest leads a candle-lighting service at Easter. *Why is Easter an important holy day throughout the Mediterranean for Roman Catholic and Greek Orthodox members?*

The Hagia Sophia in Istanbul, Turkey, was an Orthodox Cathedral before becoming a Muslim mosque in the fifteenth century. *How did the Orthodox Church influence Mediterranean Europe?*

represented the beliefs in the East. In Greek, Orthodox means "correct belief."

Later, Orthodox Christian missionaries took their Church farther east into the Balkans and Russia. The Catholic Church and later, the Protestant Reformation, spread throughout Western Europe.

Greece

"To be Greek is to be Greek Orthodox." That saying is true, as more than 98 percent of Greeks are Greek Orthodox. The remaining 2 percent are Muslims, Jews, Roman Catholics, and Protestants.

The Greek Orthodox Church has no pews. Instead of sitting, the priest and people stand or walk around chanting the rituals. In some rural churches, men stand on the right and women stand on the left. Services may last up to three hours.

Easter is the most important holiday of the church year. The celebration includes feasts, processions with lighted candles, fireworks, elaborate family meals, music, and dancing. The Greek Orthodox Church also celebrates Christmas, although people traditionally exchange gifts on January 1.

WORD ORIGINS

The word **mass** comes from the Latin phrase *Ite, missa est,* which means "Go, it is ended." In the early Latin mass, the priest dismissed the congregation with these words as an encouragement for the people to go forth and continue God's work in the world.

Italy and Vatican City

Almost all Italians are Roman Catholic. Until 1985, Roman Catholicism was the official religion of Italy. Now other religions have legal protection.

The pope leads the Catholic Church from Vatican City, an independent country located entirely within the city limits of Rome. Vatican City, one of the smallest countries in the world, mints its own coins and prints its own newspaper. It has its own flag and diplomatic officers. The Swiss Guard once protected the pope. Its purpose now is mostly ceremonial. Michelangelo designed the Swiss Guard's uniforms.

St. Peter's Basilica, whose great dome was also designed by Michelangelo, attracts thousands of pilgrims from all over the world. The pope celebrates mass there. Today, only about one third of Italian Catholics attend church services weekly, but nearly everyone celebrates religious holidays.

Christmas festivities begin on Christmas Eve with a large family meal and Midnight Mass. Italians exchange presents on Christmas and January 6, the feast of Epiphany, in honor of the three kings who offered gifts to the infant Jesus.

The tradition of the crèche, the re-creation of the manger scene with Mary, Joseph, and the infant Jesus surrounded by shepherds and angels, began in Italy in the early thirteenth century. St. Francis of Assisi introduced the crèche as a way of imagining the humble birth of Jesus.

Roman Catholics gather in St. Peter's Square in Vatican City. Vatican City is actually a small country. *In what city is it found? Who is Vatican City's leader?*

Spain

About 99 percent of Spaniards are Roman Catholic. Nearly 300,000 Muslims also live in Spain today.

Until recently, Roman Catholicism was the official religion of Spain. Only Catholic marriages were legal. Laws also forbade members of other religions from seeking new members. In 1978, Spain's new constitution guaranteed religious freedom to all people.

The most important religious festival in Spain occurs during *Semana Santa* (or Holy Week), the seven days before Easter. During this time, Spanish Catholics carry beautifully decorated religious statues through the streets. These solemn processions, accompanied by music and torch light, occur near sundown.

Members of Catholic organizations carry heavy gold and silver statues in a Holy Week procession in Seville, Spain. *When did Spain grant religious freedom to its citizens?*

Portugal

Nearly 97 percent of Portuguese are Roman Catholic. Until the early 1900s, the Catholic Church was actually part of the Portuguese government. In 1911, the church and government separated. Even now, in rural areas, Catholic priests play an important role in education, social life, and local government.

Portuguese Catholics enthusiastically celebrate *romarias,* or religious processions. In Portugal, every town and village honors its own saint on the appropriate feast day with a romaria, which ends with a fireworks display.

LESSON 2 REVIEW

Fact Follow-Up
1. In what ways are Mediterranean Europe's major holidays linked to religious celebrations?
2. To what religious denominations do most people of Mediterranean Europe belong?
3. What caused the Christian church to split into Roman Catholicism and Greek Orthodoxy?

Think These Through
4. Do differences in holidays among Mediterranean countries seem to be influenced more by national traditions or religious beliefs? Why?
5. What challenges might be faced by a non-Christian living in Mediterranean Europe?

LESSON 3 Food and Leisure

Two young women work out at their local gymnasium. One stretches her muscles, a discus clasped in her hand. The other flexes with hand weights. Of course, this scene might occur today at any of the fashionable spas or luxury resorts located along the Mediterranean coast.

These two Roman gymnasts appear in a mosaic that is 1,600 years old. A mosaic is a work of art pieced together from tile or glass. Archaeologists unearthed it while digging in Sicily.

Sport and Leisure

Two gymnasts working out 1,600 years ago is scarcely surprising. Sport has been an important part of life in the Mediterranean region for hundreds of centuries. The Greeks organized the first Olympic Games in 776 B.C.

The Mediterranean region offers a variety of ways to have fun. Most people in the Mediterranean take their vacations right at home. They appreciate the beauty of the land and enjoy local sports and leisure activities. Tourists flock to the region to join in the fun.

Imported Sports

Some of the most popular games and leisure activities have been imported into the region. Professional soccer games draw huge crowds as they do in the British Isles, Western Europe, and South America. Soccer stars are popular heroes. One of the most popular comic books in Greece—*Eric Castel*—tells the story of a soccer player.

Basketball, a game imported from the United States, has become popular in the region. Stars from colleges and universities

LESSON PREVIEW

Key Ideas
- Most sport and leisure activities reflect the special character of the region.
- Although the food produced in the Mediterranean region does not differ much among the nations, each has its own distinctive ways of preparing the food.

This Roman mosaic shows that keeping fit is not a new idea. Roman female athletes competed in sports and won palm branches. *In what sports did they compete?*

in the United States are recruited to play in Italy and Greece, sometimes for large salaries. Many city neighborhoods have basketball goals. Pickup games between neighborhood kids keep them in constant use.

Finally, United States-style theme parks are making their way into the Mediterranean. Spain will build parks such as Disneyland Paris and others in Western Europe that draw large crowds.

Mediterranean Sports

Water Sports People who enjoy water sports find the Mediterranean's climate and warm waters inviting. Many Europeans head for beaches in southern France. Beaches in the four Mediterranean countries are equally popular.

The coasts and islands of Greece offer great opportunities for all kinds of water sports—sailing, waterskiing, and windsurfing. Scuba diving is also popular, but the government strictly controls where people can dive.

Hundreds of ancient ships lie on the bottom of Greek coastal waters. To protect them, the government discourages treasure hunters. If divers find anything of value, they must report it to Greek government officials.

Bullfighting is popular in both Spain and Portugal. *How do bullfights end in each country?*

Bicycling Italy's flat regions are perfect for bicycling, and the most dedicated cyclists climb high into the mountains as well. Many young cyclists train all year for the Giro d'Italia bicycle race in the spring. The three-week race follows a course all through the country. Racers must endure southern heat as well as mountainous terrain.

Bullfighting The Spanish have given the world bullfighting. Bullfighting angers many in the United States and Europe. It is a contest between a matador (the bullfighter) and a bull that has been trained to attack. Critics are outraged by the bloody nature of the contest. The bull will certainly die and the matador is sometimes seriously injured or killed.

Bullfighting draws huge crowds in Spain and Portugal as well as in regions settled by the Spanish—Middle and South America. These fans see bullfighting as a test of the matador's courage and artistry.

The matador approaches the angry bull with cape and sword. Every time the bull charges, the matador steps aside at the last moment. After tiring the animal, the matador stabs the bull between the shoulders. When the matador kills the bull, everyone cheers and throws flowers.

Portugal's bullfighting is easier on the bull. The crowds, like those in Spain, enjoy watching the fight, but they do not expect to see the bull killed. Instead, the fight ends when the bull is subdued, or tamed, by the men in the ring.

Jai Alai In the Pyrenees, the Basque people developed the sport jai alai (HIGH lie). Jai alai means "joyous festival" in their language. The sport began as a simple kind of handball, with players hitting a ball against a wall. Now that game is much faster and more complex.

Today, jai alai players hit the ball off three walls instead of one. The game is usually played within a concrete court, and players wear long, curved baskets on their arms to return the ball quickly. Although the sport began in Spain, many of the best players move to Miami, Florida, where they can earn high salaries.

Skiing Both Spain and Italy have high mountains where snow comes early and offers fine skiing. Usually there are several weeks during the year when people in the mountains are skiing while at the same time others along the beaches are enjoying the sun and warm water.

Food

The peoples of the Mediterranean can rely on their region to provide them with an abundance of seafood, fruit, and vegetables. The meals may be simple, but the quality of Mediterranean food is excellent and healthful.

Pamplona, Spain, draws young people from all over the world who want to "run with the bulls." They run ahead of the bulls in the narrow streets of the city. *Why do you think they do that?*

◆◆◆◆ **GAMES** ◆◆◆◆
People Play

Running of the Bulls
At a festival in Pamplona, Spain, young men running with the bulls risk injury or even their lives. Many want to demonstrate to themselves and the crowds watching them that they, like matadors, have the courage to let angry bulls come close. Some save themselves by jumping into alleys or up onto balconies.

◆ ◆ ◆ ◆ ◆ ◆ ◆ ◆ ◆ ◆ ◆ ◆ ◆ ◆

Because Mediterranean afternoons can be very hot, people avoid cooking and eating at that time of the day. Instead, most Mediterranean families gather for dinner very late, to take advantage of the cool evenings.

Greece Most Greeks begin the day with a simple breakfast of coffee and a roll with honey. Greeks gather for the main meal at about 2:00 P.M. The meal begins with appetizers, followed by meat or fish and salad, topped off with a dessert of fruit and yogurt or walnuts and pastry.

Greeks sit down to dinner about 10:00 P.M. Because dinner is so late, Greeks regularly eat snacks in the early evening. These may include olives, cheeses, bread, and tidbits of lamb and fish.

EYEWITNESS TO HISTORY

Ernest Hemingway on the Italian Front

A tragic chapter in Italian history was described vividly by American novelist and short-story writer Ernest Hemingway (1899-1961). Hemingway served with the American Red Cross in Italy during World War I. His 1929 novel, A Farewell to Arms, *was based on his war experiences.*

In May 1918, while working as a reporter for the *Kansas City Star,* the young Hemingway (left) volunteered to serve as an ambulance driver for the Red Cross. He was soon shipped out to Italy and served on the Italian front, near Milan. There he volunteered to work in the Red Cross canteens, carrying special treats to the soldiers in the trenches.

Italian soldiers pose near their artillery.

Many traditional Greek dishes are popular in the United States. Perhaps you have tried *souvlaki,* meat grilled on a skewer, or the honey and nut-filled pastry called *baklava.*

Italy Italian immigrants brought many of their favorite foods with them to this country. Pasta became as much of a favorite in the United States as in Italy where it originated. Other Italian foods you may know are specialties of different regions. Salami, the spicy sausage, comes from Bologna. Parmesan cheese is made in Parma, in the North.

Spain A Spanish meal represents a delicious expression of many different cultural influences. Spain's long partnership

Greek food can be found in restaurants in many American cities. *Can you identify any of the foods that Greeks enjoy?*

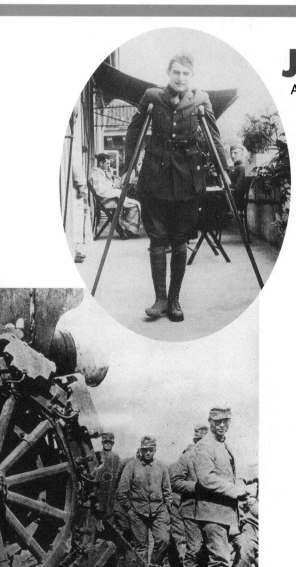

Just before Hemingway's nineteenth birthday, in July 1918, an Austrian mortar shell wounded him in the legs (left). Despite his injuries, he carried a wounded Italian soldier to safety. Then he went to the hospital for treatment of his own wounds.

A *Farewell to Arms* (right) vividly describes the battlefield. "The road here was below the level of the river bank and all along the side of the sunken road there were holes dug in the bank with infantry in them. The sun was going down.... There was one smashed bridge across the river. They were going to put over another bridge when the bombardment started...."

Society and Culture **339**

with the sea provides the half-dozen kinds of seafood that enrich a hearty stew. The saffron rice and spices come from the country's Moorish past. The tomatoes, potatoes, peppers, and even the chocolate for dessert reflects Spain's early trade with the Americas.

Breakfast and lunch in Spain tend to be light, because people save their appetites for *tapas* in the early evening and a large dinner much later. A dinner may be simple yet filling, like *tortilla de patata,* a potato omelet served cold. Spanish families particularly enjoy this dish on picnics.

Portugal Because few families in Portugal owned refrigerators and freezers, the Portuguese grew accustomed to shopping every day at the local market. There they can make their choice among the fruit and vegetables in season, the meats preserved with spices, and the fish caught that morning.

Fish from the Atlantic Ocean dry on a Portuguese beach. Fish and a dessert are the main ingredients for a Portuguese meal. *How do Portuguese and Spanish cooks prepare fish?*

With simple ingredients, Portuguese cooks create fine meals. A favorite is *caldo verde,* a delicious soup made of cabbage, broth, spiced sausage, potatoes, and onions. *Caldeirades,* or seafood stews, include a variety of fresh fish, always available in Portugal.

The Portuguese enjoy desserts, especially *arroz doce,* a cold rice pudding with eggs, sugar, and cinnamon. From the Moors, the Portuguese learned to sculpt almond paste into flowers, birds, and other decorative shapes.

LESSON 3 REVIEW

Fact Follow-Up
1. Describe the daily diet of a person living in Greece.
2. How do the foods of Mediterranean Europe reflect the long coastlines of the region?
3. Compare the popular sports of the four nations of the region.
4. Why are water sports popular?

Think These Through
5. Do you think bullfighting should be banned or encouraged? Explain.
6. Which sport of the region would you most like to see or play? Explain.
7. Of all the foods described in this lesson, which would you most like to sample? Explain why.

Demonstrating Skills in Constructive Interpersonal Relationships and Social Participation

Resolving Tensions Among Different Religions

Have you ever had an argument with a friend or a family member? How did you resolve it? Or, have you ever wanted something—more television time, a new video game, some new clothing—that your parents didn't think you should have? What did you do? In both cases, you probably thought up as many arguments as you could to support your own point of view in the conflict.

In an argument or conflict, did you ever think about the other person's point of view? Sometimes, thinking of the arguments on the opposing side can help you come up with better arguments to support your own point of view.

Sometimes, as well, if you look at the arguments for both points of view, it will be easier to resolve the conflict. By looking at arguments for both points of view, you can often find some areas on which both sides can agree.

Think of a conflict you have had or one you may have in the future. What are some arguments on both sides of the conflict? Transfer the chart (right) to a sheet of paper and use it to note arguments for both sides of the issue or conflict.

Some conflicts are both complex and serious. They may even threaten the peace and stability of societies. In Mediterranean Europe, for example, each nation has a dominant religion. In Greece, more than 98 percent of the people are Greek Orthodox. Nearly all Italians are Roman Catholic. Spain

Issue/Conflict	
Muslims	**Others**

(99 percent) and Portugal (97 percent) are also mainly Roman Catholic.

Yet there are increasing numbers of immigrants from North Africa and Southwest Asia in all four nations. These immigrants are mostly Islamic, and they generally settle in urban areas.

Already tensions are rising. Difficulties are rooted in different religious faiths. Trouble also comes from differences in social customs—the way people dress, the food they eat, or the ways they live. Sometimes conflict is tied to jobs. Immigrants may work for lower wages.

How would you try to stop the tensions from rising? After you have listed the arguments on each side, try to develop a list of *possible solutions.* For example, should nations try to stop Muslim immigration? insist on immigrants adopting their nation's customs? set aside areas where immigrants may follow their own customs? convert to the dominant religion? Compare and discuss your list with a classmate.

Chapter 17 Review

LESSON 1   Athens, Rome, and Madrid each have many structures—columns, plazas, castles, and squares—dating from their ancient pasts. These stand alongside modern buildings. The mix shows part of the character of Greece, Italy, and Spain and highlights Mediterranean culture.

LESSON 2   The Roman Catholic Church and Greek Orthodox Church (part of the Eastern Orthodox Church) were once part of a single church. They split away from each other long ago. Since the split they have developed different beliefs and practices.

LESSON 3   Sport, leisure activities, and unique styles of preparing food help identify the Mediterranean as a distinctive European region. The four large nations in the region are different from one another. Yet their cultural characteristics identify them as countries having much in common.

FACT FOLLOW-UP

1. What are the national capitals of Mediterranean Europe? Why are their locations important?
2. Which national capital has most religious importance?
3. What are the two dominant religions in Mediterranean Europe?
4. What are some cultural characteristics of Madrid?

5. Compare popular foods in Spain and Greece.
6. What is the most popular sport of the region?
7. Compare religious observances in Italy and Greece.
8. How did Picasso's *Guernica* become a famous modern painting?
9. What is the subject of the novel *A Farewell to Arms*? Who was the American who wrote this famous novel?
10. What are some special rites and festivals of the Roman Catholic Church in Mediterranean Europe?
11. Compare Greek and Italian Christmas customs.
12. How do the physical characteristics of the region influence eating habits in Mediterranean Europe?
13. How do the large cities of Mediterranean Europe deal with problems of pollution?
14. What are some differences between older and newer parts of the city in Athens and Rome?

THINK THESE THROUGH

15. Why do you think people of Mediterranean Europe eat and rest when they do?
16. Why do people in nations so close to each other celebrate religious holidays so differently? Give examples.
17. Which large city in Mediterranean Europe do you think is most like a large city in the United States? Explain.
18. Imagine that you could taste foods from any one nation in Mediterranean Europe.

Which nation's foods would you choose? Explain why.

19. What aspect of American sports do you think a visitor from Mediterranean Europe would find most unusual? Explain why.

20. Which do you think is more important in explaining the way of life in Madrid: physical or cultural characteristics of place? Explain.

21. In which religious observance, festival, or sporting activity of Mediterranean Europe would you most like to participate? Explain your choice.

22. Imagine that you have the opportunity to spend a year in one of the cities described in Chapter 17. Which city would you choose? Explain your choice.

SHARPENING SKILLS

23. Choose a local controversy or conflict in your own community. Use the chart to lay out arguments for both sides of the local conflict. Plan a debate.

24. How can some conflicts or controversies have more than two sides? Explain your answer.

25. Do you think a chart like the one in the skill lesson is more useful for resolving personal or social conflicts? Explain your answer.

26. How would you improve the chart?

PLACE LOCATION

Use the letters in the map key to locate the following places. Name the nations as you locate them.

27. The nation in Mediterranean Europe where the dominant church split away from the Catholic Church centuries ago. What is the name of this church?

28. The country and city in which the headquarters of the Catholic Church is located. What is the name of this church's headquarters?

29. The peninsula that was once mostly under Muslim control and where Islam exercised considerable influence. Name and describe the relative location of the nations that now occupy this peninsula. What church is now predominant in these nations?

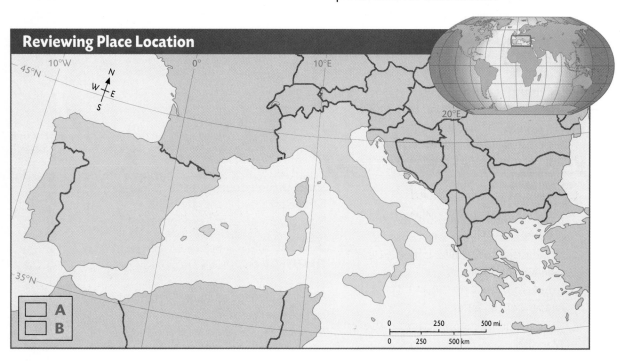

Reviewing Place Location

The Region of Eastern Europe

Throughout Eastern Europe brightly costumed dancers step lively to toe-tapping music. The dances and music are old, part of each nation's traditions.

Folk music is considered to be different from classical music in the United States. In Eastern Europe the two musical forms have often been combined. Many of the most famous classical composers have incorporated folk music into their compositions. Classical composers have been patriots. They have joined folk musicians in expressing pride in their homelands.

UNIT PREVIEW

CHAPTER 18
People and Lands
Eastern Europe is notable for the diversity of its people. The land is also diverse, and the climate changes from moderate Marine West Coast to harsh Humid Continental.

CHAPTER 19
People and Environment
The Agricultural and Industrial Revolutions reached Eastern Europe late. Urban life and industrial pollution have mostly come in the twentieth century.

CHAPTER 20
Government and Economy
Communist dictatorships and the Soviet Union's domination of Eastern Europe collapsed in the late 1980s. New governments and economies have been formed.

CHAPTER 21
Society and Culture
The diversity—and antiquity—of Eastern Europe is reflected in three major cities, religions, and variety in food and sport.

Hungarian State Folk Ensemble

CHAPTER 18

People and Lands

In 1972, while digging a deep ditch near Varna, Bulgaria, a workman noticed a shiny gleam in the mud. Looking closer, he saw an object that looked like a human figure.

Archaeologists at the National Museum told the workman that he had found a statue (left) of a woman. People living in Bulgaria 5,000 years ago carved the figure and covered it with gold! Here was proof that people began communities in Eastern Europe long ago.

Bulgaria and other Eastern European nations today are more than countries with ancient roots. They are also nations struggling to recover from their recent domination by the Soviet Union. Communist rulers, for example, tried to stamp out religion. As the Cold War ended, monasteries (below) and churches of the Eastern Orthodox faith have been rebuilt and reopened.

CHAPTER PREVIEW

LESSON 1
People of Eastern Europe
Eastern Europe's people are diverse. This diversity is an obstacle to cooperation.

LESSON 2
Lands of Eastern Europe
The region's geography has contributed to rivalry among ethnic groups. Mountains have isolated groups. Eastern Europe's access to the open seas is limited.

LESSON 3
Climate and Vegetation
Unlike Western Europe's moderate marine climate, most of Eastern Europe has a harsher continental climate.

Eastern Europe–Political/Physical

NORWAY

SWEDEN

DENMARK

North Sea

GERMANY

Baltic Sea

ESTONIA
Tallinn

Riga
LATVIA

LITHUANIA
Vilnius

RUSSIA

RUSSIA

Minsk
BELARUS

NORTHERN EUROPEAN PLAIN

Oder R.

Warsaw

Vistula R.

POLAND

Kiev

Dnepr R.

Prague
CZECH REPUBLIC

CARPATHIAN MTS.

Bratislava
SLOVAKIA

UKRAINE

Dniester R.

MOLDOVA

SWITZERLAND

AUSTRIA

Budapest

HUNGARY

Chisinau

SLOVENIA
Ljubljana

CROATIA
Zagreb

ROMANIA

Bucharest

Black Sea

BOSNIA -
HERZEGOVINA

Belgrade

Danube R.

Adriatic Sea

Sarajevo

DINARIC ALPS

SERBIA-
MONTENEGRO

BALKAN MTS.

BULGARIA

ITALY

Skopje
Sofia

Tiranë

BALKAN PENINSULA

TURKEY

ALBANIA   MACEDONIA

10°E   20°E   30°E   40°E

50°N

40°N

N
W   E
S

| 0 | 250 | 500 mi. |
| 0 | 250 | 500 km |

Land Elevation

Feet		Meters
13,333		4000
6,667		2000
3,333		1000
1,667		500
667		200
0		0

Nations of Eastern Europe

Estonia	Czech Republic	Croatia*
Latvia	Slovakia	Bosnia-Herzegovina*
Lithuania	Hungary	Serbia-Montenegro*
Belarus	Romania*	Bulgaria*
Poland	Moldova	Albania*
Ukraine	Slovenia*	Macedonia*

These nations are often called "the Balkans."

People of Eastern Europe

LESSON PREVIEW

Key Ideas
- Eastern Europe's ethnic diversity comes from many different people who settled the region.
- The region's languages also reflect the people's diversity.
- Yugoslavia's breakup and warfare reflect the tragic results of the region's diversity.

Key Terms
Balkans, balkanize

Scientists continue to find evidence of the antiquity, or great age, of Eastern Europe's societies. Ask Dr. Peter Veres of the Hungarian Ethnographical Institute about the origin of his Hungarian ancestors. He points to a map.

"Here is the place, just east of the Urals (yoor ulls), in western Siberia," he explains. "The region was then a pine forest, the people were hunters and fishermen.

"Between the twelfth and tenth centuries B.C. (about 3,000 years ago) a change in climate took place in western Siberia. The groundwater began to rise, the area became a sort of marsh, and the people had to move."

The ancestors of the Hungarians moved south, abandoned their lives as hunters and fishermen, and became nomadic shepherds. Over a period of 2,000 years, they moved west, arriving in Hungary in the tenth century A.D.

Hungarians honor their ancestors by wearing traditional clothing. *From where did ancestors of many Hungarians come?*

A Heritage of Diversity

The story of movement to Hungary is similar to the stories of other Eastern European nations. The ancestors of almost everyone living in the region today came from somewhere else.

As ancient land and climate changed, people migrated to more comfortable places. Today, Eastern Europe's 18 nations are filled with the descendants of such migrants. Magyars, Slavs, Balts, Bulgars, and even Romans are the ancestors of Eastern Europeans.

Magyars The Hungarians' ancestors who moved from Siberia were called Magyars. Their closest European relatives—the Estonians, Finns, and Lapps—came from the same part of Siberia. All speak languages similar to Hungarian.

Slavs Slavic groups make up the heritage of some East Europeans. Some 5,000 years ago the Slavs were concentrated in an area that is now a part of today's Ukraine (yoo·CRANE) and Poland. From there, some people migrated eastward into Russia. Others moved westward to places we now know as Poland, the Czech (CHECK) Republic, Slovakia (slow·VAH·kee·uh), and the Balkans (see chart and map, page 347).

Balts, Bulgars, and Romans Native Latvians and Lithuanians, who live along the Baltic Sea, trace their origins to ancient people known as the Balts. Another nomadic group called the Bulgars settled near the Black Sea about 1,300 years ago, where they intermarried with Slavic people. They are the ancestors of modern-day Bulgarians.

Modern-day Romania's population comes from a variety of ethnic groups. About 2,000 years ago the country was occupied by forces of the Roman Empire. The occupation did not last long, but Roman customs became a dominant force uniting a diverse people.

Other conquerors—Turks, Germans, and Russians—have come and gone. Each has left behind people, customs, and religions.

Weddings sometimes show the diversity of Eastern Europe's people. The bride and groom wear traditional clothing at their wedding in Slovakia. *What would such costumes look like from your family?*

♦♦♦♦ GAMES ♦♦♦♦
People Play

Voice Disguise In a country with limited resources, young people play traditional games that cost little money.

In Poland a popular game for six or more people uses voice disguise. A person in the center of a circle is blindfolded while everyone moves around singing. Then they stop. The person in the center points to the outer ring and tries to guess the identity of the singer. That person disguises his or her voice to try to keep the person in the center from guessing the correct name.

♦♦♦♦♦♦♦♦♦♦♦♦♦♦♦♦

Ethnic Differences Remain

What would **YOU** do?

Early in the 1990s, Bosnian Serbs began heavy artillery attacks on Sarajevo. In the middle of this terrible destruction, a group of young Serbs and Muslims—all studying to be actors and actresses—decided to stage theatrical productions.

They wanted to provide some entertainment for Sarajevo's people. Even more, they wanted to show that Serbs and Muslims could work together in peace.

Would you have attended such performances? Why or why not?

Centuries of living in Eastern Europe have not brought these diverse people together. Many years ago large numbers of Jews had migrated to Eastern Europe. Prior to World War II, Jewish people made up a substantial part of the region's population. As you have read, Germany's Nazi rulers killed millions of Jews throughout the European countries. The slaughter of Jews was especially heavy in Eastern Europe.

German troops also rounded up and killed hundreds of thousands of Eastern Europeans known as Gypsies. These people had migrated to Europe from northern India. Wherever they settled, Gypsies remained fiercely independent. They built their own villages and roamed through the countryside, earning their living as musicians, dancers, metalworkers, and horse traders. Gypsies are still to be found in the region, but their numbers are fewer.

Today, life in the region continues to multiply differences. Look at the map labeled "Eastern Europe—Major Languages" on page 409. It shows that most people in the region speak a Slavic (SLAH·vick) language.

The Slavic language is not a unifying force, though, because of its varying forms. The Slavic spoken by Polish people differs from the language spoken by the Czechs. The Czech language in turn is different from the language of neighboring Slovakia.

Differences among Eastern Europeans extend into other

Gypsies, a group originally from northern India, kept to themselves after moving to Europe hundreds of years ago. *What happened to Gypsies during World War II?*

Eastern Europe–Ethnic Groupings

ESTONIA
LATVIA
LITHUANIA
RUSSIA
BELARUS
POLAND
CZECH REPUBLIC
SLOVAKIA
HUNGARY
SLOVENIA
CROATIA
BOSNIA-HERZEGOVINA
SERBIA-MONTENEGRO
MACEDONIA
ALBANIA
ROMANIA
MOLDOVA
UKRAINE
BULGARIA

Baltic Sea
Adriatic Sea
Black Sea

0   100   200 mi.
0   100   200 km

Legend:
- Magyars
- Albanians
- Romanians
- Turks
- Germans
- Estonians
- Poles
- Czechs
- Slovaks
- Slovenes
- Croats
- Muslims
- Bulgars
- Macedonians
- Serbs and Montenegrins
- Latvians
- Lithuanians
- Byelo-Ruthenians
- Ukrainians
- Russians
- No group over 50%

Place Many different ethnic groups live in Eastern Europe. *What areas within the region have the most diversity? the least? How has the amount of diversity affected those areas?*

areas of daily life. People embrace a variety of religious faiths—Protestant Christianity, Roman Catholicism, Eastern Orthodoxy, Judaism, and Islam.

Every ethnic group celebrates its own history and customs. Many of these ethnic groups want to have nations of their own. This determination to build nations as homes for different ethnic groups dates back to the 1800s. Eastern European people resisted interference from the great European powers. They worked to have their own nations.

As you have read, a Serbian nationalist, Gavrilo Princip, assassinated the heir to the Austrian-Hungarian throne in 1914 and touched off World War I. Princip had no intention of starting a great war. He acted to keep Austria-Hungary out of his people's affairs.

The Hungarians wanted an end to Soviet control of their country. They tried, but failed, to force Soviet forces out of their country in the 1950s.

Sarajevo, Bosnia-Herzegovina, is a city of many places of worship, including the Grand Mosque (above, with tower). *What are other examples of religious diversity in Eastern Europe?*

WORD ORIGINS

Balkan is a Turkish word meaning "mountains." It referred originally to a specific mountain chain that is now called the Balkans. The word eventually became the name for the entire mountainous area of the southern part of Eastern Europe between the Adriatic Sea and the Black Sea.

The Balkans

Opposition to the big powers has been only one source of conflict in Eastern Europe. In many places different ethnic groups have been thrown together. This is especially true in the mountainous southern part of Eastern Europe between the Adriatic Sea and the Black Sea (see map, page 347) called the **Balkans** (BAWL·kuns). Sometimes Christians and Muslims live in the same towns. Sometimes one group occupies an area that is surrounded on all sides by another.

Living together has not made these groups good neighbors. They have developed conflicting ambitions, jealousies, and even deep hatreds. The people of the Balkans have often fought.

This kind of fighting has added a new word to the English language—**balkanize**. It means "to break up into small, mutually hostile political units." During the 1990s, Yugoslavia (yoo·goh·SLAH·vih·uh) demonstrated this word with warfare that tore apart the country.

L E S S O N 1 R E V I E W

Fact Follow-Up
1. To which five groups can most people of Eastern Europe trace their ancestry?
2. In which nations do Slavs now live?
3. To which groups do the Latvians and Lithuanians trace their ancestry?
4. To which group do Hungarians trace their ancestry?

Think These Through
5. How have the physical characteristics of place influenced people of Eastern Europe?
6. What influences have united people of Eastern Europe? What has separated them?
7. Apply the geographic theme of movement to the settlement of Eastern Europe.

Lands of Eastern Europe

Long ago, the Slavic people settling in one place were much like those settling in another. Differences developed over time as people settled in the mountainous regions of Eastern Europe.

These settlements developed their traditions and laws without much influence from beyond the mountains. Later, invaders and missionaries brought new religions and ideas to the region.

Slavs in some places became Roman Catholic. Other settlements took up the Eastern Orthodox faith. The Turks arrived in the 1500s from the Muslim-dominated Ottoman Empire and converted other settlements.

Barriers in the Balkan Peninsula

These settlements did not exchange ideas with each other, but through time became firmly tied to their own way of doing things. The barriers to these settlements' movement and

LESSON PREVIEW

Key Ideas
- Eastern Europe's geography has strengthened the people's diversity.
- The region has two prominent landforms. The North has the Northern European Plain. The South has rugged mountains as well as plains.
- Eastern Europe has limited access to the world's oceans.

Makarska, Croatia, is located both in the Dinaric Alps and on the Adriatic Sea. *How does such a location affect movement in the town and throughout the region?*

exchange of ideas in the Balkan Peninsula came in the form of mountains.

The wild and rugged Dinaric Alps run from the Northwest toward the South. They lie near the coast of the Adriatic (ay·dree·AT·ick) Sea. Few people lived in these mountains, but some people lived along the narrow coastal plain. Both groups were separated from the Danube River valley.

Farther east in Bulgaria, the Balkan Mountains stretch toward the Black Sea. That chain isolates the Balkan Peninsula from Greece and the Mediterranean Sea.

Land along the Danube River contained the best farmland and attracted settlers from throughout Eastern Europe and today's Russia. When they came, each group brought their own

The Danube

A classical tune called the "Blue Danube Waltz," by Johann Strauss, pays tribute to an important river in Eastern Europe. Starting in the Black Forest of Germany, two swiftly flowing streams, the Breg and the Brigach, form the Danube, which wanders 1,770 miles (2,850 km) through Eastern Europe.

The Danube flows by a Balkan castle

People of the countryside and the cities watch the Danube slide by. Slavs and Magyars once sailed on it as they settled southeastern Europe. Later forces, such as Roman legions, used it as an invasion highway. Downstream, below Belgrade, you can see where the Roman Emperor Trajan had troops build a road in the cliffs to reach what is today Romania.

The Danube at Budapest, Hungary

particular ideas and beliefs. Conflicts grew as more people settled in the peninsula.

Other Mountain Barriers

Just as in the Balkan Peninsula, geographical barriers throughout Eastern Europe isolated groups of people and contributed to differences among them. Farther north, the Carpathian (kar·PAY·the·uhn) Mountains form part of the frontier between Romania (roh·MAIN·ee·yuh) and Ukraine. These two countries are inhabited by different ethnic groups.

The Tatras Mountains and the western portions of the Carpathians divide Poland, the Czech Republic, and Slovakia.

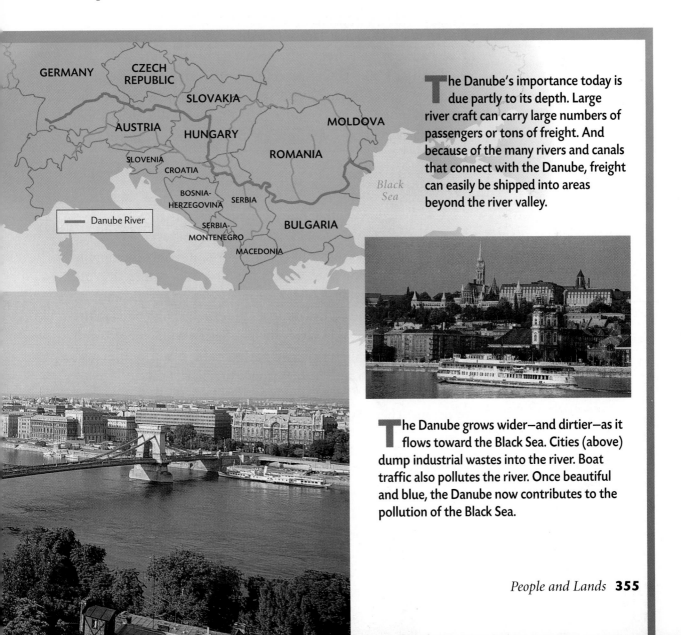

The Danube's importance today is due partly to its depth. Large river craft can carry large numbers of passengers or tons of freight. And because of the many rivers and canals that connect with the Danube, freight can easily be shipped into areas beyond the river valley.

The Danube grows wider—and dirtier—as it flows toward the Black Sea. Cities (above) dump industrial wastes into the river. Boat traffic also pollutes the river. Once beautiful and blue, the Danube now contributes to the pollution of the Black Sea.

The fertile Northern European Plain in Poland attracted people who built farms and cities. *What other parts of Eastern Europe contain the plains?*

There the mountains kept Slavic-speaking groups apart, contributing to the distinct forms of that language spoken in those countries.

The Northern European Plain

The Northern European Plain stretches through Western Europe, Poland, the Baltic states, and Belarus (bella·ROOS). It swings southward into Ukraine.

The good farmland of the plain drew a large population of early settlers, especially to Poland and Ukraine. Farms, towns, and then cities grew in river valleys. Eventually, the wealth of the area led to competition among neighboring peoples. Armies also could move easily over the plain's flat lands. For these reasons this portion of Eastern Europe has frequently been a battleground.

South of the plain lies another flat and fertile area in Hungary. Stretching for 20,000 square miles (52,000 sq km) and irrigated by rivers, the Hungarian Plain covers the eastern half of Hungary. It is one of Europe's richest farming regions.

Limited Access to Oceans

Compared with other European regions, Eastern Europe has limited access to the world's oceans (see map, page 347). Some Eastern Europe nations can reach the Atlantic only by moving through connecting seas. Others rely on rivers connecting the region's interior with seas and ocean.

Poland and the Baltic countries border the Baltic Sea. To the south, Croatia, Bosnia-Herzegovina, Serbia-Montenegro, and Albania have small ports on the Adriatic Sea. To the east, Ukraine, Bulgaria, and Romania face the Black Sea.

Other Eastern European countries have no direct links to seas or oceans. These countries conduct trade using railways or rivers.

Rivers

Eastern Europe does not have as many rivers and canals as Western Europe. Nevertheless, modern engineering has opened several rivers in the region to freight and passenger vessels.

The Danube River rivals the Rhine River as a transportation artery. The Danube flows through nearly all of Eastern Europe on its path to the Black Sea. Some of the region's largest cities grew because the river made them inland ports.

The interior areas of Belarus, Ukraine, and Moldova (moal·DOH·vuh) gain access to the Black Sea by the Dnepr (duh·NYEPP·er) River (formerly spelled Dnieper). This river, which flows out of Russia, is the second longest in Europe. Large dams built along the river have created lakes that provide water for generating electricity. The river is deep enough for freight-carrying barges. Navigation is possible along most of its 1,420-mile (2,286-km) length.

Poland has the Vistula (VIST·yullah) River. Shorter than either the Danube or Dnepr, it connects Warsaw to world trade routes. The Vistula flows north and empties into the Baltic Sea. Canals connect the Vistula with the Oder River on Poland's western border and the Dnepr River to the east.

In contrast with the British Isles and Western Europe, Eastern Europe's inland waterways are usually blocked by ice for two or three months every year. When spring comes and ice thaws, the rivers and canals fill with boats, barges, and ships that connect Eastern Europe with the world.

The Dnepr River water power plant produces hydroelectricity for Ukraine. *What other benefits does the river provide Eastern Europe?*

LESSON 2 REVIEW

Fact Follow-Up
1. What are the most important landforms in Eastern Europe? Where are they?
2. What coastal waters allow people of Eastern Europe to trade with other world areas?
3. Explain the importance of the Danube River to the region.
4. What areas are served by the Vistula and Dnepr Rivers?

Think These Through
5. How has Eastern Europe been influenced by the several mountain ranges in the region?
6. How has Eastern Europe been influenced by the Northern European Plain and Hungarian Plain?
7. What would happen to Eastern Europe's economy if the Danube River were to be blocked by an earthquake?

Climate and Vegetation

LESSON PREVIEW

Key Ideas

- Although Eastern Europe has a variety of climates, most of the region has a harsh continental climate.
- Winds blowing off the Atlantic Ocean drop much of their moisture before reaching Eastern Europe. The region is drier than lands to the west.
- Vegetation varies according to elevation and climate.

Andrzej Krawiec is a forester in the Tatras Mountains south of Kraków, Poland. "I first went to the mountains with my father when I was three years old and cannot remember a time when I did not love them or want to work in them," he says. "The mountains are like a friend to me. I have special places where I like to sit, and if I feel a bit depressed, I go there and talk to them just as I would to a friend."

Climates: The Baltic to the Black Sea

The Tatras Mountains run along Poland's border with Slovakia. They are about 350 miles (564 km) south of the Baltic Sea. Andrzej Krawiec can ski there on winter weekends, but if he lived farther north on the Baltic coast, he would not have as many chances to enjoy the sport.

Snow falls in the Tatras Mountains, partly because the altitude causes temperatures to drop. The mountains also are a long distance from the moderating influence of the sea.

This pattern is typical of Eastern Europe. Areas facing warm waters enjoy moderate climates. Other areas—some of them only short distances away—face greater temperature extremes. Winters become colder as you move away from the Baltic.

Yalta, Ukraine, on the Black Sea is a resort city. Its warm waters attract visitors from throughout Eastern Europe. Check the map on page 359. *What is the climate of southern Ukraine?*

Eastern Europe–Climate Regions

Legend:
- Mediterranean
- Humid Subtropical
- Marine West Coast
- Humid Continental
- Semiarid

Human-Environmental Interaction Location near the sea and elevation influence the climates of Eastern Europe. *What kinds of climates do the countries inland from the Adriatic Sea experience? How do those climates affect peoples' lives?*

Southwestern Poland is much colder in the winter than countries farther north in Northern Europe.

The coasts of Denmark, Germany, and Poland are on the northern edge of Europe. Yet winds blowing over the warm North Atlantic Drift keep winter temperatures from falling too far. In fact, winter temperatures in northern Poland average about 26° F (–3.3° C). Average summer temperatures are in the 70s.

Along the Adriatic Sea, Croatia, Bosnia-Herzegovina, and

Albania experience a Mediterranean climate. As in Greece, Italy, Spain, and Portugal, the summers are dry and warm, the winters cool and rainy. Nearby Slovenia enjoys a humid subtropical climate (see map, page 359). Southern Ukraine, near the Black Sea, has warm winters and hot summers.

Inland, Eastern Europe's climate changes. The farther you go eastward from the warm sea winds, the harsher the climate becomes. In Romania, for example, the climate is humid continental. Summer temperatures average 66°F (19°C). Winters are cold, averaging 21°F (−6°C).

Except for Eastern Europe's western edges, these summer and winter extremes are typical. Eastern Europe is where Europe's climate begins to change. The moderate climate of Western Europe and the British Isles fades.

LIVING IN LATVIA

Winter Tales

Josip lives in the northern Baltic country of Latvia in a small town outside Riga. The town's location in a far northern latitude means the sun rises late and sets early in winter. In summer, light stays so long that it is called the "midnight sun."

Josip hangs out with friends on long summer evenings after chores. Riga is a bus ride of an hour and a half away. Nearby are lakes and forests which offer swimming, fishing, and hiking. Twenty hours of daylight leave time for family chores and lots of fun. Josip enjoys the national parks and exploring the old castles within hiking distance.

Winter darkness slows everything down. Fewer tourists come riding through town. Snows make travel more difficult. Josip's favorite winter evening activity is listening to his grandfather tell stories about local legends. Josip likes the story of the Werewolf Pine, a tree that is said to change a person into a werewolf if that person can crawl through its roots saying the right words on a night with a full moon.

Riga, Latvia

Rainfall and Vegetation

The winds blowing off the Atlantic Ocean reach only part of Eastern Europe. Before moving too far eastward, the winds drop most of their moisture. So Eastern Europe is drier than the British Isles and Western Europe. Much of the remaining moisture is dropped when the winds hit the Carpathian Mountains. The Hungarian Plain receives little rain.

Long ago, Eastern Europe's plains and mountains were covered by forests. Settlers cut the trees from lands that they could farm. Today, nearly half of the region has been cleared for planting crops or grazing animals. In recent years, these once rural areas have grown into cities.

Forests still grow in the Baltic states. Nearly one half of Latvia is forested. About one quarter of Lithuania is covered with evergreen woodlands.

Vegetation elsewhere in the region varies depending on elevation. Beech, oak, and pine trees thrive on the plains and lower mountain slopes. Higher in the mountains, grow pine and spruce trees. Ferns, nettles, and cow parsley cover the clearings. Above the timberline, Alpine flowers bloom, including gentians, saxifrage, and edelweiss. On the high peaks, only lichens and mosses can grow in the cold and rocky soil.

A forest in Poland includes pine trees and grasslands of the Northern European Plain. Alpine flowers, such as gentian, grow in highland areas of Eastern Europe. *What other kinds of vegetation does the region contain?*

LESSON 3 REVIEW

Fact Follow-Up
1. Describe the climate of the Baltic nations.
2. How does location near water influence climate in northern areas of Eastern Europe? How does elevation influence climate there?
3. How does location near water influence climates in southern areas of Eastern Europe? Describe the influence of elevation there.
4. Describe vegetation patterns in the southern part of Eastern Europe.

Think These Through
5. Which is more important for nations in northern areas of Eastern Europe: location relative to water or elevation? Explain.
6. Which theme of geography is more essential for understanding Eastern Europe: relative location or the physical characteristics of place? Explain.

*Acquiring Information from a Variety of Sources
and Demonstrating Skills in Constructive Interpersonal
Relationships and Social Participation*

Learning About Boundaries from Maps

You have already learned much about how the physical characteristics of places affect the lives of people who inhabit them. You have seen that physical barriers such as mountains can help unite people living behind those barriers and set them apart from outsiders. Barriers within nations—deserts, mountains, and large bodies of water—can threaten national unity.

As you have read, drawing boundaries in the Balkans has been especially difficult. Many Balkan nations have high mountain

barriers inside them. Such barriers make working together difficult. Where can boundaries be drawn so that people in the same nation are not divided from one another?

You have also learned that several ethnic and religious groups inhabiting the same geographic area sometimes come into conflict. Differences among Catholics, Muslims, Protestants, and Jews have caused persecution and even wars. In this chapter you have studied the ways ethnic tensions in Eastern Europe have divided people. Where can

The Western Balkans—Political/Physical

boundaries be drawn that will not put rival ethnic groups in the same nation?

Look at the map on page 362 that shows both political and physical features of the Western Balkans. Remember that physical features such as mountains, rivers, and seas have often divided people in the past. Examine the map carefully. Note both physical features and political boundaries. Now, make two lists of the nations shown on the map. Label one list "Likely to Remain United." Label the other "Unlikely to Remain United."

Once you have placed all the nations on one list or the other, compare your lists with a classmate's. Discuss which nations are more likely to remain united and which are likely to fall apart *based just on their physical characteristics.* Save your lists.

Next, look at the map below that shows ethnic groups living in the same areas. Which of these nations have the greatest variety of ethnic groups? Which areas shown on the map appear to have the most united population? Which ethnic groups in the nations shown on the map seem most and least likely to get along with each other?

Now, reexamine the lists you made earlier of nations likely to remain united because of physical characteristics. Beside the name of each nation listed, write the names of the ethnic groups living in that nation.

Now consider the variety of ethnic groups living in each of these nations. Do you think you need to revise your earlier lists? Make any revisions you want to, and compare your lists with a classmate's lists. Do ethnic groupings have a stronger influence than physical characteristics on a country's unity?

The Western Balkans—Ethnic Groupings

Legend:
- Slovenes
- Croats
- Muslims
- Macedonians
- Serbs and Montenegrins
- Magyars
- Albanians
- No group over 50%

Chapter 18 Review

TIME FOR TERMS

Balkans   balkanize

FACT FOLLOW-UP

1. What are the largest nations of Eastern Europe? What are the smallest?
2. What nations share the Northern European Plain?
3. What nations border the Danube River?
4. What nations are Slavic in origin?

5. How do religious beliefs both unite and separate peoples of Eastern Europe?
6. How do nations of Eastern Europe gain access to international waterways?
7. Describe major landforms of Eastern Europe.
8. Through which nations does the Dnepr River flow?
9. What are some advantages the Baltic Sea gives nations of Eastern Europe?
10. How does elevation influence the climate and vegetation of southern Eastern Europe?

THINK THESE THROUGH

11. What is the greatest force for unity among the people of Eastern Europe? Explain why.
12. How would closing the Danube River affect Eastern Europe?
13. Which region offers greater stability to its people: the Baltic nations or the Balkan nations? Explain why.
14. Which theme of geography is more important in analyzing Eastern Europe: movement or relative location? Explain.
15. If you could visit one nation of Eastern Europe, which would you visit? Explain why.

SHARPENING SKILLS

16. In what other regions of Europe do the physical characteristics of place make it difficult to unite nations?
17. In what other regions of Europe do the cultural characteristics of place make it difficult to unite nations?
18. How can technology help unite different ethnic groups?

19. What are some benefits of ethnic diversity, and what are some costs? Explain your answer.
20. Which is more important in uniting a nation: physical geography or a homogeneous population? Explain your answer.

PLACE LOCATION

Use the letters on the map to locate and name the following places in Eastern Europe:

21. the nations whose borders run entirely or partly along the Carpathian Mountains.
22. the seas that give Eastern European nations access to the world's oceans.
23. the Danube River.
24. the nations with fertile soil provided by the Northern European Plain.
25. the Balkan nation settled by Magyars—people related to Estonians and Finns—rather than Slavs.
26. the nations along the Adriatic Sea and Black Sea with a Mediterranean climate.

Reviewing Place Location

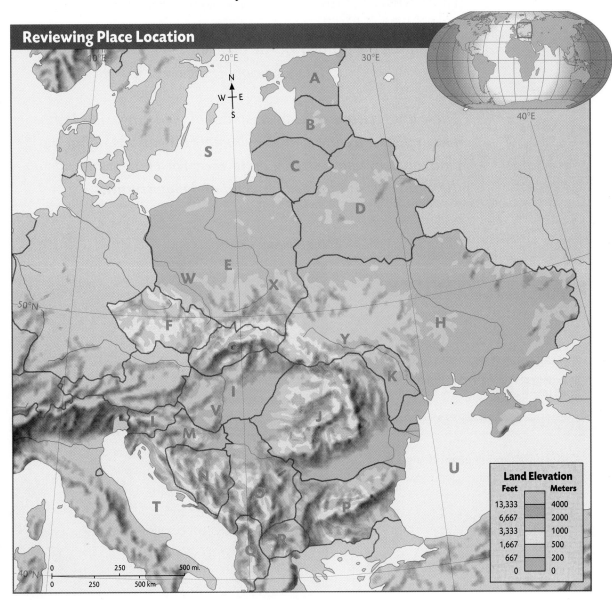

Land Elevation

Feet		Meters
13,333		4000
6,667		2000
3,333		1000
1,667		500
667		200
0		0

People and Environment

Down there, in the sea-flat regions of the Great Plain
That's where I come from, that is my world;
My eagle's soul is liberated from its prison,
When I see the infinity of the plains.

Sándor Petofi, Hungary (1823-1849)

These lines celebrate the open spaces of the Hungarian Plain. They reflect a feeling shared by many Hungarians—that the plain and sky above stretch on forever. For Hungarians, life on the plain offers unlimited freedom and opportunities.

The Hungarian Plain

CHAPTER PREVIEW

LESSON 1
Before the Coming of Industry
Human-environmental interaction changed slowly. Eastern Europe was late in experiencing the Agricultural and Industrial Revolutions.

LESSON 2
Industrialization in Eastern Europe
Cold War tensions brought changes in farming and introduced industry.

LESSON 3
Environmental Impacts of Industry
Industrialization has brought urbanization and serious pollution.

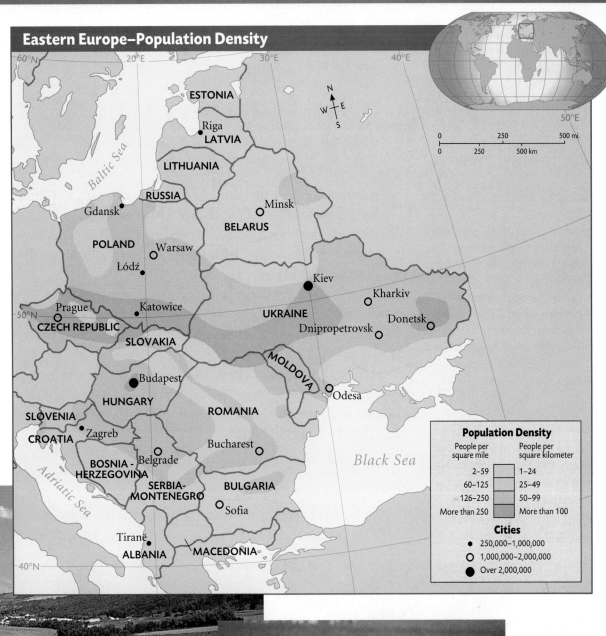

Eastern Europe–Population Density

ESTONIA

Riga
LATVIA

LITHUANIA

RUSSIA

Baltic Sea

Gdansk

Minsk

BELARUS

POLAND
Warsaw

Łódź

Kiev

Kharkiv

Prague
CZECH REPUBLIC
Katowice
UKRAINE
Donetsk
Dnipropetrovsk

SLOVAKIA

MOLDOVA

Budapest
Odesa

HUNGARY

SLOVENIA
Zagreb
ROMANIA

CROATIA
Bucharest
Black Sea

BOSNIA -
HERZEGOVINA
Belgrade

Adriatic Sea

SERBIA-
MONTENEGRO
BULGARIA

Sofia

Tiranë
ALBANIA
MACEDONIA

Population Density

People per square mile	People per square kilometer
2–59	1–24
60–125	25–49
126–250	50–99
More than 250	More than 100

Cities

- 250,000–1,000,000
- ○ 1,000,000–2,000,000
- ● Over 2,000,000

0   250   500 mi.
0   250   500 km

60°N   20°E   30°E   40°E
50°E
50°N
40°N

Hungarian cowboys

Before the Coming of Industry

LESSON PREVIEW

Key Ideas
- Farming with simple tools and some trade were the ways that early Eastern European settlers made their living.
- Eastern Europe's peasant farmers—called serfs—had fewer freedoms than those in the West.
- The Agricultural Revolution did not reach Eastern Europe.

In Hungary, as in the United States, cowboys on horseback are people of the plains. Hungarian cowboys do not lasso their livestock as cowboys do in the Americas. They snap their long-handled whips with sharp, cracking sounds as they drive thundering herds.

Hungarian cowboys dress in loose-fitting clothes well suited to their work herding cattle. Their vests and boots are carefully decorated. Traditional horsemen's broad-brimmed hats protect them from the sun.

Difficult, dangerous work marks the lives of Hungarian cowboys. They are admired, even envied, as cowboys in our country are. Perhaps that is because they enjoy the freedom of living on the endless plains.

Farming

Until recent years, most Eastern Europeans lived close to the land. Their region did not change as the British Isles, Norden,

Farmers sold crops from their wagons in city markets such as this chicken market in Bucharest, Romania. *How did living in the Danube River valley influence this way of life?*

and Western Europe did. Explorers from Eastern Europe did not venture into the world's oceans and claim foreign lands. There were no Agricultural or Industrial Revolutions in the eighteenth or nineteenth centuries. Farming remained the main economic activity. In every kind of geographical setting, most people in the region farmed.

The ancestors of modern-day Eastern Europeans first settled in the South, where mountains protected them from invaders. There, in the warm, dry soil of the Balkans, they planted grains from the Middle East.

Some settlers moved farther north and settled in the Hungarian Plain and the Danube Basin. The fertile land of the plains encouraged farming. The rolling hills and lower mountain slopes allowed for grazing.

Farming and herding also developed in the Baltic countries. Because of their location on the sea, the Baltic peoples also came to depend on fishing as a source of food.

The Northern European Plain was the last region to be settled by the ancestors of the Eastern Europeans. There they discovered forests which they cleared for farming and grazing. In time, the settlers found that hardy grains—such as wheat, barley, and rye—grew well in this region.

Amber was traded in Eastern European ports on the Baltic Sea and inland rivers. *What did Eastern Europeans trade for amber and other fine goods?*

Trade

Towns and cities did grow in Eastern Europe, because merchants and craftsmen settled where they could trade. Merchants on the Northern European Plain, especially those in Poland, traded in Western Europe. They exchanged farm products for goods not available in Eastern Europe.

Their location on the Baltic Sea or on rivers that emptied into the Baltic—the Vistula, Oder, and Elbe—helped northerners ship grain and other bulky products. Before railways or good highways, heavy freight could not be moved more than a few miles, except by water.

Medieval trade routes (see map, page 131) crossed Eastern Europe, connecting much of the region with the rest of Europe and Asia. Small items that brought high prices could be shipped overland.

For several centuries, Estonian craftspeople led Europe in the fashioning of fine metalwork. They drew their materials from Eastern Europe's rich deposits of copper and iron.

Arabs, Scandinavians, Greeks, and Romans paid high prices for Latvia's amber, a hard pine resin. People of the time used amber to make jewelry. They believed that amber cured diseases and brought good luck.

Eastern Europe's plentiful supplies of gold and silver provided other profitable trading items. Hungary became a center of this trade, shipping the precious metals up the Danube River to the merchants of Vienna and into Western Europe. By the Middle Ages, Hungary provided Europe with three fourths of its gold.

EYEWITNESS TO HISTORY

Orient-Express

The train that wound its way through the heart of Eastern Europe had its beginning in the United States. George Pullman's luxurious railroad cars inspired Georges Nagelmackers to create the Orient-Express.

Paris

FRANCE

+++ Orient-Express

The route went from Paris to Vienna, then on to Budapest and Bucharest. At Giurgiu on the Danube in Romania, passengers boarded a ferry before catching another phase of the train journey. The four-day trip ended in Constantinople (Istanbul, Turkey).

The Orient-Express

Growth of Communities

On the map of early trade routes (see page 131), look at the Eastern European cities built by commerce—Budapest, Kiev (KEE·eff), and Danzig (present-day Gdansk [guh·DAHNSK]). Other cities grew along these routes.

In contrast to Western Europe and the British Isles, Eastern Europe would not become heavily urbanized. The region remained largely rural until recent years. Towns appeared, but these were mostly small villages similar to those in the Middle Ages in the British Isles and Western Europe.

The lords of the manors and their families lived in some of these villages. Other residents included clergy and craftspeople.

(see page 131)

WORD ORIGINS

The word **serf** comes from the Latin *servus*, which means "slave." Serfs had little more freedom than slaves. They had to do whatever their master desired. Unlike slaves, they were not bought and sold but remained their entire lives in one place, working the land of their manor lord.

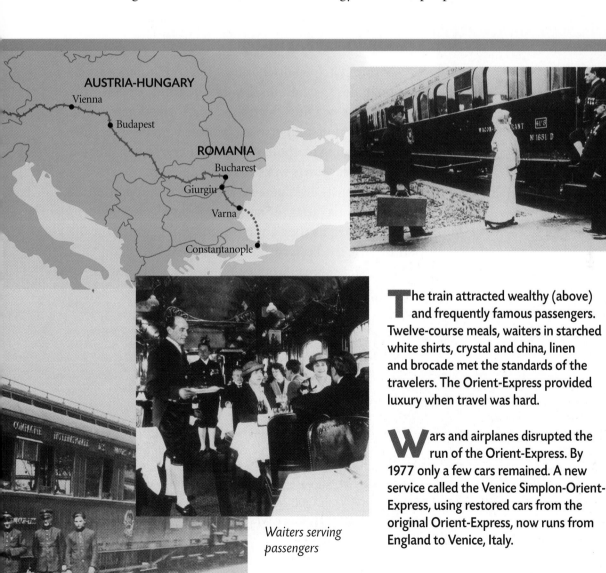

AUSTRIA-HUNGARY
Vienna
Budapest
ROMANIA
Bucharest
Giurgiu
Varna
Constantanople

Waiters serving passengers

The train attracted wealthy (above) and frequently famous passengers. Twelve-course meals, waiters in starched white shirts, crystal and china, linen and brocade met the standards of the travelers. The Orient-Express provided luxury when travel was hard.

Wars and airplanes disrupted the run of the Orient-Express. By 1977 only a few cars remained. A new service called the Venice Simplon-Orient-Express, using restored cars from the original Orient-Express, now runs from England to Venice, Italy.

Most residents were peasant farmers, or serfs who lived on the manor land.

Serfs in Eastern Europe had a daily routine similar to that of the peasants of Western Europe. Serfs, like Western European peasants, did hard farm work. Serfs were the poorest people in the villages.

The difference between peasant and serf was in personal freedom. Serfs were obliged to live their entire lives on their lord's manor. Because they could not leave, the lords treated them almost like slaves. Peasants in Western Europe could take the risk of leaving the manor if they were mistreated. The serfs of Eastern Europe and Russia had less protection against the harsh demands of their lords.

Traditional Farming Communities

Serfdom helped discourage Eastern Europe's participation in the Agricultural Revolution. Landowners introduced two new crops from the Americas—potatoes and corn—into the region. Otherwise, landowners showed little interest in new farming methods and machinery. They increased production by making serfs work harder.

In parts of Eastern Europe and Russia, serfdom continued into the 1800s, long after it had disappeared elsewhere in Europe. Serfs farmed as they always had. While farmers in the West used machinery, Eastern Europeans harvested grain with sickles. Even today, some farmers use the scythe instead of mechanical harvesters.

Farmers in Eastern Europe used simple tools to harvest their crops, even into the twentieth century. *Why were modern farming methods slow to reach Eastern Europe?*

LESSON 1 REVIEW

Fact Follow-Up
1. What does the Hungarian Plain represent for the people of Hungary?
2. Why did farming, herding, and fishing develop in Eastern Europe?
3. What resources were traded by Eastern European nations with other world areas?
4. What were obligations of serfs in Eastern Europe?
5. Why did Eastern Europe continue using traditional farming methods?

Think These Through
6. What has been the economic importance for Western Europe of trade with Eastern Europe?
7. Suppose that you were a European farmer in 1900. Would you have preferred to live in Eastern or Western Europe? Explain.

Industrialization in Eastern Europe

LESSON 2

During the Communist rule of Poland, Brunon Przewozniak worked as a manager at the Lenin Shipyards. "Gdansk has always been an important port and shipbuilding center," Przewozniak said. "But all the yards were destroyed in World War II and it was not until 1949 that the first oceangoing vessel was launched." Today, the shipyard uses up-to-date equipment. "Nowadays, not only the design but also the construction program and many of the cutting machines are controlled by computers," Przewozniak said.

Industry Comes to Eastern Europe

Most modern industries in Eastern Europe, such as the Gdansk shipyard, were built after World War II. This means that in industrial development Eastern Europe lagged 100 to 150 years behind Western Europe and the British Isles.

Industry had begun to appear in scattered places in the late 1800s. By the 1870s, large flour mills, tanneries, and breweries were springing up in a cluster of three Hungarian towns—Buda, Pest, and Obuda. As industry offered new jobs, peasants flooded in from the countryside. Soon the population of the three towns had grown together. In 1873, they united to form a single city—Budapest.

Industry also came late to what is now the Czech Republic. It developed only in places connected by rivers to Western Europe. The areas of the country that were isolated remained agricultural.

About 1918, glass and textile factories opened near Prague, in a mountainous area called Bohemia. Bohemia's access to the Elbe River and Western Europe helped export these

Cranes loom over a shipyard in Danzig (present-day Gdansk), Poland, in the 1950s. The industry of shipbuilding was one of the first in Eastern Europe. *When did most industry come to the region?*

LESSON PREVIEW

Key Ideas
- Eastern Europe's Agricultural and Industrial Revolutions occurred after World War II.
- These changes were led by the Soviet Union and the Communist governments of Eastern European nations.
- Eastern Europe's economy was changed to strengthen the Communist nations.

Key Term
collective farms

Glassmaking became an important industry in what is now the Czech Republic.
How did these products make their way to Western Europe?

products. The quality of the products earned the factories a worldwide reputation for excellence.

A few miles to the east, in Moravia, the Bata shoe factory used Henry Ford's ideas of mass production to turn out large quantities of high-quality, low-cost shoes. The Czechs also developed their own automobile industry.

Industrialization After World War II

Eastern Europe's infant industries were badly hurt by the worldwide depression of the 1930s. World War II destroyed the little that was left. The region's industry did not really begin to develop until the late 1940s, when the Soviet Union stepped in to provide leadership and financial assistance. The Soviets wanted Eastern Europe's help in a great international struggle called the Cold War.

As you have read, the United States provided aid for the reconstruction of industries in many European nations. In Eastern Europe, the Soviet Union helped Communist-led governments build industries and modernize agricultural production.

Poland's Communist leaders, for example, drew plans to develop heavy industry. The shipyards at Gdansk and government-built factories in Kraków and Warsaw became a key part of the plans. Most of the factories produced machinery and steel for Soviet industries. Poland's large coal deposits, access to the Baltic Sea, and ample labor supply helped assure the development of Polish industry.

The Soviets also succeeded in expanding industries in Czechoslovakia (now the Czech Republic and Slovakia) and Hungary. People there knew how to run industries. Those places also had the raw materials and a transportation system necessary for industrial growth.

The Soviets failed in other countries. Bulgaria's industry before World War II consisted of a few iron foundries and food processing plants. After the war, the Soviets helped improve transportation and made plans for industrialization.

Hope for change disappeared quickly. Bulgaria lacked

This steel plant uses Ukraine's rich resources of iron and oil. *What country used most of Ukraine's resources before Ukraine's independence?*

industrial resources, skilled workers, and people with management experience. Industry made little progress. The economy depended on agriculture. Bulgaria's farms produced crops, mostly for export to the Soviet Union.

After World War II, the Soviet Union contained some of the nations that are today part of Eastern Europe. Those areas felt the impact of the Soviets' efforts to rebuild and expand their own economy. These efforts brought much success in resource-rich Ukraine. Before it separated from the Soviet Union late in 1991, Ukraine supplied one fifth of the Soviet Union's food and industrial products.

The Soviets set up factories for food processing and manufacturing of agricultural equipment in Belarus. The Baltic countries of Latvia, Lithuania, and Estonia also had been a farming region. There the Soviets built new industry. Soon more people worked in manufacturing than in farming.

Collective Farms

While trying to industrialize Eastern Europe, the Soviet Union also reorganized agriculture. Communist governments seized privately owned farms. Many small farms were combined into a few large ones. Government managers decided what crops to raise, the jobs that farmers would do, and where crops were to be sold. These reorganized farms were called **collective farms**.

By the 1970s and 1980s, farm production was still low. The collective farms had failed. Young people were leaving the farms for better jobs in cities. Government officials agreed that modern farming methods were needed.

Agricultural experts began teaching farmers new ways to cultivate the land. The government also bought fertilizers and machinery and paid for irrigation projects. With these steps, the Agricultural Revolution finally began to arrive in Eastern Europe.

After World War II, Eastern Europeans began moving to large apartment buildings, such as this one in Bratislava, Slovakia. *Why did many move to the region's cities?*

Changing Ways of Life

In less than 50 years, Communist-led governments had changed Eastern Europe's ways of life. The region had become industrial and urban. Agriculture became modernized in many places.

Fewer people lived in rural villages and worked on farms. Many more lived in industrial cities and worked in factories. Throughout Eastern Europe, the people's relationship to their environment had changed dramatically.

LESSON 2 REVIEW

Fact Follow-Up
1. Outline the industrial revolution in Hungary.
2. How did World War II affect industry in Eastern Europe?
3. How did the Soviet Union change Eastern Europe's industrial development?
4. In what nations of Eastern Europe did Soviet industrial development fail?
5. List the reasons for collectivization of agriculture in Eastern Europe. What were the results of collectivization?

Think These Through
6. Why did some nations of Eastern Europe industrialize after World War II more quickly than others?
7. Was Soviet control good or bad for Eastern Europe's industrial development? Explain your answer.

Environmental Impacts of Industry

I n the Czech town of Usti Nad Labem on the Elbe River, a giant electronic scoreboard looms over the skyline. The numbers that flash on it have nothing to do with sports scores. Yet everyone in town checks the board daily. The scoreboard tracks the rise and fall of nine different toxic gases emitted into the air from nearby factories.

"We still get about 20 types of harmful substances," reported Zdenek Cerny, who is in charge of monitoring the pollution. "Suddenly half the town may get pains in the joints. Or skin problems. When these chemicals interact, it creates a kind of nerve gas."

Air Pollution

In the Soviet Union's push for industrialization in Eastern Europe, the Soviets wanted production. They gave little, if any, thought to environmental costs.

Usti Nad Labem is only a single example of how high those costs have been. It is only one of many towns and cities in an area of Eastern Europe where everything is covered with heavy layers of dark soot.

> **LESSON PREVIEW**
>
> **Key Ideas**
> - Most Eastern Europeans now live in urban environments.
> - The economic planners' failure to protect the environment has produced widespread pollution.
> - Modern agriculture and industry have not yet produced dramatic improvements in standards of living.
>
> **Key Term**
> lignite

The picture of Usti Nad Laben, Czech Republic, shows the town's heavy air and water pollution. *How did towns and cities in Eastern Europe become so polluted?*

Children in Mezibori, Czech Republic, wear masks to school to keep from getting sick from the polluted air. *Why is this part of Eastern Europe called the Black Triangle?*

The soot pours out of the chimneys of homes and factories. **Lignite**, a cheap but dirty brown coal, is the main source of energy. The area has become so unsightly that it is called the Black Triangle.

The Black Triangle includes the Czech Republic, southern Poland, and southeastern Germany (once part of Communist-led East Germany). Here the Soviets achieved their greatest successes in the drive to establish new industry. Yet these accomplishments have brought disaster. One scientist has compared industry's impact on the area's environment to the devastation in Japan after the atomic bomb was dropped there.

People experience the plague of pollution in their daily lives. In the Czech town of Mezibori, children walking to school wear pollution masks to filter the ash from nearby coal mines and coal-burning plants. Despite the masks, sulfur dioxide from the burning coal causes serious respiratory illnesses.

At the same time, air pollution has heavily damaged the Black Triangle's forests. At one time, Poland's dense woods provided camouflage for Soviet Army tanks. Years of acid rain killed many trees and thinned branches. The military moved its tanks to other hiding places.

The loss of trees has serious side effects. Mountain forests held back water and snow from the valleys. When the trees died, water rushed down the hillsides, causing erosion and flooding. Officials believe it will take decades for the forests to grow back—if the air improves.

Chernobyl

The world's greatest environmental disaster occurred on April 26, 1986, when a nuclear reactor exploded at Chernobyl, Ukraine. The explosion set off 30 fires, releasing 11 tons of radioactive particles into the air.

Ukraine was then part of the Soviet Union. At first, the Soviet

government treated the explosion as a minor incident. No warnings were issued to the people living nearby. People carried on with their daily lives, unaware of the danger.

Alarms sounded only after the winds blew radioactive materials beyond Soviet borders. When Swedish scientists found dangerously high levels, they told Swedish citizens the danger of radioactive fallout making its way into the food chain. Eating food containing radioactive material might cause cancer.

By the time the Soviet authorities evacuated the Chernobyl area, more than 100,000 people already had received massive doses of radiation. Thousands soon became seriously ill. For others, trouble came later. They developed cancers, blood diseases, and stomach ailments.

Soviet doctors and teams of cancer experts from abroad gave whatever help they could. The Ukrainian government began to send young people living in high radiation areas to Western Europe and the United States. Ukrainian authorities hoped that by moving away, these young people might get well.

No one lives in Chernobyl now. Bulldozers have buried houses and trees. A steel-and-cement building surrounds the plant. Despite the protective cover, the plant still leaks radiation. Authorities also worry that other reactors similar to the one at Chernobyl might cause trouble.

What would YOU do?

Your home won't be the same. A nuclear plant accident has caused damage to the environment. Water and food aren't safe to use. Buildings have to be bulldozed. The government will move people away. Will you choose to stay or go? Do you stay and protest so that more nuclear plants will close? Do you move away so you won't be exposed to radiation?

The nuclear plant in Chernobyl, Ukraine (left), exploded in 1986. Many Ukrainians became sick or died. An elderly woman from Chernobyl holds a picture of plant workers wearing gas masks. *How did the explosion cause the illnesses and deaths?*

Eastern Europe also has water pollution. Chemical plants dumped toxic waste for 25 years into this lagoon in the Czech Republic. *What are other sources of water pollution in the region?*

Water Pollution

People living on the outskirts of Budapest noticed that their water had an oily taste. When tests showed that the water contained kerosene, people switched to bottled water.

City officials searching for the source of the problem soon uncovered an abandoned railway freight terminal. For years tank cars carrying kerosene had been unloaded there and pipes had leaked. Now the city is busy cleaning up the groundwater. The process is costly and takes time.

You have read about water pollution in heavily industrialized Western Europe, so you know that Eastern Europe is not alone in facing this problem. Yet the region does have to deal with many more problems in its water supplies.

When the Soviets built industry in Eastern Europe, they did not require factories to clean up waste water before dumping it into rivers. Chemicals flowed into streams as more fertilizers were used on farmland.

Fishermen in the Baltic nations faced a special problem because of the Soviet dumping of outdated chemical weapons in their fishing waters. When the chemicals leaked into the water, fish frequently became unfit to eat. The fur-bearing seal population in the Baltic Sea dropped. Many of the crewmen on the fishing boats became ill.

Baltic governments are trying to clean the fishing grounds. Their efforts show a growing concern in Eastern Europe about environmental pollution. Cleaning the environment will not come quickly though, because Eastern European governments have few resources.

Environment Today

The switch from agriculture to industry has changed where people live in Eastern Europe. Before World War II, most lived on farms. With industrialization, people moved from the countryside into cities in search of factory jobs.

Compare the population density map on page 367 with the economic activity map on page 399. Note that the areas of highest population density are located near industry.

In nations such as Poland, the Czech Republic, and Slovakia, population has increased significantly. Poland's population in the mid-1990s, for example, numbered 38,655,000, an increase of nearly 9 million since 1960. Populations have not grown that much in other Eastern European nations. Poor economic

The Science Fiction of Stanislaw Lem

Stanislaw Lem started out as a physician but ended up as a science fiction writer. Lem's works are enormously popular in his homeland of Poland.

In the 1979 *Tales of Pirx the Pilot*, Lem writes about space travel by an astronaut who investigates when things go wrong on the moon. A passage from that story shows how Lem writes about technology for readers to understand how the characters feel on the cold moon's surface:

"The transition from sharp light to thick shadow made them lose sight of one another.

Soon they were braced by a nocturnal cold. Pirx felt it penetrate the layers of his antithermal suit—not a biting, bone-clamping cold, more like a mute and icy presence. The twenty-degree drop in temperature made the aluminized layers of his suit vibrate."

Another passage reveals the pilot thinking about his location in space: "...the moon, the rugged highland, glacial night alternating with blazing heat, and this ubiquitous, all-encompassing silence that reduced the sound of a human voice inside a space

helmet to something as unlikely as a goldfish on the Matterhorn."

Eastern Europeans need to eat more fruit and vegetables, such as these in Budapest, Hungary, to increase life expectancy in the region. *What does the term life expectancy mean?*

conditions have not encouraged population increases.

Finally, the coming of the Agricultural and Industrial Revolutions has not yet brought to Eastern Europeans dramatic improvements in standards of living. Life expectancy, or the average number of years people live after birth, in the mid-1990s was 67.3 years for males and 76 years for females. Those averages are lower than Western Europe. Males live six years longer, on average, in Western Europe. Females average four years more.

Experts agree that these regional differences come partly from an unhealthy environment created by air and water pollution. Other factors contribute to shorter lives in Eastern Europe—daily diets that have too much fat and not enough fruit and vegetables, too many cigarettes, and too much alcohol.

LESSON 3 REVIEW

Fact Follow-up
1. What are some long-term results of industrial pollution in Eastern Europe?
2. What were the causes and results of the Chernobyl disaster?
3. Describe the kinds of environmental damage suffered by nations of Eastern Europe. Why is it difficult to repair the damage?

Think These Through
4. Had it not been for Soviet control, what would the environment of Eastern European nations have been like? Explain.
5. What part of Eastern Europe's environment has suffered the most damage?
6. What is the most urgent environmental problem facing Eastern Europe? Why?

Participating Effectively in Civic Affairs

Controlling Environmental Damage

Are there any environmental problems in the community where you live? Of course there are. All communities have such problems.

To help you with your thinking, have you heard or read about any problems such as these? (1)Are people concerned in your community about the quality of the water supply—from home wells or the city reservoirs? (2)Are there any concerns about air pollution inside a building or out in the open? (3)Do you know of any worries about the soil in some areas being polluted? (4)If so, has anyone proposed cleaning that area before homes are built or gardens are planted?

Along the left margin of a sheet of paper list some of the environmental challenges your community faces. Label the list "Our Environmental Challenges." Beside each challenge, note what groups or individuals—including local, state, or federal government—are working to meet the challenge. If you have trouble thinking of agencies or groups, ask other students and your teacher.

Have you found that government agencies seem to work on certain types of problems? Do private groups or individuals work on others?

How many government agencies have you listed? Do you know what kind of work they do? What kind of work is done by some well-known private groups such as the National Wildlife Federation, the Sierra Club, the Nature Conservancy, and the Environmental Defense Fund? Our nation has a tradition of citizens joining together to meet challenges such as damage to the environment.

Look again at the pictures on pages 377-380. Quickly review Lesson 2 to remind yourself of why Eastern European governments seemed to pay so little attention to the environment as they pushed for industrial development.

Do you find in Lesson 3 any evidence that individuals or groups of people outside of government protested against damaging the environment in the 1950s or 1960s?

The result of environmental damage, as you read in Chapter 19, led a scientist at the University of Colorado to compare Eastern Europe's environment to Japan after the atomic bomb was dropped.

From your review of Chapter 19, list on a sheet of paper major environmental challenges faced by Eastern Europeans. Compare them to the challenges of your community. Based on what you have noted about civic action in your community to protect the environment, how can the environmental problems of Eastern Europe be tackled? Which problems can private groups and individuals work on? Which can be solved only by governments?

Based on our American traditions of civic action, is there any advice we can give Eastern Europeans as they work to solve their environmental problems?

Chapter 19 Review

LESSON 1   Eastern Europeans were slow to adopt the Agricultural Revolution that changed farming in Western Europe. Farmers there remained serfs well into the nineteenth century. Their lives were bound to the land. They led a difficult life as they raised crops with the crudest of tools.

LESSON 2   Eastern Europe's agriculture and industry remained unchanged—except in parts of Poland, Czechoslovakia, and Hungary—until after World War II. The Soviet Union led the campaign to modernize agriculture and industry. Communist governments benefited. Only a few people enjoyed improved living standards.

LESSON 3   Quick industrial development and massive agricultural change damaged the environment. Water, air, and land pollution caused by radioactive materials, industrial waste, and fertilizer runoff has led to significant health problems, including shortened life expectancy rates.

TIME FOR TERMS

collective farms   lignite

FACT FOLLOW-UP

1. What products did Eastern European countries export before the twentieth century?
2. How did the rivers of Eastern Europe affect the growth of cities?

3. Compare traditional and modern agriculture in Eastern Europe.
4. Why did farmers continue to use traditional agricultural methods in Eastern Europe?
5. How did Soviet influence affect the industrialization of Eastern Europe?
6. How did Soviet influence affect Eastern European agriculture?
7. What were some environmental results of industrialization in Eastern Europe?

THINK THESE THROUGH

8. Why did collective farms fail in Eastern Europe?
9. It has been said that the nations of Eastern Europe could not afford the luxury of being concerned about the environment. Do you agree? Give reasons for your answer.
10. What do you think is the single most important issue facing the economies of Eastern Europe today? Explain your answer.
11. Would the industrial development of Eastern Europe have been different without Soviet influence? Explain your answer.

SHARPENING SKILLS

12. How important is the work of individuals in solving such problems as environmental pollution?
13. What civic problems like environmental abuse can best be solved by private groups? Explain.
14. Are there environmental problems that only governments can solve? Explain.

15. What communications skills do citizens need in order to participate effectively in actions like saving the environment?

PLACE LOCATION

Use the map key to answer the following questions:

16. What two nations in Eastern Europe have cities with populations exceeding 2 million?

17. Using the key showing the size of cities, estimate the size of Eastern Europe's urban populations (in computing, use the low figures—250,000, 1,000,000, etc.) Which two nations have the highest urban populations? Which have the lowest?

18. Cities and high population densities in Eastern Europe usually indicate industry and commerce. Using keys to city size and population density, list three nations that seem to be most industrial and commercial. Which have the least industry and commerce?

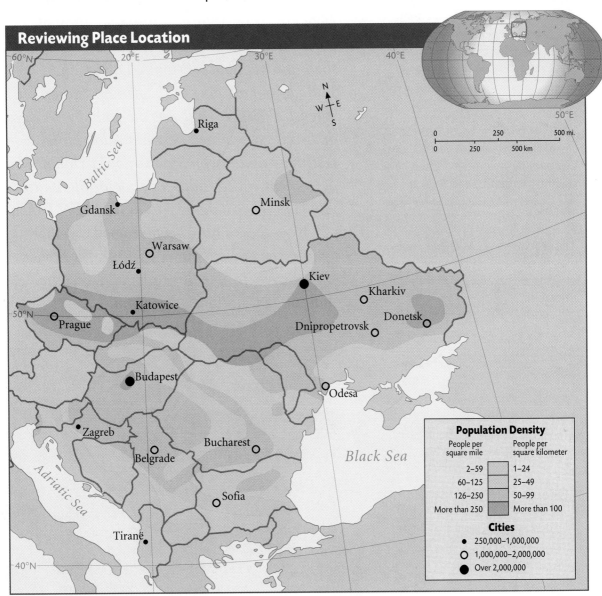

Reviewing Place Location

Population Density

People per square mile		People per square kilometer
2–59		1–24
60–125		25–49
126–250		50–99
More than 250		More than 100

Cities
- 250,000–1,000,000
- ○ 1,000,000–2,000,000
- ● Over 2,000,000

Hand in hand, arm in arm, people formed the Human Chain of Peace stretching 400 miles (644 km) from Vilnius, Lithuania, through Riga, Latvia, to Tallinn, Estonia. The people of the Baltic republics–Estonia, Latvia, and Lithuania–took part in the demonstration on August 23, 1989. That was the 50th anniversary of a secret agreement between Adolf Hitler's Germany and Joseph Stalin's Soviet Union. The agreement ended independence for the Baltic republics. They became part of the Soviet Union.

Now these Baltic peoples stood together against the Soviet Union. In 1991, the Soviet Union gave in. The three republics became independent nations once again.

Human Chain of Peace in Estonia (below and right)

HITLER · STALIN · GENOTSIID

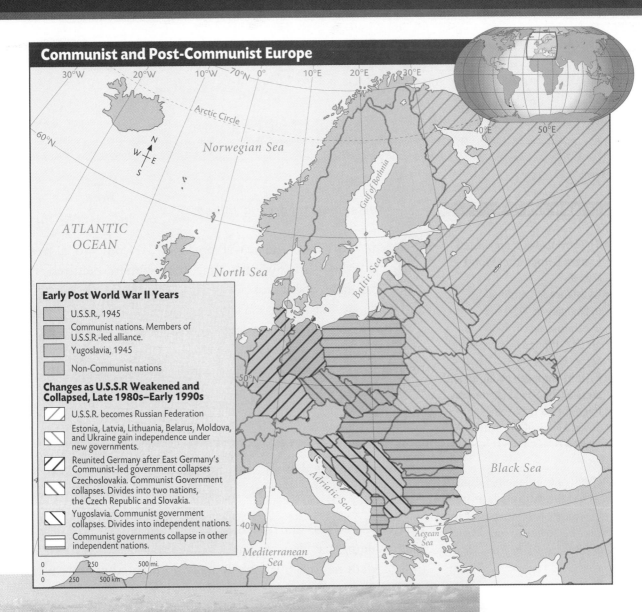

Communist and Post-Communist Europe

Early Post World War II Years

- U.S.S.R., 1945
- Communist nations. Members of U.S.S.R.-led alliance.
- Yugoslavia, 1945
- Non-Communist nations

Changes as U.S.S.R Weakened and Collapsed, Late 1980s–Early 1990s

- U.S.S.R. becomes Russian Federation
- Estonia, Latvia, Lithuania, Belarus, Moldova, and Ukraine gain independence under new governments.
- Reunited Germany after East Germany's Communist-led government collapses
- Czechoslovakia. Communist Government collapses. Divides into two nations, the Czech Republic and Slovakia.
- Yugoslavia. Communist government collapses. Divides into independent nations.
- Communist governments collapse in other independent nations.

0   250   500 mi.

0   250   500 km

The Collapse of Communism

LESSON PREVIEW

Key Ideas

- The Soviet Union dominated Eastern Europe after World War II.
- Resistance to communism in Hungary in 1956 and Czechoslovakia in 1968 was quickly stopped by a powerful Soviet Union.
- Eastern European countries and areas of the Soviet Union won freedom from a weakening Soviet Union in the early 1990s.

A 1990 rally in Tallinn, Estonia, marked the 70th anniversary of Estonia's first independence from the Soviet Union. *When did Estonia become free of the Soviet Union again?*

Valkommen till det fria Tallinn.

The words on the travel poster—"Welcome to a free Tallinn"—are Swedish, but the woman pictured is Estonian. She stands proudly in a traditional dress of red and gold.

This poster appeared in 1991 after the collapse of communism in Eastern Europe. It was the first opportunity in 50 years for Estonians to invite Western visitors to the capital city of their own independent country—a free Tallinn.

Communism in Eastern Europe

After World War II, the Soviet Union gained power throughout Eastern Europe (see map, page 387). The Soviet Union had already taken over some countries—Ukraine, Belarus, Moldova, and the Baltic republics. Other countries, such as Hungary, Poland, and Czechoslovakia, seemed to be independent nations but were actually dominated in every way by the Soviet Union.

Former British Prime Minister Winston Churchill described the result of Soviet domination in Eastern Europe. "From Stettin in the Baltic to Trieste in the Adriatic, an iron curtain has descended over the Continent," he said in a 1946 speech. Churchill's phrase, "iron curtain," became the term used to describe the barrier between free European countries and those in Eastern Europe dominated by the Soviet Union.

The Soviet Union demanded that Eastern Europe produce goods for Soviet purposes. Although the people of Eastern Europe worked hard in factories and industrial plants, they seldom enjoyed the products they made.

For 40 years, the Soviets' control of the region denied essential freedoms to the people. There was no freedom of speech, no freedom of the press, no freedom of movement, and no freedom of religion. Only Communist party members could run for election in the countries of the region.

A strong Soviet Army kept Eastern European countries and East Germany under communism. *Where did independence movements arise in the region?*

Resistance to Communism

During the era of Soviet control, some Eastern European countries did resist communism. Their opposition erupted in several uprisings—some of them bloody.

Hungary   As you have read in Chapter 5, Hungary was the site of the first major uprising against Soviet authority. In 1956, many Hungarian college students, writers, and artists demanded their human rights and freedom of expression. Street fighting broke out in Budapest, and soon the revolution swept throughout the country.

The Soviets sent troops to put down the revolution. The soldiers killed or jailed many. When the revolution failed, nearly 200,000 people fled the country.

Czechoslovakia   During the early 1960s, many people suffered from food shortages in what is now the Czech Republic and Slovakia. At the same time, Czechs demanded more freedom of expression.

In 1968, Alexander Dubcek (DOOBT · chek) became the Communist party leader and introduced reforms into the government. The changes Dubcek proposed included more freedom of the press and increased contact with Western nations. People approved of Dubcek's ideas for reform and called his movement the Prague Spring.

What would YOU do?

Hungarians tried to revolt in 1956. Shipbuilders in Poland began revolting in 1970 over food shortages. Desire for religious freedom and for democracy have been other reasons for rebellion.

Large numbers of people were treated harshly, sent to prison, or killed. Why did Eastern Europeans risk their lives? Would you have joined their fight?

The Soviet Union saw danger in the Czech reforms. If one Eastern European country reformed its government, others would demand freedom, too.

So in August 1968, the Soviet army, along with troops from Bulgaria, East Germany, Hungary, and Poland, invaded Czechoslovakia. The Prague Spring ended when Dubcek was replaced as Communist party leader, and his supporters resigned or were forced from office. Communist officials tightened their control of Czechoslovakia. Anyone opposed to the Communist-led government risked death.

Poland By the 1970s, the Polish economy was in trouble. People were paying high prices. Goods were scarce. Food shortages frequently left the stores empty. When the Communist government announced a rise in prices, riots broke out.

In 1980, the workers of Gdansk went on strike to demand higher pay, and political reforms. They wanted trade unions independent of the Communist party. They called their organization of free trade unions Solidarity. Their leader was a shipyard worker named Lech Walesa (vah·LENT·sah).

The Polish government recognized Solidarity, but economic and political problems continued. In late 1981, Solidarity was outlawed and Walesa was imprisoned. He was released almost a year later. In October 1983 he won the Nobel Prize for peace.

By 1989, political reforms had come to Poland. Solidarity was legalized again. For the first time in more than 40 years, non-Communists could run for election. Many won seats in the parliament, and a Solidarity leader became prime minister. The next year, the Polish Communist party was dissolved. In December 1990, Lech Walesa became president. Throughout Europe this election was regarded as important. It demonstrated that democracy was established in Poland. After his term ended, Walesa returned to his shipyard job. The peaceful transfer of power was another hopeful sign.

Lech Walesa led the shipyard workers of Gdansk in a strike. He went to prison for his work against the Communist party in Poland. *What political office did Walesa end up winning in his country?*

The Gdansk Seaport

By March 1945, most of Gdansk, Poland, had been destroyed by World War II battles. After the war, the people had to reconstruct their city. Rebuilding was no new experience for them. Gdansk's entire history has been one of rebuilding after conquering governments have left their marks.

In the twentieth century, for example, German, French, and Russian armies—attracted by the importance of this Baltic seaport—have destroyed Gdansk.

Today, Gdansk still ranks as an important seaport and shipbuilding city. With nearly 12,000 people employed in its shipyard, Gdansk relies on Eastern Europe's trade needs. Other countries buy fishing vessels, ferries, and container ships built there.

Lech Walesa, an engineer at the shipyard, led a movement that created Solidarity, the free trade union, in 1980. This was Poland's first step toward its freedom from the Soviet Union.

The city now draws tourists. Visitors come to the Gdansk waterfront to see the Harbor Crane, built in 1333. The ancient crane hoisted cargo and fitted masts onto ships. The crane now houses a museum.

Other shops and restaurants dot the waterfront away from the shipyards. Views of ships and ferries passing by remind people of Gdansk's importance to Poland.

Gdansk harbor crane and museum

The End of Soviet-style Communism

The Polish experience revealed a weakening Soviet Union. The Soviets did not oppose the free elections in Poland. They lacked the money and the will to use force in Poland to support Communist government. The Soviet Union had to face, for the first time since World War II, the survival of its own Communist system.

Other problems caught the Soviet Union's attention in the 1980s. The Soviet Union was tied up in an unpopular war in Afghanistan. The government could not spend the money necessary to compete with the United States in the nuclear arms race. Also, the Soviet Union was challenged by its own people's demands for freedom.

Soviet leaders, especially Mikhail Gorbachev (gor·buh·CHOF), relaxed control over countries under Soviet domination. These nations began to seek solutions to their own problems. Most Eastern European countries decided to transform their governments and economies to democracy and capitalism.

Independence for Soviet Republics

Even territories within the Soviet Union found freedom in the late 1980s and early 1990s. After nearly five decades of Soviet rule, the Baltic republics demanded and won their independence.

The Baltic Republics   The people of Lithuania, Latvia, and Estonia had many reasons to resent Soviet rule. Communism restricted business opportunities and kept the Baltic republics poorer than their Scandinavian neighbors.

Soviet planning also made certain that most of the radios, refrigerators, and other consumer goods made in the Baltics were shipped to the Soviet Union. This left the people of the area with few modern conveniences.

The thousands of Russian workers who came to live in the Baltics did not learn the local languages. Instead, Latvians, Estonians, and Lithuanians had to learn Russian in order to work in the new industries.

The Baltic peoples began opposing the Soviets in the 1980s. First they demonstrated against pollution caused by industrialization. In 1988, Baltic nationalist movements demanded

During the 1980s, people of the Baltics protested their treatment by the Soviet Union. Soon the protesters began demanding independence at rallies such as this one in Lithuania. *What had the Soviet Union done in the Baltic countries to inspire the protests there?*

self-government, and then complete freedom.

On March 11, 1990, the Lithuanian parliament declared independence from the Soviet Union. Excited crowds tore down the hammer and sickle symbol of the Soviet Union from the front of the parliament building.

Support for Baltic independence was growing, even in Latvia and Estonia, where many Russians had settled. But the Soviet Union would not allow the Baltic republics to leave the Soviet Union. In April 1990, the Soviet Union tried to punish the Baltics by cutting off shipments of oil and medical supplies to Lithuania.

International reporters brought the struggle to the attention of the world. Influenced by the world's opinion and political pressure at home, the Soviet Union finally recognized the independence of the Baltic nations in September 1991.

Ukraine, Belarus, Moldova   Ukrainians began to demand national independence in the 1980s. They especially wanted to decide economic, political, and cultural matters for themselves.

In 1990, the Ukrainian parliament approved a declaration of sovereignty. This meant that Ukrainians would follow their own laws rather than those of the Soviet Union. The parliaments of Belarus and Moldova made the same declarations at this time.

On December 1, 1991, more than 90 percent of Ukrainians voted for independence. A few weeks later, on December 25, the Soviet Union was dissolved.

The Ukrainian flag is raised at a rally to symbolize Ukrainians' desire for independence. *What event in the Soviet Union finally gained Ukraine its independence?*

WORD ORIGINS

A Transylvanian prince named Moldova. Prince Voda was hunting buffalo in the Carpathian Mountains. His dog, Molda, fell into the river and drowned. Prince Voda named the river and nearby lands Moldova, after Molda. The Soviet Union changed the name to Moldavia. With freedom, the people have chosen to return to their original name, Moldova.

LESSON 1 REVIEW

Fact Follow-Up

1. What Eastern European nations were part of the Soviet Union when World War II ended?
2. What nations of Eastern Europe came under Soviet domination following World War II?
3. Describe resistance to Soviet control in Hungary and Czechoslovakia.
4. Explain how the Baltic nations attempted to gain their independence from the Soviet Union.
5. What was the Solidarity movement in Poland? Who was Lech Walesa?

Think These Through

6. Why did nations of Eastern Europe not cooperate to push the Soviets out? Explain.
7. Which nation in Eastern Europe seemed to suffer most under Soviet control? Explain.

Governing After Communism

LESSON PREVIEW

Key Ideas

* Governing after communism has been difficult in Eastern Europe.
* Czechoslovakia peacefully split into two countries after starting a democratic government.
* Ethnic tensions have risen after communism, making it impossible to govern in the Balkans and creating an uncertain future for democracy in the region.

Crowds gathered in University Square in Bucharest, Romania. In patient silence, people waited for their turns to read every poster and paper pasted on the buildings.

It was 1989, and Romania was in the middle of a revolution. Every Romanian knew that demonstrations were challenging the authority of the Communist government and its leader, President Nicolae Ceausescu. Information could not be easily gathered because the government still controlled the press, television, and radio.

They came to University Square to read and discuss the information that was posted there. Such news was the only information that people trusted. The information from University Square served as the driving force of the democratic revolution that was sweeping Romania and the rest of Eastern Europe. Ceausescu and other leaders controlled by the Soviet Union were forced from office. Free elections began democracy in Eastern Europe.

From Communism to Democracy

In the late 1980s, Eastern Europe faced severe economic problems and such environmental disasters as Chernobyl. These events motivated Eastern Europeans to oppose their Communist governments.

As the Soviet Union faced its own strong reform movement at home, political unrest grew in Eastern Europe. The people of Poland and Czechoslovakia began to demand free elections. They demanded basic rights—freedom of speech and assembly, freedom of the press, and freedom of religion.

By the time the Soviet Union had dissolved itself as a nation in December 1991, many Eastern European countries had already outlawed the Communist party. They began building more democratic governments.

The Velvet Revolution

Czechoslovakia began its Velvet Revolution in 1989. The country transformed itself from communism to democracy in a process that was as smooth as velvet.

It started in November, when hundreds of thousands of people gathered in the streets of Prague to call for reforms in government and greater freedom. The public demonstrations had little effect. Workers went on strike to demand change. Soon people all over Czechoslovakia were expressing their anger at the Communist government.

Change came quickly. The public outcry, forced the Communist party leader to resign. The Federal Assembly then voted to end Communist rule.

In December 1989, Vaclav Havel (HAH·vuhl), a non-Communist playwright, became president of Czechoslovakia. He helped restore freedoms of religion, speech, and the press, and established closer ties with democratic nations.

Demonstrations (above and left) in Prague, Czechoslovakia, against communism included strikes and marches. *What were other ways countries in Eastern Europe became democratic?*

395

Ethnic Tensions Surface

The fall of communism brought independence to Eastern Europe, but freedom also brought new challenges. The ethnic and religious problems that had been buried during 40 years of Communist rule suddenly reemerged.

Today, many of the countries of Western and Northern Europe are finding ways to work together. Meanwhile, some countries in Eastern Europe are breaking up under the strain of ethnic conflict.

Vaclav Klaus, premier of the Czech Republic (left), and Vladimír Meciar, premier of Slovakia (right), discuss the peaceful division of Czechoslovakia into the two republics they led. *Why was the country split?*

Czechoslovakia   Peace negotiators at the end of World War I drew the boundaries of this country. The new country brought together a western area populated by Czechs and another area in the east inhabited by Slovaks. Relations between these two ethnic groups became increasingly uneasy. The country's government and politics came to be dominated by the Czechs. Slovaks resented this.

Czechoslovakia remained united under communism. After the Cold War ended, the nation's leaders were free to decide how to resolve their differences.

In 1992, Czech and Slovak leaders decided to divide the country, making two new nations. A Czech Republic would be established in the West. Slovakia would occupy the eastern half of the country. Czechoslovakia brought about this division peacefully on January 1, 1993.

Yugoslavia   Like Czechoslovakia, Yugoslavia—a name that means "Land of the Southern Slavs"—was created by the peace negotiators after World War I. Several ethnic groups lived in this new nation. The most prominent were Slovenes, Croats, Muslims, and Serbs. All were rivals.

The nation united against invading German forces during World War II. After the war, Josip Broz Tito, an heroic figure and forceful dictator, seized control of Yugoslavia. He held the country together until his death in 1980.

After Tito's death, the Serbs attempted to control Yugoslavia. Their effort led to Yugoslavia's breakup. Two rivals of the Serbs, the Croats and Slovenes, formed independent countries called Slovenia and Croatia.

Serbs armed with guns from Serbia-Montenegro—another country carved out of the former Yugoslavia—fought with Croats and Slovenes. The Serbs failed, however, to prevent either group from gaining independence. Another independent country named Bosnia-Herzegovina was formed with the support of Muslims and Albanians (see map, page 363). In Bosnia-Herzegovina a bloody civil war broke out. The war had no clear battle lines, because Bosnian Serbs and Muslims often lived next door to one another.

Serbs tried to destroy Bosnia-Herzegovina by killing or driving Muslims away. As the world's press reported horrors of this war, the United Nations and North Atlantic Treaty Organization (NATO), sent nearly 60,000 troops into Bosnia. These forces stopped the fighting and supervised elections. First steps toward forming a government began. No one, however, could predict if peace would last.

Marshall Josip Tito was the dictator of Yugoslavia until his death in 1980. *What happened to the country after he died?*

Nations Today

Some Eastern European nations are becoming more democratic. They also are strengthening their economies. European democracies and the United States have recognized these achievements. In 1997, NATO invited the Czech Republic, Poland, and Hungary to join in time for NATO's 50th anniversary in 1999. Slovenia, Romania and the Baltic nations also are taking bigger steps toward democracy. It is less easy to predict the direction of other East European nations.

LESSON 2 REVIEW

Fact Follow-Up
1. What motivated people of Eastern Europe to challenge Soviet rule in the late 1980s?
2. Describe what has happened in the area that once was Czechoslovakia.
3. Name the rival ethnic groups in the former Yugoslavia.

Think These Through
4. Which Eastern European nation do you think has been most successful in establishing its independence? Explain why.
5. Why has it been most difficult for the former Yugoslavia to establish stable and independent governments?
6. If you were an advisor to the president of the United States, what advice would you give him about relationships with Eastern European nations? Explain why.

The Economies of Eastern Europe

LESSON 3

LESSON PREVIEW

Key Ideas

- Hungary and Poland have led the region in transforming economies from communism to capitalism.
- Of the former Soviet republics, Ukraine has the strongest economy.
- Other countries in Eastern Europe are having difficulty making the transition from communism to capitalism.

Hungary's prime minister, Gyula Horn, drove up to the White House for a meeting with President Bill Clinton in June 1995. He did not come by limousine, as is usual for a visiting dignitary. Instead, he arrived in a public transit bus.

The bus, known by its Hungarian brand name, Ikarus, had been welded together in a factory in Budapest, then shipped to a plant in Alabama for completion. It was the first of a fleet of buses sold to the city of Washington, D.C. Other Ikarus buses are rolling on the streets of Baltimore, Philadelphia, and Miami.

This bus-building project was the brainchild of Peter Rona, a native of Hungary. Rona left his country after the 1956 revolution and only returned in 1989 when he began to do business there part-time. "I wanted to take a dying socialist company and save it," Rona said.

From Communism to Capitalism

Eastern Europe needs business leaders such as Rona, but it also needs large sums of money from banks to get businesses off the ground. As communism collapsed in Eastern Europe, the European Union founded the European Bank for Reconstruction and Development. The bank helps the countries of Eastern Europe transform their economies to capitalism.

Most countries in Eastern Europe saw their economic growth rate drop after the collapse of communism. Eastern Europe's economies began growing by 1994. They benefited from new profitable trade relations with other regions, especially Western Europe.

When Eastern Europe had Communist governments, everyone was guaranteed work. The Communist governments gave businesses and factories money to buy raw materials and pay their workers. Industry, in turn, gave raises and promotions based on the number of years a worker had been on the job, instead of the worker's efficiency or talent.

Under capitalism, an industry has to make a profit in order to survive. To make a profit, factories must run efficiently. Efficient factories require high productivity from workers. In

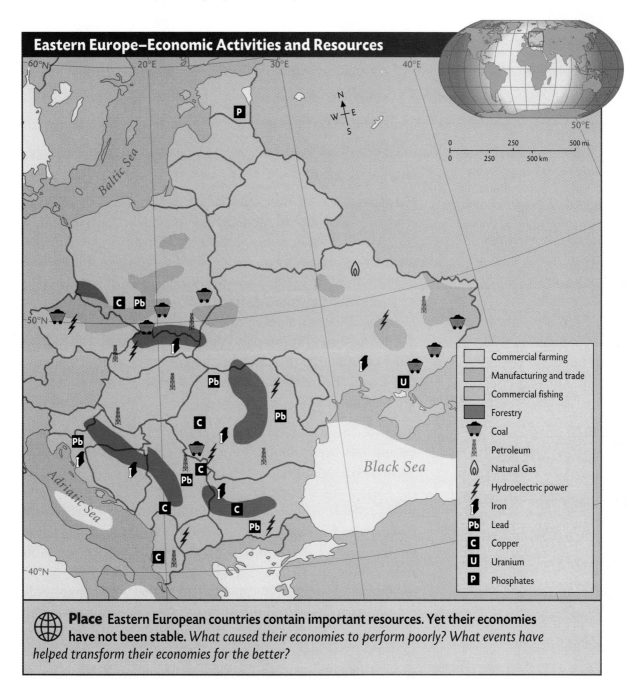

Eastern Europe–Economic Activities and Resources

☐	Commercial farming	
▨	Manufacturing and trade	
▨	Commercial fishing	
▨	Forestry	
⛟	Coal	
⛏	Petroleum	
◈	Natural Gas	
⚡	Hydroelectric power	
⬧	Iron	
Pb	Lead	
C	Copper	
U	Uranium	
P	Phosphates	

Place Eastern European countries contain important resources. Yet their economies have not been stable. *What caused their economies to perform poorly? What events have helped transform their economies for the better?*

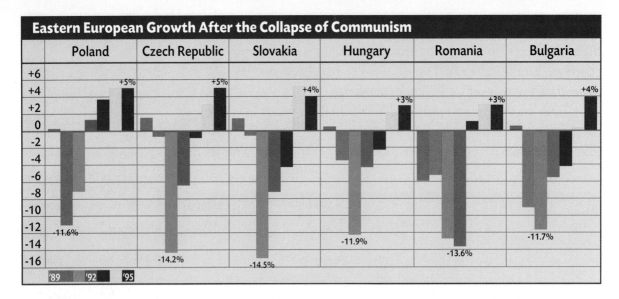

Eastern European Growth After the Collapse of Communism					
Poland	Czech Republic	Slovakia	Hungary	Romania	Bulgaria

Poland: +5%, −11.6%
Czech Republic: +5%, −14.2%
Slovakia: +4%, −14.5%
Hungary: +3%, −11.9%
Romania: +3%, −13.6%
Bulgaria: +4%, −11.7%

'89 '92 '95

Economic growth in Eastern Europe has been slow but steady after communism. *How would Western Europe and the United States benefit from a strong Eastern Europe?*

other words, to keep their jobs, workers must produce a large amount of quality goods in the shortest time possible.

Hungary   Of all the countries of Eastern Europe, Hungary enjoyed a head start in modernizing its economy. Unlike industries in other Communist countries, Hungary's government-owned businesses began setting their own wages, prices, and goals in the early 1980s. These businesses also made agreements with foreign companies, giving them contacts beyond the Soviet Union and Eastern Europe.

By the time communism collapsed, Hungary had begun to sell its businesses to private companies. The country already had established a good trading relationship with nations in Western Europe.

Poland   Since the end of Soviet control of Eastern Europe, Poland has been one of the economic leaders in the region. Western Poland especially has been flourishing.

Poland owes some of its economic success to its good roads, reliable telephone and communications systems, and its closeness to Germany. Many workers in western Poland speak German as well as Polish. That has drawn many German businesses to the area.

Poznan, the regional capital of western Poland, enjoys full employment today, and has attracted such foreign investors as AT&T. The Wrigley company has built a chewing gum factory near the city, and the German Volkswagen corporation has opened its own plant in the vicinity. Poznan officials hope to build on their success with the construction of an English-language public school.

Ukraine Ukraine once produced 25 percent of the industrial goods, 30 percent of the meat, 25 percent of other agricultural products, and 50 percent of the iron ore for the entire Soviet Union. After independence, Ukraine remains an economic powerhouse. But now the country produces goods for itself and exports the surplus for a profit.

Ukraine's future looks better than that of other former Soviet republics because it possesses raw materials and the factories to produce finished goods. Coal and iron ore are mined in the Southeast and made into steel in central Ukraine. Steel is used to produce trucks, buses, and mining equipment in northern Ukraine.

About a third of Ukraine's land is farm and pasture. The central area produces wheat, corn, and sugar beets.

Coal and iron ore from south-eastern Ukraine end up as tricycles (inset) in a former military factory. Buses (below) and other heavy machinery are also made in northern Ukraine. *Where is the steel manufactured that is used in Ukrainian industry?*

Potatoes, rye, and flax, a plant used in the making of linen, grow in the North. With the help of irrigation, farmers in the South produce vegetables and fruit. Cattle, sheep, poultry, and pigs are the most common livestock.

Ukraine also has a large supply of uranium, the material that produces energy in nuclear power plants. After the Chernobyl disaster, however, few Ukrainians support the building of more nuclear power plants. Instead, Ukraine is looking to its supply of natural gas and hydroelectric plants along the Dnepr River to meet its energy needs.

Much of Ukraine's trade still involves the other republics of the former Soviet Union. The country also has good relations with Poland and Hungary. It is reaching out to a wider trade

Coins of the Realm

Soon after governments were organized, coins, and later, paper money replaced bartering as a simpler way to conduct business. The images on money reflect what is important to the people or the rulers of a region.

Most gold coins pictured the ruler of the day. If one ruler was conquered, those coins were destroyed and newer ones minted to show the new ruler's face. Justinian appeared on a gold Byzantine coin that was called the Byzantine Solidus. The coin weighed 4.5 grams (0.16 ounce). Used widely in the Byzantine realm, the coin slowly lost value as the empire weakened.

Coins with owls on them pointed out the important role of Greek gods in ancient Greece. The Greek goddess Athena's face appeared on one side of a silver coin. An owl stared from the other side of the coin as a symbol of Athena's Wisdom.

Athenian drachma

Dutch guilder

British pence

Austrian schilling

network, including the British Isles and countries in Norden and Western Europe.

Romania For years, Romania has lagged behind other Eastern European countries. Only in the last 30 years did manufacturing pass agriculture as the leading producer of income in the country. Romania's industry remains closely tied to farming. Factories produce mainly tractors, farm equipment, and processed foods.

Since the end of communism, Romania has discovered a new source of income in tourism. Visitors come to Transylvania and the Carpathian Mountains to see villages that have remained unchanged for hundreds of years.

With the breaking apart of the Soviet Union, the Russian ruble has lost its value in the countries the Soviets once controlled. Eastern European countries have introduced their own money once again.

Polish zloty

French francs

Pfennig from the former East Germany

Czech Republic's 200 crown banknotes

Latvia may use paper money in lats, a Latvian unit, and coins called santims. The people of Ukraine spend paper money called hryvnia. In Poland you might spend a zloty, and in Slovenia you would use a Tolar. Croatia uses a Croatian dinar.

Russian rubles

Modern-day Greek drachmas

The Transition Continues

Some nations are finding the transition difficult. Albania, for example, is still largely agricultural. Bulgaria remains a developing country, its industry in need of regular financial aid every six months from the European Bank for Reconstruction and Development.

Even the most advanced of Eastern Europe's industrialized countries—Hungary, Poland, and the Czech Republic—continue to face problems. It has not been easy for them to shift from government-owned industries to private enterprise. Many factories still require government help to survive.

In 1996, the Czech Republic became the first Eastern European nation to form a special relationship with the European Union. Czech leaders hope that their new ties with the Union will speed their economic development. Like other Eastern European nations, they still recognize that their nation's economy lags behind much of Europe.

Industries such as fiberglass weaving in the Czech Republic support an improved economy in Eastern Europe. *What do these countries still need to help their economies grow?*

LESSON 3 REVIEW

Fact Follow-Up
1. What is the purpose of the European Bank for Reconstruction and Development?
2. What are some of the difficulties faced by the changing economies of Eastern Europe?
3. Describe efforts by Poland to remake its economy.
4. Why does Ukraine's economic future look brighter than that of other former Soviet republics?
5. Which nations lag behind others in remaking their economies?

Think These Through
6. If you were an advisor to Bulgaria or Albania, what advice would you give to get the economies moving? Explain.
7. Which Eastern European economy do you think is doing best now? Explain why.

*Using Information for Problem Solving,
Decision Making, and Planning*

Investing in Eastern Europe

In the wake of the fall of communism in Eastern Europe, business organizations in the United States and other nations began investing in factories and other economic interests in the newly independent nations of the region. Initially, investment—or planning to invest—in Eastern Europe was fashionable. The area was seen as a giant market for the consumer goods not available to people during the Soviet era. Some of these investments have been profitable. Others have not.

In the years since 1989, potential investors in Eastern European enterprises have become more wary. They look more deeply into information about the nations of Eastern Europe before making investment decisions.

Investors consider the economic history of nations—their industrial development before World War II and since Soviet control. For example, with what type of industry has a country had experience? Are resources still available to run the industry? What is the size and skill of the labor force? Investors also consider the political stability of each nation. Then, and only then, do they reach decisions to invest or not.

You can make some judgments about whether to invest in various Eastern European nations by completing and studying a chart like the one below.

Use information from Chapters 18, 19, and 20 to complete the chart. If you need additional information, consult a current almanac. When you have finished, compare your chart with a classmate's.

Based on the information you have gathered and organized, which nations of Eastern Europe offer the best opportunities for foreign investors? Which nations are not such good investment possibilities? Is there additional information you need? If so, what kind of information?

Investing in Eastern Europe			
Name of Nation	**Pre-World War II Industry**	**1945-1990 Industry**	**Political Stability**
Ex.: Czech Republic	Glass and Textiles	Automobiles	Stable after split from Slovakia
1			
2			
3			
4			
5			

Chapter 20 Review

LESSONS LEARNED

LESSON 1   The Soviet Union dominated Eastern Europe after World War II. Hungary and Czechoslovakia tried unsuccessfully to overthrow communist governments. In the 1980s and 1990s, Soviet influence weakened. Independence and democratic movements became successful in much of the region.

LESSON 2   Governing in Eastern Europe has been difficult. Ethnic tensions caused Czechoslovakia to peacefully split into the Czech Republic and Slovakia. In Yugoslavia those tensions caused war as independence movements spread to several republics.

LESSON 3   Hungary, Poland, and Ukraine are the economic giants of Eastern Europe. The Czech Republic has a substantial industrial base. Other countries are finding the transition from communism to capitalism more difficult.

FACT FOLLOW-UP

1. Which Eastern European nations became part of the Soviet Union before the end of World War II?
2. Which nations of Eastern Europe fell under heavy Soviet influence after World War II?
3. What was the Prague Spring? What were its results?
4. Compare the Solidarity movement in Poland with the freedom movement in Hungary and Czechoslovakia during the Cold War.

5. What are some of the problems faced by East European nations as they make the transition from communism to capitalism?
6. Hungary and Poland have been leaders in creating market economies. Why?
7. What events in the late 1980s motivated Eastern Europeans to oppose their Soviet leaders?
8. Describe the role of ethnicity in events in the Balkan countries.

THINK THESE THROUGH

9. Imagine that you work for a business that is planning to expand into Eastern Europe. With which nation do you think it would be best to do business? Explain.
10. Which nation do you think has been most successful in making the transition from communism to capitalism? Explain your choice.
11. Why do you think Czechoslovakia had a Velvet Revolution while there is still much bloodshed in the Balkans?

SHARPENING SKILLS

12. Imagine that you work for an automobile manufacturing company. Is there an Eastern European nation in which you would recommend building a factory? Which one(s)? Explain why.
13. Based on the information you have, is there an Eastern European nation in which you would recommend that no investment of any kind be made? Explain your answer.

Use letters on the map to locate and name the following:

14. An Eastern European nation that gained freedom from Russian domination and then split into two nations. What are today's names for these two nations?

15. The Soviet-dominated nation that was created as part of Eastern Europe after World War II. Today, it is part of of one of the most powerful and prosperous nations in Western Europe.

What was the nation's name just after World War II? It is part of what nation today?

16. Eastern European nations that until 1991 were part of the Soviet Union's territory.

17. The nation in the former Yugoslavia that was occupied by United Nations and NATO troops in the 1990s in an effort to stop a long, bitter war.

18. The large nation that formed most of the territory of the Soviet Union.

19. Location of Gdansk, an important port on the Baltic Sea.

Reviewing Place Location

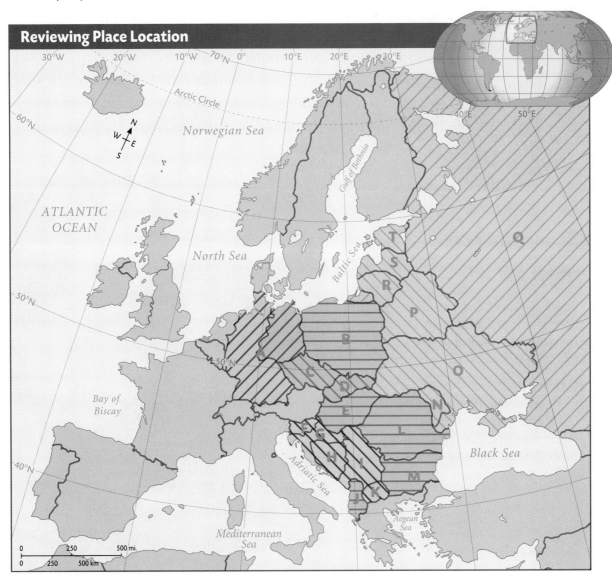

Society and Culture

On a scaffold above the streets of Prague, with only a red plastic bucket and a spatula, Jan Branda is taking on a lion.

    Branda, a stonemason and sculptor, busily repairs the cracks and crumbling edges of Prague's statues.

    "At least 80 percent of our statues and sculptures are in bad shape from assaults ranging from acid rain to mechanical damage," Vratislav Nejedly of the Culture Ministry said.

    Today, Branda touches up the mane of a royal lion with the special putty in his bucket. Tomorrow, he might reshape the chin of a cherub or restore the fingers of a saint.

Repairing Prague's statues

Stone cherub

CHAPTER PREVIEW

LESSON 1
A Tale of Three Cities
Prague, Budapest, and Warsaw, as leading cities of the Czech Republic, Hungary, and Poland, respectively, reflect the culture of Eastern Europe.

LESSON 2
Religion
Despite Communist efforts to rid the region of religion, Eastern Europeans remain faithful to a variety of religions.

LESSON 3
Food and Sports
Food and sports are important signs of culture. They reflect the land and people of Eastern Europe.

Eastern Europe–Major Languages

Estonian

Latvian

Lithuanian

Russian

Baltic Sea

Polish

Belarussian

Russian

Czech

Slovak

Hungarian

Ukrainian

Russian

Hungarian

Romanian

Slovene

German

Serbo-Croatian

Adriatic Sea

Black Sea

Bulgarian

Albanian

Turkish

Macedonian

Indo-European Languages

Slavic Languages

Romance Languages

Baltic Languages

Germanic Languages

Non-Indo-European Languages

Finno-Ugric Languages

Thraco-Illyrian Languages

Turkic Languages

0   100   200 mi.
0   100   200 km

Detail from a building column in the Czech Republic

A Tale of Three Cities

LESSON PREVIEW

Key Ideas

- Prague, Czech Republic, Budapest, Hungary, and Warsaw, Poland, are the leading cities of Eastern Europe.
- The cities reflect the cultures of their countries.

Key Terms

Warsaw Ghetto

The cities of Eastern Europe have awakened as if from a troubled sleep. After 40 years of Communist rule, Prague, Budapest, and Warsaw have led their nations in the rediscovery of their national cultures. They also are pointing the way in building modern economic systems. In the process, they are becoming truly international cities once again.

Prague

Since the end of communism, Prague, the capital of the Czech Republic, has become an important Eastern European center. The city draws people who are charmed by its traditions and attracted by its business opportunities.

Church spires mark the skyline of Prague. The many steeples earn the city its name of the City of a Hundred Spires. Prague remains one of the most beautiful cities in Europe. Its palaces and winding medieval streets fortunately escaped damage in World War II.

Prague, Czech Republic, offers visitors a view of the past in its Old Town. The capital is the home of more than 1 million people. *Why is Prague called the City of a Hundred Spires?*

Prague lies on the banks of the Vltava (VUHL·tuh·vah) River. This location has helped it grow as a city of trade since its founding 1,200 years ago. In 1348, the Holy Roman Emperor Charles IV chose Prague as the location for the first university in Eastern Europe. In the early 1400s, Prague was the headquarters for the work of religious reformer Jan Hus (HYOOS) as he challenged the Roman Catholic Church. Hus helped bring about the Reformation that swept across Europe in the 1500s.

Old Town is the historic center of Prague, dating back to the 1300s. There a monument to Hus and Tyn Church, where he preached, still stand. Nearby Old Town Hall features a famous sixteenth-century clock. As the hour strikes, statues of the 12 apostles march in procession. A skeleton figure of Death tolls the bell.

New Town is the business center of Prague. Its busiest street, Wencelas Square, includes hotels, shops, restaurants, and the Czech Republic's National Museum.

Today, more than 1 million people live in Prague, most of them on the outskirts of the city. Because of a housing shortage, the government has built new apartment buildings in the suburbs. Still, many people live closer to the center of town, in the older, more crowded areas.

Suburbs of Prague include many factories. They make aircraft and diesel engines, automobiles and streetcars, machine tools and optical instruments, processed food, chemicals, and furniture.

Budapest

Eight bridges cross the Danube River, linking the old cities of Buda and Pest to form Budapest, a capital city covering about 200 square miles (520 sq km).

The Romans founded a city on the site in A.D. 100, at an easy point for crossing the Danube. Later, Germanic, Slavic, and Hungarian tribes ruled the area. In modern times, Turks and Austrians controlled Budapest. German and Soviet forces fought over the city in World War II.

Budapest is a lively combination of old and new. Old Buda, on the west bank of the Danube, is

Budapest, Hungary, attracts young shoppers searching for concert posters and music.
What other attractions bring people to Budapest?

What would YOU do?

Rudy Vlcek was let go by his company in the United States. He moved with his wife to Prague in the Czech Republic to open a successful restaurant.

Rudy is only one of many Americans moving to Prague in the 1990s. Many young people have gone there to start businesses. The Czech language is not easy. Living there is not always comfortable. Yet some Americans have enjoyed success. Would you make such a move?

still a quiet place of wooded hills and historic churches. On Castle Hill stands the Royal Palace, within the remains of an ancient fort.

The rounded domes of old Turkish mosques are scattered through the city. Most now are Christian churches. The old State Opera House, one of Europe's great music houses, has been carefully reconstructed. It had been totally destroyed during World War II.

Tourists flocking to Budapest discover the city's cultural attractions. It has 20 museums, 25 major theaters, and several concert halls. The people living there—especially the young people—also know which stores sell the latest popular music, posters, and magazines. Rock bands from the United States, the British Isles, and Western Europe include Budapest on their tours.

Today, 20 percent of Hungary's population, more than 2 million people, live in Budapest. The city serves as more than a center of culture. Budapest is the banking and financial center for Hungary. Industrial areas surround most of the city. There, factories produce chemical products, textiles, and transportation equipment. About 75 percent of the city's population lives on the east bank of the Danube, in what was once the old city, Pest.

As the capital, Budapest contains government offices that line the river bank. The Houses of Parliament stand in the Inner City, called Belvaros.

Warsaw

In Warsaw, on the Kosciuszko waterfront, stands the statue of a siren—a mythological woman with a fish's tail, who holds a sword and shield. According to legend, this siren of the Vistula River wished to reward the hospitality of two fishermen named Wars and Sawa. So she allowed a prince to lose his way near their house on the riverbank.

The fishermen helped the prince find the path back to his castle. He was so grateful to Wars and Sawa that he gave them the land bordering the river. The fishermen founded a town, which people later called Warsaw.

In fact, Warsaw began as a Slavic settlement on the Vistula River in the 900s. By the sixteenth century, Warsaw had become the capital of the Polish kingdom.

During World War II, the Nazi Germans sealed off the **Warsaw Ghetto** where 500,000 Jews lived. This was part of the Nazi campaign to exterminate Jews. Warsaw's Jews lived under inhuman conditions. Thousands died of starvation and disease. The Nazis executed many others.

In August 1944, the people of Warsaw rose against the Germans and tried to drive them out. Soviet troops had already

CONNECTIONS

Geography & Science

Marie Curie: Discoverer of X-Ray Technology

We remember Marie Curie as a Parisian who helped discover radium and the radioactivity of uranium. She also found another element and called it polonium, in honor of her homeland.

Curie was born in Warsaw, Poland. Her given name was Manya Sklodowska. Encouraged by her father, Manya studied math and chemistry. In 1894, as a student in Paris, she met Pierre Curie. They married in 1895 and became a team. Their work earned them a Nobel Prize for physics in 1903.

It was Marie who invented the term "radioactivity." That is the property of an element in which energy is emitted

because of disintegration of the atom's nucleus. Mme. Curie earned a second Nobel Prize in 1911 for her work on radioactivity.

People were fascinated by the discovery of a new element. They wanted to know how radium worked and what it did. Marie Curie dedicated her life to finding ways radium could treat disease. During World War I, she

used the X-ray technology made possible by radium to help the wounded. She died in 1934 of leukemia, a cancer of the blood possibly caused by her work.

Curie was one of the first great physicists. She was also one of the first female scientists in any field. Her daughter Irene, became a scientist. She and her husband, Frederic, won the Nobel Prize for chemistry in 1935.

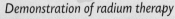
Demonstration of radium therapy

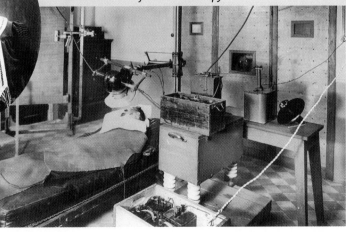

Warsaw, Poland, had to be reconstructed after World War II. *How could buildings be rebuilt to look as they had before the war?*

arrived near the city, but they did nothing to aid the revolt. After months of fierce struggle, the Poles surrendered. The Nazis completely destroyed the city.

After the war, the people of Warsaw began rebuilding their city to look as it had before the destruction. Using old paintings and prints as their guide, architects rebuilt palaces, churches, and even the thirteenth-century walls.

Modern government and business offices now rise next to the restored buildings in the city center on the left, or west, bank of the Vistula. The left bank is also Warsaw's major residential area, largely composed of high-rise apartments. More than 1.5 million people live in this city, which extends 174 square miles (452 sq km).

Besides serving as Poland's capital and chief center for culture and science, Warsaw has become an important manufacturing center. Its factories produce automobiles, electronic equipment, metals, textiles, and processed food.

LESSON 1 REVIEW

Fact Follow-Up
1. Which city is called the City of a Hundred Spires? Why is it called that?
2. Who was John Hus? Why was he important?
3. What are some cultural attractions of Budapest?
4. What is the legend about the founding of Warsaw?
5. What happened in Warsaw in World War II?

Think These Through
6. Which of the three cities would you most like to visit? Explain why.
7. Which of the three cities do you think is most important in the history of Eastern Europe? Explain your choice.
8. Which of the three cities do you think will be most important in the future? Explain your answer.

Religion

ear the city of Siauliai (shuh·lay) stands a monument to the religious faith of Lithuanians. It's not a statue or a church but thousands of crosses, some simple, some elaborately decorated. The people call it the Hill of Crosses.

During Soviet control of Lithuania, the Communist government severely restricted religious practices. Lithuanian Catholics set up the crosses as a declaration of their faith and as a silent protest against persecution.

Soviet authorities promptly destroyed the crosses, only to find that people replaced them time after time. Today, although religious restrictions have ended, the tradition continues. Every visitor to the Hill of Crosses brings a cross to leave behind.

LESSON PREVIEW

Key Ideas
- Eastern Europe is a region of many faiths, each kept alive despite efforts of the Soviet Union and local Communist governments to outlaw religion.
- The major religions in the region are Roman Catholic, Lutheran, Muslim, and Eastern Orthodox.

Key Term
Cyrillic

Religion and National Identity

You have read how religion in Eastern Europe has been a source of conflict. For centuries, religion also has played a vital role in the social and cultural life of the region.

Traditionally, the northern part of the region has been Lutheran. In the South, Muslims, Roman Catholics, and members of Eastern Orthodox churches live together. The West

The Hill of Crosses became the site of a silent protest during Soviet control of Lithuania.
What do the crosses represent? Why did Lithuanians protest?

remains mainly Roman Catholic. Elsewhere, Eastern Orthodox churches are in the majority.

Communist governments in Eastern Europe worked to restrict the influence of religion, and even tried to eliminate it altogether. By decreasing the power of religion, Communist governments in Eastern Europe hoped to increase their own power. The Soviets wanted to weaken churches to encourage people to look to Moscow for leadership.

Governments closed or tore down places of worship, forbade religious instruction of children, and imprisoned clergy. Governments kept churchgoers from entering the best schools and getting good jobs. Government-controlled media criticized religion constantly. The government scheduled the most popular

Cyrillic: An Alphabet for Religion

Eastern Europeans use different alphabets. Both Serbs and Croats speak a language called Serbo-Croatian, but they write it differently. The Croats use the Roman (or Latin) alphabet, the same one that you are reading now. The Serbs use the **Cyrillic** *(suh·RIHL·ihk) alphabet.*

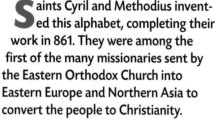
Saint Cyril

Saints Cyril and Methodius invented this alphabet, completing their work in 861. They were among the first of the many missionaries sent by the Eastern Orthodox Church into Eastern Europe and Northern Asia to convert the people to Christianity.

These Eastern Orthodox missionaries found people who had well-developed spoken languages. Cyrillic was invented so that the Bible and other Christian literature could be read by those converted to the faith.

The Cyrillic alphabet has 33 letters instead of the 26 in the Roman alphabet. When you compare Cyrillic with Greek letters, you can easily guess that Cyrillic was based largely on the writing system used by ancient Greeks.

television programs during religious services to discourage people from attending ceremonies in churches and synagogues.

Albanians probably suffered most from these anti-religious campaigns. In 1967, Albania outlawed all religions and seized property belonging to every faith. Many other people of Eastern Europe kept their traditions of faith. They protested publicly, often forcing their government to back down, or they simply continued to worship in secret. In Poland, the Roman Catholic Church was too powerful to be challenged. The Polish faithful continued church practices.

When the countries of Eastern Europe broke from Soviet rule, freedom of religion was one of the first rights to be restored. Churches reopened for worship services.

Eastern Orthodox missionaries from Constantinople (now Istanbul) carried the alphabet with them when they converted the Russians, Serbs, Bulgars, and some other Slavic people. Catholic missionaries from Rome used the Roman alphabet when they converted the Poles, Czechs, and other Slavic people.

In recent years, the Cyrillic and Roman alphabets have become entangled in politics. During the Cold War, the Soviet Union tried to force Moldovans to adopt Cyrillic, the alphabet Russians use (right). More recently, bitter differences in the former Yugoslavia have been dramatized by Balkan newspapers using two writing systems.

Poland

In the 1800s, when Russia, Prussia, and Austria divided and ruled Poland, Roman Catholicism was a source of unity for Poles. Poles could not govern their own country, or even speak Polish in their schools. Yet their religion helped to preserve cultural unity and national identity.

In the twentieth century, the Communist government tried to restrict religious life to control Polish loyalty. Communists imprisoned Stefan Cardinal Wyszynski, leader of the Catholic Church in Poland, and accused him of plotting against the government.

In 1956, Poles rioted in protest of Soviet domination of their culture and economy. The government eased off and released Cardinal Wyszynski. Poles continued to attend religious services and to teach their faith to their children, despite government disapproval.

In 1978, another Polish church leader, Karol Cardinal Wojtyla, the archbishop of Kraków, became the first Polish pope. As John Paul II, he visited Poland three times during the last years of Communist rule—in 1979, 1983, and 1987. Every time Pope John Paul II went to Poland, he spoke out for greater freedom in his native country.

Now that Poland has won its independence, freedom of religion is the right of all Poles—Protestants, Jews, and Eastern Orthodox believers, as well as Roman Catholics. Religion remains a strong bond for Poles. Religious holidays are always occasions for reunions and feasting.

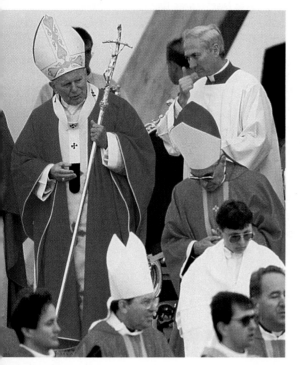

Pope John Paul II is from Poland. He is the first Polish pope. *How did his visits to Poland encourage the people to work for freedom?*

Ukraine

Most Ukrainians today belong to the Ukrainian Orthodox Church. This church is part of the Eastern Orthodox faith. As you recall, Eastern Orthodoxy consists of many national churches, each of them independent.

Since its beginnings, the Ukrainian Orthodox Church served as an important source of national identity. In the seventeenth century, however, Russia conquered Ukraine. At that time, the Russians forced the Ukrainian Orthodox Church to become part of the Russian Orthodox Church as a way of controlling Ukrainian loyalty to the czar.

Ukrainian leaders established the Ukrainian Independent Orthodox Church. It remained free of Russian control, becoming a source of religious and national unity for Ukrainians in difficult times.

The Communists also tried to destroy the Orthodox faith in Ukraine and every other place under their rule. The Ukrainian Orthodox Church continued its activities in secret. It opposed Communist rule and supported independence for Ukraine. In 1990, when the Soviet Union collapsed, the Ukrainian Orthodox Church finally became legal again. Many Ukrainians belong to the Ukrainian Orthodox Church.

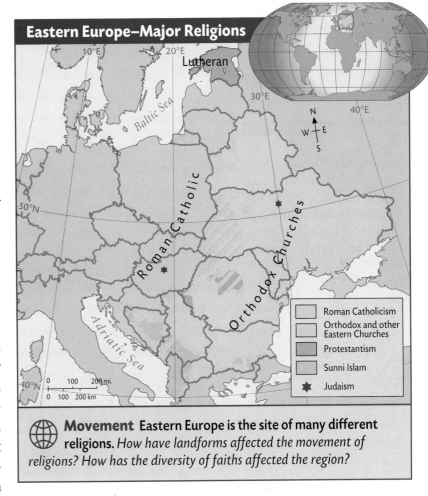

Eastern Europe–Major Religions

Legend:
- Roman Catholicism
- Orthodox and other Eastern Churches
- Protestantism
- Sunni Islam
- ★ Judaism

Movement Eastern Europe is the site of many different religions. *How have landforms affected the movement of religions? How has the diversity of faiths affected the region?*

LESSON 2 REVIEW

Fact Follow-Up

1. Describe the variety of religious beliefs in Eastern Europe. Where are the religions located?
2. Why and how did Communist governments discourage religious beliefs and practices?
3. How has Roman Catholicism served as a source of unity for Polish people?
4. Name some famous Polish religious leaders.
5. Describe religion in Ukraine under Communist rule.

Think These Through

6. Which nation of Eastern Europe do you think had the strongest religious institutions under the Soviets? Explain your answer.
7. Suppose the Soviets had not tried to suppress religion. How do you think Eastern Europe today might have been different?

LESSON PREVIEW

Key Ideas

- The influence of nearby regions—such as Mediterranean Europe, Norden, and southwest Asia—affects the kinds of food people enjoy in Eastern Europe.
- Eastern Europeans enjoy soccer and basketball.
- Also popular are mountain and water sports, depending on where people live.

. . . .

In a small village in the mountains of Bulgaria, an elderly woman keeps alive traditions of hospitality. As evening approaches, she cooks a large meal and awaits the tourists she has invited to dinner at her home.

When the minibus pulls up, the hostess is already on her doorstep. As is the custom, she greets her guests with bread, salt, and herbs, and welcomes them inside.

After a formal toast with plum brandy, the guests enjoy bowls of cold cucumber soup, then a salad of tomatoes and cucumbers with cream cheese. She then serves the main course of pork stew, bread, and red wine. The delicious dinner ends with cakes and fruit. All the while, village musicians sing and play folk songs.

In Bulgaria, as in all the countries of Eastern Europe, the food is usually simple. The ceremonies of sharing a meal can make even the simplest dinner a festive occasion.

Food

Eastern Europeans do not share the variety or abundance of food available in other regions of Europe. They make the most of the meats, grains, and root vegetables that the climate and soil produce.

Family time is important everywhere in the world. Mealtime serves as get-together time throughout Eastern Europe. *Why is this is a good custom?*

There is not one typical East European meal or cooking style. Turkey to the south, Austria and Germany to the west, and Norden to the north have affected the traditional dishes in each country of Eastern Europe.

Hungary

Hungary's traditional foods show the influence of the Magyars, Germans, and the people of the Balkans.

A meal in Hungary might begin with a spicy fish soup, called *ponty halazzle*. The best-known main course, which you may have tasted, is *gulyas* (goulash), a stew made of beef, onions, potatoes, and gravy seasoned with paprika. Hungarians also enjoy pork, usually with noodles, potatoes, or *galuska*, a kind of Hungarian pasta.

For dessert, Hungarians will serve strudel, a thin pastry stuffed with cheese or fruit. *Makos teszta*, a mixture of noodles, poppy seeds, and sugar, is another favorite.

Hungarians snack between meals, too. In the afternoon, people gather in coffeehouses to talk while they enjoy coffee and pastries.

Poland

Meals in Poland tend to be simple and filling. Hearty stews and thick beet or cabbage soup frequently appear on the table with rye bread, followed by a dessert of fresh apples.

To celebrate special occasions, Poles carefully prepare fish and elaborate pastries. The most important holiday feast, the Vigilia, occurs on Christmas Eve.

The Vigilia begins with the breaking of the *oplatek*, a thin wafer of bread, and the formal exchange of good wishes among family and guests. Then everyone shares a vegetable salad and a beet soup (*barszcz*) with mushroom dumplings (*uszki*). Fish, usually carp, forms the traditional main course. For dessert, everyone enjoys *strucla*, a poppy seed pastry.

While the family and their guests open presents, a large tray called the *bakalia* passes through the group. The bakalia offers a selection of cookies, dried and fresh fruit, nuts, and candies.

Ukraine

Ukrainian meals most often include chicken, fish, or pork. *Kasha*, cooked buckwheat, is also an important part of the Ukrainian diet.

A bakalia tray has lots of treats for a Polish family and guests on Christmas Eve. *Does your family have holiday traditions like this one?*

Marketplaces in Eastern Europe, such as this one in Bucharest, Romania, sell fresh vegetables. *What items do you recognize here?*

Kasha is a main ingredient in *holubsti*, stuffed cabbage rolls that also include meat and rice.

You may have heard of *borsch*, a Ukrainian soup of beets, cabbage, and meat served with sour cream and rye bread. Another favorite traditional food is *varenyky*, boiled dumplings stuffed with potatoes, sauerkraut, cheese, or fruit. Ukrainians serve varenyky with sour cream, fried onions, or bits of bacon.

Romania Romanians enjoy grilled meats, such as *mititei*, a kind of meatball eaten as an appetizer or a main course. *Marmaliga*, a cornmeal dish, often accompanies meats and stews.

In Romania, the principal meal is served at noon. It begins with borsch or *ciorba*, a soup with lamb, mushrooms, and leeks. The main course may be *tocana*, a pork stew with garlic and onions, served with marmaliga, and *sarmali*, cabbage leaves wrapped around rice and meat.

At dessert, Romanians enjoy ice cream, cake, or *baklava*, a thin nut-filled pastry covered with honey. Another favorite sweet is *papanasi*, doughnuts made of cream and cheese.

Serbia, Bosnia-Herzegovina, Croatia The countries that make up the former Yugoslavia cherish different traditions in preparing food, depending on their location and cultural influences.

In Serbia, for instance, the popularity of grilled meats and strong, thick coffee shows the influence of southwest Asia. Macedonian *sarma*, stuffed grape leaves, comes from Greece.

The food of Bosnia-Herzegovina includes both Turkish and Muslim traditions. *Musaka*, roasted meat with eggplant, and *kapama*, mutton with spinach and green onions, are among the favorite dinners here.

Some Croatian dishes resemble the most popular meals of Western Europe. Zagreb veal cutlet, for instance, looks and tastes much like the Austrian favorite, wiener schnitzel.

Sports

As in the rest of Europe, Eastern Europeans enjoy both playing and watching soccer. Many schools, factories, and farms organize their own teams. Professional clubs compete in the European and World Cup Soccer Championships. One of the strongest teams in Europe in the past years has been the Kiev Dynamo from Ukraine.

Basketball is also popular in Eastern Europe. Hungarians and Serbs share a strong enthusiasm for the sport.

Mountain Sports   The city of Sarajevo in Bosnia-Herzegovina was the site of the 1984 Winter Olympics. The surrounding mountains make it an ideal spot for skiing, tobogganing, and other Olympic winter sports. In the summer, the rugged highlands offer a challenging climb for hikers and hunters.

The Carpathian Mountains attract campers and hikers from the countries where the range is located. Poles, Czechs, Slovaks, Ukrainians, Romanians, and Bulgarians head for their parts of the mountains in all seasons. The crescent-shaped range is the setting for rock climbing, skiing, and tobogganing (see map, page 347).

Sarajevo, a city in Bosnia-Herzegovina, was the setting of the 1984 Winter Olympics. The stadium is now the site of a cemetery for war victims. *Who fought in the war?*

The Black Sea draws people from Eastern Europe to its coast. *What Eastern European countries are located on the Black Sea?*

◆ ◆ ◆ ◆ ◆ **GAMES** ◆ ◆ ◆ ◆
People Play

Tobogganing A large runner-less sled made of metal or laminated wood offers a broad surface to slide along powdery snow. Toboggans can hold more than one person, which makes them fun.

Take a large hill, a toboggan, a few friends, and you have an enjoyable winter's afternoon. In Eastern Europe, with its mountain ranges and snowfall, young people enjoy riding down hills. Some toboggans have runners on them, as European sleds do.

Water Sports Eastern European nations have sent medal-winning swimmers to the Olympic games. These swimmers train in indoor pools. Only a few places in Eastern Europe have open water that is warm enough for water sports.

The Black Sea is by far the most popular of these places. Its warm waters wash the beaches of Ukraine, Romania, and Bulgaria. The Adriatic Sea also draws vacationers. Lake Balaton in Hungary attracts kayakers and sailors.

People gather on beaches along the Baltic Sea to catch the summer sun or go boating. Only the brave try to swim in the cold sea.

LESSON ③ REVIEW

Fact Follow-Up

1. What are some special foods of Eastern Europe?
2. Compare the special foods of Eastern Europe with the foods you eat.
3. What are some sports that are popular all over Eastern Europe?
4. How are sports in Eastern Europe like sports in other European regions you have studied?

5. Which sports activities described in this lesson are also played in the community where you live?

Think These Through

6. Why do you think there is not one typical East European food or cooking style?
7. Of all the foods described in this lesson, which do you think would be most popular with American teenagers? Explain why.

Demonstrating Skills in Constructive Interpersonal Relationships and Social Participation

Resolving Eastern Europe's Tensions

In Eastern Europe many and varied traditions meet. Such diversity sometimes produces strife. There are misunderstandings about religion, competition for scarce resources, and conflicts rising out of long-standing ethnic resentments.

To discover how conflict might be resolved, select two ethnic groups from those mentioned in Chapter 18. Divide a sheet of paper in half lengthwise, and label each half with the name of an ethnic group you have chosen. Next, write the following categories in the left margin, allowing two to three inches between each: *geographic location, religious beliefs, economic activities, traditions,* and *political history.*

Next, skim Chapters 18 through 21 and make notes about each group. You will have created a profile—or graphic description—of two ethnic groups. Find two classmates with whom you can exchange information about each of "your" two groups. Develop as full a profile as you can on each.

Now that you have profiles of two ethnic groups, consider their similarities and differences. What can unite them? What divides them?

Working alone, decide on one unifying and one dividing feature of the ethnic groups you have chosen. Find one trait or idea the two groups hold in common and one that divides them.

For instance, most—but not all—Eastern Europeans have Slavic ancestry. Is the Slavic heritage a possible unifying factor? Most also are Christians, but their churches are not the same. Could the sharing of Christian beliefs be a force for peace, or are the differences between Roman Catholic and Eastern Orthodox faiths too great to be overcome? Do you find any evidence that people with ethnic or religious differences might have much to gain if they shared economic resources?

Once you have decided upon unifying and dividing factors, imagine that you "belong" to one of the ethnic groups. Write a short paragraph beginning with these words. "I belong to _____ group. I share (beliefs, location, etc.) with [another] _____ group. Sharing _____ can bring us together because …" Bring together as many facts as possible to argue your points. You will try to convince someone who does not agree with you.

When you have written your paragraph, find a classmate who *does not* "belong" to the same ethnic group as you. Are there some beliefs or attitudes on which you can agree? Try to work out a joint statement describing areas of agreement and disagreement between you.

Reaching common ground begins when diverse people find at least one point on which they agree. In Eastern Europe today, thoughtful citizens are searching for such points of agreement.

Chapter 21 Review

LESSON 1 Prague, Budapest, and Warsaw are the major cities of the Czech Republic, Hungary, and Poland, respectively, and of Eastern Europe. Each city has a long history of cultural leadership.

LESSON 2 Religion has been a source of conflict in the region, but it also has been a source of inspiration and strength for centuries. Despite efforts by Communist officials to stamp out religions, Roman Catholics, Lutherans, Orthodox Christians, Jews, and Muslims continued to practice their faiths.

LESSON 3 Eastern European food is influenced by nearby regions. Grilled meats, pastries, stews, and vegetables are favorite dishes. Popular sports include soccer, basketball, mountain hiking and skiing, and some water sports.

TIME FOR TERMS

Warsaw Ghetto   Cyrillic

FACT FOLLOW-UP

1. What are some similarities and differences among Prague, Budapest, and Warsaw?
2. How does the relative location of Budapest make it an important city?
3. Describe the economic leadership that Prague, Budapest, and Warsaw offer their nations.
4. What was the importance of Marie Curie?
5. What are the major religions of Eastern Europe?

6. In which area of Eastern Europe is Islam strongest?
7. Describe Soviet efforts to restrict religious practice and belief.
8. Compare the Cyrillic alphabet and the Roman alphabet.
9. How do nearby regions influence the foods enjoyed by Eastern Europeans?

THINK THESE THROUGH

10. Which city is most important to the nation that surrounds it: Warsaw, Budapest, or Prague? Explain your choice.
11. What was the importance of religion in independence and freedom movements in Eastern Europe?
12. Was it a mistake for the Communist leaders to try to control religious practices? Why?
13. Which theme of geography best explains eating habits of East Europeans? Give reasons for your answer.
14. What is the most important way in which Budapest, Prague, and Warsaw reflect the culture of Eastern Europe? Explain.

SHARPENING SKILLS

15. Which stage of the conflict resolution process was easiest for you, and which was most difficult?
16. Are there any groups in the United States or other nations (not just ethnic groups!) that might find this process helpful? Explain.
17. Which area offers the most challenge to agreement: religion or economic activities? Why do you think this is so?

Use the letters on the map to locate and name the following:

18. two Balkan nations where Roman troops long ago left people speaking Romance rather than Slavic languages.

19. nations that until 1991 were part of Russia and where Russian and the national language are spoken.

20. a nation in the Balkans and one on the Baltic where people speak Finno-Ugric languages spoken by early settlers from east of the Ural Mountains.

21. three Slavic language-speaking nations. What languages are actually spoken in these nations? Explain why they are different.

22. a nation in Eastern Europe where Turkish is spoken.

23. a nation in Eastern Europe where German is spoken.

Reviewing Place Location

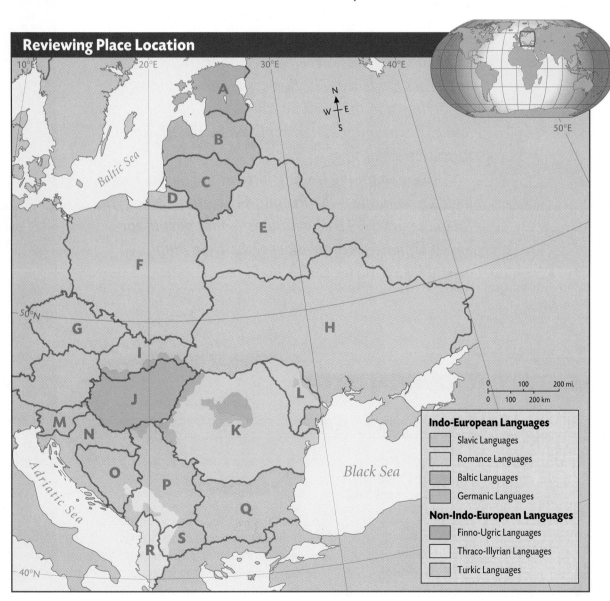

Indo-European Languages
- Slavic Languages
- Romance Languages
- Baltic Languages
- Germanic Languages

Non-Indo-European Languages
- Finno-Ugric Languages
- Thraco-Illyrian Languages
- Turkic Languages

Foundations of a Russian Empire

December 25, 1991. This was not the date of a holiday in the Soviet Union. In Moscow, Soviet President Mikhail Gorbachev signed papers that ended his government's existence. The Soviet's hammer and sickle flag flying atop the Kremlin, the capitol building, came down. It was immediately replaced by the traditional Russian tricolor flag.

Russia, once the leading force in the Soviet Union, took a new name—the Russian Federation. Along the Russian borders, 11 new nations—once part of the Soviet Union—became independent. An empire assembled centuries earlier had broken apart.

UNIT PREVIEW

CHAPTER 22
The Making and Breaking of an Empire
A huge empire stretching from Europe to Northern Asia's eastern coast is built over centuries, only to break apart in the 1990s.

CHAPTER 23
The Cultural Origins of Russia
The empire's Slavic people shaped their lives from historical experiences, a religious faith and ideas borrowed from ancient Byzantium, and contacts with an emerging Europe. Modern Russia and its neighbors today reflect these cultures.

Red Square

The Making and Breaking of an Empire

To celebrate its independence in 1991, Abkhazia, a region in Georgia, one of the new nations on Russia's southern border, issued postage stamps poking fun at the once powerful Communist party that had ruled Georgians against their will. No longer would stamps feature heroes of the Soviet Union—solemn portraits of Karl Marx, the founder of communism, or V. I. Lenin, the Russian revolutionary. Instead of Karl Marx, a new stamp featured a famous old-time United States comedian, Groucho Marx. An equally famous rock music star, John Lennon of the Beatles, appeared on another stamp.

Groucho Marx (top) and Karl Marx.

CHAPTER PREVIEW
LESSON 1
A Russian Empire Takes Shape
The rulers of Kiev organized the first Russian kingdom. Modern Russia was united by the rulers of Moscow.
LESSON 2
The Formation of the Soviet Union
A Russian empire was governed by absolute monarchs called czars. Czarist Russia fell in 1917. Communist dictators came to power.
LESSON 3
The Collapse of the Soviet Union
Russia emerged as a superpower after World War II. Communist dictators lost power, and their empire collapsed in 1991.

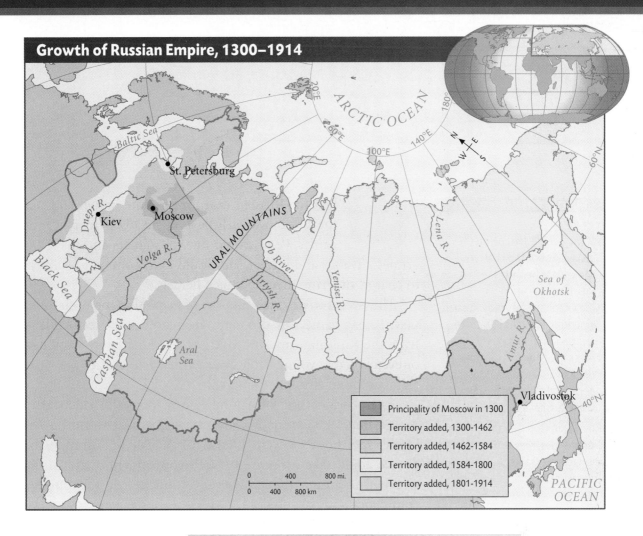

Growth of Russian Empire, 1300–1914

ARCTIC OCEAN

Baltic Sea

St. Petersburg

Днепр R.

Kiev

Moscow

URAL MOUNTAINS

Volga R.

Ob River

Irtysh R.

Yenisei R.

Lena R.

Black Sea

Caspian Sea

Aral Sea

Sea of Okhotsk

Amur R.

Vladivostok

PACIFIC OCEAN

	Principality of Moscow in 1300
	Territory added, 1300-1462
	Territory added, 1462-1584
	Territory added, 1584-1800
	Territory added, 1801-1914

0   400   800 mi.
0   400   800 km

Similar last names, but worlds apart: John Lennon (left) and V. I. Lenin.

АҦСНЫ 500

ДЖОН ЛЕННОН
JOHN LENNON

431

A Russian Empire Takes Shape

LESSON
1

LESSON PREVIEW

Key Ideas

- Slavic people settling on the plains west of the Ural Mountains became the first Russians.
- Kiev, capital of an early Russian kingdom, brought Byzantine civilization to Russia.
- After the Mongols destroyed the Kievan kingdom, Moscow became the leader, building a huge Russian empire.

Key Terms

czar, steppes, Kievan Russia, Mongols, Cossacks, Turkestan, Transcaucasia

When the Russian **czar**, or absolute monarch, Peter the Great was a little boy, he loved to play war games. Peter would line up soldiers and make his armies advance and retreat. He would even command soldiers to charge, ordering them to attack fiercely.

This seems to describe the sort of game that many children play. Peter's game was different. He played with real soldiers from the Russian army, not toys. Some soldiers were wounded or even killed in young Peter's war games. The "game" was early training for an absolute monarch.

Peter became one of a long line of powerful rulers who built a huge Russian nation and made Russia a world power. These czars, however, were often cruel and corrupt. In time, the people could take no more of such government. Early in the twentieth century, the czarist government lost the public's confidence and collapsed.

The Beginnings of Russia

By the time that Peter the Great became czar (1682-1725), Russia had already become a large empire. In size and power, Peter the Great's Russia was different from the small kingdoms from which it grew.

Slavic people who settled on the steppes west of the Ural Mountains became the first Russians. **Steppes** are flat, temperate grasslands. The Russians lived at first in small, scattered communities, farming the grasslands. Then powerful leaders drew these communities together into larger political units.

The first leaders were Vikings from Sweden. As you have read, Vikings from Norden ventured into many parts of Europe seeking wealth. To reach the lands that became Russia, Viking ships crossed the Baltic Sea and followed rivers southward

(see map, page 455). These rivers, especially the Dnepr River, connected the Viking homelands through Russia with the Black Sea and the riches of Constantinople and the Byzantine Empire.

The trade proved so valuable that the Vikings built defenses around cities. Novgorod (the name means "new city") anchored the northern end of the Vikings' route. Kiev became the passage's southern base. The city's location on the Dnepr River enabled it to command trade moving along the river to the Black Sea.

Both Novgorod and Kiev became headquarters of small kingdoms called *Rus.* Slavic people living in these kingdoms picked up the name and began calling themselves Russians (see map, page 455).

In time, the kingdoms in the north and south united. Together they occupied a large territory—often called **Kievan Russia**—west of the Ural Mountains. Russians replaced Vikings as leaders of this new European country.

Slavic Russians later became the leaders of an even larger region that would be called Russia. This first Russian kingdom maintained connections with Constantinople that had been established by the Vikings. Russia imported parts of the Byzantine Empire's civilization. Russians converted to Eastern Orthodox Christianity. Byzantine art, architecture, and political practices shaped modern Russia.

Visitors from Overseas shows Viking ships sailing across the Baltic Sea to the rivers of Russia. The ships carried warriors who sought wealth and land. *Where did the Vikings first settle in Russia?*

♦♦♦♦ **GAMES** ♦♦♦♦
People Play

Toy Soldiers In earlier centuries, children played with wooden soldiers. They came in all shapes and sizes. Painted tin and iron ones were favorites in the 1800s. Boys all over the world liked to play with tin soldiers painted with their country's uniforms. Today, those tin soldiers are collector's items.

♦ ♦ ♦ ♦ ♦ ♦ ♦ ♦ ♦ ♦ ♦ ♦ ♦ ♦

The Mongol Invasion

Despite its size and strength, Kievan Russia was challenged in the thirteenth century by invading forces from the East. On the Mongolian plains, an extraordinary military leader, Genghis Khan, built armies of horsemen that conquered an immense empire. All of China, itself one of the world's largest empires, fell to Genghis Khan's invading **Mongols**.

The Mongols also pushed deep into lands that later would become large parts of the Russian Empire. As the Mongols moved west, they seized lands ruled by Islamic forces in Central Asia.

The Mongols swung northward, conquering nearly all of Kievan Russia. The Mongols controlled these lands as feudal territories. The lands north of Kiev, including a Russian kingdom called Moscow (see map on page 431), remained unconquered.

The Mongols ruled Russia from the 1200s through the 1400s. During that time, Russians remained isolated from the rest of Europe and the events taking place there. As you remember, this was when the Renaissance spread from Italy throughout Europe. Russians did not share in the Renaissance ideas that changed Europe.

Mongol rule had another important result. The invasion destroyed Kievan Russia's power. Meanwhile, the leaders of Moscow strengthened their powers. When Mongol

Genghis Khan and his sons (below) invaded Russia in the thirteenth century. Their army conquered Kiev and took over Kievan Russia. Russians were forced to pay tribute to Khan's army (below, right). *What people did Genghis Khan lead? Where did they come from?*

rule ended because of weakening leadership, Moscow was ready to claim leadership of the Russian people.

Expansion Under the Czars

Ivan IV (remembered as Ivan the Terrible), Grand Prince of Moscow, became Russia's czar in 1547. He began a pattern followed by other czars. He strengthened the power of the throne and expanded Russia's lands.

Ivan's power grew when the Eastern Orthodox Church moved its Russian headquarters from Kiev to Moscow. The Church supported his claim to absolute authority.

Russian nobles—in return for lands and control of the peasants living on them—also supported the czar. Ivan IV claimed supreme authority by ruthlessly murdering anyone who dared oppose him.

Ivan IV had taken the throne determined to expand Moscow's small territory. He established his rule over the Volga River basin, then began to push eastward across the Urals into Siberia.

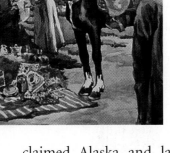

Russia's eastward expansion was led by the **Cossacks**, a small band of nomadic people from Ukraine. They wanted to make fortunes by trapping fur-bearing animals. They plunged into the eastern wilderness, fighting and defeating native people. They built forts and claimed ever-increasing amounts of new land for the czar.

Their eastward advance did not stop until 1812. By then Russia claimed territory reaching all the way to Asia's eastern coast. Russian adventurers had even crossed the water, reaching North America. They claimed Alaska and land running southward along North America's western coast as far south as today's San Francisco.

Meanwhile, Russia expanded in other directions. Finland fell to the Russians in 1809. It remained under Russian rule until the end of World War I. Russia also extended its European boundaries westward to include much of Poland.

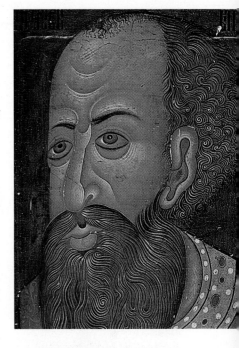

Ivan IV became Grand Prince of Moscow and czar of Russia. He ruled his court with displays of terror and wealth. *What other name did Ivan IV have?*

WORD `ORIGINS`

Cossack, from the Russian *kazak*, means "horseman." The word originated in the southern and southwestern parts of Russia, where the Cossacks first moved from Ukraine. Later, the word referred to a police officer in a strikebreaking force.

Russia sent explorers to Alaska. Remnants of a Russian colony remain, such as this church on Kodiak Island, Alaska. *Where else did Russians settle during the eighteenth and nineteenth centuries?*

In the 1800s, Russia seized a large area in Central Asia called **Turkestan**, located between the Caspian Sea and lands claimed by China. Other lands known as **Transcaucasia**, south of the Caucasus Mountains and between the Caspian and Black Seas, were conquered at about the same time.

You read earlier about Western European countries building colonial empires. Spain and Portugal had led the way. Other European countries, especially the United Kingdom, France, and Germany, followed. By 1914, Europe ruled millions of non-European people in many parts of the world.

Except for their claims in North America, Russia did not look overseas for lands to conquer. Russia advanced mainly beyond the territory that surrounded its home base west of the Ural Mountains.

By the late 1800s, Russia's czars had brought together lands that stretched from Europe, across the Urals, and all the way across Northern Asia. The region included Asians as well as Europeans. It also was the home of people of great religious diversity. Christians, Jews, Muslims, and members of many other faiths lived in the Russian Empire.

LESSON 1 REVIEW

Fact Follow-Up
1. Who were the first Russians? Who were their political leaders?
2. What river was an early trading route in Russia?
3. What was the Mongol invasion? How did it affect Russia?
4. Describe Russian territorial expansion up to 1914.

Think These Through
5. Which influence on Russia was more important: Byzantine or Mongol? Explain.
6. Russia did not experience the Renaissance ideas that changed Europe. Would the Renaissance have made Russia more like Europe?
7. Why did Russia seek a land empire rather than an empire across the seas?

The Formation of the Soviet Union

LESSON 2

On the evening of July 17, 1918, Communist party guards called Czar Nicholas II, Czarina Alexandra, and their five children from the rooms where they were imprisoned. The guards hurried the Russian royal family downstairs, and there, in the dim light of a small cellar, they opened fire, killing the last czar and his wife and children.

For 74 years, no one knew for certain how or where the royal family had died. Then, in 1992, investigators found several shallow graves. DNA tests proved that the bones were the remains of the czar, the czarina, and three of their daughters. The bodies of their son and another daughter have never been found.

Under communism, no Russian would have dared to suggest honoring the slain royal family with a ceremonial burial. By the mid-1990s, however, the Communists no longer ruled. The imperial family were to be reburied in St. Petersburg.

The Russian royal family—Czar Nicholas II, his wife Czarina Alexandra, and their children—met an ugly fate in 1918. *Why were they killed?*

The Czar's Fading Support

The murder of Russia's royal family ended government under the czars. Although Czar Nicholas II and other royalty are still remembered fondly today by some, dissatisfaction with both the czar and his government led to the Russian Revolution in 1917.

During the 1800s, the czars faced a bitterly divided country. Russia was changing. Many people wanted the country to become more like Europe's modern nations where people enjoyed more freedom and had a voice in government. There were demands that Russia should build industry and modernize agriculture.

Czar Alexander II, who ruled in the 1800s, tried to change the government. *Which changes succeeded? Which failed?*

The Russian nobility stood firmly against these changes. The czarist government could not decide what to do. Sometimes it favored change. At other times, the government opposed change. In the end, the czars lost almost everyone's support.

Reform Fails

One of Czar Nicholas's predecessors, Czar Alexander II, was one of the first to find himself caught between people with different ideas. Czar Alexander decided to meet demands for more freedom. In 1861, he freed the serfs, Russia's peasants. Serfs lived and worked on land belonging to noble families. The serfs enjoyed little freedom and were terribly poor. Alexander II believed that freedom for serfs brought more liberty to all Russians.

Alexander II also built railroads, set up a modern banking system, and introduced reforms in government. He increased freedom of the press and established a jury system in Russian courts.

Alexander II's reforms drew different reactions. Some people believed the czar had taken important first steps in modernizing the nation. Others complained that the reforms did not go far enough. They believed that Russia should become a republic with a constitution. Still others—extremists called **anarchists**—believed that people would not be truly free until all governments were destroyed.

Collapse of Czarist Russia

The Russian nobility was outraged, because this privileged class opposed any kind of change. This group failed to see any good coming out of economic or governmental reform. The nobility thought that a strong czarist government served Russia best.

The nobility looked for opportunities to reverse the reform program. Their chance came in 1881 when a terrorist's bomb killed the czar. Government support for continuing reform faded away. Those in power believed that Alexander II's reforms had not solved problems. Reforms had brought trouble, so they had to be stopped.

Ẅhat would **YOU** do?

You are a leader in your country. You have been to other countries and have seen cities with better roads and services, representative governments, and thriving businesses. You begin to make changes. How would you encourage the people of your country to accept those changes?

Demands for change, however, did not die. Russian people called for still more freedom. Bad harvests caused famine. Discontent among the poor increased. By 1894, some Russians spoke openly of removing the czar and instituting a Western-style parliamentary government.

The discontent grew. Thousands of Russians went on strike and staged protest marches. In response, Czar Nicholas II tried to find a compromise that would please everyone. He established the **Duma**, an elected parliament.

The Duma pleased some of the protesters at first. It soon became clear, however, that the Duma would not change how decisions were made. The czar and his ministers were unwilling to share power with representatives elected by the people.

Meanwhile, the writings of German philosopher Karl Marx inspired other Russians, such as V. I. Lenin. Lenin emerged as a leader of Russia's Communist party. **Communists** believe that government should own all manufacturing, agricultural, and transportation operations. They claim that such a system provides freedom and gives everyone an equal share of the wealth.

The Fall of the Czar

During World War I, military defeats and economic hardships stirred up more anger toward the czar and the nobility. In March 1917, shortages of bread and coal led to a revolt in the capital.

Angered by the uprising, Nicholas II ordered the Duma to stop meeting, but the parliament refused. The representatives in the Duma formed their own government. They forced the czar to give up his throne. This elected government did not last long.

People of Moscow wait in line for bread in 1929. Food shortages caused difficulties for Russians before and after the Communist revolution. *Why did such shortages continue after the revolution?*

Railroad cars brought food to hungry Russians during World War I. The war was fought outside of Russia among major powers. The Russian Revolution brought war within Russia. *Who was fighting inside the country?*

The Communists Capture Russia

In November 1917, Lenin and his followers overthrew the elected government. Lenin promised that the Communists would give the Russians "Peace, Land, and Bread." He signed a peace treaty with Germany. Then revolutionaries under his command imprisoned Czar Nicholas and his family. The Communists killed them and buried them in secret.

The Communists controlled the Russian capital, but they did not control the countryside. Between 1918 and 1920, Communist armies battled non-Communists for control of Russia. When the Communists won, they established a new government in the territories of the old Russian Empire. The new government was called the Union of Soviet Socialist Republics (USSR)—or Soviet Union, as it came to be known.

Communist Dictatorship

Soviet is a Russian word that means "revolutionary council." The Communist ideal was that councils throughout the country would make decisions. So the new government in theory was democratic. For that reason the Soviet Union called local governments led by these councils "republics."

Yet the Communist leadership had not created a real democracy. The Communist party led a dictatorship. The government became the owner of all land, factories, and transportation.

Political and economic decisions were made by a few leaders of the Communist party in Moscow. Local council leaders were put in power by Moscow. They were loyal to the Communist party and carried out their decisions.

Stalin

When Lenin died in 1924, Joseph Stalin rose to power. By 1929, he was sole dictator of the Soviet Union. He used three tools to maintain power: the Communist party, the **KGB**, or national secret police force, and the Soviet army.

Stalin set out to industrialize the Soviet Union and modernize its farms. To remove opposition to the Communists, he waged war on the Russian Orthodox Church. He did not totally destroy the Church, once a major force in Russian politics, but he badly weakened it.

Soviet Union in the 1930s

Territory lost by Soviets after 1917	
Union of Soviet Socialist Republics, 1939	

Region The territory of the Soviet Union changed between 1917 and 1939. *In what regions did the government lose territory? Why?*

Joseph Stalin became the leader of the Soviet Union in 1929. *How did Stalin gain power and keep power?*

Stalin also attacked the many ethnic groups within the Soviet Union. Everyone was to speak Russian and to live according to Soviet ideals. Other cultural groups were supposed to abandon their religions, languages, and traditions.

During the 1920s and 1930s, Russia changed rapidly. The Communists brought small farms together into giant ones called collectives. They forced the people to build factories, railways, and dams. The Communist party leadership demanded that everyone work and obey them. Millions of citizens tried to resist. They were sent to prison or labor camps in Siberia, east of the Ural Mountains, or they were killed.

The Soviet Union During World War II

In the early part of World War II, the Soviet Union signed an agreement with Germany saying that neither country would attack the other. Under this agreement, Germany and the Soviet Union invaded Poland and divided the nation between them. But their agreement soon broke down when Germany decided to invade the Soviet Union. German and Soviet forces began fighting each other in some of the most brutal battles of the war.

Winston Churchill of Great Britain, Franklin D. Roosevelt of the United States, and Stalin led their countries as Allies during WW II. *Whom did they oppose?*

During the rest of World War II, the Soviet Union fought on the side of the United Kingdom, the United States, and other Allies. The Soviets suffered enormous casualties. More than 10 million troops were killed, 5 million more wounded. Millions of civilians died from starvation and disease. Despite these terrible losses, the Soviet Union came out of the war in 1945 as the most powerful nation in Europe.

The Cold War

As you have read, the Soviets occupied Eastern Europe after World War II,

pushing communism by force into the region. The resulting division of Europe led to the Cold War. The distrust between East and West rose even higher when both the United States and the Soviet Union became nuclear superpowers.

The Communist dictatorship and the Cold War greatly restricted the lives of people in the Soviet Union. They could not vote in free elections. Their government denied them the freedoms of press, speech, and religion. The government ran newspapers, radio, and television. Churches were used as museums instead of places of worship.

KGB officials often arrested and imprisoned people they suspected of having ties to the United States or Western Europe. Soviet officials banned books. Writers who would not cooperate with Soviet policies could not publish their work.

Western Soviet Union, 1945

Soviet Union before WWII
Areas added to the Soviet Union

Location The western borders of the Soviet Union changed after World War II. *Which countries became part of the Soviet Union? Which lost territory (see map, page 441)?*

Geography & the Arts

Photographing War: The Work of Yeugeny Khaldei

The Soviet Union used its news bureau, called TASS, to distribute information to the West. TASS decided what news and what pictures would be transmitted to the rest of the world.

In World War II, a young twenty-three-year-old photographer, Yeugeny Khaldei, worked for TASS. Until recently, few people in the western world saw his pictures. The New York Times Magazine showed several of Khaldei's war photos in its World War II commemorative issue.

Khaldei, at seventy-eight, can say that he has photographed some of the important events in his country. Since the war, Khaldei has also taken pictures of every Soviet leader.

Khaldei photographed Berlin after Soviet forces occupied it (right). One of his most famous photos is of a Red Army soldier waving the Soviet flag (below).

The Russian Revolution claimed the ideals of equality and freedom. The Soviet Union did not fulfill this promise. In many ways, life there was just as cruel and unjust as it had been under the czars.

LESSON 2 REVIEW

Fact Follow-Up
1. Why did the czarist governments lose the support of the Russian people?
2. How did World War I contribute to the collapse of the czar?
3. Who was V. I. Lenin? Why was he important? Who was Joseph Stalin? Why was he important?
4. How was Russian society changed by Communist rule?

Think These Through
5. Did the Duma and Soviets contribute to democracy? Explain your answer.
6. Who was more important to Russian history—Lenin or Stalin? Explain.
7. Which was more important to Russia—World War I or World War II? Explain.

The Collapse of the Soviet Union

LESSON 3

When Urkash Mebetalyev was fourteen years old, he had an extraordinary dream about the mythical warrior called Manas, the national hero of Kyrgyzstan (CUR·jis·tan).

This dream told young Urkash he had a job to do. He must learn to tell a story—a 1,000-year-old chanted epic of heroic adventure. The story contained thousands of lines and took hours to tell.

The dream came to Urkash at a dangerous time. Under Soviet rule in Kyrgystan, the Manas storytellers could be beaten or imprisoned. Their national tale aroused the people against Soviet rule. Still, Urkash remained true to his dream, telling the tale of Manas throughout the years of Soviet domination.

Now, at age sixty, Urkash is free to celebrate heroic adventures of Manas. After the breakup of the Soviet Union, his audiences are eager to hear the story of their legendary warrior-king.

LESSON PREVIEW

Key Ideas

- After World War II, the Soviet Union became a superpower.
- Yet the Soviet Union was in trouble as people lost confidence in their government.
- In 1991, the Soviet Union was dissolved. The new Russian Federation lost territories along its western and southern frontiers.

Key Terms:
détente, *perestroika*, *glasnost*

As Soviet leader in the 1960s, Nikita Khrushchev wanted his country to become a world power. *How did the Soviet Union try to achieve that goal?*

The Soviet Union After World War II

After World War II, the Soviet Union tried to match the success it had experienced against the Germans. It began to strive for achievement as a world power.

It pushed its borders (see map, page 443) westward into Europe. The Soviet Union tried to extend its influence worldwide. Stalin and his successors wanted governments around the world to adopt communism.

Leaders of the Soviet Union wanted to build a stronger economy than the economy in the United States. They worked to transform the country into an industrial giant.

Soviet leaders did not understand that their system

was in trouble. They had put nearly all of the nation's resources into building its military power. Soviet forces were among the largest in the world. Its best scientists and engineers worked hard to build nuclear weapons and make the nation first in the space race.

Yet the Soviet government failed to make its people's lives better. Most Russians lived in poor, crowded apartments. Food, clothing, soap, and other basic goods seemed always in short supply. Citizens spent hours in line hoping to purchase these necessities.

The Russian people learned about growing prosperity elsewhere, even in Communist countries of Eastern Europe. They became less willing to support their own government.

EYEWITNESS TO HISTORY

The Russian and American Space Race

The Soviet Union shocked the United States in 1957 by launching Sputnik, the world's first satellite. The countries then began a space race, competing to get the first human in space, then the first person on the moon.

The Soviets won the first phase. In 1961, Soviet Cosmonaut Yuri Gagarin (right) rode the *Vostok I* in space for 108 minutes. But in 1969, Neil Armstrong (middle right) fulfilled President John F. Kennedy's goal of having an American walk on the moon before the end of the decade.

The Soviet Union sent the *Salyut 1* into orbit ten years after Gagarin's flight. This was the world's first space station. The United States built Skylab and successfully had Americans on board in 1973. The Soviet Union responded with two more space labs in 1977 and 1986. The 1986 crew lived in space for 366 days, a record.

Sputnik I

Détente

Because of bad harvests and poor planning in the 1960s, the Soviet Union had to buy wheat from the United States to feed its people. At the same time, the Soviet Union was losing its influence in Eastern European affairs.

Dependence on the United States for food and the rise of reform movements in Eastern Europe began to influence Soviet citizens. As ideas from the West filtered into the country, many Soviets began to question the plans and goals of their government.

By the middle of the 1970s, **détente**, an easing of world tensions, led to more Soviet ties with Western nations. The Soviet

Space shuttles became the next arena for competition. The United States began with *Columbia* (right) and the Soviet Union built *Buran*.

With the end of the Soviet Union, the space race has changed. The United States and Russia now work together in space. Astronauts and cosmonauts meet in the Mir space station (below) for scientific experiments. The goal of the twenty-first century is for cooperation in space. The countries will race together.

447

The Orengoi pipeline in Siberia transports natural gas to Western Europe. *What did its completion mean to the relationship between the Soviet Union and the rest of the world?*

Union hoped to buy advanced technology as well as food. When the Orengoi natural gas pipeline from Siberia to Western Europe was completed, cooperation increased between the Soviet Union and democracies beyond the Communist world.

Under détente, more political ideas about freedom came to the Soviet Union from the West. Leaders in Ukraine, Georgia, and along the Baltic Sea began to strive for independence from the Soviet Union.

Other non-Russian people, such as those living in Central Asia and Transcaucasia, did not feel loyalty toward the Soviet Union. They thought of themselves as conquered people because the Soviets would not allow them to practice their religious or cultural traditions. Non-Russians never shook that feeling, despite more than 50 years as Soviet citizens.

All over the Soviet Union, artists and writers protested the government's control over people's lives. In response, the Soviet Union arrested the critics. Many were sent to prisons and mental hospitals to punish them and silence their protests. Citizens became more resentful of police power in Soviet society.

Many Western nations, including the United States, spoke out against these dictatorial actions. They also decreased their trade with the Soviet Union. They wanted the Soviet Union to improve its treatment of its people. The United States responded to the Soviet Union's invasion of Afghanistan by leading a boycott of the Olympic games hosted by Moscow in 1980.

Perestroika and Glasnost

By the 1980s, several conditions inspired a new generation of Soviet leaders. The people were unhappy with the economy. They distrusted the KGB. Leaders faced rebellion in Eastern Europe and worldwide condemnation of the Soviet invasion of Afghanistan. Officials began to govern differently. The most important of these leaders was Mikhail Gorbachev.

When Gorbachev became leader of the Communist party, he introduced reforms to solve those challenges facing the Soviet Union. He knew the Soviet Union could not afford to pay for its role in the arms race. It could no longer spend large amounts of money on weapons and armed forces. Gorbachev withdrew Soviet troops from Afghanistan in February 1989. He made large cuts in the size of the forces in 1989 and 1990.

Gorbachev worried that poverty and restless minority groups could cause more problems. He began *perestroika*, a restructuring of the Soviet economic and political system. He also advocated *glasnost*, or openness, a policy that would permit people the freedom to express and debate ideas about Soviet society and politics. This had not happened in more than 60

The woman's T-shirt encouraging peace between the Soviet Union and the United States is a political statement that could not have been expressed before Gorbachev came to power. *What policy of Gorbachev's allowed freedom of expression?*

Gorbachev, a popular leader in the eyes of the world, had to resign as president of the Soviet Union. *What was one reason for that resignation?*

years. In the Soviet Union's first free election, Gorbachev became its president.

Gorbachev tried to find ways of holding the Russian Empire together. He faced, however, growing resistance to Moscow's rule, especially in the republics along the Soviet Union's borders. He tried to win the republics' loyalty by offering them more freedom. The republics were not satisfied with the president's offer. The Communist party also opposed the idea and tried to overthrow the president.

On December 25, 1991, Gorbachev resigned. The Soviet Union officially dissolved itself as a nation the next day. The empire built by the czars and taken over by the Communist party broke into several nations.

Russia and Neighboring States

The largest of these nations is the Russian Federation. It stretches from Europe all the way to Northern Asia's eastern coast. Smaller independent nations—once part of the Soviet Union—lie along Russia's western and southern borders.

You have already read about some of these nations—the Baltic Republics, Belarus, Moldova, and Ukraine. They are now part of the region of Eastern Europe. In the pages ahead you will read about eight other nations in Transcaucasia and Central Asia.

LESSON 3 REVIEW

Fact Follow-Up
1. Describe Soviet aims after World War II.
2. What was the space race?
3. What was détente?
4. Who was Gorbachev? How did his policies change Russia?
5. Describe the events that led to the end of the Soviet Union.

Think These Through
6. After World War II, how was the Soviet Union able to become a world power?
7. If you were living in Moscow, what would be your opinion of Gorbachev and his reforms? Explain.

Using Information for Problem Solving, Decision Making, and Planning

Using a Time Chart to Organize Information

Chapter 22 takes you through more than a thousand years of Russian history. You are introduced to Russian czars and Communist leaders with whom you associate important events. You trace the expansion and collapse of the Russian Empire. To gain command of all of this, you need to do more than just read the text.

In an earlier skill lesson you created a multidimensional time line. You might want to turn to the skill lesson in Chapter 11 (page 219) to review how such organizers are made. Another kind of time line, called a T[ime]-chart can help you remember events in this chapter on Russian expansion.

To make the T-chart, take a sheet of paper and crease it lengthwise. Draw a line along the crease. Across this line you will list in chronological order the political leaders of Russia at various periods. Remember that these leaders are sometimes individuals and sometimes groups of people.

Scan this chapter carefully for the leaders associated with the events included below on the left side of the T-chart. When did these leaders rule? On the right side, you will describe the territorial expansion of Russia. Where did Russia add territory?

Take care that the areas into which Russia expanded are accurately linked to the leaders listed on the T-chart. Your chart should look something like the one below.

Another way of displaying the same information is a simple data retrieval chart similar to the one used to organize dates and events (see page 210).

Compare your chart with a classmate's. How are they similar? How are they different? Make another T-chart on how the Russian government changed through time.

Graphic Organizer: Time Chart		
Events	**Ruler and/or Date**	**Territorial Expansion and Collapse**
Kiev forms kingdom	Prince Vladmir	[describe size and location of territory]
Moscow begins expansion	1300	[describe size and location of territory]
Moscow expands east of Urals	[ruler and dates?]	[describe size and location of territory]
Russia acquires Islamic territories in Central Asia	[ruler and dates?]	[describe size and location of territory]
Soviet Union adds territory after WW II	[ruler?] 1945	[describe size and location of added territory]
Soviet Union collapses	[ruler?] 1991	[describe territories lost]

Chapter 22 Review

LESSONS LEARNED

LESSON 1 An early Russian kingdom was built by rulers in the city of Kiev. This Kievan empire was important for bringing Byzantine civilization to Russia's Slavic people. Mongol invaders helped build the tradition of authoritarian government among Russians and limited Russian contacts with Europe. After the Mongols, Moscow's leaders began to build a huge empire under the harsh rule of czars.

LESSON 2 The Communists overthrew the czarist monarchy during World War I. Communism replaced the harsh authoritarian rule of the czar with an equally harsh dictatorship. The Communists established their rule over most of the old Russian Empire.

LESSON 3 The Soviet Union emerged from World War II as a superpower. Yet the Russian people lost confidence in their government. In the 1990s, the Soviet Union was dissolved. Republics along the former Soviet Union's borders broke away. The new Russian Federation took steps toward democracy.

TIME FOR TERMS

czar
Kievan Russia
Cossacks
Transcaucasia
Duma
Soviet
détente
glasnost

steppes
Mongols
Turkestan
anarchists
Communists
KGB
perestroika

FACT FOLLOW-UP

1. Who were the first Russians? How were they governed?
2. What Russian cities were founded by Vikings? Why were they built?
3. How did the coming of the Mongol invaders affect Kievan Russia?
4. How did Moscow become the center of Russian life?
5. Compare the importance to Russia of Ivan the Terrible and Alexander II.
6. How did the coming of communism change Russian ways of life?
7. What was the Cold War? How did it affect the lives of the Russian people?
8. Compare the theories and effects of détente and perestroika.
9. Compare the leadership of Stalin and Gorbachev.
10. Describe the collapse of the Soviet Union. Explain why this happened.

THINK THESE THROUGH

11. Which was more important in influencing Russia: Byzantine or Mongol rule? Explain your choice.
12. Suppose the Mongol invasion had not occurred. How might Russia have developed differently?
13. Most European nations built overseas empires in the late nineteenth century, but Russia's empire was created by expanding over land areas. Explain why.
14. In which period of Russian history described in this chapter would you have most liked to live? Why?
15. Could anything have prevented the breakup in the 1990s of the Soviet Union? If so, what?

If not, why not? Explain your answer in detail.

16. Who do you think was the most important and influential Russian leader described in this chapter? Why was this person the most important?

17. Which do you think had most influence on Russian culture—Europe, Asia, or Byzantium? Explain why.

SHARPENING SKILLS

18. What are some other ways of organizing the information in this chapter?

19. Based on the T-chart you created, at which time period was the territorial expansion of Russia greatest and least? What effects did the leadership of Russia have on this expansion?

20. Which do you think is better for showing chronological information: the data retrieval chart or the T-chart? Why?

PLACE LOCATION

Use the letters on the map to name and locate the places described below:

21. principality of Moscow, which led Russian expansion.

22. territories added by Moscow in the 1300s and 1400s.

23. non-Slavic territory added, 1600s-1700s.

24. far eastern territories added in the 1800s.

25. mostly Muslim territories added in the 1800s.

Reviewing Place Location

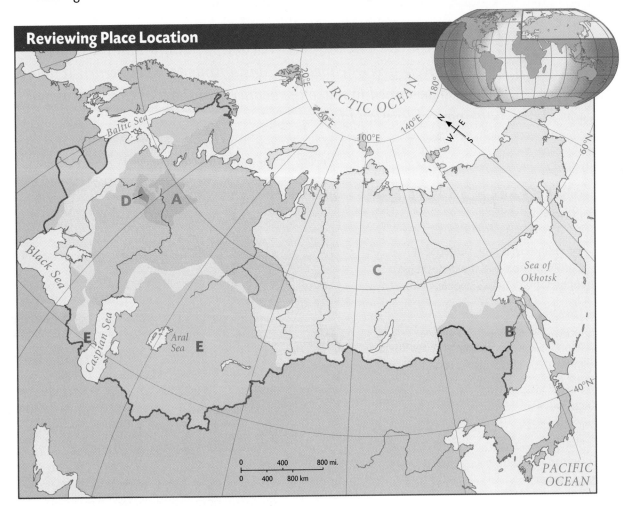

The Making and Breaking of a Russian Empire **453**

The Cultural Origins of Russia

Grand Prince Vladimir I

In the tenth century, Grand Prince Vladimir and his nobles began a voyage from his capital of Kiev. They sailed south on the Dnepr River to Constantinople (see map, page 455).

The Russians brought slaves, furs, grain, amber, and lumber to sell. The authorities in Constantinople did not trust the strangers. The officials ordered them to sell their merchandise quickly and go home.

Despite the poor welcome, Vladimir and the nobles were overwhelmed by Constantinople. They returned home determined to make the beauty and spirit of Constantinople part of Russian life.

Istanbul, Turkey (formerly Constantinople)

CHAPTER PREVIEW

LESSON 1
Byzantine Influences
Byzantine civilization centered at Constantinople was the first foreign influence on Russia's people.

LESSON 2
Mongol Influences
Mongol invaders reaching Kievan Russia in the 1200s became a second foreign influence.

LESSON 3
Opening the Window on the West
Two powerful czars led efforts to reform Russia by linking their country to Europe.

Kievan Russia and Byzantium, about A.D. 1000

Uppsala
KINGDOM OF SWEDEN
North Sea
Gulf of Finland
Lake Ladoga
Baltic Sea
Volkhov R.
Novgorod
W. Dvina R.
Smolensk
KIEVAN RUSSIA
Kiev
Dnepr (Dnieper) R.
Black Sea
Adriatic Sea
Constantinople
Aegean Sea
Mediterranean Sea
BYZANTINE EMPIRE

→ Route of Varangians (Vikings)

0   250 mi.
0   250 km

Baptism of Prince Vladimir

Byzantine Influences

LESSON PREVIEW

Key Ideas

- One thousand years ago, the Byzantine Empire—centered at Constantinople—became a key influence shaping Russian culture.
- Although related to the civilizations of ancient Greece and Rome, the Byzantine influence helped set Russia apart from Europe.

Key Terms

Byzantine, chronicles, icons

n 988, Grand Prince Vladimir accepted Christianity by being baptized in the Dnepr River. To unite Kievan Russia, he ordered that his subjects also be baptized. For his conversion, Vladimir later was declared a saint of the Russian Orthodox Church, an independent branch of the Eastern Orthodox Church of Constantinople.

The earlier trading expedition had led to a lasting connection between Russia and Constantinople. The first Russian ambassadors to the city described the scene in *The Story of the Passing Years,* a chronicle of the visit. "We did not know whether we were in heaven or earth for upon earth there is no such sight or beauty; we only know that there, God is present among men."

Shaping Russian Culture

Grand Prince Vladimir's decision to embrace the Eastern Orthodox faith changed Russia's culture. Close ties grew between Kievan Russia and Constantinople, a city that was the center of Byzantine culture and the Eastern Orthodox Church.

Russia's earliest years had been much like those of its Eastern European neighbors. Slavic people settled on the Northern European Plain west of the Ural Mountains. They farmed the

The buildings of Kiev show the influence of Byzantine architecture. *From where did Byzantine culture come to Russia?*

steppes, the flat, temperate grasslands of the Northern European Plain. They carried on trade along the Dnepr and Volga Rivers. Their language was a version of modern Russian.

The Russians began to shape a tradition of their own. The czars built a country that reached from Europe all the way across Northern Asia. No other European country became so large or claimed so many different people. Moreover, no other country accepted authoritarian rule for such a long time.

Byzantine Culture

In the ninth century, Constantinople remained one of the world's most important cities. After the fall of Rome, Constantinople became the capital of what remained of the Roman Empire. The Roman Empire under Constantinople was not the same as Rome's.

Constantinople's civilization was a mixture of classical Greek culture, Christianity, Roman law, and Asian art. The culture of the city is called **Byzantine** (BIH·zuhn·teen), after the city's earlier Roman name, Byzantium.

Grand Prince Vladimir's contacts with Constantinople brought to Russia a new religious faith and the Byzantine culture. The distinctive Byzantine art, architecture, music, and literature assured that Russia's culture would develop differently from Western Europe.

This is a page from a Cyrillic manuscript in the Moscow Museum of History. Based on Greek letters, the Cyrillic alphabet became the method of writing the language spoken by Slavs in Russia. *Who began the Cyrillic alphabet?*

The Cyrillic Alphabet Once Russians reached Constantinople in the ninth century, Byzantine art and thought began to flow into the towns and cities of the steppes.

For example, the Cyrillic alphabet became the way of writing the Slavic language spoken in Russia. In the ninth century, Eastern Orthodox missionaries Cyril and Methodius introduced the Slavs to the Cyrillic alphabet. As you remember, the alphabet was based on Greek letters.

Byzantine Writing The connection to Constantinople also brought Byzantine literature to the Slavs. At first, most of it was religious. Clergy copied sermons, hymns, and biographies of saints. Few works featured details of life in Russia.

By the late 900s, Russian writing had branched out to include the **chronicles**, the records of important events in public life. Each community had its own chronicle, and many included political discussions. Some chronicles emphasized the importance of cooperation among the communities. Later, the chronicles argued that Moscow should unite all of Russia under its authority.

In the 1100s, an anonymous writer wrote *The Lay of Igor's Campaign*. In beautiful language, this Russian poem describes the defeat of a Russian prince by an Asian tribe. The story came true in the next century when the Mongols invaded Russia.

Byzantine Music and Art Eastern Orthodox church services introduced Byzantine hymns to Russia. This music mingled with ancient Slavic folk music was performed at fairs and festivals.

Byzantine art is characterized by painted wood icons and

Icons

*In the candlelit cathedrals of Russia, you will find beautiful works of art. These works, called **icons**, represent the special relationship between Russian Christians and their faith.*

Kremlin cathedral exterior

I cons hang in most Orthodox churches. The word "icon" comes from the Greek word *eikon*, which means "image." Icons came to Russia from the Byzantine Empire. Artists of that era painted the Virgin Mary and Jesus (left) and various saints on wood. The wooden shapes were square, rectangular, and triangular.

Interior of Russian cathedral

colored mosaics on gold backgrounds. These are displayed within Orthodox churches that feature golden domes and marble walls.

Byzantine Beliefs   The bishops of Constantinople taught Russians to believe in the teachings of the Eastern Orthodox Church. One teaching was that each nation should have its own Orthodox Church. The Russian Orthodox Church was influenced, but not controlled, by far-off Constantinople.

Eastern Orthodox belief also made the ruler of each nation the protector of that nation's Orthodox Church. The czar demanded that the clergy and all believers in the Russian Orthodox Church be loyal to him. The Church then received the government's full support.

The artists used brilliant colors to draw the viewer into the images. Viewing the art was part of the spiritual experience of going to church. Brilliant midnight blue shaded Mary's cloak. Crimson colored Jesus' clothing. St. Peter often had a cloak of yellow and light blue, and St. Paul a deeper blue and claret-red. Gold leaf reflecting candlelight gave the impression of a holy light shining on the subjects.

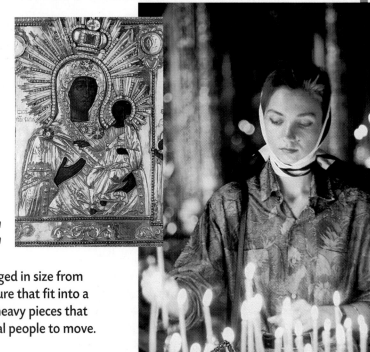

Golden icon

Icons ranged in size from a miniature that fit into a pocket to heavy pieces that took several people to move.

After communism outlawed churches, the faithful could carry small wooden icons and golden crosses (right). These could be hidden from authorities, who had made religion illegal. Individuals could have experiences of faith without group ceremonies.

459

Byzantine mosaic art—colorful ceramic tiles formed into designs—decorated Russian churches. *What religion was brought to Russia through the influence of Byzantine culture?*

In Western Europe, this practice of churches and governments supporting each other had not been followed. Europe's kings usually regarded the Roman Catholic Church as a rival. As you have read, monarchs in countries such as England and Sweden supported the Protestant Reformation, because they wanted to end the Roman Catholic Church's interference in politics. In czarist Russia, Protestant reformers were not welcome.

The Russian czar used another Byzantine influence to protect himself. Spies and secret police were used to control enemies. This practice became the basis for strict governmental control in Russia.

LESSON 1 REVIEW

Fact Follow-Up

1. Explain the movement of Byzantine culture into Russia.
2. What parts of Byzantine culture did Russia adopt?
3. What was important about the relative location of Kiev?
4. What are icons? What has been their importance for Russia?

Think These Through

5. What was the most important Byzantine influence on Russia? Explain your answer.
6. Why may it have been easier for Eastern Orthodox Churches to form close relations with governments than it was for the Roman Catholic Church?

Mongol Influences

he chroniclers of thirteenth-century Russia wrote of the invading Mongols. "There have come peoples, about whom no one knows anything for certain—who they are, whence they came, what tongue they speak, what tribe they belong to, what faith they preach."

Under attack, Prince Yuri of Ryazan pleaded with neighboring princes to save his city from "an army so great that it darkened the skies and made the Earth tremble under horses' hooves." Help never arrived. The Mongols soon swept through most of Russia, conquering city after city.

Some people said the fierce, pitiless warriors would "drink dew, ride the wind, and devour human flesh on the battlefield." Others saw the approaching armies as a sign from God. They wrote, "The end of the world is at hand."

LESSON PREVIEW

Key Ideas
- In the 1200s, Mongol armies invaded Kievan Russia. The Mongols ruled for 200 years.
- The Mongols did not destroy Byzantine culture. Their rule reinforced Byzantine influences, isolating Russia from Europe.
- The Mongols also strengthened a growing tradition of rulers who exercised absolute authority.

Key Terms
yurt, Khans

Nomadic Life

The Mongols were nomads of the grassy steppes of today's Mongolia (see map, page 463), where they herded sheep and horses. They carried everything they needed with them. Their food included the sheep they herded.

The nomads of Tajikistan and other countries of Central Asia are herders, as were the Mongols when they invaded Russia in the thirteenth century. *What are nomads?*

Their shelter was the **yurt**, a tent they could fold up and transport easily on horseback. The yurt became a lasting part of Asia's nomadic culture. Today, animal herders living along Russia's southern borders from Mongolia westward into Central Asia still live in yurts. The national emblem of Kazakhstan, for example, features a *shaneraq,* the wooden wheel that forms the frame of the yurt.

The Mongol Invasion

Toughened by the rigors of nomadic life, the Mongols were perhaps the fiercest warriors the world has ever seen. Mongol armies drove westward into Central Asia. In the 1200s, they turned northward to conquer Kievan Russia. They held that country for the next 200 years.

The Mongol leader, Genghis Khan, organized his army brilliantly. As a result, his relatively small force could break up much larger military formations.

Mongol leaders organized their army into groups of 10, 100, 1,000, and 10,000. Each unit of ten was responsible for every man in it. If one warrior in a unit fled in battle, the other nine would be executed.

WORD ORIGINS

Nomads are people who move to survive. The word comes from the Greek *nomas*, or roaming to find pasture.

The Mongols ruled Russia for 200 years. This scene shows the royal court of the leader who led the Mongols into Russia. *Who was that leader?*

The Mongols' use of horses in battle gave them a great advantage over defenders who fought on foot. Stirrups, a Mongol invention, increased the stability of the horse-warriors so they could shoot their arrows while riding at a full gallop. They also employed a system of signals in battle, so that large groups could turn or attack in a single moment. The combination of organization, speed, and constant attack made the Mongols seem invincible.

Russians learned these new methods of warfare when the Mongols forced them to serve in their army. They received training in horsemanship, strategy, and weapons.

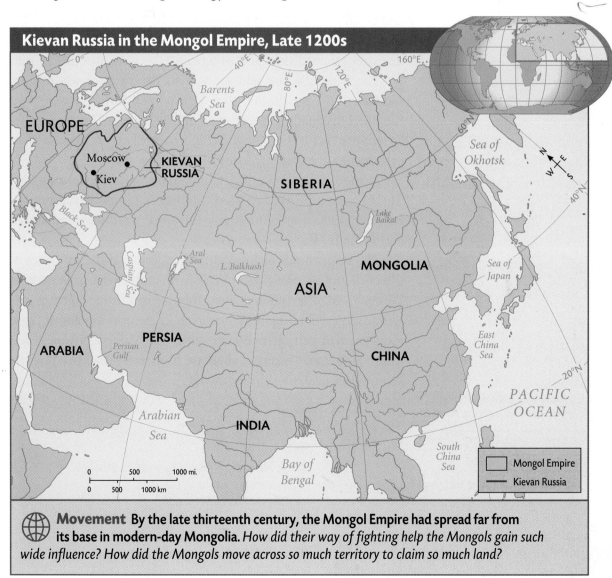

Kievan Russia in the Mongol Empire, Late 1200s

Movement By the late thirteenth century, the Mongol Empire had spread far from its base in modern-day Mongolia. *How did their way of fighting help the Mongols gain such wide influence? How did the Mongols move across so much territory to claim so much land?*

Mongol Rule in Russia

Under Mongol occupation, Russia experienced a government of total authority. Early Slavic kingdoms had shared power among their leaders. Customarily, the eldest prince held the greatest power, but the honor circulated regularly among all the kingdoms. The Slavic kingdoms also included assemblies where the nobles and landowners could advise the prince.

Under the Mongols, however, Russian princes ruled only by permission of the Khan. The Mongol **Khans**, or leaders, regularly chose a local favorite—the one who was most likely to cooperate—and gave him power over other Russian nobility. Distrust and rivalry grew among Russian leaders. The Mongols used the rivalry to strengthen their own rule. Among Russians, the practice strengthened the habit of a prince to claim absolute power.

The Mongols also did away with the people's assemblies, reducing the possibility that democracy could develop in Russia. This made princes even more powerful in their own kingdoms. As for the Mongols, their control over strong Russian princes made it easier to control all the people.

Mongol rule also cut Russian contacts with Western Europe during an important period in that region's development. Between 1200 and 1400, many Europeans rediscovered Greek and Roman ideas.

The importance of individual freedom and the practices of direct democracy and republican forms of government grew in Western, Mediterranean, and Northern Europe during the Renaissance. The Russians, however, knew nothing about these ideas until much later. By the time the Mongol invaders left Russia, the czar—a single, absolute monarch—had become the key figure in Russia's government.

LESSON 2 REVIEW

Fact Follow-Up
1. What type of life did the Mongols lead? How did this help them conquer territory?
2. How long did the Mongols rule Russia?
3. What methods of warfare did Russians learn from the Mongols?
4. How did Mongol rule affect Russia's connection with Europe?

Think These Through
5. Why were the Mongols able to conquer Russia?
6. What was the most important Mongol influence on Russia? Explain your choice.

Opening the Window on the West

"**H**e came this winter over to England and stayed some months with us," wrote Bishop Gilbert Burnet, recalling his meeting with the young czar from Moscow, Peter the Great.

"He is mechanically turned and seems by nature rather to be a ship-carpenter, than a great prince," the bishop observed. "This was his chief study and exercise, while he stayed here: he [built] much with his own hands, and made all about him work at the models of ships."

Bishop Burnet also recognized the Russian monarch's plans for his native country. "He was resolved to encourage learning, and to polish his people, by sending some of them to travel in other countries, and to draw strangers to come and live among them." Peter's year abroad would influence the history of Russia for centuries.

Peter the Great

As a young ruler in the late seventeenth and early eighteenth centuries, Peter the Great first explored his growing interest in Europe by frequently visiting the foreign quarter of Moscow. There he made friends with soldiers and business people, most of them German, and heard about life in the cities beyond his kingdom.

Westernization

After visiting Europe for himself in 1697, Peter the Great returned to Russia full of ideas for **westernization**, which meant changing Russia to be more like Europe.

Peter began with the nobles at his court. He ordered them to shave their long beards and to shorten the sleeves

Peter the Great encouraged his people to learn about Europe and become more like Europeans. *What was this process of change called?*

Turn to page 50?

The Cultural Origins of Russia **465**

Peter wanted Russians to follow European fashion by cutting their beards. *What more important changes did he want to make in Russia?*

of their shirts and coats, according to the European fashion. As czar, Peter wanted to make certain that when Russians visited abroad or entertained guests at home, they would not look "strange" or "foreign" to Europeans.

The czar also reformed the Russian government to be more European. Peter ended the old system of departments headed by a single minister. He used Sweden as a model for organizing departments for tax collection, foreign affairs, economy, and war. Involving more people with several ideas, Peter hoped, would improve his government's administration.

To introduce Western ideas, Peter invited European engineers, surgeons, and business people to Russia. He asked European writers and artists to visit Russia. In imitation of Western Europe, he began elementary schools and founded an Academy of Sciences to encourage learning.

Economic Development

To catch up with Europe economically, Peter began developing an iron industry in the Ural Mountains. By 1750, Russia would be the largest producer of iron in Europe.

Government efficiency, new technology, and a good supply of iron made it possible for Peter to improve his military. After fighting Sweden, Russia secured ports on the Baltic Sea, nearer to the Western European cities Peter admired.

Iron ore helped Peter begin an iron industry, which helped Russia's economy and improved its military. The industry spread throughout Russia. Blast furnaces, such as this one in Siberia, help turn iron ore into steel. *Where was the ore found?*

St. Petersburg

In 1712, St. Petersburg became the new capital of Russia. The city on the Baltic Sea was Peter's "window on the West." The czar built the city according to European models. He even

LIVING IN ST. PETERSBURG

Czar Peter's City

Spread out over 150 square miles (390 sq km), this city sits on the water's edge. It is located in the mouth of the Neva River on the Baltic Sea. Czar Peter began building his city on an island. He wanted a port on the Baltic. He also wanted an island fortress that his forces could easily defend. The czar named the city after himself. Petersburg means "Peter's city."

Today, lights make the imperial palaces shine in the dark nights of winter. The Neva River and other waterways crisscross the city. After the rivers freeze in late fall, people walk and skate on their frozen surfaces.

Peter wanted this city to be modern, to look European—and it does. St. Petersburg also combines East and West. The city has Russian-style monuments and cathedrals that hold Byzantine art.

Constructed in the 1600s, the city turned its back on Moscow to face Europe. Peter planned the city with geometric lines and Western-style architecture.

Now tourists arrive in St. Petersburg by boat, train and bus. They come to the Palace Square, where in 1917 Communists stormed the czar's Winter Palace and where in 1991 people held an all-night vigil to demonstrate their support for democracy.

In the summer, people stroll through gardens, attend puppet shows in amusement parks, and watch fountains shoot sparkling jets of water into the sky.

St. Petersburg's name has been changed several times. The city was renamed

Petrograd during World War I (Petersburg sounded too much like a German name). After the Communists took over, they changed the name to Leningrad in honor of V. I. Lenin. The city's name reverted to St. Petersburg after democracy came to Russia in 1991.

The city today has had many problems. Fewer goods for purchase, poorly repaired streets, and long lines at grocery stores have shown the confusion of political change. Despite the changes, the beauty of the city by the Baltic has remained.

The Winter Palace

ordered his nobles to build town houses in the European style rather than the Russian style.

St. Petersburg was much more than a beautiful city, or even a major port. For the Russians and their czar, St. Petersburg represented a new Russia, one that looked westward to Europe for its inspiration and its identity, as well as to its Slavic history.

Catherine the Great

Empress Catherine II came to the throne in 1762. She had long experience in both Western Europe and Russia. She was born a German princess and was familiar with the culture of Western Europe. Catherine had spent 20 years in the Russian court observing royal life. Then, as czarina, Catherine eagerly brought European ideas of reform to her adopted country. She became known as Catherine the Great.

European Political Philosophy

Catherine read the writings of the eighteenth-century European philosophers who supported democratic principles. The czarina even wrote letters regularly to Voltaire, a French philosopher whose work she admired.

In 1767, Catherine took the first step in introducing modern ideas of government to Russia. She called together 500 delegates from all walks of Russian life. They formed a Legislative Commission to advise her in reforming the government.

Before the commission met, Catherine sent them her own ideas. These were influenced by the philosophers of Western Europe. In time, the Legislative Commission proposed some reforms. These included a plan to give more control to nobles in local matters. Catherine tried to combine Western European and Russian ideas to solve problems.

Development of Trade

Catherine continued the economic practices begun by Peter the Great. She lowered taxes on trade to encourage imports from Europe. Russian merchants exported grain and furs.

Empress Catherine II was not born in Russia. As a native of Germany, Catherine was familiar with western ways. *In what ways did she improve Russia?*

During Catherine's reign, Russian cities prospered from trade.

Trade depended on transportation by sea. Northern Russian ports remained frozen part of the year, so Catherine waged war with the Ottoman Empire to gain an ice-free port. By 1783, Russia captured the Crimea on the Black Sea (in today's southern Ukraine), giving it a connection by sea to Europe all year-round.

By the end of the eighteenth century, then, Russia was being shaped by more than Slavic heritage, Byzantine culture, and Mongol influences. Russia also was becoming more European in trade, travel, and ideas. Europe, in turn, was beginning to be influenced by Russian music, ballet, and literature.

Russia's Golden Age of Music and Ballet

At the turn of the eighteenth century, Peter the Great had introduced Western music to Russia. He invited European musicians to perform at his court. The nobility imitated the czar. German and Italian musicians performed in their homes.

During the reign of Catherine the Great, Russians built opera and concert halls in St. Petersburg for the performance of Western music. At the same time, Russian composers revived traditional Slavic folk music.

Music Mikhail Glinka (1786–1880) was the first to mix Slavic folk music and European classical music to create uniquely Russian musical compositions. He composed the first Russian operas, including *Ivan Susanin* ("A Life for the Czar"), which opened in 1842 at the Bolshoi Theatre in Moscow. The structure and orchestration of the opera were European. Yet the work differed from anything heard in Vienna or Paris. Glinka featured a Russian story and included the Slavic tradition of bell-chiming in the work's "Glory Chorus."

Nikolai Rimsky-Korsakov (1844–1908) continued the practice of mixing Russian tradition with European musical orchestration. In his symphony *Scheherazade,* the composer drew on narrative and musical themes inspired by Russia's Mongol past. In *Russian Easter,* he used church songs familiar to Russians through their Russian Orthodox faith. As you have read, those songs contain Slavic folk music. So Rimsky-Korsakov drew upon all influences on Russian culture.

Russian culture influenced Europe through ballet and music during the eighteenth and nineteenth century. The Kirov Theatre (right) in St. Petersburg is the headquarters of the Kirov Ballet, an internationally famous ballet company. *What leading Russian composer wrote music for ballet?*

Perhaps the most famous Russian composer of the nineteenth century was Pyotr Tchaikovsky, who wrote music for operas, ballets, and symphonies. Tchaikovsky, too, added traditional Slavic themes to his musical compositions. His *1812 Overture* and *Marche Slav* especially highlight the enduring power of Slavic folk and Russian Orthodox Church traditions.

Emergence of Russia

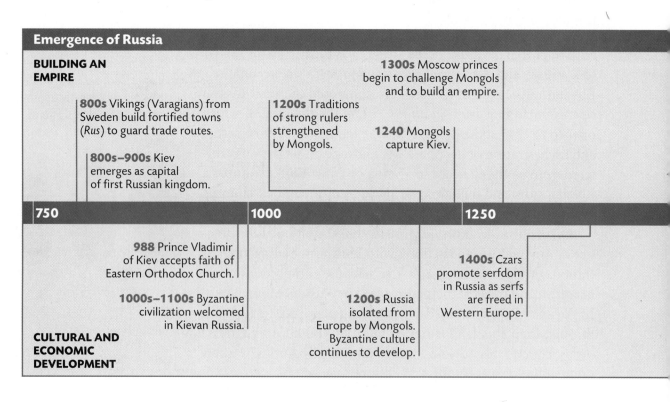

BUILDING AN EMPIRE

800s Vikings (Varagians) from Sweden build fortified towns (*Rus*) to guard trade routes.

800s–900s Kiev emerges as capital of first Russian kingdom.

1200s Traditions of strong rulers strengthened by Mongols.

1240 Mongols capture Kiev.

1300s Moscow princes begin to challenge Mongols and to build an empire.

750

1000

1250

988 Prince Vladimir of Kiev accepts faith of Eastern Orthodox Church.

1000s–1100s Byzantine civilization welcomed in Kievan Russia.

1200s Russia isolated from Europe by Mongols. Byzantine culture continues to develop.

1400s Czars promote serfdom in Russia as serfs are freed in Western Europe.

CULTURAL AND ECONOMIC DEVELOPMENT

Dance   Peter the Great brought Western dance—including ballet—to Russia when he invited German, French, English, and Polish dance companies to perform in St. Petersburg.

Russian audiences appreciated ballet as a form of art before Western audiences did. During the eighteenth century, ballet schools opened in St. Petersburg and Moscow. During Catherine's reign, French and Italian ballet teachers moved to Russia. They found ways of blending Western European and Russian themes into dances performed to music by Russian composers.

Their efforts produced such works as *Sleeping Beauty, The Nutcracker,* and *Swan Lake* with music by Tchaikovsky. These works gave ballet the form we recognize today—beautifully costumed dancers moving gracefully to the rich sounds of a great orchestra.

Russian ballet made its impact on Europe in 1909, when the Ballet Russe toured the continent. Audiences wildly cheered the productions, which featured Russian choreography, dancers, composers, and artists. A French critic praised the Russians. "Like a great gust of fresh wind, dance has come back to us from the north."

What would YOU do?

You are a writer in a country where the government decides what you can and cannot write. You know there are wrongs in your country and you know stories about people that would highlight the injustices. If you write these stories, you might be sent to prison or executed. Would you write them anyway? If you had a story to tell and you lived in this country, how would you tell it?

1500s Ivan the Terrible (1533–1584) strengthens royal authority and pushes Russian rule east of Urals.

1800s Russia acquires additional territory along Asian coast, lands in Central Asia, and Transcaucasia; Finland annexed.

1930s Communist rulers develop modern heavy industry; begin to modernize farming.

1991 Soviet Union ended; border territories annexed by the czars before 1917 break away.

1700s Russian expansion into Siberia continues; empire extends to Pacific and into North America by 1800.

1914-1919 World War I; czarist government collapses; Communists gain control of Russian Empire.

1500   1750   2000

1700s Peter the Great (1682–1725) and Catherine the Great (1762–1796) open Russia to Western Europe.

1800s Age of great achievements in literature, music, and dance. Tchaikovsky, 1840–1893 Rimsky-Korsakov, 1844–1908

1940s Nazi Germans attack Russia; much property is destroyed.

1930s Soviet government rules as harsh dictatorship; strict control of the arts.

1980s Russia attempts to shift to private enterprise and democracy.

Russian Literature

Fyodor Dostoyevsky was one of Russia's great novelists. He used European styles to tell Russian stories. *What was the subject of his great book,* The Brothers Karamazov?

Western readers know Russian literature through poetry and novels. Russian writers borrowed European literary forms. Their poems and stories, however, came out of the Russian people's lives and experience.

Alexander Pushkin Russia's first great poet, Alexander Pushkin, wrote in the 1820s. In many of his works, Pushkin emphasized the connections between Russia and Europe. Pushkin's play *Boris Godunov,* for example, celebrates a Russian historical hero in the English style. In this poetic drama, Pushkin imitates the historical plays of William Shakespeare.

In his narrative poem *The Bronze Horseman,* Pushkin deals with Russia's westernization under Peter the Great. The poem examines both the good and bad effects of Western cultural influence on the Russian people.

The Russian Novel Later in the century, Russian novelists used popular European fictional styles to tell Russian stories of moral conflict and religious redemption. Fyodor Dostoyevsky, influenced by English novelist Charles Dickens, wrote *Crime and Punishment,* the story of a murderer haunted by his crime. A later novel, *The Brothers Karamazov,* explored the breakdown of family and the search for the meaning of life.

Leo Tolstoy, the best known of nineteenth-century Russian novelists, described Napoleon's invasion of Russia in *War and Peace.* Much of the story also involves people struggling to make decisions in their personal lives.

LESSON 3 REVIEW

Fact Follow-Up
1. Make a chart showing the westernization efforts of Peter the Great and Catherine the Great.
2. Describe Peter's plan for the construction of St. Petersburg.
3. Describe important developments in Russian literature, music, and dance. Who were some of the leaders of these parts of Russian culture?

Think These Through
4. Compare the importance to Russia of Catherine and Peter.
5. Was it wise for Peter to establish St. Petersburg as the capital of Russia? Explain.
6. How effective was westernization under Peter the Great? Catherine the Great? Explain.

Acquiring Information from a Variety of Sources

Comparing the Influence of Cultures

Chapter 23 examines the influence of three different cultures on Russia—Byzantine, Mongol, and European. The three cultures mixed in Russia, where they changed an ancient Slavic culture. In what way did each of these three foreign cultures contribute to the shaping of Russia? Which of these foreign cultures influenced Russia most?

To answer these questions, you need first to analyze the way each of these cultures influenced Russia.

To make such an analysis, web or spider charts are useful. On a sheet of paper, make three charts like the one shown above.

Once you have drawn the charts, write something like "Byzantine Influences" in the center of one chart, "Mongol Influences" on the second chart, and "European Influences" on the third.

Then review the information in Chapter 23 in order to label as many legs of the "spider" as you can. When the charts are complete, examine them for similarities and differences. For example, did all three cultures influence Russia similarly in the area of religion? Or was

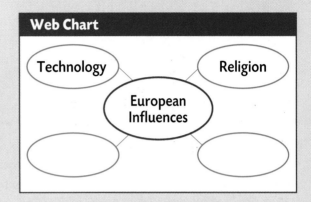

one culture clearly more influential?

You can take another step to help you compare the influence of the three cultures. Transfer the information from each spider or web chart to a data retrieval chart like the one shown below. (You may remember using a data retrieval chart in Chapter 13.)

After you have transferred the information to a data retrieval chart, you will have arranged the influences coming into Russia side by side. Does this help you see clearly how each foreign culture influenced Russia? Can you say which culture was most influential?

Which of the two graphic organizers will be most useful in helping you decide which culture was most influential in shaping Russia?

Data Retrieval Chart			
Influence	**Byzantine**	**Mongol**	**European**
government			
religion			

The Cultural Origins of Russia **473**

Chapter 23 Review

LESSON 1 Russia was built upon a foundation laid by Slavic people, who migrated into the Northern European Plain west of the Ural Mountains. The earliest outside cultural influence came from Byzantine civilization centered at Constantinople. Russia's Kievan kingdom encouraged development of Byzantine influences.

LESSON 2 Mongol invasions in the 1200s destroyed the Kievan kingdom. Mongol rule reinforced Byzantine influence by continuing to isolate Russia from Western Europe.

LESSON 3 Two powerful monarchs, Peter the Great and Catherine the Great, opened Russia to the West. In the years following their rule, Russian literature, music, and dance flourished and influenced the arts in Western Europe.

TIME FOR TERMS

Byzantine	chronicles
icons	yurt
Khans	westernization

FACT FOLLOW-UP

1. Compare Byzantine and Mongol influences on Russia.
2. What methods of political control and warfare did Russians learn from Byzantine and Mongol rulers?
3. What was the connection between the Russian Orthodox Church and the government? Explain.
4. What were the aims of Peter the Great, and why did he have those aims?
5. Describe the new capital city of St. Petersburg built by Peter the Great.
6. How did the arts and literature flourish under Peter and Catherine?
7. Russia had three capital cities: Kiev, Moscow, and St. Petersburg. Explain the cultural influences found in each city.
8. How did Byzantine, Slavic, and Mongol culture spread into Russia?

THINK THESE THROUGH

9. Which cultural influence on Russia was greatest: Slavic, Byzantine, Mongol, or European? Explain your answer.
10. How would Russia have been different had it been more influenced by Germany than by Constantinople?
11. Which capital city was more "Russian": Kiev, Moscow, or St. Petersburg? Explain why.
12. What was the most important Byzantine influence on Russia? Explain your answer.
13. Would westernization have occurred without Peter the Great? Explain.

SHARPENING SKILLS

14. Can you devise a way of organizing information and making decisions other than the one suggested in the skill lesson? How well does it work using information from Chapter 23?
15. When are web charts more useful than data retrieval charts?

16. When do you think it might be better to use data retrieval charts than web or spider charts?

17. Is it always useful to create graphic organizers when you need to make decisions based on information? Give reasons for your answer.

Use the letters on the map to locate and name the places described below:

18. a civilization that shaped Russian culture.

19. the cultural center of that civilization.

20. river that was an early Russian trade route.

21. an early Russian kingdom.

22. the capital of that early kingdom.

23. a northern kingdom outside of Russia whose people conducted trade along rivers crossing Russia from north to south.

24. Catherine the Great waged a war to gain an ice-free port on this sea. Why did the czarina want this port?

25. Peter the Great built his capital city on this sea. Why did he choose this location?

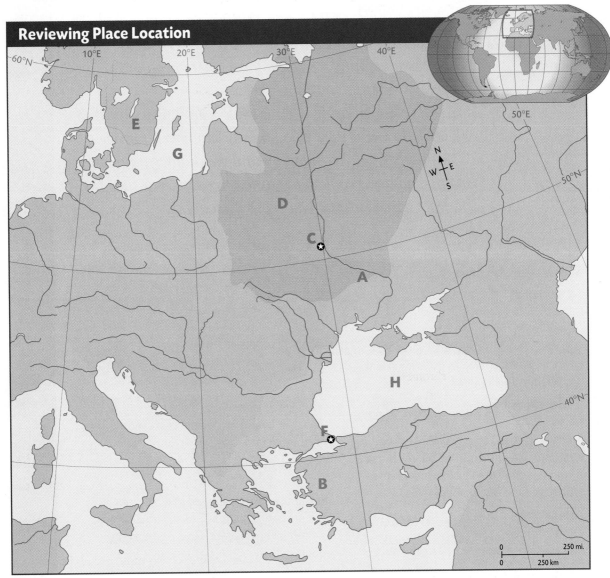

Reviewing Place Location

UNIT 7

Russia and Its Neighbors Today

Late in 1995, Russians elected members to their Duma, or parliament. Candidates for office had campaigned freely. People had been free to vote as they wished. This was something new in a land where people had been allowed little freedom.

The election came when people were uneasy and divided. So when they voted, many supported former Communists. Others stood behind candidates promising democracy. People had gained freedom, but they had not agreed on their nation's direction.

UNIT PREVIEW

CHAPTER 24
Land and People
Despite rich resources, Russia's northern location, harsh climate, and landlocked territory have limited its population and economic development.

CHAPTER 25
People and Environment
Russia has been an agricultural nation. Industry strengthened the nation under communism, but industrial growth has damaged the environment.

CHAPTER 26
Economy and Government
Russia and its neighbors are rich in resources. Russians have more freedom than ever before. Its neighbors are mostly ruled by dictators.

CHAPTER 27
Society and Culture
Russia's culture is captured in three cities. The Russian Orthodox Church and Islam are regaining influence. Food, sport, and leisure activities reflect geography.

Voting in Moscow

Land and People

How would you like to rent a Russian military helicopter to go sightseeing, or explore the controls of an abandoned Russian army tank, or ride a cog railway up a steep hill to watch ships in a crowded harbor?

All of these things are possible in Vladivostok, Russia's major port opening on the Pacific Ocean. Nowhere in Russia are the collapse of the Soviet Union and the end of the Cold War more dramatic than in that city. For 45 years, Vladivostok was closed to all foreigners. Even Russians had to have special permits to visit.

Today, it is wide open to foreigners.

Docked Russian naval vessels (below) and harbor cargo cranes (right) in the port of Vladivostok

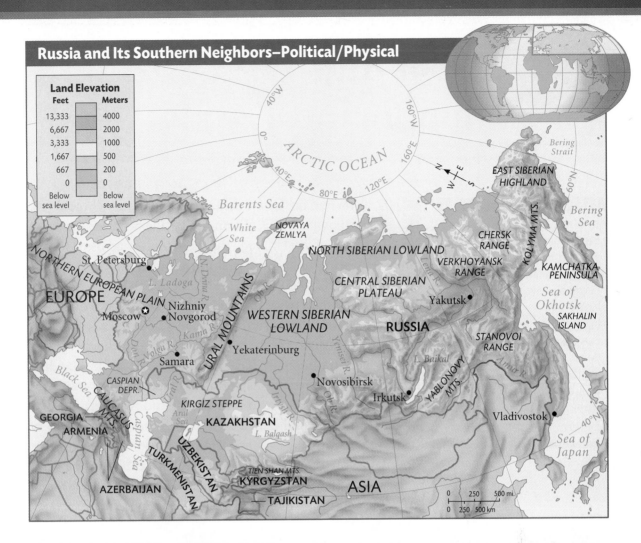

Russia and Its Southern Neighbors—Political/Physical

Land Elevation

Feet	Meters
13,333	4000
6,667	2000
3,333	1000
1,667	500
667	200
0	0
Below sea level	Below sea level

ARCTIC OCEAN

Barents Sea

White Sea

NOVAYA ZEMLYA

NORTH SIBERIAN LOWLAND

EAST SIBERIAN HIGHLAND

CHERSK RANGE

Bering Strait

Bering Sea

KOLYMA MTS.

VERKHOYANSK RANGE

KAMCHATKA PENINSULA

St. Petersburg

NORTHERN EUROPEAN PLAIN

L. Ladoga

N. Dvina R.

EUROPE

Moscow

Nizhniy Novgorod

Kama R.

Volga R.

Don R.

Samara

Ural R.

URAL MOUNTAINS

Ob R.

WESTERN SIBERIAN LOWLAND

Yekaterinburg

CENTRAL SIBERIAN PLATEAU

Lena R.

Yakutsk

RUSSIA

Sea of Okhotsk

SAKHALIN ISLAND

STANOVOI RANGE

Yenisei R.

Novosibirsk

Irtysh R.

Ob R.

L. Baikal

Irkutsk

YABLONOVY MTS.

Amur R.

STANOVOI RANGE

Vladivostok

Sea of Japan

Black Sea

CAUCASUS MTS.

GEORGIA

ARMENIA

AZERBAIJAN

Caspian Sea

CASPIAN DEPR.

Aral Sea

KIRGIZ STEPPE

KAZAKHSTAN

L. Balqash

TURKMENISTAN

UZBEKISTAN

TIEN SHAN MTS.

KYRGYZSTAN

TAJIKISTAN

ASIA

| 0 | 250 | 500 mi. |
| 0 | 250 | 500 km |

Russia and Neighboring Lands

Russia remains by far the largest nation in the world (see map on page 479). From the Bering Sea near Alaska to the Gulf of Finland, Russia stretches across 11 time zones. Its northern lands lie well north of the Arctic Circle. Its southern borders reach the same latitude as Salt Lake City, Utah. Russia is more than twice the size of the United States or China.

The Ural Mountains run more than 2,000 miles (3,220 km) from near Russia's northern coast to its southern border. Geographers traditionally have used the Urals as the dividing line between Europe and Asia. Russia's lands west of the Urals are part of Europe. Those to the east fall into Northern Asia.

The former republics of the Soviet Union that lie south of Russia in Transcaucasia are also in Asia. The Caucasus Mountains form another border between Asia and Europe. That range runs west to east from the Black Sea to the Caspian Sea. It separates Georgia, Armenia, and Azerbaijan (ah·zur·bye·ZHAN), from Russia.

Five other former Soviet republics extend south of the Siberian Lowland into **Central Asia**. Kazakhstan (kah·ZAK·stan), Uzbekistan (uz·bek·ih·STAN), Turkmenistan (turk·MEN·ih·stan), Tajikistan (tah·jik·ih·STAN), and Kyrgyzstan (cur·gih·STAN) reach from the Caspian Sea to the western border of China.

The Caucasus Mountains, shown here in Georgia, form a border between the continents of Asia and Europe. *What seas lie at the western and eastern ends of the ranges?*

The gentle slopes of the Ural Mountains are irrigated for agriculture. *What plain extends from Europe's Atlantic shores to the Ural Mountains? What plain stretches east from the Urals to the Pacific Coast?*

Landforms and Agriculture

The landforms in Russia differ from those in its former republics south of the Caucasus Mountains and in Central Asia.

Russia   Unlike other regions of Europe, which contain a variety of landforms in a small area, Russia's landscape is unchanging for thousands of miles. The greatest part of the nation consists of plains. The Russian world for plains is steppes.

The steppes extending from Russia's western borders to the Ural Mountains are part of the Northern European Plain. This plain spreads from Europe's Atlantic shores eastward through Poland, Belarus, Ukraine, and then into Russia. As in Eastern and Western Europe, these plains provide Russia its best farmland.

The Ural Mountains appear on maps to be an overpowering feature of Russia's landscape. They are in reality an old, eroded mountain range that rises some 3,000 to 4,000 feet (900 to 1,200 m). They present few barriers to movement. Travelers often find the slopes so gentle that they are unaware of having left the plains and entered the Urals.

East of the Ural Mountains, low plains and a higher plateau make up a vast region known as Siberia. The Siberian flatlands form the largest unbroken plains in the world, reaching eastward from the Ural Mountains almost to Russia's Pacific coast.

Near Russia's eastern coast, rugged mountains erupt from

the landscape. These are a jumbled mass of volcanic peaks and steep valleys standing between the flatlands and the ocean. Locate on the map on page 479 the Kamchatka Peninsula that extends from Russia's northeastern coast. Some of the peaks in this land tower more than 15,000 feet (4,500 m).

Few parts of these lands east of the Urals attracted settlers. Despite Siberia's flat lands, people chose to avoid it because the climate is much too cold for agriculture. Instead, settlements grew west of the Urals, where the weather is mild enough for raising crops.

Georgia, Armenia, and Azerbaijan These three republics gained independence from the Soviet Union in 1991. They are

EYEWITNESS TO HISTORY

Vitus Bering and the Bering Strait

Siberia

A Danish explorer, Vitus Bering (1681-1741), served in the Russian Navy. He charted the Siberian coast of the Arctic Ocean. He sailed through what is now called the Bering Strait, and mapped most of the Alaskan coast for the first time.

Bering Island

O n his return in 1741, Bering's ship *St. Peter* lost its way in heavy fog. Shipwrecked on an unknown island (now named Bering Island), Bering died on December 8 from scurvy, a disease caused by lack of vitamin C, and exhaustion.

*Bering's shipwreck (above)
and the Bering Sea (right)*

located in what is called Transcaucasia (meaning "across the Caucasus") between the Black and Caspian Seas. They are not large, but they provide valuable agriculture resources.

Western Georgia along the Black Sea, eastern Azerbaijan along the Caspian Sea, and the Aras River valley of Armenia contain fertile high plains. The area produces so much food it is called "the southern breadbasket." Sheep, goat, and cattle herding are the main agricultural activities of the central mountains.

Azerbaijan is dry, but irrigation has made it an agriculturally rich nation. Mountains cover Armenia, but rich topsoil of the river valley makes the country a major producer of orchard fruit, wheat, and potatoes. Georgia also grows wheat and fruit, as well as tobacco, corn, and tea.

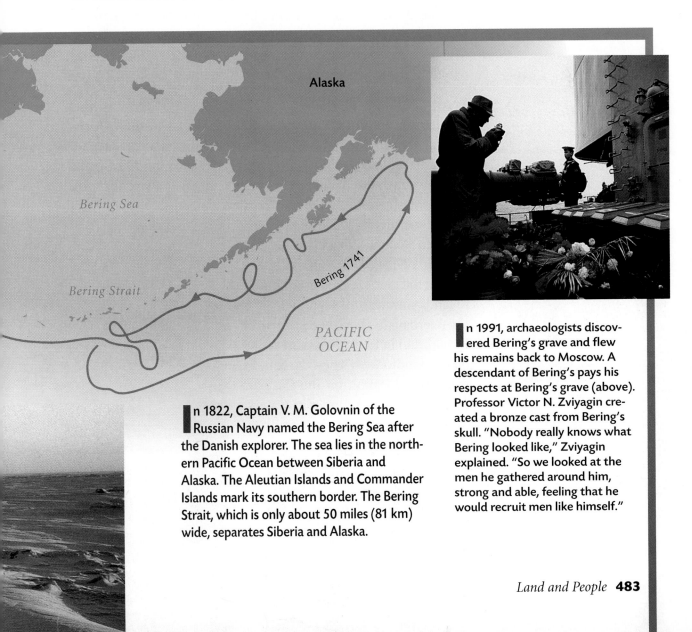

Alaska

Bering Sea

Bering Strait

Bering 1741

PACIFIC OCEAN

In 1822, Captain V. M. Golovnin of the Russian Navy named the Bering Sea after the Danish explorer. The sea lies in the northern Pacific Ocean between Siberia and Alaska. The Aleutian Islands and Commander Islands mark its southern border. The Bering Strait, which is only about 50 miles (81 km) wide, separates Siberia and Alaska.

In 1991, archaeologists discovered Bering's grave and flew his remains back to Moscow. A descendant of Bering's pays his respects at Bering's grave (above). Professor Victor N. Zviyagin created a bronze cast from Bering's skull. "Nobody really knows what Bering looked like," Zviyagin explained. "So we looked at the men he gathered around him, strong and able, feeling that he would recruit men like himself."

Central Asian Republics Nature provides little rain for the high plateaus of Central Asia. The Soviet Union built irrigation projects that made farming possible. The people had been herders of sheep, cattle, yaks, and camels before irrigation. Herding still continues in the eastern Tien Shan Mountains along the border with China and in the Kara Kum Desert of Turkmenistan.

Waterways and Movement

Compared to Western Europe, Russia and its neighbors are nearly landlocked. These lands have little direct access to the seas by way of rivers or ports.

The Arctic Ocean coastline, the region's longest, remains frozen most of the year, leaving ports unusable for months. Much of the Pacific Coast is also too cold for regular traffic, except in the southernmost ports.

Seas Ports on the Baltic and Black Seas offer entry to the Mediterranean and the Atlantic. Russia's access to these ports became limited when the Baltic countries—Estonia, Latvia, and Lithuania—plus Ukraine and Georgia broke away in 1991. Russia can now reach the Baltic Sea through territory it owns north of Estonia. Kalingrad is the main port of the territory which is located between Poland and Lithuania (see the map on page 347). Russia's openings on the Black Sea are now limited to lands southeast of Ukraine.

Azerbaijan, Turkmenistan, and Kazakhstan in Central Asia are completely landlocked. They do benefit from their location on the Caspian Sea. Because oil lies under its waters, the Caspian Sea will bring wealth to these countries.

Rivers In expressing their deep emotional attachment to the land, Russians frequently refer to their country as *rodina,* or motherland.

They speak similarly of the Volga River, which is affectionately called *Matushka*—"Dear Little Mother."

"The Volga flows in the heart of every Russian," explained a Moscow riverboat captain. For him, the Volga is the soul of Mother Russia. It is the longest and most important waterway of the region.

The Volga rises northwest of Moscow and winds 2,400 miles (3,864 km) before flowing into the Black Sea. The river also connects by canals to the Baltic Sea and remains open to shipping for nine months of the year.

The Volga is the chief transportation route of Russia, moving cargo into the ports of Europe and the rest of the world. In addition, the river irrigates the fertile steppes along its banks and produces energy through its system of hydroelectric plants.

Most rivers in the region outside Russia are not navigable. They are valuable in the farming valleys of Armenia and Georgia but they are too shallow for navigation.

Lake Baikal Lake Baikal, west of the Yablonovy Mountains of southern Siberia, is the deepest lake in the world. Nearly 5,315 feet (1,595 m) from surface to bottom, the lake holds about one fifth of all the fresh water in the world (see the map on page 479). Russians feel the same awe about the size and beauty of

The Caspian Sea provides resources to the nations surrounding it. Baku, Azerbaijan (left), is a port city for the oil the country pumps from beneath the sea. Huge sturgeon are among the many fish caught in the Caspian. *What countries benefit from their location on the sea?*

The Siberian city of Irkutsk sits on the edge of Lake Baikal (top of photo). *What is the importance of this lake to Siberia and to Russia?*

Lake Baikal that Americans feel about the Grand Canyon.

Lake Baikal has existed for more than 25 million years and is one of the oldest bodies of water in the world. By contrast, Lake Superior in the United States is only 10,000 years old. Because Lake Baikal is so ancient, many forms of aquatic life that do not live in other parts of the world continue to thrive in its waters.

Fishing boats pull good catches from the lake. Few people and little freight, however, are transported on its waters. Unlike the Great Lakes in North America, Lake Baikal has only one city—Irkutsk—and only a few people along its edges. There is little need in the area to move goods. A major hydroelectric project has been developed north of Irkutsk. This is on Angara River, the stream carrying water out of the lake.

LESSON 1 REVIEW

Fact Follow-up
1. Describe the size of Russia.
2. What former Soviet republics lie south of the Caucasus? Which are in Central Asia?
3. Describe the landforms and waterways of Russia. Describe the landscape and waterways of Russia's southern neighbors.

Think These Through
4. Is Russia fortunate or unfortunate to be so large? Explain your answer.
5. Is the relative location of Russia an advantage or a disadvantage? Explain.
6. How has being nearly landlocked been both a help and a hindrance to Russia?

Climate and Vegetation

LESSON 2

According to a folktale, the people of Georgia have enjoyed their green landscape and mild climate since the eighth day of creation. On that day, the story goes, God divided the land among all people. On his way home, God found the Georgians eating and drinking at a table by the side of the road. He scolded them for not coming to receive their land.

"But we were toasting you," the Georgians explained. "We wanted to thank you for making such a beautiful world." According to the legend, God was so pleased by their gratitude that he gave them the part of the world that most resembled paradise.

LESSON PREVIEW

Key Ideas

- Climates in Russia and neighboring lands reflect the region's northern location. Much of the region is located in cold latitudes.
- Much of the region is also distant from oceans that warm the air and bring rain.
- The cold and dry climate limits vegetation. A variety of vegetation grows in the region's milder climates.

Climate

Georgia enjoys a mild Mediterranean climate. Russia and its other neighbors endure the extremes of many climate zones—from the Arctic cold in the North to the desert heat of Central Asia (see the climate map on page 501).

Russia Because much of Russia is flat and far from large bodies of water, it generally has a continental climate, with freezing winters and hot summers. Snow buries the ground in most areas for six months of the year.

The Siberian plains endure the widest range of temperatures in the world. It is one of the coldest regions, with winter temperatures occasionally dropping as low as −90°F (−67.8°C), although the average temperature tends to stay around −50° (−45.6°C). In contrast, on a typical summer day in Siberia, temperatures might rise to 60° F (15.6°C) and sometimes even top 100° (37.8°C).

Navy cadets harvest carrots north of Moscow. Growing seasons are short in Russia. *What climate causes Russia's cold winters and hot summers?*

The western part of Russia enjoys a more moderate climate. Winter days usually average around 10° F (−12.2°C). Summers are short and warm. Western Russia also receives a moderate amount of rainfall, while the East remains dry most of the year.

In years ahead, the rich resources that lie beneath the ground in Siberia—even in the far North of the region—may draw a higher population. To this point, however, the long, dark winters and extreme cold have limited what people may do. Rivers and lakes remain frozen much of the year. The range of

LIVING IN SIBERIA

The "Sleeping Land"

Siberia covers three quarters of Russia yet claims only 23 percent of the country's population. Siberia gets its name from the Mongol dialect word *Sibir,* which means "sleeping land." With frozen tundra, icy wastelands, thin soil, snow depths up to 50 inches (127 cm) in the North and as little as 1 inch (2.5 cm) in the South, Siberia indeed sleeps. People have difficulty surviving in Siberia, but people do live in that vast land. Western Siberia contains the most population in the sparsely settled area.

Thirty nationalities have settled Siberia. Mongols live in regions east and west of Lake Baikal. Samoyeds and Ugrians live in the central and northern parts of western Siberia.

Many young college graduates find their way to Siberia because the government offers extra pay and housing to those willing to work in the frozen wastelands. Young people work, meet, and marry there. Some stay because of the relative freedom in the area. They work in logging camps, mines, steel mills, or at natural gas and petroleum wells.

Irkutsk started as a small fort and became a city in 1684. It served as a starting point for exploration to Alaska. Enemies of the government were sent to Irkutsk. Their punishment was "banishment to Siberia."

Irkutsk is no longer a remote outpost. Its population has grown to well over a half million. The city has become a center with factories and a variety of businesses. These support efforts to develop Siberia's rich resources.

Siberian landscape

vegetation that can survive is limited. This is why so much of Russia is so thinly populated.

Central Asia   In Central Asia, the climate varies with elevation. The mountains are much colder in the winter than are the plains or the valleys. In some of the highest areas, snow remains on the mountains all year long. Summers are hotter and drier in the low-lying plains and valleys.

Deserts cross much of Central Asia. Extreme heat and cold alternate with the seasons. In the summer, desert temperatures rise between 95° and 122°F (35° and 50°C), and the winter temperatures can drop as low as –32°F (–49.8°C).

Georgia, Armenia, and Azerbaijan   Extremes in hot and cold within a relatively small area characterize the climate of Georgia, Armenia, and Azerbaijan. Snow remains all year-round on some high mountain peaks. The Black Sea coast enjoys the mildness of the Mediterranean climate. The Southeast near the Caspian Sea experiences heat and desert dryness.

The Caucasus Mountains protect the area from severe Russian winters. The western coast also benefits from the warm, moist air of the Black Sea, but inland areas are drier and hotter. In the East, only the mountains receive heavy rainfall, and the valleys and plains remain dry.

Central Asia contains many deserts, including the Kyzul Kum Desert, an extension of the Kara Kum Desert. Look at the map on page 490. *What countries have deserts?*

Vegetation

From its frozen North to its much warmer South, Russia and its neighbors are located in lands that produce a great variety of vegetation (see map below).

Tundra   Russia is where the coldest lands are found. Its North consists of tundra, a bitterly cold, treeless, and mostly uninhabited zone. About half of it is permafrost, soil that remains frozen all year. Only low shrubs and mosses can survive the harsh life of the tundra.

Subarctic   South of the tundra grow subarctic forests. Coniferous forests, with cedar, fir, pine, and spruce trees grow south of the

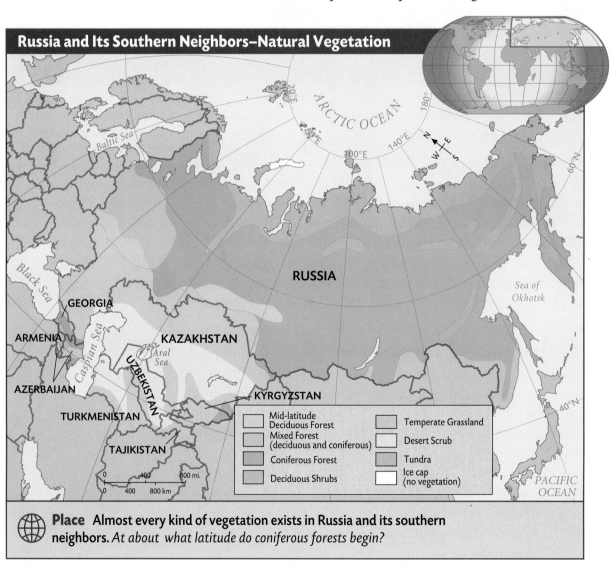

Russia and Its Southern Neighbors–Natural Vegetation

- Mid-latitude Deciduous Forest
- Mixed Forest (deciduous and coniferous)
- Coniferous Forest
- Deciduous Shrubs
- Temperate Grassland
- Desert Scrub
- Tundra
- Ice cap (no vegetation)

Place Almost every kind of vegetation exists in Russia and its southern neighbors. *At about what latitude do coniferous forests begin?*

The steppes of Kazakhstan are dry plains. Other steppes include wooded areas and meadows. *In what part of the steppes is farming most successful?*

tundra. Although the trees thrive here, the soil is too poor for farming.

Farther south are forests of conifers and deciduous trees, including aspen, birch, elm, maple, and oak. The soil and mild, moist climate of the southern subarctic can support some crops.

Steppes Even farther south lie the steppes, a great expanse of grassy plains. The northern steppes include some wooded areas and meadows. In the South, the steppes consist of treeless prairie stretching in all directions. The steppes offer the best soil for agriculture in the region.

Most farming in the steppes occurs in the West, in Russia and south of the Caucasus Mountains. A moderate amount of rain falls in these western areas. On the drier steppes of Central Asia, farming succeeds only with irrigation.

Desert In the semidesert and desert zones of Central Asia and Azerbaijan, low brush is the only vegetation. The deserts of the South contain rocks, sand, and wasteland.

LESSON 2 REVIEW

Fact Follow-Up
1. Describe the several climates of Russia.
2. What has Siberia contributed to Russia?
3. Describe the variety of vegetation in Russia.
4. Describe the climate and vegetation of Transcaucasia and Central Asia.

Think These Through
5. If you were to live in the area now under Russian authority, where would you choose to live? Explain why.
6. How has climate been both a benefit and a burden for Russia? for Transcaucasia? for Central Asia?

Land and People **491**

People

More than 80 percent of Russia's people are descendants of early Slav settlers. *What are other ethnic groups in Russia?*

On a lonely plateau in Kazakhstan, where the wind carries the scent of wild sage, Marat Imashev watches over his 650 sheep. Like an American cowhand, he roams freely under the blue sky as a *shaban,* or shepherd.

With his horse and two camels, Imashev will guide his flock of sheep across the plateau to the mountains. He has been traveling for a month, and still has 60 miles (97 km) to go in the next two weeks.

"I know the way without a map," he says. "Kazakhs have been grazing sheep on this plateau for centuries."

From the farmers of Georgia and the Aleuts of Siberia to the Slavs of Russia, this huge region contains a rich variety of people and ethnic identities. In Russia, most people are Russians. Russians are a minority in Central Asia and in the countries south of the Caucasus Mountains, despite Soviet control there for more than 70 years.

Russians

About 83 percent of Russia's people are descendants of the early Slavs. The population also includes more than 100 other nationalities. Some are Asiatic Mongols, whose ancestors invaded Kievan Russia. Others are Ukrainians, Belarusians, Germans, and Turks.

The Slavic ancestors of the Russians settled in a forested area in what is now Ukraine. It offered good farmland, plentiful hunting, and fishing. They soon spread out into other forested regions in Russia and Eastern Europe.

The far North in Russia is home to many small communities of Aleuts, Chukchi, Inuit, and Koryaks. Each group differs in ancestry and language. Yet their ways of life are similar to one another because of the common challenges

Russia and Its Southern Neighbors—Ethnic Groups

Armenian
Caucasian
Iranian
Mongolian

Slavic
Russian
Ukrainian

Sparsely populated

Finno-Ugric
Karelian
Other Finno-Ugric

Turkic
Azeri
Kazakh
Kyrgyz
Turkmen
Uzbek
Yakut
Other Turkic

ARCTIC OCEAN

Baltic Sea

20°E

Black Sea

GEORGIA

ARMENIA

AZERBAIJAN

Caspian Sea

TURKMENISTAN

TAJIKISTAN

UZBEKISTAN

Aral Sea

KAZAKHSTAN

RUSSIA

Sea of Okhotsk

KYRGYZSTAN

100°W
140°W
180°
140°E
100°E
60°N
40°N

0   400   800 mi.
0   400   800 km

Place **Most Russians belong to Slavic ethnic groups.** *What ethnic groups live in the Asian nations south of Russia? What ethnic groups live in Armenia, Georgia, and Azerbaijan?*

of cold and isolation. Some of these people are related to Native Americans of Alaska.

Georgians, Armenians, and Azerbaijanians

The people of Georgia, Armenia, and Azerbaijan live where Europe meets Asia. Many different people and cultures have settled there and sometimes fought with one another in this area south of the Caucasus Mountains.

Over the centuries, various Asian people, Turks, Mediterranean people, Vikings, Arabs, and the Mongols invaded. Russians settled in the area after the Soviet Union was formed. The most

The people of Transcaucasia—Armenia (top), Georgia, and Azerbaijan (bottom)—speak a total of more than 80 languages. *Why is there such great diversity in this area?*

WORD ORIGINS

Some people think **Georgia** comes from a Greek word meaning "people who work the earth." Others believe it derives from the ancient Persian word for the people of the area, "Gurj." In any case, it is only a coincidence that the country shares its name with the state of Georgia in the United States, which was named for an English king.

recent newcomers are Muslims moving from Iran and Turkey. Because of this diversity, the people speak more than 83 languages.

Armenians Armenians came from across the Euphrates River in the eighth century B.C. By 600 B.C., they had formed a nation and had established one of the earliest centers of civilization in the world. At the end of the third century, Armenia became the first nation to adopt Christianity. The Armenian language is an ancient branch of Indo-European.

Georgians The people of Georgia began mining copper, gold, and silver around 3500 B.C. The trade in precious metals attracted the Greeks, who might have created the myth of the Golden Fleece based on their voyages to an ancient Georgian kingdom. Then, as now, Georgians farmed their rich land and fished in the rivers and along the Black Sea coast.

The Georgian language is unlike any other in the world. It has its own alphabet, which may be related to Eastern Aramaic of the Middle East.

Azerbaijanians Azerbaijan's people are the descendants of very early settlers and Persians who moved into the lowlands about 3,500 years ago. In the eleventh century, the Turks of Central Asia invaded and brought their culture, including the Muslim religion, to the Azerbaijanians.

The major language of Azerbaijan is Azeri. The language combines an eastern dialect of Turkish with some Persian and Russian words.

Central Asians

As you read in Chapter 22, the czarist government took over vast stretches of land east of the Ural Mountains in the 1700s and 1800s. At the time, much of this land was thinly populated. Most of the people living in this new Russian territory were not related in any way to the Slavic Russians. They were Asians who practiced Islam.

The nomads of Kazakhstan were once citizens of the Soviet Union in an area called Turkestan. Stalin divided Turkestan into five republics. *Why did Stalin do this?*

Turkestan was one of the largest of such areas. At the time the Russians annexed it, the area had no definite borders. It was land bounded on the west by the Caspian Sea and on the east by China's Tien Shan Mountains. Modern-day Iran, Afghanistan, and Pakistan lie along its southern edges. The region was called Turkestan because it had been inhabited by various Turkish groups since the early 500s.

After coming to power, the Communist-led Soviet Union made serious efforts to establish Moscow's authority in the area and to win the people's loyalty. Soviet leader Joseph Stalin divided the area into five republics: Kazakhstan, Uzbekistan, Turkmenistan, Kyrgyzstan, and Tajikistan. The separate republics had less power than a united Turkestan, so the Soviets could control the region more easily.

The Soviets sent Russians into the republics. In this way Moscow could control government. Moscow's representatives also campaigned to suppress local customs, languages, and the people's devotion to Islam.

These efforts brought change to the area. Since the Soviet Union's collapse in 1991, the Central Asia republics have shown little interest in giving up their individual identities. Local leaders have taken control of each republic's government and seem determined to retain their independence.

What would YOU do?

Archaeologists can only discover how people lived in the past if they are permitted to dig. If you think of some place as holy or sacred, should others be allowed to come in and explore that place by digging? We can learn from the past. We learn about people's lives and someday may uncover something that helps us live today. Yet we also believe some places should not be disturbed. What would you do? Would you allow an archaeologist to dig in a sacred place or not?

The republics also want to continue some of the economic changes started by the Soviet government. When Soviet officials arrived in Central Asia, they found land that was flat and sandy in the northwest. Mountains rose in the southeast. None of the area received much rainfall. Rivers flowed out of the mountains toward the interior, where they disappeared in desert sands.

For hundreds of centuries most people of Turkestan had lived as nomadic herders or merchants. The Soviets built irrigation projects and began to develop the region's mineral resources. This opened new jobs in agriculture and industry. The independent governments now want to keep these jobs for their citizens.

Different ethnic groups live in the countries of Central Asia.
What forces may draw these groups apart?

Many people gave up lives as nomadic herders and began working on large farms. Irrigation had opened millions of acres to production of wheat, rice, millet, oats, and cotton.

Other people of the Central Asian republics went to work in construction, mining, or petroleum production. Cities grew as these industries developed. Many began working in businesses related to those industries.

Economic development was not enough to bond Central Asia with today's Russia. In the 1990s, Central Asia has experienced an Islamic revival. Mosques have opened and people are returning to Islamic worship and life. This religious revival is causing Central Asian republics to turn away from Russia and toward the Islamic Middle East.

LESSON 3 REVIEW

Fact Follow-Up
1. Describe the ethnic character of the Russian people.
2. Describe the diversity of the Transcaucasians.
3. Describe the diversity of the population in the Central Asian republics.
4. For Russia, what have been some advantages and disadvantages of ethnic diversity?

5. What Soviet programs did the Central Asian republics want to maintain? Why?

Think These Through
6. Suppose Russia had not annexed territory in Central Asia. How might the course of history have been changed?
7. Why did Soviet efforts to change the traditions of Central Asia fail? Explain.

*Using Information for Problem Solving,
Decision Making, and Planning*

Using Geography's Themes to Organize Information

The information presented in Chapter 24 can be organized in different ways. Applying geography's themes is one way. To refresh your memory of the five themes, review the skill lessons for Chapters 1 through 6.

In this lesson you will concentrate on the themes of location, place, human-enviromental interaction, and movement. You will use the themes to help analyze conditions in three places. Imagine that you can choose to live in one of these places for two years. By using geography's themes to draw information together and to analyze it, you will be able to make a good decision about where you will live.

First, select the places you will consider: one from Russia, one from Central Asia, and one from Transcaucasia. You will need to use the maps in this unit and data from the reading. In addition, you may want to use other reference works, such as almanacs or encyclopedias. Now you are ready to begin your analysis. First, construct a data retrieval chart like the one shown below.

After you have gathered your data, ask yourself questions such as these: (1) Would I prefer one location—considering location in both absolute and relative terms—more than others? Why? (2) Are there physical or cultural aspects that would be more appealing than another? Why? (3) How will aids or barriers to movement help in making my decision? Now, where will you live? Can you explain the factors that influenced your decision?

Data Retrieval Chart: Choosing Where to LIve			
Theme	**Place 1**	**Place 2**	**Place 3**
1. Location			
a) Absolute			
b) Relative			
2. Place			
a) Physical			
b) Cultural			
3. Human-Environmental Interaction			
4. Movement			
a) Aids			
b) Barriers			

Chapter 24 Review

LESSONS LEARNED

LESSON 1 Modern-day Russia remains by far the largest nation in the world. Much of its land, however, consists of huge plains. In contrast with Western Europe, Russia has few navigable rivers and has limited access to the world's oceans. Its neighboring republics to the south have more varied landforms, but they also have few rivers and limited access to open oceans.

LESSON 2 Much of Russia has limited rainfall, and temperatures are low much of the year. The nations south of Russia also live in dry climates. These patterns in climate reflect these nations' northern location. They also are distant from oceans that might bring moisture and warmer air.

LESSON 3 The core of Russia's population is composed of Slavic people. Modern-day Russia, however, has a mix of many ethnic groups. A mixture of ethnic groups is typical of some of Russia's neighboring republics. But most people in these countries are Muslims.

TIME FOR TERMS

Central Asia

FACT FOLLOW-UP

1. Describe the size of Russia, explaining the advantages and disadvantages of its large territory.
2. Compare the climate and vegetation of Russia with that of Central Asia and Transcaucasia.
3. What waterways serve Russia?
4. Describe the ethnic diversity of Russia.

5. What has been the importance of the Volga River for Russia?
6. Describe the climate and resources of Siberia.
7. What are the physical characteristics of place in Transcaucasia and Siberia?
8. What ethnic groups are dominant in Transcaucasia?
9. Which is more ethnically diverse: Transcaucasia or Central Asia?

THINK THESE THROUGH

10. Would governing Russia be easier if the nation were not so large? Explain.
11. Is the Russian climate a friend or foe to Russians? Explain.
12. After World War II, the Soviet Union promised young engineers extra pay if they would settle in Siberia and help develop the region's resources. Explain why you would or would not have taken such an offer.
13. Is the Volga River as important as it once was? Explain.
14. The Soviet Union spent money improving navigation on such rivers as the Volga and Dnepr. Why was so little work done on the long rivers running through Siberia?
15. Are ethnic conflicts unavoidable in Russia? Explain.
16. In which area described in this chapter would you most like to travel? Explain why.
17. How has being nearly landlocked and having only limited access to the world's oceans influenced the economic and political development of Russia?
18. Is Russia too ethnically diverse? Explain.

19. What sources of information did you use in deciding where to live? Which was most useful?
20. Which of the geographic themes was easiest for you to use? Why?
21. What other questions could you ask to make generalizations from your information?
22. Which of the themes do you think is most important in explaining life in this area? Explain your answer.

Use the letters on the map below to locate and name the places described below:

23. two mountain ranges considered the dividing lines between Europe and Asia.
24. Russia's best farmland first settled by ancestors of modern-day ethnic Russians.
25. vast flat lowlands and plateau that is thinly populated.
26. inland sea valuable both for fishing and oil.
27. place where Russia and the United States nearly meet.
28. one of the largest bodies of freshwater in the world.
29. river flowing into the Caspian Sea that is honored by Russians much as Europeans honor the Danube.

Reviewing Place Location

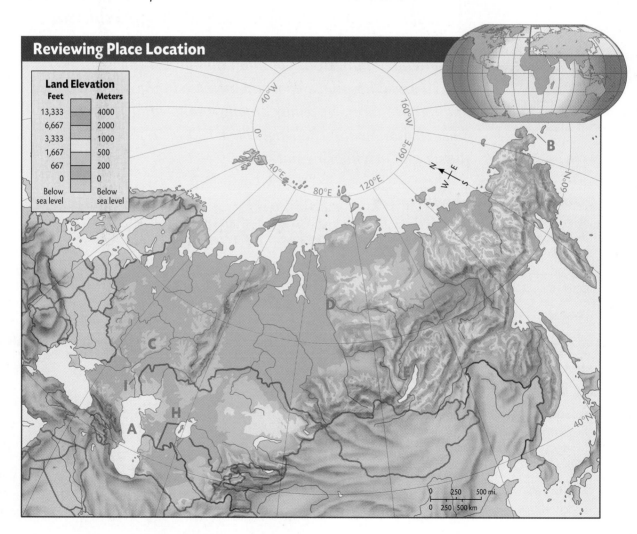

Land Elevation

Feet	Meters
13,333	4000
6,667	2000
3,333	1000
1,667	500
667	200
0	0
Below sea level	Below sea level

Land and People **499**

People and Environment

CHAPTER 25

Irrigation equipment

Around the Aral Sea, a body of water lying between Uzbekistan and Kazakhstan, a 30-year irrigation project has created unexpected results.

Engineers pumped water from streams feeding the Aral Sea to nearby farms. The irrigation reduced the Aral Sea to half its original size. The loss of water has made the sea saltier. The salt and pesticides from nearby farms have produced dangerous pollution in and near the sea.

Local hospitals report an increase in infectious disease and throat cancer, especially among infants and children. Such environmental challenges have become a problem in Russia and neighboring nations.

CHAPTER PREVIEW

LESSON 1
Before the Coming of Industry
Most Russians lived in small villages and farmed, using simple tools until the early twentieth century.

LESSON 2
Industrialization
When modern industry reached Russia, people moved to cities. Industrialization did not improve living standards.

LESSON 3
Environmental Impacts of Industry
Modern agriculture and industry changed Russian lives. These changes also brought serious environmental problems.

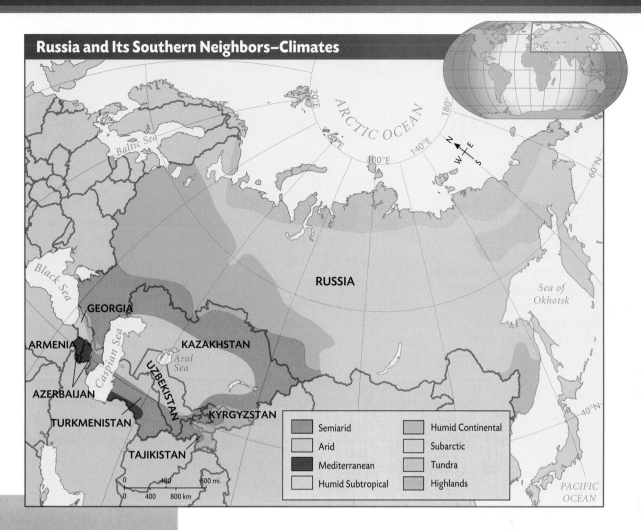

Russia and Its Southern Neighbors—Climates

ARCTIC OCEAN

20°E
40°E
100°E
140°E
180°

Baltic Sea

RUSSIA

Sea of Okhotsk

Black Sea

GEORGIA

ARMENIA

Caspian Sea

Aral Sea

KAZAKHSTAN

AZERBAIJAN

UZBEKISTAN

TURKMENISTAN

KYRGYZSTAN

TAJIKISTAN

PACIFIC OCEAN

60°N

40°N

	Semiarid		Humid Continental
	Arid		Subarctic
	Mediterranean		Tundra
	Humid Subtropical		Highlands

0   400   800 mi.

0   400   800 km

Ships of the Aral Sea are stranded in sand (left).
The changes in the Aral Sea have made living conditions
difficult on its shores (above).

Before the Coming of Industry

LESSON PREVIEW

Key Ideas

- The Agricultural Revolution did not reach czarist Russia.
- The majority of the people were serfs, or peasants, who worked with simple tools, lived in poverty, and were often mistreated by the nobility.

For the first time I looked closely at all the household gear of a peasant hut," wrote Alexander Radishchev in his book *A Journey from St. Petersburg to Moscow.* "The upper half of the four walls and the whole ceiling were covered with soot; the floor was full of cracks and covered with dirt at least two inches thick."

A quick look around the hut revealed the harsh life of Russian serfs. Because there was no smokestack for the oven, smoke filled the hut, and the single candle appeared "as though shrouded in mist." Instead of glass panes, "stretched bladders" served as windows, admitting only "a dim light at noon time."

The living conditions were more fitting for animals than humans. A feeding trough filled one corner of the hut. At night, the family slept together with their farm animals.

Radishchev published *A Journey from St. Petersburg to Moscow* in 1790. The book outraged Russian authorities. They sent him to Siberia.

The Last Serfs

In Russia, serfdom continued well into the nineteenth century—long after it had disappeared from the rest of Europe. Because of serfdom, the Agricultural Revolution that swept the British Isles and Western Europe did not reach Russia until the twentieth century. As long as there was plenty of peasant labor, landowners were not interested in changing ways of farming.

The czar and the nobility ruled Russia and were rich and powerful. They owned the fertile farmland west of the Ural Mountains and controlled the peasants who farmed it.

Peasants were born into serfdom. The nobles thought of them as a form of property, as a part of the land itself. Serfs became attached to an estate simply by being born there.

Vastly different styles of living in Russia between serfs (left) and nobles (right) created problems in Russia. *How did nobles treat the serfs?*

Russian landowners treated the serfs as though they were farm animals. Nobles beat serfs, traded them, even wagered them in card games. Some landowners punished rebellious serfs by branding them on the face.

Russian landowners did not have to buy the latest farm machinery or try new methods of farming. They tried to increase production by forcing serfs to work harder. Harsh treatment failed to increase crop yields in the Russian interior. The eastern edge of the Northern European Plain lies far from the warm and moist winds of the North Atlantic Drift. Growing seasons shortened by early winters or late springs could ruin a year's crop. When that happened, landowners lost profits. Serfs lost their lives to starvation.

The Abolition of Serfdom

In reaction to mistreatment by nobles, Russian serfs rose against the landowners. The czar's troops violently put down more than 500 revolts between 1825 to 1854.

In 1855, Czar Alexander II came to the throne. He believed that the Russian nobility could no longer hold the serfs in their power. In 1861, Alexander freed 20 million serfs. This step eventually brought great changes to Russia. Freeing the serfs, however, did not improve their lives.

When the czar freed the serfs, he also promised to give them some land of their own to farm. Land reform did not turn out as the former serfs hoped. Serfs usually received only a small portion of the land they had worked all their lives. Some had to pay the landlord for the small amount granted them. At times, an entire village rather than individuals received a share of land. As the village population grew, the amount of land given each person became smaller.

Because of these complex rules, Russian nobles still owned much of the land. The serfs were free, but they had few hopes of better lives. Families had little land to farm. So even in good years, when the Russian climate was favorable, they would not have much to eat or sell.

Russian farmers lived in rural villages and tilled the land just

Farming in Russia

Technology has changed farming life in Russia, but farmers have rarely enjoyed the fruits of their labors.

RUSSIA

The plow changed the way medieval Europeans farmed, but Russian serfs farmed with hand tools. As the English and French kingdoms dropped feudalism, the Russian nobility turned to it. Russian peasants found their lives even more difficult than any of their European counterparts.

Commercial Farming
Subsistence Farming
Livestock Raising

Russian milk seller

Landowners used serf labor to produce crops. Whatever the serfs grew belonged to the landowners. Little was left over for the serfs. Many children died in infancy and adults' lifespans were short. Smoky, dirty huts and poor diets made disease a constant companion.

as the farmers of Western Europe had hundreds of years earlier. Farm life did not change much until Communists came to power in 1917.

LESSON 1 REVIEW

Fact Follow-Up

1. Describe the lives of serfs.
2. Why did the Agricultural Revolution not reach czarist Russia?
3. How did the abolition of serfdom affect the lives of serfs?

Think These Through

4. Suppose that you were a Russian landowner in czarist Russia. How would you justify the way serfs lived?
5. Why were the lives of serfs not much improved by abolition of serfdom?

PACIFIC OCEAN

When the Communists seized power, modern farming methods and machinery became more common (right). Farmers still received little for their work.

Harvesting tobacco by horse (above) and by hand (left) still occurs in Russia.

Much of the land of the former Soviet Union is still government-owned, but private farms are appearing. Hay (above) is harvested on a private farm in Ukraine, the former breadbasket of the Soviet Union.

Industrialization

LESSON 2

LESSON PREVIEW

Key Ideas
- Czarist Russia began to industrialize late in the nineteenth century. Under communism, industry grew at a rapid pace.
- Communist leaders hurried to modernize agriculture in the 1930s at the same time that they were building industry.

Key Terms
Five-Year Plan

Russians in the early days of industry put up with difficult working conditions, such as in this textile mill near Moscow. *How did factory managers treat the workers?*

"Punishment in the factory was meted out by lashing," remembered R.V. Gerasimov. He had worked as a child in a factory before the Communist revolution in 1917. "Once I accidentally broke a broom, which earned me 25 lashes, and another time I received 50 lashes for riding the elevator from the fourth to the third floor. They beat me with such force that not a white spot remained on my back; it turned all black."

He recalled even worse treatment of child workers in the factory. "I was myself witness of a beating which a certain assistant foreman administered to a girl, who died the very following day in the hospital." Gerasimov joined the Communist revolution because of what he saw.

Industry came late to Russia—almost 100 years after the Industrial Revolution changed the British Isles and Western Europe. Textile factories and railways arrived in Russia not long after the serfs became free. Peasants working in factories were technically free, but the managers regarded these workers as their property. "In a word, they dealt with them any way they wished," Gerasimov said.

Early Industrialization

In the second half of the nineteenth century, Russia began to industrialize rapidly. By freeing the serfs, Czar Alexander II provided a large pool of workers. When the former serfs found that they had little or no land of their own, many moved to the cities to start work in the new factories. The life they found in the factories was scarcely better than on the farm.

Factory work was usually dirty and often dangerous. The pay was low and the hours long. Russian factory workers spent from 11 to 14 hours a day at their machines. Some worked 20 hours a day.

A Russian worker described labor conditions for his family at the time. "I earn four rubles [about two dollars] a month.... My time is all spent in the [cotton] mill—from five o'clock in the morning until eight o'clock at night. My wife and two daughters work on the field belonging to [a noble] five days every week in the summer. They get no wages. In winter they do any kind of work required of them. My son (who is seventeen) works also in the mill and gets two rubles a month."

Because factory owners provided only crowded and expensive housing, many workers simply slept beside their machines, just as the serfs slept beside their farm animals. For both former serfs and new industrial workers, there was no relief from the grind of harsh working conditions.

Communism Comes to Russia

Russia's defeats in World War I increased the despair of factory and farm workers. Soon hundreds of thousands were demanding "Peace, Land, and Bread," the slogan of Communist leader V. I. Lenin. Such widespread discontent produced the Russian Revolution of 1917. Government by the czar ended in March. By November, Russian Communists had seized power. Russian workers hoped that the new Communist-led government would take them out of the war and bring them better working conditions. They hoped for real freedom.

In the nineteenth century, Russian children worked in such early industries as shoe making. They worked the same hours as adults but earned less. *How long was the workday in Russia during the nineteenth century?*

WORD ORIGINS

The term **Bolsheviks** came into use during Lenin's takeover of the Russian government. Lenin assigned the name Bolsheviks, which means majority, to a small group of people who were to lead the Communist Revolution. In November 1917, the Bolsheviks stormed the czar's palace.

V. I. Lenin led the Communist Revolution in 1917. Here he addresses a crowd in Moscow in 1919 during the civil war that followed the revolution. *What slogan did he use to inspire his followers? What did it mean?*

A Red Army armored train heads for Volgograd to face opponents of the Communist Revolution during the Russian Civil War. *How did the Communists win the war?*

The workers soon lost hope again. After the Communist revolution, the average Russian worker saw little change. Peasants on the land and industrial workers in the factories still had nothing to call their own. The new Communist government did not allow citizens to own property.

The majority of Russians remained powerless. The Communist government replaced the landowners and factory owners by taking ownership of all the farms and the factories in the country. The government forced everyone between the ages of sixteen and fifty to work.

Not everyone accepted the changes brought by communism. After Russia had pulled out of World War I, civil war soon began in Russia. The Communists were opposed by a variety of groups, including the Allied powers of World War I. The fighting caused social chaos. Millions of Russians wandered homeless and sick. Many starved or died of widespread disease.

A total of 7 million Russians died during the revolution. In 1921, when drought caused starvation in the farmland, 5 million more died. At the same time, Russia lost 1.5 million more people who left the country because of the revolution and civil war.

The Communists' Red Army won the civil war in 1921. Their opponents' armies failed to unite against them. Even more important was their opponents' failure to rally people behind them. Forces opposing the Communists often treated people cruelly. Many feared the Communists' enemies would bring back the czar.

In 1921, British writer H. G. Wells visited Petrograd, formerly St. Petersburg (renamed Leningrad after Lenin died

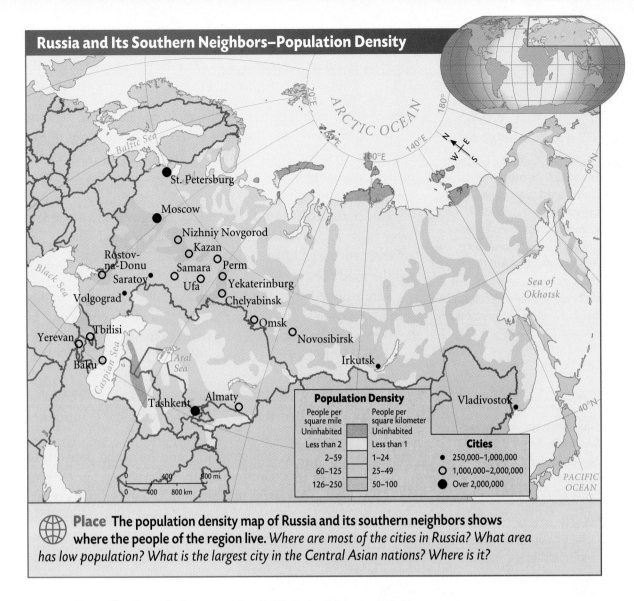

Russia and Its Southern Neighbors–Population Density

Population Density

People per square mile	People per square kilometer
Uninhabited	Uninhabited
Less than 2	Less than 1
2–59	1–24
60–125	25–49
126–250	50–100

Cities

- ● 250,000–1,000,000
- ○ 1,000,000–2,000,000
- ● Over 2,000,000

Place The population density map of Russia and its southern neighbors shows where the people of the region live. *Where are most of the cities in Russia? What area has low population? What is the largest city in the Central Asian nations? Where is it?*

in 1924). Wells found the once beautiful city devastated by revolution, war, and famine. Petrograd was "an astonishing

spectacle of desolation," Wells wrote. "Nothing had been repaired for four years. There were great holes in the streets; not a shop was open, and most were boarded up over their broken windows."

Petrograd's residents were also in a terrible state. "The scant drift of people in the streets wore shabby clothing, for there were no new clothes in Russia, no new boots," Wells reported.

Stalin and Agriculture

The Communist goal was to modernize Russia and make the country competitive with Western Europe. Yet the Communist leaders did not want to rely on the methods of free enterprise that had transformed the West. When Lenin led the Soviet Union, he supported the New Economic Policy (NEP) to encourage production.

Under the NEP (1921-29), the Soviet government backed away from earlier attempts to control farm production. The government taxed farm crops, but allowed workers to keep or sell the food they grew.

Lenin hoped that the NEP would help Russia by getting farms operating again after the destruction of the civil war. The Soviet leader allowed farmers to manage their own crops. This was not strictly part of communism, but Lenin accepted it to prevent starvation.

When Lenin died in 1924, Joseph Stalin came to power. Within five years he rejected the NEP. He ordered local Communist leaders to seize grain stored by the peasants.

Stalin began a process of taking land from the peasants to introduce large-scale collective farming everywhere. The government gathered small farms into large units and claimed ownership of rural land throughout Russia. Leaders in Moscow managed agriculture for the entire country.

Between 1929 and 1933, the peasants fought back by slaughtering more than 100 million of their horses and cattle, rather than let the Soviet leadership get their hands on them. Government forces killed as many as 10 million peasants and shipped millions more to Siberia. Stalin won the battle for control of the farmlands, but the outcome did not solve the problem of production.

Lenin with the Peasants of Shunshenskaye shows the Soviet leader talking to peasant farmers. *What program did Lenin begin to improve farming?*

Stalin and Industrialization

Stalin also set Russia on a course of rapid industrialization under strict central control. Stalin proposed a **Five-Year Plan** for the Soviet Union. Under the plan, the government would take over all private business to increase production and expand heavy industry within five years.

To meet the goals of the Five-Year Plan, factories had to run 24 hours a day. Stalin forced managers to produce at high levels or face imprisonment themselves. No one could complain or suggest changes without risking arrest and execution.

Even farm workers played a part in the plan to expand industry. Peasants sold their crops to the government at low prices. The cheap produce fed factory workers and gave the government farm products to trade with other countries for industrial machinery.

Stalin's Five-Year Plan introduced great changes in Russia. In the 1930s, Russia built 500 new factories. Steel production increased. Many people moved to cities to work in factories (see map, page 509). New oil wells and coal pits supplied more energy for factories.

Stalin's harsh measures resulted in the deaths of millions of citizens. Stalin wanted to make Russia a world industrial power, no matter the sacrifice. In this, he was successful.

Stalin's Five-Year Plan forced the Soviet Union to rapidly industrialize. The Molotov auto plant at Gorky produced cars similar to the Ford automobile of the United States. *What did the Five-Year Plan include? How successful was it?*

LESSON ② REVIEW

Fact Follow-Up

1. Describe Russian factory labor in the nineteenth century. Did it change under communism? Why or why not?
2. What was the NEP? How well did it work?
3. How did Stalin treat the peasants? How did the peasants respond?
4. What were the results of Stalin's Five-Year Plan?

Think These Through

5. Would you have preferred to be a Russian factory worker in czarist or Communist times? Explain.
6. Did Stalin gain or lose by abolishing the NEP and collectivizing agriculture? Explain.
7. Suppose that you had been Stalin's economic advisor. Would you have recommended the Five-Year Plan? Why or why not?

Environmental Impacts of Industry

LESSON PREVIEW

Key Ideas

- The Agricultural and Industrial Revolutions engineered by the Soviet Union have created environmental disasters.
- Almost every area of the former Soviet Union suffers from air, water, and soil pollution.
- Partly as a result of this pollution, life expectancy is dropping and babies are being born with serious defects.

Steel manufacturing in the Soviet Union created problems for the environment. *How did that industry and others hurt the environment?*

"Let's say you decide to get away from it all in Siberia," proposed Alexei Yablokov, a Russian environmentalist who advised Russian President Boris Yeltsin. "You travel up the Yenisey River toward the Arctic. You look across the empty tundra and think you are alone in nature, miles upon miles from the nearest person, and you decide to stretch out on the river bank."

The vision of an untouched paradise would deceive you. "Unfortunately, you are lying in sands contaminated by plutonium from three reactors whose radioactive wastes have been carelessly dumped for over 40 years."

The Cost of Industrialization

"We've inherited an ecological disaster," declared Boris Yeltsin, shortly after the collapse of the Soviet Union.

Stalin and later Soviet leaders built Russian industry rapidly, without concern for environmental safeguards. Russian power plants, weapons factories, and huge, industrialized farms produced dangerous waste for decades. The Russian people now suffer the worst consequences of industrialization but enjoy few of its benefits.

Some environmental problems stem from wasteful energy use. The average Russian uses 90 percent less energy than a Westerner because of smaller homes and fewer appliances. Yet Russian industry uses more energy than American and Western European factories. Production of this energy pollutes air and water.

Every major river in the region is polluted. One fourth of the water is unfit for humans to drink. Thirty-five million people breathe unsafe air.

This pollution is taking its toll on the Russian people. Only one fourth of Russian schoolchildren are in good health. Russians, on average, do not live as long as before industrialization.

Lake Baikal

Russians have treasured Lake Baikal, the Blue Eye of Siberia, for its enormous size and great beauty. It contains a huge supply of fresh water.

According to legend, if you swim in Lake Baikal, it will make

CONNECTIONS

Geography & Math

Russian Life Expectancy Rates

In most industrialized countries, life expectancy has been going up, as people live healthier lives. But in Russia, life expectancy has taken a sudden, dramatic drop.

In 1991, Russian men lived an average of 63.5 years. By 1994, life expectancy for Russian men had dropped to 57.7 years. How fast is the life expectancy rate falling? In three years it dropped 5.8 years. What is the average drop per year? If life expectancy continues to drop at the same rate, what would be the life expectancy of Russian men in 2000?

From 1991 to 1994, life expectancy for Russian women also dropped, from 74.3 to 71.3 years. Is the life expectancy rate falling more quickly for women or for men? Give reasons for your answer.

In contrast, life expectancy in the United States is 72 years for men and 79 years for women.

At the same time, the birth rate in Russia has been decreasing. In 1984, the birth rate was 16 babies per 1,000 Russians. By 1994, that number had dropped significantly, to fewer than 10 per 1,000.

In every one of Russia's 79 districts, the population has been shrinking because of fewer births and earlier deaths.

A drop in population may come from a poor Russian diet, a high rate of alcoholism, or the stress of economic and political turmoil. Experts believe this is also a consequence of pollution and industrialization.

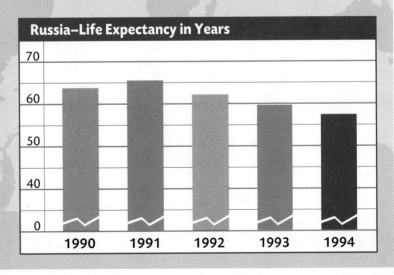

Russia–Life Expectancy in Years

you look a year younger. Folklore aside, scientists explain that a species of crustacean maintains the purity of the lake's waters by eating dangerous bacteria.

But Lake Baikal now shows signs of pollution from Russian industry. The southern end of the lake contains factory waste that has begun killing organisms at the deepest level. In time, these chemicals will poison the lake's entire food chain.

This pollution comes from a factory built in 1961. Soviets designed the plant to use Baikal's pure waters in the production of jet aircraft tires. The Russians knew that Americans were making similar jet tires, and they felt they had to compete.

When the Soviet leader Nikita Khrushchev learned of the plan, he declared, "Baikal too must work." The government sacrificed a great natural resource to the military and industrial competition of the Cold War.

Nuclear Reactors and Radiation

As you have read, the nuclear disaster in Chernobyl caused widespread damage in Ukraine and surrounding areas. Experts pointed to the poor design of the Chernobyl reactor as the cause of the explosion. That poor design is used in 19 of the nuclear reactors that are in former republics of the Soviet Union. The reactors are slow to cool down. During an emergency their cores may explode. That was the cause of the Chernobyl accident.

Russian nuclear scientists worry about the poorly designed nuclear plants. A total of 37 reactors produce about 12 percent of the energy in Transcaucasia. Many scientists believe it is just a matter of time before one of the older reactors causes another environmental disaster.

What would YOU do?

Nuclear reactors supply Russian people with energy. Many of those reactors are in bad shape. A disaster such as Chernobyl could happen again. One response would be to shut down all the reactors to make them safe. If that happened, then people in many areas would be without electricity. Also, the costs would be enormous. Many factories and other businesses would have to close. This would cause still more hardships for the Russian people. What would you do about the nuclear reactors?

Nuclear Weapons and Waste

The Soviet Union tested and produced many nuclear weapons. Although the Cold War has passed, dangers resulting from weapon production still remain.

Chelyabinsk (see map, page 509) was once a secret nuclear weapons production site. Since the 1950s, it also has served as a dumping ground for atomic waste. The radioactivity level has remained so high that even now a visitor will receive a lethal dose of radiation in less than an hour.

Soviet engineers tried to contain the radioactive pollution in the nearby Techa River by surrounding it with a fence. The fence did not work. Scientists discovered radiation 100 miles (161 km) away, where the Techa empties into the Arctic Ocean.

The island of Novaya Zemlya (see map, page 479) served as a nuclear weapons testing range and then as a radioactive waste dump. The military abandoned eight marine reactors in the bays surrounding the island. Although the reactors are encased in steel, radiation might leak into the water.

Beginning in 1964, the Soviet Union also dumped 17,000 barrels of nuclear waste off the shores of Novaya Zemlya. When the barrels would not sink, sailors shot holes in them. The radioactive waste leaked into the water.

Nuclear energy facilities, such as a radiochemical mill in Siberia (left) and a reactor still in operation at Chernobyl, contaminate the water, land, and air of Russia. *How does this happen?*

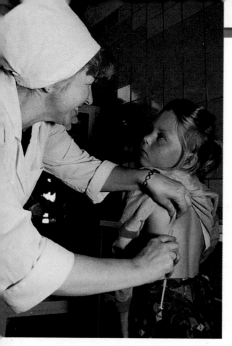

Doctors in Russia vaccinate children against diphtheria and other infectious diseases. There is no way of protecting humans against sickness caused by nuclear pollution. *Why are children most affected by the health problems caused by pollution?*

Poor Health After Industrialization

Many scientists see environmental pollution as the source of failing Russian health. They cite the poor health of children, especially the rise in birth defects.

"Back in the early 1960s our eminent geneticists warned about the genetic damage to the Russian population," said the Russian head of a United Nations committee on ecological health and safety. "No one believed them. Now congenital deformities [birth defects] are increasing faster than any other health problem."

More than 10 percent of Russian children now suffer from birth defects, and half have chronic diseases. The Russian Education Ministry reported that 35 percent of the first graders in 1994 needed treatment for serious health problems. By 2000, the ministry predicts that only 5 percent of Russian high school graduates will enjoy good health.

"The question is how long are we going to accept these numbers," said Marina Cherkasova, director of a Russian environmental health group. "Are we going to sit here for another 50 years and wonder [if the] diseases can be prevented?"

Russian authorities are attacking these problems. They have assigned scientists and engineers to clean the worst pollution sites. These scientists have come to the United States to study our own environmental challenges. United States experts have gone to Russia to help.

Everyone agrees that the problems are too large to solve right away. No one is sure how Russia can pay the high costs required to clean the massive environmental mess.

LESSON ③ REVIEW

Fact Follow-Up
1. Describe the environmental consequences of Russia's rapid industrialization.
2. Describe the condition of Lake Baikal.
3. What environmental dangers are posed by some of Russia's nuclear reactors?
4. How would you describe the health of the Russian people today?

Think These Through
5. Imagine that you are an advisor today on Russia's health problems. What five or more recommendations would you make and why?
6. Do you think the Russians can solve their environmental problems? Why or why not? If they fail, should any other people be concerned? Why or why not?

Reviewing Human-Environmental Interaction by Region

Chapter 25 describes changing human-environmental interaction in czarist, Communist, and post-Communist Russia. Earlier chapters have described similar changes in the British Isles and Norden (Chapter 7), Western Europe (Chapter 11), Mediterranean Europe (Chapter 15), and Eastern Europe (Chapter 19).

Russia's Agricultural and Industrial Revolutions came later than those in the British Isles, Norden, and Western Europe. As a result, Russia today is facing difficult environmental problems that other regions faced earlier and have tried to solve. Is there anything in the experiences of those regions of Europe that Russians might try to help them resolve their problems? To answer this question, you will need to gather information summarizing the experience of other nations.

Here are some questions that you might ask as you review for each region:

(1) What new discoveries changed ways people farmed or made goods?

(2) In what ways did these changes alter where people lived, how they lived, or the quality of their lives?

(3) Did the changes in people's lives create problems that needed to be solved? If so, were solutions found?

A graphic organizer, such as the one below, will help you draw together information and start analyzing it.

Dig into earlier chapters, looking for changes in agriculture and industry that might be similar to those in Russia. What problems in human-environmental interaction did those changes bring? What solutions have been tried? After you have entered this information in the proper colums, examine it. Develop a list of things the Russians might try based on the experiences of other regions. Which options should be tried immediately? Which problems can be solved later?

Graphic Organizer: Problems in Human-Environmental Interaction			
Regions	**Environmental Problems**	**Effect on People's Lives**	**Solutions/ Continuing Problems**
British Isles			
Norden			
Western Europe			
Mediterranean Europe			
Eastern Europe			

Chapter 25 Review

LESSONS LEARNED

LESSON 1   Russia remained a land of nobility and peasant farmers until the late nineteenth century. Farming continued in Russia much as it had throughout Europe in the Middle Ages. As a result, Russia's peasants (serfs) continued to live almost as slaves and suffered lives of poverty.

LESSON 2   Some industry reached Russia in the late nineteenth century. After the Communists seized Russia, they pushed hard to modernize agriculture and build modern industry. Communist efforts brought change that strengthened the nation, but millions of people died as the Communists changed the economy.

LESSON 3   Changes in Russia's economy have also been costly in environmental damage. Soil, water, and air have been seriously polluted all over the country. Recently, the Russian government announced that widespread pollution was contributing to the decline in the people's health and life expectancy.

TIME FOR TERMS

Five-Year Plan

FACT FOLLOW-UP

1. Compare Russian agriculture before and after the Communist revolution.
2. How has Russia's location—absolute and relative—affected its agricultural production?
3. Many freed serfs worked in Russia's new industries. How were their lives changed?
4. Compare the working conditions in Russia's factories before and after the Communist revolution.
5. How has industrialization in Russia affected human-environmental interaction?
6. Describe the Russian people's health today.
7. List some of the challenges faced by the economy of Russia today.

THINK THESE THROUGH

8. Were Russian peasants (serfs) better off under the czars or Communist government? Explain your thinking.
9. If you could magically solve what you believe to be Russia's worst environmental problem, which problem would you choose? Why?
10. Reexamine the evidence on Stalin's programs for boosting agricultural and industrial production. What did his programs achieve? What were their costs? Now weigh the achievements against the costs. How do you rate Stalin's leadership? Was he a success or a failure?

SHARPENING SKILLS

11. What do you think is the most important lesson Russians today can learn from other industrialized European nations? Explain your thinking.
12. In what ways did the graphic organizer suggested in the skill lesson help you draw together and analyze data from several locations? Can you think of other ways of

organizing data that might have been even more useful? If so, describe the way(s).

13. Do you think that it is possible for people in one nation to learn from the experience of others? If so, cite examples of such learning. If not, explain why experience is so difficult to transfer.

PLACE LOCATION

Have you learned the location of Russia's major climate areas? The map shows these climate areas accurately. Labels, however, have been removed from the key, and new labels for each climate color have been given in questions 14 through 20. Based on your studies, is each new label "True" or "False"?

14. **A**—Semiarid regions that can be farmed; warm winters and hot summers.

15. **B**—Arid region, some parts of which can be farmed with water pumped from the Sea of Okhotsk.

16. **C**—Mediterranean climate similar to that of the southern French coast.

17. **D**—Humid subtropical is typical of the area around Moscow.

18. **E**—Humid continental offers uncertain rainfall and growing seasons, but this is Russia's largest and best farming land.

19. **F**—Vast subarctic region with rich soils and areas of good farm land.

20. **G**—Arctic tundra, mostly barren land that remains frozen all year.

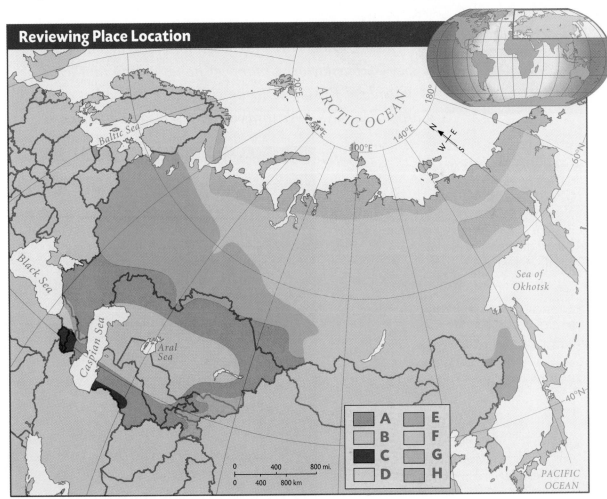

Reviewing Place Location

People and Environment **519**

Economy and Government

Workers in a St. Petersburg factory once produced equipment for the Soviet Union's navy. Their work, of course, was top secret. Now the Soviet Union is gone. Russia no longer spends as much money on the navy as the Soviet government did. So these workers (left) have taken on a different assignment. Instead of naval equipment, they are building large tractors. Some of these machines are used on farms. Others are purchased for construction projects. The factory's manager hopes to find markets outside of Russia. "Our machines are as good as any in Europe," he says. "We think we can sell some there."

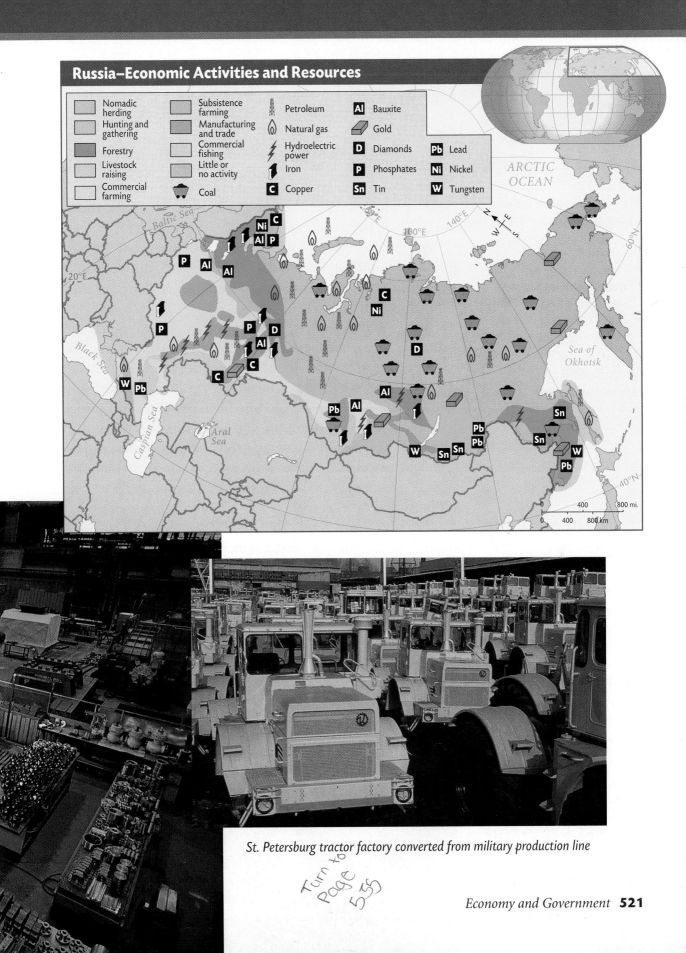

Russia–Economic Activities and Resources

Nomadic herding
Hunting and gathering
Forestry
Livestock raising
Commercial farming
Subsistence farming
Manufacturing and trade
Commercial fishing
Little or no activity
Coal

Petroleum
Natural gas
Hydroelectric power
Iron
Copper

Al Bauxite
Gold
D Diamonds
P Phosphates
Sn Tin
Pb Lead
Ni Nickel
W Tungsten

ARCTIC OCEAN

Baltic Sea
Black Sea
Caspian Sea
Aral Sea
Sea of Okhotsk

St. Petersburg tractor factory converted from military production line

Turn to Page 535

Economy and Government **521**

The Russian Economy

LESSON PREVIEW

Key Ideas
- Private enterprise is replacing government ownership and management of Russia's economy.
- The sudden move to private enterprise has been accompanied by confusion.
- Russia has the resources to become a major industrial power.

Key Term
foreign investments

Since 1990, Russians have been lining up daily at the world's busiest fast-food restaurant in Moscow's Pushkin Square. The restaurant is part of a famous hamburger chain from the United States.

For a while, it seemed that Americans in Russia had the fast-food business all to themselves. Then in 1995, just across the street from the American restaurant, another restaurant started competing, Russian-style.

Russkoye Bistro offers fast food with a cultural difference. Customers here place their orders with uniformed workers at the cash register, just as they do in the American place. They do not order hamburgers, though. Instead, their platters are filled with traditional Russian food: vegetable-filled pastries called pirogi, mushroom soup, and strong tea with lots of sugar, all for less than a dollar. A typical meal across the street costs nearly three dollars.

"This place is just great," said a customer after trying the pirogi. "The food is fresh, it's quick, and it's cheap. I'll be here for lunch five times a week."

Russkoye Bistro serves about 1,000 customers a day, many fewer than the American restaurant. This comparison is a little

Workers serve customers at Russkoye Bistro, a Russian fast-food restaurant. *What do the presence of fast-food restaurants suggest about the economy of Russia?*

unfair, according to the bistro's manager. "They sell hamburgers, but this food is in the Russian blood."

From Communism to Capitalism

Under communism, the Soviet government took ownership of farms and factories. Russia modernized its farms and expanded its industry.

Yet as you have read, communism failed to create a successful economy. Collective farms did not produce enough to feed the people. The Soviet Union had to import grain, especially after severe winters or prolonged droughts.

Soviet industry successfully made weapons and heavy equipment, but did not provide the people with consumer goods, such as telephones, automobiles, and refrigerators.

Russians knew that their housing was poor and their food lacked variety. Western products brought illegally into the Soviet Union were vivid reminders of Russian poverty. The people knew they had much less than people living in the United States, Canada, and democratic Europe.

One reason for communism's collapse was this failure of the Soviet economy to meet its citizens' needs. Soviet leaders promised people a better life, but they did not keep their promise.

With the end of the Soviet Union, Russia has begun a transformation from communism to capitalism. The change has been difficult, because workers and managers have no experience in how to make private enterprise work. They are learning how a free market affects the prices of goods and how personal goals among factory workers and farmers improve productivity.

After communism, Russians had to deal with confusion in the factories. Many lost their jobs. Communism had offered guaranteed employment to Russian workers. In the new Russian economy, workers could no longer just show up to collect a paycheck. Managers began paying employees according to how well they did their jobs. They fired workers they did not need.

After communism, Russians also faced a puzzling market. Private businesses began producing a wider variety of goods. Yet these newly available goods were often expensive.

Under capitalism, independent Russian car sellers can offer more choices to buyers. *How is this different from the past, under communism?*

WORD ORIGINS

Sometimes people take words from one country to another. **Bistro** is a Russian word for "Fast!" The French adopted this word after hearing Russian soldiers shout impatiently for food in Parisian cafés. The Russians had chased a French army unit back to Paris. At a small café, or bistro, today, Parisians get quick service.

A 1980s street scene in Moscow offers a view of Russian daily life under communism as opportunities for free expression began to grow. *Where do you see examples of this in the photograph?*

The Communist government had kept prices artificially low. After prices were no longer regulated, they rose rapidly. Wages stayed low. Few people were able to buy new products. Private businesses had not learned to respond to the needs and income of Russians.

One of the biggest tasks facing Russia is improving transportation and communication connections within the country. Russia rapidly industrialized before and after World War II. Yet Russia's communication and transportation systems have remained underdeveloped. Russia now seeks foreign investors who may help pay for up-to-date transportation equipment. That equipment is necessary to take advantage of Russia's wealth of natural resources.

Russia's Natural Resources

Russia's abundant natural resources offer economic hope. These resources, if used efficiently, could make Russia an economic giant (see map on page 521).

Russia is an energy superpower. The country produces 22 percent of the world's oil, 16 percent of the world's coal, and 40 percent of the world's natural gas. Siberia especially contains rich deposits of oil and gas. Recent discoveries in northwestern Russia could yield 4 billion barrels of oil. Many international energy companies are working with Russian companies to tap these abundant supplies.

Russia also possesses the world's largest forest reserves. In contrast to the United States, which has less than 5 percent of its ancient forests, Russia has 25 percent of its original forests. Russian business leaders want to sell some of this timber abroad to earn money.

Siberia is also the main source of Russia's supply of minerals—diamonds, gold, iron ore, silver, and bauxite, the key substance used in making aluminum. Western mining companies have joined Russians in prospecting for these minerals.

These resources are located in cold and remote areas. Russia must expand its transportation system to reach these valuable resources.

Agriculture and Fishing

Only 13 percent of Russia's land is devoted to farming. The best farming regions are the western plains, the Volga River basin, the northern Caucasus Mountains, and western Siberia. Farmers grow barley, corn, cotton, oats, potatoes, and wheat. Cattle and sheep also graze in grassy regions.

Russia's short growing seasons, droughts, and inefficient farming methods reduce crop yields. The country often must import wheat to feed its people. Even so, Russia is one of the world's largest grain producers.

With communism gone, the government has begun to divide huge collective farms into smaller, privately owned farms. Russians hope that these farms will be more productive than the collective farms. Private owners are sometimes having trouble. They often need money from the government to stay in business.

Much of Russia's food also comes from the sea. Fishing crews in northern coastal waters haul in cod, haddock, herring, and salmon. The Caspian Sea produces sturgeon, whose eggs—called caviar—bring high prices on world markets.

Oil workers drive pipe on a platform in northwestern Russia. Russia has rich sources of energy, including natural gas, coal, and petroleum. *What areas of Russia contain large deposits of oil?*

What would **YOU** do?

You advise the Russian government on **foreign investments** (where one country allows business people from foreign countries to set up businesses or buy into its own companies). You know that Russia needs money to create new business. You welcomed foreign-owned hamburger restaurants, but Russia needs large investments to develop natural resources. Will you advise allowing foreign companies to own Russia's basic resources?

Manufacturing

As you remember, Russian manufacturing produces more heavy industrial goods than consumer products. Moscow, St. Petersburg, and their industrial suburbs today serve as centers for most heavy industries. Factories produce tractors, electrical equipment, and steel.

Other plants in Moscow concentrate on chemicals, electronics, and processed foods. St. Petersburg plants specialize in shipbuilding and industrial equipment. Factories in the Urals process metals and refine oil.

The dream of Communist leaders that Russian manufacturing would lead the world never succeeded. Inefficient factories of the Soviet era caused much of that region's environmental problems. Many are now closed. Other factories need new machinery. Here, too, Russians are looking for foreign investors to provide financial backing that will make Russian goods competitive in world markets.

Russian manufacturers continue to produce more heavy equipment, such as tractors, than consumer goods, such as televisions. *Where are these products of heavy industry produced?*

Service Industries

In most industrialized countries, the economy includes jobs in service industries. Service industry workers include restaurant waiters, teachers, lawyers, computer programmers, and health care providers.

Service industries made up only a small part of the Soviet economy. Service workers had little training and earned low pay. Now the service industry is growing in Russia. Individuals and families are starting small businesses to respond to the demand for restaurants, taxis, and personal services.

The Future of Russia

If Russia can gain access to its resources through an improved transportation system (see maps, pages 521 and 527), its economy will grow. Despite the challenges that Russia faces,

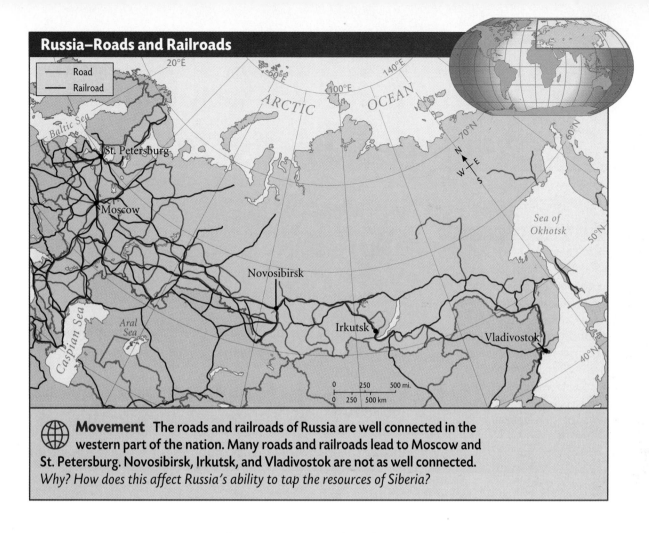

Russia–Roads and Railroads

Road
Railroad

ARCTIC OCEAN

St. Petersburg
Moscow
Baltic Sea
Caspian Sea
Aral Sea
Novosibirsk
Irkutsk
Vladivostok
Sea of Okhotsk

0   250   500 mi.
0   250   500 km

Movement The roads and railroads of Russia are well connected in the western part of the nation. Many roads and railroads lead to Moscow and St. Petersburg. Novosibirsk, Irkutsk, and Vladivostok are not as well connected. *Why? How does this affect Russia's ability to tap the resources of Siberia?*

many Russians are optimistic. They are eager to take advantage of the new opportunities in a changing Russian economy. Big businesses may need assistance from foreign investors. Many Russians, however, have raised the money needed to start smaller businesses on their own.

LESSON 1 REVIEW

Fact Follow-Up

1. In what ways was the Communist economy successful? In what ways was it a failure?
2. How did agricultural shortages help weaken the Communist government?
3. What are some of the economic problems faced by Russia as it changes from communism to capitalism?
4. What are some difficulties Russia faces in gathering its natural resources?

Think These Through

5. In what areas do you think Russia should concentrate in order to have a successful economy? Explain.
6. If you were to begin a new business in Russia today, what would it be? Explain your choice.

Economies of Central Asia and Transcaucasia

LESSON 2

LESSON PREVIEW

Key Ideas
- Herding farm animals was a common way of life in the countries of Transcaucasia and Central Asia.
- Under the Soviet Union, these countries developed modern farming and some industry.
- Valuable resources will help these countries continue with modern development.

"We decided to go on our own for the future of our children," Murat Iskakov told a visitor in 1993. "They'll be good farmers." Iskakov is a private farmer in newly independent Kazakhstan. He owns land with his four brothers.

The Iskakovs originally leased their land from the Red Flag State Farm in 1989. With a loan of 800,000 rubles, they bought cattle and planted wheat.

Now, with the loan repaid, the Iskakovs have invested their profits in farm machinery. They own five combines, five tractors, trucks, wagons, and horses. "And now we're rich," Iskakov proudly explains. "We bought combines for 17,000 rubles. Now they sell for more than a million."

Economies Under the Soviet Union

Under the czars, the Central Asian states (Kazakhstan, Tajikistan, Turkmenistan, Kyrgyzstan, and Uzbekistan) relied on herding as a way of life. Later, the Soviet Union made farming possible through irrigation.

The Transcaucasian republics of Georgia, Azerbaijan, and Armenia also expanded agriculture through irrigation after becoming part of the Soviet Union in the 1920s.

The Soviets also built factories, roads, and hydroelectric dams to encourage industrial growth in Central Asia and Transcaucasia. Transcaucasia produces oil and minerals.

Farms in Kazakhstan are run by Kazakh farmers who have planted wheat and bought new combines. *Who owned the farms before Kazakhstan's independence?*

During World War II, the Soviet government sent many Russians to Central Asia. They built heavy machinery, textiles, chemicals, petroleum, and food processing industries.

Central planners in the Soviet Union controlled the economies of Central Asia and Transcaucasia. Georgian food products, Kazakhstani textiles, and Uzbekistani minerals were manufactured for the entire Soviet Union, not just those republics.

Economies After Communism

Now independent, the nations of Central Asia and Transcaucasia can make use of their resources as they wish (see map on page 530). They can decide how best to sell their products.

Industry Countries bordering the Caspian Sea—Kazakhstan, Turkmenistan, and Uzbekistan, as well as the Transcaucasian nation of Azerbaijan—share the possibility of enormous wealth. They could profit from one of the largest untapped oil and natural gas sources in the world.

Experts predict that the Caspian Sea and land around it could become the second largest supplier of oil and gas, after the Persian Gulf. If the oil and gas reserves are developed and sold on world markets, then the Caspian Sea countries could become rich. They already have begun some exploration.

Another important energy source is the huge Nurek Dam in Tajikistan. This hydroelectric energy runs the factories that produce the country's textiles and processed foods. Mineral resources of coal, gold, lead, zinc, and copper are found in Central Asia and Transcaucasia. Semidesert regions produce sand and limestone for building materials.

Georgia processes food instead of petroleum or minerals. Many Georgian crops from the country are shipped to the city

Water is a precious resource in Transcaucasia and Central Asia. A farmer near the Aral Sea fills his water tank that is transported by donkey. *How did the Soviet Union change agriculture in the regions?*

◆◆◆◆ GAMES ◆◆◆◆
People Play

Buz kashi In the far reaches of Central Asia, a popular sport reflects the rugged lives of the herders. Buz kashi, played by young men on horseback, combines skill, strength, and daring. They circle a calf's carcass filled with sand. One reaches from his horse, grabs it from the ground, and races to a pole about a mile away. All chase after the one who has the carcass and try to take it away—while at full gallop.

◆◆◆◆◆◆◆◆◆◆◆◆◆◆

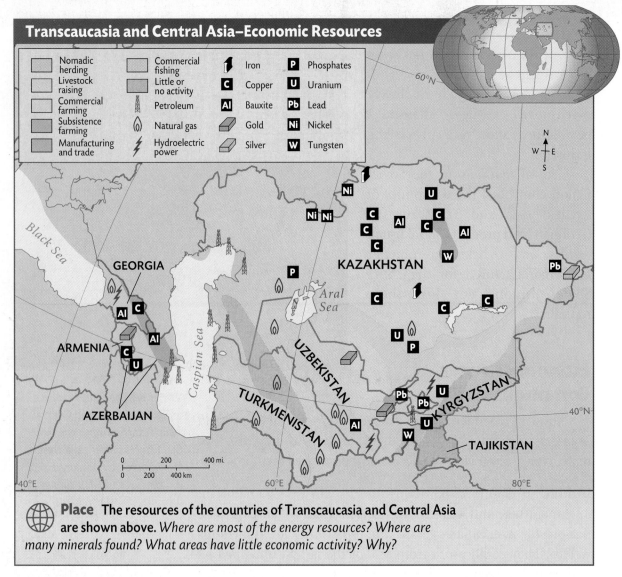

Transcaucasia and Central Asia—Economic Resources

Legend:
- Nomadic herding
- Livestock raising
- Commercial farming
- Subsistence farming
- Manufacturing and trade
- Commercial fishing
- Little or no activity
- Petroleum
- Natural gas
- Hydroelectric power
- Iron
- Copper (C)
- Bauxite (Al)
- Gold
- Silver
- Phosphates (P)
- Uranium (U)
- Lead (Pb)
- Nickel (Ni)
- Tungsten (W)

Place The resources of the countries of Transcaucasia and Central Asia are shown above. *Where are most of the energy resources? Where are many minerals found? What areas have little economic activity? Why?*

for processing and end up as products for export.

Georgia's location on the Black Sea supports commerce in the country. Georgian ports have long been a center for shipping in the region. They are important warm-weather outlets to the Mediterranean.

Resorts along the Black Sea, popular since the time of the czars, attract thousands of vacationers each year. Tourism could be a valuable industry in Georgia. Ethnic conflicts and the danger of war must stop before tourists will feel safe to visit.

Agriculture Farmers throughout Central Asia and Transcaucasia are becoming accustomed to crop production without the pressure of central planning. Armenian farmers quickly made the change to private farming. They grow cotton, grapes, and grain.

Because of fertile soil and a warm climate, agriculture remains the most vital part of Georgia's economy. Farmers in the western areas produce citrus fruit, tea, and tung oil (a waterproofing agent). Farther inland, crops include tobacco, wheat, grapes, and corn. Herders raise sheep and cattle in the mountains.

Herding prevails throughout the mountains of Central Asia and the Transcaucasia. Herders raise cattle, goats, sheep, and yaks, a type of oxen.

Herders in Uzbekistan and Turkmenistan raise Karakul sheep for their fine wool. Cattle and goats also produce plentiful milk for Uzbeks. Turkmen also raise camels and horses. Many of Kyrgyzstan's people herd sheep, cattle, and goats for their milk, meat, and wool.

Cotton is the most important crop in Azerbaijan and Central Asia. About half of the farmland in Turkmenistan produces cotton. Crops in these dry areas still depend on the irrigation projects begun by the Soviet Union.

Less than 10 percent of Kyrgyzstan's land is good for growing crops. Farmers produce cotton, poultry, fruit, grains, and vegetables in irrigated areas of Kyrgyzstan.

For years, the Soviets encouraged the growing of cotton in Uzbekistan. Today, cotton is the country's chief crop. But overplanting cotton has harmed the soil. Farmers also raise grapes, melons, rice, and vegetables.

Azerbaijan has a warm climate and fertile soil for cotton production. Its location on the Caspian Sea helps trade. *What other economic benefits does Azerbaijan enjoy?*

LESSON 2 REVIEW

Fact Follow-Up
1. Describe the economies of Central Asia and Transcaucasia under the Communists.
2. What natural resources can be developed to benefit the economies of this area?
3. Describe the economies of Transcaucasia today.
4. Describe the economies of the now independent Central Asian republics.

Think These Through
5. What do you think is the greatest economic challenge facing the area? Explain why.
6. If you could choose to start a business in any country mentioned in this lesson, which would it be? What kind of business would you start? Explain.

Government and the People

LESSON PREVIEW

Key Ideas

- In the 1990s, Russia took significant steps toward democracy. Free speech and elections became common. Russian politics, however, did not run smoothly.
- With some exceptions, Russia's neighbors continued to be governed under dictatorships.

Democratic changes meant opportunities for free speech in Moscow. *How has the free exchange of information helped Russia and other countries of the former Soviet Union?*

"The KGB came to arrest the Xerox machines," remembered an aide to President Mikhail Gorbachev. That happened in 1991, when some Soviets intent on maintaining a Communist government tried to overthrow Gorbachev. They held the Soviet president prisoner in his vacation home in the Crimea.

Meanwhile, back in Moscow, Boris Yeltsin had decided to resist the coup. He stayed in the parliament building, named the White House. To tell the people of Moscow that Gorbachev's government still had control, he faxed the President's office. The aide, in turn, photocopied Yeltsin's statements and had them distributed as leaflets throughout the city.

Thousands of Soviet citizens rallied to Yeltsin's cause and gathered around the parliament building. Yeltsin addressed the crowd of supporters from the top of a tank positioned to defend the White House. At the same time, Moscow's Pizza Hut sent carloads of pizzas to feed the crowds that had gathered to resist the coup and defend the beginnings of democracy in Russia.

The Beginnings of Democracy

As you have read, the movement toward democracy in Russia began with Mikhail Gorbachev's perestroika. To Gorbachev, perestroika meant "a thorough renewal of every aspect of Soviet life." He introduced reforms that would change Russia's government-controlled economy to one of private enterprise. He also introduced glasnost, or openness. This brought freer speech, a clearer look at the Western world, and more choices to the Russian people.

Some traditional Communists objected to Gorbachev's reforms. That is when they took him prisoner. The Communists planned to seize the government and reestablish their control over Russian society. The Communists failed. Popular support favored Gorbachev's reforms.

The Russian people later chose Boris Yeltsin as president in their first free election. He received 60 percent of the votes. In 1996, Yeltsin was reelected president.

Boris Yeltsin addresses the crowd gathered around the parliament building during an attempted coup against Soviet president Mikhail Gorbachev. From his perch atop a tank, Yeltsin told the people of Moscow and the world that the elected president's government still had control. *What helped the coup fail?*

The Russian Government Today

The new government's official name is the Russian Federation. The Russian president, elected by the people, serves a four-year term. The president appoints the prime minister, who forms a cabinet and works with them to run the daily affairs of government.

Russia's parliament is called the Federal Assembly. In the lower house, or Duma, 450 elected representatives of many parties work together to create laws. The upper house, or Federation Council, consists of 178 citizens appointed to serve by local governments. The Federation Council makes government appointments and decides on matters of war and peace. Members of both houses serve four-year terms.

Democratic Changes in Russian Society

Under communism, only a small percentage of people had the right to vote. Even then, their choices were limited to candidates of the Communist party. Today in Russia, every adult may vote for a candidate of any party running for office.

The Russian people now know more about the debates and decisions of their government. Russians can watch sessions of the Federal Assembly on television. Political leaders and representatives regularly answer reporters' questions at press conferences, a practice that never occurred during communism.

In addition to freedom of the press, Russians now enjoy many other rights. Citizens may gather in assemblies to protest government policies. They may speak and write without risking arrest. This freedom is extended to Communists, who speak of the need to return to the old dictatorship. Russians of all faiths may worship freely without fear of persecution.

EYEWITNESS TO HISTORY

The Kremlin

Kremlins were Russian fortresses built in medieval times. The Kremlin in Moscow is the seat of Russia's government. Other cities, such as Novgorod, Smolensk, and Rostov, were built around old kremlins.

Built of wood at first, and later of brick and stone, the structures came with a moat, towers, and battlements. The Moscow Kremlin is usually referred to as "the Kremlin." Built in 1156, the wooden fortress played a role in protecting the city. The Kremlin lost its importance as a fortress after the Mongol invasions ended.

In Red Square, on the east side of the Kremlin, Soviet troops marched during May Day parades (right).

G.U.M. (State department store)

Red Square

The Palace of Congresses

Kremlin Museum

Government in Central Asia and Transcaucasia

Moscow no longer governs Central Asia. After the Soviet Union collapsed, each of the republics that had been established by Moscow in Central Asia (Turkestan) proclaimed its independence. Since 1991, Kazakhstan, Tajikistan, Turkmenistan, and Uzbekistan have fallen under the harsh rule of dictators. Only Krygyzstan's government is a democratic republic.

In Transcaucasia, Georgia, Armenia, and Azerbaijan have faced ethnic conflict since independence. Armenia and Azerbaijan fought over land settled by Armenians but claimed by Azerbaijan. After a cease-fire in 1994, Armenian voters

The Kremlin reflects stages of Russian history. Onion-shaped domes (inset) illustrate Byzantine influences. Greek and Roman columns reflect Western architecture. Inside the Kremlin are cathedrals that contain both Italian and Byzantine designs.

Palaces of white stone or brick now house treasures of the czars. The Grand Kremlin Palace (above) seats 6,000. The Communist government used the palace for meetings and theatrical performances.

Also along Red Square, facing the Kremlin, is G.U.M., the State Department Store (left). Customers line up outside hoping to buy goods.

Disappearing Ways of Life

Aleksander Asoskov, his wife, and their two children have moved to a tiny village north of Moscow.

The Asoskovs run a small store. Mr. Asoskov bakes bread to sell. He is thinking of making pasta as well. The family's food comes from a garden.

The villagers like Asoskov's goods, but they have difficulty buying much. Little money filters into the village.

In some ways not much has changed since villagers built their small white church 400 years ago. Families plant gardens and farm a few acres. They walk or ride in wagons over unpaved roads. Cattle still share rooms with people.

But things are changing. Young people leave for education and never come back. Half the town's population of 750 is older than sixty-five. Such Russian villages are disappearing.

approved a constitution.

The government in Azerbaijan has been unstable since independence because of the war with Armenia. A military dictatorship took power from a democratically elected government in 1993.

Georgia has also been torn by ethnic violence. Troops help keep peace after a cease-fire was signed in 1994. Despite the upheaval, Georgia elected a president and council.

LESSON 3 REVIEW

Fact Follow-Up
1. Using an outline or a graphic organizer, show the organization of the Russian government.
2. What kinds of governments are there in Central Asia? in Transcaucasia?
3. Describe life today in a typical Russian village.

Think These Through
4. Could it be said that Gorbachev's policies of glasnost and perestroika "lost the battle but won the war"? Explain your answer.
5. Do you think political and religious freedoms are more important to Russians than to Americans? Explain.
6. Which nation in Central Asia and Transcaucasia do you think has changed least in recent years? Explain.

What Is an Effective Citizen?

With the collapse of Communist governments, the citizens of Russia have begun to build open and democratic political institutions. There has been increased contact between citizens of our own nation and Russian citizens. There have been exchanges of teachers, business leaders, scientists, and everyday citizens.

One issue that has been discussed repeatedly is how to build democratic governments that will last. A part of this issue is the question, "How should we educate the next generation for effective citizenship?" Can you answer this question in ways that might help Russian leaders?

What is an effective citizen? To begin, think of people in your community who are effective citizens. What are the characteristics of these people? To help you start thinking, look at the two short lists on the right. They contain some of the activities of one student that made her an effective citizen. Can you put those activities in categories, such as "Keeping Informed" or "Environmental Awareness"? What other kinds of categories do those activities fit? List the ones you find.

When you have finished your list, exchange it with a classmate and discuss your ideas. If your discussion produces new ideas, revise your list.

Next, think about what happens in your school—in such subjects as social studies as well as in extracurricular activities—to build citizenship or civic skills. What in your school experience has helped you grow as a citizen? Make a list of these school experiences similar to those listed in the first chart.

What activities do you do in your community that make you an effective citizen? Make a list of these community experiences similar to those listed in the second chart. Again, discuss your list with a classmate and improve your list. Your two lists of school activities and community activities show how those kinds of experiences build good citizens.

Begin your letter with your description of an effective citizen. Then make specific recommendations on what a Russian school might do to encourage effective citizenship.

Join several classmates in exchanging letters. Now revise your letter to include all of the best ideas.

School–Making An Effective Citizen

- headed T-shirt sale–funds helped clean stream near school
- member, volunteers from school to deliver meals for homeless
- student volunteers to rid school grounds of trash

Community–Making an Effective Citizen

- reads local and national news every day
- active in her political party's precinct
- PTA volunteer in school

Chapter 26 Review

LESSON 1 During the 1990s, Russia began turning its economy into a private enterprise system. Some successful businesses appeared, and progress was made in developing the nation's rich natural resources. The changeover from a government-owned and government-managed economy, however, caused confusion and hardship.

LESSON 2 Under the Communist rule from Moscow, the republics of Central Asia and Transcaucasia saw their economies changed. Agriculture became more modern, and some industry was built. As independent nations in the 1990s, these republics are continuing to build their economic strengths.

LESSON 3 In the 1990s, Russia replaced a harsh dictatorship with the beginnings of democracy. Most of the breakaway republics south of Russia, however, remained under dictators.

TIME FOR TERMS

foreign investments

FACT FOLLOW-UP

1. What natural resources can be tapped to improve the Russian economy?
2. Describe the natural resources of Central Asian and Transcaucasian areas.
3. Describe the change from a Communist economy to private enterprise in Russia.
4. What economic challenges do Russia, Central Asia, and Transcaucasia face today?
5. How is the government of Russia organized?
6. What freedoms do the Russian people enjoy today that they did not have under czarist and Communist governments?
7. What political changes have taken place in the former Soviet republics in Transcaucasia and Central Asia?
8. What new kinds of businesses are having success in Russia and its neighboring republics today?
9. Describe agriculture in Russia today.
10. Describe transportation and communications systems in Russia today.

THINK THESE THROUGH

11. If you could start a new business in Russia today, what kind of business would it be? Why would you choose this business?
12. Why do you think the Russian transportation and communications systems were not more fully developed under communism?
13. What physical characteristics of geography's theme of place may benefit the Russian economy in the future? Explain why.
14. Do you think it is possible or desirable for Russia to become independent in agriculture? Explain your answer.
15. Is the economic future of Russia brighter than that of the Central Asian and Transcaucasian republics? Give reasons for your answer.
16. How is government in Russia today different from government under communism?
17. If you were a political leader of Russia, what

would be your greatest challenge? Explain.

18. What do you think is the most important way schools teach citizenship skills? Which skill is most important? Why?
19. How can extracurricular activities build the skills of effective citizenship?
20. What suggestions would you make to encourage the development of effective citizenship skills in your own school?
21. Why do you think Russians might want to discuss how to "make" effective citizens with people living in the United States?

Use the map key to locate and name the relative locations where the following resources are found:

22. fuel resources (coal, natural gas, and oil).
23. manufacturing and trade.
24. commercial farming.
25. hydroelectric resources and gold.
26. forestry.
27. hunting and gathering.
28. subsistance farming.
29. little or no economic activity.
30. iron.
31. nomadic herding.
32. commercial fishing.

Reviewing Place Location

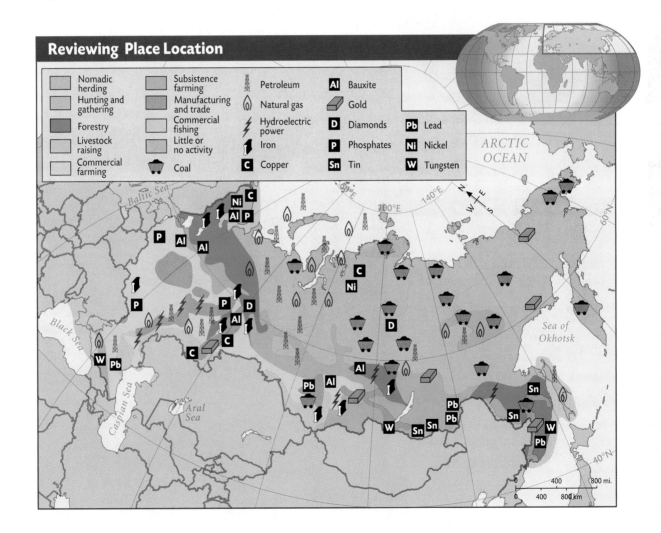

Economy and Government **539**

Society and Culture

Living in Moscow, twelve-year-old Masha gets to school by underground train—or the Metro, as it's known. Her mother rides with her and comes to pick her up after school. The trip one way is 45 minutes, but Masha doesn't mind.

She goes to a school that teaches dance as well as regular schoolwork. Besides Russian grammar, Masha's language lessons include English and French. In the afternoons, Masha studies ballet.

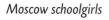

Moscow schoolgirls

Moscow Metro

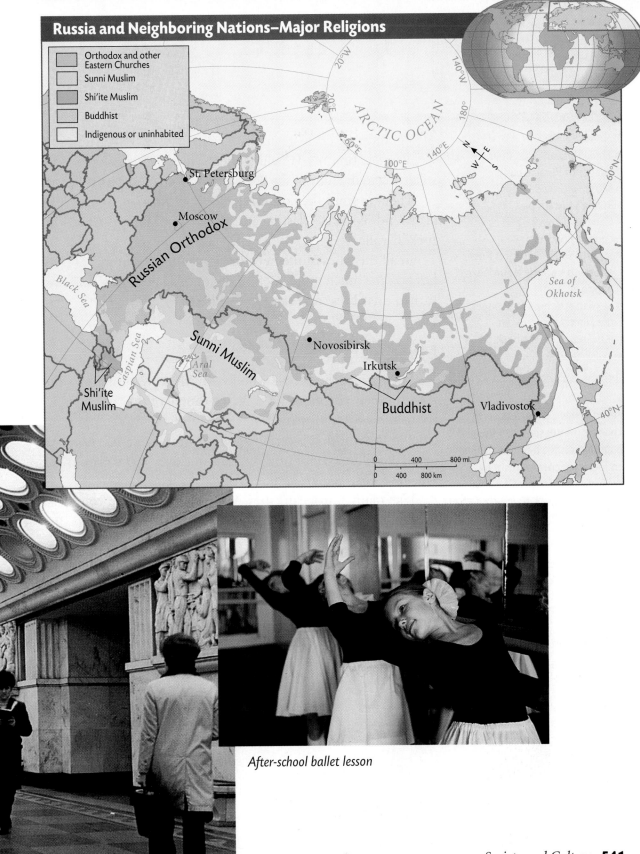

Russia and Neighboring Nations—Major Religions

Legend:
- Orthodox and other Eastern Churches
- Sunni Muslim
- Shi'ite Muslim
- Buddhist
- Indigenous or uninhabited

ARCTIC OCEAN

St. Petersburg

Moscow

Russian Orthodox

Black Sea

Caspian Sea

Aral Sea

Sunni Muslim

Shi'ite Muslim

Novosibirsk

Irkutsk

Buddhist

Vladivostok

Sea of Okhotsk

20°W 20°E 60°E 100°E 140°E 180° 140°W

60°N 40°N

0   400   800 mi.
0   400   800 km

After-school ballet lesson

A Tale of Three Cities

In Moscow's Red Square, elderly women called *babushkas*—"grandmothers"—regularly sweep the cobblestones with wooden brooms. Watching them, you might think you were still living in the time of the Soviet Union—or even czarist Russia.

Then, around the corner, stride three Russian teenagers in jeans and T-shirts. Blasting from their boombox is American rock 'n' roll.

In all the cities of the new Russia, change is coming. Society has become much more open, and—once again—Russians have turned their eyes (and ears) to the West.

Moscow

Muscovites, the people who live in Moscow, pronounce the name of their city *mosk-VAH*. As the capital of the largest country in the world, Moscow ranks as one of the most important cities in the world. It is certainly one of the largest. It is home to nearly 9 million people and spreads out over 400 square miles (1,040 sq km).

Like many European cities, Moscow is a study in contrasts. Old and new live side by side in the capital. For example, the heart of the city, Red Square, contains 400-year-old St. Basil's Cathedral, with its eight colorful, onion-shaped domes. Nearby stands the Palace of Congresses, constructed of glass and aluminum in 1960. Many Muscovites believe the modern building is out of place. They call it a "giant aquarium."

The city is shaped like a wheel, with the Kremlin at its hub. Streets stretch out from the center like spokes to meet two circular boulevards divided by a green belt. The shape shows how the city has grown

All ages have experienced the changes in Russia. Even the *babushkas* have begun to adjust to life after communism by selling items for profit. *Why would this have not occurred during communism?*

outward in all directions from the Kremlin, which serves as the center of Russian government.

The liveliest sections of the city lie near the Kremlin. Many businesses and administrative offices have their headquarters there. It is also the location of a huge department store complex called G.U.M.—the initials in Russian for State Department Store. Originally built in 1894 and refurbished in the 1950s, G.U.M. is a three-story shopping mall containing 150 shops.

Most Muscovites live in high-rise apartment buildings. Much of the housing is relatively modern, but the apartments are small. A family of four might have only one bedroom. In older buildings, several families share a kitchen and bathroom.

These city dwellers enjoy outings in Gorki Park, a favorite spot for relaxing on the weekend. Covering more than 300 acres (120 sq hm), the park includes an outdoor theater and an amusement park. Muscovites go there for boating, tennis, and ice skating.

Muscovites can get to the park by the Metro. Electric trains speed along 140 miles (225 km) of track and arrive every minute during rush hour at one of the 135 stations. The Metro offers a quick and easy way to get around the city.

The Metro is also the most beautiful subway system in the world. Built in the 1930s, the subway stations look like the halls

More than 9 million people live in Moscow, Russia's largest city. Like most large cities, it has its beauty and its problems. *What are some of the attractions of Moscow?*

◆◆◆◆◆ **GAMES** ◆◆◆◆◆
People Play

School Festival Young people in every country go to school. Many young people look forward to the first day of school because they know education is one way to learn and become good at something. This helps their country later on when they become adults.

Russians celebrate the first day of school! Music, banners, and parades mark that day for many Russian children. How do you celebrate the first day of school?

◆◆◆◆◆◆◆◆◆◆◆◆◆◆◆◆◆

of a palace, complete with paintings, statues, and stained glass. Some stations even include chandeliers.

St. Petersburg

St. Petersburg, Russia's second largest city with nearly 5 million people, is Russia's most European city. As you remember, Peter the Great founded the city in 1703 as his "window on the West."

It has had three different names—St. Petersburg, Petrograd, and Leningrad. During times when Russia wanted to maintain connections to Europe and the West, the city was called St. Petersburg. In 1991, with the decline of communism, the people of the city voted to restore its original name—Sankt (St.) Petersburg.

The Hermitage

During her reign, Catherine the Great needed a place for her huge art collection. She ordered the construction of the Hermitage. The Hermitage (far right) is a treasure of St. Petersburg, one of the world's finest museums. Only 7 percent of the 3-million-item collection is displayed.

Catherine began the collection as part of her effort to introduce European culture and reforms to Russian nobility. She built the Hermitage as an addition to Peter the Great's Winter Palace.

Hermitage exhibit

Western art (above) is the foundation of the Hermitage's collection. Western paintings fill 141 rooms of the museum. Other styles include Asian art (middle right).

The city lies on a marshy delta consisting of 40 islands where the Neva River empties into the Gulf of Finland and the Baltic Sea. Finland is only 90 miles (145 km) away.

Peter designed his new capital to resemble the cities he had visited in Europe. Like Venice, St. Petersburg features many canals and bridges. Its elegant street lamps and architecture remind some people of Paris.

The Summer Palace, Peter the Great's residence outside the city, looks much like the Palace of Versailles, where French kings held court. Peter even insisted that his nobles move to St. Petersburg and build town houses in the European style. Many of these beautiful buildings still stand in the center of the city.

The center of the city lies on the southern bank of the Neva.

The Hermitage staggers the imagination with its size and grandeur. The museum contains 1,050 rooms, 117 staircases, 1,886 doors, and 1,945 windows. Italian architect Rastrelli and Scottish architect Charles Cameron incorporated silk, agate, jasper, and white marble in their design of the interior (left and below right).

But the Hermitage has suffered. To raise cash, Stalin sold treasures to American and British museums. German bombs damaged the roof during World War II. During the winter the roof leaks, and the old walls need reinforcing.

Tibetan Buddha

At the end of the Communist era, museum officials began using Western-style means of raising money to refurbish the museum. Images of objects were printed onto posters (above), calendars, and catalogs. The Hermitage went into the gift and souvenir business.

In 1995, the Hermitage opened a controversial show. The museum displayed 74 paintings taken from Germany after World War II. Paintings by Cézanne, Degas, Gauguin, and van Gogh belonged to German collectors. Russia believes the art repays some of the damage caused by Nazi Germany.

A water taxi along the Neva River offers a stunning view of St. Petersburg's riverfront. *Who planned the building of St. Petersburg?*

What would **YOU** do?

After communism, Russians gained freedom to move. If you were Russian, where would you most want to live?

Would you prefer Moscow because it is the center of government? Or would your choice be St. Petersburg, on a sea coast and more European? Or how about Novosibirsk, a developing frontier city?

This main business district includes many of the eighteenth-century buildings first built in St. Petersburg. Most residents live on the outskirts, in modern apartment buildings. St. Petersburg's shipbuilding industry provides jobs for many city dwellers.

Because St. Petersburg lies so far north, it experiences the extremely long days of summer that are found in Norden and the Baltic nations. In June, St. Petersburg has "white nights," when the sun stays up until midnight. During these long sunlit evenings, St. Petersburgers celebrate with music and theater performances. The festivities end with a spectacular display of fireworks.

Novosibirsk

Novosibirsk (novo · see · BEERSK) means "new Siberia." Founded as a railroad town on the Ob River in 1893, the city is now the largest in Siberia, with a population of nearly 1.5 million.

Novosibirsk sees itself as the Siberian Chicago. In the United States, Chicago has played a major role in developing the resources of the American West. Novosibirsk's leaders believe that their city will play the same role in Russia. Siberia offers rich natural resources, including diamonds, gold, coal, and petroleum.

Novosibirsk has served as a transportation and industrial center for mining and drilling operations. Factories in the city also have manufactured heavy machinery.

The city hopes to expand these economic activities. A United States government-sponsored agency—called the American Business Center—was welcomed when it opened an office there. The American Business Center brings American and Russian business people together. The center also helps make contracts that provide for imports from the United States, purchase of Russian raw materials, and construction of industrial plants. Through the center, the Siberian Trade Bank of Novosibirsk opened connections with large banks in Russia and the United States.

Just outside Novosibirsk is another city called Akademgorodok (ah · kuk · DYEM · roh · DOCK), or Science City, founded in 1958 as a research center. In Akademgorodok, scientists have conducted research in computers, genetics, nuclear physics, medicine, and space technology.

Because Novosibirsk is a relatively new city, its streets follow a checkerboard or gridiron design—straight up and down, back and forth. The buildings are modern, and the subway has been open only since 1985. The city includes a large opera house, a sports arena, and a theater. The Novosibirsk music academy owns the only pipe organ in Siberia.

Novosibirsk, the largest city in Siberia, manufactures many of Siberia's natural resources. This clearing unit for coal production processes 4,500 tons of coal daily. *Name other natural resources in Siberia.*

LESSON 1 REVIEW

Fact Follow-Up
1. What are some contrasts of old and new in Moscow?
2. What are some differences between Novosibirsk and St. Petersburg?
3. What is the importance of the Hermitage?
4. Describe the relative locations of Moscow, St. Petersburg, and Novosibirsk.

Think These Through
5. Which of the cities described in this lesson will be most important 25 years from now? Explain your choice.
6. Which of the three cities enjoys the best location? Why?

LESSON 2 · Religion and Tradition

LESSON PREVIEW

Key Ideas

- Communist rulers failed to stamp out religion.
- The Russian Orthodox Church is again influential.
- Jews, persecuted by both the czars and Soviets, now live under fewer restrictions.
- Muslims, once a large segment of the Russian Empire's population, now live mostly in republics on Russia's southern borders.

The Cathedral of Christ the Savior was built by a czar and destroyed by a dictator. *What does the church represent to Russia today?*

The Cathedral of Christ the Savior has risen once again on the banks of the Moscow River. Czar Alexander I commissioned the world's largest Orthodox church in 1839. It took 44 years and 15 million rubles to construct the church.

In his attempt to replace Russian religion with communism, Joseph Stalin ordered the Cathedral of Christ the Savior dynamited in 1931. After the rubble was cleared, the Communist government used the land for a large swimming pool. Standing over the rubble, Lazar Kaganovich, builder of the Moscow Metro, declared, "Mother Russia is cast down!"

The Cathedral stands again. The huge cross atop the central dome rises 335 feet (101 m) above the street. The cathedral is the home church of the Russian Orthodox Church.

The Reemergence of Religion

Under communism, the people of Russia and Northern Asia were forbidden to practice their religions or honor their ethnic traditions. In 1975, for example, the largest Russian Orthodox cathedral in St. Petersburg was turned by the Communists into a Museum of Atheism (a museum honoring the belief that there is no God).

Now Russians and other peoples of the region are rediscovering their unique cultures and faiths, and celebrating them publicly without fear. Today, all Russian Orthodox churches—including the cathedral in St. Petersburg—have been returned to leaders of the faith. An American reporter traveling near Lake Baikal witnessed an Orthodox priest baptizing a group of young people.

Russian Orthodoxy   For the first time in decades, Christmas is now a national holiday in Russia. The Russian Orthodox Church celebrates Christmas January 7 with church services. As in all Russian Orthodox rituals, Christmas prayers are chanted and sung, not spoken.

At Christmas time, Russian children look forward to the arrival of a man with a red suit and a long, white beard—*Dyed Maroz*, or Grandfather Frost. Dyed Maroz brings presents on New Year's Day.

CONNECTIONS

Geography & the Arts

Easter Egg Decorating

Proudly, nine-year-old Masha presented an American guest in her home with a special Easter gift—a *pysanky*, or decorated egg. The egg painted with religious symbols—crosses, stars, and a fish—glowed with color.

"It's really simple to make," Masha explained. "You just melt some beeswax from a candle onto the egg. Then you carve the designs with a *kistka* (a sharp-pointed tool). Dip the egg in dye. The more designs you carve, the more layers of wax and dye you use."

"We like them so much," Masha added, "that we display them all year long."

The Russian Orthodox Church celebrates Easter as its most holy day. Masha makes the eggs because they represent the resurrection. They also symbolize the return of spring.

In the 1800s, a Russian artist took up the idea of the symbolic eggs and turned them into priceless art.

Peter Carl Fabergé made Easter eggs for the czar from 1870 until the revolution in 1917. Using 500 people to design, carve, and enamel the eggs,

Decorating Easter eggs

Fabergé egg and portrait inside

Fabergé created unique works of art. The eggs now are owned by collectors around the world.

Diamonds, rubies, and gold adorn the eggs. Inside the eggs are the tiniest of jeweled flowers, picture frames, and the famous 3-inch replica of Nicholas and Alexandra's coronation coach.

You might use wax crayons to make designs on plain eggs and then dip the eggs into dye. Try geometric patterns to create your unique work of art.

Russian president Boris Yeltsin and Russian Orthodox Church Patriarch Alexy II mark the beginning of the Russian Orthodox Christmas. *When is the holiday celebrated?*

In Russia, the season leading up to Christmas lasts 12 days, from December 25 through January 6. Russians call this time the Winter Festival, when people compete at winter games and many families go to carnivals or the circus. Everywhere, Christmas trees are displayed.

Judaism Russian Jews celebrate Hanukkah (HAH·nah·kah) in December. The eight-day festival recalls the victory of the Maccabees in Jerusalem and the freeing of the Temple. Children receive gifts each day at sunset.

Other Jewish holidays include Yom Kippur (yom ki·POOR), a day of fasting and atonement. Rosh Hashanah is the beginning of the New Year. In the spring, Passover commemorates the captivity of the Jews in Egypt and their departure into Israel.

Under communism, Jews suffered persecution. Many Russian Jews wanted to leave the country to resettle in Israel. The Soviet government refused. Now Russian Jews are not only free to practice their traditions, but those who want to leave for Israel or elsewhere can do so without any restrictions.

Islam Before it dissolved, the Soviet Union was the largest Islamic country in the world. People living in Central Asian republics and Transcaucasia—then the Soviet Union's territory—are mostly Muslim. The Soviets tried to stamp out Islam as they did other faiths. Here, too, the Soviets failed. Since the Soviet Union's collapse, Islam has been enjoying a revival along Russia's southern borders. Islam is weakening the republics' ties with Russia. The republics are forming links with other Islamic countries.

Muslims celebrate Ramadan, a month of prayer and meditation when adults fast from sunrise to sunset every day. At the end of the month, everyone celebrates with feasts and gifts.

In Central Asia and Transcaucasia, there is a mixture of Islamic, Western, and nomadic ways of life. Some men may wear Western suits. Others continue to dress in traditional style. Muslim women wear black shawls and some add their own colorful, embroidered touches to the traditional clothing.

Families are close, and several generations may live together in one house. Most families in the same village are usually related to one another in some way. Closely related families belong to the same clan. Senior clan members offer leadership in local communities. Clans sharing a common ancestor cooperate with each other. These larger groups send leaders to hold positions in the national government.

Many Central Asians who live in rural areas keep the tradition of the yurt, the portable tent that serves as a house. Constructed of a wooden frame with a felt covering, the yurt dates back to the time of the Mongols. Because it is so easily

Muslims visit Tamerlane Mosque in Samarkand, Uzbekistan. *How has Islam affected life in Central Asia and Transcaucasia?*

Islamic women prepare a young bride for her wedding ceremony in Turkmenistan. While modern in their work, young people hold on to traditional practices. *Why?*

folded and packed away for moving, the yurt is an important link to the Central Asian nomadic past.

Sometimes parents still arrange marriages for their children. Wedding traditions in the region include the *Kalym*, a gift of money that a Kazakh groom must pay to his bride's family. In Turkmenistan, a bride must remain silent on her wedding day, keeping her eyes lowered with a handkerchief pressed to her lips.

While maintaining ancient traditions, the people of Central Asia also add modern ones. The government of Turkmenistan, for example, gives newlyweds a traditional gift of flour and oil as well as two weeks paid vacation.

The Turkmenistan government also proposed a way to continue the tradition of early marriage while supporting women's education. By eliminating a year of school, the government made it possible for a woman to finish college by the age of twenty. Under this arrangement, a Turkmen woman can enter a traditional marriage and still be prepared for a professional life.

LESSON 2 REVIEW

Fact Follow-Up
1. What are some similarities and differences in Russian and American Christmas celebrations?
2. What are the three most prominent religions in Russia, Transcaucasia, and Central Asia?
3. Describe Jewish and Islamic religious holiday celebrations.
4. What are some traditional family activities of Central Asia and Transcaucasia?

Think These Through
5. If you were a Russian Jew, would you remain in Russia or leave? Explain why.

Food and Recreation

LESSON 3

In July 1991, a few weeks before the political coup in the old Soviet Union, a dozen writers and editors left Russia's national sports daily *Sovetskii Sport* to start their own publication. They were tired of writing only about government-sponsored Olympic sports, such as track and field, weight-lifting, and archery. Instead, they wanted to write about sports the people were more interested in—basketball, soccer, and hockey.

They founded *Sport Ekspress* and started publishing. The editors worked in one another's kitchens to write the magazine. They delivered the issues in one editor's car to any newsstand that would sell them.

"We'd published for three days when the coup began," Vladimir Kuchmi recalled. "All newspapers were closed down, but I was so obsessed I forgot the danger. Our printing plant was surrounded by troops, but I begged a soldier to let me pass with our layouts. He could have shot me, but he waved me by."

Within four years, the circulation of *Sport Ekspress* had risen to more than 800,000.

Sports and Leisure

Soon after he successfully defended his title as world chess champion in 1995, Russian Garry Kasparov sat down in Munich, Germany, to play again. He competed in ten games of chess at one time.

Many grand masters play several games at once, but Kasparov's opponents were in New York, Denmark, Germany, Israel, England, France, Switzerland, and India. Kasparov played the ancient game of chess over the global Internet computer connection. Global computer communication is sometimes called "cyberspace." Kasparov made chess a "cybersport." Later, Kasparov lost his first match to a computer programmed to play chess. In a match against a computer called "Big Blue," Kasparov won one match, then lost again.

LESSON PREVIEW
Key Ideas
- Despite the Soviet emphasis on Olympic sports, other sports now are more popular in Russia.
- Chess is a leading leisure activity in Russia.
- Central Asians enjoy gymnastics, horseback sports, and traditional folk singing.
- Geography and resources affect the kinds of food enjoyed in the region.

Young men play volleyball in St. Petersburg along the Neva River. *What other sports are popular in Russia?*

Chess is a popular sport in Russia. Many international chess masters, including Garry Kasparov, are Russian. *How does Russia encourage mastery of chess?*

Russia   One of every four Russians plays a sport, and many more watch amateur and professional competitions. Soccer draws the most attention, but gymnastics, hockey, and basketball remain popular. Many Russians are also discovering tennis as a challenging sport for children and adults.

Russian schools teach physical education every day from the first grade onward. Children who play a sport particularly well may transfer to a special sports school at age ten. The students attend regular classes in the morning and then concentrate on athletic training in the afternoon.

Competition in chess, called *shakh-maht* in Russian, attracts as much interest as championship games in sports. Russian children learn to play chess in kindergarten, and instruction continues through the early grades. By the fifth grade, boys and girls study the *gambits,* or strategies, of the world's great chess champions, many of them Russian.

Those who reach a high level of achievement in chess can become chess masters. Masters compete with the best chess players in the world in special competitions sponsored by the International Chess Federation. More than 4,000 Russian children have qualified as chess masters.

Central Asia   Most Central Asians enjoy soccer, volleyball, wrestling, and gymnastics. Uzbeks also have a particular fondness for tightrope walking. Both Kazaks and Uzbeks play *ulaq,* a game in which players on horseback compete to drag a dead sheep across a goal.

In addition to playing and watching sports, Central Asians also take part in traditional pastimes, like folk-dancing and singing. Kazaks particularly enjoy the *aitys,* a singing competition. Throughout Central Asia, the telling of folk legends provides entertainment and strengthens local culture.

Transcaucasia   Georgians, Armenians, and Azeris all enjoy basketball. Favorite outdoor sports are swimming, soccer, and tennis.

Because Transcaucasia is so beautiful and the climate mild, the people often vacation close to home. Armenians travel to their own Lake Sevan every summer. Resorts on the Black Sea also attract many visitors for water sports.

Food

Nine-year-old Olga Surikova lives in the town of Suzdal, 150 miles (242 km) east of Moscow. Every year she enjoys helping her mother cook a special meal for her father on his birthday.

This evening she's chopping four small apples for *pirog,* a Russian apple pie. After chopping, Olga will spread butter in a pie pan and place the apples in it. Then she'll pour sugar, flour, and eggs over the apples and put the *pirog* in the oven until the top is golden brown. To Olga, *pirog* tastes especially good with a tall glass of cold milk.

Diet throughout the region changes according to geography and resources. Central Asian herding families enjoy roasted goat

Women at a market in Namangan, Uzbekistan, sell yogurt to a young boy. *Why are dairy products so common in Central Asia?*

Society and Culture **555**

and lamb. The food of Transcaucasia shows Greek and Turkish influence. Russian diet is varied but is affected by the economy. Russian cooks learned to make do with few available foods.

Russia The Russian diet is hearty and simple. Varieties of foods often cannot be bought, so cooks must create different tasting dishes that share similar ingredients.

At breakfast, Russians enjoy eggs, sausage, bread, butter, and jam. The main meal of the day at noon includes a cucumber salad and *borscht* (beet soup), followed by meat or fish, with either potatoes or *kasha* (cooked buckwheat). A dessert of fruit or pastries ends the meal. In the evening, most Russians eat a light supper.

Bread is served with every meal. Strong, sugary tea stays warm for the family in a samovar all day. Another favorite drink, *kvass,* is made from black bread.

Russians frequently enjoy *blinis,* thin pancakes stuffed with fish, vegetables, or fruit. *Piroshki,* dumplings with meat or vegetables, often appears at the main meal. You might have heard of a dish called beef stroganoff, strips of beef cooked with onions and mushrooms in sour cream.

Russians often use different types of food to describe people. For example, Boris Yeltsin, president of Russia, likes especially a

WORD ORIGINS

A **samovar** is a large container Russians use to boil water for tea and other hot beverages. The urn has a spigot at its base so the contents can be easily poured.

The word samovar comes from two Russian words that describe the function of this combined pitcher and pot. *Samo* means "self" and var is from *varit,* meaning "to boil." So Russians can heat and serve beverages in the self-boiling samovar.

Piroq?

Tea served from a *samovar* **(above) plus boiled eggs and pastries make a welcome afternoon treat.** *What kinds of snacks do you and your family enjoy?*

simple meal of herring and boiled potatoes. To many Russians, the president's taste for such food demonstrates that he is a direct and down-to-earth man. In contrast, Russians say of someone who thinks he is more important than anyone else that he has "*s zhiru besitsya*"—gone mad from eating rich food.

Kasha—cooked buckwheat—also plays an important role in Russian conversation. When Russians say "*kashu maslom ne isportish*" (you can't spoil kasha with too much butter), they mean you can't have too much of a good thing. Someone who speaks unclearly has *kasha* in his mouth. If you make a big mistake and have to fix it, then you must "*raskhlyobyvat kashu*" (eat up the kasha).

Children in Tashkent, Uzbekistan, sell fresh produce at a farmers market. *What other foods are eaten in Central Asia?*

Central Asia Central Asian dishes often include lamb, goat, or beef because many families herd these animals. Cheeses and noodles or rice round out the meals. Tea and *kumiss,* or mare's milk, are favorite beverages.

Kazaks enjoy *besh barmak,* a dish of sliced meat and noodles boiled in broth. Turkmen frequently serve *chorba,* a spicy meat soup, followed by *chishlik,* meat roasted on a skewer, with *pilaf,* a savory rice dish. Uzbeks eat *nan,* a flat, round bread, with their meals. People in Kyrgyzstan enjoy *shurpa,* a thick soup of mutton and vegetables.

Transcaucasia Because Transcaucasia lies so near Greece, you will find many similarities to Greek foods and ways of cooking.

Armenians like to prepare *shish kebab,* pieces of meat and vegetables grilled on a skewer. They also enjoy bean salads and *lavash,* a thin bread. Like the Greeks, Armenians often serve *dolma,* cabbage or grape leaves wrapped around rice and meat.

Georgians also serve a shish kebab that they call *shashlik.*

Mealtime in the Caucasus might include *shish kebab, lavash,* or *dolma*. *Have you ever eaten one of these dishes? Describe it.*

Family gatherings often feature chicken *tabaka,* chicken that is pressed then fried before serving.

Azeris frequently make meals of grilled lamb, goat, or beef with *pilaf. Bozartma,* an Azeri specialty, is a hearty mutton stew. *Dovga,* a lighter dish, combines yogurt, meat, and herbs in a soup. Tea or wine accompanies most meals.

Have you noticed that many of the favorite dishes in different countries are made of similar ingredients? The people in each country, however, combine these ingredients into unique meals. In recent years, immigration from these countries to Europe or the Americas has introduced some of these unique foods to the world.

LESSON 3 REVIEW

Fact Follow-Up
1. Use a Venn diagram or other graphic organizer to compare Russian recreational activities with those in Transcaucasia and Central Asia.
2. Compare food and drink in Central Asia with food and drink in Russia.
3. How do geography and natural resources affect diet in these areas?

4. What is a samovar? Explain the word's origin.

Think These Through
5. Which food traditions described did you find most interesting? Why?
6. If a student from Russia came to visit your community, what foods would you share and describe as "typically North Carolinian"? Explain why you would share these foods.

Using Information for Problem Solving, Decision Making, and Planning

Comparing Cities in Europe and Northern Asia

You are now at the end of your sixth-grade study of nations and peoples of Europe and Northern Asia. This is a good time to examine the diversity of life and culture in the world areas you have studied. One way is by studying the cities of this world area.

Chapter 27 describes three famous Russian cities: Moscow, St. Petersburg, and Novosibirsk. Earlier chapters in the text described London, Stockholm, and Copenhagen (Chapter 9); Paris, Berlin, and Vienna (Chapter 13); Athens, Rome, and Madrid (Chapter 17); and Prague, Budapest, and Warsaw (Chapter 21). The authors of the text chose these cities as illustrative of their nations and regions.

Since it would take too much time to compare all the cities mentioned above, you will need to choose one city each from Chapters 9, 13, 17, 21, and 27 to analyze. You might want to review the information in the chapters before choosing the five cities you will analyze.

Once you have chosen "your" cities, draw a data retrieval chart on a sheet of paper. The chart should have six columns. Write the name of your cities at the top of five of these columns.

Next, you have to decide what characteristics of these cities to analyze. Will you include art, architecture, music, recreation, food, holidays? It's up to you! The characteristics you choose will be written in the far left column. Your chart should be similar to the example below.

At this point you have decided the cities you will analyze and the characteristics you will compare. Review the information in Chapters 9, 13, 17, 21, and 27 to complete the chart. Now you have a solid basis for comparing these great cities.

Do you recall reading about the ways Europeans have helped shape the United States? Now you have the information to compare the United States with Europe. Discuss two things from your chart that one or more European countries share with the United States.

Data Retrieval Chart: Comparing Great Cities					
Cultural Characteristics	**city 1**	**city 2**	**city 3**	**city 4**	**city 5**
Art and Architecture					
Music and Performing Arts					
Food					
Sports and Recreation					

Chapter 27 Review

LESSON 1 Important features of Russia's character are captured by three cities. Moscow, one of the nation's capital cities, tells us about the politics, economy, and culture of the czars and Communists. St. Petersburg captures Russia's attempts to become more like Western Europe. Novosibirsk reflects Russian eastern expansion.

LESSON 2 Religions are reemerging after years of repression by Soviet authorities. In Russia the Orthodox Church is again becoming the major focus of worship. Russian Jews are an important minority. Muslims, another important minority in czarist and Soviet Russia, are now members of the majority of people living in the republics south of Russia.

LESSON 3 People living in Russia and neighboring republics share in the international enthusiasm for such sports as soccer. However, geography and tradition continue to influence popular choices in many leisure activities and in food.

FACT FOLLOW-UP

1. Compare the architecture of Moscow and St. Petersburg.
2. Describe the relative locations of Moscow, St. Petersburg, and Novosibirsk.
3. In what ways are Novosibirsk and Akademgorodok similar and different?
4. What are the three major religions in Russia and neighboring republics? How are they alike and different?
5. In which geographic areas are Russian Orthodoxy, Judaism, and Islam most represented?
6. What is Russian government policy toward religion today? How is it different from Communist policy?
7. How are foods in Russia and the neighboring republics affected by landforms and climate?
8. Describe the importance of sports in Russia.
9. In what ways are Russian sports and entertainment influenced by geography and traditions?
10. Describe why the Hermitage is important for Russia and the world.

THINK THESE THROUGH

11. Which city described in this chapter do you think best illustrates Russian culture? Explain your choice.
12. How might Russia be different today had there been Protestant and Roman Catholic religious traditions instead of the ones it has had? Explain.
13. Which Russian city or landmark would you most like to visit? Why?
14. Which Russian city do you think would be most attractive to a young Russian business owner? a young artist? Explain.
15. Which foods that you eat regularly are most like those eaten in Russia? are least like them? Give reasons for your choices.
16. If you were going to introduce a new sporting activity into Russia, what would it be? Explain why.
17. Which Russian city described in this chapter best illustrates geography's theme of place? Explain your choice.

18. What characteristics of cities did you choose to compare? If you were to do this activity again, would you choose different characteristics?

19. Did you find more similarities or differences among the cities you compared?

20. In which ways are the five cities most alike? most different?

Use the letters on the map to locate and name the following:

21. major port giving Russia access to the Pacific Ocean.

22. center of activities associated with Russia's expansion into Siberia and a leader in seeking foreign capital investment.

23. Czarist capital that reflected Russia's desire for closer conections with the West. The Hermitage is located here.

24. major Siberian city near one of the oldest and deepest bodies of fresh water in the world.

25. Russia's transportation hub, longtime capital, and headquarters of the Russian Orthodox Church.

26. the dominant religion of Russia.

27. the dominant religion of Central Asia.

28. the dominant religion of Transcaucasia.

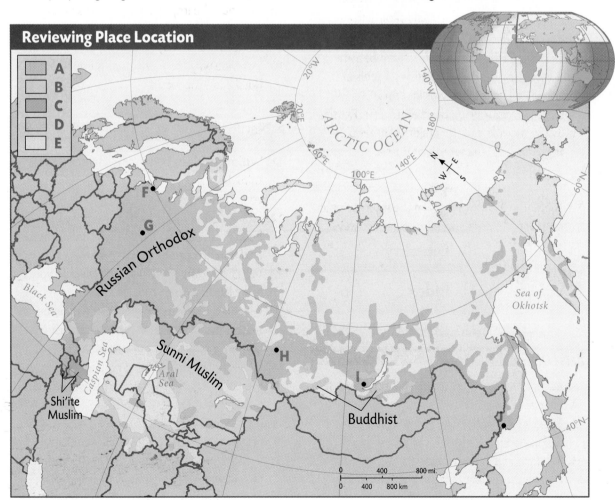

Reviewing Place Location

A
B
C
D
E

ARCTIC OCEAN

Russian Orthodox

Black Sea

Caspian Sea

Aral Sea

Sunni Muslim

Shi'ite Muslim

Buddhist

Sea of Okhotsk

F

G

H

I

Appendix

Atlas Key

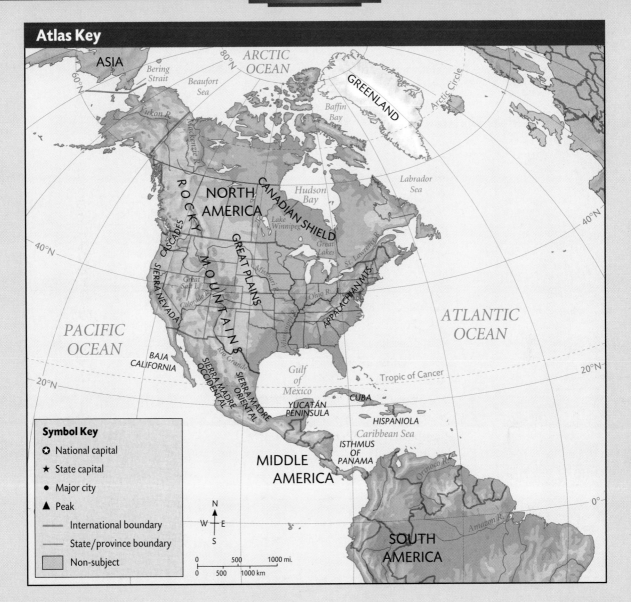

ASIA

ARCTIC OCEAN

60°N

80°N

Bering Strait

Beaufort Sea

Yukon R.

Mackenzie R.

GREENLAND

Arctic Circle

Baffin Bay

ROCKY MOUNTAINS

NORTH AMERICA

CANADIAN SHIELD

Hudson Bay

Labrador Sea

40°N

CASCADES

Lake Winnipeg

Great Lakes

St. Lawrence R.

GREAT PLAINS

SIERRA NEVADA

Great Salt L.

Colorado R.

Missouri R.

Mississippi R.

Ohio R.

APPALACHIAN MTS.

ATLANTIC OCEAN

40°N

PACIFIC OCEAN

20°N

BAJA CALIFORNIA

Rio Grande

SIERRA MADRE OCCIDENTAL

SIERRA MADRE ORIENTAL

Gulf of Mexico

Tropic of Cancer

20°N

YUCATÁN PENINSULA

CUBA

HISPANIOLA

Caribbean Sea

ISTHMUS OF PANAMA

MIDDLE AMERICA

Orinoco R.

0°

SOUTH AMERICA

Amazon R.

Symbol Key

✪ National capital

★ State capital

● Major city

▲ Peak

— International boundary

— State/province boundary

▨ Non-subject

N
W E
S

| 0 | 500 | 1000 mi. |
| 0 | 500 | 1000 km |

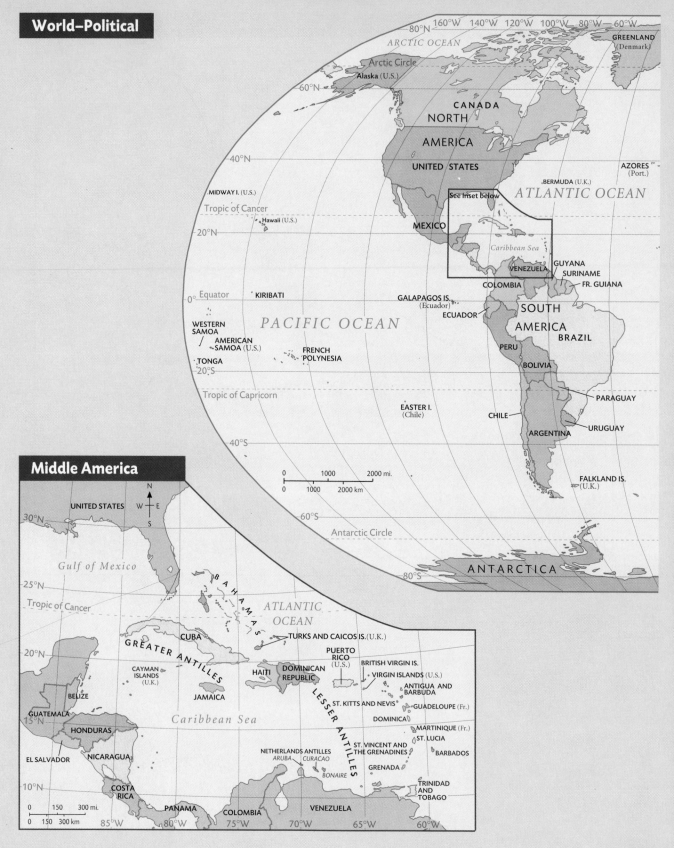

World–Political

80°N · 160°W · 140°W · 120°W · 100°W · 80°W · 60°W

ARCTIC OCEAN

GREENLAND
(Denmark)

Arctic Circle

60°N

Alaska (U.S.)

CANADA

NORTH

AMERICA

40°N

UNITED STATES

AZORES
(Port.)

BERMUDA (U.K.)

ATLANTIC OCEAN

MIDWAY I. (U.S.)

See inset below

Tropic of Cancer

20°N

Hawaii (U.S.)

MEXICO

Caribbean Sea

GUYANA

VENEZUELA

SURINAME

FR. GUIANA

COLOMBIA

0° Equator

KIRIBATI

GALAPAGOS IS.
(Ecuador)

SOUTH

ECUADOR

AMERICA

PACIFIC OCEAN

WESTERN
SAMOA

BRAZIL

PERU

AMERICAN
SAMOA (U.S.)

FRENCH
POLYNESIA

BOLIVIA

TONGA

20°S

PARAGUAY

Tropic of Capricorn

EASTER I.
(Chile)

URUGUAY

CHILE

40°S

ARGENTINA

0 · 1000 · 2000 mi.

0 · 1000 · 2000 km

FALKLAND IS.
(U.K.)

60°S

Antarctic Circle

80°S

ANTARCTICA

Middle America

N
W · E
S

UNITED STATES

30°N

Gulf of Mexico

25°N

BAHAMAS

ATLANTIC
OCEAN

Tropic of Cancer

CUBA

TURKS AND CAICOS IS. (U.K.)

GREATER ANTILLES

PUERTO
RICO
(U.S.)

BRITISH VIRGIN IS.

20°N

CAYMAN
ISLANDS
(U.K.)

HAITI

DOMINICAN
REPUBLIC

VIRGIN ISLANDS (U.S.)

ANTIGUA AND
BARBUDA

BELIZE

JAMAICA

Caribbean Sea

ST. KITTS AND NEVIS

GUADELOUPE (Fr.)

GUATEMALA

LESSER ANTILLES

DOMINICA

15°N

HONDURAS

MARTINIQUE (Fr.)

ST. LUCIA

EL SALVADOR

NICARAGUA

NETHERLANDS ANTILLES
ARUBA   CURACAO

ST. VINCENT AND
THE GRENADINES

BARBADOS

GRENADA

BONAIRE

10°N

COSTA
RICA

TRINIDAD
AND
TOBAGO

0 · 150 · 300 mi.

0 · 150 · 300 km

PANAMA

COLOMBIA

VENEZUELA

85°W · 80°W · 75°W · 70°W · 65°W · 60°W

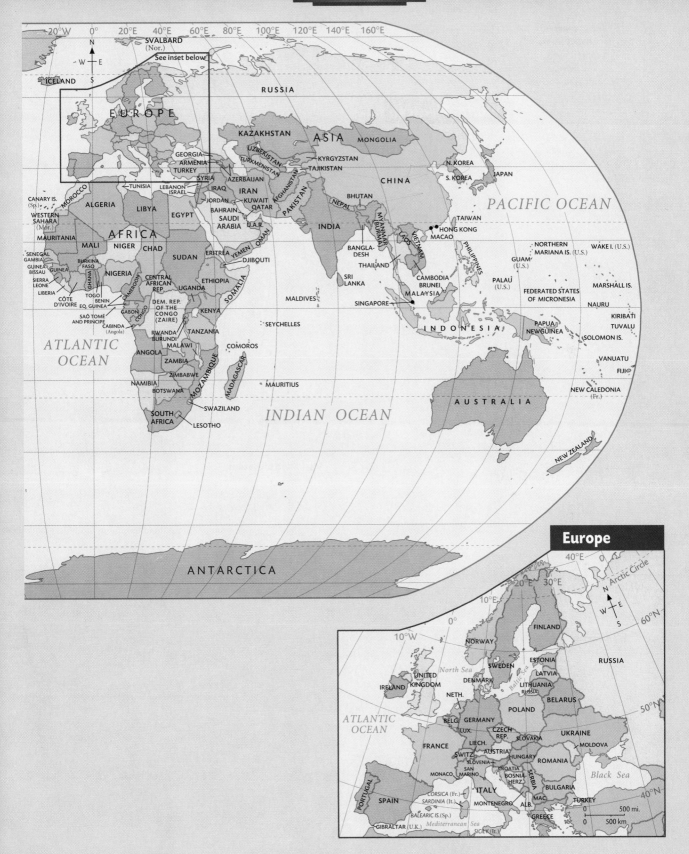

20°W 0° 20°E 40°E 60°E 80°E 100°E 120°E 140°E 160°E

SVALBARD
(Nor.)
See inset below

ICELAND

N
W E
S

RUSSIA

EUROPE

ASIA

KAZAKHSTAN

MONGOLIA

UZBEKISTAN
GEORGIA
ARMENIA
TURKEY

KYRGYZSTAN
TURKMENISTAN
TAJIKISTAN

N. KOREA
S. KOREA JAPAN

AZERBAIJAN
SYRIA

CHINA

PACIFIC OCEAN

TUNISIA
LEBANON
ISRAEL
IRAQ
JORDAN

AFGHANISTAN

BHUTAN

CANARY IS.
(Sp.)
MOROCCO

ALGERIA

LIBYA

EGYPT

IRAN
KUWAIT
QATAR
BAHRAIN
SAUDI
ARABIA
U.A.R.

PAKISTAN
NEPAL

INDIA

MYANMAR/BURMA
LAOS

TAIWAN

HONG KONG
MACAO

VIETNAM

NORTHERN
MARIANA IS. (U.S.)

WAKE I. (U.S.)

WESTERN
SAHARA
(Mor.)

MAURITANIA

MALI NIGER CHAD

AFRICA

SUDAN

ERITREA
YEMEN

OMAN

BANGLA-
DESH
THAILAND

GUAM
(U.S.)

MARSHALL IS.

SENEGAL
GAMBIA
GUINEA
BISSAU GUINEA
SIERRA
LEONE
LIBERIA
CÔTE
D'IVOIRE

BURKINA
FASO
GHANA
TOGO
BENIN

NIGERIA

CENTRAL
AFRICAN
REP.

DJIBOUTI

ETHIOPIA

UGANDA

SRI
LANKA

CAMBODIA
BRUNEI
MALAYSIA

PHILIPPINES

PALAU
(U.S.)

FEDERATED STATES
OF MICRONESIA

NAURU

KIRIBATI

SAÕ TOME
AND PRINCIPE
EQ. GUINEA
CAMEROON
GABON
CONGO
CABINDA
(Angola)

DEM. REP.
OF THE
CONGO
(ZAIRE)

KENYA

RWANDA
BURUNDI

TANZANIA

SOMALIA

MALDIVES

SINGAPORE

INDONESIA

PAPUA
NEWGUINEA

SOLOMON IS.

TUVALU

ATLANTIC
OCEAN

ANGOLA

MALAWI

ZAMBIA

ZIMBABWE

MOZAMBIQUE

MADAGASCAR

SEYCHELLES

COMOROS

MAURITIUS

INDIAN OCEAN

AUSTRALIA

VANUATU

FIJI

NEW CALEDONIA
(Fr.)

NAMIBIA
BOTSWANA

SOUTH
AFRICA

SWAZILAND

LESOTHO

NEW ZEALAND

ANTARCTICA

40°E
20°E 30°E

N Arctic Circle
W E
S

10°E

60°N

0°

10°W

NORWAY

FINLAND

North Sea

SWEDEN

ESTONIA
LATVIA

RUSSIA

IRELAND
UNITED
KINGDOM

DENMARK

Baltic Sea

LITHUANIA
RUSSIA

BELARUS

NETH.

POLAND

50°N

ATLANTIC
OCEAN

BELG.
LUX.

GERMANY

CZECH
REP.
LIECH.
SWITZ.

SLOVAKIA

UKRAINE

FRANCE

AUSTRIA

HUNGARY

ROMANIA

MOLDOVA

SLOVENIA
SAN
MARINO

CROATIA

BOSNIA-
HERZ.

SERBIA

BULGARIA

Black Sea

40°N

MONACO

PORTUGAL

SPAIN

CORSICA (Fr.)

SARDINIA (It.)

ITALY

MONTENEGRO

MAC.
ALB.

TURKEY

GREECE

0   500 mi.

BALEARIC IS.(Sp.)

GIBRALTAR
(U.K.)

Mediterranean Sea

SICILY (It.)

0   500 km

World–Physical

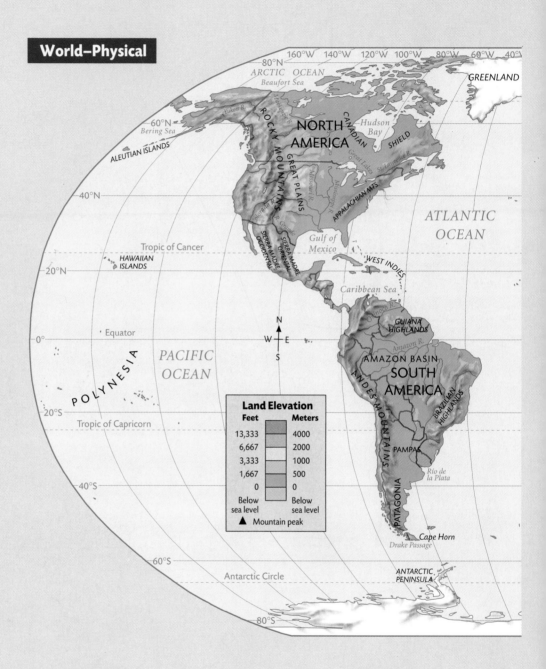

80°N
ARCTIC OCEAN
Beaufort Sea
GREENLAND
160°W 140°W 120°W 100°W 80°W 60°W 40°W

60°N
Bering Sea
Yukon R.
Mackenzie R.
ROCKY MOUNTAINS
NORTH AMERICA
CANADIAN
Hudson Bay
SHIELD
Great Lakes
St. Lawrence R.

ALEUTIAN ISLANDS

GREAT PLAINS
Missouri R.
Mississippi R.
APPALACHIAN MTS.

40°N
ATLANTIC OCEAN

Colorado R.
Rio Grande

Tropic of Cancer
SIERRA MADRE OCCIDENTAL
SIERRA MADRE ORIENTAL
Gulf of Mexico
WEST INDIES

HAWAIIAN ISLANDS
20°N

Caribbean Sea

Orinoco R.
GUIANA HIGHLANDS
Amazon R.

0° Equator

N
W E
S

PACIFIC OCEAN

AMAZON BASIN
SOUTH AMERICA

P O L Y N E S I A

ANDES MOUNTAINS
BRAZILIAN HIGHLANDS

20°S
Tropic of Capricorn

PAMPAS

Land Elevation

Feet	Meters
13,333	4000
6,667	2000
3,333	1000
1,667	500
0	0
Below sea level	Below sea level

▲ Mountain peak

Rio de la Plata

40°S
PATAGONIA

Cape Horn
Drake Passage

60°S
Antarctic Circle
ANTARCTIC PENINSULA

80°S

20°W   0°   20°E   40°E   60°E   80°E   100°E   120°E   140°E   160°E

ARCTIC OCEAN
Arctic Circle

SCANDINAVIAN
PEN.

SIBERIA

KOLYMA
RANGE

BRITISH
ISLES

North
Sea

URAL MTS.

Volga R.

Ob R.

Yenisei R.

Lena R.

KAMCHATKA
PENINSULA

NORTHERN EUROPEAN PLAIN

WEST
SIBERIAN
PLAIN

EUROPE

ALPS

IBERIAN
PEN.

BALKAN
PEN.

CAUCASUS
MTS.

Black Sea

Caspian Sea

Aral
Sea

ASIA

ALTAI MTS.

TIAN SHAN

Baikal

Amur R.

GOBI
DESERT

NORTH
CHINA
PLAIN

ATLAS MTS.

Mediterranean
Sea

Nile R.

ZAGROS MTS.

PLATEAU
OF IRAN

KUNLUN SHAN

TIBETAN
PLATEAU

Huang He

SAHARA

ARABIAN
PEN.

Tigris R.

Persian
Gulf

Indus R.

HIMALAYAS

Ganges R.

▲ Mt. Everest
29,028 ft.
8,848 m

Yangtze

Tropic of Cancer

SUDAN

DECCAN
PLATEAU

AFRICA

ETHIOPIAN
PLATEAU

Arabian
Sea

Bay of
Bengal

South
China
Sea

PHILIPPINE
ISLANDS

PACIFIC
OCEAN

MICRONESIA

Zaire R.

L. Victoria

INDIAN
OCEAN

SUMATRA

BORNEO

CELEBES

EAST INDIES

NEW GUINEA

MELANESIA

ATLANTIC
OCEAN

MADAGASCAR

AUSTRALIA

GREAT DIVIDING RANGE

KALAHARI
DESERT

Darling R.

Cape of
Good Hope

0   1000   2000 Miles
0   1000   2000 Kilometers

ANTARCTICA

Western Hemisphere–Political

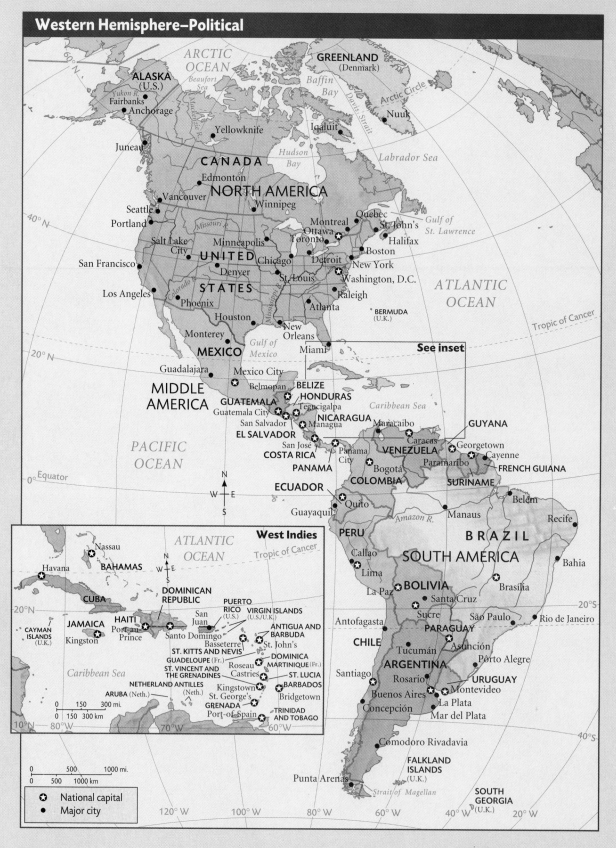

ARCTIC OCEAN

GREENLAND
(Denmark)

ALASKA
(U.S.)

Beaufort Sea

Fairbanks
Anchorage

Baffin Bay

Yellowknife

Iqaluit

Davis Strait

Arctic Circle

Nuuk

Juneau

CANADA

Hudson Bay

NORTH AMERICA

Labrador Sea

Edmonton

Mackenzie R.

Vancouver

Winnipeg

Quebec

Montreal
Ottawa
Toronto

St. John's

Gulf of St. Lawrence

Seattle

Missouri R.

Portland

Halifax

Salt Lake City

Minneapolis

Boston

UNITED

Chicago

Detroit

New York

San Francisco

Colorado R.

Denver

St. Louis

Washington, D.C.

STATES

Los Angeles

Phoenix

Mississippi R.

Atlanta

Raleigh

ATLANTIC OCEAN

Houston

New Orleans

BERMUDA
(U.K.)

Tropic of Cancer

Monterey

MEXICO

Gulf of Mexico

Miami

See inset

Guadalajara

Mexico City

MIDDLE AMERICA

Belmopan

BELIZE

HONDURAS

Caribbean Sea

GUYANA

GUATEMALA

Tegucigalpa

Guatemala City

NICARAGUA

Maracaibo

San Salvador

Managua

Caracas

VENEZUELA

Georgetown

EL SALVADOR

San José

Panama City

Paramaribo

Cayenne

PACIFIC OCEAN

COSTA RICA

PANAMA

Bogotá

SURINAME

FRENCH GUIANA

ECUADOR

COLOMBIA

Belém

Equator

Quito

Amazon R.

Manaus

Recife

Guayaquil

PERU

BRAZIL

Callao

SOUTH AMERICA

Bahia

Lima

BOLIVIA

Brasília

La Paz

Santa Cruz

São Paulo

20°S

Antofagasta

Sucre

Rio de Janeiro

PARAGUAY

Tucumán

Asunción

Pôrto Alegre

CHILE

ARGENTINA

URUGUAY

Santiago

Rosario

Montevideo

Buenos Aires

La Plata

Concepción

Mar del Plata

Cómodoro Rivadavia

FALKLAND ISLANDS
(U.K.)

SOUTH GEORGIA
(U.K.)

Punta Arenas

Strait of Magellan

West Indies

ATLANTIC OCEAN

Nassau

BAHAMAS

Tropic of Cancer

Havana

DOMINICAN REPUBLIC

PUERTO RICO
(U.S.)

VIRGIN ISLANDS
(U.S./U.K.)

CUBA

San Juan

ANTIGUA AND BARBUDA

CAYMAN ISLANDS
(U.K.)

JAMAICA

HAITI

Port-au-Prince

Santo Domingo

St. John's

Kingston

Basseterre

DOMINICA

ST. KITTS AND NEVIS

Caribbean Sea

GUADELOUPE (Fr.)

Roseau

MARTINIQUE (Fr.)

ST. VINCENT AND THE GRENADINES

Castries

ST. LUCIA

NETHERLAND ANTILLES
(Neth.)

Kingstown

BARBADOS

ARUBA (Neth.)

St. George's

Bridgetown

GRENADA

Port-of-Spain

TRINIDAD AND TOBAGO

0   150   300 mi.
0   150   300 km

0   500   1000 mi.
0   500   1000 km

⊗ National capital
•   Major city

568

Western Hemisphere–Physical

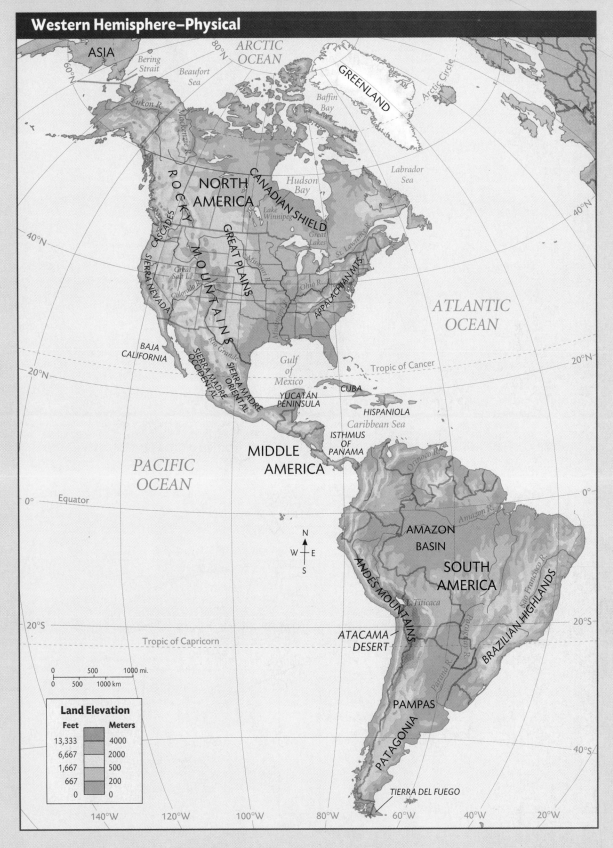

ASIA

ARCTIC OCEAN

Bering Strait

Beaufort Sea

Yukon R.

GREENLAND

Arctic Circle

Baffin Bay

Labrador Sea

ROCKY

NORTH AMERICA

CANADIAN SHIELD

Hudson Bay

Lake Winnipeg

CASCADES

Great Lakes

M O U N T A I N S

GREAT PLAINS

St. Lawrence R.

40°N

SIERRA NEVADA

Great Salt L.

Missouri R.

Colorado R.

Ohio R.

APPALACHIAN MTS.

40°N

ATLANTIC OCEAN

BAJA CALIFORNIA

Rio Grande

Gulf of Mexico

Tropic of Cancer

20°N

20°N

SIERRA MADRE OCCIDENTAL

SIERRA MADRE ORIENTAL

Mississippi R.

CUBA

YUCATÁN PENINSULA

HISPANIOLA

Caribbean Sea

MIDDLE AMERICA

ISTHMUS OF PANAMA

PACIFIC OCEAN

Orinoco R.

Equator

0°

0°

N
W   E
S

AMAZON BASIN

Amazon R.

SOUTH AMERICA

São Francisco R.

ANDES MOUNTAINS

L. Titicaca

20°S

BRAZILIAN HIGHLANDS

20°S

ATACAMA DESERT

Tropic of Capricorn

Paraná R.

| 0 | 500 | 1000 mi. |
| 0 | 500 | 1000 km |

PAMPAS

Land Elevation

Feet		Meters
13,333		4000
6,667		2000
1,667		500
667		200
0		0

PATAGONIA

40°S

TIERRA DEL FUEGO

140°W   120°W   100°W   80°W   60°W   40°W   20°W

60°N

80°N

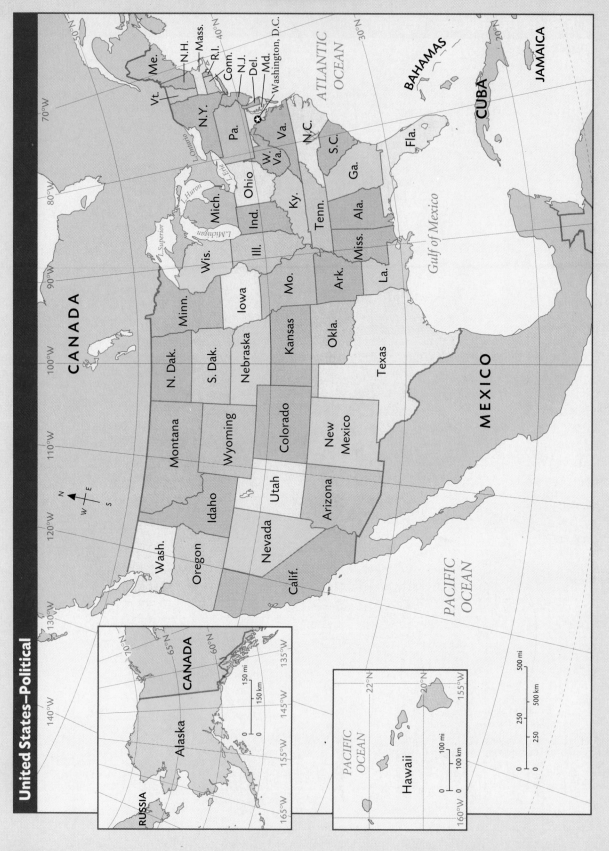

United States–Political

CANADA

RUSSIA

Alaska

CANADA

Hawaii

PACIFIC OCEAN

PACIFIC OCEAN

MEXICO

Gulf of Mexico

BAHAMAS

CUBA

JAMAICA

ATLANTIC OCEAN

Wash.
Oregon
Calif.
Nevada
Idaho
Utah
Arizona
Montana
Wyoming
Colorado
New Mexico
N. Dak.
S. Dak.
Nebraska
Kansas
Okla.
Texas
Minn.
Iowa
Mo.
Ark.
La.
Wis.
Ill.
Ind.
Mich.
Ohio
Ky.
Tenn.
Miss.
Ala.
Ga.
Fla.
S.C.
N.C.
Va.
W. Va.
Pa.
N.Y.
Me.
Vt.
N.H.
Mass.
R.I.
Conn.
N.J.
Del.
Md.
Washington, D.C.

L. Superior
L. Michigan
L. Huron
L. Erie
L. Ontario

150 mi
150 km
0

500 mi
500 km
250
0
0

100 mi
100 km
0
0

N
E
S
W

570

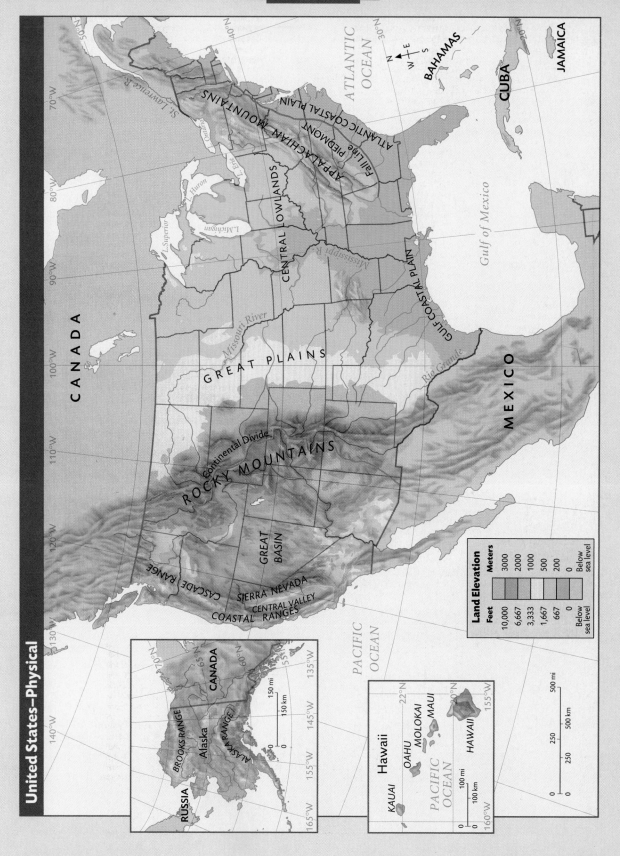

United States–Physical

CANADA

St. Lawrence R.

L. Ontario

L. Erie

L. Huron

L. Michigan

L. Superior

ATLANTIC OCEAN

APPALACHIAN MOUNTAINS

PIEDMONT

Fall Line

ATLANTIC COASTAL PLAIN

CENTRAL LOWLANDS

Mississippi R.

Missouri River

GREAT PLAINS

GULF COASTAL PLAIN

Rio Grande

Gulf of Mexico

BAHAMAS

CUBA

JAMAICA

MEXICO

Continental Divide

ROCKY MOUNTAINS

GREAT BASIN

CASCADE RANGE

SIERRA NEVADA

CENTRAL VALLEY

COASTAL RANGES

PACIFIC OCEAN

N
E
W
S

Land Elevation

Feet	Meters
10,000	3000
6,667	2000
3,333	1000
1,667	500
667	200
0	0
Below sea level	Below sea level

RUSSIA

CANADA

Alaska

BROOKS RANGE

ALASKA RANGE

150 mi

150 km

Hawaii

KAUAI

OAHU

MOLOKAI

MAUI

HAWAII

PACIFIC OCEAN

100 mi

100 km

500 mi

500 km

Europe–Political

30°W · 20°W · 70°N · 10°W · 0° · 10°E · 20°E · 30°E · 40°E

Barents Sea

Reykjavik **ICELAND**

Arctic Circle

60°N

FAROE IS.
(Den.)

SHETLAND IS.
(U.K.)

Norwegian Sea

FINLAND

Helsinki

St. Petersburg

NORWAY

Oslo

Stockholm

Tallinn

RUSSIA

SWEDEN

ESTONIA

Moscow

*ATLANTIC
OCEAN*

Scotland

No. Ireland

North Sea

Riga **LATVIA**

LITHUANIA

DENMARK

Copenhagen

Vilnius

Minsk

Dublin

**UNITED
KINGDOM**

RUSSIA

50°N

IRELAND

Wales

England

NETHERLANDS

Amsterdam

Berlin

POLAND

Warsaw

BELARUS

Kiev

London

The Hague

Brussels

GERMANY

BELGIUM

LUXEMBOURG

Prague

Paris

CZECH REP.

SLOVAKIA

UKRAINE

FRANCE

LIECHTENSTEIN

Bratislava

Vienna

Budapest

MOLDOVA

Kishinev

*Bay of
Biscay*

Bern

SWITZ.

AUSTRIA

HUNGARY

ROMANIA

Ljubljana

SLOVENIA

Zagreb

MONACO

CROATIA

ANDORRA

SAN MARINO

Adriatic Sea

**BOSNIA–
HERZEGOVINA**

Belgrade

Bucharest

*Black
Sea*

40°N

PORTUGAL

Madrid

CORSICA
(Fr.)

ITALY

Sarajevo

SERBIA

BULGARIA

Lisbon

SPAIN

Rome

MONTENEGRO

Podgorica

Sofia

Istanbul

ALBANIA

Skopje

MACEDONIA

TURKEY

SARDINIA
(It.)

Tiranë

BALEARIC IS. (Sp.)

GREECE

*Aegean
Sea*

*Strait of
Gibraltar*

Gibraltar (U.K.)

Mediterranean Sea

SICILY
(It.)

Athens

30°N

MALTA

CRETE (Gr.)

⊛ National capital

— International boundary

0 · 250 · 500 mi.

0 · 250 · 500 km

AFRICA

Gulf of Bothnia

Baltic Sea

Europe–Physical

30°W 20°W 70°N 10°W 0° 10°E 20°E 30°E 40°E

Barents Sea

ICELAND

Arctic Circle

N
W · E
S

60°N

Norwegian Sea

FAROE IS.

SHETLAND IS.

KJÖLEN MOUNTAINS

SCANDINAVIAN PENINSULA

Gulf of Bothnia

ATLANTIC
OCEAN

Baltic Sea

North Sea

JUTLAND
PENINSULA

BRITISH ISLES

50°N

Thames R.

English Channel

Ruhr
Valley

NORTHERN EUROPEAN PLAIN

Elbe R.

Oder R.

Vistula R.

Rhine R.

Dnepr R.

Bay of
Biscay

Seine R.

Loire R.

CARPATHIAN MTS.

Dniester R.

Garonne R.

Danube R.

A L P S

Po R.

Danube R.

Black
Sea

PYRENEES

Rhône R.

40°N

IBERIAN PENINSULA

Ebro R.

APENNINES

ITALIAN PENINSULA

Adriatic
Sea

DINARIC ALPS

BALKAN MTS.

Bosporus

CORSICA

BALKAN PENINSULA

Tagus R.

Guadiana R.

PINDUS MTS.

Dardanelles

BALEARIC
ISLANDS

SARDINIA

Aegean
Sea

ASIA MINOR

Strait of
Gibraltar

M e d i t e r r a n e a n   S e a

Ionian
Sea

SICILY

CRETE

AFRICA

Land Elevation

Feet		Meters
13,333		4000
6,667		2000
3,333		1000
1,667		500
667		200
0		0

30°N

0   250   500 mi.

0   250   500 km

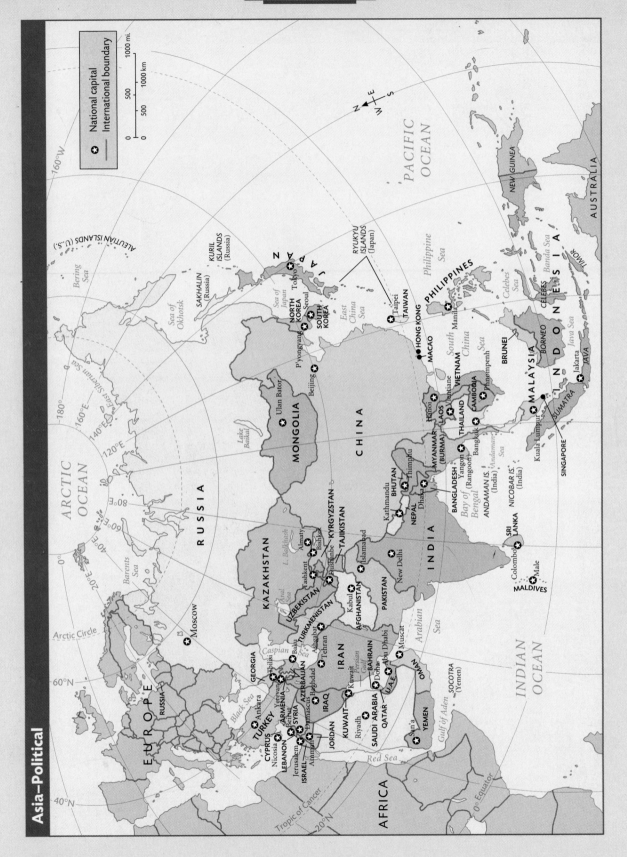

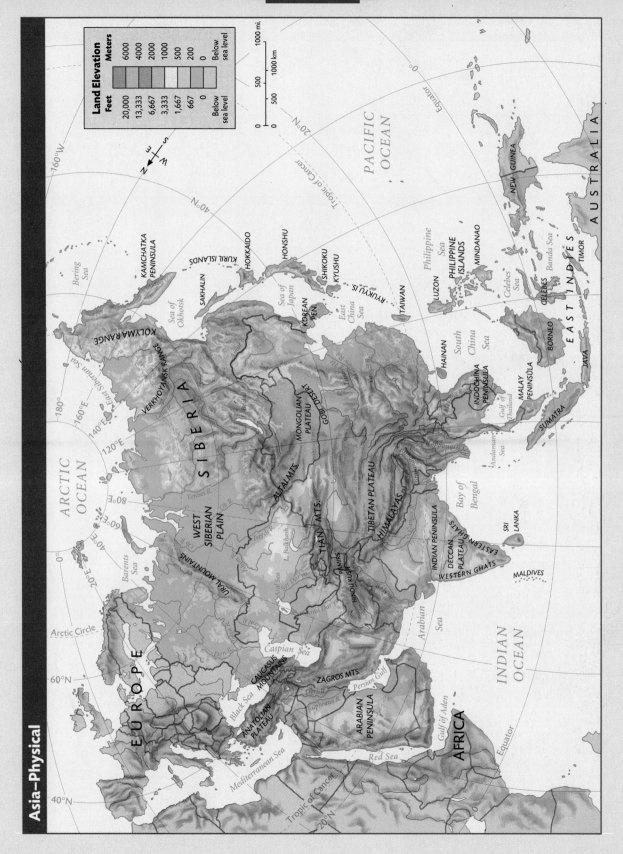

Asia–Physical

Land Elevation

Feet	Meters
20,000	6000
13,333	4000
6,667	2000
3,333	1000
1,667	500
667	200
0	0
Below sea level	Below sea level

1000 mi.

1000 km

500

500

0

0

ARCTIC OCEAN

EUROPE

SIBERIA

KOLYMA RANGE

VERKHOYANSK RANGE

Bering Sea

KAMCHATKA PENINSULA

KURIL ISLANDS

SAKHALIN

Sea of Okhotsk

HOKKAIDO

HONSHU

Sea of Japan

SHIKOKU

KYUSHU

KOREAN PEN.

East China Sea

RYUKYU IS.

TAIWAN

PACIFIC OCEAN

Equator

20°N

Tropic of Cancer

40°N

NEW GUINEA

AUSTRALIA

EAST INDIES

TIMOR

Banda Sea

CELEBES

Celebes Sea

MINDANAO

PHILIPPINE ISLANDS

Philippine Sea

LUZON

BORNEO

South China Sea

JAVA

SUMATRA

HAINAN

INDOCHINA PENINSULA

Gulf of Thailand

MALAY PENINSULA

Andaman Sea

MONGOLIAN PLATEAU

GOBI DESERT

ALTAI MTS.

TIEN MTS.

TIBETAN PLATEAU

HIMALAYAS

PAMIRS

HINDU KUSH

WEST SIBERIAN PLAIN

URAL MOUNTAINS

Aral Sea

L. Balkhash

Amu Dar'ya

Syr Dar'ya

Yenisei R.

Ob R.

Irtysh R.

Lena R.

INDIAN PENINSULA

DECCAN PLATEAU

EASTERN GHATS

WESTERN GHATS

SRI LANKA

MALDIVES

Bay of Bengal

Arabian Sea

INDIAN OCEAN

Equator

Tropic of Cancer

20°N

40°N

60°N

Arctic Circle

Barents Sea

East Siberian Sea

Caspian Sea

Black Sea

CAUCASUS MOUNTAINS

ZAGROS MTS.

ANATOLIAN PLATEAU

Mediterranean Sea

Tigris R.

Euphrates R.

Persian Gulf

ARABIAN PENINSULA

Gulf of Aden

Red Sea

AFRICA

160°W

180°

160°E

140°E

120°E

80°E

60°E

40°E

20°E

0°

0°

20°N

40°N

575

Africa–Political

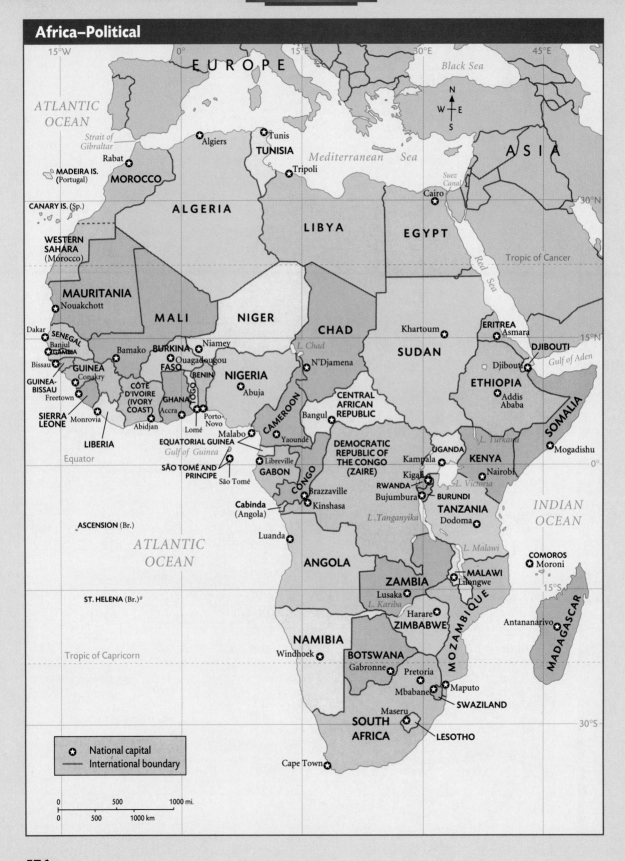

15°W   0°   15°E   30°E   45°E

EUROPE

ATLANTIC
OCEAN

Black Sea

N
W   E
S

ASIA

Strait of
Gibraltar

✪ Algiers

✪ Tunis
TUNISIA

Mediterranean Sea

Suez
Canal

✪ Tripoli

Rabat ✪
MOROCCO

MADEIRA IS.
(Portugal)

CANARY IS. (Sp.)

WESTERN
SAHARA
(Morocco)

ALGERIA

LIBYA

Cairo ✪

EGYPT

30°N

Red Sea

Tropic of Cancer

MAURITANIA

✪ Nouakchott

MALI

NIGER

CHAD

Khartoum ✪

ERITREA
Asmara ✪

15°N

DJIBOUTI

Dakar ✪
SENEGAL

✪ Niamey

L. Chad

SUDAN

Djibouti □

Gulf of Aden

Banjul ✪
GAMBIA

Bamako ✪

BURKINA
FASO

N'Djamena ✪

ETHIOPIA

Bissau ✪

GUINEA

✪ Ouagadougou

NIGERIA

Addis
Ababa ✪

GUINEA-
BISSAU

Conakry ✪

BENIN

Abuja ✪

CENTRAL
AFRICAN
REPUBLIC

SOMALIA

SIERRA
LEONE

Freetown ✪

CÔTE
D'IVOIRE
(IVORY
COAST)

GHANA

TOGO

Monrovia ✪

Accra ✪

Porto-
Novo ✪

CAMEROON

Bangui ✪

L. Turkana

LIBERIA

Abidjan ✪

Lomé ✪

Malabo ✪

Mogadishu ✪

Equator

EQUATORIAL GUINEA

Yaoundé ✪

DEMOCRATIC
REPUBLIC OF
THE CONGO
(ZAIRE)

UGANDA

KENYA

0°

Gulf of Guinea

Kampala ✪

SÃO TOMÉ AND
PRINCIPE

Libreville ✪

São Tomé

GABON

CONGO

Kigali ✪

L. Victoria

Nairobi ✪

RWANDA

INDIAN
OCEAN

ASCENSION (Br.)

Brazzaville ✪

Bujumbura ✪

BURUNDI

Cabinda
(Angola)

Kinshasa ✪

TANZANIA

Dodoma ✪

ATLANTIC
OCEAN

L. Tanganyika

Luanda ✪

L. Malawi

COMOROS
✪ Moroni

ST. HELENA (Br.)

ANGOLA

ZAMBIA

MALAWI

Lilongwe ✪

15°S

Lusaka ✪

L. Kariba

MOZAMBIQUE

Antananarivo ✪

Harare ✪

MADAGASCAR

NAMIBIA

ZIMBABWE

Tropic of Capricorn

Windhoek ✪

BOTSWANA

Gaborone ✪

Pretoria ✪

Maputo ✪

Mbabane ✪

SWAZILAND

Maseru ✪

SOUTH
AFRICA

LESOTHO

30°S

| ✪ | National capital |
| — | International boundary |

Cape Town ✪

0   500   1000 mi.

0   500   1000 km

576

Africa–Physical

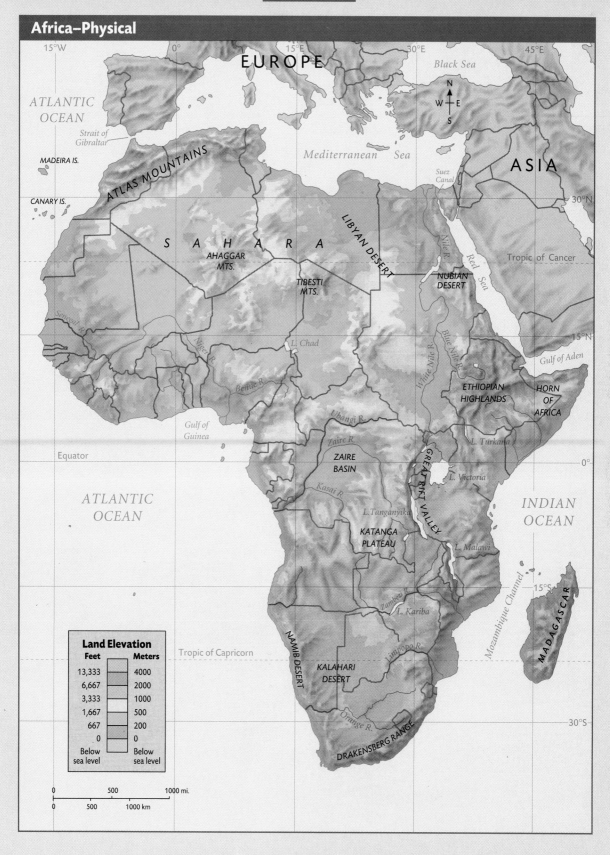

EUROPE

ATLANTIC
OCEAN

Black Sea

N
W E
S

Strait of
Gibraltar

Mediterranean Sea

ASIA

MADEIRA IS.

ATLAS MOUNTAINS

Suez
Canal

CANARY IS.

30°N

S A H A R A

AHAGGAR
MTS.

LIBYAN DESERT

NUBIAN
DESERT

Tropic of Cancer

Red Sea

Nile R.

TIBESTI
MTS.

Blue Nile R.

15°N

Gulf of Aden

Senegal R.

Niger R.

L. Chad

White Nile R.

ETHIOPIAN
HIGHLANDS

HORN
OF
AFRICA

Benue R.

Gulf of
Guinea

Ubangi R.

Zaire R.

L. Turkana

ZAIRE
BASIN

GREAT RIFT VALLEY

L. Victoria

Equator

0°

Kasai R.

ATLANTIC
OCEAN

L. Tanganyika

INDIAN
OCEAN

KATANGA
PLATEAU

L. Malawi

MADAGASCAR

Mozambique Channel

15°S

Zambezi R.

L. Kariba

Land Elevation	
Feet	**Meters**
13,333	4000
6,667	2000
3,333	1000
1,667	500
667	200
0	0
Below sea level	Below sea level

Tropic of Capricorn

NAMIB DESERT

Limpopo R.

KALAHARI
DESERT

Orange R.

DRAKENSBERG RANGE

30°S

0   500   1000 mi.

0   500   1000 km

15°W   0°   15°E   30°E   45°E

The Pacific Realm–Political/Physical

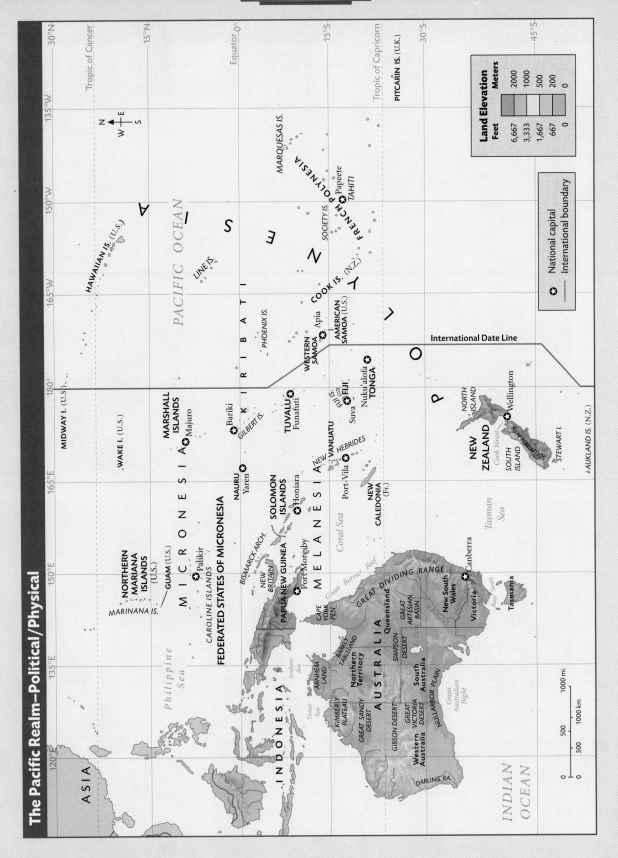

Land Elevation

Feet	Meters
6,667	2000
3,333	1000
1,667	500
667	200
0	0

✪ National capital
— International boundary

N
W ← → E
S

30°N Tropic of Cancer 15°N Equator 0° 15°S Tropic of Capricorn 30°S 45°S

PITCAIRN IS. (U.K.)

PACIFIC OCEAN

POLYNESIA

MARQUESAS IS.

FRENCH POLYNESIA
Papeete
TAHITI
SOCIETY IS.

HAWAIIAN IS. (U.S.)

LINE IS.

COOK IS. (N.Z.)

PHOENIX IS.

American
SAMOA (U.S.)
Apia
WESTERN SAMOA

International Date Line

MIDWAY I. (U.S.)

WAKE I. (U.S.)

MARSHALL ISLANDS
Majuro

Bariki
GILBERT IS.

KIRIBATI

TUVALU
Funafuti

Nuku'alofa
TONGA

FIJI
Fiji IS.
Suva

NORTH ISLAND
NEW ZEALAND
Wellington
Cook Strait
SOUTH ISLAND
STEWART I.
AUKLAND IS. (N.Z.)

NORTHERN MARIANA ISLANDS (U.S.)
GUAM (U.S.)
Palikir
MICRONESIA
MARINANA IS.
CAROLINE ISLANDS
FEDERATED STATES OF MICRONESIA

NAURU
Yaren

SOLOMON ISLANDS
Honiara

NEW VANUATU
NEW HEBRIDES
Port-Vila

NEW CALEDONIA (Fr.)

MELANESIA

BISMARCK ARCH.
NEW BRITAIN
PAPUA NEW GUINEA
Port Moresby

Coral Sea

Tasman Sea

Canberra

ASIA

Philippine Sea

INDONESIA

Arafura Sea

Timor Sea

CAPE YORK PEN.
GREAT DIVIDING RANGE
Queensland

ARNHEM LAND
Northern Territory
KIMBERLY PLATEAU
GREAT SANDY DESERT

BARKLY TABLELAND
SIMPSON DESERT
GREAT ARTESIAN BASIN
New South Wales
Victoria
Bass Strait
Tasmania

AUSTRALIA
South Australia
GIBSON DESERT
GREAT VICTORIA DESERT
Western Australia
NULLARBOR PLAIN
Great Australian Bight

DARLING RA.

Great Barrier Reef

INDIAN OCEAN

1000 mi.
1000 km
500
500
0
0

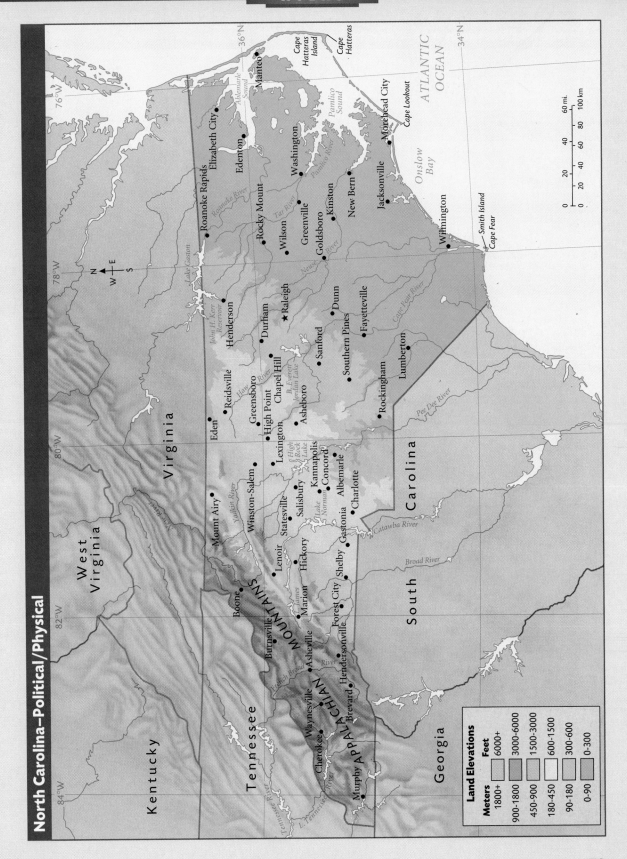

North Carolina–Political/Physical

Europe and Northern Asia–Climate

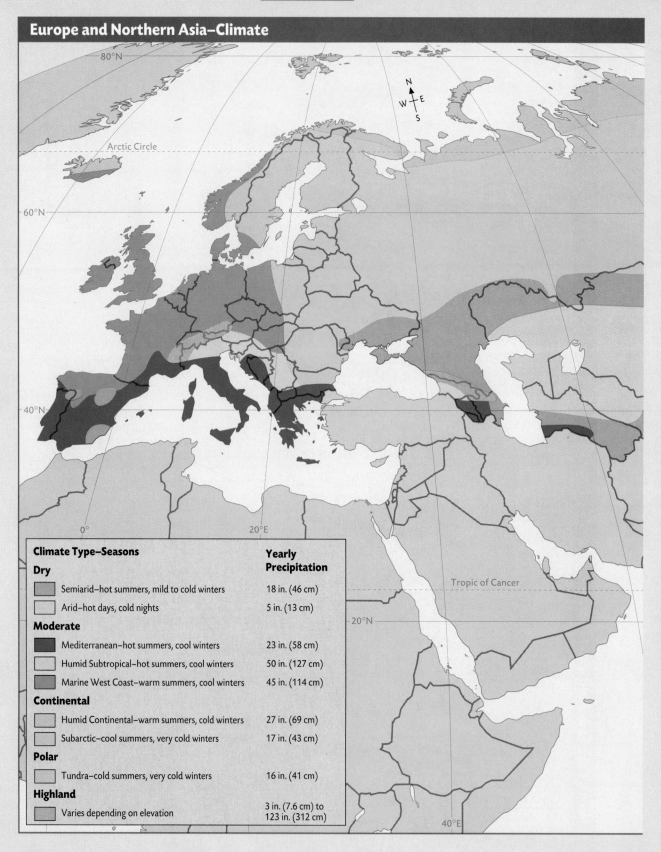

80°N

Arctic Circle

60°N

40°N

0°   20°E

20°N

Tropic of Cancer

40°E

N
W E
S

Climate Type–Seasons | **Yearly Precipitation**

Dry

Semiarid–hot summers, mild to cold winters — 18 in. (46 cm)

Arid–hot days, cold nights — 5 in. (13 cm)

Moderate

Mediterranean–hot summers, cool winters — 23 in. (58 cm)

Humid Subtropical–hot summers, cool winters — 50 in. (127 cm)

Marine West Coast–warm summers, cool winters — 45 in. (114 cm)

Continental

Humid Continental–warm summers, cold winters — 27 in. (69 cm)

Subarctic–cool summers, very cold winters — 17 in. (43 cm)

Polar

Tundra–cold summers, very cold winters — 16 in. (41 cm)

Highland

Varies depending on elevation — 3 in. (7.6 cm) to 123 in. (312 cm)

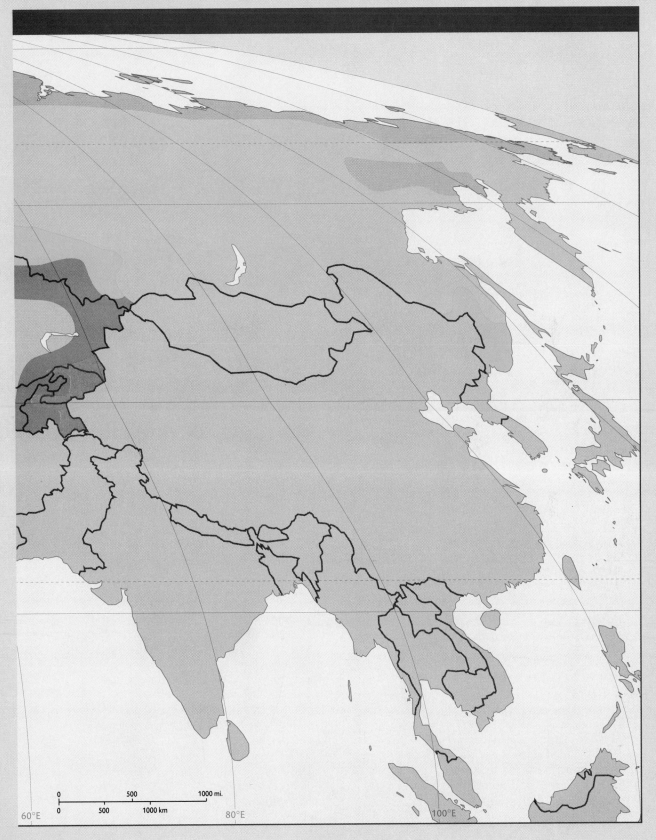

60°E

80°E

100°E

0   500   1000 mi.

0   500   1000 km

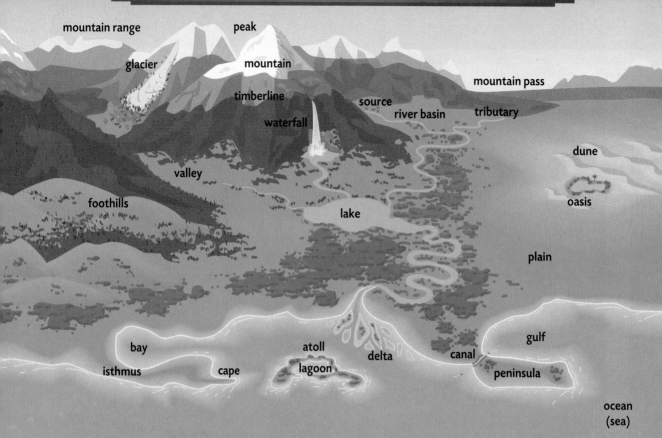

archipelago (ar·kee·PELL·ah·goh) A large group or chain of islands.

atoll A ring-shaped coral island or string of islands surrounding a lagoon.

basin An area of low-lying land surrounded by higher land. *See also* **river basin**.

bay Part of an ocean, sea, or lake extending into the land. Usually smaller than a gulf.

beach The gently sloping shore of an ocean or other body of water, especially that part covered by sand or pebbles.

butte (beyoot) A small, flat-topped hill. A butte is smaller than a plateau or a mesa.

canal A waterway built to carry water for navigation or irrigation. Navigation canals usually connect two other bodies of water.

canyon A deep, narrow valley with steep sides.

cape A projecting part of a coastline that extends into an ocean, sea, gulf, bay, or lake.

cliff A high, steep face of rock or earth.

coast Land along an ocean or sea.

dam A wall built across a river to hold back the flowing water.

delta Land formed at the mouth of a river by deposits of silt, sand, and pebbles.

desert A very dry area where few plants grow.

dune A mound, hill, or ridge of sand that is heaped up by the wind.

fjord (fyord) A deep, narrow inlet of the sea between high, steep cliffs.

foothills A hilly area at the base of a mountain range.

glacier (GLAY·sher) A large sheet of ice that moves slowly over some land surface or down a valley.

gulf Part of an ocean or sea that extends into the land. A gulf is usually larger than a bay.

harbor A protected place along a shore where ships can safely anchor.

hill A rounded, raised landform, not as high as a mountain.

island A body of land completely surrounded by water.

isthmus (ISS·muss) A narrow strip of land bordered by water that connects two larger bodies of land.

lagoon A shallow body of water partly or completely enclosed within an atoll. Also, a shallow body of sea water partly cut off from the sea by a narrow strip of land.

582

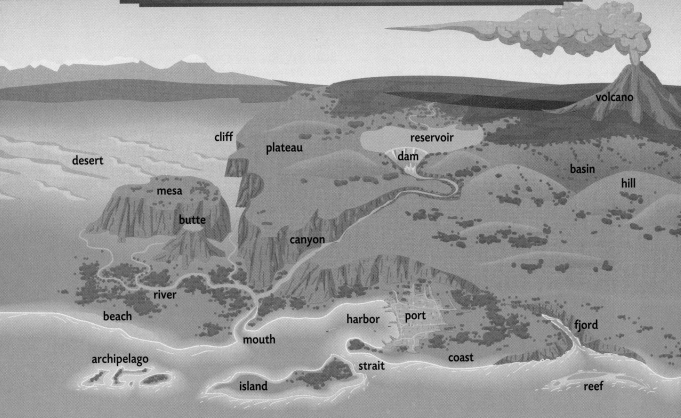

desert mesa butte cliff plateau reservoir dam volcano basin hill canyon river beach mouth harbor port fjord archipelago island strait coast reef

lake A body of water surrounded by land.

mesa A high, flat landform rising steeply above the surrounding land. A mesa is smaller than a plateau and larger than a butte.

mountain A high, rounded or pointed landform with steep sides, higher than a hill.

mountain pass An opening or gap through a mountain range.

mountain range A row or chain of mountains.

mouth The place where a river empties into another body of water.

oasis A place in the desert made fertile by a steady supply of water.

ocean One of the earth's four largest bodies of water. The four oceans are really a single connected body of salt water that covers about three fourths of the earth's surface.

peak The pointed top of a mountain or hill.

peninsula A body of land nearly surrounded by water.

plain A large area of flat or nearly flat land.

plateau A high, flat landform that rises steeply above the surrounding land. A plateau is larger than a mesa or a butte.

port A place where ships load and unload goods.

reef A ridge of sand, rock, or coral that lies at or near the surface of a sea.

reservoir A natural or artificial lake used to store water.

river A large stream of water that flows across the land and usually empties into a lake, ocean, or other river.

river basin All the land drained by a river and its tributaries.

sea A large body of water partly or entirely surrounded by land. Another word for ocean.

source The place where a river or stream begins.

strait A narrow waterway or channel connecting two larger bodies of water.

timberline An imaginary line on mountains above which trees do not grow.

tributary A river or stream that flows into a larger river or stream.

valley An area of low land between hills or mountains.

volcano (vol·KAY·no) An opening in the earth through which lava, rock, gases, and ash are forced out.

waterfall A flow of water falling from a high place to a lower place.

583

Aberdeen–Carpathian Mountains

A

Aberdeen A large seaport city in Scotland on the North Sea.

Adriatic Sea An arm of the Mediterranean Sea between Italy and the Balkan Peninsula.

Aegean Sea An arm of the Mediterranean Sea between Greece and Turkey.

Albania A nation of Eastern Europe on the Balkan Peninsula. Its west coast faces the Adriatic Sea.

Alps A major south-central European mountain system that extends through France, Italy, Switzerland, Austria, and the western Balkan Peninsula. Highest mountain system in Europe.

Amsterdam A seaport city and capital of The Netherlands. Connected to North Sea by ship canal.

Andorra A tiny nation in the Pyrenees between France and Spain.

Apennines A mountain system extending the length of Italy and continuing into Sicily.

Aral Sea A landlocked saltwater sea in Kazakhstan and Uzbekistan.

Arctic Ocean The chiefly ice-covered ocean at the North Pole.

Ardennes Deciduous-forested region in northeastern France, western Luxembourg, and southeastern Belgium east of the Meuse River.

Armenia A nation of Transcaucasia in southwestern Europe south of the Caucasus Mountains. Once part of the Soviet Union.

Arno River One of the longest rivers in Italy. Flows west from the Apennines through Florence into the Ligurian Sea.

Austria A nation in Western Europe south of the Czech Republic and north of Italy.

Athens The capital city of Greece, located near the Saronic Gulf and enclosed on three sides by hills.

Atlantic Ocean One of the world's largest bodies of water, separating North and South America from Europe and Africa.

Azerbaijan A nation of Transcaucasia in southwestern Europe south of the Caucasus Mountains. Once part of the Soviet Union.

B

Baikal Mountains A mountain range in southern Siberia, Russia, on the western shore of Lake Baikal.

Balearic Islands Islands off the east coast of Spain in the Mediterranean Sea.

Balkan Mountains A mountain range in central Bulgaria extending from the border with Serbia-Montenegro to the Black Sea.

Balkan Peninsula A peninsula in Eastern Europe bounded by the Adriatic, Aegean, and Black Seas.

Baltic Nations The Eastern European nations of Estonia, Latvia, and Lithuania. All border the Baltic Sea.

Baltic Sea An almost landlocked sea north of Germany and Poland and southeast of Sweden. The Eastern European nations of Poland, Lithuania, Estonia, and Latvia face this sea.

Belarus (formerly Byelorussia) A nation of Eastern Europe east of Poland and west of Russia. Once part of the Soviet Union.

Belfast The capital and seaport city of Northern Ireland.

Belgium A nation of Western Europe north of France and west of Germany. Northwest coast is on the North Sea.

Benelux A short name for three nations of Western Europe: Belgium, Netherlands, and Luxembourg.

Bering Strait The body of water separating Asia and North America, located west of Alaska and east of Russia.

Berlin The capital city of Germany, replacing Bonn, which had been the capital of West Germany. Capital of Germany prior to the nation's split after World War II. Divided into East and West Berlin during the Cold War.

Birmingham An industrial city of England northwest of London.

Black Sea A landlocked sea between Europe and Asia, connected to the Mediterranean Sea by the Bosporus Strait.

Black Forest A region of deciduous forests in southwest Germany along the upper Rhine River.

Bosnia-Herzegovina A nation of Eastern Europe on the Balkan Peninsula. Once part of Yugoslavia.

Bristol A city in central England located where the Avon and Frome Rivers meet.

Britain An island of the British Isles that contains Scotland, England, and Wales. Located west of the North Sea.

British Isles A region of Europe that contains the United Kingdom, the independent Republic of Ireland, and numerous small islands. It is located northwest of the mainland of Europe.

Brussels The capital city of Belgium on the Senne River.

Bucharest The capital of Romania on the Dîmbovita River.

Budapest The capital city of Hungary on the Danube River.

Bulgaria A nation of Eastern Europe on the Black Sea south of Romania.

C

Cardiff The capital and seaport city of Wales.

Caribbean Sea Part of the southern Atlantic Ocean between North and South America. Enclosed by the Lesser Antilles to the east, the Greater Antilles to the north, and Yucatán Peninsula to the west.

Carpathian Mountains A major mountain system of Eastern Europe in southern Poland and southern Ukraine.

Caspian Sea Inland sea of Central Asia, bordered by Azerbaijan, Russia, Kazakhstan, Turkmenistan, and Iran.

Caucasus Mountains A mountain range extending west to east from the Black Sea to the Caspian Sea.

Charlotte, North Carolina The largest city in North Carolina, located in the Piedmont Region in southwestern North Carolina.

Chernobyl A city in central Ukraine abandoned after 1986 nuclear accident.

Constantinople An ancient city, eastern capital of the Roman Empire, and seat of the Orthodox (Christian) Church. Located in present-day Turkey and called Istanbul.

Copenhagen The capital city of Denmark.

Córdoba Capital of Córdoba province on the Guadalquivir River in southern Spain. Once the Muslim capital of Iberia.

Cork City in southwest Republic of Ireland. The second largest city in Ireland.

Corsica A French island in the Mediterranean Sea west of Italy and north of Sardinia.

Croatia A nation of Eastern Europe on the Balkan Peninsula. Once part of Yugoslavia.

Czech Republic A nation of Eastern Europe north of Austria, south of Poland, and east of Germany. With its eastern neighbor, Slovakia, formed the former nation of Czechoslovakia.

D

Danube River A major river of Western and Eastern Europe, flowing from Germany east through Austria, Hungary, Serbia, along the Romanian-Bulgarian boundary, then into the Black Sea.

Danzig *See* Gdansk.

Denmark A nation of Norden north of Germany and south of Norway and Sweden along the North Sea.

Dnepr River (formerly spelled Dnieper) One of Russia's longest, navigable rivers. Flows from near Moscow to the Black Sea.

Douro River A river in Portugal and Spain that flows west into the Atlantic Ocean.

Dublin Port city and capital of the Republic of Ireland. Located at the mouth of the Liffey River on Dublin Bay.

E

Eastern Europe A region in Europe that includes the following nations: Albania, Belarus, Bosnia-Herzegovina, Bulgaria, Croatia, Czech Republic, Estonia, Hungary, Latvia, Lithuania, Macedonia, Moldova, Poland, Romania, Serbia-Montenegro, Slovakia, Slovenia, and Ukraine.

Ebro River Second longest river in Spain. Rises in the Cantabrian Mountains and flows east-southeast into the Mediterranean Sea.

Edinburgh The capital city of Scotland on the Firth of Forth River.

Elbe River A river in the Czech Republic and Germany that flows to the North Sea.

England Formerly independent nation now part of the United Kingdom. Located in the British Isles south of Scotland on the island of Britain. *See* United Kingdom.

English Channel A body of water between England and France, connecting the Atlantic Ocean and the North Sea.

Estonia A nation of Eastern Europe east of the Baltic Sea and west of Russia. One of the Baltic nations that was part of the Soviet Union.

Europe The world's second smallest continent. A peninsula of the landmass bounded by the Arctic Ocean, the Atlantic Ocean, the Mediterranean Sea, and Asia.

F

Finland A nation of Norden east of Sweden and west of Russia.

Flanders A region in northern Belgium.

Florence A large city at the foot of the Apennines in north-central Italy on the Arno River.

France A nation of Western Europe north of Spain and southwest of Germany.

G

Gascony A southwestern region of France.

Gdansk A seaport city in northern Poland. Formerly known as Danzig.

Georgia A nation of Transcaucasia in southwestern Europe south of the Caucasus Mountains. Once a part of the Soviet Union.

Germany A nation of Western Europe west of Poland and northeast of France.

Glasgow A city in central Scotland on the Clyde River. The largest city in Scotland.

Great Britain *See* United Kingdom.

Greece A nation of Mediterranean Europe in the southwestern part of the Balkan Peninsula and east of Italy. Includes many islands in the Mediterranean and Aegean Seas.

Greenland Island in North Atlantic off northeast North America belonging to Denmark. The largest island (other than Australia) in the world.

Gulf Stream Warm ocean current in the North Atlantic Ocean that flows north along the North American coast from the Gulf of Mexico through the Florida Straits, then northeast to the Grand Banks of Newfoundland. Merges with North Atlantic Drift current, which flows northeast to the Barents Sea and influences climate of Western Europe, the British Isles, and Norden.

Greenwich The city in England through which the prime meridian runs.

Gulf of Corinth Inlet of the Mediterranean Sea in central Greece northeast of the Peloponnesus.

Gulf of Patras Inlet of the Ionian Sea on west coast of Greece. Joined by narrow strait to the Gulf of Corinth.

H

Hague, The The seat of government in The Netherlands, headquarters of the International Court of Justice.

Helsinki The capital city of Finland.

Hungary A nation of Eastern Europe north of the Balkan Peninsula and west of Romania.

I

Iberian Peninsula A peninsula in southwestern Europe, shared by Spain and Portugal, which is bordered by the Mediterranean Sea, the Atlantic Ocean, the Bay of Biscay, and France.

Iceland An island nation of Norden in the North Atlantic Ocean northwest of the British Isles and southeast of Greenland.

Ionian Sea An arm of the Mediterranean Sea, between Greece and southern Italy.

Ireland, Republic of An independent nation of the British Isles on the island of Ireland lying west of Great Britain in the Atlantic Ocean. The island also contains Northern Ireland, a part of the United Kingdom.

Irkutsk A city in Russia on the western edge of Lake Baikal in Siberia.

Istanbul A seaport city in northwestern Turkey on the Bosporus Strait. Formerly called Constantinople.

Italian Peninsula A peninsula extending into the Mediterranean Sea that contains the nation of Italy.

Italy A nation of Mediterranean Europe that covers the Italian Peninsula. Includes the islands of Sicily and Sardinia.

J

Japan A nation of East Asia between the Sea of Japan and the Pacific Ocean.

Jerusalem Israeli and Arab city in the eastern Mediterranean, northwest of the Dead Sea. A holy city for Christians, Jews, and Muslims.

K

Kaliningrad A port city opening on the Baltic Sea. The city and some surrounding territory are between Lithuania, to the north, and Poland, to the south. Retained by Russia after the Baltic nations became independent.

Kara Kum A desert in the Central Asian nation of Turkmenistan.

Kazakhstan A nation of Central Asia south of Russia and north of Kyrgyzstan. Once part of czarist Russia and the Soviet Union.

Kiev A city in Ukraine. Capital of Kievan Russia before 1200.

Kyrgyzstan A nation of Central Asia south of Kazakhstan and west of China. Once part of czarist Russia and the Soviet Union.

L

Lake Baikal A huge freshwater lake, the deepest in the world, in southern Siberia in Russia.

Lapland A region occupied by Lapps that crosses the boundaries of Norway, Sweden, Finland, and Russia in the most northerly portion of the Scandinavian peninsula.

Latvia A nation of Eastern Europe east of the Baltic Sea. One of the Baltic nations that was part of the Soviet Union.

Le Havre The major French port on the English Channel.

Liechtenstein A small nation of Western Europe between Switzerland and Austria bordering on the Rhine River.

Lisbon The capital and seaport city of Portugal.

Lithuania A nation of Eastern Europe east of the Baltic Sea. One of the Baltic countries that was part of the Soviet Union.

Liverpool A major port city in northwest England on the Mersey River estuary.

Loire River The longest river in France. Rises in southeastern France and empties into the Bay of Biscay.

London The capital city of the United Kingdom.

Luxembourg A nation of Western Europe north of France and southeast of Belgium.

M

Macedonia A nation of Eastern Europe on the Balkan Peninsula. Once part of Yugoslavia.

Madrid The capital city of Spain.

Malta A tiny island nation in the Mediterranean Sea, south of Sicily.

Marseilles A major seaport city in southeastern France.

Mediterranean Sea Inland sea enclosed by Europe to the west and north, Asia to the east, and Africa to the south.

Mediterranean Region The region of southern Europe near the Mediterranean Sea. Major nations are Greece, Italy, Spain, and Portugal. Andorra, Malta, Vatican City, and San Marino—four of the world's smallest nations—are in this region.

Meseta plateau Tableland shared by Portugal and Spain.

Milan A commercial and industrial city in northwestern Italy.

Moldova (formerly spelled Moldavia) A nation of Eastern Europe south of Ukraine. Once part of the Soviet Union.

Monaco A nation of Western Europe on the Mediterranean Sea between France and Italy.

Moscow The capital and largest city in Russia.

Munich A city in southeastern Germany on the Isar River.

N

Netherlands A nation of Western Europe north of Belgium and west of Germany.

Norden A region in northern Europe that includes the nations of Norway, Finland, Denmark, Sweden, and Iceland.

North America The world's third largest continent. The landmass north of the Isthmus of Panama that includes Mexico, Canada, and the United States.

North Atlantic Drift The warm ocean current that extends from the Gulf Stream in the Atlantic Ocean and affects the climates of Norden, the British Isles, and nations south of the Baltic Sea.

North Italian Plain The largest flat region of Italy.

North Sea An arm of the Atlantic Ocean between Great Britain and the European mainland.

North Sea Canal One of the world's deepest and widest canals. Links the port of Amsterdam to the North Sea.

Northern European Plain Extends from the Atlantic Ocean through Western Europe and Eastern Europe to the western edge of the Ural Mountains in Russia.

Northern Ireland The nation once part of Ireland that is now part of the United Kingdom. Located in the British Isles, on the island of Ireland. *See* United Kingdom.

Norway A nation of Norden west of Sweden and east of the Norwegian Sea.

O

Oder River A river on Poland's western border.

Oslo The capital city of Norway.

P

Paris The capital city of France.

Po River The longest river in Italy. Flows from the Alps to the Adriatic Sea.

Poland A nation of Eastern Europe east of Germany and west of Belarus and Ukraine.

Portugal A nation of Mediterranean Europe that shares the Iberian Peninsula with Spain.

Prague The capital city of the Czech Republic.

Prussia A former nineteenth-century kingdom that included parts of today's Poland and Germany.

Pyrenees A mountain range in southwestern Europe forming the border between France and Spain.

R

Raleigh The capital of North Carolina, an eastern coastal state in the United States.

Reykjavík The capital city of Iceland.

Rhine River A river in Western Europe rising in Switzerland and flowing north through Germany to the Netherlands.

Riga The capital city of Latvia on the Gulf of Riga.

Rhône River A river in Western Europe that rises in the Swiss Alps and flows south through France into the Mediterranean Sea.

Romania A nation of Eastern Europe on the Black Sea north of Bulgaria and south of Ukraine.

Rome The capital city of Italy. Seat of the ancient Roman Empire.

Rotterdam The second largest city in the Netherlands.

Ruhr Valley A region in Germany with iron ore resources.

Russia A nation of Europe and Asia west of Finland, Estonia, Latvia, Belarus, and Ukraine and north of China and Mongolia. The largest nation in the world.

Russian Realm A term often used to identify the parts of Europe and Asia that once were ruled by czarist Russia and the Soviet Union.

S

San Marino A tiny Mediterranean nation on the east coast of Italy.

Sardinia An Italian island in the Tyrrhenian Sea west of the Italian mainland and just south of Corsica.

Scandinavia A part of Norden consisting of Norway, Sweden, and Denmark.

Scandinavian peninsula A peninsula that juts into the North Sea and Baltic Sea. Contains the nations of Norway and Sweden.

Scotland Formerly independent nation now part of the United Kingdom. Located in the British Isles north of England on the island of Britain. *See* United Kingdom.

Seine River A major river in France that flows through Paris and on into the English Channel.

Serbia-Montenegro A nation of Eastern Europe on the Balkan Peninsula. Once part of Yugoslavia.

Siberia A resource-rich region of Russia that extends from the Ural Mountains east to the Pacific Ocean. The Siberian plains are the largest unbroken plains in the world.

Sicily The largest island in the Mediterranean Sea, located west of the extreme southern point of the Italian peninsula. Separated from the mainland by the narrow Strait of Messina and from Africa (Tunisia) by part of the Mediterranean.

Slovakia A nation of Eastern Europe north of Hungary, south of Poland, and west of Ukraine. With its western neighbor, the Czech Republic, formed the former nation of Czechoslovakia.

Slovenia A nation of Eastern Europe on the Balkan Peninsula. Once part of Yugoslavia.

Soviet Union A Communist nation founded in 1917 that ceased to exist in 1991. Consisted of Russia, Estonia, Latvia, Lithuania, Byelorussia, Ukraine, Moldavia, Georgia, Armenia, Azerbaijan, Kazakhstan, Uzbekistan, Tajikistan, Kyrgyzstan, and Turkmenistan.

Spain A nation of Mediterranean Europe. Occupies the Iberian Peninsula with Portugal.

Stockholm The capital city of Sweden.

St. Petersburg A city in Russia at the mouth of the Neva River founded by Peter the Great. Once called Petrograd and, in honor of the Soviet Union's first leader, Leningrad.

Sweden A nation of Norden west of Finland and east of Norway.

Switzerland A nation of Western Europe north of Italy, south of Germany, west of Austria, and east of France.

T

Tallinn A port city in Estonia on the Gulf of Finland opposite Helsinki.

Tatra Mountains A mountain range in Eastern Europe along Poland's border with Slovakia. Part of the Carpathian Mountains.

Tiber River A river in Italy that flows through Rome and empties into the Tyrrhenian Sea.

Transcaucasia The nations south of the Caucasus Mountains that were part of the Soviet Union: Georgia, Armenia, and Azerbaijan.

Turkestan Territory between the Caspian Sea and China that the Soviet Union organized into five republics. The five republics are now independent nations of Central Asia: Kazakhstan, Kyrgyzstan, Tajikistan, Turkmenistan, and Uzbekistan.

Turkey A nation in southeast Europe and southwest Asia.

Turkmenistan A nation of Central Asia south of Uzbekistan, north of Iran, northwest of Afghanistan, southeast of Kazakhstan, and east of the Caspian Sea.

Tyrrhenian Sea The part of the Mediterranean Sea west of the Italian mainland, north of Sicily, and east of Sardinia and Corsica.

U

Ukraine A nation of Eastern Europe on the north coast of the Black Sea. Once part of the Soviet Union.

United Kingdom A nation of the British Isles off the northwestern coast of Europe. Contains the once independent nations of England, Scotland, Wales, and Northern Ireland. Official name is the United Kingdom of Great Britain and Northern Ireland. Sometimes called Great Britain.

Ural Mountains A mountain system in Russia that forms part of the border between Europe and Asia.

Uzbekistan A nation of Central Asia southeast of Kazakhstan and north of Turkmenistan. Once part of the Soviet Union.

V

Vatican City The nation within the city of Rome. The administrative and spiritual center of the Roman Catholic Church.

Venice A large city in northeastern Italy. That country's third largest port.

Versailles The French palace built by King Louis XIV in northern France, near Paris. Site of peace negotiations ending World War I.

Vienna The capital city of Austria on the Danube River.

Vistula River A river in Poland that connects Warsaw with the Baltic Sea.

Vladivostok A city in eastern Russia on the Sea of Japan. A major port and naval base.

Volga River A river in Russia that rises near Moscow and flows into the Caspian Sea. The Russian people have a strong sentimental attachment to the river.

W

Wales Formerly independent nation now part of the United Kingdom. Located in the British Isles west of England on the island of Britain. *See* United Kingdom.

Warsaw The capital city of Poland.

Western Europe The region of Europe that includes Germany, France, Belgium, The Netherlands, Luxembourg, Switzerland, Monaco, Liechtenstein, and Austria.

Y

Yugoslavia *See* Bosnia-Herzegovina, Croatia, Macedonia, Serbia-Montenegro, and Slovenia.

This glossary will help you pronounce and understand the meanings of the Key Terms in this book. The page number at the end of the definition tells where the word or phrase first appears.

A

"a single Europe" Expressed goal of European Community (forerunner of the European Union), whereby Europe's nations would become part of a larger governmental system. (p. 237)

absolute monarch The principle of an absolute monarch, given a right to rule by God, was extensively used in Europe during the seventeenth and eighteenth centuries. (p. 158)

acropolis The elevated stronghold in ancient Greek city-states used as a gathering place. The Acropolis of Athens contains the ruins of the Parthenon and surrounding complexes, built there during the days of the Athenian empire. (p. 39)

Age of Exploration Time of European exploration of North America, South America, Asia, and the coasts of Africa, from 1450 to 1750. (p. 71)

alliances Agreements between two or more countries to come to each other's assistance in the event of war. During the Cold War, tensions between the Communists and non-Communist nations prompted the creation of military alliances: NATO for the West (1949) and the Warsaw Pact for the East (1955). (p. 82)

Allies World War II alliance of the United Kingdom, France, the Soviet Union, and the United States that fought the Axis countries of Germany, Italy, and Japan. (p. 87)

anarchists Anti-government extremists. Czar Alexander II was assassinated by anarchists in 1881. (p. 438)

antiquity Ancient times, especially before the Middle Ages. (p. 348)

Appian Way A main thoroughfare through the ancient Roman Empire. (p. 286)

Axis World War II alliance—Germany, Japan, and Italy—that fought the Allies—the United Kingdom, France, the Soviet Union, the United States, China, and 45 other nations. (p. 87)

B

balkanize To break up a region or group into smaller and often hostile units. An example is Yugoslavia during the 1990s. (p. 352)

Balkans Countries of Eastern Europe occupying the Balkan Peninsula bounded by the Adriatic, Aegean, and Black Seas: Albania, Bosnia-Herzegovina, Bulgaria, Croatia, Macedonia, Serbia-Montenegro, and Slovenia. Also includes Greece and part of Turkey. (p. 352)

barter To exchange one commodity for another. Bartering was a common practice in the Middle Ages. (p. 53)

Benelux countries Western European countries of Belgium, The Netherlands, and Luxembourg. (p. 189)

Blitz, the The devastating bombing raids on England by the Germans during the early years of World War II. (p. 148)

Byzantine (BIH•zuhn•teen) A visual arts and architecture style that originated in the fourth century in Byzantium (the capital of the Eastern Roman Empire, later named Constantinople) and spread to Italy, the Balkans, and Russia, where it survived for many centuries. (p. 457)

C

cathedral The principal church of a bishop or archbishop. Most cathedrals were built in the Middle Ages. (p. 20)

cereal crops Wheat, barley, and rye, which grow well in the Northern European Plain. (p. 369)

Central Asia The five former republics of the Soviet Union located between the Caspian Sea and China: Kazakhstan, Kyrgyzstan, Tajikistan, Turkmenistan, Uzbekistan. (p. 480)

chronicles Written records of important events in public life. (p. 458)

city-state Independent area organized around and including a city. Democracy grew out of the Greek organization of these political units. (p. 38)

clans Close-knit groups of related families. (p. 495)

Cold War Dangerous rivalry between United States and Soviet Union from 1945 to 1990. (p. 91)

collective farms Agricultural management system established by the Soviet Union in the 1930s. Many small farms were combined into a few large ones and were controlled by the government. (p. 375)

colonies Areas settled in one country by people from another country. (p. 73)

comedy Dramatic form invented by the Greeks that poked fun at famous people, ideas, or social customs. (p. 42)

Common Market. *See* European Union.

Communists Followers of German philosopher Karl Marx and Russian revolutionary V. I. Lenin who believe in government ownership of industrial and agricultural production. (p. 439)

constitutional government Government ruled by law, one that is regulated by the principles of a constitution. (p. 47)

constitutional monarch Sovereign whose powers are defined or limited by law. Duties are mainly symbolic and ceremonial. An example is Queen Margrette II, the monarch of Denmark. (p. 158)

containment The policy, process, or result of preventing the expansion of a hostile power or ideology. After World War II, the United States' policy was to contain the expansion of the Soviet Union. (p. 92)

convents Religious communities for women. (p. 175)

Cossacks Nomadic frontiersmen of southern Russia (originally runaway serfs) organized as cavalry in the czarist army. (p. 435)

cottage industry System of work in the Middle Ages. Labor force consisted of family units or individuals working at home with their own equipment. (p. 132)

covenant A written agreement or promise between two or more parties. (p. 48)

crop rotation Practice of growing different crops in succession on the same land chiefly to preserve the productive capacity of the soil. (p. 127)

Cyrillic Alphabet invented by Eastern Orthodox missionaries in the ninth century. Used throughout Eastern Europe. (p. 416)

czar Absolute monarch in Russia. "Czar" was the imperial title from 1547 to 1721, although it continued in popular use until the 1917 revolution. (p. 432)

D

democracy Government by the people, usually through elected representation. (p. 160)

détente The relaxation of strained relations or tensions between nations. An example was the easing of tensions between the United States and the Soviet Union. (p. 447)

dialects Regional variations of languages. (p. 24)

Diaspora The dispersal of the Jews, initially from Palestine after the Roman sacking of Jerusalem (A.D. 70) and crushing of the Jewish revolt in 135. The term has come to refer to all Jews living outside Israel. (p. 48)

dictator Person who heads a government that exercises total authority over its people. An example was Adolf Hitler. (p. 317)

direct democracy A government in which the supreme power is given to the people and exercised by them directly through periodically held free elections. (p. 40)

diverse Differing from one another. Europe, for example, is diverse because it has many different ethnic groups and its peoples speak more than 50 different languages. (p. 24)

division of labor In the factory system, workers specializing in different tasks to create a finished product. Led to mass production. (p. 133)

Duma Elected parliament established by Czar Nicholas II in 1905 in an unsuccessful effort to pacify the discontented Russian people. Today, it is the lower house of Russia's latest parliament, the Federal Assembly. (p. 439)

E

empire Territory under a single sovereign authority filled with people speaking many different languages and living different ways of life. (p. 66)

enclosure Fencing in private farms and grazing lands. An innovation of the sixteenth through eighteenth centuries. (p. 208)

established church A church recognized by law as the official church of a nation or state and supported by civil authority. (p. 65)

ethical Refers to questions of rightness, fairness, and equity (freedom from bias or favoritism). (p. 48)

ethnic group People with the same cultural background, united by language, religion, or ancestry. (p. 24)

European Community. *See* European Union.

European Parliament Parliament of the European Union, which meets in Strasbourg to comment on legislative proposals of the European Commission. (p. 237)

European Union (until 1994 called the European Community) Political and economic alliance consisting of the European Coal and Steel Community (1952), the European Economic Community (EEC, popularly called the Common Market, 1957), and the European Atomic Energy Commission (Euratom, 1957). Aims include the expansion of trade, reduction of competition, the elimination of restrictive trading practices, the encouragement of free movement of capital and labor within the community, and the establishment of a closer union among European people. There are 15 members: Austria, France, Germany, Italy, Belgium, Netherlands, Luxembourg, Denmark, Republic of Ireland, Sweden, Finland, the United Kingdom, Greece, Portugal, and Spain. (p. 97)

F

factory system Brought about by the Industrial Revolution. An efficient combination of workers and power-driven machinery that replaced cottage industries. (p. 133)

Fascist party An organization that exalts nation and often race above the individual and that stands for a centralized autocratic government headed by a dictatorial leader. An example was Mussolini's party in World War II. (p. 87)

Fascists Those who follow a political ideology (fascism) that denies all rights to individuals in their relations with the government. Examples of Fascist leaders were Francisco Franco of Spain and Benito Mussolini of Italy. (p. 317)

feudalism The main form of social organization in medieval Europe. A system based primarily on land, it involved authority, rights, and power that extended from the monarch downward. An intricate network of duties and obligations linked royalty, nobility, lesser gentry, free tenants, and serfs. The system declined from the thirteenth century, partly because of the growth of a money economy, with commerce, trade, and industry, and partly because of the many peasants' revolts, 1350–1550. Feudalism ended in England in the sixteenth century, but lasted in France until 1789 and in the rest of Western Europe until the early nineteenth century. In Russia it continued until 1861. *See also* serfs. (p. 54)

Five Themes of Geography Location, Place, Human-Environmental Interaction, Movement, and Region—the concepts used to describe a place on earth and the people who live there. (p. 14–15)

Five-Year Plan A course of rapid industrialization set for the Soviet Union by Joseph Stalin. The government took over all private businesses and expanded heavy industry to increase production. (p. 511)

fjords small inlets—most notable in Norway—with steep sides carved by glaciers during the Ice Age. (p. 111)

Flemish Language spoken primarily in northern Belgium. It is similar to Dutch. (p. 189)

foreign investments Where one country allows other countries to set up businesses or buy into its companies. In the mid-1990s, Russia—resource rich and money poor—desperately needed foreign investors to provide financial support as it moved from communism to capitalism.(p. 525)

G

geothermal energy Energy extracted from natural steam, hot water, or hot dry rocks in the earth's crust that is used for heating and the generation of electricity. A major energy source in such volcanic areas as Iceland and New Zealand. (p. 139)

glasnost Mikhail Gorbachev's policy of openness to allow freedom of expression and debate about Soviet society and politics. (p. 449)

Gospels Christian sources about the life, death, and resurrection of Jesus. Divided into four books—Matthew, Mark, Luke, and John—within the New Testament of the Bible. (p. 49)

Greens, the European political party noted for its environmental concerns. (p. 218)

gross national product The total value of the goods and services produced by the residents of a country during a specified period. (p. 307)

Gulf Stream (North Atlantic Drift) Ocean current carrying warm water from the Gulf of Mexico to the western coast of Europe. (p. 30)

H

heresy Saying or doing something contrary to acceptable beliefs. (p. 64)

Holocaust The mass slaughter of 6 million Jews and countless other Europeans during World War II by the Nazis. (p. 253)

Human-Environmental Interaction One of the Five Themes of Geography. Describes a place in terms of the environment's effect on humans who live there and how humans affect that environment. (p. 15)

I

Iberians Forefathers of present-day Spanish and Portuguese. Lived as far back as 5,000 years ago. (p. 269)

icon (EYE•kahn) A conventional religious image typically painted on a small wooden panel and used in the devotions of Eastern Christians. (p. 458)

Industrial Revolution The sudden acceleration of technological and economic development that began in Britain in the eighteenth century and spread throughout the world. The traditional farming economy was replaced by one dominated by machinery and manufacturing. This transferred the balance of political power from the landowner to the industrial capitalist and created an urban working class.(p. 133)

iron curtain Popular term first used by Winston Churchill to describe barrier between free Western Europe countries and Soviet-dominated ones in Eastern Europe. (p. 92)

irrigation Artificial water supply for dry agricultural areas by means of dams and channels. Irrigation has been practiced for thousands of years, in Europe and Asia as well as the Americas. (p. 288)

K

kaiser Title used by the Holy Roman emperor, Austrian emperors (1806-1918), and German emperors (1871-1919). The word, like the Russian "czar," is derived from the Latin *Caesar*. (p. 82)

KGB The national secret police force of the Soviet Union from Stalin's time to the end of the Cold War. The KGB had at least 220,000 border guards, with reinforcements of 80,000 volunteer militia members. (p. 441)

Khans Mongol leaders. (p. 464)

Kievan Russia An early kingdom of Russia west of the Ural Mountains that combined smaller kingdoms centered at Kiev and Novgorod. (p. 433)

knights Noblemen in feudal times who served as mounted warriors. (p. 54)

L

Lapps A seminomadic herding people who live in a region of Europe within the Arctic Circle in Norway, Sweden, Finland, and the Kola Peninsula of northwestern Russia. (p. 118)

Latin The language of ancient Italy that has passed through four influential phases: as the language of (1) republican Rome, (2) the Roman Empire, (3) the Roman Catholic Church, and (4) Western European culture, science, philosophy, and law during the Middle Ages and the Renaissance. The direct influence of Latin in Europe has decreased since Renaissance times, but both the language and its classical literature still affect many modern languages and literatures. (p. 268)

legions Roman army units of about 6,000 men each, which were divided into smaller, more mobile units. (p. 45)

life expectancy The average life span. (p. 215)

lignite Cheap brown coal. The main source of energy in Eastern Europe. (p. 378)

Location One of the Five Themes of Geography. Describes a place by its nearness to other places (relative location) or by its exact latitude and longitude (absolute location). (p. 14)

lord A feudal nobleman with military power whose right, title, and power came directly from the king. (p. 51)

M

manor Village community in the Middle Ages consisting of the lord's house and cultivated land,

591

land rented by free tenants, land held by villagers, common land, woodland, and waste land. (p. 129)

Middle Ages Period between the decline of Rome in the 400s and the beginning of the modern world (the Renaissance) in about 1450. Among the period's destinctive features were the unity of Western Europe within the Roman Catholic Church, the feudal organization of political, social, and economic relations, and the use of art for largely religious purposes. (p. 51)

monasteries Religious communities for men. (p. 175)

Movement One of the Five Themes of Geography. Describes a place by its movement of people, goods, and ideas. (p. 15)

Mongols Genghis Khan's armies of armed horsemen that conquered an immense empire. (p. 434)

N

nation An area inhabited by people who occupy territory defined by borders, controlled by a central government, and that inspires a sense of belonging to its citizens. (p. 68)

nationalism Citizens' sense of pride in their nation's history and culture. (p. 69)

NATO (North Atlantic Treaty Organization) An alliance established in August 1949 between the United States, Canada, and ten Western Europe countries. All agreed that an armed attack by the Communists against one or more of them would be considered an attack against all. (p. 92)

navigable Waters deep enough and wide enough for boats to travel. (p. 275)

Nazis National Socialist political party founded in Germany by Adolf Hitler. (p. 87)

New Economic Policy (NEP) Introduced in 1921, Lenin's plan to energize Russian farm production. The government taxed farm crops but allowed workers to keep or sell the food they grew. The policy was ended in 1928 by Stalin's first Five-Year Plan, which began the collectivization of agriculture. (*See* collective farms.) (p. 509)

New Monarchies Powerful monarchs in the 1500s and 1600s who replaced the feudal system of the Middle Ages with strong, central governments. (p. 66)

Nobel Prize Awarded to individuals by Sweden and the Nobel Foundation for lifetime achievements in literature, medicine, and science. (p. 171)

nomadic Refers to pastoral people who have no fixed residence, who move from place to place frequently and aimlessly. (p. 48)

P

patriots People who take pride in their nation. (p. 70)

peasants Common laborers and farmers in feudal times. (p. 129)

peninsula A body of land surrounded by water on three sides. (p. 25)

perestroika (peh•reh•STROY•kuh) Mikhail Gorbachev's policy of restructuring Soviet economic and political systems. (p. 449)

philately The hobby of collecting stamps. (p. 209)

philosophers People who seek wisdom or enlightenment (understanding something by using reason). (p. 41)

Place One of the Five Themes of Geography. Describes a spot on the earth by its physical (landforms, climate, and vegetation) and human (culture, government, and economy) characteristics. (p. 14–15)

polder Area of flat fertile farmland that used to be covered by a river, lake, or the sea. Polders have been artificially drained and protected from flooding by building dikes. They are common in The Netherlands, where the total land area has been increased by nearly one fifth since A.D. 1200. (p. 209)

pope The bishop of Rome, the head of the Roman Catholic Church. (p. 50)

Protestants Christians not of a Roman Catholic or Eastern Orthodox church. (p. 64)

Q

quarried Stone that is dug from the earth. (p. 287)

R

Reformation A sixteenth-century religious movement marked by the rejection or the change of some Roman Catholic doctrine and practice. The movement was a challenge to the authority of the Roman Catholic Church throughout Europe. It led to the establishment of the Protestant churches. (p. 64)

Region One of the Five Themes of Geography. Describes a place in terms of its shared characteristics that distinguishes it as part of a broad geographical area. (p. 15)

Reichstag (RIKE•stahg) Huge Berlin building that housed the parliament of the unified German empire. (p. 236)

Renaissance Meaning "rebirth" in French. The transitional movement in Europe between medieval and modern times beginning in the fourteenth century in Italy. Renaissance thinkers, particularly in the fifteenth century, emphasized knowledge and learning not based on religious sources. (p. 62)

republic A country with a republican form of government in which elected representatives are chosen by citizens to run the government. The chief of state is not a monarch and in modern times is usually a president. (p. 46)

republican governments Governments in which the heads of state are not monarchs, either by heredity or elected, but are usually presidents whose roles might include political functions. (p. 160)

Romance languages French, Spanish, Portuguese, and Romanian, all of which came from Rome and Latin. (p. 268)

S

Scandinavian peninsula Long, narrow stretch of land with jagged coastlines in Norway and Sweden. (p. 110)

scythe Agricultural implement composed of a long curving blade fastened at an angle to a long handle. An improvement on the sickle. (p. 207)

Second Industrial Revolution The redesigning and reequipping of Europe's industries after World War II. (p. 225)

secular Not specifically religious. Concerned with earthly affairs. (p. 64)

serfs Peasant farmers legally obligated to live and work for the nobility. They worked the land in return for their lord's protection. (p. 54)

service industries Businesses that supply services such as retailing, banking, and education. (p. 155)

sickle Agricultural implement that has a curved metal blade with a short handle. (*See* scythe.) (p. 207)

single Europe A political union of Europe to be created out of the European Union. Many members of the E. U. oppose the idea. (p. 237)

sirocco A wind from the Sahara Desert in Africa that blows north during the summer, bringing dry, hot weather to the Mediterranean region of Europe. (p. 277)

Soviet A Russian word that means "revolutionary council." (p. 440)

standard of living In economics, the measure of consumption and welfare of a country, community, class, or person. Individual standard-of-living expectations are heavily influenced by the income and consumption of other people in similar jobs. (p. 215)

steppes The vast treeless, flat, temperate grasslands of Europe and Asia. (p. 456)

summer solstice In the Northern Hemisphere, June 21, the first day of summer. The longest day of the year. (p. 172)

Swedish Modern architecture Nationalistic style with simple lines, built in brick and granite, used in many public and residential buildings. (p. 170)

T

terrace farming Marked by a series of horizontal ridges made in a hillside to increase arable land, conserve moisture, or minimize erosion. Perfected by Italian farmers during days of the Roman Empire. (p. 288)

three-field system Method of farming that improved crop yields. Farmers grew different crops in two fields and left one field fallow. *See* crop rotation (p. 126)

toxins Any chemical substance that is capable of injuring health or destroying life. Despite the legal efforts of many countries, industrial and agricultural toxins are regularly dumped into waters and onto lands, entering the food chain and poisoning people and the planet. (p. 216)

trade deficit When one country buys more goods from other countries than it sells. (p. 308)

tragedy Dramatic form invented by the Greeks in which a major character suffers a disaster. (p. 42)

Transcaucasia The republics of Georgia, Armenia, and Azerbaijan. (p. 436)

trenches Deep ditches from which soldiers on both sides fought during World War I. (p. 83)

Turkestan Central Asian region between the Caspian Sea and China formerly part of the Soviet Union. Stalin created five republics out of the area. (p. 436)

U

urbanization Process by which the proportion of a population living in or around towns and cities increases through migration as the agricultural population decreases. A relatively recent phenomenon, dating back only about 150 years to the beginning of the Industrial Revolution. (p. 137)

V

vassals People who held land under the protection of feudal lords to whom they vowed loyalty. (p. 54)

Vikings Norwegians, Swedes, and Danes who plundered settlements along the coasts of Europe in the eighth to tenth centuries. In their narrow, shallow-draft, highly maneuverable longships, the Vikings were able to penetrate far inland along rivers. (p. 116)

W

Walloon French dialect spoken primarily in southern Belgium. (p. 189)

Warsaw Ghetto Area of Warsaw, Poland, where Nazi Germans isolated 500,000 Jews during World War II. (p. 413)

Warsaw Pact Alliance established in 1955 between Eastern European Communist countries and the Soviet Union. All pledged to protect one another from NATO forces. Dissolved in 1991. (p. 92)

Western Civilization Special combination of ideas, institutions, religious faiths, and ways of life brought together by Europeans. (p. 31)

westernization Reforming Russia to be more like Western Europe. Energetically promoted by Peter the Great and Catherine the Great. (p. 465)

winter solstice In the Northern Hemisphere, December 21, the first day of winter. The shortest day of the year. (p. 172)

Y

yurt Mongol tent made of felt and sheep's wool that could easily be transported on horseback. (p. 462)

Acknowledgements

20, Excerpt from "Utopia, Limited" by W.S. Gilbert and Sir Arthur Sullivan in *The Savoy Operas*. Copyright © 1973 by MacMillan Publishing; 70, Excerpt from *Richard II*, Act II by William Shakespeare; 124, Excerpt from *A Social History of England* by Asa Briggs. Copyright © 1983 by Viking; 128, Excerpt from *The Vikings* by Michael Gibson. Copyright © 1976 by Silver Burdett Press (Simon & Schuster Education Group); 164, Excerpt from *The National Geographic*, "The Living Tower of London," October, 1993. Copyright © 1993 by *The National Geographic*; 206, Excerpt from *The National Geographic*, "Bordeaux: Fine Wines and Fiery Gascons," August, 1980. Copyright © 1980 by *The National Geographic*; 222, Information courtesy of Kees Rijnos, Rector and Professor of Economics, Erasmus University, Rotterdam, The Netherlands; 269, Excerpt from *The National Geographic*, "The Dead Do Tell Tales at Vesuvius," May, 1984. Copyright © 1984 by *The National Geographic*; 339, Excerpted with permission of Scribner, a Division of Simon & Schuster, from *A Farewell To Arms* by Ernest Hemingway. Copyright © 1929 Charles Scribner's Sons. Copyright renewed © 1957 by Ernest Hemingway; 358, Excerpt from *We Live in Poland* by Ewa Donica and Tim Sharman. Copyright © 1989 by the authors. Reprinted by permission of Wayland Publishers Limited; 373, Excerpt from *We Live in Poland* by Ewa Donica and Tim Sharman. Copyright © 1989 by the authors. Reprinted by permission of Wayland Publishers Limited; 377, Excerpt from "East Europe Still Choking on Air of the Past" by Marlise Simons, *The New York Times*, Section A1, November 3, 1994. Copyright © 1994 by *The New York Times*. Reprinted by permission of *The New York Times*; 381, Excerpt from *Tales of Pirx the Pilot* by Stanislaw Lem, translated by Louis Iribarne. Copyright © 1979 by Harcourt Brace & Company. Reprinted by permission of Harcourt Brace & Company; 408, "Prague Journal: For Statues, the City's Soul, a Very Wearing Time" by Jane Perlez. *The New York Times*, Section A4, July 12, 1995. Copyright © 1995 by *The New York Times*. Reprinted by permission of *The New York Times*; 456, Excerpt from *Moscow-Leningrad Handbook: Including The Golden Ring* by Masha Nordbye. Copyright © 1991 by Moon Publications; 461, Excerpt from *The Insider's Guide to Russia* by Gleb Uspensky. Reprinted by permission of Hunter Publishing; 465, Excerpt from *The Heritage of World Civilizations* by Craig et al. Copyright © 1990 by Simon & Schuster. Reprinted by permission of Simon & Schuster (MacMillan College Division); 487, Excerpt from *Places and Peoples of the World: Soviet Georgia* by Michael Boyette and Randi Boyette. Copyright © 1989 by the authors. Reprinted by permission of Chelsea House; 502, Excerpt from *The Russian Revolution* by John M. Dunn. Copyright © 1994 by Greenhaven Press; 506, Excerpt from *The Russian Revolution* by John M. Dunn. Copyright © 1994 by Greenhaven Press; 507, Excerpt from *The Russian Revolution* by John M. Dunn. Copyright © 1994 by Greenhaven Press; 508, Excerpt from *The Russian Revolution* by John M. Dunn. Copyright © 1994 by Greenhaven Press; 512, Excerpt from *Time*, "The Tortured Land," September 9, 1995. Copyright © 1995 by Time-Life Syndication; 516, "Plunging Life Expectancy Puzzles Russia" by Michael Specter. *The New York Times*, Section A1, August 2, 1995. Copyright © 1995 by *The New York Times*. Reprinted by permission of *The New York Times*; 520, Excerpt from *The National Geographic*, "A Broken Empire," March, 1993. Copyright © 1993 by *The National Geographic*; 522, "Borscht and Blini To Go: From Russian Capitalists, an Answer to McDonald's" by Michael Specter. *The New York Times*, Section DI, August 9, 1995. Copyright © 1995 by *The New York Times*. Reprinted by permission of *The New York Times*; 528, Excerpt from *The National Geographic*, "Kazakhstan: Facing the Nightmare," March, 1993. Copyright © 1993 by *The National Geographic*; 553, "Home-Grown Capitalism Delivers the Wide World of Sports to Russian Fans" by Robert Edelman. *The New York Times*, Section D9, December 4, 1995. Copyright © 1995 by *The New York Times*. Reprinted by permission of *The New York Times*.

Maps

Mapping Specialists Limited

Illustrations

DECODE, Inc.: 5, 30, 33, 39, 46, 47, 56, 57, 63, 72, 77, 98, 99, 104, 107, 120, 121, 134, 159, 185, 191, 210, 219, 239, 259, 265, 280, 291, 294, 298, 301, 341, 347, 400, 416, 470, 517, 537; Precision Graphics: 3, 4, 7, 8, 11, 13, 14, 22, 52, 54, 68, 94, 128, 131, 136, 141, 149, 191, 208, 215, 227, 268, 288, 290, 318, 338, 355, 371, 417, 482, 504, 534, 544.

Photographs

xiv, (l) David Levenson/Black Star, (r) Jim Alchediak/NCSU; xiv-1, A. B. Joyce/Photo Researchers; 1, (ml) Robert Harding Picture Library, (mr) Jim Alchediak/NCSU; 2, (t) Richard Dunoff/The Stock Market, (m) Mark Boulton/Photo Researchers, (b) Rafael Macia/Photo Researchers; 2-3, Philippe Brylak/Gamma Liaison; 3, (t) Tony Stone Images; 4, (bl) Courtesy of ARCTCO, Inc., (mr) Courtesy of Tubbs Snowshoe Company; 4-5, Bryan F. Peterson/The Stock Market; 5, (t) Les Todd/Duke University Photography, (b) John Gabb/AP/Wide World Photos; 6, (t) Sonya Jacobs/The Stock Market, (ml) Jim Alchediak/NCSU; 6-7, Kevin Galvin/The Stock Market; 7, (tr) Herve Donnezan/Photo Researchers, (m) Jim Alchediak/NCSU, (br) Tony Stone Images; 8, (tl) Jose Fuste Raga/The Stock Market, (m) Jim Alchediak/NCSU, Courtesy of Anna Morosoff, (b) Harvey Lloyd/The Stock Market; 9, (t) Giulio Veggi/Photo Researchers, 10, (t) Explorer/Photo Researchers, (b) Explorer/Photo Researchers, (mr) Tony Stone Images, (bl) Jim Alchediak/NCSU, Courtesy of Darwin Braund; 10-11, Sovfoto; 11, (r) Lee Malis/Gamma Liaison; 12, (bl) Robert Semeniuk/The Stock Market, (mr) Hutchison Library; 12-13, John O'Hagan/Photo Researchers; 13, (t) ZEFA (UK)/The Stock Market, (m) Jim Alchediak/NCSU, Courtesy of Myrna Schwartz, (br) Tim Crosby/Gamma Liaison; 16-17, Jane Faircloth/Transparencies, Inc.; 18, N. C. Travel; 20, Chris Hildreth/Duke University Photography; 21, "Queen Charlotte," by Allan Ramsay, Mint Museum of Art, Charlotte, North Carolina, Gift of Frank Ryan Harty; 22, (ml) N. C. Travel, (mr) N. C. Museum of History; 22-23, N. C. Travel; 23, (m) Courtesy of the Museum of Early Southern Decorative Arts, (b) N. C. Travel; 25, Jalil Bounhar/AP/Wide World Photos; 26, (t) Alon Reininer/ Woodfin Camp, (m) French Government Tourist Office; 28, Marty Reichenthal/The Stock Market; 30, (l) Tom Sobolik/Black Star, (r) Will & Deni McIntyre/Photo Researchers; 31, Frank Fournier/Woodfin Camp; 36, Carl Purcell/Photo Researchers; 36-37, Hamilton Wright/Photo Researchers; 38, N. C. Museum of Art; 40, (b) William Hubbell/Woodfin Camp, (inset) Jim Alchediak/ NCSU; 41, Scala/Art Resource; 42, Erich Lessing/Art Resource; 43, Scala/Art Resource; 45, Adam Woolfitt/Woodfin Camp; 46, (ml) Greek National Tourist Organization, (mr) Nimatallah/Art Resource, (bl) The Granger Collection, (br) Scala/Art Resource; 47, (ml) Alanari/Art Resource, (mr) Scully/Migaiolo, (bl) Scala/Art Resource, (br) William Hubbell/Woodfin Camp; 48, Jewish Museum/Art Resource; 50, Bettmann Archive; 51, Glasgow Museums: The Burrell Collection; 52, Giraudon/Art Resource; 52-53, Pierpont Morgan Library/Art Resource; 53, (m) Giraudon/Art Resource; 55, David Ball/The Stock Market; 57, Scala/Art Resource; 60, (t) Scala/Art Resource, (b) Alinari/Art Resource; 61, Scala/Art Resource; 62, N. C. Museum of Art; 62-63, Erich Lessing/Art Resource; 64, N. C. Museum of Art; 66, Erich Lessing/Art Resource; 68, (l) Giraudon/Art Resource, (r) David Ball/The Stock Market; 69, (t) C. Ursillo/Photo Researchers, (m) G. Dagli-Orti, (b) Rapho Agence/Photo Researchers; 70, Alabama Shakespeare Festival; 72, Portuguese National Tourist Office; 73, (t) "First Landing of Christopher Columbus," by Frederick Kemmelmeyer, National Gallery of Art, Gift of Edgar and Bernice Chrysler Garbisch, (b) Scala/Art Resource; 74, Jim Alchediak/NCSU; 76, Hulton/Deutsch/Woodfin Camp; 80, (t) AP/Wide World Photos, (m) The Granger Collection; 80-81, Archive Photos; 82-83, Culver Pictures; 83, (r) Bettmann Archive; 84, (t) Archive Photos, (m) The Granger Collection; 85, National Portrait Gallery, Smithsonian Institution/Art Resource; 86, Bettmann Archive; 87, AP/ Wide World Photos; 88, Archive Photos; 90, Hayne Palmour; 91, 92, 93, & 94, AP/Wide World Photos; 94-95, Archive Photos; 95, (t) German Tourist Information Center, (ml, inset) Archive Photos, (r) AP/Wide World Photos; 96, European Community Delegation, New York; 98, State Archives of North Carolina; 102-3, Courtesy of the British Tourist Authority; 104, (inset) Courtesy of Mr. Thorsten Persson; 104-5, Moller/Swedish Travel & Tourism Council; 106, Homer Sykes/Woodfin Camp; 107, Finnish Tourist Board; 108, Norwegian Tourist Board; 110, Max Schmid/Woodfin Camp; 112, H. P. Merten/The Stock Market; 113, Danish Tourist Board; 114, G. Dagli-Orti; 115, (t) Tony Stone Images, (inset) British Tourist Authority; 116, The Granger Collection; 116-17, Robert Harding Picture Library; 117, (t) Art Resource, (mr, br) Canon's Yeoman & the Wife of Bath, Ellesmere Manuscript, Private Collection, Bridgeman Art Library, London; 118, Jim Alchediak/NCSU; 119, Finnair/Finnish Tourist Board; 124, (t) N. C. Museum of History; 124-25, Nelson-Atkins Museum of Art, Kansas City, Missouri, Purchased by the Nelson Trust; 125, (r) Frank Fournier/Woodfin Camp; 126, (t) The Granger Collection, (b) ZEFA (UK) /The Stock Market; 127, The Granger Collection; 129, Tony Stone Images; 130 & 130-31, Giraudon/Art Resource, (inset) Bodleian Library, Oxford; 132, Archive Photos; 134, (tl) Archive Photos, (t, br) Bettmann Archive, (bl, tr) The Granger Collection; 137, Archive Photos; 138, Iceland Tourist Board; 139, Finnish Tourist Board; 140, Lawrence Migdale/Photo Researchers; 144-45, Norwegian Tourist Board; 145, Allen Green/Photo Researchers; 146, Archive Photos, 146-47, Tony Stone Images; 148, (l, bl) Hulton/Deutsch/Woodfin Camp, (tr) UPI/Bettmann; 148-49, Culver Pictures; 149, (r) ZEFA (UK)/The Stock Market; 150, (l) Adam Woolfitt/Woodfin Camp, (r) Courtesy of Glaxo Wellcome Inc.; 151, Ned Haines/Photo Researchers; 152, AP/Wide World Photos; 153, Allen Green/Photo Researchers; 155, (t) Courtesy of Saab Automobile AB, (b) FINNPAP/Helsinki; 156, Janerik Henriksson/Pica Pressfoto; 157, SPL/Photo Researchers; 158, "King George III," by Allan Ramsay, Mint Museum of Art, Charlotte, North Carolina; 160, Jerry Bergman/Gamma Liaison; 164, British Tourist Authority; 164-65, Will & Deni McIntyre/Photo Researchers; 165, British Tourist Authority; 166, Tony Stone Images; 167, ZEFA (UK)/The Stock Market; 168, (l, b) Tivoli Museum, Copenhagen; 168-69, Explorer/ Photo Researchers; 169, (t) Danish Tourist Board, (m) Richard Rowan/Photo Researchers, (b) Tony Stone Images; 170, Danish Tourist Board; 171, (t) Swedish Travel and Tourism Council, (b) Janerik Henriksson/Pica Pressfoto; 172, Swedish Travel and Tourism Council; 173, B. & C. Alexander/Photo Researchers; 174, Courtesy of the Royal Collection, Her Majesty Queen Elizabeth II; 175, Courtesy of the Board of Trinity College, Dublin; 176, Finnish Tourist Board; 177, Bettmann Archive; 178, Ted Spiegel/Black Star; 182-83 & 183, QA Photos Ltd.; 184, (t) Jim Alchediak/NCSU, Courtesy of Sabina Leuppi; 184-85, Sabina Leuppi; 185, Bern (Switzerland) Department of Public Instruction; 186, Karen Kasmauski/Woodfin Camp; 187, Gerald Buthaud/Woodfin Camp; 188, Bill Bachmann/Photo Researchers; 189, (t) Jim Alchediak/NCSU, (b) Swiss National Tourist Office; 190, (t) AP/Wide World Photos, (b) Raphael Gaillarde/Gamma Liaison; 191, (t) Les Todd/Duke University Photography, (b) European Union Delegation, New York; 192, AP/Wide World Photos; 193, (l) ZEFA-Rossembach/The Stock Market, (r) B. Hemphill/Photo

Researchers; **194,** German Information Center; **196,** Netherlands Board of Tourism; **197,** Mike Yamashita/Woodfin Camp; **199,** David Cup/Woodfin Camp; **200,** (t) Leroy H. Mantell/The Stock Market, (b) Swiss National Tourist Office; **204,** Adam Woolfitt/Woodfin Camp; **204-5,** Joe Bator/The Stock Market; **205,** Adam Woolfitt/Woodfin Camp; **206,** Snowdon/Hoyer/Woodfin Camp; **207,** Culver Pictures; **208,** Nathan Benn/Woodfin Camp; **208-9,** Tony Stone Images; **209,** (inset) Explorer/Photo Researchers, (r) Netherlands Board of Tourism; **211,** French Government Tourist Office; **212 & 213,** Archive Photos; **214,** Giulio Veggi/Photo Researchers; **215,** Eric Grave/Photo Researchers; **216,** Explorer/Photo Researchers; **218,** Tom McHugh/Photo Researchers; **222,** Courtesy of Professor Kees Rijnvos; **222-23 & 223,** AP/Wide World Photos; **224-25,** Mike Yamashita/Woodfin Camp; **226,** (l) "Registring Immigrants," [sic] from *Frank Leslie's Illustrated Newspaper* (1866), Museum of the City of New York, Gift of Andreas Feininger, (m) Archive Photos, (r) Jeff DeBooy/AP; **227,** (t, b) German Information Center; **228,** Gilles Bassignac/Gamma Liaison; **228,** Douglas T. Mesney/The Stock Market; **230,** UPI/Bettmann; **230-31,** Patrick Piel/Gamma Liaison; **232,** Farrell Grehan/Photo Researchers; **233,** Tony Stone Images; **234,** Sabina Leuppi; **235,** Michael Rosenfeld/The Stock Market; **236,** Regis Bossu/Sygma; **237,** Raphael Gaillarde/Gamma Liaison; **238,** Agency Vienna Report/Sygma; **242 & 242-43,** Bernard Annebicque/Sygma; **243,** Tony Souter/Hutchison Library; **244,** David Sailors/The Stock Market; **245,** Bill Bachmann/Photo Researchers; **246 & 247,** Austrian National Tourist Office; **248,** German Information Center; **249,** Serge Sibert/Matrix International; **251,** Courtesy of Martine & Gary Smith; **252,** (l) The Granger Collection, (r) "Der Rabbiner," by Rembrandt van Rijn, photo by Lutz Braun/Bildarchiv Preussicher Kulturbesitz; **252-53,** Alfredo Dagli Orti/Bildarchiv Preussicher Kulturbesitz; **253,** (b) Bildarchive Preussicher Kulturbesitz, (r) Jewish Museum, New York/Art Resource; **254,** J. Alex Langley/Photo Researchers; **255,** Robert Harding Picture Library; **256 & 257,** Switzerland Tourism; **258,** Massimo Mastrorillo/The Stock Market; **262-63,** Dale Boyer/Photo Researchers; **264,** Bettmann; **264-65,** "Eruption of Mt. Vesuvius," by Pierre Volaire, N. C. Museum of Art; **266,** Jose Fuste Raga/The Stock Market; **267,** Explorer/Photo Researchers; **268,** (l) Robert Frerck/Woodfin Camp, (r) Borromeo/Art Resource; **269,** (l) Scala/Art Resource, (r) Art Resource; **271,** Joachim Messerschmidt/The Stock Market; **272,** Ronny Jaques/Photo Researchers; **272-73,** John de Visser/Black Star; **274,** Robert Frerck/Woodfin Camp; **275,** Noboru Komine/Photo Researchers; **276,** (t) Andy Levin/Photo Researchers, (b) Portuguese National Tourist Office; **277,** Michele Burgess/The Stock Market; **278,** Tony Stone Images; **279,** Loren McIntyre/Woodfin Camp; **284,** Jim Alchediak/NCSU; **284-85,** George Holton/Photo Researchers; **285,** Jean Anderson/The Stock Market; **286,** N. C. Museum of Art; **287,** National Geographic Society; **288,** Bo Zaunders/The Stock Market; **290,** (l) Metropolitan Museum of Art, Gift of Edith Macy Schoenborn-Bucheim, in memory of Valentine E. Macy, Jr., (r) Metropolitan Museum of Art, Cora Timken Burnett Collection of Persian Miniatures and other Persian Art Objects, photo by Schecter Lee; **291,** (l) A. Ramey/Woodfin Camp, (r) Pierpont Morgan Library/Art Resource; **292,** The Granger Collection; **293,** Herve Donnezan/Photo Researchers; **294,** William Hubbell/Woodfin Camp; **296,** S. Grandadam/Photo Researchers; **297,** Roger Hutchings/Woodfin Camp; **298 & 299,** Robert Harding Picture Library; **300,** (l) Linda Bartlett/Photo Researchers, (r) Scully/Migaiolo; **304,** Robert Frerck/Woodfin Camp; **304-5,** National Geographic Society; **305,** Herve Donnezan/Photo Researchers; **306,** Explorer/Photo Researchers; **307,** Hutchison Library; **308,** Italian Government Tourist Board; **309,** Robert Frerck/Woodfin Camp; **310,** John D. Cunningham/Visuals Unlimited; **311,** Tomas Friedmann/Photo Researchers; **312,** European Community Delegation, New York; **313,** AP/Wide World Photos; **315,** Barry Sweet/AP/Wide World Photos; **316,** Archive Photos; **317,** UPI/Bettmann Newsphotos; **318,** (t) The Granger Collection, (b) Michos Tzovaras/Art Resource; **318-19,** G. Dagli-Orti; **319,** (l) Scala/Art Resource, (inset) Robert Harding Picture Library; **320,** Reuters/Bettmann; **324,** Farrell Grehan/Photo Researchers; **324-25 & 325,** Tony Stone Images; **326-27,** Joachim Messerschmidt/The Stock Market; **327,** (r) Robert Harding Picture Library; **328,** Cesare Gerolimetto/The Stock Market; **329 & 330,** Giraudon/Art Resource; **331,** Adam Woolfitt/Woodfin Camp; **332,** Will & Deni McIntyre/Photo Researchers; **333,** Robert Harding Picture Library; **334,** Robert Frerck/The Stock Market; **335,** Erich Lessing/Art Resource; **336,** Explorer/Photo Researchers; **337,** Brooks Kraft/Sygma; **338,** The Granger Collection; **338-39,** UPI/Bettmann; **339,** (l) Jim Alchediak/NCSU, (ml) The Granger Collection, (mr) Duke University Special Collections Library; **340,** Leroy H. Mantell/The Stock Market; **344-45,** Interfoto MTI/Eastfoto; **346,** (t) Erich Lessing/Art Resource, (b) Tony Stone Images; **348,** Contact Press Images/The Stock Market; **349,** Momatiuk Eastcott/Woodfin Camp; **350,** Corbis-Bettmann; **352,** D. Glaubach/Photo Researchers; **353,** Noboru Komine/Photo Researchers; **354,** (l) Duke University Special Collections Library, (r) Adam Woolfitt/Woodfin Camp; **354-55,** Bill Bachmann/Photo Researchers; **355 & 356,** Adam Woolfitt/Woodfin Camp; **357,** ITAR-TASS/Sovfoto; **358,** Josef Polleross/The Stock Market; **360,** Tony Stone Images; **361,** (t) Lee Malis/Spectrum Pictures, (inset) J. Gerlach/Visuals Unlimited; **366-67,** Bill Weems/Woodfin Camp; **367,** Tierbild Okapia/Photo Researchers; **368,** UPI/Bettmann; **369,** Aldo Tutino/Art Resource; **370,** The Granger Collection; **370-71 & 371,** Compagnie des Wagons-Lits; **372,** Archive Photos; **373,** AP/Wide World Photos; **374,** Corbis-Bettmann; **375,** Sovfoto; **376,** AP/Wide World Photos; **377,** Miroslav Hucek/Spectrum Pictures; **378,** Lee Malis/Spectrum Pictures; **378-79 & 379,** Hutchison Library; **380,** Petr Berger/CTK/Eastfoto; **381,** Jim Alchediak/NCSU; **382,** Bill Weems/Woodfin Camp; **386 & 386-87,** Sovfoto/Eastfoto; **388,** E. Tarkpea/ITAR-TASS/Sovfoto; **389,** Archive Photos; **390,** AP/Wide World Photos; **391,** Courtesy of Darwin G. Braund; **392,** Nikolai Ignatiev/ Matrix International; **393,** Erica Lansner/Black Star; **394-95,** Chip Hires/Gamma Liaison; **395,** Reuters/Bettmann; **396,** Igor Zehl/CTK/Eastfoto; **397,** UPI/Bettmann; **401,** Gerd Ludwig/Visum Archiv der Fotografen; **402-3,** All coins by Les Todd/Duke University Photography, except Athenian drachma by Culver Pictures; **403,** (r) Tomas Novak/CTK/Eastfoto; **404,** Lee Malis/Spectrum Pictures; **408,** (t) Robert Harding Picture Library; **408-9,** Martina Storek/New York Times Pictures; **409,** Robert Harding Picture Library; **410,** Tim Crosby/Gamma Liaison; **410-11,** Kwok Leung Paul Lau/Gamma Liaison; **412,** Sovfoto/Eastfoto; **413,** The Bettmann Archive; **414,** Tony Stone Images; **415,** Chip Hires/Gamma Liaison; **416,** (l) Erich Lessing/Art Resource, (r) Duke University Special Collections Library; **417,** Peter Dejong/AP/Wide World Photos; **418,** Laski Diffusion/Gamma Liaison; **420,** Stephanie Maze/Woodfin Camp; **421,** Les Todd/Duke University Photography; **422,** Robert Harding Picture Library; **423,** (b) Wally McNamee/Woodfin Camp, (inset) Lester Sloan/Woodfin Camp; **424,** Tony Stone Images; **428-29,** Tony Stone Images; **430,** (t) Jim Alchediak/NCSU, (b) AP/Wide World Photos; **431,** (l) Jim Alchediak/NCSU, (r) AP/Wide World Photos; **433,** Scala/Art Resource; **434,** Bridgeman/Art Resource; **434-35,** Sovfoto; **435,** The Granger Collection; **436,** Jeff Gnass/The Stock Market; **437,** AP/Wide World Photos; **438,** The Granger Collection; **439,** ITAR-TASS/Sovfoto; **440 & 442,** AP/Wide World Photos; **444,** Sovfoto; **445,** AP/Wide World Photos; **446,** (l) SPL/Photo Researchers; **446-47,** Science Source/Photo Researchers; **447,** (l) NASA/Wide World Photos, (br) AP/Wide World Photos, (tr) Mark M. Lawrence/The Stock Market; **448,** Sovfoto; **449,** Tomas Oneborg/Pica Pressfoto; **450,** AP/Wide World Photos; **454,** (r) Culver Pictures; **454-55,** Tony Stone Images; **455 & 456,** Sovfoto; **457,** Scala/Art Resource; **458,** (l) Jim Alchediak/NCSU, (t) Lyn Hughes/Gamma Liaison; **458-59,** Lyn Hughes/Gamma Liaison; **459,** (r) Alexander Zemlianichenko/AP/Wide World Photos, (inset) Cyril Le Tourneur/Gamma Liaison, (br) Jim Alchediak/NCSU, Courtesy of Anna Morosoff; **460,** Erich Lessing/Art Resource; **461,** Ned Gillette/The Stock Market; **462,** "Genghis Khan Dividing his Empire among his Sons," Metropolitan Museum of Art, Francis M. Weld Gift Fund; **465,** The Granger Collection; **466,** (t) The Granger Collection, (b) Bilderberg/The Stock Market; **467,** J. Greenberg/Photo Researchers; **468,** Erich Lessing/Art Resource; **469,** Jim Alchediak/NCSU, Courtesy of Myrna Schwartz; **470,** (l) Sovfoto, (r) Saola/Gamma Liaison; **472,** Culver Pictures; **476-77,** ITAR-TASS/Sovfoto; **478,** Tim Crosby/Gamma Liaison; **479,** Tim Crosby/Gamma Liaison; **480,** Serguei Fedorov/Woodfin Camp; **481,** Tony Stone Images; **482,** (l) Culver Pictures; **482-83,** Ron Levy/Gamma Liaison; **483,** Sarah Leen/Matrix International; **484-85,** Robert Nickelsberg/Gamma Liaison; **485,** Sovfoto; **486,** Jeremy Nicholl/Matrix International; **487,** Alexander Zemlianichenko/AP/Wide World Photos; **488,** Hutchison Library; **489,** Ned Gillette/The Stock Market; **491 & 492,** Wolfgang Kaehler/Gamma Liaison; **494,** (t) Bill Wassman/The Stock Market, (b) Alexander Zemlianichenko/AP/Wide World Photos; **495,** Bill Swersey/Gamma Liaison; **496,** AP/Wide World Photos; **500,** (l) Hutchison Library; **500-1,** Alexander Zemlianichenko/AP/Wide World Photos; **501,** Josef Polleross/The Stock Market; **503 & 504,** Culver Pictures; **504-5,** Robert Semeniuk/The Stock Market; **505,** (ml, mr) Robert Semeniuk/The Stock Market, (tr) AP/Wide World Photos; **506,** ITAR-TASS/ Sovfoto; **507,** The Granger Collection; **508,** Culver Pictures; **508-9,** ITAR-TASS/Sovfoto; **510,** The Granger Collection; **511,** Sovfoto; **512,** John Launois/Black Star; **514-15,** ITAR-TASS/Sovfoto; **515,** Gerd Ludwig/Visum Archiv der Fotografen; **516,** Sergei Karpukhin/AP/Wide World Photos; **520 & 521,** Gerd Ludwig/Visum Archiv der Fotografen; **522,** Gleb Kosorukov/New York Times Pictures; **523,** M. Bertinetti/Photo Researchers; **524,** Tomas Oneborg/Pica Pressfoto; **525,** Sovfoto; **526,** Howard Sochurek/Woodfin Camp; **528,** Sovfoto; **529,** Hutchison Library; **531,** Sovfoto; **532,** Tomas Oneborg/Pica Pressfoto; **533,** Sovfoto; **534,** Vlastimir Shone/Gamma Liaison; **535,** (l) Jose Fuste Raga/The Stock Market, (inset) Diana Walker/Gamma Liaison, (b) Stock Photos/The Stock Market; **536,** Sovfoto; **540,** Jurek Holzer/Pica Pressfoto; **540-41,** Sovfoto; **541,** Hannele Rantala Lehtikuva/Woodfin Camp; **542,** Jurek Holzer/Pica Pressfoto; **543,** M. Bertinetti/Photo Researchers; **544,** (l) Ed Lallo/Gamma Liaison, (inset) Daniel Sheehan/Black Star, (r) Jurma Jormanainen/Woodfin Camp; **545,** (l) Kurgan-Lisnet/Gamma Liaison, (tr) Henri Matisse, "The Dance," Scala/Art Resource, (m) Shakyamuni Buddha (Tibeto-Chinese, late 17th century), John Bigelow Taylor/Art Resource, (br) Kurgan-Lisnet/Gamma Liaison; **546,** Blaine Harrington III/The Stock Market; **547,** ITAR-TASS/Sovfoto; **548,** Dr. Robert Fearn; **549,** (l) David MacDonald/Gamma Liaison, (r, inset) Virginia Museum of Fine Arts, Richmond, Va., Bequest of Lillian Thomas Pratt, photos by Katherine Wetzel; **550,** Andrei Tyapchenkov/AP/Wide World Photos; **551,** Dr. Robert Fearn; **552,** Sovfoto; **553,** Janerik Henriksson/Pica Pressfoto; **554,** David R. Swanson/Gamma Liaison; **555,** Contact Press Images/The Stock Market; **556,** (l) Jim Alchediak/NCSU, Courtesy of Myrna Schwartz, (r) J. Greenberg/Photo Researchers; **557,** Dr. Robert Fearn; **558,** Wally McNamee/Woodfin Camp.